THE MINUTES OF
THE DARTMOUTH, MASSACHUSETTS
MONTHLY MEETING OF FRIENDS
1699–1785

* * *

VOLUME II:
MEN'S MINUTES 1773–1785
WOMEN'S MINUTES 1699–1782

THE MINUTES OF
THE DARTMOUTH, MASSACHUSETTS
MONTHLY MEETING OF FRIENDS
1699–1785

*   *   *

VOLUME II:
MEN'S MINUTES 1773–1785
WOMEN'S MINUTES 1699–1782

THOMAS D. HAMM

EDITOR

BOSTON · 2022
COLONIAL SOCIETY OF MASSACHUSETTS
IN COOPERATION WITH
THE DARTMOUTH HISTORICAL AND ARTS SOCIETY

DISTRIBUTED BY
THE UNIVERSITY OF VIRGINIA PRESS

Dedication
To
DAN SOCHA

Printed from the Income of the Sarah Louisa Edes Fund

CONTENTS

VOLUME TWO

ILLUSTRATIONS

BOOK III: 1762–1785

Note:
Continued from Volume 1.

2ᵐᵒ 1773   At a Monthly Meeting held in **Dartmouth** yᵉ 15: 2ⁿᵈ ᵐᵒ 1773
the Representatives are **Samuel Smith** and **James Davis** present

Jos Russell Ju   **David Sheepherd [Shepherd]** Reports that he attended the Marraige of **Joseph**
marriage   **Russell** & **Mehetable Howland** According to Appointment which
was Consomated Orderly & Sᵈ **David** has rend[e]red a Excuse for his
not making Report Last monthly meeting

Shearman   The Committee appointed to treat with **Sherman Craw** Report
Craw give   that they have treated with him and he gave them a good Degree
in a paper   of Satisfaction, and Sᵈ **Craw** hath given in a paper to this meeting
Signifying his Sorrow, Therefor the matter is Referᵈ under the
Cair [care] of the above Sᵈ Committee and **Paul Russell** is ad[d]ed to them
for a further Trial of his Sencerity and they to Report ~~to next meeting~~
when they think Necessary

     The Committee appointed to inquire into the matter Respecting
T. Almy   **Thoˢ Almy**, have Draughted a Certificate on his behalf, to the mᵒ
Certificate   meeting of **Acoakset** which was Signed by the Clerk in behalf
Signᵈ   of this meeting

Complaint   The Committee appointed Respecting the Complaint of **Wᵐ Barker**
against David   and **Daniel Cornal [Cornell]** against **David Smith** for Reporting that Some
Smith   of the Overseers were false men, Report as followeth and is Accepted
To the Monthly Meeting of **Dartmouth** – –
Agreeable to your Appointment last monthly meeting we have made
Inquirey into the Grounds of the Complaint of **Wᵐ Barker** & **Daniel
Cornel** Against **David Smith** and we find by undoutted Evidences
Judgment   that Sᵈ **David Smith** has Publickly Reported that Some of the
against   Overseers of our Meeting were false men to the Defamaing of
D. Smith   them therefore our Judgment is that Sᵈ **David Smith** Ought as
Publickly to Condemn the Same, as he Reported the Scandel – –
Given forth by your Comᵗᵉ   **Nicholass Howland**
this 10ᵗʰ the 2ᵐᵒ 1773   **John Ricketson**
                                               Benjᵃ Taber
                                               Wᵐ Wood
                                               Benjᵃ Howland 2ⁿᵈ

     David Smith Requests a Coppy of the Complaint of **Wᵐ Barker**
& **Daniel Cornel** against him which is granted
D:S appeal   Lik[e]wise Sᵈ **David** Requests an Appeal from the afore Sᵈ Judgment
granted   to the Quarterly meeting which is granted – –

Settled   The Committee Appointed to Settle Accounts with the Treasurer
accoump with   Report that they have Settled Sd Accoumpts and Remain in the
Treasurer   Stock 23£ : 1ˢ : 2ᵈ old tennor – –

account of meetings debt   The S^d Committee also Inform that they have Collected the Chief
Debts against this meeting which amount to 35$^£$ – 12^S – 2^d; L[awful]: mon[ey]
this meeting Collected the Sum of - – 13$^£$ – 12^S – 2^d Old tennor

Order on Treasurer   and the Treasurer is Ordered to Deliver £2:0-0 Lawfull money
to the Overseers of the poor for the Use of the poor – –
and S^d Treasurer is Ordered to pay **Wm Anthony J^u** 1$^£$ – 2^S – 2^d L. money
for Repairing the meeting house – –

money to be raised   **Samuel Smith** is Appointed to Draught Subscriptions for to
Raise money to Defray the above S^d Debts and bring them
to the Adjournment of this meeting, this meeting Adjourns
to the Last forth Day in this month

2mo 1773   At a Monthly Meeting meet by Adjournment 24th : 2mo : [1]773
the Representatives were Called **Samuel Smith** present

The case of Dav Smith   this meeting has further Consid[e]red the matter Respecting **David Smith**
and do appoint **Prince Allen Seth Sherman Abraham Tucker** to Show
him the Judgment that was Read and Accepted at the first sitting
of this meeting in Consequence of the Complaint of **Wm Barker**
and **Daniel Cornal** and to Labour with the S^d **David** to Comply
therewith- and make Report to the next monthly meeting

Commit to correct ye minutes   **Thos Hicks Samuel Smith Job Russell Wm Anthony J^u** are
appointed to Correct the monthly meeting minutes in order to
be Put on Record And also to Inspect the papers and they to burn[?]
them that appear to be of no Use or Service and make Report
to next M^o Meeting – –

Papers for Subscrip= =tions   **Samuel Smith** hath Drafted papers for Subscriptions agreeable
to Appointment And **Caleb Russell Prince Allen Gideon Howland
William Mosher Timothy Russell** & **Jonathan Hussey** are appointed
to Communicate S^d papers to Each member of this meeting that
are able) in order for them to Subscribe thereto & S^d Committee
to Receive the money and pay the Same into the Treasury
of this meeting and make Return of their doings, and the
Sum total So Collected to this meeting as Soon as they Can
with Conveniency

J: Hussey overseer of ye buring ground   **Jonathan Hussey** is appointed to have the Oversight of
the Buriing [Burying] Ground ~~belonging~~ing belonging to this meeting
in the Room [place] of **Daniel Russell** Deceas^d

3mo 1773   At a Monthly Meeting held in **Dartmouth** the 15th y^e 3mo 1773
the Representatives are **William Mosher** & **William Wood** present

Treasurer paid out money   the Treasurer Reports that he hath paid the Overseers of the poor
£2 – 0^S – 0^d Lawfull money also paid **Wm Anthony J^u** 19[?]$^£$ – 2^S – 2^d L money
as Ordered last monthly meeting – –

Report of Com^tee
on David
Smith case

　　The Committee appointed to Shew **David Smith** the Judgment
in Consequence of the Complaint of **Daniel Cornal** & **Wm Barker**
against Said **David**, and to labour with him to Comply therewith
Report as followeth which is Accepted

　　Agreeable to appointment we have Shewed **David Smith** the
Judgment of the Committee appointed to Judge & Determine between
Said Smith and the Overseers of our Meeting which was read and
Accepted in our Last monthly Meeting (**David Smith** present)
we have Likewise laboured with S^d **Smith** to Comply with Said
Judgment which he Refusses to do and Still Insisted upon his
appeal to the Quarterly meeting
Dated **Dartm°** ye 15th 3mo 1773

⎰ **Abraham Tucker**
⎱ **Seth Sherman**
⎰ **Prince Allen**

To correct
Miniutes &
Record them

　　The Committee appointed to Correct the Monthly Meeting
minuets & Inspect the loos[e] papers & burn those that appear
to be of no Use or Service Report that they have fulfilled their
appointment & **Sam^ll Smith** & **Wm Anthony J^u** is to Record S^d Mi:

Step: Merithew
desires a
Certificate

Stephen Mearithew [**Merithew**] hath Removed within the Compass of
Sandwich Monthly Meeting and Desires a Removel Certificate
therefore we Appoint **John Williams** & **James Davice** [**Davis**] to Inquire
into his Life and Conversation & also to see if his Outward
affairs be Set[t]led to Satisfaction and Draught a Certificate
for him if they find things Clear and Report to next mont[hly] meeting

Report of
Com^tee ab°ut
yearly meet
ing

　　The Committee appointed to Consult with **Acoakset** M° Meeting
about the Alteration of our yearly meeting Report as followeth
which is Accepted

　　We the Committee appointed by the Moonthly Meetings of **Dartmouth**
and **Accoakset** , Persuaht [Pursuant] to appointment we have Weightily
Consid[e]red the matter in R[e]gard to an Alteration in our yearly

agreed y^t
Coakset
& Aponig^st
yearly
meetings
be two
Distinct
meetings

meeting, And have Agreed that S^d yearly meeting be two distinct
meetings the better to Accomodate the Select meeting and
that they both be held at the Same time as heretofore and
that the time of meeting be first as followeth (viz)
The first day of said meeting to begin at the twelfth
hour the Second Day at the Eleventh hour & the last Day at y^e
tenth hour **Dartmouth** the 10th of ye 3mo 177[3?]

Joshua Davel	**Joseph Tucker**
Same^l Smith	**Abraham Tucker**
Paul Russell	**Jon^a Hussey**
Leomuel Sisson	**Joseph Tripp**
	Job Russell

The Queries hath been answer^d in this meeting and an Epistle

Represe: to ye Q: meeting — Signed to the Quarterly meeting and order^d forward by the Repre: who are **Wm Mosher Samuel Smith Barzillia Tucker Prince Allen** & **Job Russell** and Likewise S^d Representatives are to Procure Such papers & Coppies as shall appear Necessary and Report to next Monthly Meeting

4mo 1773 — At a Monthly Meeting held in **Dartmouth** ye 19th ye 4mo 1773 the Representatives are **Thos Hicks** & **James Davice** [Davis] Present

Certificate for Step Merithew — This meeting hath signed a Removal Certificate for **Stephen Mearithew** [Merithew] to the Monthly Meeting of **Sandwich** – –

Report from Quart meeting — The friends appointed to attend the Quarterly Meeting Report that they all Attended according to Appointment and have Produced an Epistle from the Same which hath been read and well Accepted

J: Case Desires a Certificate — **Job Case** Informs that he is about to Remove to the **Oblong** and Desires a Removal Certificate for himself and Children, therefore do Appoint **Prince Allen** & **Daniel Cornal** [Cornell] to Inquire into his life and Conversation and see that his Outward affairs be Sett[l]ed to Satisfaction and Draw a Certificate for them if they find things Clear and bring it to next monthly meeting – –

The friends appointed to have the Oversight of that meeting at **Bedford**, Report that they attended S^d meeting which was kept in a good Degree orderly, And the friends at **Bedford**

Meeting at Bedford Continued — Request that the weekday meeting there be Continued as here= =tofore untill the Monthly Meeting in the tenth month Next, which is granted and **David Sheepherd** [Shepherd] & **James Davice** [Davis] are appointed to have the Oversight of S^d meeting to see that it be kept orderly & in the Authority of truth and Report to the tenth Month next – –

H. Cook admited a member — The Women friends Inform that they have Admitted **Hannah Cook** A member of our Society which this meeting approveth

Some meetings discontinued in New Town — The friends at **Newtown** inform that they think it Necessary to Drop Several meetings held on week Day there namely the meeting held on that week our youths meeting is, and also the meeting on that week our Monthly meeting is held therefore S^d meetings are Discontinued for time to come

S: Craw paper Accepted — The Report Respecting **Sherman Craw** being Satisfactory therefore this meeting accepts of his paper Condemning his marr[y]ing out of the Unity of friends

This meeting is Informed by the Epistle from the Quarterly Meeting that said ^{meeting} has Confirmed the

Judgment againᵗ David Smith confirmed by Quar meeting — the Judgment of this Meeting against **David Smith** therefore we appoint **Abraham Tucker Prince Allen** and **James Davice [Davis]** to Labour with Said **Smith** to Comply with Said Judgment, and they to Report to next monthly meeting

Received Extracts from yᵉ Q meeting — This Meeting has Received 330 Extracts of Epistles from the Quarterly Meeting which were Lat[e]ly Reprinted and are to be Distributed among friends in generall – – ~

Money Recd by Subscrip =tions Order on Treasurer — **William Mosher** Reports that he has Received by way of Subscription £40 " 12ˢ " 2ᵈ old tennor which he paid into the Treasurey, And Sᵈ Treasurer is orderᵈ to pay Sᵈ Sum to them that has Demands on this meeting and Report to next mᵒ Meeting – – Collected at this meeting £6 "18ˢ " 0 Old <u>Ten</u>

5ᵐᵒ 1773 — At a Monthly Meeting held in **Dartmouth** yᵉ 17ᵗʰ 5ᵐᵒ 1773 the Representatives are **Thoˢ Hicks** & **Samˡˡ Smith** present

on the case of Job Case — the friends appointed to Inquire into **Job Casse**s Conversation and Settlement of his outward affairs and prepare a Certificate for him, Report that Sᵈ **Cases** affairs are not all Settled therefore they have not prepared one for him, and they are Continued in that Service and to Report when ready – –

David Smith Case — The Committee appointed to Labour with **David Smith** Reports ~~as followeth~~ that he is not willing to comply and Sᵈ matter is Referᵈ to next monthly Meeting for Sd Smiths further Consideration under the Same friends care as heretofor and then they to make Report

order on Treasurer — The treasurer reports that he hath paid part of the money as orderᵈ last Monthly meeting, therefore he is Still Continued to pay as Orderᵈ and Report to ~~next Mᵒ meeting~~ when he thinks Necessary

J. Howland Requests Certificate — **John Howland** Requests a Certificate to the mᵒ meeting of **Rhod Island** Certif[y]ing his Clearness Respecting marraig and Conversation, And we appoint **David Shepherd** and **James Davice** to take the necessary Care Care on that account and Draw a Certificate if they think proper and bring to next monthly meeting

friends Request to build a Meet house at Bedford — Friend Living at **Bedford** Request the Liberty to build a Meeting House there Therefore we appoint **Joseph Tucker Abraham Tucker Joseph Barker John Potter Benjᵃ Smith Jᵘ Thoˢ Hicks** & **William Anthony Jᵘ** To Consider wheather it be best to build a house there or not, and if they think best to build to agree on what Size to build, and Report to next mᵒ meeting

M: Stratton
Receiv^d a
member &
Susan^h Wing

The women friends Inform that they have minueted [minuted] **Margaret Stratton** and **Susanah Wing** under their Care which this meeting Approveths of – –

D. Cornel
Complaind
of Tho Smith

Daniel Cornal [Cornell] hath Exhibitted a Complaint against **Thoˢ Smith** for accusing him of being a falls [false] man and saying he Could prove it, which is Refer^d to next mᵒ meeting by Reason of S^d **Smith** not being present and **John Potter** is appointed to Inform S^d **Smith** and Report to next mᵒ meeting this Meeting Collected £7 " 6ˢ " 2^d old tennor

6mo 1773

At a Monthly Meeting held in **Dartmouth** yᵉ 25: 6mo 1773 the Representatives are **Prince Allen** & **Wᵐ Anthony Jᵘ** Present

        the Committee appointed to have the Care of that matter Respecting **David Smith** Report that he Refusses to Comply with the Judgment of this Meeting and friends being Clear from further Labour with him Do hereby Deny the Said

Da. Smith
Denied

David Smith from being a member of our Sosiety [Society] and **Prince Allen** is Appointed to Inform s^d **Smith** of his Denial and Report to next mᵒ meeting – –

J: H obtaind
Certificate

        This Meeting has Signed a Certificate for **John Howland** to the monthly meeting of **Rhod Island** Certifing his Clearness Respecting maraige & Conversation

Thoˢ Smⁱth
Case

The Referance of Last Monthly Meeting Respecting **Daniel Cornal [Cornell]** and **Thoˢ Smith**, Now Coming under notice and we appoint, **David Sheepherd [Shepherd] Abraham Howland James Davice [Davis] Seth Russell Joseph Barker** to Inquire and here [*sic*] and Determine between them in behalf of this meeting & Report to next Mᵒ Meeting

Wm Mathews
visited
this
meeting

        Our friend **William Mathews** hath Visited this meeting with his Certificate from the Monthly Meeting of **Worrington [Warrington]** in theCounty of **York** in **Pennsilvania** Dated the fifth month last, Whose labour and Service in the Truth is well Accepted[13] Likewise our friend **John Willis** hath Visited us with a few Lines of Concur[r]ence from the yearly Meeting of **Flushing** held the first of the 6mo 1773 whose Visit was Kindly accepted – –

R:B & wives
Certificate

        This Meeting hath Received Removals Certificates form [from] **Rice Baker** and Wife from the Monthly Meeting of **Acoakset** which is Accepted

Meetings
to begin
at the 11
hour
adjourn

        This Meeting hath Concluded for friends to meet at the Eleventh hour in the fore noon at all our meetings for worship Except our yearly Meetings – – this meeting Adjourns to the first Six Day in next month

13. William Mathews (1732-1792), a native of Stafford County, Virginia, lived in York, Pennsylvania.

mett At a Monthly Meeting held according to adjournment
the 2ⁿᵈ day of the 7ᵐᵒ 1773 the Representatives both present

Wᵐ Anthony Juʳ Clerk   **William Anthony jᵘʳ** is Chosen Clerk for this day and untill
Job Russell Shall be able to attend the business

The Committee appointed to Consider about building a meeting

Building Bedford mee[t]ing house referᵈ to Quar meeting answers Epistles & Representa House at **Bedford**, Report that they think it might be well
to build a House there, yet that matter is Referᵈ to the
Quarterly Meeting for further advice, An Epistle to yᵉ Quarterly meeting
was Signᵈ Sent with yᵉ answer to the Queries by our Representatives who are
Thos Hicks Barzillia Tucker Caleb Russell Seth Russell & Nicholas Howland

---

7ᵐᵒ 1773 At a Monthly Meeting held at **Dartmouth** ye 19ᵗʰ yᵉ 7ᵐᵒ 1773
the Representatives are **Wᵐ Mosher & Samuel Smith** present

Luthan Wood proposal of marriage and Ben Sawdy L.W & S. W published **Luthan Wood** and **Susannah Wing** Declearᵈ their Intentions of
marraige, also **Benjamin Sawdy & Hannah Cook** Declerᵈ
Their Intentions of marriage (they having produced their parents
Consent in writing to Satisfaction) and were Desirᵈ to wait till
next monthly meeting for their Answer, And **Prince Allen** and
Joseph Barker are appointed to Inquire into **Luthan Wood**s Clearness
Respecting marraige and Conversation, And **Barzillia Tucker** and
Wᵐ Wood are appointed to Inquire into **Benjᵃ Sawdie**s Clearness Respectⁱⁿᵍ
marriage & Conversation and Report to next mᵒ meeting – –

D Smith in= =formed of his denial **Prince Allen** Informs that he Informᵈ **David Smith** of his Denial
as orderᵈ Last mᵒ meeting

Tho Smiths Case referᵈ The Committee appointed on Account of **Thoˢ Smith & Daniel Cornal**
Report that they han had an opportunity to Discharge themselves
therefore the matter is Referᵈ under their Care and they to make
Report to next monthly meeting – –

Return from Qur meeting The friends appointed to attend the Quarterly Meeting Report that
they all attended Except **Seth Russell** & he hath Renderᵈ an Excuse
which is Accepted, Said friends have Produced an Epistle from
Said Quarterly meeting which hath been Read and kindly Ac-
=cepted and Likewise the **London** Printed Epistle of last year
which hath been Read in this meeting & the moving & whol[e]som[e]
advice therein Earnestly Recommended to the Notice of Each

Received 6 books from yᵉ Q meeting Individual, The Quarterly Meeting hath Sent this meeting Six books
part whereof was wrote by **Ambrose Rigg**, Entitled, a Brief & Serious
warning to Such as are Concerned in Commerce & Tradeing &C¹⁴ [etc.] – –

14. Ambrose Rigge (1634–1704) was an English Friend. His *A Brief and Serious Warning to Such as Are Concerned in Commerce and Trading, Who Go under the Profession of Truth, to Keep within Bounds thereof, in Righteousness, Justice and Honest towards All Men* was first published as a broadside in London in 1678. A new edition was published by Mary Hinde in London in 1771.

The other part being the Advices of Several yearly meetings in **London**, which books are Recommended to friends Perusal – –

Received T. W: Certifi: appeal granted to David Smith Received a Removel Certificate from **Acoakset** Monthly meeting on behalf of **Thos Willcox** Dated ye 7th month 1773 which is Accepted This meeting grants **David Smith** an Appeal to the Quarterly meeting and **Prince Allen** is Appointed to Inform Sd **Smith** thereof

money collected **Caleb Russell** Informs that he hath Collected by way of Subscription according to appointment £45 " 4s " 0 old tennor **Prince Allen** Reports likewise that he hath Collected Sd Subscription as appointed 20£ – 14s – 9d all which they paid into the treasury this meeting Collected 12£ – 3s – 0 old tennor

order on Treasurer The Treasurer is ordered to pay **Joseph Tucker** 1£ – 15s – 0 old tennor for Shewing friends horses

The treasurer is ordered to pay **Timothy Russell** five Dollars for half years ke[e]ping the meeting house

overseer of ye meetinge Land This Meeting appoints **Prince Allen** & **Thomas Hicks** to Oversee the Meeting House & to Inspect the meeting house Lot, in the Room [place] of **John Potter** (who is Dismised) & **Seth Sherman** Deceasd

16th ye 8mo 1773 At a Monthly Meeting held in **Dartmouth** ye 16th ye 8mo 1773 the Representatives are **Thos Hicks** & **Barzillia Tucker** both Present

Lut Wood and Ben Sawdy Clearness The friends appointed to Inquire into **Luthon [Luthan] Wood**s and **Benja Sawdy**s Clearness Respecting marraige & Conversation make Report that they find nothing to hinder their Proceeding

Luthan Wood and Ben Sawdy Answer **Luthon [Luthan] Wood** & **Susanah Wing** appeard at this meeting for their Answer Likewise **Benja Sawdy** and **Hannah Cook** appeared for their Answers whose Answers ware, that Each Couple might Proceed to take Each other in marraige [marriage] in Some Convenient time before next monthly meeting Advising with the Overseers that this meeting Shall appoint for that purpose and **Joseph Barker** & **Prince Allen** are appointed to See **Luthon Wood**s marraig Consomated Orderly and **William Wood** and **Peleg Gifford** is appointed to See **Benja Sawdie**s marriage Consomated orderly and they to make Report to next mo meeting

Tho Smith Case continud The Committee Appointed on Account of **Daniel Cornal [Cornell]** & **Thomas Smith** Report that Sd **Smith** Refuses to make answer thereto until he have a Coppy of the Complaint Exhibeted against him which this meeting grants Provided Sd **Smith** Obligate him= =self that he make no other Use thereof but for his own Defence in the Society, And the afore Sd Committee are Continued in that Service and make Report to next monthly meeting

Treasurer paid out money   The treasurer Reports that he hath paid **Timothy Russell** 5 Dollars as Order^d Likewise **Joseph Tucker** 35/ as order^d

C: Hoag visited this meeting   **Comfort Hoag** hat[h] Visited this meeting with a Certificate from the Monthly Meeting held at **Hamton** in the **Province** of **New – – hamshier** in **New England** baring Date ye 17th ye 6mo 1773 which kindly Accepted – –

The Committee appointed to have the Care of **Abner Russell** Some months past Report that one of them hath had an oppertunity of Conferrence with him and he gave him no Satisfaction on that account, and that he had fallen into the like Disorder again and is Obsconded So as friends hant Opertunity as with him, and *A. Russell Denied* this meeting Apprehending they are Clear hath Signed a paper of Denial against him and the Clerk is Ordered to Read S^d paper at the End of a first Days meeting & Return S^d papere to next monthly meeting

J:Howland Ju Request   **James Howland J^{ur}** Desires to come under the Care of friends therefore we Appoint **Jonathan Hussey Barzillia Tucker** and **John Williams** to take an Oppertunity of Solid Conferrence with him in Order to Discover the motive of his Request and Report to next monthly meeting – –

order to give D:S Coppy of denial   The Clerk is Ordered to gave **David Smith** a Coppy of the minute of his Denial made Against him Agreeable to his Request

This meeting Collected £6 " 0^s " 4^d old tennor

Prince Allen Reports that he Informed **David Smith** that his Appeal is granted

Disorder in Loitering round the meeting house   This meeting Discovers Disorders by People^s Companying Round the meeting house and talking in Companies before meeting and after the time of Day for meeting both for Worship and Disapline – Therefor do appoint our friend **Joseph Tucker Thos Hicks Joseph Barker Prince Allen** & **Wm Anthony J^u** and **Wm Mosher** to Inspect into the above Disorder and Advise as they Shall think proper in that Respect and they to be Continued in that Service one year and then make Report to this meeting

9mo 1773   At a Monthly Meeting held in **Dartmouth** ye 20th ye 9mo 1773 **William Mosher** and **Samuel Smith** appear as Representatives from the Preparative meeting – –

meeting adjourns by request   This meeting Conclud[e]s to adjourn to the 21 Instant by the Request of a Committee which was appointed by the Quarterly meeting to Visct the Monthly Meetings – –

mett   This Meeting being meet by adjournment yᵉ 21 yᵉ 9ᵐᵒ 1773
the Representatives being Called both present – –

Lu Wood   The friends appointed to See **Luthan Wood**s & **Susanah Wing**'s
and
Ben Sawdy   marriage Consomated, Also the friends Appointed to See **Benjᵃ**
marriage   **Sawdie**s [**Sawdys**] & **Hannah Cook**ˢ marriage Consomated All made report
to this meeting that they Discharged themselves according to
appointment on those Accounts and Saw nothing but Sᵈ mar=
=riages was Consomated orderly – –

A: Russel   The Clerk Reports that he hath Read the paper of Denial against
paper   **Abner Russell** as orderᵈ and Returnᵈ Sᵈ paper to this meeting
Read   which is as followeth – –

From our Monthly Meeting of friends held in **Dartmouth**
the 16ᵗʰ Day of yᵉ 8ᵐᵒ 1773 – –

Testimony   Whereas **Abner Russell** having had his Education among
against   friends, But by not giving heed to the grace of God in his
A: Russel   own heart, a Measure whereof is given to Every man to
profit withall, has So far been lead away through the
Stratagems and Tem[p]tations of the Enemy of mans felicity,
as to be Accused and Charged on Oath by **Mary Anthony** of
being the father of her Bastard Child, And friends having
Bestowed Some Labour with him in Order to bring him to a
Sense of his Transgression that he by an Unfeigned Repe=
=ntance might be Restored to the way of truth again but his Conduct
& Behaviour Sense [Since?] Sᵈ Labour was bestowed on him Seams to Demon=
=strate it had not its Desired Effect, Friends therefore thinking they
are Clear from Any further Labour with him think we can do no
less for the Clearing of truth, than to Testify against him & hereby do
Disown the Sᵈ **Abner Russell** from being a member in Unity with our
Society, Nevertheless hoping & desiring that yᵉ Almighty by the Riches of
his grace & mercy may yet bring him to a Sight & Sense of yᵉ Evil of his ways
& by unfeigned Repentance witness his peace to be made with him and
Restored to yᵉ way of truth
          Signed in and on behalf of our Sᵈ meeting by **Wᵐ Anthony Jᵘ** Clerk

James   The friends Appointed to take an Opportunity of Solid Conferrance
Howlanᵈ   with **James Howland junor** Report that they have had Some Confer[ence]
Case referd   with him and he gave them Some Satisfaction and Sᵈ **Howland**
is now gone to See [Sea?] and the matter is Referᵈ under the Care of Said
Committee and they to make Report as Soon as the[y] Can with Conve=
=n[i]ency – –

D Smith Recᵈ   The Clerke Reports that he gave **David Smith** a Coppy of the
a Coppy of   minute of his Denial as orderᵈ – –
miniut.

The Case of Thom Smith Continued   The Committee appointed on Account of **Daniel Cornal [Cornell]** & **Thomas Smith**, Reports that they are not Ready to make full Return of their Appointment therefore the matter is Referd under their Care, and Said Committee Desire Some addition therefore this meeting adds **Giles Slocum Wm Wood Barzillia Tucker** and **Joseph Howland** to the afore S^d Committee and they to make Report to the next monthly meeting – –

money Collected   **Gideon Howland** Reports that he hath Collected 29^£ " 7^s " 6^d O-Tenno^r by way of Subscription as appointed Some months past and has ^paid Said money into the Treasurer – –

Represent^a to the Q meeting   The Queries were read in this meeting and Answers thereto prepar^d, Likewise an Epistle prepar^d and Signed by the Clerk for the Quarterly meeting and Ordered forward to Said Quarterly by the Representatives, who are **Caleb Russell Barzillia Tucker William Anthony J^u Wm Barker Prince Allen** and **Samuel Smith** and they to make Report to next m° meeting

appointing overseers Refer^d   The appointing Overseers both of the meeting & of the Poor is Refer^d to next monthly meeting

---

10mo 1773   At a Monthly Meeting held in **Dartmouth** 18th 10mo 1773 **Jonathan Hussey** & **Thos Hicks** Appears as Representatives from the Preparative meeting – –

overseers for yearly meeting   This meeting thinks proper to Appoint Some friends to have the Care and Oversite of the Lofts & Other Seats at our Ensuing yearly meeting to Prevent Indecencies among the youth & others and therefor Do Appoint our friends **Wm Barker Wm Sandford Jon^a Hussey Joseph Raker Thos Hicks Samuel Smith Wm Anthony J^ur Abraham Howland** and **Benj^a Chase** for that purpose and they to make Report to the next monthly meeting – –

adjourn   This Meeting adjourns to the 25th Instant after ye meeting for worship which is to begin at ye Eleventh hour – –

mett   This Meeting meet by Adjournment ye 25th ye 10mo 1773 – – the Representatives are **Jonathan Hussey** and **Thos Hicks** present

Tho Smith Case Referd   The Committee appointed on account of **Daniel Cornal [Cornell]** and **Thomas Smith** Reports that they are not ready to make Return therefore the matter is Refer,d under their Care and they to make [report?] to next monthly meeting – –

Epistle Received from ye Q. meet   The Representatives to the Quarterly meeting being Called upon Report that they all attended S^d meeting and Produced An Epistle from the Same which was read in this meeting & Kindly Excepted – –

Overseers in the Society This Meeting appoints our friends **Thos Hicks Wm Mosher William Anthony Ju Benja Howland 2nd James Davice [Davis]** as Overseers in the Society for the year Insewing

Overseers of ye Poor This Meeting appoints our friends **Joseph Barker Caleb Russell Barzillia Tucker Abraham Howland David Shepherd John Williams** & **Gideon Howland** Overseers of the Poor for the year Ensuing – –

The friends Appointed to have the Oversight of ye meeting at **Bedford** made Report that they generally Attend Sd meeting which was kept in a Good Degree Orderly And Sd friends at

meeting at Bedford Still Requested **Bedford** Still Requests to hold their meeting on first Days & week Days as Uusal [Usual] untill ye monthly meeting in ye 3d mo next, which is granted and **David Shepherd** & **James Davis** Are Appointed to have the Oversight of Sd meeting & make Report at ye Expiration thereof.

J: Wing Intention of marriage **Jonathan Wing** and **Ann Wood** Decleard their Intentions of marriage and were desired to wait till next mo Meeting for their Answer, The Sd **Wing** having Produced a Certificate from **Acoaksat** Mo Meeting Respecting marriage

This meeting Collected £14-7s-2[d] Old tennore [tenor]

11th mo 1773 At a Monthly Meeting held in **Dartmouth** 15th ye 11mo 1773 the Representatives are **Jonathan Hussey** & **Barzillia Tucker** – –

overseers of yearly meeting Report The friends appointed Last monthly meeting to have the Oversight of the Lofts and Other Seats at our yearly meeting made Report that they all attended Sd meetings ∧Except **J. Barker** & **B. Chase** and Measurable Dischargd themselves in that Respect and that Said meeting was Conducted in Some good Degree orderly on that account

Case of Tho Smith referd The Committee appointed in the Case between **Daniel Cornel [Cornell]** and **Thomas Smith** not being Ready to make report, one of them being Sick, its therefore Refered to next monthly meeting

Transcrips read The Transcrip[t]s Received from the Quarterly meeting in ye 7 month last hath now been Read and the Whol[e]som[e] Advice therein Conta= ined is Earnestly Recommended to friends Obsersvation & notice

B. L & wifs paper **Barker Little** and **Elisabeth** his wife hath given in a paper to this meeting Condemning their falling into the Sin of Fornication therefore we appoint **Prince Allen** and **Philip Allen** and **Jonathan Hussey** to have an Oppertunity of Conferrance with Sd **Little** also to Inquire into his life & Conversation in order to Discover his Sincerity and make report to next monthly meeting

Complaint against Ebenezer Mosher This Meeting is Informed from the Preparative meeting that **Ebenezer Mosher** Neglects attending our meetings for which Disorder he hath been labour^d with and gave no Satisfaction on that Account and Desires to be Disowned by friends, And we appoint **Abraham Tucker** & **Joseph Tucker** to have the Care of that matter and Labour as they may find freedom & make Report to next m^o meeting – –

Complaint against R: Peckha^m This Meeting is Inform^d that **Richard Peckham** hath Married his first Cousen & Married out of the Unity of friends and his wife hath had a Child Soon after Marriage and he hath been Labour^d with and Declines making Satisfaction and we appoint **Joseph Gifford David Sheaphard** [Shepherd] and **John Williams** to have the Care of y^t [that] matter and Report to next monthly meeting – –

W: Brigg Certificate Return^d **Wesson Briggs** and family hath Return^d their Certificate to this meeting Dated y^e 12mo 1770 which this meeting Accepts

J. Wing Receiv^d his answer **Jonathan Wing** and **Anna Wood** appear^d for their Answer which was that they might Proceed to take Each other in Marriage in Some Convenient time before next m^o meeting Advising with the Overseers that this meeting Shall app= =oint for that purpose, and **John Potter** and **William Mosher** are appointed to See their marriage Consomated in good order and make Report to next Monthly Meeting – –

This meeting Collected the Sum of £8-4^s-4^d old tennor [tenor]

meetings begin at y^e 12 hour This Meeting Concludes that all our meetings for Worship only (Except at **Bedford**) begin at the twelfth hour

---

12 mo 1773 At a Monthly Meeting held in **Dartmouth** 20th ye 12mo 1773 the Representatives are **Prince Allen** and **Samuel Smith** present

Case of Barker Little refer^d The Committee Appointed Last monthly meeting to confer with **Barker Little** in order to Discover his Sincerity Report that they think proper to wait a while Longer before we Accept his paper therefore the matter is Refer^d under the Same friends Care as heretofore and they to make report to next m^o meeting

overseers of yearly meeting report **Joseph Barker** and **Benjamin Chase** makes report that they attended the yearly Meeting According to Appointment and Saw nothing but what was in tolerable good order and they have both Render^d an Excuse for their not Reporting to Last monthly meeting which is Accepted

Tho Smith Case referd The Committee Appointed on Account of **Daniel Cornal** [Cornell] and **Thos Smith** Inform that they are not Ready to make Report

therefore the matter is Refer^d one month longer under their
Care and then they make Report

The friends Appointed to treat with **Ebenezer Mosher** report
that they have Discharg^d themselves on that account and
he gave them no Satisfaction and this meeting Apprehending
they have fully Discharged themselves therefore his Request is
granted and we do hereby Disown him the S^d **Ebenezer Mosher**
from being a member of our Society and **Abraham Tucker** is
appointed to Inform him of his Denial

E: Mosher Denied

The friends Appointed to have the Care of that matter Respecting
Richard Peckham Report that they have had an Oppertunity
with him and he Declines Condemning his Disorders to friends
Satisfaction, and the Same friends are Appointed to Draw a paper
of Denial against him and to Shew [Show] him the Same and labour
with him as they may find freedom and make Report to next
monthly meeting – –

friends to Draw a paper of Denial against R=Peckham

The friends Appointed to See **Jonathan Wing**s and **Anne Wood**s
marriage Consomated Report that they Attended S^d marriage and
Saw nothing but what it was Consomated in good Order – –

J: W & A. W marriage Consomated

William Russell hath given in a paper to this meeting Condemning
his marr[y]ing out of the Unity of friends and we Appoint **Samuel
Smith** and **Abraham Howland** to have an Oppertunity of Conferrance
with him in order to Discover his Sencerity on that Account and
make Report to next monthly meeting – –

W. Rusell gave in a paper

This meeting is Inform^d that **Frances [Francis] Allen** and his Son
Thomas hath taken the Oath in form before a Majestrate [Magistrate]
they having been labour^d with on that account and S^d **Frances** hath
Appeared in this meeting & Condemned the S^d Offence and Also
his two much Neglect in Attending meeting, which Seems to be
Some Degree of Satisfaction, but it being the mind of his meeting
that S^d Offence ought to be Condemned Publeckly therefore
this meeting do Appoint our friends **Barzillia Tucker** and
John Williams to assist the S^d **Frances** and to labour with
his Son as they may find freedom & make Report to next mo
meeting   this meeting Collected 9^£–5^s–6^d old theror [tenor] – –

Complainst Francis Allen and Son Thos

This meeting Adjourns to the last forth day in this month
after the meeting for worship which begins at ye 11th hour

meeting Adjourn^d

This meeting being meet by Adjournment ye 29th ye 12mo 1773
the Representatives are **Prince Allen** & **Samull [Samuel] Smith** present
The Queries were read in this meeting and Answers thereto

mett

prepair^d and an Epistle read and Singed [Signed] for the Quarterly
meeting and order^d forwar^d by our Representatives who are

Representa
to ye Q meeting

**Prince Allen William Anthony J^u William Wood Nicholass
Howland** and **Thomas Hicks** and they to make Report to next
monthly meeting – –

The young Couple that Appear^d at this meeting ~~for their~~
to Lay their Intentions of marriage being Consid[e]red and friends
not being Unanim[o]us in let[t]ing them pass by reason of their
being So nigh in kind therefore S^d matter is Refer^d to next
monthly meeting – –

R. Smith
under
Dealing

This meeting being Inform^d from the Preparative meeting
that **Ruben Smith** hath been and Contracted marriage
with a young woman not of our Society that belong^d
to a Distant Land and brought her home with him
wherein his Conduct Appears Very Disagre[e]able to friends
principals and he being Labour^d with by one of the
Overseers and not giving Satisfaction for S^d misconduct
therefore we do appoint **Prince Allen** & **Jonathan Hussey**
to have the Care of that matter and Labour with him
as they may find freedom & make Report when they
have Discharged themselves

order on
Treasurer

The treasurer is Ordered to pay **Timothy Russell** 5 Dollars
for half a years keeping the Meeting house and make
Report to next m^o meeting

1mo 1774

At a Monthly Meeting held in **Dartmouth** 17th ye 1mo 1774
the Representatives are **Wm Barker** & **Jonathan Hussey** present

Bark Little
case refer^d

The friends appointed to have the Care of that matter Respecting
Barker Little, Report that they are not fully Satisfyed in
that matter therefore S^d matter is Refer^d Under their Care one
month Longer and then they to make Report – –
all but one of the Committee Appointed in that Care between
Daniel Cornal [Cornell] & **Thos Smith** Report that Said **Smith** Ought
Publickly to Condemn his Reporting that **Daniel Cornel** was
a fals[e] man, which Report being Ac[c]epted & is as followeth
Agreeable to the Appointment of the monthly meeting we have

Report of
ye Committee
Respecting
D.C & T.S

heard the matter Depending Between **Daniel Cornal** & **Thomas
Smith** Respecting S^d **Smith**s Accusing S^d **Cornal** of Being a fals[e]
man and that he could prove it – –
We having hear^d Each parties pleas & Allegations Respecting
Said affair and it is our Judgment that the affore S^d

Accusation of **Thomas Smith** against **Daniel Cornal** is with
out Sufficient grounds – And that therefore S^d **Smith** Ought
publickly to Condemn his Accusing S^d **Cornall** of Being a
fals[e] man – –
given forth and Dated
this 27 Day ye 12 ^mo 1773   **Joseph Barker　Giles Slocum**
                    Seth Russell　Wm Wood
                 Joseph Howland　Abraham Howland
                 James Davis　Barzillia Tucker

Tho Smith offender Therefore Said **Thomas Smith** is now looked upon as an
offender therefore we do Appoint our friends **Abraham Tucker**
Wm Sandford Joseph Tucker & **John Williams** to Labour
with him in order that he may Condemn his Disorder
and they to make Report to next m^o meeting

*Testimony against Richard Peckam is Recorded in page 305 The friends Appointed to have the Care of that matter Respecting
Richard Peckham Report that they Discharg^d themselves on
that Account and they have Draughted a paper of Denial *
against S^d **Peckham** which was Signed by the Clerk & the
Clerk is order^d to Read S^d paper at ye Close of a first Days meeting
for worship before next monthly meeting & then make Report *

Eben Mosher Case **Abraham Tucker** Informs that he Desires to be Continued one
month Longer in Discharging himself with **Ebenezer Mosher**
as appointed – –

Wm Russel give in a paper The friends Appointed to take an Oppertunity with **Wm Russell**
Report that he gave them a Degree of Satisfaction yet the
Receiving his paper is Refer^d to next Monthly Meeting

Frac Allen & Son Tho give in a paper **Francis Allen** & his Son **Thomas** hath given in a paper to this
meeting Condemning their taking the oath in form, which is Accepted
provided they Cause S^d paper to be Read publickly at the Close of a
first Days meeting before next monthly meeting & Return S^d paper
and Report of its being Read – –

Representa Report The friends Appointed to attend the Quarterly Meeting Report
that they all Attended Except **Thos Hicks,** and he Sent his Excuse
which was Accepted – And they have Produced an Epistle
from S^d Quarterly meeting which hath been Read and the
Moving and Salutary advice therein Earnestly Recommended to
friends Notice & Observation – –

Tim Russel paid The treasurer reports that he hath paid **Timothy Russell** 5 Dollars
as order^d – –

G. H. & C. S. Published **Gideon Howland** and **Catheren [Catherine] Slocum** appear^d in this meeting
in order to Lay their Intentions of taking Each other in marriage

and the matter of their being nigh in kind hath been weightely
Consid[e]re^d and the Circumstances Relating thereto, And as they have
So far Contracted in that Relation before our yearly meeting minutes
of 1772 was made in Regard to marriage of nigh in kind, And
they were Ignorant / as they Say that it was Conterary to the order of
friends when they So Contracted and that they Cannot now willingly
Desist therefore this meeting doth permitt them to pass tho it is
not fully Satisfactory to this meeting neither is it me[a]nt to be a presedent [precedent]
but is at this time Suffer^d for the Reasons aforeS^d therefore

Gideon How =land 2ᵈ proposal of marriage **Gideon Howland** ² and **Catherin Slocum** Declar^d their Intentions
of taking Each other in marriage and were Desir^d to wait till
next monthly meeting for their Answer and **Benjamin Slocum**
and **William Barker** are appointed to Enquire into the young mans
Clearness respecting marriage and Conversation & Report to next
monthly meeting

E. Russel Complaind of **Deliverance Smith** hath Exhibeted a Complaint against **Elijah**
Russell for Refusing to Submit a Controvercy to men, therefore
we do Appoint **William Barker** and **Prince Allen** to labour
with him as they may find freedom & Report to next monthly meeting
The Committee Appointed to Viset those friends that possess
Slaves made Report to this meeting which is Accepted and is
as followeth – – We the Subscribers Persuant to Appointment
of the monthly meeting have Again Viseted those friends
that Possess Slaves and Labour^d with them to do Justice to their
fellow Creatures, by Disc[h]arging them from a State of bondage
and Slavery, And **William Sandford** hath Accordingly freed his
Negro. **Joseph Russell** yet Refusses to Comply with our advice
Peleg Slocum Keeps his Negroes yet in bondage, but Saith that
he Shall free them at the age of 26 years, they Providing afterwar^d
and Laying up a Certain Sum yearly to Secure his Estate,
John Russell thath one that is under age that is now in a

Report of yᵉ Committee about Negroes masters State of Slavery, but he gave Encourag[e]ment he Should free her at
a Suitable age & **Isaac Howland** hath given Good Encouragement
to free his Negro – –
Given forth by your Committee this 17th yᵉ 1ᵐᵒ 1774

> **Benjᵃ Howland 2ⁿᵈ**
> **Barzillia [Barzillai] Tucker**
> **Samull [Samuel] Smith**
> **James Davis**

advice to
Negro masters
And those friends mentioned in the above Said Report that
Continue Slaves in bondage are Desir^d to Comply with the
tenth Query in that case and if not they may Expect to be
Disown[e]d, and we appoint our friends **Joseph Gifford William
Sandford William Anthony j^u** and **Joseph Tucker ju^r** to let them
know the mind of this meeting & make report to next m^o meeting
This meeting Collected 8£ " 16^s " o Old tennor [tenor]

2mo 1774
At a Monthly Meeting held in **Dartmouth** 21st ye 2mo 1774
the Representatives are **William Mosher** & **Samuel Smith** both present

Barker
Little
Case refer^d
the friends that had the Care of that matter Respecting **Barker
Little** Report that they are not fully Satis[f]ied to Receive his
paper yet therefore they are Still Continued in that Service
and to make Report to next monthly meeting

R. Peckh
paper Read
The Clerk Reports that he hath Read the paper of Denial against
Richard Peckham as order^d

Wm Russell
case refer^d
The Receiving of **Wm Russell** paper is Refered one month
Longer in order to Discover his Sincerety & **Samu[e]l Smith** and **William
Anthony j^{ur}** are Appointed to have the Care of that
matter and make Report to next monthly meeting – –

Tho Smith
disowned
The Committee appointed to Labour with **Thomas Smith**
Report that he gave them no Incouragment of Condemning
his Disorder agre[e]able to the Judgment of this meeting
therefore we do hereby Disown the Said **Thos Smith** from
being a member of this meeting, and we do Appoint our
friends **Thomas Hicks** & **Prince Allen** to Draught [Draft] a paper
of Denial against S^d **Thos Smith** and bring it next m^o meeting
and likewise Inform S^d **Smith** of his Denial & his Right of appeal
and Report to next monthly meeting

Eben Mosher
inform^d
of denial
Abraham Tucker Reports that he fully answer^d his Appointment by Informing **Ebenezer Mosher** of his Denial

Francis
Allen &
Thos Case
referd
Frances [Francis] Allen & **Thomas Allen** made no Report of their paper
being Read as order^d therefore the matter is Refer^d one month
Longer and **James Davice [Davis]** is appointed to Inform them of their
Neglect on that Account and to Inform them that the meeting
Expects them to make Report as order^d last m^o meeting

G: H & C. S:
not to have
their answer
Sent to ye Q: mee
for Advice
This Meeting not being Unanimo[u]s in let[t]ing **Gideon Howland** and
Catherin Slocum have their Answer by reason of their being nigh
in kind therefore we Conclude to Send the matter to the Quarterly
meeting for advice – –

E: R. Submits Controvercy to men The Committee appointed to labour with **Elijah Russell** Reports that he Concludes to leave S^d Controvercy to men and S^d Committee are Continued to See that it is Completed, and make Report to next monthly meeting

Com^t on Slaves Continued The Committee appointed to Labour with those friends that possess Slaves Desire to be Continued one month longer and thos[e] friends are looked upon as offenders that hath not Compli[e]d with ye tenth Query This meeting Collected 9^£ " 1^s " o old tennor

3 ^mo 1774 At a Monthly Meeting held in **Dartmouth** 21st 3mo 1774

The Representatives are **Wm Sandford** & **Benj^a Howland** 2nd present

The matters Respecting **Barker Little** & **William Russell** is Refer^d one month Longer under the Same friends Care as heretofore in order to Discover their Sencerity – –

*T: Smith Denied *Testimony Recorded in page 299* The Committee Appointed to Draw a paper of Denial against **Thomas Smith** and Inform him of his Denial & Right of appeal Report that they Discharg^d themselves according to their appointment and this meeting hath Signed a paper* of Denial against **Thos Smith** and the Reading S^d paper publickly is Refer^d by Reason

Thos Smith Appeal S^d **Smith** Requests an appeal to the Quarterly meeting, which this meeting grants, and **Thos Hicks** is appointed to Inform him that we grant him an Appeal to S^d Quarterly meeting and Report to next m^o meeting

James Davis Reports that he Inform^d **Franiecs [Francis] Allen** as order^d and they have not made Report at this meeting therefore the matter is Refer^d one month longer under the Care of **James Davis** and then he to make report

The matter Respecting **Elijah Russell** being not fully Set[t]le^d therefore it is Refer^d as heretofore and the Committee to make Report when Ready – –

the matter Respecting those friends that Possess slaves is Refer^d one month longer under the Care of the Same friends as heretofore and then they to make Report – –

4th Day meeting Discontinued This Meeting Concludes to Discontinue the meeting that was held on the fourth day Preceeding **Sandwich** yearly meeting when it happeneth in the Same week with the monthly meeting

meeting begin at ye 11 hour This meeting Concludes that all our meetings for Worship begin at the Eleventh hour

this meeting Collected 5^£ " 8^s " 0^d – –

adjourn This meeting adjourns to the first Six Day in next m^o after the meeting for Worship – –

mett This Meeting meet by Adjournment y{e} 1{st} Day y{e} 4{mo} 1774
the Representatives being Called both Present
The friends appointed to have the Oversight of that meeting
at **Bedfor**{d} made Report that they generally Attended
S{d} meeting And that it was kept up in Some good Degree
Orderly, And the friends at **Bedford** Still Request to hold
a meeting for worship there which this meeting grants as followeth

meeting at Bedford Still Continued Said meetings to be held on Every first Day of the week
and on Every Sixth day of the week, Except in those weeks
that our Monthly meeting Preparative & youths meetings
are and to Continue till the third month next, and
David Sheepherd [Shepherd] and **James Davice [Davis]** are Appointed to have
the Care and Oversight of S{d} meeting & make Report at the
Expiration thereof

J: Chase Requests Certificate **Jacob Chase** Requests a Removal Certificate for him Self and
Children to the Monthly Meeting of **Acoakset**, and we do appoint
Barzillia Tucker & **Barnabus [Barnabas] Mosher** to make the Necessary Inquiry
in that matter and Draw one for him if the[y] think proper and
bring it next monthly meeting

Charles Russel paper **Charles Russell** hath given a paper to this meeting Condemning
his falling into the Sin of fornication therefore we appoint
Samu{ll} [Samuel] Smith & **Prince Allen** to have the care of that matter
in order to Discover his Sencerity and Report to next m{o} meeting

Ephraim Trip paper **Ephrim [Ephraim] Tripp** hath given in paper to this meeting Condemning
Some misconduct of his therefore we appoint **Barzillia Tucker**
and **Prince Allen** to have the Care of that matter in Regard
to the young mans Cencerity [Sincerity] in that matter & Report to next
monthly meeting

Gideon Gifford paper **Gideon Gifford** hath given in a paper to this meeting Condemning
his marr[y]ing out of the Unity of friends and we Appoint our friends
Abraham Tucker & **Joseph Tucker** to take an Oppertunity of
Solid Conferrance with him in order to Discover his Sencerity
and Report to next monthly meeting – –

J: Allen Requests Advice **Jedediah Allen** Informs that he hath thoughts of Sel[l]ing and
Removing from hence and Desires the Advice of this meeting
and we do Appoint our friends **Prince Allen** & **Nicholass Howland**
to Advise with him as they may think proper
The Queries were Read & Answers thereto prepar{d} and an Epistle
to the Quarterly meeting was Read & Sign{d} by the Clerk and
Sent with S{d} Answers to the Quarterly meeting by our Representa={tives}

Representaˢ to the Quarterly meeting — who are **Jonathan Hussey Barzillia Tucker Wᵐ Anthony jᵘʳ Thoˢ Hicks Wᵐ Sandford & Prince Allen** and they to make to next mᵒ meeting

To review Miniuts — **Samuel Smith Thoˢ Hicks Prince Allen & Wᵐ Anthony jᵘʳ** are appointed to Review & Correct the monthly meeting minutes in order that they may goe to Record and make Report to next mᵒ meeting

---

4ᵗʰ mo 1774 — At a Monthly Meeting held in **Dartmouth** yᵉ 18ᵗʰ yᵉ 4ᵗʰ ᵐᵒ 1774 the Representatives are **Thomas Hicks & Samuel Smith** both Present

Bar Little and Wm Russell case referᵈ — The matters Respecting **Barker Little & Wᵐ Russell** is Refered one month longer under the Same friends as heretofore in order to Discover their Cincerity & also to See if they dyly [duly] attend meetings and then they to make Report – –

Tho Smith Informed — **Thomas Hicks** Reports that he Informed **Thoˢ Smith** as orderd last monthly meeting

F:Allen & Tho Allen paper returnᵈ — **Francis Allen** made Report of his paper & his Son **Tho**ˢᵉˢ being Read and is Returnᵈ

[middle third of page is blank]

Respecting Slaves — The matter Respecting those friends that Possess Slaves is Referᵈ one month Longer under the Same friends care as heretofore

Jacob Chase Certificate — This meeting hath Signed a Removal Certificate for **Jacob Chase** and Children to the monthly meeting of **Acoakset**

Charles Russell case referd — The matter Respecting **Charles Russell** is Referᵈ to next mᵒ meeting under the care of the Same friends ‸as before they not having Discharged themselves ~~care,~~ for a further proof of his [?] and they to make Report to next mᵒ meeting

Eph Tripp case referd — The matter of Receiving **Ephrim [Ephraim] Tripp**s paper is also Referᵈ to next mᵒ meeting under the care of the Same friends for a further proof of his Sincerity and they to make a Report to Sᵈ meeting

Gid: Gifford case referd — The friends appointed to Confer with **Gideon Gifford** Report that he gave them Some Degree of Satisfaction but the Receiving his paper is Referᵈ to next monthly meeting under the Same friends as heretofore & then they to make Report

Representa tives Report from Q: meeting — the friends Appointed to attend the Quarterly meeting, Report that all attended Except **Jonathan Hussey** & he Sent his Excuse for his not Attending which was Accepted, And they have produced an Eppistle from Sᵈ meeting which was Read & well accepted and the Salutary advice therein Carefully observed and Rec= commended to Each Individual

minutes Corected The friends appointed to Revise and Correct this meetings minutes in order to goe on Record Report, they have fullfilled their Appointment and left them with **Wm Anthony J^u** to goe on Record

Clerk appointed This Meeting Appoints our friend **William Anthony J^u** Clerk of this meeting in the Room of our Esteemed friend **Job Russell** Deceas^d, And we do hereby Rattify and Confirm what S^d **Anthony** hath done as Clerk Since the Deceas[e] of S^d **Job Russell**

P: Rusell Complain^d of The Overseers have Inform^d that **Paul Russell** hath been guilty of Abusive behaviour in the night Season at **Roger Mosher**s also a being with an Unbecoming Company at **Prince Potter**s and S^d Overseers have Laboured with him for Said misconduct and he hath given in a paper Condemning the Same and we do appoint our friends **Abraham Tucker Joseph Tucker Joseph Barker** & **Jonathan Hussey** to have the care of that matter and make Report to the next monthly meeting

friends Remov^d Whereas there hath Divers friends Removed and about to Remo^{ve} within the Compass of the **Nine=partners** monthly meeting (Namely **Jonathan Smith** and **Phebe** his wife **Benj^a Russell** famely [family] **Stephen Smith** & Children **David Anthony** & famely, and it appearing Necessary that they have Certificates therefore we do Appoint our friends **Jonathan Hussey Prince Allen Samu[e]l Smith William Anthony J^u Thos Hicks** to Join the women & make the Necessary Inquiry on that account and Draw Certificates if they find things Clear and bring them to next m^o meeting

D. Cornel wants advice **Daniel Cornal [Cornell]** Informs that he Desires Some Advice in Regard to his Selling & Removing from home, And we do appoint our friends **Thomas Hicks William Sandford** and **Joseph Gifford** for that purpose

To Settle with Treasurer We appoint **Prince Allen** & **William Anthony J^u** to Settle Accounts with the Treasurer & also with **Thos Smith** in behalf of this meeting & Report to next monthly meeting, they are also to Receive & Examine all accounts that Sands [Stands?] against this meeting and bring the Sum total to nex^t monthly meeting
This meeting hath Collected ten pounds four Shillings & 7^d old tennor [tenor]

5 mo 1774 At a Monthly Meeting held in **Dartmouth** ye 16th ye 5mo 1774 the Representatives are **Thos Hicks** & **Samuel Smith** both present

Case of Bar Little and Wm Russell refer^d The matters Respecting **Barker Little** & **William Russell** is Refer^d to next monthly meeting under the Same friends care as heretofore and then they to make Report – –

Pero manimitted — **Isaac Howland 2ⁿᵈ** hath Signed a bill of Manimission]Manumission] for his Negro man **Pero** and Deliverᵈ to this meeting which this meeting accepts

Concerning Pel: Slocum and John Russel Slaves and J Russell — The matters Respecting **Peleg Slocum** & **John Russell** in Regard their freeing their Slaves is Referᵈ by reason of Some Incouragment of Comply[ing] one month Longer under the Same friends case as heretofore – – and also the matter Respecting **Joseph Russell** in regard to his holding his Negro in Bondage is Referᵈ by the Request of his Son & **Abraham Tucker** & **John Potter** and they to make Report ~~to next mo meeting~~ when Said Russell Returns home from his Journey

Case of Cha Russel referᵈ — The matter Respecting **Charles Russell** is Referᵈ under the Care of the Same friends as heretofore and they to make report ~~next mo meeting~~ when Ready as Sᵈ **Russell** is gone from home – –

Eph Tripp Gid Gifford And Paul Russel Cases referd — The matters Respecting Receiving **Ephrim [Ephraim] Tripp**ˢ & **Gideon Gifford** paper is Referᵈ one month longer under the Same friends care as heretofore and then they to make Report
The matter Respecting **Paul Russell** paper is Referᵈ one month longer under the Same friends care as heretofore 5 month

Certificates Signᵈ J. Smith D. Anthony Wife & childreⁿ — This meeting hath Signᵈ Certificates for **Jonathan Smith** & Wife and **David Anthony** & Wife & Children to the Monthly meeting of the **Nine=Partners** – –

Prince [Allen] & **William Anthony Jᵘ** made Report to this meeting as followeth which is Accepted
According to Appointment we have Set[t]led Accoumpts [Accounts] with the Treasurer and Remain in the Stock- – – – – – – – – £8 " 0ˢ " 0ᵈ old tennʳ
Due to **Benjᵃ Allen** – – –   11 " 14 " 4 £ mo

Settlement of Accoumpts — Due to **Benjᵃ Smith Jᵘʳ** for keeping **Alice Smith** from the 25ᵗʰ yᵉ 10 ᵐᵒ 1773 to the 4ᵗʰ yᵉ 4 ᵐᵒ 1774 – – – } 5 – 7 – 4 £ mo
Due to **Thomas Hicks** for Repa[i]ring meeting house   3 – 3 –11 £ mo
Due to **Timothy Russell** – – – – – – – – – – – – 0 – 4 – 0
and also we have Set[t]led with **Thoˢ Smith**   20 – 9 – 7 £ mo
and paid him in full of all his Demands
Dartmouth the 16ᵗʰ yᵉ 5ᵐᵒ 1774   [fr?]

                         William Anthony Jᵘ
                         Prince Allen

a few Lines Jonthan Hussey — This meeting Signed a few lines for **Jonathan Hussey** by way of Certificate to the **Oblong** & **Nine partners** as he is abought [about] to travel to them parts

To draw Certiᵗᵉ for Ben Russel & Stephen Smith — We Continue the Same friends as heretofore to Draw Certificates for **Benjᵃ Russell** & **Stephen Smith** and their Children and make Report when Ready – –

This meeting Collected　　　　　　　　　　£12　11 – 4 O:T.

order on Treasurer The Treasurer is Order^d to pay **Benj^a Allen**　　£20 old tennor [tenor]
and Report to next m^o meeting

6th mo 1774 At a Monthly Meeting held in **Dartmouth** ye 20th ye 6mo 1774
the Representatives are **Jonathan Hussey** & **Prince Allen**
both present

Barker Little and Wm Russel case refer^d The matter Respecting **Barker Little** and **William Russell** is
refer^d to next monthly meeting for further Consideration under
the Care of the Same friends as heretofore

Ephra Tripp case referd The matter in Regard to **Ephrim [Ephraim] Tripp** is Refer^d to next monthly
meeting for further proof of this Sincerity under the care of **Prince
Allen** & **Barzillia Tucker** and then they to make Report

Gid Gifford case refer^d Likewise the Case of **Gideon Gifford** is Refer^d to next monthly
meeting under the care of **Joseph Tucker** & **Abraham Tucker**
and then they to make report

Case of John Russell & Peleg Slocum freeing Negros referd The matters Respecting **John Russell** & **Peleg Slocum** in regard
to their freeing their Negroes is Refer^d one month Longer under
the care of **Joseph Gifford William Sandford** and **Samuel Smith** by
reason of Incouragment of Compliance and then they to make Report

Ben Allen paid the treasurer reports he hath paid **Benj^a Allen** the money as ordered
last m^o meeting

R: Walker viset Our friend **Robert Walker** hath Visited this meeting with a
Certificate from the monthly meeting of **Brighouse** in the
County of **York**, Dated the 19th y^e 3mo 1773 also one from y^e Quarterly meeting
held at **york** the 24th & 25th y^e 3mo 1773 with a Concur[r]ing one from
the yearly meeting of ministers & Elders held in **London** from
the 29th y^e 5mo to the 7th of y^e 6mo 1773 all which were read to Satis=
faction and his Viset Kind accepted – –

Case of Paul Russel referd The matter in Regard to **Paul Russell** is Refer^d to next monthly meeting
under the care of the Same friends as heretofore for a further proof of
his Sincerity and then they to make Report

H: Smith 2 Requests Certificate **Humphry Smith 2nd** Informs that he is about to Remove with his
fammily to **East Hoosuck**[15] and Desires our Certificate therefore
Joseph Barker Prince Allen & **Samuel Smith** are appointed to make the
Necessary Inquiry and draw one for him if think proper and bring
it to next monthly meeting – –

Micajah Wood paper **Micajah Wood** hath given in a paper Condemning his marrying
out of the Unity of friends & we do appoint our friends **Barzillai
Tucker** & **Wm Mosher** to Confer with him on that Account in order

15. East Hoosick Monthly Meeting was in Berkshire County, Massachusetts.

order to Discover his Sincerity and make Report to next
monthly meeting

E: Robert^{son} Viset — Our friend **Elisabeth Robinson** hath Viseted this meeting
with a Certificate from the monthly meeting of **Richmond** in
Yorkshire bearing date yᵉ 4th yᵉ 3ᵐᵒ 1773 with one of Concurrence
from the Quarterly meeting held at **York** yᵉ 24 & 25 of the 3ᵐᵒ 1773
with another of Concurrance from the Yearly meeting of ministers
and Elders held at **London** from yᵉ 29ᵗʰ yᵉ 5ᵐᵒ to the 7ᵗʰ of yᵉ 6ᵗʰ mo
1773 all which were Read to Satisfaction and her Viset and
Testimony well accepted[16] – –

S: Light^{foot} viset — Likewise our friend **Susanah Lightfoot** hath viset us with
her Certificate from the monthly meeting held at **Urchlon [Uwchlan]**
Chester County in **Pensylvania** Dated the 9ᵗʰ of the 6ᵐᵒ 1774
whose Visit was Kindly Accepted[17]

The Queries and Answers thereto were read and an Epistle

Representa: to yᵉ Q: meeting — Sing^d [signed] for the Quarterly meeting and Order^d forward to S^d
meeting by our Representatives who are **Thoˢ Hicks James**
Davice [Davis] Barzillai Tucker Wᵐ Anthony Jᵘ & Joh[n] Williams
and they to make Report to next monthly meeting

2 meetings a Day at Bedford — The friends at **Bedford** Request to hold two meetings for
Worship on first days which is Granted untill the monthly
meeting in the tenth month next, Said meetings to begin
in the forenoon at the 10 hour and in the afternoon at
the 3ʳᵈ hour – –

Giles Slocum give in a paper — **Giles Slocum** hath Given in a paper to this meeting Condem=
=ning his falling into the Reproachfull Sin of fornication
and we appoint our friends **Samuel Smith Joseph Gifford Joseph**
Barker Wᵐ Barker Seth Russell to take an Oppertunity of
Conference with Said **Slo[c]um** in order to Discover his Sincerity
and make Report to next monthly meeting

This meeting Collected £12 – 0ˢ – 9ᵈ old tenor

7ᵗʰ mo 1774 — At a Monthly Meeting held in **Dartmouth** yᵉ 18ᵗʰ yᵉ 7ᵐᵒ 1774
the Representatives are **Jonathan Hussey** & **Prince Allen** both present

Case of Wᵐ Russell referd — The matters Respecting **William Russell** is Refer^d one month
Longer under the Care of the Same friends as heretofore & then they
to make Report

16. Elizabeth (Hoyle) Robinson (1729–1804) was a native of Lancashire with a reputation for a formidable presence. See Larson, *Daughters of Light*, 309.

17. Susanna (Hudson) Hatton Lightfoot (1720–1781) traveled widely as a minister. See Larson, *Daughters of Light*, 327.

Case of Bar Little referd	The matter Respecting **Barker Little** is Refer[d] to next m[o] meeting under the care of the Same friends as heretofore and then they to make Report – –
Case of Eph Tripp referd	The matter Respecting **Ephrim [Ephraim] Tripp** is Refer[d] to next monthly meeting under the Care of **Prince Allen** & **Barzillai Tucker John Potter** & **Caleb Russell** and they to Report next monthly meeting
Case of Gid Gifford referd	The matter Respecting **Gideon Gifford** is Refer[d] to next monthly meeting under the care of the Same friends as heretofore and then they to make Report – –
Case of John Russel and Peleg Slocum freeing Negroes referd	The matters Respecting **John Russell** & **Peleg Slocum** freeing their Negroes, not being fully Compleated therefore its Refer[d] to next monthly meeting under the Care of the Same friends as heretofore and then they to make Report
Case of Paul Russel referd	The matter in Regard to **Paul Russell** is Refer[d] to next monthly meeting under the Same friends Care as heretofore and then they to make Report – –
Case of Hum Smith referd	The friends appointed to prepare a Certificate for **Humphry Smith** Report that they hant Compleated S[d] Business therefore they are Still Continued for that purpose and to make Report to next monthly meeting
Case of Micajah Wood referd	The matter Respecting **Micajah Wood** is Refer[d] to next m[o] meeting under the care of the Same friends as before and then they to make report – –
Return from Quarterly meeting	The friends appointed to attend the Quarterly meeting Report that all attended and have Produced an Epistle from the Same which was Read & well Accepted – –
London Epistle	The **London** Printed Epistle of Last year was read in this meeting and as it Contains much Good Advice & Instruction Pertinant to the Present times it is order[d] to be Publickly Read at the close of our meeting for worship – –
Transcip yearly meeting Epistle	A Transcrip[t] of our Last yearly meeting Epistle was Read and Kindly Accepted S[d] Transcrip[t] Informs the yearly meeting
David & Thomas Smiths Case	Confirm[d] the Judgment of the Quarterly meeting against **David** and **Tho[s] Smith** and as to the matter of **Gideon**
Gid Howland marriage not allowed	**Howland** & **Katherine Slocum** marriage, it is Recommended that we Strictly adhear to the Rules of the Society in that Respect
Transcrip of London Written Epistle	A Transcript of the **London** Written Epistle for the Last year was Likewise read in this meeting and the Salutory advice

therein well Received Also a Transcript of the Epistle from

Epistil from Philidel[a] the yearly meeting of **Philidelphia** was read to good Satisfaction

Giles Slocum case referd The matter in Regard to **Giles Slocum** is Refer[d] to next monthly meeting under the care of the Same friends as heretofore and **Jonathan** & **Daniel Cornal [Cornell]** & **Joh [John] Williams** are ad[d]ed to them and they to make Report to next m[o] meeting

Sewel History paid for The Treasurer Reports he hath paid two Dollars it being the Remainder for one of **Sewels** History

Denial to be draw[d] against David Smith We appoint our friend **Samuel Smith** & **Prince Allen** to Inspect the minutes made against **David Smith** and Draught [Draft] a paper of Denial Against him if they think proper when S[d] minutes is inspected and bring it to next monthly meeting

Clement Beedle proposal marriage **Clement Biddle** of **Philidelphia** and **Rebecca Cornal** Declared their Intentions of taking Each other in marriage and were Desir,[d] to wait untill the next monthly meeting for their Answer

D: Conel Requests Certificate **Daniel Cornal** Desire[d] a Removal Certificate for him Self and Children under age ˄to the m[o] meeting of the **Ninepartner** therefore we appoint **Thos Hicks** and **William Anthomy Jur** to make the necessary and to Draw one for him if they think proper and bring it to next monthly meeting

This meeting hath Concluded to come to a Subscription

Subscription to Raise money being in Debt nearly to the amount of twenty five pounds Lawfull money, and our friends **Caleb Russell Prince Allen William Wood Abraham Howland** & **Benj[a] Slocum** are appointed to Receive & to pay the Same into the treasury of this meeting and make Report of their Doings with the Sum total as Soon as they Convenient can

This meeting hath Collected £13"1s"3d old tennor

Three books Receiv,d This meeting hath Received three Books of **Robert Barkley [Barclay]** & **William Penn**s works from our yearly meeting which is for the Use of friends in General

8th mo 1774 At a Monthly Meeting held in **Dartmouth** 15th the 8 [mo] 1774 the Representatives are **Prince Allen** & **Tho[s] Hicks** present

Wm Russell case referd The matter Respecting **William Russell** is Refer,[d] to next monthly meeting under the care of the Same friends as here-tofore, and they are Desir,[d] to Inform him that friends are not willing to Receiv his paper by reason of his Slackness of attending meetings

B Little
case referd

The matter Respecting **Barker Little** is Refer,d to next
mo meeting under the Care of **Jonathan Hussey** & **Seth Russell**
and then they make Report – –

Ephraim Tripp
Case refer,d

The matter Respecting **Ephrim Tripp** is Refer,d to
next monthly meeting under the Same friends care as heretofore and then to make Report – –

Gideon
Gifford's
case refer,d

The friends that had the Care of that matter in regard to
Gideon Gifford Desire the matter Refer,d one month longer
therefore s^d matter is Refer,^d under s^d friends and then they to
make Report

John Russell &
Peleg Slocum
Case referd

The matter in Regard to **John Russell** & **Peleg Slocum** freeing
their Negroes not being yet fully Compleated therefore s^d
matter is Refer,^d one month Longer under the Same friends
Care as heretofore and then they to make report

H. Smith
Certificate

This meeting hath Signed Removal Certificate for
Humphry Smith 2nd his Wife and Children to the monthly
meeting at the **Ninepartners**

Paul Russell
Case refer,^d

The matter Respecting **Paul Russell** is Refer,^d to next
monthly meeting under the Same friends Care as hereto=
fore and then they to make Report

Micaj Wood
Case refer,d

The matter in regard to **Micajah Wood** is Refer,^d under
the care of **Barzillia Tucker Benjamin Rider** and **John
Williams** to next monthly meeting & then they to make
Report

Giles Slocum
Case refer,d

The Committee that had the care of that matter Respecting
Giles Slocum Desire the matter to be Refer,d which is Refer,d
to next monthly meeting & then they to make Report

Testimony
against
D. Smith
Recorded in
page 299

This meeting hath Signed a paper of Denial against
David Smith and the Clerk is order,^d to read sd paper
Publickly at the Close of first days meeting for
worship and make Report to next monthly meeting

Clement Biddle
Certificate

Clement Biddle hath Produced a Certificate from
the monthly meeting of **Philidelphia** Certifying that he
is a member of their meeting & Clear of marriage Entanglements Engagments as far as they know

C:B &
R: C
Receiv,d
their answer

Therefore **Clement Biddle** and **Rebecca Cornal** appear,d
for their answer which was that they might Proceed
to take Each other in marriage in Some Convenient time
before next monthly meeting advising with the Overseers
this meeting Shall appoint for that purpose and

Caleb Russell and **Jonathan Hussey** is appointed for to
See their marriage Consomated in good order and make
Report to next monthly meeting

D Cornel Certificate Sing,d This meeting hath Signed a Removal Certificate to the
Monthly Meeting of **Ninepartners** for our friend **Daniel
Cornal** and his Children under age

Certificat to be given all moved in the Verge of Ninepart-ners month -ly meeting We appoint our friends **Thomas Hicks Prince Allen William
Anthony J**ᵘ and **Samuel Smith** to Draw Removal Certificates
for all the friends that have Removed to **Sarhatoga** that
they on Inquiry Shall think proper and make report to
next monthly meeting and also to Draw one for
Jedidiah Allen his wife and Children all to be Directed
to the monthly meeting of **Ninepartners**

Order on Treasurer The Treasurer is order,d to pay **Timothy Russell** five dollars
for half years keeping the meeting house
This meeting hath Collected £11"10s"11d old tennor

1774 9ᵗʰ mo At a Monthly Meeting held in **Dartmouth** 19ᵗʰ the 9ᵗʰ mo 1774
the Representatives are **William Sandford** & **Thoˢ Hicks** present

Wᵐ Russell case referd The matter Respecting **Wᵐ Russell** is Refer,d to next monthly
meeting under the Care of the Same friends as heretofore
and then they to make Report

Bark Little case refer,d The matter Respecting **Barker Little** is Refer,d to next mo
meeting under the Care of the Same friends as heretofore
and then they to make Report

E: Tripp Denied Whereas **Ephraim Tripp** hath long been under Dealing and the
matter having been under the care of a Committee for a long time
and now Said Committee Report that they have found no Satisfaction
therefore we hereby Disown the Said **Ephraim Tripp** from being
a member of our Society and **Prince Allen & Thos Hicks** is appointed
to Draw a publick Testimony against him and bring it to next
monthly meeting and also to Shew him a Copy of the minute
made against him

Gid Gifford's case referd The matter Respecting **Gideon Gifford** is Referd to next monthly
meeting under the Care of **Joseph Tucker** & **William Mosher** and
then they to make report

manimition from John Russell **John Russell** hath Signed and Deliver,d to this meeting Two
Bills of Manumition one for a Negro Woman Named **Luce**
and one for a negro gall Named **Vilot** which this meeting

Peleg Slocum case referd Accepts. And **Peleg Slocum** Not fully Complying with
friends Request in Regard to freeing his Negroes, therefore the

matter is Refer,^d under the Same friends care as heretofore, to next
monthly meeting & then they to make Report

P: Russel
Denied

Whereas **Paul Russell** having been under Dealing and the
matter hath been Long under the Care of a Committee & now the
greater part of Sd Committee (the other being absent) Report that
they found no Satisfaction therefore we hereby Disown the Said
Paul Russell from being a member of our Society and **Prince
Allen** & **Thomas Hicks** are appointed to Draw a publick Testimony against **P. Russell** & bring it to next monthly meeting
& also Shew him a Coppy of this minute

Certificates
Sing,^d for
Several friends
Zephaniah
Anthony
Wife & Children
&c

This meeting hath Sign,^d Removal Certificates to the monthly
meeting at the **Ninepartners** for the following friend (viz)
Shadrac Dennice his Wife and Children, **Zephania Anthony** with
his Wife and Children

B Biddle
Certificate
Sign,^d

This meeting hath also Signed a Removal Certificate to
the monthly meeting of **Philidelphia** for **Rebeca Biddle**
wife of **Clement Biddle**

Micaj Wood
case referd

The matter Respecting **Micajah Wood** is Refer,^d to next mo
meeting under the Care of **Barzillia Tucker, Benja Rider Joseph
Barker** & **Prince Allen** and then they to make Report

Giles
Slocum
case referd

The Committee appointed on account of **Giles Slocum** Desire
the matter to be Refer,^d which matter is Refer,^d to next mo
meeting and then they to make report

T: & D: Smith
Testimony
Read

The Clerk Reports that he hath Read the testimonies against
David and **Thos Smith** as orderd

This meeting Collected – – £11 00s 00d old tennor

This meeting adjourns to the Last first in this month after
the meeting of worship

This meeting meet acccording to adjournment the 28th the 9 ^{mo} 1774
the Representatives being called both Present

Clement
Biddle
marriage

The friends appointed to See **Clement Biddle** & **Rebecca
Cornel** marraige Consomated, Report that Said marraige was
Consomated orderly Except the young womans appearing with
her bonet on in time of marriage, which appears that She did
it Inadvertantly therefore friends advise for the futer on Such
Occations women take off their bonets

manimitions
from J:R

Joseph Russell hath free,d his Negro men from the State
of Slavery, Namely **Quash** and **Pero**, and their Manu-
missons hath been Read in this meeting & accepted

Tim Russel
is paid

The Treasurer Reports he hath paid **Timothy Russell** five
Dollars for keeping the meeting house half a year as orderd

The Queries were read in this meeting and answers thereto
and approv,ᵈ & Sent with the Epistle, which was Sign,ᵈ in this

F. Rider
Recommended
as a Minister

meeting to the Quarterly meeting, and our friend **Freborn
Rider** was Recommended as a member of the Quarterly meeting
of ministers & Elders

money sent
for the Y: M
Stock

The Treasurer is orderᵈ to hand three Dollars to the Representatives
to the Quarterly for the yearly Stock and Report next mo meeting

Representatives
to the Q:
Meetig

Our friends **Thomas Hicks Barzillia Tucker Wᵐ Barker Wᵐ An[thony]**: ʲᵘ
are appointed to attend the Quarterly meeting and present the
Epistle with the answers to the Queries and make report next mo Meeting.

10ᵗʰ ᵐᵒ 1774

At a Monthly Meeting held in **Dartmouth** the 17th of 10 ᵐᵒ 1774
the Representatives ar **Joseph Barker** & **Prince Allen** both present

Wᵐ Russell
case referd

The matter Respecting **Wm Russell** is Refer,ᵈ to next mo meeting
under the care of the Same friends as heretofore and then they
to make Report

Barker Little's
case referd

One of the Committee appointed on account of **Barker Little** Reports
that they hant had an oppertunity with him and Desire the matter
Refer,ᵈ therefore Sᵈ matter is Refer,ᵈ untill next mo meeting under
their Care and then they to make Report

Testimony
Signed against
E:T & P: R

Prince Allen & **Thoˢ· Hicks** hath answer,ᵈ their appointment
and brought Testimonies against **Ephrem Tripp** & **Paul Russell**
which were Sign,ᵈ by the Clerk and Sᵈ Clerk is order,ᵈ to read
Sᵈ Testimonies at the Close of a first Days meeting at Some
Convenient time after the time of appeal is out & then make Report

Gideon Gifford
paper accepted

The Committee appointed on account of **Gideon Gifford**
Report that they have So much Satisfaction as they are willing
to Receive his paper Therefore this meeting Concluds to accept
Sᵈ paper which is as followeth

G: Giffrd
paper

To the Preparative & Monthly meeting of friends
Whereas I have Married Out of the Unity of friends & therein
broak the good order Established among them, which broack
of Disorder I am Sorrow for and do Condemn the Same and
Desire friends So far to pass by mine offence as to let me
Remain under their Care from your friend
Dartmouth the 3 the 3 ᵐᵒ 1774　　　　　**Gideon Gifford**

P. Slocum
case referd

The Committee appointed in the affair of **Peleg Slocum**, made no
Report therefore the matter Respecting **Peleg Slocum**ˢ freeing his Negroes is
Refer,ᵈ untill next monthly meeting under the care of the Same friends as
heretofore & **Joseph Tucker** & **Abraham Tucker** is aded to them and they to
Report to next monthly meeting

M: C
& E: T
Deni,[d]   The women Inform that they have Signed papers of Denial against
Mary Cornal & **Elisabeth Tucker** which this meeting approveth of &
the Clerk hath Signed S[d] papers also – –

M: W
Deni,[d]   Whereas **Micajah Wood** hath been under Dealing for marring out of the
Unity of friends, and the matter been under the Consideration of a Committee
for a long time, and they Report that Said **Woods** Conduct hath been
Disagreeable, in Reporting a Scandeclos Story about **Edieth Smith** wife
of **Humphry Smith** the 2[d] and not Inclining to Condemn the Same to friends
Satisfaction therefore we hereby Disown him the Said **Wood** from being
a member of our Society and **Benj**[a] **Rider** & **Prince Allen** are appointed
to Draw a Testimony against him & bring it to next <u>mo</u> meeting
also to Shew him a Coppy of this minute and Inform of his Right
of appeal and make Report to next monthly meeting – –

G Slocum
Case referd   The Committee appointed on account of **Giles Slocum** Desire
the matter Refer,d which is Refer,d under the Same friends Care
as heretofore unto next monthly meeting & then they to make Report

money
paid by
Treasurer   the Treasury Reports that he hath paid the money to the Representatives
as order,[d] last monthly meeting

Return
from the
Q: meeting   The Representative Report that they all attended the Quarterly
meeting, also we Received an Epistle from S[d] meeting with an
Printed one from **Philidelphia** which were read & kindly accepted

D Shephers
Ju[r] *desires*
a Certifi   **David Sheepherd j**[ur] Requests a few lines to the <u>mo</u> meeting
of **Smithfield** Certifying his Clearness Respecting marriage and
Conversation & **Caleb Russell** & **John Williams** are appointed for that
purpose & they to Report to next <u>mo</u> meeting. Likewise
Elias Slocum Requests one of the like to the <u>mo</u> meeting of
Coakset & **Prince Allen** & **Thos Hicks** are appointed to take
the necessary Care on that account & Report next monthly meeting
This meeting Collected 8£-5s-5d old Tennor

Testimony
against
David Smith
Should have
been Recorded
in page 293   (Whereas **David Smith** of **Dartmouth** in the **County of Bristol**
in the Province of the **Massachussets Bay** in **New England**
having Long made Profession with us & been a member
of our monthly meeting of **Dartmouth**, But for want ^of due
watchfulness, and Giving way to a Contentious mind, has
So far Deviated from our Profession as to Publickly Report
that Some of the Overseers of our meeting were fals men, to
the Defaming of them, and friends having Labour,[d] with
him in much Love in order to Retract & Condemn the same
and Restore him to unity with his Brethren again, But
he Refusing to Comply therewith therefore for the Clearing

of truth and friends from the Reproach of Such a Con=
=tentious Person This meeting is Concerned to Give this
forth as a Publick Testimony against him, and hereby
Disown him the Said **David Smith** from being a member
of our Society untill by Repentance he shall be Restor^d to the
way of truth – – Given forth at our s^d <u>mo</u> meeting held on
the 15th day of the 8th month – 1774
Signed in and on behalf of S^d meeting by **Wm Anthony ju^r** Clerk)

Testimony against T: Smith Should have been Recorded in page 285

(Whereas **Thomas Smith** Son of **David Smith** had his Education
among friends & Disregarding the testimony of truth So for as to
Publickly Declare that **Daniel Cornel** was a fals man & he could
prove it, and he hath failed of his assertion, and friends hav=
=ing Repeatedly Labour,^d with him in Love in order to restore
him to the way of truth, but our Labour of love not having
the Desire,^d Effect to friends Satisfaction therefore for the clearing
of truth and friends from the Reproch of Such practices this
meeting is Concerned to Give this forth against him & do hereby
Publickly Disown him the s^d **Thos Smith** from being one
society and from under the care of friends Nevertheless Des=
=iring if it be agreeable with Divine pleasure that he may
yet be Restor,^d from the Evil of his way & by unfeigned Repen-
-tance Return to the way of truth – –
Given forth at our Monthly Meeting held in **Dartmouth**
the 21st Day of the 3 <u>mo</u> 1774. And Signed in & on behalf of S^d
meeting by – – **Wm Anthony j^ur** Clerk

11th mo 1774

At a Monthly Meeting held in **Dartmouth** the 21st of the 11th <u>mo</u> 1774
the representatives are **Jonathan Hussey** & **Wm Mosher** both Present

Wm Russel case referd

The matter Respecting **William Russell** is Refer,d to next <u>mo</u>
meeting under the Care of the Same friends as heretofore and then
they to make Report
Some of the Committee that had the care of that matter Respecting

Barker Little case referd

Barker Little report that they hant fully Disharg,^d themselves
on that account therefore the matter is Still Refer,^d to next mo
meeting under their care & then they to make Report

manimition from P.S Receiv,d

Peleg Slocum hath Signed & Deliver,^d to this meeting two
Bills of Manimission one for a Negro man named **Cesor** & one
for a Negro man Named **London** which this meeting accepts

Testimony against M: Wood

This meeting hath Signed a Testimony against **Micajah**
Wood and the Clerk is orderd to read S^d paper at the Close of a
first Days meeting for Worship at Some Convenient time before

next monthly meeting & then make Report S^d Testimony is
as followeth – –

Whereas **Micajah Wood** hath had his Education amongst
friends and Disregarding the testimony of truth So far as
to marry out from amongst friends and also Reporting a
Scandalos Story about **Edieth Smith** wife of **Humphry Smith**
all which friends having Laboured with him in love in order
to Restore him to the way of truth, but our Labour of love
not having its Desired Effect to friends Satisfaction there
fore for the Clearing of truth and friends from the Reproach
of Such Practices this meeting is Concern,^{d} to give this forth
against him the Said **Micajah Wood** and do hereby Publickly
Disown him from being one of our Society and from under
the Care of friends Nevertheless Desiring if it be agreeable
with Divine Pleasure that he yet may be Restored from
the Evil of his ways and by unfeigned Repentance Return
to the way of Truth – –

Given forth at our monthly meeting held in **Dartmouth**
the 21 Day the 11th month 1774 and Signed in
and on behalf of S^d meeting by

Wm Anthony j^{ur} Clerk

manimited negroes informed   We appoint our friends **Prince Allen Joseph Gifford** and
Caleb Russell to Inform all the Negroes Manimited by friends
belonging to this meeting that they are Set at liberty and
advise with them as they think proper

G Slocum's case referd   The Committee appointed on that affair of **Giles Slocum** Desire
that matter Refer,d one month longer as they are not fully ready
to make Report therefore S^d matter is Refer,^{d} to next mo meeting
under their Care & then they to make Report

D: Sheepherd^{ju} Certificate   This meeting hath Signed a Certificate for **David Sheepherd** j^u
to the monthly meeting of **Smithfield** Certifying his Clearness Resp-
ecting marriage, Also one of the like kind for **Elihu Slocum** to the
monthly meeting of **Acoakset**

This meeting hath Signed a Removal Certificate for **Jededi-^{ah}**
J: A Certificate   **Allen** his wife and Children to the Monthly meeting of the **Nine
Partners** Likewise one for **Isaac Sandford** & Children to S^d mo meeting
and Likewise one for **Benj^a Russell** his wife & Children to S^d mo- meeting
Likewise one for **Stephen Smith** & Children to S^d mo meeting – –

The year being Expired of the Service of the Overseers, Likewise
the Overseers of the Poor yet the Same are Still Continued in that

Service till next monthly meeting and the Choice of S⁴ Overseers
is Refer,ᵈ to next mo meeting

meetings This meeting Concluds that all our meetings for worship only
begin at Begin at the twelveth hour Except at **Bedford**, and to Continue
12 hour So untill the monthly meeting in the fourth month next, and then
all our meetings to Begin at the Eleventh hour untill our
yearly meeting in the faul – –

C: G & J: S The Overseers Inform that **Caleb Green**, and **Joshua Sherman** = ᴶᵘ
under Dealing hath married out of the Unity of friends and that S⁴
Green hath married his first Cousin and the overseers having
Labour,ᵈ with them for the Same (altho they were not
Previsously Cautioned to Desist) and they Decline
to Condemn their Transgression therefore we do Refer,ᵈ matter
to next monthly meeting – –

The Overseers Inform that **Isaac Smith** hath married out
I. Smith of the Unity of friends and he having been Precautioned to
Denied Desist, Therefore we do Disown him the said **Isaac Smith**
from being in membership & from under the Care of this meeting
This meeting Collected £5 " 1s " 11d O:T

12thᵐᵒ At a Monthly Meeting held in **Dartmouth** the 19ᵗʰ of the 12 ᵐᵒ 1774
1774 The Representatives are **Thoˢ Hicks** & **Barzillia Tucker** both present

overseers Our friends **William Mosher Thomas Hicks Benjamin Howland** and
appointed **James Davis William Anthony jᵘ** are appointed Overseers for
the year Ensuing and **John Williams** and **Prince Allen** is nominated
and Desire to Consider of the matter one month – –

Our friends **Joseph Barker Gideon Howland Abraham Howland**
Overseers of **Caleb Bassell Barzillia Tucker David Sheepherd Philip Allen Benjamin**
the poor **Rider** are appointed Overseers of the Poor for the year Ensuing

E. B The Women friends Inform that they have Received **Elizabeth**
admitted a **Briggs** a member of our Society which we Concur with – –
member The matter Respecting **Wᵐ Russell** is Refer,ᵈ to next mo meeting
under the Care of **Samuel Smith** & **Prince Allen** and then they
to make Report – –

B: Little This meeting hath Concluded to accept of **Barker Little** and
paper Wifes paper Provided they Cause S⁴ paper to be Read publickly
accepted at the End of a first days meeting for Worship and Return
Said paper to next mo meeting

M: Wood The Clerk reports that he hath Read **Micajah Woods** paper as
paper order,ᵈ
Read
This meeting Collected – – £8"14s"0 old Tennor

FIG. 9: *The Allen's Neck Meeting House was first built in 1758 and rebuilt in 1873.*
© Copyright Jean Schnell

order on the Treasurer is order,[d] to pay **Timothy Russell** 5 Dollars for half years
Treasurer keping the meeting house

This meeting adjourns to the 28th this Instant

This meeting meet by adjournment the 28th the 12th <u>mo</u> 1774 – –

the Representatives being Called **Barzillia Tucker** present and

Tho[s] Hicks Sent his Excuse for not being here which this meeting accepts

case of Giles The Committee appointed on account of **Giles Slocum** made Report
Slocum continu[d] to this meeting which Report this meeting being not willing

to accepts by Reason the matter is not fully Setled then for

the Same Committee is Still Continued and hereby Impower

them to Settle the whole affair in behalf of this meeting and

make Report to next monthly meeting – –

Case of Caleb The matter Concerning **Caleb green** and **Jorshua Sherman ju**
Greene and being Refer,[d] Last monthly meeting to this meeting therefore
Joshua
Shearman we appoint our friends **John Williams Caleb Russell** and

Benjamin Rider to Labour further with them and make

Report to next monthly meeting Likewise to Inform **Isaac**

Smith of his Denial and his right of appeal and Report
to next monthly meeting

D: Russell
Requests
Certificate
David Russell Desires a Removal Certificate to the
monthly meeting of **Coakset** and **William Mosher** and
Barzillia Tucker are appointed to take the Necessary Care
on that account and Draw one for him if they think proper
and bring to next monthly meeting – –

on Title of
meeting house
Lands
This meeting Concluds it Necessary that there be an Inspection
into the Title of our meeting house Lands but this meeting
being Small therefore the Chusing a Committee on that
account is Refer'd to next monthly meeting – –

J: Wood
under
Dealing
This meeting being Inform,ᵈ that **John Wood** hath been found
in the Reproachful Evil of Joining with other in Stealing
of watermillions from **John Sheepherd** also in Gatherin with a
Tumultious Company by way of Riot very unbecoming the truth
Likewise he is Published out of the Unity of friends and Likewise

W: Haden
under
Dealing
the Overseers inform that **William Hoden [Hayden]** hath also been Conside=
rate in Stealing Said Sheepherds watermillion all which matters
Said Overseers hath Labour,d with them for and we appoint
our friends **Caleb Russell Prince Allen Barzillia Tucker** to Labour
further with them on those accounts and Report next mo meeting

1 ᵐᵒ 1775
At a Monthly Meeting held in **Dartmouth** the 16ᵗʰ of the 1ˢᵗ mo 1775
the Representatives are **Jonathan Hussey** and **John Williams** present

Prince Allen
John Wᵐˢ
proposed
overseers
Prince Allen and **John Williams**, not being fully willing to be appointed
Overseers at present therefore they are Still Desir,ᵈ to Consider of the matter
one month Longer and then they to make Report – –

W: R paper
accepted
This meeting accepts of **William Russell**ˢ paper, the Committee
on that account ~~on that account on that amount~~ making Somewhat
a Satisfactory Report Concerning him – –

B Littles
paper
not read
Barker Little and wives paper not being Read by Reason of
Disappointment therefore the matter is Refer,ᵈ and he is Desir,ᵈ to
Cause Sᵈ paper to be read as order,ᵈ before and Return it to next mo meeting

Tim Russ
is paid
Timothy Russell Informs that the Treasury has paid him the money
as order,d Last mo meeting

Giles Slocuᵐ
case referd
The matter Respecting **Giles Slocum** is Refer,d to next mo meeting
under the Care of the Same Committee as heretofore by their Request
and then they to make Report

Caleb Green
J Shearman
case referᵈ
The Committee appointed on account of **Caleb Green** and **Jorshua**
Sherman Desire the matter Refer,ᵈ which is Referd to next mo
meeting and **Caleb Russell** is Dismised from that Service by

Reason of being nigh in kind & **Benjᵃ Taber** is aded in his
Room and they to make Report next <u>mo</u> meeting

D: Russel
Certificate
Sign,d Removal Certificate for friends **David Russell** & his wife to
Acoakset monthly meeting were Signed at this meeting – –

J: H & M: A
Received
their
answer **Jonathan Howland** and **Mary Allen** Declar,ᵈ their Intentions of
marriage and were Desired to wait till next monthly for their answer
and **Joseph Barker** & **William Anthony ju** are appointed to Inquire into
the young mans Clearness Respecting marriage & Conversation and
make Report to next monthly meeting – –

Our friends **Prince Allen Wᵐ Anthony ju Samuel Smith**
Barzillia Tucker are appointed to Inspect into the Title of our
Committee
to Inspect
the title
of meetingᵉ
Land meeting house land and where they find any defect to mend
and Strengthen the Same as they may think best and make
Report when they have Accomplished the Same – –

Report from
Quarᵗ meeting The Representative Report that they all attend the Quarterly
meeting According to appointment & have Produced an Epistle
from the Same which hath been Read & kindly Accepted – –

John Wood &
Wᵐ Haden
case referd The matters Respecting **John Wood** and **Wm Haden** are Referd
to next monthly meeting on the account the Committee have not
had opportunity to fulfill their appointment therefore they are
Continued in that Service & to make Report to next mo meeting

This meeting Collected 11£"os"od old tennor which is Sent to the
treasury by **Benjamin Smith jur** – –

(The following paper of **Richard Peckhamˢ** Should have been Recorded
in page 278 – –

Testimony
against
R: Peckham Whereas **Richard Peckham** a member of this meeting, hath for
want of adhearing to the measure of Light and Grace in his
own Heart, So far Deviated from the good order Established
amongst us as to fall into the Sin of fornication as appears by
his wives having a Child Soon after marriage, and Likewise
hath married his first Cousin the which he Declines to Condemn
to friends Satisfaction, and after our Labour of love we think
we are Clear do disown the Sᵈ **Richard peckham** from being a
member of our Society Untill it may please God to Shew him his
Error and by an unfeigned repentance he may Return, is our
hearty Desire, Given forth at our monthly meeting held in
Dartmouth – – the 17ᵗʰ Day of the first month – – 1774 – –
Signed in and on behalf of Sᵈ meeting by – –

          William Anthony jur Clerk —)

2 mo
1775

John Wⁿˢ
overseer
B Littles
paper read

At a Monthly Meeting held in **Dartmouth** the 20ᵗʰ the 2ⁿᵈ mo 1775
the Representatives are **Jonathan Hussey** & **Barzillia Tucker** present
John Williams is appointed Overseer in order to Join the Rest
in that Service – – This meeting is Inform,ᵈ that **Barker Little**
and wives paper hath been read as orderd & Returnd to this
meeting and is as followeth

The monthly meeting of friends to be holden at **Dartmouth** the
15ᵗʰ the 11ᵗʰ month 1773

B: Little
and wifes
paper

Friends whereas we through the Infirmation of the adversary
have fallen into the gross Sin of fornication and brought a great
Scandal upon our Profession for which we are Sorry for and do
Condemn hoping God will forgive us and friends So for pass by
this Offence with all other our offences as to lett us Still Remain
under their Care – –   **Barker Little**
                                                      Elisabeth Little

Case of
Caleb Green
J Sherman
& I Smith

The Committee appointed on account of **Caleb Green** & **Joshua
Sherman jur** & **Isaac Smith** Report that they Inform,ᵈ Sᵈ **Smith** as
order,ᵈ and that **Caleb Green** gave them Some Satisfaction and
Sᵈ **Green** & wife gave in a paper to the meeting Condemning
their misconduct they likewise Report in Regard to **Joshua
Sherman** that they had an oppertunity of Conferrance with him
and he gave them no Satisfaction and this meeting Concluds
to Refer the matters Respecting ^Sᵈ **green** & **P. Sherman** Under the
Care of **Benjᵃ Taber John Williams** & **Benjᵃ Rider** and they to make
Report next monthly meeting – –

The friends appointed to Enquire into the Clearness of
Jonathan Howland Report that they have made Inquiry and
find nothing So material as to hinder his Proceeding – –

J. H &
M A
Receiv,ᵈ
their
answer

Jonathan Howland and **Mary Allen** appear,ᵈ for their Answer
which was that they might proceed to take Each other in
marriage in Some Convenient time before next mo meeting
advising with the Overseers we Shall appoint for that purpose
and **Joseph Barker** & **Wᵐ Anthony jᵘ** to See their marriage Consoma
in good order & make Report next monthly meeting – –

T: M &
R: H
Publish,ᵈ

Thomas Mott and **Rhoda Hathaway** Declar,ᵈ their
Intention of taking Each other in marriage & were Desir,ᵈ
to wait untill next monthly meeting for their Answer and
William Wood & **Barzillia Tucker** are appointed to Inquire into
Sᵈ **Motts** Clearness in Regard to marriage & Conversation & make
Report next monthly meeting

John Wood &
Wm Haden
Case referd

The friends appointed to Labour with **John Wood** and **Wm Haden** Report they have not fully Discharged themselves in that matter and Desire it to be Refer,^d which is Refer,^d to next monthly meeting and then they to make Report

J Davis
Requests Certif-
icate

James Davis Desires a Certificate Signifying his Clearness Respecting marriage & Conversation to the Monthly meeting of **Smithfield** therefore **David Sheeherd** and **Benjamin Taber** are appointed to take the Necessary Care on that account and bring one to the next monthly meeting if they find him Clear

David Hart
gave in a
paper

David Hart hath given in a Paper to this meeting Condeming his marring out of the Unity of friends, and we appoint **Joseph Tucker William Mosher** & **William Wood** to take an Oppertunity of Conferrance with him in order to Discover his Sincerity, and Report to next monthly meeting – –

Charles Russel
case

The Committee appointed Some months past on Acount of **Charles Russell** Report that he gave them no Satisfaction and that S^d **Russell** is about to marry out of the Unity of friends and **Samuel Smith** & **Prince Allen** are appointed to Draught a Testimony against S^d **Russell** and bring it to next <u>mo</u> meeting also to Inform him of his Right of an Appeal – –

money paid
to the treasury

Caleb Russell Reports that he hath Reciv,^d by way of Subscription as order,^d Some months past the Sum of Eight pounds Eleven Shillings & four pence Lawfull money and paid into the Treasury This meeting Collected £13"7s"4d old tennor which is Sent to the treasury by **Prince Allen**

order on Treasur^er

The Treasury is order,^d to pay **Benjamin Allen** his Demand on the meeting also those that have Demand for Reparing the meeting house and make Report next mo meeting

J: Hussey
Requests a
Certificate

Jonathan Hussey Desires a Removal Certificate for him self his Wife & Children to the monthly meeting of **Ninepartners** and we appoint **William Sandford Wm Anthony j^r** and **John Potter** to take the Necessary Care on that account and bring one to next <u>mo</u> meeting if they think proper – –

adjourn

This meeting adjourns to the first Day of next month

mett

This meeting meet by Adjournment the 1st Day: 3 <u>mo</u> 1775 the Representatives are **Jonathan Hussey** and **Barzillia Tucker** present

P Russell
denial read

The Clerk Reports that he hath read the Testimony against **Paul Russell** & **Ephrim Tripp** as order,^d Some months past and Return,^d Said Testimonies to this meeting **William Barker** and **William Sandford** are Appointed to have

Wm Barker
Wm Sanford
oversite
of Bury
=ing ground
the Oversight of the Burying Ground in the Room of **Jonathan Hussey** who is about to Remove from hence, and they to Join with **Abraham Tucker** & **Joseph Tucker** in that Service – –

Order on Treasurer
The Treasury is order,^d to pay **Benjamin Smith j^ur** his bill against this meeting which was Inspected and allow,^d Some time past and Report to next monthly meeting

Testimony against P: Russell
Whereas **Paul Russell** Son of **Paul Russell** having had his Education among friends and Disregarding the Testimony of of Truth So far as to be found in Some abusive behavour with **Roger Mosher** in the Night, and Likewise in Resorting with a Rude Company at **Prince Potter**s house all which plainly appears by his own Confession and friends having Repeatedly with him in Love in order to Restore him to the way of Truth but our Labour of Love not having the Desir,^d Effect to friends Satisfaction, therefore for the Clearing of Truth and friends from the Reproach of Such practises this meeting is Concern,^d to give this forth against him and do hereby publickly Disown him the S^d **Paul Russell** from being one of our Society and from under the Care of friends yet Nevertheless Desiring if it be agreeable with Divine pleasure that he may yet be Restor^d from the Evil of his ways and by Unfeigned Repentance Return to the way of Truth Given forth at our monthly meeting held in **Dartmouth** the 17th the 10 ^mo 1774 – –

and Signed in & on behalf of S^d meeting by

Wm Anthony j^r Clerk

Testimony against E: Tripp
Whereas **Ephriam Tripp** Son of **Wm Tripp**, Having had his Education amongst friends and Disregarding the Testimony of Truth So far as to be found in Some abusive behaviour with **Roger Mosher** in the Night Season and Likewise in Resorting with a Rude Company at **Prince Potter**s house all which appears by his one Confession, and friends having Repeated Laboured with him in love in order to Restore him to the way of Truth, but our labour of Love not having the Desir,^d Effect to friends Satisfaction therefore for the Clearing of Truth and friends from the Reproach of Such Practices this meeting is Concerned to give this forth against him & Do hereby Publickly Disown him the Said **Ephrim Tripp** from being one of our Society and from under the Care of friends yet Nevertheless Desiring

if it be agreeable with Divine Pleasure that he may yet
be Restored from the Evil of his ways and by unfeigned
Return to the way of Truth – –
Given forth at our Monthly meeting held in **Dartmouth**
the 17th Day the 10 mo 1774 and Signed in & on behalf of Sd
meeting by – –

William Anthony jr Clerk

Bill for keeping Alice Smith The Overseers of the Poor hath handed in a bill from
Benjamin Smith Ju for keeping **Alice Smith** to the amount
of £4"6s"8d Lawfull money which is accepted – –

Case of James Howlands Request **Caleb Russell** & **Seth Russell** are appointed in the room
of **Jonathan Hussey** to **Jaine Barzillia Tucker** in having the
Care of that matter Respecting **James Howland J**u who
Requested to Come among friends and make Report
when ready

Content Tucker Receiv,d the women Inform that they have minutes **Content Tucker**
under their Care which this meeting approveth

J: H and C. T: Publish,d **Jonathan Hussey J**u & **Content Tucker** Declar,d their Intention
of marriage and were Desir,d to wait till next monthly
meeting for their answer and **William Sandford** and **John
Potter** are appointed to See into the young mans Clearness
Respecting marriage and Conversation and Report to next mo Meeting

3 mo 1775 At a Monthly Meeting held in **Dartmouth** the 20th 3 mo 1775
the Representatives are **Benj**a **Howland 2**nd & **Samuel Smith** present

Caleb Green J Shearman case referd The Committee appointed on Account of **Caleb Green** & **Joshua
Sherman j**u Desires them matters Refer,d as they have not
fully Discharged themselves on those Accounts therefore
Sd matters is Refer,d under their Care of the Same Committee
and **W**m **Mosher** & **Barzillia Tucker** are aded to them in that
Service and they to make Report next mo meeting

Case of Giles Slocum referd The matter Respecting **Giles Slocum** not being fully
Setled to friends Satisfaction therfore Sd matter is Referd
under the Care of the Same Committee as heretofore and
the to make Report to next monthly meeting

Jona Howland marriage One of the friends Appointed to See the marriage of
Jonathan Howland & **Mary Allen** Consomated, Report
that he attended Sd marriage and Saw nothing but what
it was Consomated in a Degree Orderly the other friend hath
Render,d a Reasonable Excuse for his non Attendance

Tho Mott Clearness The friends appointed to Inspect into the Clearness of **Tho**s
Mott Respecting marriage and Conversation Report that

they find nothing to hinder his Proceeding in marriage

Jona¹ Hussey
Clearness

The friends appointed to Inquire into **Jonathan Hussey Ju** Clearness
make the Like Report that they find nothing to hinder

Tho⁵ Mott &
Jona¹ Hussey
answer

Thomas Mott and **Rhoda Hathaway**, and **Jonathan Hussey jᵘʳ**
& **Content Tucker** Appear,ᵈ for their Answer, which was that
Each Couple might Proceed to take Each other in marriage
in Some Convenient time between this & the next monthly
meeting advising with the Overseers this meeting Shall Appointe
for that purpose and **Adam Gifford** & **Barzillia Tucker** are Appointed
to See the marriage of **Tho⁵ Moot** & **Rhoda Hathaway** Solamnised
orderly, and **Wᵐ Sandford** and **John Potter** are Appointed for the
Same Service with the Other Couples – – and all to make
Report next mo meeting – –

John Wood &
Wᵐ Haden
case referd

The matter Respecting **John Wood** and **William Haden** are
Refer,ᵈ to next monthly meeting under the Care of the Same
friends as before, and they to make Report next monthly meeting

James Davis
Certificate

A Certificate was Signed as this meeting for **James Davis** to the
Monthly meeting of **Smithfield** Signifying his Clearness in regarᵈ
to marriage and Conversation – –

F. Rider
Recommend
to the Select
meeting

This meeting hath Signed and Sent to the Quarterly meeting
of Ministers and Elders a minitue Recommending **Freburn**
Rider as a minister and member of the Select meeting

The friends appointed to have the Oversight of the meeting at
Bedford Report that they have Generally attended Sᵈ meeting
and that it was held and Conducted in a Good Degree orderly
and that they think it might be advantagious to Continue
the Same, and the friends Living there do Generally Request
it to be Continued one year Longer which is granted accordingˡʸ

two meeting
a Day
at Bedford

and they to hold Two meetings ∧on first∧ Days untill the monthly meeting
in the tenth month then one meeting on first Day and one on
the Sixth day of the week and Sᵈ meeting to begin on the 10ᵗʰ hour
and on the 3ʳᵈ hour on the first day & at the 11ᵗʰ hour on 12th Day
and our friends **David Sheepherd James Davis** and **Caleb**
Russell are appointed to have the Oversight of Sᵈ meeting &
and to make Report at the Expiration therof – –
This meeting Collected £6"11s"6d old tennor

adjourn

This meeting adjourns to the 29ᵗʰ Instant after the meeting of worship

3 ᵐᵒ mett
1775

This meeting being meet by Adjournment the 29ᵗʰ the 3ʳᵈ mo 1775
the Representatives are **Benjamin Howland** & **Samuel Smith** present

David Hart
case referd

Two of the friends appointed on account of **David Hart** Report
that he gave them Some Satisfaction, yet they Desire the matter

Refer,d which is also Refer,d under their Care and they to make
Report next monthly meeting – –

Treasurers report   The Treasury Reports that he hath not paid all the money as order,d Last monthly meeting therefore he is Still Desird to accomplish that business and make Report to next <u>mo</u> meeting

Testimony against C: Russel Sign,d   This meeting hath Signed a Testimony against **Charles Russell** and the Clerk is order,d to Read Sd Testimony at the Close of a first Days meeting for worship before next <u>mo</u> meeting and then make Report – – Sd Testimony is as followeth – –

Whereas **Charles Russell** having had his Education among friend, but Thro, Unwatchfulness and Disregarding the Testimony of truth in his own heart hath So far departed therefrom as to be found Guilty of the Reproachful Sin of fornication and also hath married out of the unity of of friends and we having timely Labour'd with him in Love in order for his recovery but friends Labour not having the Desir,d Effect to friends Satisfaction therefore this meeting is Concern'd for the maintaining of our Christian Testimony and the Preservation of the Professions thereof from the Reproach of Such Enormous practices Do hereby Publickly Disown him the Sd **Charles Russell** from being a member of our Religious Community and from under our the Care of this meeting Untill by Unfeigned Repentance he shall Return to the way of truth & find mercy with the Lord Given forth & Sign,d in & on behalf of our <u>mo</u> meeting held in **Dartmouth** by adjournment 29th the 9 <u>mo</u> 1775 by **Wm Anthony jur** Clerk

Answers Epistle and Representative to the Q: meeting   The Queries have been Read and Answer,d in this meeting and an Epistle to the Quarterly meeting Read and Sign,d & Sent with sd answers to Sd Quarterly meeting by our Representatives who are **Caleb Russell Barzillia Tucker James Davis John Williams Wm Mosher Wm Barker & Wm Anthony jur** who are appointed to attend the Quarterly meeting and make Return next <u>mo</u> meeting

adjourn   This meeting adjourns to the 7th Day of next month – –

mett   This meeting being meet by Adjournment the 7th Day of the 4 <u>mo</u> 1775 the Representatives are **Benja Howland 2nd & Samuel Smith** present **Job Howland** hath Exhibited a Complaint against **Wm Wood** wherein he Requests Sd **Wood** to Leave an affair to men Subsist-
=ing between him & Sd **Wood** and the Overseers Inform that they have had them together and Advis,d Sd **Wood** to submitt Sd matter to men but he Declines the Same and this meeting being Small therefore the Chusing a Committee is Refer,d to next <u>mo</u> meeting This meeting hath Signed a Removal Certificate to the mo

J: Hussey *Certificate* *Sign,d*	meeting at the **NinePartners** for our friend **Jonathan Hussey** and **Hepzibah** his wife and **Sylvenus** & **Rachal** their Children and their Grandaughter **Elisabeth Hussey** – –
Jonaⁿ Hussey Ju *request a Cer-* *tificate*	**Jonathan Hussey J^u** Requests a Removal Certificate to S^d meeting and **Wm Sandford** & **Wm Anthony J^u** are appointed to Draw one for him if they on Inquiry Shall think Proper and bring it to next m<u>o</u> meeting

4mo
1775
no Representa
tive from
preparitive
meeting
At a Monthly Meeting held in **Dartmouth** the 17th the 4mo 1775
There not appearing any Representative from the Preparative
meeting the Reason alledged being the Severity of the
weather that day that there was no meeting held, yet this
meeting Concluds to goe forward as Usual, yet fear the
Coolness and want of True Zeal for the Cause of Truth
was too much the Primary Cause of the afore S^d Neglect

Caleb Green &
J Shearman Ju^r
case referd
The Committee that had the Care of them matters Respect-
=ing **Caleb Green** and **Joshua Sherman J^{ur}** Report that
they have Received Some Satisfaction, yet this meeting
meeting thinks proper to Refer S^d matter under the Care of
the Same Committee and they to make Report to next mo. meeting – –

G. Slocum
paper
Accepted
This meeting Concluds to accepts of **Giles Slocums** paper
Condemning his falling into the Sin of Fornication with
Ruth Russell provided he Cause S^d pape to be publickly Read at
the Close of a first Days meeting for worship before next monthly
he being present and Report to next monthly meeting and return
S^d paper and **Prince Allen** is appointed to Serve S^d **Slocum** with a
Copy of this minute
Said paper is as followeth – –

    To the Monthly meeting of friends in **Dartmouth**
Whereas I have Gave way to the Ensenuation of the adversary so
far as to be guilty of the Sin of fornication with **Ruth Russell**
Whereby She Charged me of being father of her bastart Child
which Reproachful Sin I am Sorry for & do hereby Condemn Desiring
forgiveness from the Almighty and that friends may do far
pass by mine offence as to let me Remain under their Care
from your friend   **Giles Slocum**
Dartmouth the 16th the 4mo 1774

Tho Mott
J Hussey Ju
marriage
The friends appointed to See **Thos Mott** and **Rhody Hathaway**
and **Jonathan Hussey j^u** and **Content Tucker** marriage Consomated
all made Report that they attended S^d marriages and Saw nothing
but that they was Consomated orderly – –

John Wood
Wm Haden
case referd

The Committee Appointed on account of **John Wood** and
'**William Haden** Desire them matters Refer'd which is Refer'd
which is Refer,d under the Care of the Same Committee and they to make
to next monthly meeting – –

Treasurer
report

The Treasurer Reports he hath not paid the money as order'd Last
monthly meeting Therefore he is yet Continued to pay S^d mony as
order'd and make Report next monthly meeting

C Russell Testi-
mony
Read

The Clerk Reports that he hath Read the testimony against
Charls Russell as order'd – –

Return
from the
Quarterly
meeting

The Representatives to the Quarterly meeting being Called upon
Report that four of them attended but **Caleb Russell** & **James**
Davis did not attend the whole of s^d meeting bur renderd a reason
therefor which was Accepted
and they have Produced an Epistle from S^d Quarterly meeting which
hath read and well Accepted

Case of Wm Wood

The appointing a Committee at the Last Adjournment on that
affair of **William Woods** being Omitted by reason of the Smallness
of the meeting therefore we now Appoint our friends **Adam Gifford**
Benj^a Slocum Benj^a Chase Philip Allen to Labour with S^d **Wood**
to submit S^d matter to men Agreeable to our Dissipline – –

J. H j^u
Certificate
Signd

This meeting Signed a Removal Certificate for **Jonathan Hussey**
J^u and **Content** his wife to the monthly meeting of the **Ninepartners**

Report
Wm Smith case

The Committee appointed Some time past to Labour with **Wm Smith**
Report as followeth We the Subscribers being appointed Some
time past to Labour with **Wm Smith** for taking too much Spiritous
Liquor Soon after which Appointment he Removed up the
Country Nevertheless two of us had an Oppertunity to Speak
with him on that Account and Labour,^d with him According
to our Ability, but Receiv,^d no ^real Satisfaction and after a long
time of Tryal we are Inform,^d by Credible Information and
undoubted Evidence that he yet Continues in the Same practice
of taking Spiritous Liquor therefore we think best that he be Denied
by friends –   from your friends   **Philip Trafford**
                                                 Samuel Smith
Dated the 19th the 3mo 1775 –   **John Potter**
Which is accepted therefore this meeting Doth Disown the S^d

W: Smith
Deni,d

Smith from under the Care of friends and **Samuel Smith** is appoint
ed to Draw a testimony against him and bring it to next <u>mo</u>
meeting also to Serve him with a Copy of this minute

Jemimah
Davis
Certificate

This meeting hath Signed a Removal Certificate for **Jemimah**
Davis to monthly meeting at the **Oblong**–

This meeting Collected – – £8-8ˢ-5ᵈ old tenor – –

To Revise Correct & record meetings minutes This Meeting appoints **William Anthony Jᵘ Samuel Smith Thomas Hicks Barzillia Tucker** to Revise Correct and Record this meetings minutes and also to Settle Accounts with the Tresurer and make Report next monthly meeting

5 mo 1775 At a Monthly Meeting held in **Dartmouth** the 15ᵗʰ of the 5ᵐᵒ 1775 the Representatives are **Caleb Russell** & **Nicholass Howland** present – –

Case of C Green & J Shearman referᵈ The Committee that had the care of the matter Respecting **Caleb Green** and **Joshua Sherman Jᵘʳ** hath made Report which is Somewhat Satisfactory yet they not being present Said matters are Refer,d to next monthly meeting under the Same friends and then they to make Report.

G S paper accepted report that been made that **Giles Slocum** paper hath been read and Returned to this meeting as orderd.

D.H.ˢ paper accepted The Committee that had the Care of that matter Respecting **David Hart**, made Report that was so Satisfactory to this meeting that we Conclude to accept **D. Harts** papers as Satisfactⁱⁿ

Wᵐ Wood case referd The Committe that had the Care of that matter Respecting **Wᵐ Wood** Report that Said **Wood** Still Declines to leave Controvercy to men yet by his request the matter is Referd to next monthly meeting for further Consideration and then he to make report – –

J.W. and Wᵐ Haden matter Referd The Committee that were appointed in the Case Respecting **John Wood** and **Wᵐ Haden** Report that they have been in a Progress but have not fully Compleated the Same to their Satisfaction & Desire it Continued which is Cont= inued Accordingly under the Same friends care as before and they to make Report when they Shall accomplish sᵈ matter

Wᵐ Smith Paper A Testimony against **Wᵐ Smith** was Signed in this meeting by the Clerk and he is order,ᵈ to read it Publickly as usual & make Report to next monthly meeting which is as followeth

Wᵐ Smith denial Whereas **William Smith** Son of **Jonathan Smith** & **Phebe** his wife Late of **Dartmouth**, but now a Resident in **East Hoosuck** in the Province of the **Massachussets Bay** in **New England** having been Educated and made profession with friends but hath So far Departed there from as frequently to fall in to the Repro achful Evil of taking too much Spiritous Liquor, to his own Prejudice of his Family, and a Reproach to that holy pro= fession and name that he hath Pretended to make Profession of and friends having from time to time in Love Labour,ᵈ with him for his Recovery in hopes he would Refrain from apra[?]

So Obviously Destructive to mankind, but friends Labour
of Love not Obtaining the Desired End, But he Continuing
therein therefore for the Clearing of truth and the Testimony
we bear from Such Reproachful Evils this meeting is Concerned to give this forth as a Publick Testimony against him,
and do hereby Disown him the Said **William Smith** from
being a member of our Society untill by Repentance
and Reformation he Shall Return from the Error of his
way and be Restored to the way of Truth – –
Given forth & Signed in and by order of our monthly
meeting of friends held in **Dartmouth** the 15ᵗʰ of 5ᵐᵒ 1775

by Wᵐ Anthony Jᵘ Clerk

Committee to Correct the minutes — The Friends to Revise Correct & Record this meetings minutes
Report that they have Revised & Corrected Sᵈ minutes and left
them with **William Anthony Jᵘ** to Record but they Report
they have not Setled with the Treasurer by Reason Some
Subscriptions that are gone out & not made up & Completed

To Settle with Treasurer — and **Wᵐ Anthony Jᵘ** and **Prince Allen** are appointed to Settle with
Said Treasurer and make Report next monthy meeting

Ruben Smith case — One of the friends appointed Some time past to Labour with **Rubin
Smith** being Removed from hence. This meeting appoints **Abraham
Howland** to Join **Prince Allen** in that matter and to make Report
next monthly meeting

J. Howland Recevᵈ under friend Care — The Committee appointed Sometime past on account of **James
Howland Jᵘ** Request to come under friends made Report to this
meeting that he gave them a Degree of Satisfaction therefore we
accept of Said **Howland** to be under the Care of this meeting

Obediah Allen desire a Certificate — **Obediah Allen** Requests a Removal Certificate for him Self his wife
and Children to the monthly meeting of the **Nine Partners** and we
appoint **Thos Hicks** & **Philip Allen** to Join the women and take the
necessary Care if they think proper
This meeeting collected £9"11s"0d old tenor – –

*Certificate for **Rhoda Allen** & **Meribah Allen*** — Removal Certificates for **Rhoda Allen** & **Meribah Arnold**
Directed to the monthly meeting of the **Nine Partners** were Signed
in this meeting

---

6 mo 1775 — At a Monthly Meeting held in **Dartmouth** 19ᵗʰ of 6ᵗʰ mo 1775
The Representatives are **William Mosher** & **Samuel Smith** both present

James Howlanᵈ proposal of marriage — **James Howland** and **Meribah Sheepherd** Declared their Intentions of
of taking Each other in marriage and were Desired to wait till next
monthly meeting for their Answer, and **Seth Russell** & **John**

Williams are appointed to Inquire into the young mans Clearness
Respecting marriage and Conversation & make Report to next
monthly meeting

The Committee that had the care of that matter Respecting

J.S. paper
accepted

Joshua Sherman Jᵘ made Report to this meeting which was
So Satisfactory as we Conclude to Accept of Sᵈ **Sherman**s paper
for Satisfaction but **Caleb Green** not being present by reason
of his being Unwell therefor that matter Respecting **Caleb Green**
is Refer.ᵈ to next monthly meeting under the Same friends care
as heretofore & then they to make Report

Matter
Between
J:H and
Wᵐ W:

William Wood made no Report to this meeting wheather he
would Submit that matter to men Subsisting between himself
and **Job Howland**, or not therefore the matter is Refer,ᵈ under:
the Care of **Adam Gifford Philip Allen Benj**ᵃ **Chase Benj**ᵃ
Slocum & **Joseph Gifford** and they to Labour with Said **Wood**
to leave the matter to men & make Report to next mo meeting

The Clerk Reports that he hath Read the testimony against
Wᵐ Smith as order.ᵈ

S Slocum
Certificate
from ***Coakset***

The women Inform that they Received a Removal
Certificate in behalf of **Sarah Slocum** from monthly
meeting of **Coakset**

Certificate for
Obediah Allen
Wife & Children

A Removal Certificate on behalf of **Obediah Allen**
His Wife & Children Directed to the monthly meeting of the
Nine Partners was Signed in this meeting

The Committee that had the Care of that matter Respecting

R: Smith
Deni,ᵈ

Rubin Smith made Report that he gave them no Satisfaction
for his misconduct therefore we do Disown him the Said **Rubin
Smith** from being under our care and **Abraham Howland**
is appointed to Inform him of his Denial and make Report
to next monthly meeting

money raisᵈ

The Treasurer Reports that the Committee Appointed Some
time past to Rais money by way of Subscription have rais,ᵈ
and paid to the Treasury the sum of £9–10ˢ–2ᵈ Lawfull money

The Committee Appointed to Settle with the Treasurer mad[e]
the following Report which is accepted

We the Subscribers having Settled accounts with the
Treasurer according to Appointment as followeth --

Settlement
with the
Treasurer

The money Collected and into the Treasury by order
of the monthly meeting Sinse the 16ᵗʰ the 5ᵐᵒ 1774

amounts to in Lawfull money ———————— 33[£] 16^s　0^d

Treasurer paid out ————————————— 24　15　11

Remains in the Stock ———————————　9　0　1

Dartmouth the 17th the 6<u>mo</u> 1775 for **Prince Allen**

W<u>m</u> Anthony J<u>u</u>

Jos Trafford Diswown,^d We are informed that **Joseph Trafford** is Inlisted in to the war or militia and been Labour,^d with by one of the overseers and not Retracting therefrom and for the Clearing of truth we do Disown him from being under our care and we appoint **Abraham Howland** and **Benj^a Howland 2nd** to Serve Said **Trafford** with a Coppy of this minute when they have and Opportunity, & the Clerk is order'd to Read this minute Publickly as Usual & Report to next <u>mo</u> meeting

R: Russell Disown,d The Women Inform that they have Disowned **Rebeckah Russell** wife of **Jethrow Russell**, and **Mary Wing** wife of **Giles Wing** which this meeting Concurs with

Queries answer.^d The Queries were Read in this meeting and Answers thereto which were approved and Sent by our Representatives to the Quarterley meeting with our Epistle to S^d meeting which was Sign.^d by the Clerk and Sent by our Representatives who are

Represen tatives **Thomas Hicks Samuel Smith Benj.^a Howland 2nd Caleb Russell William Anthony J<u>ur</u> Barzillia Tucker**

This meeting Collected ———————— £10--2^s--3^d old Ten

Order on Treasurer The Treasurer is ordered to pay **Timothy Russell** 5 Dollers for half years keeping the meeting house

7 <u>mo</u> 1775 At a Monthly Meeting held in **Dartmouth** the 17th 7<u>mo</u> 1775 the Representatives are **W<u>m</u> Mosher** & **Benj^a Smith J<u>u</u>** present The friends appointed to Inquire into **Jones Howland** Clearness Respecting marriage & Conversation Report that they dont find nothing to hinder their proceeding

J.H & M.S. had their answer **James Howland J<u>u</u>** and **Meribah Sheapherd** appear^d at this meeting for their Answer which was that they might Proceed to take Each other in marriage in Some Convenient time before next monthly meeting. Advising with the Overseers that this meeting Shall appoint for that purpose and **Caleb Russell** and **Seth Russell** are appointed for ~~that purpose~~ to See their marriage Consumated orderly and make Report next m<u>o</u> meeting.

C:G & wivs paper The Committee that had the Care of that matter Respecting **Caleb green** made Report which was So Satisfactory to this meeting that we Conclude to accept of **Green** & wives

paper provided They Cause Said paper to be publickly read
at the Close of a first Days meeting and for worship they being
present before next monthly meeting and then Return
Said paper & Report of its being Read

The Committee that had the Care of that matter Respect-

J:H: & W:W matter Refer,ᵈ ing **William Wood** Report that Said **Wood** hath Concluded
to Submit the Controvercy Insisting Susisting between himself
and **Job Howland** to men and the Same Committee are
Continued to See that it be Completed.

Abraham Howland Report that he Inform.ᵈ **Rubin
Smith** of his Denial as order,ᵈ – –

The Representatives to the Quarterly meeting made
Report that they all attended and have brought an Epistle

Return from the Q. meeting from Said meeting with Divers transsrips(viz) one from
the Last yearly meeting of **Rhodyland**, one from the yearly
meeting in **Landon [London]** one from the yearly meeting a
one from the yearly meeting at **flushing** & a Number of
Printed Epistles from **London** all which were read in this
meeting and the Salutary Advice therein, is Recommended
to Each Individuals Observation and notice

It is Recommended in P.Quarterly meeting Epistle
that the Queries be Answer,ᵈ by & in the Open preparative

Advis,ᵈ yᵗ Queries be answer.ᵈ in yᵉ meeting meeting for the future, its also Recommended for this
meeting to rais the Sum of five pounds ten Shillings Law-
full money to Supply out yearly meeting Treasury, and
Convey it to the Treasurer of sᵈ meeting as Soon as may be
which this meeting Complies with – –

Treasurer report The Treasurer Reports that he hath paid **Timothy Russell**
five Dollars as order,ᵈ S.ᵈ Treasurer also Reporth that
he hath paid **Benjᵃ Smith Jᵘ** ten pounds Eight Shilling
Lawfull money for the keeping **Alice Smith** which this
meeting approveth – –

Subscriptioⁿ for Bar Apology **Thomas Hicks** is appointed to take in Subscriptions for **Barkleyˢ
[Barclay's]** Apology agreeable to the Directions of the Quarter[ly] Meeting
This meeting Collected – – 11£ 6ˢ 80ᵈ T

8 ᵐᵒ 1775 At a Monthly Meeting held in **Dartmouth** 25ᵗʰ the 8 ᵐᵒ 1775
the Representatives are **William Mosher** & **Benjᵃ Howland 2ⁿᵈ**
both present

Shubel Bunker Certificate **Shubel Banker [Bunker]** Brought a Certificate from the mo̲ meeting
on **Nantucket** Certifying his having a Birth right of membership
there & Clearness Respecting marriage.

S:B *& L:G* *publish.ᵈ*	**Shubel Banker** and **Lydia Gardner** Declar.ᵈ their Intentions Of taking Each other in marriage and were Desir.ᵈ to wait till the next monthly meeting for their Answer
James Howland Ju marriage	The friends appointed to See **James Howland Ju** ‸**& meribah**: [Sharp?]: marriage Consomated Report that they attended Said marriage and Saw nothing but that it was Consomated orderly. – –
Caleb Green paper read	Report hath been made of **Caleb Green** & Wives paper being read and return,ᵈ to this meeting as order,ᵈ, Said ‸paper is Recorded in page 354.
Committee to rais money	We appoint our friends **William Barker Gideon Howland Giles Slocum Isaac Howland Jᵘ** & **John Allen** to rais money by way of Subscription to Supply our yearly meeting Stock and ‸pay the money into the treasury and make Report of their Doings with the Sum total to next mo meeting. This meeting Collected 8£"7ˢ"7ᵈ old tennor
J.H. had a Certific: to London Certifiate for John Williams	This meeting Sign.ᵈ a Certificate in favour of **Joh[n] Howland** to friends in **London** also one in favour of **John Williams** to friends in the West[w]ard Provinces as they were about to go there on account of business

9 mo 1775-	At a Monthly Meeting held in **Dartmouth** the 18th the 9thmo 1775 – – The Representatives are **Wᵐ Barker** & **Thoˢ Hicks** both present
Shubel Bunkers answer	**Shubel Bunker** & **Lydia Gardner** appear.ᵈ for their answer which was that they might proceed to take Each other in marriage before next monthly meeting Advising with the Overseers that this meeting Shall appoint for that purpose and **Seth Russell** & **Wᵐ Barker** are appointed to see their marriage Consomated orderly and make to next mo meeting
Money Rais,ᵈ	The Committee appointed Last monthly meeting to raise money by way of Subscription Report that they have rais.ᵈ and paid into the treasury the Sum of Eight pounds three Shillings & four penies Lawfull money and the Treasurer is
money order to the yʸ meetig	Is order.ᵈ to pay into the treasury of our yearly meeting the Sum of five pounds ten shillings Lawfull money & Report to the next mo meeting
	The Overseers Inform that **Jedediah Allen** hath married out of the Unity of friends, They Likewise
J.Allen Disown.ᵈ	Inform that they Precautioned him Therefore this meeting Doth Disown him the Said **Jedediah Allen** from under our Care, and **Irvine Allen** is appointed to Inform him of

his Denial and Report next monthly meeting – –

Jonathan Russell Gave in a paper to this meeting Condemning
his Reporting & Exercising with a Company of men in
the military order which is Refer.[d] to next mo meeting

Committee to fence the Land round y meet. house Friends Conclude it best to fence our Land around our
and we appoint our friends **W[m] Barker W[m] Sandford Thomas
Hicks W[m] Anthony J[u] Timothy Russell Benj[a] Rider** and
Caleb Russell Elishap Smith & Samuel Smith to Confer
together and Cause S.[d] Land to be fenced when and
after what manner they shall think proper.– –

P Russell Disown.[d] The Women Inform that they have Denied **Patience
Russell** wife of **Stephen Russell** which this meeting
Concurs with – –

H: Hicks Receiv[d] They also Inform that they have minuted **Hannah Hicks**
Under their Care which this meeting Concurs with –

Anna Wing Certificate We Likewise Sign,[d] a Certificate to the mo meeting of
Acoakset for **Anna Wing** wife of **Jonathan Wing**
This meeting Collected – – L 8"17[s]"10[d] old tennor

meeting adjourns This meeting Adjourns to the 27 Instant after the meeting
for worship

mett This meeting meet by Adjournment the 27th the 9[mo] 1775-
the Representatives being Called both present
The Queries were Read in this meeting and Answers
thereto prepar,[d] and Likewise an Epistle Sign.[d] by the
Clerk and orderd forward to the Quarterly meeting by

Representi to the Quarterly mee: our Representatives who are **Joseph Tucker Thomas
Hicks Caleb Russell W[m] Mosher W[m] Anthony J[u]** and
William Sandford to attend S[d] Quarterly meeting and they
to make Report to next monthly meeting.

10[mo] 1775 At a Monthly Meeting held in **Dartmouth**
the 16th the 10th mo 1775
The Representatives are **Wm Mosher & Thos Hicks** present
Samuel Smith Chosen Clerk for this time
W[m] Barker & Seth Russell Reports they attended the

Shubel Bunker marriage the marriage of **Shubel Bunker & Lydia Gardner**
which was accomplished orderly

Report of Treasurer The Treasurer Reports he hath not paid the money
to the yearly meetings Treasurer therefore he is now order'd
to pay the Same with two pounds Lawfull money more
which is now aded by the Quarterly meeting, and make

Report next mo meeting

Jedediah Allen not inform of his denial **Prince Allen** Reports he hath not Inform,ᵈ **Jedediah Allen** of his Denial as order,ᵈ

J.Russell paper accepted This meeting Doth Accept **of Jonathan Russell**s paper Condemning his Exercising with the militia, for satisfaction

Return from the Q. meeting The Representatives to the Quarterly meeting Reports they all attended Agreeable to Appointment and have Produc,d an Epistle from the Same which was Read & well Accepted

Epistle Receiv,ᵈ Two Printed Epistles from the Last yearly meeting of our friends in **London** were read in this meeting and the Salutory, Pirtenant & Necessary Advice therein Contain,ᵈ kindly Accepted and Recommended to Each members

J:Wood under Dealing The Overseers Inform that **Josiah Wood** hath been in the Practice of firing up and mending Guns for the Use of war and that they Labour,ᵈ with him therefor but he still persisteth therein. Therefore **Joseph Barker Abraham Howla**nd and **Samuel Smith** and Benjª ~~Howland 2nd~~ **Rider** are appointed to Labour further with him and make Repot next monthly meeting

meetings to begin at the 12 Hour This meeting Concluds that all our meetings for worship only Except at **Bedford** begin at the 12 hour & all the others meetings at the 11 hour and this to Dontinue all the m̲o meeting in the 4th month next

O:Beard Recommeᵈ from Nantucket **Obediah Beard** hath Produced a Certificate from this monthly meeting at **Nantucket,** Informing us that he had a Birthright among them when he Removed from them which is Accepted

Debo: Davic[e] and S. Shephard Certificates Removal Certificates for **Deborah Davice [Davis]** wife of **James Davice**, And **Sarah Sheepherd** wife of **David Sheepherd Jᵘ** from the monthly meeting at **Smithfield** was Read in this meeting and Accepted

F.R. going to Sandwich Our friend **Freeborn Rider** Informs us of her Intention to Visit **Sandwich** Quarterly meeting which this meeting taking into Consideration Concurs with and have Unity with her therein and the Clerk is order,d to Give her a Copy hereof – –

C:Cassel Disown,ᵈ The women Informs they have Denied **Comfort Castle** wife of **Daniel Castle** which this meeting Concurs with this meeting Collected – – £9"13ˢ-9ᵈ old tennor

11 mo 1775   At a Monthly Meeting held in **Dartmouth** the
20th the 11 mo 1775.

the Representatives are **William Barker** and **Joseph Barke[r]**
both present

A.A. & P.K publis.d   **Abraham Allen** and **Phebe Kirby** Declard their Intention
of taking Each other in marriage and were Desir,d
to wait till next monthly meeting for their answer.

and **Prince Allen** and **Thos Hicks** are appointed to Inquire
into the young mans Clearness Respectin marriage & Conversation
and make report next monthly meeting – –

Treasurer Report   The Treasurer Reports that he hath not paid the money
into the yearly meeting treasury as order,d, therefore he is
Continues to pay it as Soon as he can Conveniently and
Report next mo meeting

J.W. matter Refer,d   The Committee that had the Care of that matter Respecting **Jessiah [Josiah]
Wood** Report that they have Labour,d with him and Desire the
matter Refer,d therefore Said matter is Refer,d to next mo meeting
under the Care of the Same friends as heretofore and then they
to make Report

S:Wilcox Disown,d   The women Inform that they have Disown.d **Sarah Wilcox**
Wife of **William Wilcox** which this meeting Concurs with

Job Anthony hath Return.d a Removal Certificate for him=
=self and famely which was Given out from this meeting

J. Anthony Certificate Return,d   the 17th of the 8th mo 1761 which was Directed to the monthly
meeting of **Rhodssland** . And not Deliver.d but now Return.d
he as afore S.d And now he Living in the Compass of the **Coakset**
meeting which was then apart of this meeting therefore the
Clerk is order.d to Transmit a Coppy hereof to S.d **Coakset** meeting

Benjamin Smith jur hath brought a bill to this meeting

B.S. bill given in   fo keeping **Allice Smith** as pr Agreement with the Overseers
of the poor to the amount of £4"17s"1 Lawfull mony
which this meeting approveth and the Treasurer is order.d to
pay Said bill as Soon as he can ~~with~~ and make Report to
this meeting

The Overseers Inform that **James Cornal** hath married
out of the Unity of friends and was timely precautioned

J.Cornal Disown.d   by the Overseers therefore friends Apprehending they are Clear
and do hereby Disown the Said **James Cornal** from being
under our Care and **Barnabas Mosher** is appointed to Inform

him thereof and make Report to next mo meeting

This meeting Collected £4"12^s"11^d old Tennor

To repair meeting house Stable friends Concluds to Repair the meeting house Stable and **Thos Hicks** and **William Anthony j^u** to See it Compleated and make Report next mo meeting

---

12 ^{mo} At a Monthly Meeting held in **Dartmouth** the 18th the 12 ^{mo} 1775

1775 the Representatives are **Caleb Russell** and **Samuel Smith** pres[ent]

Abra Allen Clearness The friends appointed to Inquire into **Abraham Allens** Clearness and Conversation Respecting marriage Report that they have taken the Necessary Care and find nothing to hinder their proceeting

Abraham Allen and **Phebe Kirby** appear,^{d} for their Answer

A:A.& P K had their answer which was that they might proceed to take Each other in marriage in Some Convenient time before next mo meeting advising with the Overseers that this meeting shall appoint for that purpose and **Prince Allen** and **Thomas Hicks** are appoint[ed] to See S^d marriage Consomated orderly and make next mo meeting.

Treasurer Report The Treasurer Reports that he hath not paid the money into the yearly meeting treasury therefore he is Desired to pay Said money as Soon as he Conveniently can and Report to next mo meeting

The Treasurer Reports that he hath paid $^£$4"17^s"1^d to **Benja^m Smith j^u** as order,^{d} last monthly meeting

Stable Repar.^{d} The friends appointed to Repair the meeting house Stable Report that it is Copleated – –

The Committee that had the Care of that matter Respecting **Jesiah Wood** Report that Notwithstanding their Repeeted Labour with him he Still Continues in the Same practice of mending & Repairing guns for the Use of war which is Inconsistant with the profession we make therefore this meeting

J.W. matter Refer.^{d} doth Conclude to Disown him if he doth not Imediately Desist therefrom and the Same Committee are still Continued to Inform him hereof and Draw a paper of Denial against him if do not Comply with the Judgment of this meeting and they to make Report next mo meeting

Barnabus Mosher Reports that he hath Inform,^{d} **James Cornal** of his Denial as order,^{d}

Our well Esteemed friends **Aaron Vail** and **David Sands** were

A.V: and David Sands visited us at this meeting with their Certificates from the monthly meeting of the **Nine Partner** Dated the 17th of the 11 ^{mo} 1775 whos Visit

Testimon and Labour of Love was Kindly Accepted among us[18]
The Queries were Answer,^{d} ad an Epistle Signed in this
meeting and orderd forwar.^{d} to the Quaterly meeting by our
Representatives who are **Thomas Hicks Wm Mosher Barzillia**

Representa^s to the Q: meeting **Tucker Samuel Smith Abraham Howland & Wm Barker** and
they to make Report next <u>mo</u> meeting

order on Treasur^{er} The Treasurer is orderd to pay **Timothy Russell** five Dollars
for Keeping the meeting house half a year and make Report
next mo meeting
This meeting Collected 8$^£$"2^s"0^d old tenor

---

1 ^{mo} At a Monthly Meeting held in **Dartmouth** the 15th the 1 <u>mo</u> 1776

1776 the Representatives are **Benj.^{a} Howland 2.nd & Joseph Tucker ju**
both Present
one of the friends appointed to see **Abraham Allen** and

A Allen Married **Phebe Kirb**made Report that he
attended Said marriage and Saw nothing but what it was
Consomated orderly & the other friend Render,^{d} a Reasonable
Excuse for his not attending S.^{d} marriage

Report of Trea surer The Treasurer Reports that he hath paid the money as orderd
into the yearly meeting Treasury
The Committee that had the Care of that matter Respecting
Jesiah Wood Report that he gave them Incouragment of

J.W. matter Referd Desisting from mending guns for the ~~we of~~ Sogers therefore
the matter is Refer,^{d} under the Care of the Same
Same Committee as heretofore and they to Inform Sd **Wood** that
tis the mind of this meeting that he ought to Condemn his past
misconduct in that matter and **Prince Allen** is aded to s^d Committee
and they to Report to next monthly meeting
The Representatives to the Quarterly meeting Report that

Return from the Q meeting they all attend agreeable to appointment and have Produced
an Eppistle from the Same which hath been read to Satisfaction
and therein Inform that **Smithfield [Rhode Island]** monthly meeting hath
been at the Expence of £294"6"1 Lawfull money in building
a meeting house which is recommended for Contrebution
as they in their Freedom Shall see fit

Report from Treasurer The Treasurer Reports he hath paid **Timothy Russell**
five Dollars as order.d – –

18. David Sands (1745–1818), a native of Long Island, traveled extensively among Friends, including a visit to the British Isles from 1795 to 1804. See *Journal of the Life and Gospel Labours of David Sands, with Extracts from His Correspondence* (London: C. Gilpin, 1848).

B.H. 3rd under Dealing We are Inform,^d from the Preparative meeting that
Benjamin Howland the 3rd hath been Aiding or Assisting
with a Company of men in taking away guns from from
friends and others and hath been Labour,^d with by the
Overseers and not Condemning it to friends Satisfaction
therefore we appoint our friends **Joseph Barker** & **Samuel
Smith** to Labour further with him and Report to next mo meeting

Jos Trafford informd of denial **Benjamin** ∧Howland **the 2**nd Reports he hath Served **Joseph Trafford** with
a Coppy of his Denial Agreeable to Appointment
there was a Certificate Sign,^d in this meeting for our Traveling

Certificate for Trave[l] friends friends **Aaron Vail** & **David Sands** to the mo meeting
of the **Ninepartners**
this meeting Collected 3£"16^s"3^d old tenor

---

2 ^{mo} 1776 At a Monthly meeting held in **Dartmouth** 19th the 2 mo 1776
the Representatives are **John Potter** & **Gideon Howland** both present

J.R and Sarah M publish.^d **John Ricketson** and **Sarah Morell** Declar,^d their Intention
of taking Each other in marriage and were Desir,^d to wait
till next monthly meeting for their answer and **Thomas Hicks**
and **Philip Allen** are appointed to Inquire into Said **Ricketson**s
Clearness Respecting marriage and Conversation and make
Report next monthly meeting

Josiah Wood gave in a paper The Committee that had the Care of that matter Respecting
Jesiah Wood Report that they have Discharg,^d their trust in
that matter & S.^d **wood** gave in a paper to this meeting as follow^{eth}

J:Williams Confession **John William** appear,^d in this meeting and Confer,^d
that he Some time past Inconsiderately fixed and sold
Some Straps for the use of Solder in Corring [Carrying?]their warlike
Stoves [Stores?] but going uneasy therein Desisted from Suppling them
in any such matters also **P.Williams** verbilly Condemned
his misconduct therein which this meeting Accepts for Satisfaction

Ben Howlands Case referd The Committee that had the Care of that matter Respecting
Benj^a **Howland 3.**rd Reports that they have made Some progress
in that matter and **B. Howland** gave in a paper to this meetg
Condemning S.^d misconduct but friend not Reseiving full Satisfaction
Satisfaction on account of S^d **Howland**^s not going to the
parsons from which the guns was taken, therefore the matter
is Refer^d to next monthly meeting under the Care of the Same
Committee as heretofore and then they to make Report
We are informed by the Overseers that **Elijah Sandford**
hath married his first Cousin & out of the Unity of friends

and been Labour^d with by s^d Overseers & not Inclining to
to Condemn his misconduct in that matter therefore
this meeting concluds that for the Clearing of truth we

E.S. can do no less than Disown him therefore we hereby Disown
Disownd the S^d **Elijah Sandford** from under our Care and the Clerk
is orderd to read this minute at the Close of a first days
meeting before next monthly meeting and then make report
and **William Barker** is appointed to Inform S^d **Sandford** of his
Denial and report to next monthly meeting

The Overseers inform that **Daniel Smith** Son of **Humphy**
hath been in the Practice of taking Spiritous Liquors
to access also neglects attending meetings for which they

D.Smith have Labour^d with him and he not Condeming it to
under
Dealing Satisfaction therefore we appoint **John Potter** and
Abraham Howland to Labour further with him on that
account and Report to next mo meeting – –
This meeting Collected – – £6"8ˢ"11ᵈ old T

adjourn This meeting Adjourns to the 28th Instant – –
mett Meeting met by Adjournment ye 28th of 2nd mo 1776
The Representatives are **John Potter** & **Gideon Howland** Present

B. Sherman   We are Inform^d by the Overseers from the preparative
under
Dealing meeting that **Benjamin Shearman** hath been to a place
of frallicking and measureably join^d with those that
that were therein very unbecoming a friend also neglects
attending meeting & the Overseers having Labour^d with him
and he not Condeming it to Satisfaction Likewise the
Overseers Inform that Divers of our young friends hath
been in the practice of going to places Publick revort where
very undue Liberty is taken Evin of musick and
dancing and other Lacivious and unbecoming conduct to
the Reproach of truth and a Grief to Solid friends. Some
of which hath been Labour^d with by S^d Overseers and this
meeting taking it into Consideration thinks proper that
they be further Labour^d with, therefore do appoint **Joseph
Tucker and William Sandford Barzillai Tucker Samuel
Smith Wm Barker Benjamin Rider** for that purpose
with the Assistance of the Overseers and make Report to
next mo meeting

3 mo At a Monthly Meeting of friends held in **Dartmouth**
1776 the 18th of 3rd month 1776 – –

The Representatives are **William Mosher** and **Saml Smith** present
Notwithstanding **Jesiah Wood** gave in a paper Last
monthly meeting Condemning his misconduct in mending
guns, yet this meeting as Inform^d by part of the
former Committee that had the care of that matter
that he Still Continues in the practice of mending

J.W. yet under Dealing guns in this time of publick Commotion which we apprehend
brings a Reproach upon friends therefore this meeting
Concluds that **J.Wood** Desist from mending or making any more
guns at present and the former Committee is appointed
to Inform **J.Wood** of the Conclution of this meeting and
S^d Committee to Draw a paper of Denial against him
if he Dont Emadiately Desist and bring it to next mo
Meeting

Ann Gifford Visit to Sandwich **Anne Gifford** Inform,^d this meeting that She has thoughts
of attending **Sandwich** Quarterly meeting and Desires
our Concurence therein and this meeting having Unity with
her Intended Visit She being in unity with us and her
Publick Testimony approv^d of among us and the

Clerk to give a coppy of this minute Clerk is order.^d to gave her a Coppy of this minute
The Clerk Reports that he hath read the minute against

Elij. Sanford inform.^d of denial **Elijah Sandford** as order.^d also **Wm Barker** Reports that
he Inform.^d S^d **Sandford** of his Denial as order.^d – –

L.S Confession **Leamuel Smith** gave in a paper to this meeting Condemning
his marrieng out of the Unity of friends which this meeting accepts
This meeting Collected £4"2^s"8^d old tennor

Adjourn this meeting adjourns to the Last forth Day in this month
after the meeting for worship which is to begin at ye 11 hour

Mett This meeting meet by Adjournment the 27th ye 3 ^mo 1776
the Representatives are **Wm Barker** & **Samuel Smith** present
The Committee that had the Care of that matter Respecting
Daniel Smith Reports that they have Discharg.^d their trust
in that matter and find no Satisfaction Therefore this meeting

D.Smith Disown.^d Apprehending we have Discharg.^d our Duty towards him
Do Disown the Said **Daniel Smith** from under our Care
and **Abraham Howland** & **Gideon** are appointed to Inform
him of the Conclution of this meeting and Draw a testimony
against him & bring it to next mo meeting

Case of Benj Shearman referd The Committee that was appointed to Join the Overseers in
Labouring with **Benjamin Sherman** & Some of our young friends
for going to places of frollicking Report that they havent

Completed S^d business therefore they are still Continued
in that Service & to make Report next <u>mo</u> meeting

Case of B Howland 3rd refer^d

The Committee that had the care of that matter Respecting
Benj.^a Howland 3.rd Report that that matter is not fully settled
therefore S^d matter is Refer.^d to next <u>mo</u> meeting under their Care
and then they to make Report – –

The friends that were appointed to Inquire into **John
Rickertson,^s** Clearness Respecting marriage Reports that
they find nothing So materal as to hinder their Proceeding
in marriage

J.R. had his Answer

John Ricketson and **Sarah Morell** appear.^d for their
answer which was that they might Proceed to take Each
other in marriage in Some Convenient time before next
monthly meeting advising with the friends that this meeting
appoints for that purpose and **Thomas Hicks** & **Wm Barker**
are appointed to See their marriage Consomated orderly
and make report next <u>mo</u> meeting

M:Wing under Dealing

A former minute of this meeting made in 8th <u>mo</u> 1753
Respecting **Mary Wing** was read in this meeting whereby
it appears She had been Under Dealing and had not
"Received her as a friend in full Unity but Suspended
the matter for Some further Proof of her Sincerity"
And this meeting taking the matter into Consideration
do appoint **William Anthony ^ju Gideon Howland Sam.^el Smith**
to Inquire into her Life and Conversation where She hath
Lived, for a further Proof of her Sincerity and make
Report next mo meeting

H.Smith Confession

Henry Smith gave in a Paper this meeting Condeming
Some Expressions he made in his Pation to Oder [?]
which this meeting Accepts

J.Slocum Complain.^d of

Thomas Hicks hath Exhibited a Complaint against
Jonathan Slocum for Refusing or Neglecting to pay
his Rate for the year 1768 therefore this meeting
doth Appoint **Benj.^a Smith ^ju Benj^a Slocum** & **George
Smith** to Enquire into the Reason of ^ye **Slocum**s Refusing
to pay S^d rate & Report next <u>mo</u> meeting

G.H. & wives Confession

Gideon Howland the 2nd with his wife **Catherin** Gave in
a paper to the Preparative meeting Condemning their falling
into the Sin of fornication and marrying Nigh of kind, but by
Reason of S^d paper being mislaid & not brought to this meeting

the matter is Refer,^d to next <u>mo</u> meeting and the Clerk is Desir,d
to Brouse[?] Said paper to S^d meeting

The Queries were answer,^d in this meeting and an Epistle
Sign.^d for the Quarterly meeting and order,^d forward to S.^d Quarterly

Repre: sentatives to ye Q. meeting   meeting by our Representatives who are **Barzillia Tucker William Anthony j^u James Davis** & they to make Report next <u>mo</u> meeting

---

4 <u>mo</u> 1776   At a Monthly Meeting held in **Dartmouth** the 15th ye 4th month 1776

the Representatives are **Caleb Russell** & **Joseph Barker** present

Josiah Wood Disown,d   The Committee Appointed to Labour with **Jesiah Wood** Reports they have fulfilled their appointment therein and that he Refuses to Comply with the advice & Judgment of this meeting there: =fore the Clerk hath Sign.^d a paper of Denial against him

Daniel Smith Disown,d   Also the Committee appointed on account of **Daniel Smith** Report they have fulfiled their appointment and have Drafted a paper of Denial against him which was also Sign,^d by the Clerk and the Clerk is order,^d to Read both the afore S,^d papers Publickly at the Close of a first Days meeting for worship and make Report next <u>mo</u> meeting

B.Shear= =man & o case refer,d   The friends appointed to Join the Overseers in Labouring with **Benj^a Shearman** & Some young People for going to places of frollicking, Report that they have not fulfilled their appointment in that matter therefore they are Still Continued in that Service and to Report next <u>mo</u> meeting

Ben Howland case referd   The Committee appointed on account of **Benj^a Howland 2nd** Report that they have made Some progress in that matter but finding things things not fully setled to friends Satisfaction therefore Said matter is Still Continued Under their Care and they to Report to next monthly meeting

J.Ricketson married   One of the friends appointed to See the marriage of **John Ricke- =tson** and **Sarah Moral** consomated Report that he attended Said marriage and did not see but that it was Consomated in good order, the other friend Reports that he was Detain,^d by Sickness and did not attend S^d marriage

Case Mary Wing referd   The Committee appointed on account of **Mary Wing** Reports that they ~~gave~~ have made Some progress and this meeting thinks proper that they Inform S,^d **Mary Wing** of their appoint= =ment therefore S,^d matter is Refer,^d under their Care one month Longer and then they to make Report – –

Case of Jonathan Slocum Settled — The Committee appointed on Account of **Jonathan Slocum** Reports that Said **Slocum** hath paid his Rate to **Tho.ˢ Hicks** and the the matter is Setled – –

Return from yᵉ Q. meeting — The friends appointed to attend the Quarterly meeting Report that they all attended and have produced an Epistle from S.ᵈ meeting which was read and well Accepted – – they Define in Said Epistle Some Assistance towards Defraying the Charge of building the meeting house at **Smithfield** therefore this meeting Appoints **Caleb Russell Thoˢ** ~~Hicks~~ **Russell Tho.ˢ Mott Giles Slocum & Wᵐ Barker** to Draw Subscriptions & Sign them in behalf of this meeting and

Committee to raise money — Receive the money of Each member as they in their freedom Shall See fit and **Caleb Russell** is order,ᵈ to pay the Same to the Said **Smithfield** meeting and they to make Report of the Sum So Collected to next mo meeting

Gideon Howland and wife paper — **Gideon Howland 2.ⁿᵈ & Catherine** his wife gave in a paper to this meeting Condemning their falling into the Sin of fornication and marring[marrying] nigh in kind, Therefore we appoint **Benjᵃ Taber John Williams** and **Joseph Barker** to Join the women and take an Oppertunity of Conference with them in order to Discover their Sincerity in that matter and make Report next mo meeting

Committy to Revise yᵉ minut — We appoint **W.ᵐ Anthony Jⁿ Samuel Smith Gideon Howland** and **Thomas Hicks** to Revise and Correct the monthly meeting minutes in order to goe on Record, Also to Settle Accounts with the Treasurer and make Report next monthly meeting – –

Chusing overseer referd — The Chuising Overseers is Refer,ᵈ to next monthly meeting and the former ones is continued untill there be a new Choice

meetings to begin 11 hour — it.ˢ Concluded that all our meetings Except at **Bedford** begin at the Eleventh hour untill the monthly meeting in the tenth month next

P.Giff under Dealing Baptice — The Overseers Inform that **Peleg Gifford jᵘʳ** hath been to a Baptice meeting and undertook to Emitate them in Singing which we think very unbecoming one of our profession – – and tis the mind of this meeting that S.ᵈ **Gifford** aught to publickly Condemn S.ᵈ misconduct therefore we appoint **Abraham Howland Benjᵃ Smith jᵘ Philip Allen** to Labour with him on that account and make Report next monthly meeting – –

order to pay Tim Russell for hay — The Treasurer is order,ᵈ to pay **Timothy Russell** 9ˢ/£:m: to pay for hay which was Expended at our Quarterly meeting last faull – –

A.Rick
Disown,d

The Committee appointed Some time past to have the care of that matter Respecting **Abraham Ricketson** Report that they have had S^d matter under Consideration and now Inform that they have no Satisfaction from S^d **Ricketson** therefore we hereby Disown the S^d **Abraham Ricketson** from under our Care and **Thos Hicks** is appointed to Inform Him thereof

This meeting Collected £7"3^s"4^d old tennor—The Treasurer

T.R. paid

reports that he paid **Timothy Russell** the above 9^s/ as order,^d

---

5mo 1776

At a Monthly Meeting held in **Dartmouth** the 20th the 5th mo 1776

The Representatives are **Joseph Barker** & **Thos Hicks** present

G. Handy
Publish,^d

George Handy and **Mary Potter** Declared their Intentions of taking Each other in marriage and were Desired to wait till next monthly meeting for their answer, and **Samuel Smith** and **Abraham Howland** are appointed to Inquire into the young mans Clearness Respecting marriage and Conversation and Report to next monthly meeting – –

Choosing
Overseers
refer,^d

The Choosing of Overseers is Refer,^d to next monthly meeting

The Clerk Reports that he hath Read the testimony against **Jesiah Wood** and **Daniel Smith** as order,^d. Said Testimonies are as followeth

J.Wood
Denial

Whereas **Jesiah Wood** having made Profession with us, and under the care of this meeting, yet hath so far Departed from the Principal of Truth and the Testimony thereof as to be found in the practice of mending or Repairing Guns, or fire arms (So called) for the use of war and friends having Labour,^d with him Repeatedly in much Love in order to Discover to him the Evil thereof, and to Reclaim him there from, but friends Avice and Admonision not having the Desired and he Continuing in the Said Practice to the Dishonour of Truth and Grief of faithfull friends, Therefore for the maintaining of our Testimony herein, This meeting is Concern,^d to Give this forth as a Publick Denial Against him, and do hereby disown him the S^d **Jesiah Wood** from being a member of our Society, and from under the care of this meeting. Desiring Nevertheless that he may Return from the Error of his way, and by an unfeigned Repentance and Acknowledgement of the Evil thereof, Return to the way of truth Given forth & Signed in & on behalf of our monthly meeting held in **Dartmouth** the 15th ye 4th mo 1776 by – **Wm Anthony jur** Clerk

Dan Smith
denial

Whereas **Daniel Smith** Son of **Humphry Smith** of **Dartmouth** in the County of **Bristol** in the Province of the **Massachusets** Bar in **New England**, having been Educated and made Profession with friends but hath so far Departed therefore

as to frequently take too much Spiritous Liquors to the Reproach of that holy
and name that he hath protended to make profession of also hath much
neglected attending of meetings, and friends having Labour^d with him in
Love for his Recovery but our Labour not having its Desir,^{d} Effect therefore
for the Clearing of truth and the testimony we hear from such Practices this meeting
is Concern.^{d} to give this forth as a Publick testimony against him & do hereby
disown him the S.^{d} **Daniel Smith** from being a member of our Society untill
by a Reformation he Shall Return from the Error of his ways & be Restored
to the way of truth Given forth & Signed in and by order of our monthly meeting
of friends held in **Dartmouth** the 15th ye 4th m̲o̲ 1776 by **Wm Anthony ju** Clerk

Benj
Howland 3
case referd

The Committee appointed on account of **Benjamin Howland 3rd** Report that
the matter is not fully Setled therefore Said matter is Refer,^{d} to next
monthly meeting under the Care of the Same Committee as heretofore
and then they to make Report

The Committee appointed on account of **Mary Wing** Report that they
have fulfilled their appointment therein and by Enquiry they do not
find her Life and Conversation hath Manifested a Sincear Repen-

M.Wing
Disown,d

=tance in Respect to her Crimes for which She was under Dealing
therefore this meeting Concluds to disown her from being a member
of our Society and the Same Com,^{tee} are appointed to Draw up a
paper against her and bring it to the next monthly meeting

R.Case
Receiv,^{d}

The women Inform that **Rachel Case** wife of **John Case** is Receiv,^{d}
as a member among them they also Inform they Receiv,^{d} a Removal Certificate for **Phebe Beard** Daughter of **John Beard** which is accepted

Ben Sher=
=man case

The Committee appointed to Laboure with **Benj^a Sherman** Reports
They have fulfilled their appointment and he Acknowledges his Desit[Deceit]
in not attending our meetings, but they do not find upon full Inquiry
that he Join,^{d} with those in a frolick but hapened there on
the account of Business which Report is accepted

young peo=
=pel case
refer^d

The Committee appointed to Joine or assist the overseers in Labouring
with the young people Reporte they have not gone through with
S^d Service they are therefore Still Continued in that Service and
to make Report next monthly meeting

Report on
Collecting
money

The Committee appointed to Draw Subscriptions & Collect money
for the use of **Smithfield** meeting Report they have made Some
Progress therein but not finished it they are Continued for that
Service and to Report next monthly meeting.

P.Gifford jn^r
gave in a
paper

Peleg Gifford j^u gave in a paper to this meeting Condemning
his misconduct which is Refer,^{d} to next mo meeting by reason
the Committee appointed on that account are not fully

Satisfied and they are Continued in that Service and to Report next monthly meeting

C:Green Paper accepted **Tho.ˢ Hicks** Reports he hath Inform,ᵈ **Abraham Ricketson** of his Denial as order,ᵈ

Caleb Green hath given in a paper to this meeting Condemning his Procuring the Printing of a Small Pamphlet on the Subject of paying Taxes that was not Discovered by the yearly meetings Committee for Viewing manuscripts which paper is accepted for Satisfaction[19]

Dan Wood request a Certificate **Daniel Wood** Requests a Removal Certificate to the monthly meeting of the **Oblong**, and this meeting appoints **James Davis** and **Caleb Russell** to Enquire into his Circumstances and draw one for him if they think proper and bring it to next mo meeting

Gid Howland case referd The Committee Appointed to Confer with **Gideon Howland 2ⁿᵈ** Report that he gave them a Degree of Satisfaction but the but the Receiving his paper is Refer,ᵈ to next mo meeting under the care of the Same Comittee & then they to make report

Settlement with yᵉ treasury The Committee appointed to Revise & Correct this meetings minuts Report they have fulfilled their Appointment also Setled Accounpts with the treasurer and there Remains in the Stock £6"5ˢ"9ᵈ Lawfull money – –

C.Russell Request **Charles Russell** Gave in a paper to this meeting Condemning his falling into the Sin of fornication for which transaction he wa Denie,ᵈ and Requests to be Receiv,ᵈ again under friends care Therefore this meeting appoints **Prince Allen** & **Benjᵃ Smith jⁿᵉʳ** to take an oppertunity of Solid Conference with him in order to Discover his Sincerity and to make Report next mo meeting

Report of yᵉ meeting at Bedford The friends Appointed to have the Oversight of the meeting at **Bedford** Report that Sᵈ meeting hath been held & Kept as orderly as Usual and they Still Request Sᵈ meeting may be Continued as heretofore untill the monthly meeting in the forth month next year which is granted and **Caleb Russell** and **Seth Russell** & **James Davis** are Appointed to have the oversight thereof and to make Report at the Expiration thereof – –

19. Any Friend wishing to publish a work on Quaker beliefs and practices was expected to have the work reviewed and approved by the Meeting for Sufferings, which functioned as the equivalent of an executive committee for the yearly meeting. The "Small Pamphlet" was almost certainly Timothy Davis, *Letter from a Friend to Some of His Intimate Friends on the Subject of Paying Taxes* (Watertown, Mass.: B. Edes, 1776). See below, n. 23.

B Smith
bill

Benj^a Smith j^u gave in a bill for doing for the poor
to the amount of £6"14^s"8^d Lawfull money which is accepted
and the treasurer is order^d to pay S^d money & Report next
mo meeting – –
This meeting Collected – – £6"2^s"11^d old tennor

6 month
1776

At a Monthly Meeting held in **Dartmouth** the
17th the 6mo 1776 - **Thomas Hicks** is appointed Clerk for this Day
the Representatives are **Wm Sandford** & **Nicholas Howland** present
This meeting Adjourns to the 24th Instant after ye meeting
of worship – –
This meeting meet by Adjournment ye 24th 6mo 1776
the Representatives being Called both Present
The friends appointed to Inquire into **George Handy**^s Clearn[ess]
Respecting marriage and Conversation Report that they
have taken the Necessary care on that account and find
nothing to hinder their Proceeding

G Handy
Answer

George Handy and **Mary Potter** appear^d for their Answer
which was that they might Proceed to take Each other in
marriage in Some Convenient time before next monthly
meeting Advising with the Overseers that this meeting
Shall appoint for that purpose, and **Abraham Howland**
and **Samuel Smith** are appointed to See their marriage
Consomated orderly and Report next mo meeting

Overseers
appointed

Our friends **Joseph Barker Thomas Hicks Wm Barker**
James Davis & **Wm Anthony j^{ur}** are appointed Overseers
for the year Ensuing

appointing
overseers of
poor referd

The appointing Overseers of the poor is Refer^d to next
monthly meeting

~~Gid~~ Benj
Howlands
case refer^d

The Committee appointed on account of **Benj^a Howland 3rd**
made Somewhat a Satisfactory Report on that account
yet the Receiving of S^d **Howland**^s paper is Refer^d to next
monthly meeting under the Care of the former Committee
and **Prince Allen** & **Wm Barker** are ad[d]ed to them and they
to Report next mo meeting

Mary Wing
case refer^d

The Committee appointed on account of **Mary Wing** have
Prepar^d a paper agreeable to Appointment, yet that mat[t]er
is still Continued to next monthly meeting under Care of
S^d Committee

Visit of
D F and
J - Perry

Our Beloved friends **David Faris** and **John Pery [Perry]** have
attended this meeting with their Certificates from the monthly

meeting of **Willminton** [**Wilmington**] in the **County of New Cassell** [**New Castle**]
on **Dillewar** [**Delaware**] [*originally written on one line*]
Dated the 15th of the 5th month 1776 – which were Read to Satisfact[ion]
and their Visit well Accepted

Visit of
R W and
P- Yarnall

Also our Beloved friends **Phebe Yarnall** and **Rebecca Wright**
were at this meeting with their Certificates, the former from
the monthly meeting held at **Concord** in **Chester County Pennsyl**
vania the 7th of the 2nd mo 1776[20] The Latter from the monthly
meeting held at **Chesterfield** the 2nd day of ye 5th mo 1776, which
were read to Satisfaction & their Visit Kindly Accepted – –

on account of
young people

The Committee Appointed to Assist the Overseers in Labouring
with Some of the young People, Report they have made Some
further Progress therein and that they Beleive it to be of
Service therefore they are Continued to Proceed further in that
matter as they may find themselves Engaged therein and to make
Report thereof to the next monthly meeting

Queries
Answerd

The Queries have been Read and Answers thereto Read &
approved . –   This meeting is Informed that **Thomas Allen**
(Son of **Francis**) hath married out of the Unity of Friends
Notwithstanding his being Previously Cautioned to desist

T -Allen
Disownd

therefore this meeting doth Disown him the Said **Thomas Allen**
from being a member of our Religious Society & **Benja Taber**
is appointed to Inform Said **Allen** of his Denial & Report next
monthly meeting

This meeting Collected – –   £10 " 5s " 9d old tennor

Adjourn This meeting Adjourns to the 26 Instant after the meeting for worship

mett This meeting meet by adjournment the 26th ye 6th mo 1776
the Representatives both Present

Peleg Gifford Ju
case referd

The Committee that had the Care of that matter Respecting
Peleg Gifford Ju Report that they Satisfied on that [*next word is faded*]
but the Receiving Sd **Giffords** paper is Referd to next mo meeting
by Reason he is not [*smudged*] present

D-Wood
Certificate

A Removel Certificate of **Daniel Wood** Directed to the monthly
meeting at the **Oblong** was Signed in this meeting – –

Case of Gid
Howland 2
referd

The Matter Respecting **Gideon Howland 2nd** is Referd to next
monthly meeting under the Care of the former Committee who
are then to make Report

M Wing
Certificate
wife of Giles

A Removal Certificate Directed to the monthly meeting
of the **Nine Partners** for **Mary Wing** wife of **Giles Wing** was

20. Several women named Phebe Yarnall were members of Philadelphia Yearly Meeting at this time.
Rebecca Wright (1737–1811) later traveled in the British Isles. See Larson, *Daughters of Light*, 333.

Signed in this meeting

Cha^r Russel case referd — The Committee Appointed to Confer with **Charles Russell** Report that he gave them a Degree of Satisfaction but his not being present Said matter is Refer^d to next mo meeting under the care of S^d Committee who are then to make Report

The treasurer Reports that he hath paid the money to **Benjamin Smith J^u** as order^d last monthly meeting

Treasurer report — The Treasurer is order^d to pay **Timothy Russell** five Dollars for half year^s keeping the meeting house and Report next monthly meeting

mony Rais^d for Smith-field — The friends appointed to Collect money for the Use of **Smithfield** monthly meeting and pay to **Caleb Russell** for that purpose Report (**Giles Slocum**) Excepted) [*sic*] that they have Collected and paid Said **Russell** the Sum of – – £7 " 3^s " 7^d Lawfull money

A Wilcox under Dealing — Whereas **Amos Willcox** having a birthright among friends but we finding his Conduct & Conversation being very Inconsistant with our Profession (viz) going to frollicks, bad Language and not attending meetings and he having been Labour^d with by the Overseers but he Continuing therein and we appoint **Benjamin Howland Prince Allen** to Labor with him as they find freedom and Report next mo meeting

Representa: to ye Q: meeting — There was an Epistle Signed in this meeting to the Quarterly meeting we appoint our friends **Caleb Russell Thomas Hicks Wm Anthony J^u** to attend the Quarterly meeting and present the Epistle and Answers to the Queries and Report next mo meeting

---

7mo 1776 — At a Monthly Meeting held in **Dartmouth** 15th ye 7mo 1776 The Representatives are **Wm Barker** & **Prince Allen** present

George Handy marriage — The friends appointed to See **George Handy** and **Mary Potter^s** marriage Consomated Report that they attended S^d marriage & Saw nothing but that it was Solemnised orderly

overseers of ye Poor — We appoint our friends **Abraham Howland Prince Allen Philip Allen Joseph Tucker J^ur Caleb Russell** & **Benj^a Rider** Overseers of the Poor for the year Ensuing. – –

E. Taber Disownd — One of the Overseers Inform that **Edward Taber** is married out of the Unity of friends after being precaution^d Therefore we do Disown him the Said **Edward Taber** from being one of our Society and **John Williams** is appointed to Inform him of his Denial and Report to next monthly meeting

Case of Benja Howland 3 refered — The matter Respecting **Benjamin Howland** 3^d[?] is Refer^d to next mo meeting under the Same friends care as heretofore & then they to make Report. – –

Case of young people refer^d   The Committee that was to Joine the Overseers in Labouring with Some young People, Report they have not Compleated S^d business therefore they are Still Continued & **Prince Allen** is ad[d]ed to them and they to Report next mo meeting

Mary Wing case referd   The Matter Respecting **Mary Wing** is Refer^d to next mo meeting *ration* under the care of the Same Committee as heretofore for further Conside

Peleg Gifford J^ur case referd   The matter Respecting **Peleg Gifford J^ur** is Refer^d to next mo meeting under the care of the Same Committee as heretofore they being not fully Satisfied[?] and then they to make Report

C: Russel accepted   The Commit[t]ee that had the care of that matter Respecting **Charles Russell** made a Satisfactory Report on that account therefore this mee[ting?] Accepts of S^d **Russell** to be one under our care provided he cause the paper [he?] gave into the meeting to be Read publickly at the Close of a first day and he being present befor[e] next <u>mo</u> meeting & then Return S^d paper & Report its being read

Treasurer Report   The Treasurer Reports he paid **Timothy Russell** five Dollars as order[ed] last mo meeting

A Wilcox case referd   The Committee appointed to Labour with **Amos Willcox** Report that they have not fulfilled their Appointment by reason when they went to [his?] place of abode he was not at home therefore they are Still Contin[ued?] in that Service & to make report next mo meeting – –

Report from ye Quarterly meeting   The friends Appointed to attend the Quarterly meeting Report they all Attended S^d meeting And Produc^d an Epistle from the Same [which?] was Read and well Accepted, Together with a Transcript of Our last yearly meeting Epistle together with a number of Epistles from the yearly meeting & meeting of Sufferings in **London** which Said Epistle[s] have been Reprinted and Distributed among most of friends famelies of this meeting for their perusial [perusal]

T Hicks appointed Elder   This meeting appoints **Thos Hicks** an Elder and Refer the appointing more to next mo meeting

Gid How= =land 2 case referd   The matter Respecting **Gideon Howland 2nd** is Refer^d to next <u>mo</u> meeting by reason the women have non [a]ccepted his wives paper

This meeting Collected – – £8   1^s   8^d

---

8 month 1776   At a Monthly Meeting held in **Dartmouth** y^e 19th the 8th mo 1776 the Representatives are **John Williams** present **Benj^a Smith J^u** not present by Reason of his attending funeral

Edw Taber not inform^d of denial   **John Williams** Reports that he hath not Inform^d **Edward Taber** of his Deniel as order^d therefore he is Continued to Compleat S^d apointment And make Report next monthly meeting – –

Tho Allen informd   **Benjamine Taber** Reports that he hath Informed **Thomas Allen** of his Deniel [Denial] as ordered

Part of the Committy that had the car[e] of that matter Respecting

Ben How=
=land 3
case referd
Benjamine Howland 3ʳᵈ Reports that have made Some progress but desire
the matter Referd therefore Sᵈ matter is Referd under their Care and they to
Report to next monthly meeting – –

young people
case continued
Some of the Committee that was to Join the Overseers in Labouring
with Some of the young People Report that they have made Some
progress and Desire Sᵈ matter to be Continued therefore its Continue[d] to
next mo meeting & then they to make Report

M. Wing
Disownd
This meeting Signᵈ a paper of Deniel against **Mary Wing** and the
Clerk is orderᵈ to Read Sᵈ paper at the close of a first days meeting before
next <u>mo</u> meeting & then they to make Report and **Wᵐ Barker** is appointed
to Inform her of her Denial & Report next <u>mo</u> meeting Said paper is as followeth

her paper of
denial
Whereas **Mary Wing** Some years past was under Dealing by this
meeting (as appears by our Records) and altho She Gave in a paper
Condemning her Misconduct, yet the meeting did not Receive her
into full Unity but Suspended the matter for further Proof of her
Sincerity. Now this meeting (of late) having made Enquiry into her
Conduct and Conversation and Likewise have had Conference with
her on that matter and do‸ᶰᵒᵗ find a Sufficient Proof of a Sincear Repentan[ce?]
but Rather the Contrary therefore this meeting doth deny her the
Said **Mary Wing** from being a member of our Religious Society
untill by a Sincear Repentance and Return from the Evil of her
ways as a Sure token thereof to the way of Truth & well doing
Signᵈ in and on behalf of our monthly meeting held in
Dartmouth the 19ᵗʰ yᵉ 8ᵗʰ month 1776 - by **Wᵐ Anthony Jᵘ** Clerk
　　　　　　　　　　　　　　　Susana Smith C[l]erk

report on Peleg
Giffords case
The Committee that had the care of that matter Respecting **Peleg**
Gifford Jᵘʳ Report that he gave them a Degree of Satisfaction
therefore this meeting Accepts of Sᵈ **Gifford** paper for Satisfaction
provided he cause Sᵈ paper to be publickly Read at the Close of a
first Days meeting (he being present) before next <u>mo</u> meeting & then
Return Sᵈ paper & make Report　　Sᵈ paper is as followeth

P .Gifford
paper
To the monthly meeting of friends to be held in **Dartmouth** on the
20 yᵉ 5<u>mo</u> 1776 – – Dear friends being in A Sense of my misconduct
when being at a meeting of another Society, in Singing Psalms
with them, which I am Sorry for Considering it was not according
to the Constitutional principles of our Profession So to do Desiring
friends and all others therein Concernᵈ to pass it by that I may
Remain under the care of this meeting is the Desire of your
friend – –　　　　　　　　　　**Peleg Gifford Jᵘʳ**
Dartmouth 14 yᵉ 5ᵐᵒ 1776

Charles Russell paper not read   Report hath been made that **Charles Russell**s paper hath not been Read therefore he is Defer^d to Accomplish the Reading S^d paper as order[ed] and make report next mo meeting

case of Amos Wilcox referd   The matter Respecting **Amos Willcox** is Refer^d to next mo meeting by the Request of the Committee and then they to make Report . – –

Mary Spoo= =ner deni^d   The women Inform that they have Deni[e]^d **Mary Sponer** [**Spooner**] wife to **Simson Spooner**

This meeting collected – –   £9   8^s 3 old te[nor]

adjourn   This meeting Adjourns to next Second Day at y^e 11th hour – –

mett   Meet by Adjournment y^e 26 y^e 8^{th mo} – 1776

The Representatives being called both present

Case of Gidi How =land 2 referd   The matter Respecting **Gideon Howland 2nd** is Refer^d to next mo – meeting by reason the women are not Ready to Receive his wifes paper the Chusing of Elders is Refer^d to next mo meeting – –

A G Certificate   **Ann Gifford** Signified to this meeting that She hath a mind to visit **Sandwich** monthly meeting and Desir^d our Concurance therein, And we approving of her Intended visit She being a member of this meeting and her Publick Testimony well Accepted among us And the Clerk is ordered to give her a Coppy of this minute

R. Hath Disownd   This meeting is Inform^d that **Richard Hathaway** Son of **Caleb Hathaway** hath Inlisted & gone into the war very Conterary to our profession therefore for the Clearing of truth friends thinks proper to Disown him, hereby Denying the Said **Richard Hathaway** from under our care and **John Williams** is appointed to [*smudge*] Inform him of his Denial when he [has] an oppertunity and Report to this meeting

D. Chase acknow: ledg^d   It appears that **David Chase** hath been under Dealing for [Some?] Time for marr[y]ing out of the Unity of friends, And now part of the Committee that had the care of that matter ~~Report~~ Making a Satisfactory Report on that account and friend Concludes to accept of his acknowlegment for Satisfaction

A:S and E:Gifford under Dealing   We are Inform^d that **Abraham Smith** hath been Assisting or fit[t]ing warlike Implements also paid money towards building a fort and hath been Labour^d with by friends and Rather Jus--tifies S^d Conduct – – Likewise **Elihue Gifford** hath Join^d with a Military Company in their Exercise by way of training & hath been labour^d with also, and not Condemning S^d Conduct therefore we appoint our friends **Caleb Russell John Williams William Mosher** & **Joseph Tucker** [**J^{ur}?**] to Labour further with S^d **Smith** and **Gifford** and make Report next mo meeting

J. Case Certificate   There was a Removal Certificate Sign^d in this meeting to the monthly meeting of the **Oblong** for **Job Case** & his children

List of those Lately Removed within the bounds of Nine partners monthly meeting

This meeting hath Collected a List of the names of all the persons who have Latterly Removd within the bounds of the **Nine partner[s]** monthly meeting and inclosd the Same in a letter Directed to Sd mo meeting of ye **Nine partners** ‸the names of ye persons in Said List is as followeth

(Viz) **Jonathan Smith** & **Phebe** his wife, **Jonathan Hussey** and **Hepzabeh** his wife & **Selvenus** & **Rachel** their Children & their Granchild **Elisabeth Hussey Jonathan Hussey Ju** & **Content** his wife, **Benja Russell** and **Anna** his wife and **Patience** & **John** Their Children; **Stephen Smith** and his Children namely **Jonathan Elihue** and **hannah, Elisabeth Smith** wife of **Wm Smith** & their Children namely **Gideon Zadock Judith Rebecca Catherin Caleb Noah ann** & **Elisabeth**; **David Anthony** & **Judith** his wife & their Children namely ‸**Elihu Humphry Susana** & **hannah**; **Humphry Smith** and **Edieth** his wife and their Children namely **ann Neomy abigail Mary Mager Humphry** & **Peleg**, all the above at present & there abouts, **Zephaniah Anthony** & **Wait** his wife and their Children namely **Ase[?]** and **Mary, Hannah Dennice[?]**, wife of **Thos Dennice, Lillis Baird** wife of **David Baird, Obediah Allen** & **Phebe** his wife & their Children **Ebenezar, Jonathan** & **James Daniel** Children **Thos Abigail Benja Elisabeth** & **John, Shadrick[?] Dennice[?]** & **abiel**

Cornal & his his wife & of John Allen & thereabouts walter Ruth & Children and Gideon

their children **Hephzebah, Paul Noah** & **Jonathan, Rhoda Allen** wife & **Mary Wing** wife to **Giles wing**, there to **Saratoga**, orter **Crick** & to **Whit Cricks Jedediah Allen** & **Eunice** his wife & their children **Matilda Sarah Polina wilson Pamela** & **Keziah, Isaac Sandford Oyman Kethrine[?], Neomy Sisson** wife to **John Sisson** at **Hoosack Bowdish** who hath Removd to **Saratoga** without Requesting one or informing friends thereof[21]

---

9 ᵐᵒ 1776

At a Monthly Meeting of friends held in **Dartmouth** the 16th ye 9th mo 1776 – – The Representatives are **Wm Moshe[r]** and **Thomas Hicks** both present

Edw Taber informed of denial

John Williams Reports that he hath Informd **Edward Taber** of his Denial as orderd – –

case of Ben Howland 3 referd

The matter Respecting **Benjamin Howland 3rd** is Referd to next moly meeting under the care of the Same Committee as hereto[fore] and then they to make Report – –

Case of young people referd

The Committee appointed to Joine the Overseers in Labouring with Some young People Desires that matter Referd therefore its Refer[d] to next mo meeting & then they to make Report – –

21. This mass granting of certificates of removal shows how common it was for Friends to move without first procuring a certificate.

Mary Wing denial not read The Clerk Reports that he hath not Read **Mary Wing**s Deniel, and **Wm Barker** Reports that he Inform^d **mary wing** of her Denial [and?] Likewise Informs that S^d **mary Wing** Desires an appeal to the Quarterly meeting in the Winter Quarter – –

P. G. & C. R papers been Read **Peleg Gifford J^u** and **Charles Russell** having Caus^d Each of their papers to be Read as order^d or Requir^d by last <u>mo</u> meeting and have Return^d S^d papers to this meeting S^d papers as followeth

To the Preparative and Monthly meetings of friends in **Dartmouth** Whereas I have gave way to the Ensenuations [Insinuations] of the Adversary So far at [*sic*] to be guilty of the Sin of fornication with [**Jenifer?**] **Lumber** whereby She Charg^d me on oath of being father of her basterd Child which Reproachfull Sin I am Sorrow for & do hereby Condemn Desiring forgivness from the Almighty and that friends m^ay So far pass by mine offence as to let me Remain under their Care from your friend – – **Charles Russell** **Dartmouth** ye 15th [3?] ^mo 1774[?]

A:Wilcox paper **Amos Willcox** hath given a paper to this meeting Condemning his misconduct for which he hath been under Dealing but friends not being fully Satisfied of his Sincerity the matter is therefore Continued under the care of the Same Committee as heretofore for their Inspection and a proof of his Sincerity & **Wm Sandford** is ad[d]ed to S^d Committee – –

Gid. Howland 2 [&] wife paper accepted This meeting Conclud[e]s to Accept of **Gideon Howland 2^d** and wives paper Condemning their fal[l]ing into the Sin of fornication & marriing nigh in Kind for Satisfaction Provided they cause S^d paper to be publickly Read at the Close of a first Days meeting he being present She being unwell & Return it to next monthly meeting & Report of it being Read There was Subscriptions Sign^d in this meeting to rais[e] money for the yearly meeting Stock and we appoint our friends **Caleb Russell**

Committee to raise money **John Smith 2nd Daniel Gifford George Handy Joseph Tucker J^u Wm Sandford** to Receive the money of Each member and pay the Same into~~tal~~ the Treasury and Report to next monthly meeting of the Same total So Collected & paid in

This meeting Collected – –   8 – 1 – 8 o.T. [old Tenor]

adjourn This meeting Adjourns to the 23 Day of this Instant at ye 11th hour

mett Met by Adjournment the 23rd ye 9mo 1776 – – The Representatives being Called both present – –

The Overseers have Communicated a Complaint to this meeting

E: Russell Complain^d of under the hand of **Sarah Davis** against **Elijah Russell** for Refusing to Submitt a matter of Differance to men as the

Overseers Inform for which they Labour^d with him and he
Refuses as afores^d We appoint **Prince Allen Wm Mosher Wm Sandford**
to Inquire into the above S^d matter & Labour with S^d **Russell**
as they may find freedom and make Report next mo meeting

[Ch]useing
Elders refer^d The Chusing of Elders is Referd to next <u>mo</u> meeting

Abra. Smith & The greater part of the Committee appointed to Labour with
Elihu Giffords
case refer^d **Abraham Smith** and **Elihu Gifford** Report that they
have Discharg^d themselves in that matter and S^d **Smith**
and **Gifford** Justifies their Conduct therein therefore **Sam^{ll}**
Samuel Smith is appointed to Draw a Testimony against
them & bring to next mo meeting and **Caleb Russell** is appoin[ted]
to Inform them thereof & Report next mo meeting

Compl[a]int We are Inform^d that **Abraham Wood** is in practice of fit[t]ing
against
Abra Wood guns for the use of war, And friends having Labour^d with him
to Desist but he Still Continues therein – –

Complaint Also we are Inform^d that there is a Negro man held in a State
against
Isaac How of Slavery by **Isaac Howland 2nd** & **Joseph Russell J^u** and friend
land 2 & having Labour^d with them on that account therefore we appoint
Jos Russel Ju **Benjamin Smith J^u Benjamin Howland 2nd Joseph Tucker J^u**
Samuel Smith & **William Sandford** to Labour further with S^d **W^{ood}**
on that account Likewise with **Isaac Howland** & **Joseph**
Russell J^u on that account & make Report next <u>mo</u> meeting

tives
The Queries were Answer^d in this meeting and an Epistle Signd
*Representa^* to the Quarterly and order^d forward by our Representatives
to Q meeting who are **Joseph Tucker Sam^{ll} Smith Wm Barker** and they to
Report next <u>mo</u> meeting

---

10 ^{mo} At a Monthly Meeting held in **Dartmouth** 21st ye 10 ^{mo} 1776
1776 The Representatives are **Wm Barker** & **Joseph Barker** presen[t]

B Howlan^d this meeting Accepts of **Benjamin Howland 3rd** paper for Satisfac^{tio[n]}
paper
Accepted Condem[n]ing his going in Company with men that took away
guns for the Use of war, Provided he cause S^d paper to be
Publickly read at the Close of a first Days meeting for worship
he being present before next mo meeting & then Return S^d paper
and Report of its being read

Gid Howland Report hath been made of **Gideon Howland 2nd** & wives paper
paper read being Read as order^d & is Returned to this meeting

                            Said paper is as followeth

G.H. & wifes To the Preparative and Monthly Meeting of **Poneganset**
paper to be held the 13th & 18th Days of the 3 ^{mo} 1776
Dear friends Whereas we through unwatchfulness have

fallen into the Sin of fornication as appears by our having
a child So Soon after marriage for which we are Sorry
Desiring the Lord may forgave us and friends pass it
by together with our marr[y]ing nearer in kin than is
allowable among friends hoping for the futer through
Divine Assistance we may be Enabled to walk more
Circumspect that friends would Still Continue us under
their Care   **Gideon Howland 2**
Dated this 13th ye 3 mo 1776   **Catherin Howland**

Case of Labouring with youths Con= tinued The Committee appointed to Join the Overseers in Labouring
with Some of our youth Desire that matter Refer[d] therefore
S[d] matter is Refer[d] to next mo meeting & then they to make Report

Raising money for yearly meeting referd The Committee appointed to rais[e] money for the yearly
meeting Stock Desire S[d] matter to be Continued therefore its
Refer[d] to next mo meeting and then they to make Report

Elisª Russell case referd The Committee appointed to Labour with **Elisabeth Russell**
Report that they have Inquir[d] into S[d] matter as order[d]
and Labour[d] much with S[d] **Russell** to Settle with **Sarah**
Davis or leave the matter to men all w[^]hich S[d] **Russell**
Intirly [entirely] Refuses to Comply with yet by the Request of
Benjamin Smith it is Refer[d] one month longer under the
Care of the Same Committee and then they to make Report

appointment of Elders Refer[d] The Appointing of Elders is Refer[d] to next mo meeting
Caleb Russell Reports that he Inform[d] **Abraham Smith** and
Elihu Gifford of their Denial as order[d] and there was a
testimony Sign[d] against S[d] **Smith** & **Gifford** & the Clerk is order[d]
to read S[d] Testimonies Publickly as usual -& Report next mo meeting
/ To the Monthly Meeting of friends in **Dartmouth** to be [held?]
the 20th day of 2nd month 1775

                    Whereas we have gone Conterary to
good order with friends in marrying near of kin, and [f...?]

C Green and wives paper among friends And as we have offended in both these
things which we are Sorry for and do Condemn an[d]
as we are truly Desirous to remain under your care [we?]

[illegible words written vertically in this column] hope you can find it clear with yourselves on deliberat[e]
thought and tenderness towards us to pass by this fault
Praying the Allwise Director may So order our Steps
for the future in the paths of truth that henceforth we
may justly be called your Affectionnate friends
                                    Caleb Green
                                    Elisabeth Green

Isa: Howland
Jos Russel
Abra Wood
cases refer^d

The friends appointed to Labour with **Isaac Howland 2ⁿᵈ** and
Joseph Russell Jᵘʳ & Abraham Wood, not having
Compleeted the matter It is therefore Refer^d to next <u>mo</u> meeting
and Said friends Continued for that Service & then to make Report

Return
from yᵉ
Qu meeting

The Representatives to the Quarterly meeting Report they all
attended S^d meeting and have Produc^d an Epistle from the
Said meeting which was read and well Accepted

Certificate
for A:Allen

This meeting Sign^d a Certificate for **Abraham Allen** to the
monthly meeting of the **nine partners,** as he is a going to viset [visit]
his friends within the coᵐpass of S^d meeting

Ben Smith
Bill

Benjamin Smith Jᵘ gave in a bill for keeping **Else Smith**
to the amount of £36 " 8ˢ old tennor which the Treasurer is
order^d to pay & Report next <u>mo</u> meeting
This meeting Collected £1 " 4s " [0?] Lawfull money

11ᵐᵒ
1776

At a Monthly Meeting held in **Dartmouth** 18ᵗʰ 11ᵐᵒ 1776
the Representatives are **Wᵐ Barker & Wᵐ Mosher** Present

Sam Howland
Certificate

Receiv^d a Certificate from **Coakset** monthly meeting Seting [forth?]
Samuel Howlandˢ Clearness Respecting marriage – –

Sam Howland
proposal of
marriage

Samuel Howland & Mary Smith Declar^d their Intentions of
marriage and were Desir^d to wait till next <u>mo</u> meeting for
their Answer

BenHowland3
paper read

Report hath been made of **Benjamin Howland 3ʳᵈ** paper
being Read and is Return^d to this meeting S^d paper is as
followeth

         Dartmouth the 14ᵗʰ of the 2ⁿᵈ month 1776
To the Monthly Meeting of **Dartmouth**
Beloved friends
         I hereby Condemn my Going in Company with

Ben Howland
paper

those that took Guns in order to be used in the millitary Service
with all my misconduct in that matter hoping thro Divine
Assistance to be preserved from the Like behaviour in future
and I Desire friends So far to pass by this mine offence as to
Let me Remain under their Care, freely Acknowledging friends
Kindness Extended towards me in this matter and much Desir=
=ing that for time to come I may So walk as to be Justly Called your
beloved friend – –   **Benjamin Howland 3ʳᵈ**

Labouring with
youths left to
overseers

Most of the Committee Appointed to Join the Overseers in
Labouring with Some of our youth Report that altho they
have not Proceeded So fully as Intended yet they think it
best that the matter be Left with the Overseers and they

Dismiss[d] which is agreed to by this meeting and the Overseers
are Desir[d] to watch Over the youth in a more particula[r]
manner and where Any transgress to bring their names
with their Respective Crimes to this meeting

Epistles
Receiv[d]　This meeting Receiv[d] Some Printed Epistles from the yearly
meeting at **Philidelphia** which is Destributed among friends
also one from the yearly meeting of Ministers & Elders, both
which were Read & Kindly Accepted – –

This meeting Collected £0 – 13[s] – 2[d] Lawfull money – –

adjourn　This meeting Adjourns to the 27th Instant after the meeting of
worship which is to begin at the 11th hour

mett　This meeting meet by Adjournment the 27 of the 11[mo] 1776
the Representatives being Called both Present – –

Raising
money
referd　The Committee appointed to rais[e] money for the yearly meeting
Stock, not being Ready to make Report therefore the matter
is Refer[d] to next <u>mo</u> meeting and then they to Report

Case of
Elijah
Russell　The Committee appointed to Labour with **Elijah Russell** Report
that they have had a nother Oppertunity with S[d] **Russell** (**B: Smith**
Present) and he Declines Submitting the matter to men agreeable to
the Advice of S[d] Committee, therefore this meeting taking S[d] matter
into Consideration, It is Our Sense & Judgment that he the S[d] **Russe[ll]**
ought to Settle the Same with **Sarah Davis** before the next
<u>mo</u> meeting or Submit S[d] matter to men and the S[d] Committee
are Desir[d] to Inform him hereof & to make Report next <u>mo</u> meeting

Chusing
Elders
referd　The matter of Chusing [Choosing] Elders is Refer[d] to next mo meeting

denial of
to be Sign[d]
& read　Whereas the Testimony against **Abraham Smith** & **Elihu Gifford**
that was brought & Read at Last mo meeting not being Sign[d] by
an Omition of the Clerk he is therefore now order[d] to Sign the
Same & Read it as order[d] before & make Report next <u>mo</u> meeting

Case of
I:Howls
J:Russ[Ju]
refer[d]
A Wood
deny[d]　The Committee Appointed to Labour with **Isaac Howland** and
Joseph Russell J[u] and **Abraham Wood** Report that they have
fulfill[d] their apointment therein & Said **Wood** Refuses to Comply
with friends A[d]vice but Continues to mend guns for the Use of
war therefore this meeting doth Deny S[d] **Wood**
from being a member [of] our Society and S[d] Committee is order[d] to
Draw a Testimony against him & bring it to next <u>mo</u> meeting they
also Report that **Isaac Howland** & **Joseph Russell** have ~~of Late~~ not
fully Compli[d] with friends Advice in Regard to the Negro, the matter
is therefore Refer[d] to next month[l]y meeting under the care of S[d] Committee
and then they to make Report – –

J A
[confessiᵒ]

Jedediah Allen gave in a paper Condem[n]ing his misconduct and Requests[?] to Come under friends Care again, And we appoint **Joseph Barker** and **Wᵐ Barker** to have an Oppertunity of Conferrance with Sᵈ **Allen** in order to Discover the Sencerity and motive of his Request and Report next monthly meeting

C Rus
paper
accept
ed

Caleb Russell Gave in a paper to this meeting Condem[n]ing his having a hand in Conveying Some Goods Called prise Goods and being with those that Sold Such Goods & Drinking with them; which this meeting Accepts‸for Satisfaction Provided he Cause the Same to be Publickly Read at the Close of a first Days meeting for worship (he being Present) between this and next <u>mo</u> meeting and then Return Sᵈ paper

[f]ence
round
meeting
house

The Committee appointed to fence the Land round the meeting house Report that they have Compleated Sᵈ matter and Repa[i]rᵈ the meeting house and brought in their bill whis [which?] is – £5 " 4ˢ " 4ᵈ L:[lawful] money Exclusive of those that gave work – –

Little
House

This meeting Conclud[e]s to build a Little house for the Use of friends at our meeting house, And we appoint **William Sandford** to Comput[e] Sᵈ business as Soon as he can with Convenency & bring in his account The Treasurer Reports he hath paid **Benjᵃ Smith Jᵘ** £36 - 8ˢ old tennor as orderᵈ

12ᵐᵒ
1776

At a Monthly meeting held in **Dartmouth** yᵉ 16ᵗʰ 12ᵗʰ ᵐᵒ 1776 the Representatives are **Wᵐ Sandford** & **Samuel Smith** present

Samˡ
Howland
answer

Samuel Howland and **Mary Smith** appearᵈ for their Answer which was that they might proceed to take Each other in marriage in Some Convenient time before next monthly meeting [advising?] with the friends that Shall be appointed for that purpose and we appoint **Wᵐ Mosher** and **Joseph Gifford** to See their marriage Consomated in good order and make Report next <u>mo</u> meeting

Case of
Elij Russ
Settled

The Committee that had the Care of that matter Respecting **Elijah Russell** Reports that Sᵈ **Russell** and **Sarah Davis** hath Set[t]led Sᵈ matter or Controvercy

Testimony
against
Abr Wood
Signd -

There was a Testimony Against **Abraham Wood** Signᵈ in this meeting by the Clark and he is orderᵈ to Read it Publickly at the Close of a firs[t] Days meeting for worship and make Report next mo meeting

Case of
I. Howland
J Russel Ju
referᵈ

The Committee appointed to have the Care of that matter Respect= =ing **Isaac Howland** & **Joseph Russell Jᵘ** freeing his Negro Report that Said friends have not Compleated Sᵈ matter therefore the Same Committee are Still Continued in that Service & to make Report next mo meeting – –

Jede:Allen
Receiv^d

The Committee that had the Care of the matter Respecting
Jedediah Allen^s Requesting to Come under friends Report that
they have had an oppertunity of Conferrance with him and
Receiv^d a Degree of Satisfaction therefore Said **Allen** is Received
under friends Care – –

money
Rais^d

The Committee appointed to raise money by way of Subscription
for the yearly meeting Stock Report that they have Rais^d and
paid into the Treasurer · – £12 – 3^s – 6^d Lawfull Money

Abra Smith
Elihu Giff
denial

the Clerk Reports he hath Read the testimony against **Abraha[m]**
Smith & Elihu Gifford as order^d Last m<u>o</u> meeting S^d paper is
as followeth

Whereas **Abraham Smith & Elihu Gifford** having ma[de]
Proffession with us & under the care of this meeting, But have So far
Departed from the way of Truth and the Testimony thereof as to be
found in joining with & measurably Supporting of war or preparation
for the Same particularly the S^d **Smith** hath paid money towards
the building a fort & also in fit[t]ing Some war like Impl[e]ments
and they having been Tenderly Labour^d with by friends to Desist
from & Condemn their S^d Conduct but our Labour therein not
obtaining the Desir^d Effect, But they Still Justifying the Same this meet[in]g
therefore being Concern^d for the maintaining our Testimony against all outward worst
fighting and preparations for the Same do give this forth as a testimony against them
hereby Disowning them the S^d **A:Smith & E:Gifford** from being members of our Society
and from under the care of this meeting Untill by unfeigned Repentance & Return
from the Error of their ways they Shall be Restor^d to y^e [the] way of truth Given forth and
Signed on behalf of our mo meeting held in **Dartmouth** 21st 10mo 1776 by

William Anthony J^ur Clerk

Caleb Russell hath Caus^d his paper to be read as order^d and Returnd is as
followeth – –

To the Preparative and Monthly meetings of friends next
to be held in **Dartmouth**
Dear friends

C Russell
paper

Being under a Sense of my Error in having a Concern or
hand in those Goods Called Prize Goods, So far as to assist in Carting or
Conveying Some of them a Small distance & being with them that
Sold Such goods & Drinking with them Some wine & water, and having
found my ~~self~~ mind Troubled therewith am real[l]y and heartily Sorry
for it not thinking it according to the principales of our profession
to have any hand in Such Goods Desiring friends will pass this by
and that I may be more watchfull for the future from your ^affectionate friend

Dartmouth 12ᵗʰ of 11ᵐᵒ 1776   Caleb Russell – –

Caleb Rus Ju Davi Sheph & paper accepted — Caleb Russell jᵘʳ and David Sheepherd Jᵘʳ gave in papers to this meeting Condemning their misconduct, the first in Carting of Prise Goods the Latter for going as Pilot in a Prise Vessell which this meeting Accepts for Satisfaction – –

Divers friend condemn their misconduct — Also **Giles Slocum Elihu Slocum Timothy Howland** & **Jonᵃ [Jonathan] Tucker** have appearᵈ in this meeting and Verbally Confes[s]ed & Condem[n]ᵈ their having been Concernᵈ in buying Carting or Conveying of prise Goods which this meeting also Accepts for Satisfaction – –

Order on Treasurer — The Treasurer is orderᵈ to pay **Timothy Russell** five Dollars for half years keeping the meeting house and Report next mo meeting This meeting Collected 17ˢ/5ᵈ - Lawfull money – –

adjourn — This meeting adjourns to the 30ᵗʰ Day of this Instant at yᵉ 11 hour

mett — Meet by Adjournment the 30ᵗʰ yᵉ 12ᵐᵒ 1776 the Representatives being Called both present – –

Chusing Elderˢ referᵈ — The Chusin[g] of Elders is Referᵈ to next mo meeting – –

Complaint against Divers friends — The Overseers Inform that **David ~~Shepherd~~ Briggs Jonathan howland Nicholass Lapham** hath purchased prise Goods and **Joseph Russ[ell] David Allen Elezer Allen Jonathan Allen** & **Thoˢ Akin** hath been Carting prise goods and **Joseph Russell Jᵘ** has taken Charge of Such goods when bid of at Vandue & Stord & Shipt them again all which Sᵈ Overseers Report they have Labourᵈ with them but they have not Condemnᵈ Sᵈ misconduct to friends Satisfaction therefore we appoint **Wᵐ Mosher Samuel Smith Philip Allen Benjᵃ Howland 2ⁿᵈ John Williams** to Labour further with the above Sᵈ friends and Report next monthly meeting

Queries Answerᵈ — The Queries were Answerᵈ in this meeting and an Epistle Signᵈ for the Quarterly meeting and orderᵈ forward to Sᵈ Quarterly meeting

Representativ[e]s — by our Representatives who are **Thoˢ Hicks Benjᵃ Howland 2ⁿᵈ Wᵐ Anthony Jᵘ Wᵐ Mosher** and they to Report next mo meeting – –

Paper of denial to [drawᵈ?] against John Wood & Wᵐ Haden — The friends Appointed Some time past to Labour with **John Wood** and **Wᵐ Haden** for their misconduct Report that they have fulfil[led] their Appointment therein but they Gave them no Real Satisfaction therefore Sᵈ friends are Appointed to Draw a paper of Denial against them & bring it to next mo meeting

A Pass for Representaᵉ — This meeting Signᵈ a Certificate for our Representatives to the Quarterly meeting Directed to the Commanding Offeser [Officer] of this Melitary [Military] Service Desiring their Leave for Sᵈ Represen[ta]tives to pass on their way to Sᵈ Quarterly meeting

1 mo
1777

At a Monthly Meeting held in **Dartmouth** the
20th the 1st mo 1777
the Representatives are **Prince Allen** & **Joseph Barker** Present – –

Case of those concernd in prize goods

The Committee appointed Last mo meeting to Labour
with those friends that Purchasd prise [prize] goods Report that
they Lab[o]urd with Sd friends, and **Nicholass Lapham David Brigg[s]**
Jonathan Howland gave in papers to this meeting Condemning
Sd misconduct which is Accepted provided they Sign a Testimon[y]
against Such proceedure according to the Conclution of this
meeting   And this meeting Conclud[e]s / Notwithstanding the
minute of Last mo meeting, That all those friends that
hath Condemnd Sd misconduct Sign a testimony against Such
Such proceedure to be publickly read as Usual in order to take
of the Report from the Society, and Said Committee are Desird
to Draw a Testimony for that purpose and Desire all those
friends that have ~~no~~ transgressd as aforeSd to Sign the Same
if they find freedom and bring to next mo meeting – –
and said Committee is Desird to Draw up Testimonies against
those friends that Decline making Satisfaction and bring
to next mo meeting – –

Complaint a gainst Ralph Allen

We Understand that **Rhalf Allen** Son of **Benjamin Allen**
hath Inlisted & gone on bo[a]rd of a Vessell of war which being
Conterary to our profession therefore we hereby Disown the Sd

Ralph Allen disownd

Rhalf Allen from being under our Care & the above Committee
is Desird to Draw a testimony against him & bring to next
mo meeting

Wm Russell Son of Tim disownd

Likewise we Understand that **Wm Russell** Son of **Timothy**
Russell hath Inlisted into the war & Cannot well be Spoake
with therefore we Disown the Sd **Wm Russell** from being
under our Care and the afore Sd Committee is orderd to
Draw a Testimoney against Sd **Russell** and bring it to
next mo meeting – –

Certificate for Thos Allen

This meeting Signd a Certificate for **Thos Allen** to
the mo meeting of the **Nine partners** as he is a going there
to Visit his friends
This meeting Collected – –   £1   6S   1d
                                                  L. [lawful] money

adjourn

This meeting Adjourns to the 29th Instant after the
meeting for Worship which is to begin ye 11th hour

mett

Meet by Adjournment ye 29th ye 1 mo 1777 – –
The Representatives being Called both Present

Samuel Howland Marriage The friends appointed to See the Marriage of **Samuel Howland** and **Mary Smith** Report that they attended S.ᵈ marriage and Saw nothing but that it was orderly Accomplished

The Clerk Reports that he hath read the Testimony against

Testimony against Abra Wood **Abraham Wood** as order,ᵈ Last mo meeting Sᵈ paper is as followet Whereas **Abraham Wood** the Son of **Jesiah [Josiah] & Hannah Wood** Having had his Education Amongst friends, But by Departing from the Testimony of truth hath So far gone astray as to be found in the Practice of mending & Preparing of guns and Instruments of war and friends having Labour,ᵈ with him in love in order to Reclaim him from a Practice So Inconsistant with the Profession he hath made but he Continuing in Said Practice. This meeting therefore doth Give this forth as a Testimony against him hereby Diso- wing him the Said **Abraham Wood** from being a Member of our Society untill by an Unfeigned Repentance & Acknowldgement of the Error of his way he Shall be Refer,ᵈ to the way of Truth -- Given forth & Signd in & on behalf of our monthly meeting of friend. held in **Dartmouth** the 16ᵗʰ the 12 ᵐᵒ 1776   By – –

                      William Anthony Jᵘ Clerk

Case of Isaac Howland Ju refer.d **Isaac Howland 2ⁿᵈ** gave in a bill to this meeting Manimiting a Negro man named **Primus** but yet Some friends Doubting wheather S.ᵈ Negro is fully free,ᵈ therefore S.ᵈ matter is Refer,ᵈ under the care of the Same Committee as heretofore & they to Report next mo meeting

Treasurer report The Treasurer Reports that he paid 5 Dollars to **Timothy Russell** as orderᵈ Last mo meeting

The Chusing of Elders is Refer,ᵈ to next mo meeting

Return from Q meeting The Representatives to the Quarterly meeting Report that they all attended Except **Benjᵃ Howland 2ⁿᵈ** who Sent a Reasonable Excuse. They also brought an Epistle from S.ᵈ meeting which was Read and well Accepted

Treasurer report The Treasurer Reports that he hath Sent the money that was rais,ᵈ to Supply the yearly meeting Stock according to the Direction of the yearly meeting which this meeting approves

paper of denial brought against J Wood & Wᵐ Haden The friends Appointed to draw a paper of Denial against **John Wood** and **William Hayden** have brought S.ᵈ paper which was Sign,ᵈ by the Clerk, who is order,d to read the Same as Usual & make Report next mo meeting S.ᵈ friends also Inform that they have Inform,ᵈ Sᵈ **Wood & Hayden** of their Denial

John Howland Certificate from London **John Howland** being Return,d from England hath Produc,ᵈ a Certificate from the two weeks meeting held in **London** the

25th the 3rd mo 1776 Certifying his Good Conversation while there
and his Clearness from marriage Engagements which hath been
Read & well accepted

Job Gifford Luthan Wood Barker Little purchase prize goods The Overseers Inform that **Job Gifford Luthan Wood & Barker Little** have Purchas,d Prize Goods, and they have Treated with
them for their misconduct, and the matter is put under the
Care of the Same Com,tt that were appointed to Deal with
the others under the Same Transgressions & to Report of them
with the others

Case of Wm Rus= =sell Tim Son referd This meeting having Reconsider,d the minute made at the
first Seting of this meeting Respecting **Wm Russell** Son of
Timothy Russell and do defer the denying of him untill
a further Confirmation of his being inlisted into the war

money to be raisd **Joseph Gifford Philip Allen John Williams and Obediah
Beird** are appointed to raise money by Subscriptions to pay
the Cost of fencing in our Land Round the meeting house and
make Report next mo meeting

2 month 1777 At a Monthly Meeting held in **Dartmouth** the
17th the 2nd mo 1777
The Representatives are **Philip Allen** & **Joseph Tucker Ju** present

Testimony Signd against Jos Russell Jur David Allen Ebenez Allen Jonat Allen Ralph Allen The Testimonies against **Joseph Russells jur David Allen
Elezer Allen Jonathan Allen And Rhalf Allen** were Sign,d
in this meeting by the Clerk who is order,d to read the Same
Publickly as Usual & report next mo meeting & **John Williams**
is appointed to Inform them of their Denial & Report next mo meeting

John Akin manimitt Indian boy named Hazzard A Manumition was Read in this meeting Signed by **John
Akin** thereby manumiting an Indian boy Named **Hazzard**
which is accepted for Satisfaction

Papers accepted of Divers friends concerned in prize goods The Committee appointed to Labour with those friends that
were transgressions in being Concern.d with Prize goods
brought Testimonies to this meeting Sign,d by **Barker Little
David Briggs Elihu Slocum Jonathan Howland** & **Timothy
Howland David Sheepherd Ju** and **Thos Akin** which Testimony
are Accepted for Satisfaction provided they Cause them to be
Publickly read as Usual & Returnd & Report made to next
mo meeting thereof – and Said Committee are Still Contin[ued?]
to Labour with those Transgressors on them accounts who have
not yet Complid with friends Advice, also to Draw testimony again[st]
them that Decline making Satisfaction and Report next mo meeting.

Case of Isaac Howland Ju refrd The Committee that had the case of that matter Respecting
Isaac Howland Ju freeing his Negro, Desires s.d matter Continued

therefore its Refer.ᵈ to next mo. meeting and then they to Report

Wᵐ Mosher an Elder — This meeting Appoints **William Mosher** an Elder

John Wood Wᵐ Haden denial — The Clerk Reports he hath the Testimonies against **John Wood** and **Wᵐ Haydon** as orderᵈ S.ᵈ Testimonies is as followeth –

Whereas **John Wood** & **Wᵐ Haydon** has had their Education amongst friends yet by Giving way to the Insinuations of the adversary – they have been found guilty of Stealing watermillions from **John Sheepherd** likewise yᵉ sᵈ **wood** has appeard with a Tumultuous Company by way of Riot very unbeco= ming the truth which we profess. Likewise Sᵈ **Wood** & **Haden** has Proceded in Marriage out of the Unity of friends, all which they have been Labour,ᵈ with for in order to Convince them of the Evil of their ways but our Labour of love not having the Desirᵈ Effect to friends Satisfaction therefore for the Clearing of truth and friends from Such Evil Practises do hereby Disown the S.ᵈ **John Wood** & **Wᵐ Haden** from being members of our Religious Society and from under the care of this meeting Desiring If it be Consistant with Divine goodness they may come to Sight & Sence of their outgoings and by unfeigned Repentance be [returned?] to the way of [truth?]

Given forth at our mo meeting held in **Dartmouth** the [?1]ˢᵗ Day 1ˢᵗ mo 1777 and Signed in and on behalf S.ᵈ meeting by – **Wᵐ Anthony** [Ju] Clerk

Wᵐ Russells denial confirmᵈ — This meeting being now Confirmᵈ of **Wᵐ Russell** having been in the wars therefore Do confirm the Denial of Sᵈ **Russell** and the Committee Continued to Draw a Testimony against him as ordered Last mo meeting and Inform him thereof & Report next mo meeting.

Friends to raise money not ready to report — The Committee appointed to rais money, not being fully Ready to make Return therefore they are Continued in that Service & to Report next mo meeting –

Complaint a gainst Walter Wood he is denid — We are Inform,ᵈ that **Walter Wood** hath married out of the Unity of friends after being Precautiond by one of the [?] Therefore we Deny him the Said **Walter Wood** from being under the care of friends and **Joseph Tucker** Jᵘ is appointed to Inform him thereof & Report next mo meeting

Complaint a gainst Benj Russellson of Benj referᵈ — This meeting being Inform,ᵈ that **Benjᵃ Russell** Son of **Benjᵃ Russell** Son of **Benjᵃ** hath purchas,ᵈ or partook of prise goods and been Labour,ᵈ with, but not appearing to make Satisfaction therefore S.ᵈ matter is Refer,ᵈ under the Care of the Committee appointed to Labour with transgressors of that [kind?] – –

Complint a gainst Stephen Mott referd — This meeting is Informᵈ that **Stephen Mott** hath Inlisted into the war and we Appointed **Caleb Russell** and **John Williams** to treat with him and Draw a paper of Denial aganst him if he Declines to make Satisfaction and make Report next <u>mo</u> meeting – –

Jos Mott deny^d This meeting is Informed that **Joseph Mott** hath Remov^d
away a far distance from hence and married out of the
Unity of friends and as he cannot will be Labour,^d with by
Reason of his being gone away as afore S^d. Therefore this meeting
doth deny him from being a member of our Society.

Amos Wilcox disown^d The Committee that had the Care of that matter Concerning
Amos Willcox made Report that he hath Given them no
Satisfaction but Still Continues in this Transgressions therefore
this meeting doth deny him from being in membership
with us & S^d Committee are order,^d to draw a paper of Denial
against him & bring to next <u>mo</u> meeting also to Inform him of his Denial.

Case of Simeon Gifford The Clerk hath Signed a Certificate or Recommendation to the
monthly Meeting of the **NinePartners** for **Simeon Gifford**, who
hath Remov^d there & married out of the Unity of friend^s. Request-
-ing them to take the matter with him under their Care.

To Inspect into the Right of Member--Ship It hath been moved in this meeting to Consider the matter in [respect?]
to our members who Stand as members & who hath a proper ᴀ[Birth?] Right
by the Rules of our Society & who not therefore **Prince Allen W^m
Anthony J^u Thos. Hicks Benjamin Smith J^u & Samuel Smith** are
appointed as a Committee to Consider thereof and if they think
there needs a further Explanation to our yearly meeting minutes
in that Respect they are Desir^d to Draw up what they think
needfull in writing and bring it to next mo meeting – –
This meeting collected – –   0^L 16^s 1^d
                                                      L_mony

---

3 month 1777 At a Monthly Meeting held in **Dartmouth** y^e 17th 3<u>mo</u> 1777
the Representatives are **Prince Allen** & **Benj^a Howland 2nd** present

Testimony against Jos Russell Ju & the Allens not read The Clerk Reports he hath not Read the Testimony^s against
Josep Russell J^u & the Sons of **Benj^a Allen** as order^d Last <u>mo</u> mee[tin]g
therefore he is Still Continues for that Service & to Report next <u>mo</u> meeting
The friends (viz) **Barker Little David Briggs Elihu
Slocum Jonathan Howland, Timothy Howland David Shepherd J^u
Thos Akin** hath Caus^d their Testimonies to be read Publickly as
order^d Last mo meeting & Return^d them to this meeting S^d Testimony

Confession of Several Traders in Prize goods are as followeth
To the Monthly Meeting of **Dartmouth**
Beloved Friends
        We the Subscribers having Inconsiderately or unduly Purchased
or Carted Some Small Quantity of those goods called Prize goods taken by

war and Violence Which Said Conduct of ours after a Matter of
Consideration thereof we do Utterly condemn and are Sorry
for it hereby Testifying to friends, and Publickly Declaring
Declaring to all People to whom these Presents may come
that as our conduct herein is Inconsistant with the Religious
Profession we make, So we would take the Reproach thereof to
ourselves, and Clear the truth and the Professors thereof from the
Same Desiring forgiveness from the Divine goodness and that
friends would So far pass by this our misconduct as to let us
Remain Under their care hopin in future through Divine
Assistance to be Preferred from the Like misbehavour – –
from your friends Dated ye 29th of the 1st month AD: 1777

Thos. Akin	**Barker Little**
Timothy Howland	**David Briggs**
	Elihu Slocum
David Shepherd J^u	**Jonathan Howland**

Job Gifford
Nick Lapham
Luthon Wood
papers
accepted
Job Gifford Nicholass Lapham & **Luthon Wood** gave in
Papers to this meeting Condemning their Purchasing Some
Prise goods which is Accepted, Provided they Cause them to be
Publickly Read as Usual & Report & Return S^d paper to next
<u>mo</u> meeting – And the Same Committee are Still Continu^d
to Labour with those that are transgressors on account of
being Concern^d with Prize goods & to Report next <u>mo</u> meeting
and Draw testimonies against those that Decline making
Satisfaction if any there be & bring to next <u>mo</u> meeting – –

Isaac
Howland Ju
case refer'd
The Committee Appointed to Labour with **Isaac Howland J^u**
on account of his freeing his Negro Report that they have
not Discharg,^d themselves on that account therefore they
are Still Continued in that Service & to Report next <u>mo</u> meeting

Walter Wood
not Inform'd
of denial
Joseph Tucker J^u Reports that he hath not Inform,^d **Walter
wood** of his Denial as order,^d therefore he is Continued for
that Service & to Report next <u>mo</u> meeting

Testimony a
gainst Stephen
Mott Signd
There was a Testimony against **Stephen Mott** Sign,^d in
this meeting by the Clerk who is order,^d to Read it Publickly as
Usual & Report next <u>mo</u> meeting & **John Williams** is appointed
to Inform S^d **Mott** of his Denial ˄& Report next <u>mo</u> meeting

Report of
money rais^d
The Committee appointed to rais money by way of Subsim
ption Report that they have Rais,^d the Sum of 5^ℓ 17^s 6^d
of which is paid to the Committee that fenced the land
round the meeting house the Sum of – ^£5 4^s 4 ½

and the remainder is Deliver,^d to the treasurer which is 12 /9

Testimony Signd a gainst Amos Wilcox There was a Testimony Sign,d in this meeting by the Clerk against **Amos Willcox** & the Clerk is order,d to read it publick[ly] as Usuel & Report next mo meeting

This meeting Collected – –   1£ 8s 1d £m

Adjourn This meeting Adjourns to ye 26th Instant after the meeting of worship which is to begin at ye 11th hour

mett Meet by Adjournment ye 26th ye 3rd mo 1777 – – the Representatives being Caled both present

Concerning Birth right of members The friends Appointed who hath a Proper Birthright by the Rules of Discipline &c Report that they have mett and and Consider,d but are not ready for a Report in full therefore they are Still Continued for that Service & to make Report next mo meeting

Jonathan Willbor & Wife desir to come un der friend care **Jonathan** & **Huldy Willbur** gave in a paper Requesting to Come under friends Care with their Children and our friends **Philip Allen** & **Prince Allen** are appointed to Join the women and take an Oppertunity of Solid Conferrance with them in order to Discover the motive of their Request and Report next mo meeting – –

Abiel Gifford reques to come under friends care **Abiel Gifford** Requests to come under friends Care and we appoint **Wm Mosher** & **Wm Baker** to take an oppertun[it]y of Solid Conferrance with him in order to Discover the motive of his Request & Report next mo meeting

Certificates J Barker J Howland Ju J Hart There was Certificates Sign,d in this meeting for **James Bark[er]** **Job Howland Ju** & **Jonathan Hart** the two first to the mo meeting of ye **Ninepartners** the Latter to the mo meeting o **Smithfield** they being a going there to make some [?]

Wm Barkers accompt **Wm Barker** gave in an account to this meeting for hay- which he Procur,d at our Quarterly meeting in the 10th mo Last which is Allowed & the treasurer is order,d to pay the Same with is £1 = 4s £-12[?] and make Report next mo meeting – –

To Revise miniutes **William Anthony Jun Samuel Smith Prince Allen** and **John Williams** are appointed to Revise and Correct this meeting minutes in order to goe on Record and Report next mo meeting – also to Settle accounts with the treasurer

Friend appoint ted Elder The Women Inform that they have Appointed **Sussanah Smith Deborah Haden** & **Deborah Hicks** in the place of Elders which this meeting Concurs with and they with

our friends **Wm Mosher** & **Thos Hicks** is Recommended
as Elders to the Quarterly meeting – –

Queries answer^d The Queries was Answer,^d in the meeting and Said Answers
together with a Epistle which was Sign,^d in this meeting
was order,^d forward to the Quarterly meeting by our Repr-

Representativ^es esentatives who are **Caleb Russell Wm Mosher Thos Hicks**
John Williams & **William Anthony J^u** and they to make
Report next monthly meeting

4 month　At a Monthly Meeting held in **Dartmouth** 21st the
1777　4th mo 1777

Testimony　The Representatives are **Caleb Russell** & **James Davis** Present
red against　　　The Clerk Reports he hath Read the Testimonyes
Jos Russell Ju^r
& Sons of against **Joseph Russell J^u** & the Son^s of **Benjamin**
Benj Allen **Allen** as order,d Last mo meeting S.^d testimonies are
as followeth

Testimonies　Whereas **Joseph Russell** the Son of **Caleb Russell**
against　and **David Allen Jonathan Allen** & **Elezer Allen**
J: R
D: A　being the Sons of **Benj^a Allen** all having had their
J: A　Education amongst friends, but by Departing from
E: A　their Education and the Testimony of Truth have So far
gone astray as to be Concern,d in Receiving buying Cart[ing]
or otherwise Concern,^d in those goods taken in the w[ar]
Testimony of　by fors of armes, being those good Called Prisse goods
Ralph Allan
Recorded　and friends and friends having Labour,^d with Each often
in page　in order to Discover to them the Evil of Such a pract[ice]
390　but friends Labour of Love not having its Desir,^d Effect
these are therefore Given forth as a Publick Testimony
against them the S.^d **Joseph Russell** [&?] **David Allen Jonatha[n]**
Allen & **Elezer Allen** hereby Denying & Disowning
them from being members of our Society & from under
the Care of this meeting untill by unfeigned Repentance
and Acknowledge of the Error of their ways. they shall
be Restor.^d to the way of Truth.　　Given forth and
Sign,^d in and on behalf of our S^d meeting of friends held
in **Dartmouth** y^e 17th the 2nd mo 1777 by
　　　　　　　　　　　Wm Anthony J^u Clerk

Luthan Wood **Luthan Wood Job Gifford Nicholass Lapham** hath Cast
Job Gifford
Nick Lap=　their papers to be Publickly Rea.d & Return^d to this mat[ter]
=ham Confessi　as order,^d last mo meeting S.^d papers is as followeth – –
on　To the Monthly Meeting held 17th Day 3 mo 1777

[written through margins]
Whereas Sometime past, We ₍Inconsiderately₎ purchas.ᵈ Some Goods Called Prise good
and upon a further Consideration find it is Conterary to the Principals of
truth which we are Sorry for and do Condemn and Desire friends
to pass it by and let us Remain under their Care from your friend.

Luthon Wood
Job Gifford
Nicholas Lapham

Jos Russell & Part of the Committee appointed to Labour with those
Ben : Russell friend that are transgressors on account of being Concern,ᵈ with
Case Concerning
Prize goods Prise goods Report that **Joseph Russell** and **Benjᵃ Russell**
Declines Condeming their Conduct in that matter to friends
Satisfaction therefore the Same Committee are Continued to
Labour further with them & if they find no Satisfaction
to Draw testimonies against them & bring to next <u>mo</u> meeting

Wm Russell There was a Testimony Sign.ᵈ in this meeting by the Clerk
Son of Tim against **Wᵐ Russell** Son of **Timothy Russell** & the Clerk
[be] disownd is orderᵈ to Read it publickly as Usual & Report to
next <u>mo</u> meeting.

Treasurer The Treasurer Reports that he has paid £1 – 4[?] £ mo
report to **Wᵐ Barker** as order,ᵈ last <u>mo</u> meeting – –

Isaac Howland This meeting not being fully satisfied on account of **Isaac**
case Sent to **Howland** freeing his Negro and being Somewhat Different-
Q: meeting for
advice ly minded in that affair Conclude to ask the advice of
the Quarterly meeting therein – –

Walter Wood **Joseph Tucker Jᵘ** Reports that he hath Inform,ᵈ **Walter Wood**
inform d of his Deniel as order,ᵈ Last <u>mo</u> meeting

Testimony a The Clerk Reports that he hath Read the testimony against
gainst Ste **Stephen Mott** as orderᵈ Sᵈ Testimony is as followeth
pen mott
Whereas **Stephen Mott** Son of **Jacob Mott** having had a birth
Right of Membership with us but hath So far Deviated from our princip[les]
as to inlist himself a Solder & having been Labourᵈ with in love for his
misconduct in order to Reclaim him from the Evil of his ways but
friends Labour not having its Desir.ᵈ Effect therefore for the Clearing
of truth from Such practices we give this forth as a Publick testimony
against him & do deny him from being a member of this meeting
Nevertheless Desiring if it be Consistant with Divine Pleasure that he may
Come to a Sight of his Outgoings & Returned, Signed in on behalf of our <u>mo</u> meeting
held in **Dartmouth** yᵉ 17ᵗʰ 3ʳᵈ mᵒ 1777 by **Wᵐ Anthony Jᵘ** Clerk

Stephen Mott
not informd
of de[n]ial

John Williams not having Inform,[d] **Stephen Mott** of his Denial
as order,[d] he is Still Continued for the Service & to make Report
next mo meeting

Mary How
= land Certi
= ficate

There as a Removal Certificate Sign[d] for **Mary Howland**
wife of **Samuel Howland** to the mo meeting of **Coakset**

Letter to
Greenwich

This meeting Signed and Directed a Letter to **greenwick** mo
meeting Desiring their Assistance to Labour with the family
of **Charles Slocum** he being Deceas,[d] – –

The Clerk Reports that he hath Read the testimony against
Amos Willcox as order,[d] Last mo meeting S.[d] testimony is as followeth

Testimony
against
Amos Wilcox

Whereas **Amos Willcox** Son of **W**[m] **Willcox** Deceas[d] and
Dorrity his wife of **Dartmouth** in the **County of Bristol** &
Province of the Massac[h]usetts Bay in **New England** having
has a birthright with us the People Called Quakers, yet
through unwatchfullness and a Disregard to the testimony of
truth in himself hath been found in the practice of Using
bad Language, going to places of frollicking and Neglects
attending of meetings, which conduct being Reproachfull
and Scandalous to our Profession and friends having Labour[d]
with him in love in order to bring him to a Sight of his
Errors but their Labour Proving Inafectual and he Continuing
in S.[d] Practices. therefore for the Clearing of truth and friends
from the Reproach thereof this meeting is Concern[d] to Give this
as a Publick Testimony against him Disowning him the S[d]
Amos Willcox from being under our care yet Desiring if it be
Agreeable with Divine goodness that he may yet Come to a Sight
of the Evil of his ways and through Unfeigned Repentance
find mercy.
Given forth at our Monthly meeting held in **Dartmouth**
the 21 Day of y[e] 4 mo 1777 and Signed in and by order of S.[d] meeting
by **W**[m] **Anthony** Clerk

Case of Birth=
=right of Chil
dren gone to
yearly meet
ing

We understand the matter in Regard to what Children have
Proper Birth Rights & who not by the rules of our Society is
gone from the Quarterly meeting to the yearly meeting for an
Explanation thereof therefore the Committee appointed in our
meeting for that Service is Dismised.

Abiel Gifford
accepted

The friends appointed to have an opportunity with **Abiel
Gifford** Report that he gave them good Satisfaction therefore we
accept of the S.[d] **Gifford** to be under our Care – –

Case of
Jonat Wilbor
referd

The Committee appointed to have an Oppertunity of Conference with **Jonathan Willbur** Report the S.ᵈ Willbur gave them good Satisfaction but he not being present therefore S.ᵈ matter is Refer,ᵈ to next <u>mo</u> meeting under the care of the Same Committee as heretofore

Martha Allen
Received

The Women Inform that they Received into membership **Martha Allen** wife of **Jonathan Allen** & their two Daughters **Mary** & **Isbil** which this meeting Concurs with – –

Return from
Qar meeting

The friends Appointed to Attend the Quarterly meeting Report that they all attended S.ᵈ meeting but have not Produc.ᵈ their Epistle by Reason it was not Transcrib,ᵈ Two Epistle from **London** and one from the meeting of Sufferings in **Philadelphia** were Read in this meeting to good Satisfaction & the Clerk is order'd to read them severally at his Deferassion [Deposition?] at the Close of some of our Publick meetings of worship – –

Charles Slocum
& Ebenezer
Slocum
Sons of Charles
Slocum disowned

This meeting is ^informd that **Charles Slocum** & **Ebenezer Slocum** Sons of **Charles Slocum** Deceas.ᵈ who Remov.ᵈ from hence Some years past, & having a right among friends but they having been lately visited & treded[traded?] with by two friends of this meeting who Report that S.ᵈ **Slocum**ˢ owned them -selves to have been Concernᵈ in military matters & not Discovering in them any Disposition of a Return on Reformation therefore we do Disown them from being member of our Society and **Benjᵃ Howland Samˡˡ Smith** to Draw a Testimony against them & bring to next <u>mo</u> meeting and **Caleb Russell** is Appointed to Inform them of their s.ᵈ Denial a Soon as he Convenient can & Report to this meetg.

Miniuts not
revisd

The Committee appointed to Revise and Connect this meetg minutes not having Compleated it they are Still Continued for that Service & also to settle account with yᵉ treasurer & Report next <u>mo</u> meeting

Giles Slocum
request a
Certificate

Giles Slocum Requests a Certificate to the <u>mo</u> meeting of **Sandwich** Certifying his Clearness Respecting marriage & Conversation therefore **Nicholas Howland** & **Samˡˡ Smith** are Appointed to Inspect into S.ᵈ matter and Draw one if they think proper & bring to next <u>mo</u> meeting – –

Meetings
Graⁿᵗᵉᵈ at
Bedford

The friends appointed to Oversee the meeting at **Bedford** make Report that S.ᵈ meeting hath been kept up as orderly as Usual heretofore and they Request the Same may be Continued as heretofore for the year Ensuing which is

Granted and **Caleb Russell** & **Seth Russell** & **James Davis** is Appointed to Oversee the S.^d meeting to see it be kept up according to the Good order of truth & to make at the Expiration thereof – –

This meeting Collected £1 – ^s10 – ^d8 £. money

---

5 month 1777 At a Monthly Meeting held in **Dartmouth** the 19th the 5th mo 1777

The Representatives are **Benj^a Howland 2nd** & **Abraham** [Howland?] Present

Received an Epistle from our Last Quarterly meeting which was read and the Advise therein well Accepted

Case concerning Prize good Good refer'd The Committee Appointed on the amount of those friends Concern^d in Prise Goods made Report that they have not fully gone through with the matter they are therefore Continued in the Same Service & to make report next monthly meeting

Stephen Mott Informed of his denial **John Williams** Reports he hath Inform.^d **Stephen Mott** of his Denial as order^d

Testimony against Wm Russell not read The Clerk Reports he hath not Read the Testimony against **Wm Russell** According to Appointment he is therefore Continued for that Service & to make Report next mo meeting

Testimony Signed agains^t Eben Slocum & Charles Slocum There was a Testimony Sign,^d in this meeting against **Ebenezer** & **Charles Slocum** Sons of **Charles Slocum** Deceas^t and the Clerk is order,^d to Read the Same Publickly as Usual and Report next mo meeting

Miniuts revisd The Committee Appointed to Revise & Correct the meeting minutes & to Settle accounts with the Treasurer report that they have fulfilled their Appointment & Left the

Settled with Treasurer minutes with the Clerk to be Recorded and there remains in the Stock after Settlement the Sum of £5 Lawf. mony.

Giles Slocum Certificate There was a Certificate Sign.^d in this meeting on the Account of **Giles Slocum** Directed to the mo meeting of **Sandwich** Certifying his Clearness Respecting marriage

Complaint against Joshua Shearman This meeting is Inform^d that **Jorshua Sherman** hath Remov,^d out of the [?ing] of this meeting Sometime past and not applying for a Certificate also Neglects attending meeting and hath been Labour,^d with by one of ye Overseers & othe friends but they not finding Satisfaction therefore we appoint **Caleb Russell** and **John Williams** to Labour further with him for his misconduct and Report next mo meeting

Jonathan Willbor Wife & Children Recievd This Meeting in Concurrance with the womens meeting doth Accept of **Jonathan Wilbur** and **Haldah** his wife and all their Children to be members under the Care of this meeting

Prince Allen Treasurer This meeting Appoints **Prince Allen** Treasurer in the room of **Tho.ˢ Hicks** who by his Request is Dismissed
This meeting Collected – £1 – ˢ9 – 9 £. money

6 month 1777 At a Monthly Meeting held in **Dartmouth** the 16ᵗʰ the 6ᵗʰ mo 1777

The Representatives are **William Sandford** & **Prince Allen** Present
The Queries were read and Answers prepar.ᵈ in this meeting

adjourn This meeting Adjourns to the 23ʳᵈ Instant after the meeting Of worship which is to begin at yᵉ 11ᵗʰ hour, by reason if its now being the time of the yearly meeting

Mett Meet by Adjournment yᵉ 23ʳᵈ 6 mo 1777
The Representatives being Called both present

Report of Comtee Concerning Prize goods The Greater part of the Commitee appointed to Labour with those transgressors on account of prise goods Report that they have Discharged themselves in that matter and **Joseph Russell** and **Benjamin Russell** gave the Satisfaction on that account, and S.ᵈ Committee hath Draughted and brought Testimonies against them to this meeting, yet the matter is Refer.ᵈ one month Longer by the Request of **William Barker** and **Joseph Gifford** as they Express a Concern to treat further with them and they to Report next monthly meeting.

Testimonys Read The Clerk Reports he hath Read the Testimonies against **Wᵐ Russell** & **Charles** & **Ebenezer Slocum** as order.ᵈ Last mo meeting S.ᵈ Testimonies are as followeth – –

Testimony a gainst Wm Russell Tim son Whereas **William Russell** Son of **Timothy Russell**, having had a Birthright among friends and been under the Care of this meeting but hath So far Departed from our Profession as to Inlist into the wars which being So Inconsistant with our profession and Principals and Reproachfull to our Society that this meeting is Concern,ᵈ to gave this forth as a publick testimony against the Said **William Russell** hereby Disowning him from being under our Care, yet Desiring if it be Agreeable with Divine Pleasure that he may Come to Sight and Sense of the Evil of Such practices and through unfeigned Repentance find mercy Given forth at our Monthly meeting held in **Dartmouth** the 21ˢᵗ of yᵉ 4ᵗʰ mo 1777 and Sign.ᵈ in and by order of S.ᵈ meeting by – – 　　　　　　　　　　　　　**William Anthony Jᵘ** Clerk

Testimony Against Eben & Charles Slocum

Whereas **Ebenezer Slocum** and **Charles Slocum**, Sons
of **Charles Slocum** Deceas,[d] and **Sarah** his wife, having had
a Right of Membership amongst us, but they Departing
So far from the Principals we Profess as to be Concern,[d]
in Millitary or War.like matters and friends having
Treated with them on that Account, but they Discovering
no Disposition of a Return or Reformation, therefore
this meeting being Concern,[d] to maintain our Testimony
herein do hereby Publickly Disown and testifie against
them the Said **Ebenezer** and **Charles Slocum** from being
members of our Religious Society Untill by unfeign,[d] Repen
=tance & Reformation they shall be Restor.[d] to the way
of truth – – Given forth and Signed in & on behalf
of our monthly meeting of friends held in **Dartmouth**
the 19th of the 5th mo 1777 by **William Anthony J[u]** Clerk

Judith Akin & Abigail How = land

The Women Inform they have Denied **Judith Akin** and **Abigail
Howland** which we Concur with

Case of Joshua Shearmen refer'd

The Committee appointed to Labour with **Joshua Sherma[n]**
Report that they have not fully accomplished S.[d] matter
therefore its Refer.[d] under their Care and they to make
Report next mo meeting

Elizabeth Russell disowned

There was a Testimony of Denial against **Elizabeth
Russell** wife of **Benjamin Russell** Sign.[d] in this meeting
by the Clerk – –

Bethiah Eldredg Receiv'd

The women Inform they have Minuted **Bethah Eldridg**
under their Care which we Concur with – –

Representative

Our friends **Thomas Hicks William Anthony J[u]**
Benjamin Howland 2.nd and **Seth Russell** are appointed
to attend the Quarterly meeting and report next mo

answers & Epistle

meeting and present the Epistle with the Answers to the Queries – –

Chusing overseers referd

A New Choice of Overseers is Refer.[d] to next mo meeting
and the former Continued in that Service till a New Choice is made
This meeting Collected . . 2[£] '' 3[s] '' 5[d] £. money

---

7 th month 1777

At a Monthly Meeting held in **Dartmouth** 21st 7[mo] 1777
the Representative are **W[m] Barker** & **Joseph Tucker J[u]** present

John Williams proposal of marriage

John Williams and **Martha Peabody** Declar.[d] their Intents
of taking Each other in marriage and were Desir.[d] to wait
till next monthly meeting for an Answer and **Joseph
Gifford** and **W[m] Barker** are appointed to Enquire into the
Clearness of S.[d] **William** Respecting Marriage & Conversation
and make Report next mo meeting – –

Choice of Overseers referd A new Choice of Overseers both of the meeting and of ye Poor is Refer,^d to next mo meeting

Report from Quart meeting The Representatives to the Quarterly meeting Report they all Atten,d Agreeable to appointment and have

Epistils Recievd Produc,^d an Epistle from the Same with a Transcript[ion] of a written one from **London** baring Date from ye 27 the 5 mo 1776 to the 1st of ye 6th mo Enclusive with a Trans cript from **Philadelphia** with our Last yearly meeting Epistle with an Extract from Some of S.^d yearly meeting minutes all of which have been Read in this meeting to Good Satisfaction and the S.^d Trascript from **London** is order to be Publickly Read in Each of our meetings for worship – –

[J and B?] Russell disownd **Joseph Gifford** and **William Barker** made Report that they have had Conference with **Joseph Russell** and **Benj^a Russell** agreeable to their appointment and that the Said **Benj^a** did not give them Satisfaction therefore he is hereby Denied from being a member of this meeting and the Clerk hath Sign,^d a paper of Denial against him and is order,^d to read it Public^kly as Usual & make Report next mo meeting – –

Case of Joseph Russell referd And their Report Respecting **Joseph Russell** not being fully Satisfactory the matter is Refer,^d at ye Request of **John Potter**, to next mo meeting & **Nicholass Howland** is appointed to Inform **Benj^a Russell** of hi Deniel & Report next mo meeting

Case of Joshua Shearman & son Joshua referd The Committee appointed on account of **Joshua Sherman** Report that he gave them a Degree of Satisfaction for his Removing without the advice of friends & not Requesting a Certificate therefore we appoint our friends **James Davis** and **John Williams** to See if his outward affairs be Setled to Satisfaction and Draw a Certificate if they think proper. also to Draw one for **Jorshua Sherman J^ur** if they think proper and bring them to next monthly meeting

Elizabeth Howland disownd This meeting in Concurrance with the Women^s meeting have Sign,^d a Testimony Against **Elizabeth Howland** wife to **Benj^a Howland**

Jonathan Slocum disown,d This meeting is Inform.^d that **Jonathan Slocum** hath Married out of the Unity of friends after being Previously Caution,^d by the Overseers, and also hath been found Guilty of fornication as appears by his wife^s having a Child before marriage as also by his own Confession therefore this meetig doth Disown him the Said **Jonathan Slocum** and **Philip Allen** & **Samuel Smith** are appointed to Draft a paper of

Denial against him and Inform him thereof and to make
Report next mo meeting – –

Complaint against Tho.s Wilcox and Wm Sanford Jur We are Inform,[d] That **Thomas Willcox & William Sandford J**[u] hath Purchas,[d] Some Prise Goods and they have been Labour[d] with by friends for their misconduct but did not Give them Satisfaction therefore our friends **John Potter & Benj**[a] **Taber** are appointed to Labour further with them and to make rep[ort] next mo meeting

To have oversight of meeting house yard We appoint our Friends **William Barker Prince Allen John Potter Benj**[a] **Howland 2**[nd] **William Anthony J**[u] to have the Oversight & Care of the yard fenced in Round our meeting ho[use] and Indeaviour to Preserve the feed for the Use of furren[22] friends horses at the time of the Quarterly meeting and other times as they shall See Cause upon Application mad[e] to them

Penelope Trafford denyd The women Inform that they have Denied **Penelope Trafford** which this meeting Concurs with

Collected – –   £1 .. 11[s] ... 1[d] £. Money

Order on Treasurer The Treasurer is order,[d] to pay **W**[m] **Barker** 4 Dollars for half year.[s] keeping the meeting house and £1 – 3[s] for other Charge which he paid for this meeting
also S.[d] Treasurer is order.[d] to pay **Joseph Rotch** 2[£] – 8[s]– 0 for **Peter Barney** for the hire of a vessell for friend to goe to **Nantucket**

8 th month 1777 At a Monthly Meeting held in **Dartmouth** 18th 8 mo 1777
The Representatives are **Joseph Barker** & **Prince Allen** present
The Committee appointed to Inquire into **John Williams** Clearness Respecting marriage & Conversation Report that they have found nothing to hinder his proceeding – –

John William answer **John Williams** and **Martha Pebody** appear,[d] for their Answer which was that they might Proceed to take each other in marriage in Some Convenient time between this & next mo meeting Advising with the friends this meeting Shall appoint for that purpose and **Joseph Gifford & W**[m] **Barker** are Appointed to see their marriage Consuma--ted orderly & Report next mo meeting

Recd Wm Penn Epistles Receivm[d] Several Reprinted Epistles of our worthy friend **William Penn** taken from his Select works page 497, one of which being Rea[d] to Satisfaction and they are order,[d] to be Destibuted among friends to be read in their forneties [families?][23] – –

22. "Furren" here means "foreign," traveling Friends from outside the monthly meeting.
23. The reference is probably to *Select Works of William Penn, to Which Is Prefixed a Journal of His Life* (London, 1771).

Overseers of Meeting We appoint our friends **Joseph Barker James Davis Prince Allen** & **William Anthony J^{ur}** Overseers of the meeting for the year Ensuing and an Additional Choice is Refer^d to next <u>mo</u> meeting

Overseers of poor **Caleb Russell Seth Russell Benj^a Reder Samuel Smith Gideon Howland** are Appointed overseers of the poor for the year Ensuing

The Clerk Report he hath Read the Testimony against **Benj^a Russell** and **Nicholas Howland** Reports he Inform^d S.^d **Russell** of his Denial as order,^d Last mo. meeting S.^d testimony is as followeth

Testimony against Benj Russell Whereas **Benj^a Russell** (Son of **Benj^a Russell** Deceas,^d having been a Member of our Society but hath so far Depart^{ed} from our Religious Profession as to purchase Some of those Goods Called Prise Goods taken in the war, and this meeting having Labour,^d with him in Love in order to Discover to him the Evil of his S.^d Conduct but our Labour therein not being Effectual therefore for the Clearing of our testimony herein this meeting is Concern,^d to Give this forth as a Publick Testimony against him hereby Disowning him the S^d **Russell** from being a member of our Society untill by a Sincear Reformation & Return he shall be Restor,^d to the way of Truth – Given forth & Sign.^d in & on behalf of our <u>mo</u> meeting of friends held in **Dartmouth** the 21 Day of the 7th <u>mo</u> 1777 By – –

Wm Anthony J^u Clerk

Step. Gifford request a Certificate **Stephen Gifford** Requests a Certificate to the <u>mo</u> meeting of **Acoakset** Certifying his Clearness Respecting marriage and Conversation therefore **Samuel Smith** & **Thos Hicks** are appointed to take the Necessary Care on that account & make Report next <u>mo</u> meeting

Aaron Lan= =kestor and David Sands Visit Our Beloved Friends **Aaron Lankestor** and **David Sands** were at this meeting on a Religious Visit whose Testimony and Visit hath been well Accepted And **Samuel Smith** & **Wm Anthony** are Appointed to Draw Certificates for S^d friends and bring them to next [?] the Adjournment of this meeting

Adjournd This meeting adjourns to the 27th Instant after the meeting of worship

Mett Met by Adjournment the 27th ye 8 <u>mo</u> 1777

The Representatives Called both present – –

Jos Russell Case referd **John Potter** made Report Respecting **Joseph Russell** and he the **Russell** gave in a paper to this meeting which were to pretty good Satisfaction yet the matter is Refer.^d to next <u>mo</u> meeting for Same alteration in S^d paper if he Shall See fit to alter the Same

Joshua Shearman Certificate	This Meeting Sign^d Removal Certificates for **Jorshua Sherman** and **Jorshua Sherman J^u** to the mo meeting of **Sandwich** who have Remov^d their then Some time ago
Jonat Slocum denial	a paper of Denial was Sign^d against **Jonathan Slocum** and the Clerk is order.^d to Read the Same Publickly as Usual and make Report next mo meeting but ye Committee not having Inform.^d him of his Denial **Philip Allen** is order^d to Inform him of his S.^d Denial & Report next mo meeting
Jonat Green Certificate	Received a Removal Certificate from the Monthly meeting of **Greenwich** for **Jonathan Green** and **Martha Green** who have moved here & is Accepted
Easter Russell denial	A paper of Denial was Sign.^d in this meeting against **Easter Russell** wife of **Paul Russell** in Concurrance with the women meeting
Case of Wm Sanford Jur & Thos Wilcox	The Commitee Appointed to treat with **Wm Sandford J^u** and **Thos Willcox [Wilcox]** Report that they have had a Conference with them The former of which gave them a Degree of Satisfaction the Latter Apear.^d in a state of willfull blindness yet they have Each of them Given in a paper Condeming their misconduct but nither of them attended this meeting Said Committee are Still Continued to treat with them once more and to Draw a paper of Denial against S^d **Willcox** if he do not Give them Satisfaction and bring it & make Report next mo meeting
Treasurer report	The Treasurer not having paid the money to **Joseph Rotch** as orderd he is Therefore Still Continued to pay the Same & Report next mo meeting
The Time next monthly meet -ing to be held	This meeting doth Conclude at ye Request & by the Directions of our Quarterly meeting Committee to hold our next mo meeting on the next day following the preparative meeting being the fifth Day of the week and to begin at the Usual hour – –
Complaint against Nat Kirby	This meeting being inform.^d that **Nethaniel Kirby** hath appear.^d with the millitary Company as a Solger[Soldier], and been Labour.^d with by the Overseers, and Justifies S^d Conduct therefore we appoint **Peleg Slocum** & **Philip Allen** to Labour further with him and Draw a paper of Denial against him if they find no Satisfaction and bring to next mo meeting
Certificate for A Lankestor & D. Sand	Certificate for **Aaron Lankestor** and **David Sands** were Sign,^d in this meeting The former to ye mo meeting at the **Oblong** the Latter to the mo meeting of y^e **Nine partners**

9 Month 1777	At a Monthly Meeting held in **Dartmouth** ye 11th Day 9mo 1777 the Representatives are **Benj.^a Howland 2nd** & **Benj.^a Taber** present
Meeting to Be purged	This meeting hath Concluded not to Indulge any into this meeting that are not members of the Society for the future Neither at the

time of young people pasing in order for marriage nor other time

John Williams Marriage **Jo.**[s] **Gifford & W**[m] **Barker** Reports they attended the marriage of of **John Williams & Martha Pebody** and that it was Consumated orderly. an Additional Choice of Overseers Refer.[d] to next mo meeting

Step Gifford Certificate A Certificate was Signed in this meeting for **Stephen Gifford** Respecting his Clearness of marriage and Conversation Directed to y[e] mo meeting of **Accoakset.**

Case of Jos Russell refered The matter Respecting **Joseph Russell** is Refer.[d] to next mo meeting under the care of **John Potter** who is then to make Report

Jona[t] Slocums denial read The Clerk Reports he hath read the Testimony against **Jonathan Slocum** as order.[d] Last mo meeting but **Philip Allen** not having Inform.[d] him is Continued for that Service & to make Report next mo meeting – –

W[m] Sanford & Tho Wilcox refered The Committee that had the Care of that matter Respecting **W**[m] **Sandford J**[ur] and **Tho.**[s] **Willcox [Wilcox]** Report that they found Some Satisfaction with both S[d] friends yet by S.[d] Committee Request it is Refer.[d] to next mo meeting under their Care & then they to make Report

Treasurers report The Treasurer not having paid the money to **Joseph Rotch** as order.[d] he is therefore order.[d] to pay the Same & Report when it is done

Nat Kirby case referd The Committee appointed to treat with **Nathaniel Kirby** Report they have had a Conference with him and Receiv.[d] a Degree of Satisfaction, therefore the matter is Refer.[d] to next mo meeting under the Care of y[e] Same Committee as before and **Benj**[a] **Howland & Samuel Smith** is aded to them and they to Report if he do not give them Satisfaction.

To collect account of Sufering friends We appoint our friends **Samuel Smith Prince Allen John Williams Benj.**[a] **Rider** A Committee to Collect the Account of the Sufferings of friend within the Compass of this meeting & bring them to this meeting

Ben Howland's proposal of marriage **Benjamin Howland 3**[rd] and **Mary Slocum** Declar.[d] their Inten-:tions of taking Each other in marriage and were Desired to wait till next mo meeting for their answer and **W**[m] **Barker & Joseph Gifford** are Appointed to Enquire into the young man's Clearness and to make Report next mo meeting

Collected – – L9 – 6[s] – 1[d] L [mo]

This meeting to the 24th Instant after the meeting for worship

Meet by Adjournment y[e] 24 Day y[e] 9th mo 1777

The Representatives Called both present-

*Quar^t meeting
Com^tee on
Isaac Howland
case*

The Committee from the Quarterly meeting appointed to Advise
this meeting in a matter Respecting **Isaac Howland** freeing
his Negro or other matters as truth opens the way, have given
in the following in writing as their advice which is well Accepted

Dartmouth ye 11th ye 9 ^mo 1777

*Their advice
& Judgment*

We the Committee appointed by our last Quarterly meeting to
visit the <u>mo</u> meeting of friends at **Apponaganset** for the Support
of our Christian Discipline and more Especially that part
of it against Slavery Do give it as our Sense and Judgment
in the first place that the Spirit and Intention of our Rule
Discipline on that behalf be fully observ.^d and Attended unto,
But Nevertheless when any friend moved by a Principal
of Benevolence to Assist any in Bondage in order to Provide
their freedom if time & oppertunity Admitt that Such friend
before he Proceed therein lay the Same before the <u>mo</u> meeting
to which he belong & take their Advice yet if he Should for
want of time or Oppertunity Proved therein without the
advice of friends as afore S.^d we think it may be safe for
the Monthly meeting where the Benevelent Intention
is Evident by attending Circumstances to let Such fiends
Escape the Censure of Society

> **John Collins**
> **Joshua Devol[Davol]**
> **Thos Hazzard** Son of **Robert**
> **Aziel Wilkenson**

and the matter Respecting

*I Howland
Case*

Isaac Howland is Refer^d to this meeting Committee that had the
Care of that matter Last in Charge & they to Judge thereon and
make Return to this meeting when they have fulfill.^d the Same

*Answers
Epistles &*

The Queries were Answer.^d and an Epistle Sign.^d in this
meeting and order.^d forward to the Quarterly meeting by our

*Reprsenta
=tives*

Representatives who are **Joseph Tucker Samuel Smith**
& **Thos Hicks** and they to Report next <u>mo</u> meeting – –

*order on
Treasurer*

By Directions from Last Quarterly this meeting orders
the Treasurer to pay to the yearly meeting, Treasurer the
Sum of twelve pounds to Supply the yearly meeting Stock
and make Report next <u>mo</u> meeting

*10 month
<u>1777</u>*

At a Monthly Meeting held in **Dartmouth** ye 20th 10mo 1777
the Representatives are **Caleb Russell** and **Philip Allen** Present
An Additional Choice of Overseers is Refer.^d to next <u>mo</u> meeting

Jos. Russell paper accepted

Joseph Russell give in a paper to this meeting Condeming his Suffering his Team to draw Some prise Shugar, which this meeting Accepts provided he he Cause the Same to be Publickly Read as Usual & Return S.^d paper to next <u>mo</u> meeting.

Wm Sanford ^Ju & Tho Wilcox case referd

The Committee Appointed on the Case of **Wm Sanford** ^Ju and **Thos Willcox** not having Accomplish.^d their Service Define it may be Refer.^d to next mo meeting which is accordingly and then they to make Report

Nathaniel Kirby disownd

Whereas **Nethaniel Kirby** hath Sometime past taken up arms in the military Service and the Committee appointed to Labour with him therefor, hath made Report that he Gave them no Satis-=faction, Therefore for the Clearing of our Testimony herein this meeting doth Disown him from being a member of our Society and from under the care of friends, and the Clerk is order.^d to read this minute Publickly at the Close of a first Days meeting as Usual & Report next <u>mo</u> meeting

The friends appointed to Inspect into **Benj.^a Howland 3rd** Clearness Respecting marriage Report that they Don't find any thing to hinder his proceeding

Return from Q. meeting

The friends appointed to attend the Quarterly meeting Report they all Attended and have Produc.^d an Epistle from the Same which hath been Read to Good Satisfaction

Treasuresr report

The Treasurer Reports he hath Sent the money to the yearly meeting ' Treasurer Agreeable to his Appointment

Benj. Howland 3 Answer

Benj^a Howland 3rd and **Mary Slocum** Appear^d for their answer which was that they might Proceed to take Each other in marriage at Some Convenient time before next ^mo meeting Advising with the Overseers this meeting shall appoint for that purpose and **Joseph Gifford** & **Wm Sanford** are appointed to see S^d marriage Consomated orderly and Report next <u>mo</u> monthly m–

Mary Slocum Certificate

The Women Inform they have Receiv.^d a Removel Certificate for **Mary Slocum** wife of **Giles Slocum** which this meeting Concurs with They also Inform they have Receiv.d a Removel Certificate

Martha Sloc-cum

for **Martha Slocum** wife of **John Slocum** with all her Children Except the youngest which being born Since they Remov.^d which is Receiv.^d as a member at the Request of the mother of s^d Child

John Smith request a Certificate

John Smith Son of **Isaac Smith** Deceas.^d Requests a Removel Certificate to y^e <u>mo</u> meeting at the **Ninepartners** therefore we Appoint **Nicholas Howland** & **Thos Hicks** to take the necessary Care therein and Draw one for him if they find things Clear and bring it to next mo meeting

Gilbert How land request a Certificate

Gilbert Howland also Requests a Removel Certificate to the mo meeting at the **Ninepartners** therefore we appoint **Joseph Barker** and **Thos Hicks** to Draw one for him if they think proper after Enquiry & bring to next mo meeting– –

Collected – – L4 – 5ˢ – 1ᵈ – L. mo

11 month 1777

At a Monthly Meeting held in **Dartmouth** the 17ᵗʰ yᵉ 11ᵐᵒ 1777 The Representatives are **Benjᵃ Howland 2ⁿᵈ** & **Prince Allen** present

Josep Russell paper read

Joseph Russell's paper having been read as order'ᵈ and is Returnᵈ to this meeting Sᵈ paper is as followeth

To the Monthly Meeting of friends in **Dartmouth**
Respected Friends

Jos Russell paper

    Whereas Some time past I Suffer.ᵈ my Team to draw Some prise Shuger a Small Distance and thereby offended my friends for which I am Sorry and Do Condemn keeping you may So far pass it by as to Let me Remain under you Care – from your friend – **Joseph Russell** – –

Case of Wᵐ Sanford and Tho Wilcox referd

This Meeting not being fully Satisfied to accept of **Wᵐ Sandford iᵘ** & **Tho.ˢ Willcox** paper therefore the matter Respecting them is Refer.ᵈ to next mo meeting under the Same friends Care as heretofore and then they to Report

Edw Taber request

Edward Taber hath Given in a paper to this meeting Condemning his marr[y]ing out of the Unity of friends and Requests to be Receiv,ᵈ into Unity again therefore **James Davis** and **John Williams** are Appointed to tak an Oppertunity of Solid Conference with him in order to Discover his Sincerity and make Report next mo meeting

Nat Kirby informd of denial

Philip Allen Reports he hath Informᵈ **Nathaniel Kirby** of his Denial as order,ᵈ but Clerk not having read his Denial he is Continued for that Sevis[Service] and to Report next mo meeting

Ben How land's Marriage

Joseph Gifford and **Wᵐ Barker** Report they attended the marriage of **Benjᵃ Howland 3ʳᵈ** & **Mary Slocum** and Said nothing but that it was Consomated orderly

Mary Howland Certificate

This meeting Sign.ᵈ a Certificate for **Mary Howland** to the mo meeting at the **Nine partners**

Lilis Maccomber Received

The Women Inform they have Receiv.ᵈ into membership **Lilis Maccombur[Macomber]** which this meeting Concurs with

John Smith Gilbert Howland Certificates refer.ᵈ

The friends Appointed to Draw Certificate for **John Smith** and **Gilbert Howland** Report that things are not fully Clear in Regard to S.ᵈ **Smith** they are Still Continued and to advise him as they think proper and Report next mo meeting

and they have prepar.d a Certificate for **Gilbert Howland** and brought which was Sign.d in this meeting

Testimony against J Slocum recorded next page

Philip Allen Reports he hath Inform.d **Jonathan Slocum** of his Denial as order.d Some time past-

Ben Howland 2nd Bill for keeping A Smith

Benj.a Howland 2.nd hath given in an Account to this meeting for helping [**Allice**] to the amount of L4-14.s-8.d L money which is allowed and the Treasurer is order.d to pay the Same and Report next mo meeting

The Treasurer Reports he hath paid **Joseph Rotch** for **Peter Barney** – 2.L – 8.s agreeable to his appointed some time past -

Collected – 1.L – 14.s – 9.d

12th month 1777

At s Monthly Meeting held in **Dartmouth** 15.th 12.mo 1777

The Representatives are **Benj.a Taber** & **Joseph Tucker J.u** present

The matter Respecting an additional Choice of Overseers is being Consider.d in this meeting and not finding any willing to accept S.d matter is Dismissed

Tho.s Wilcox disowned Wm Sanford J.u case referd

The Committee appointed on account of **Tho̱s Willcox [Wilcox]** and **W.m Sanford J.u** Report that S.d **Willcox [Wilcox]** gave them no real Satisfaction therefore we hereby Disown the S.d **Tho.s Willcox[Wilcox]** from under our Care S.d **Sanford** gave the Committee Some Satisfaction therefore S.d Committee is Still Continued and **Abraham Howland** is aded to them in that matter & to Report next mo meeting also to Draw a Testimony against S.d **Willcox [Wilcox]** and bring to next mo meeting Likewise Inform him of his Denial

Edw Taber Rec.d

The Committee appointed on account of **Edward Taber** Report that they have received a degree of Satisfaction. Therefore we conclude to except[accept] of said **Taber** under our Care

Nat Kirby Denial read

The Clerk reports he hath read the Testimony against **Nathaniel Kirby** as ordered: Said Testimony is as followeth

Testimony against Jonathan Slocum

Whereas **Jonathan Slocum** hath made profession with us as a member of our Society but hath so far departed there from as to marry out of Unity of friends after being previously Caution.d and also fallen into the Sin of fornication as appears by his wife's having a Child before marriage therefore this meeting being conserned to maintan our Testimony herein do Give this forth as a publick Testimony against him hereby Disowning the S.d **Jonathan Slocum** from being a member of our Society untill by a Sincear Repentance & Acknowledgement of the Evil of his Conduct he shall be Restor.d to the way of Truth Given forth at our mo meeting held in **Dartmouth** by adjournment the 27.th the 8.mo 1777 & Signed in & by order of S.d meeting by – –

                                 W.m Anthony J.u Clerk

Testimony against R A should been Recorded in page 370

Whereas **Ralph Allen** Son of **Benjamin Allen** & **Allaphal** his wife
having had a Birthright among friends but hath so far Departed from our
Profession as to Inlist[Enlist] or Enter on bond of a Vessell of war Called a Privateer and
against Such Proceedings do Give this forth as a publick denial against
him & do hereby disown him the Said **Ralph Allen** from being [?]
a member of our Society & from under the Care of this meeting
Given forth & Signed in & on behalf of our mo meeting held in **Dartmouth** 17th 2mo 1777
by **Wm Anthony Ju** Clerk

Certificate for J Smith not accompli shed

The Committy appointed to draw a Certificate for **John ~~Russell~~ Smith**
Report that said matter is not accomplished. therefore said Committy
are still continued for that Service and make report when ready.

B Howland paid

The Treasurer Reports that he hath paid **Benjamin Howland** the money
as ordered the last Monthly meeting

A Gifford's Request also J Devol and Seth Huddleston

We received a paper from **Abiel Gifford** requesting his Children to
be taken under friends care. Also one from **John Devol** requesting to
come under friends care and his Son also . . . Likewise one from **Seth
Huddlestone** requesting to come under friends care with his Children,
Therefore we appoint **Joseph Barker, Thomas Hicks, Benjamin Rider**
and **William Mosher** to take an opportunity of conference with Said
Pertitioner in order to discover their Sencerity and wheather[whether] said request be
from the bottom of true Convictions and make report when ready.

Certificate for N Howland Received

We received a Certificate for **Nicholas Howland** from **Coakset** meeting
which is accepted

M Lapham Received

The Women friends Inform they have received **Mary Lapham**, Wife
of **Nicholas Lapham** under their care which we concur with
This Meeting Collected L3 – 13s – 3d

adjournd

This meeting adjorns to the 24th Instant

mett

This Meeting mett by adjornment the 24th of 12th month 1777
The Representatives being called, both present

Queries answered Friends appointed to Quarterly Meeting

The Queries were answer'd in this meeting, And an Epistle Sign'd
for the Quarterly meeting, and forwarded by our Representatives to Said
Quarterly meeting; Who are **William Mosher William Anthony Jur**
Caleb Russell and **Gideon Howland:** and they to make report to the
next Monthly meeting

Wm Anthony Ju his Bill

William Anthony Jur gave in a bill for keeping **Alice Smith**
from the 24th of the 4th month to the 28th of the 10th month 1777 which is
Six months: as by agreement with the Overseers of the poor: To the
amount of 5L – 18s – 6d Which is approv'd, and the Treasurer is order'd
to pay the Same, and report to next Monthly Meeting

1 month 1778

At a Monthly meeting held in **Dartmouth** the 19th of 1st month 1778

    The Representatives are **Benjamin Smith Ju^r** and **John Williams** Present

Report of a Committee on T.Wilcox & W. Sanford

    The Comitty appointed on the case of **Thomas Wilcox** and **William Sanford Ju^r** make report that the matter not being fully settled in regard of **Sanford**'s delinquent to be continued, therefore it is referred to next Monthly meeting under their care Who are then to make report; They also make report that they have fulfilled their appointment respecting said **Wilcox** and have drafted a paper of Denial against him, which after being read, and considered and Signed by the Clerk, who is ordered to read the Same as Usual, and make report to our next monthly Meeting

Return of Friends from Quarterly Meeting

    The friends appointed to attend the Quarterly meeting, report that they all attended except **Caleb Russel** who gave a reasonable Excuse They also produced an Epistle from said meeting which was read and kindly accepted

W Anthony Bill not paid

    The Treasurer reports he hath not paid the money to **William Anthony Ju** as ordered: therefore he is continued to pay the Same and report to the next Monthly meeting

Certificate for C. Howland

    Cornelius Howland Informed this meeting that he had some expect =ation of going to Sea, and desired a Certificate, which was granted, and one being present was Signed by the Clerk

C Peckham Disowned

    The Women friends Inform they have denyed **Katurah Peckham** which this meeting concurs with

Samuel Gifford declar'd his intention of marriage

    Samuel Gifford and **Lillis Maccomber** declared their Intentions of Taking each other in Marriag : and were desired to waite till the next Monthly Meeting for their answer: and ~~Phil~~ **Prince Allen** and **Nicholas Howland** are appointed to Inquire into the young man's Clearness and to make report next Monthly Meeting

N Lapham request for his Children

    Nicholas Lapham requests that his Children may be taken under the care of this Meeting: therefore **William Anthony Ju^r** and **Thomas Hicks** are appointed to take the needful care in that case and make report to next monthly meeting

    This Meeting Collected 5^L – 15^s – 3^d

T Russell under dealing

    Timothy Russel hath given in a paper to this meeting Condemning his Purchasing Some Prize goods: But as he hath some time past Lett out his house for the use of an Hospatal to Inocculate the Small Pox in after being advised to the contrary; which hath given uneasiness to divers friends[24] . . . Therefore this meeting doth appoint **Benjamin Taber William**

---

24. Friends did not oppose inoculation as such. The "uneasiness" was probably due to the hospital being used for military inoculations. See Robert A. Clark and J. Russell Elkinton, *The Quaker Heritage in Medicine* (Pacific Grove, Calif.: Box Grove Press, 1978), 39–40; and Ann M. Becker, "Smallpox in Washington's Army: Strategic Implications of the Disease during the Americaz Revolution," *Journal of Military History*, 68 (April 2004), 381–430.

Mosher and **Samuel Smith** to have conference with him in those matters
and give in their report and Judgment, there upon to the next Monthly
Meeting

2ᵈ *month* — At a Monthly Meeting held in **Dartmouth** the 16ᵗʰ of 2ⁿᵈ month 1778
1778

　　　　　The Representative are **William Barker** and **Benjamin Taber** Present

Report of the — 　　　　　The Committy appointed to have a conference with **John Devol**
Committee for
J Devol, Seth — **Seth Huddlestone** and their Children and **Abiel Gifford**s childrens Report
Huddleston and — that they have fulfilled their appointmen, and have found good
A Gifford
　　　　　Satisfaction. Therefore they are all accepted to be under friends Care
the name of **John Devol**'s child is **Job** . . . . **Seth Huddleston**'s Children
names are **Sarah** and **Lavinah** and **Abiel Gifford**s childrens names
are **Levi, Lilis, Gilbart, John, Jeremiah, Abiel** and **Joanna.**

The case of — 　　　　　The commity appointed on account of **William Sanford Juʳ** desire
Wᵐ Sanford Ju — that matter refered, therefore it is refered under their and they
referd
to report next Monthly Meeting

T Wilcox — 　　　　　The Clerk Reports he hath not read **Thomas Wilcox**'s Denial
Denial not
read — as ordered therefore he is continued to accomplish the same and report
to next Monthly Meeting

W Anthony's — 　　　　　The Treasurer reports he has paid **William Anthony Juᵉʳ** the money
Bill paid — as order'd last Monthly Meeting

S G reported — 　　　　　The friends appointed to Enquire into **Samuel Gifford**'s clearness
Clear — Respecting marriage report that they find nothing to hinder this proceeding
in marriage

N Lapham's — 　　　　　The friends appointed to have the care of that matter respecting
request refer'd — **Nicholas Lapham**s children being taken under the care of friends
desire it to be refered therefore said matter is refered to next Monthly
meeting

S Giffords — 　　　　　**Samuel Gifford** and **Lillis Maccomber** appeared for their answers
and L Ma — Which was, that they might Proceed ₐᵗᵒ ᵗᵃᵏᵉ ᵉᵃᶜʰ ᵒᵗʰᵉʳ in Marriage in Some Convenient
comber an
swer — time between now and next monthly meeting, advising with the
friends, that this meeting shall appoint for that purpose, and **Nicholas
Howland** and **Prince Allen** are appointed to see their said marriage
Solemnized and to make report next monthly meeting

J Roach — 　　　　　**Joseph Rotch** Requests a removal Certificate to the monthly
request a — Meeting at **Nantucket.** therefore this meeting appoints **James Davis**
Certificate — and **Seth Russel** to take the necessary care on that account, and
bring one to next monthly meeting if they think proper.

The case of — 　　　　　The matter respecting **Timothy Russel** is refer'd to next monthly
T Russell — meeting for further consideration
refer'd
　　　　　This meeting collected 2ᴸ – 8ˢ – 5ᵈ

Quarterly meeting Com^tee – visit J Howland

The Quarterly Meeting's Committy that was appointed to Visit and advise this meeting on account of **Isaac Howland**'s freeing his Negroe; have given in ~~advise~~ the following advice: which is accepted, and that matter is dismised, and this Meeting's Committy discharged there from

Their advice to Monthly Meeting

The advice of the Quarterly meeting's Commity is as followeth

We whose names are hereto Subscribed. being a Commity to advise the Monthly Meeting of **Dartmouth** Respecting a matter of **Isaac Howland**'s being concerned with a Negroe &c: Having had an oppertunity with him and said monthly meeting's Commity and considered the case, Look upon it that there is at least an appearance of weakning our Testimony against Slavery in his Conduct: Therefore think well of the care of said meeting in the case: yet we have Learnt by Strict Inquiry he had no Such intent; But reather acted from a Benevolent purpose, and has mannumitted said Negroe, therefore we advise said meeting to drop that matter

     Dartmouth the 16th day of the 2nd month 1778

> **T Hazard son of Robert**
> **Joshua Davol**
> **Moses Farnum**
> **Benj^a Buffinton**
> **David Steere**
> **Oziel Wilkinson**

3rd month 1778

At a Monthly meeting held in **Dartmouth** the 16th of 3rd month 1778

The Representatives are **Peleg Gifford** and **Benjamin Smith Ju^r** present

W Sanford's paper accepted

The Commity appointed in the case of **William Sanford Ju** Report that he hath given them a degree of Satisfaction, therefore the Paper he gave in to this meeting, condemning his purchasing Prize goods is accepted provided he cause the same publickly to be read as Usual and return Said ~~pa~~paper to next monthly meeting

The Clerk reports he hath read the paper of denial against **Thomas Wilcox** according to appointment – Which is as followeth

T Wilcox Testimony of denial

Whereas **Thomas Wilcox** hath, through unwachfulness so far deviated from the Principles of Truth: as to purchase goods, take by violence and War, And after due admonition his not condemning the Same ^to the – – Satisfaction of this Meeting: Therefore we give this forth as a publick Testimony against him, denying him the right of membership with us: With desires that he may by Sincear repentance be brought to a Sight and sense of his past life, and come to the fold of the Just, with a Sincear heart

Given forth at our Monthly Meeing, held at **Aponaganset** in **Dartmouth** The 19th day of the 1st month 1778   pr **William Anthony Ju^r** Clerk

N Lapham's request refer'd

The matter in regard to **Nicholas Lapham**'s Children is refered to next Monthly meeting

Report of N [sic] Gifford marriage

The friends appointed to oversee the Marriag of **Samuel Gifford** and **Lillis Maccomber,** report that they attended the marriage and that it was orderly accomplished

The case respecting J Roch's Certif icate refered

The friends appointed in respect of **Joseph Roch**'s Certificate Signify they have not accomplished said appointment, therefore it is refered to next monthly meeting and they continued for that Service

T Russell con demns his mis conduct

Timothy Russel hath appeared in person in this Meetinging and hath so far condemned his Conduct in Letting out his house to Inocculate the Small Pox in, as this Meeting takes up with for Satisfaction . . . This meeting also Concludes to accept of his paper Condemning his purchasing Prise goods provided he cause the Same to be publickly read as Usual and return it to next Monthly meeting

D Shepherd & Son request a removal Certi ficate

David Shepard and his Son **David** each request a removal Certificate to the Monthly meeting at **Smithfield**, for themselves and Children under age they being about to remove theighther; therefore **Benjamin Taber James Davis**, **Caleb Russell**, and **William Sanford** are appointed to inquire into their Circumstances and to draw a Certificate for them if they think proper, after due inquiry is made, and make reports and bring them to next monthly meeting

Certificates for J Allen & P Cor nel Signed

Certificate for **John Allen** and **Paul Cornel** directed to the monthly meeting at the **Nine partners** were Signed in this meeting, they bring about to take their Jerney within the compass of said meeting

J Cornel request

James Cornel hath given in a paper to this meeting Requesting to come into Unity with us agains being free to Condemn his misconduct in mariyng out of the Unity of Friends: and in paying money toward the Support of War: therefore **William Mosher** and **Abiel Gifford** are appointed to have a Sollid conference with him in order to know his Sincerity and to make Report next monthly meeting

This meeting Colected L2 – 17ˢ – 7ᵈ

Adjourn

This meeting adjourns to the 25th Instant after the meeting of Worship which is to begin att the 11th hour

mett

This meeting met by adjournment the 25th of the 3rd month 1778 The Representatives being called, both present

Complaint against C Hathway

This Meeting is Informed that **Caleb Hathway** hath so far gone out from the Order of Truth and friends as to forsake our meetings and follow Seperate meetings that are held out of the true Unity of And he having been Treated with on that acount, but Still persists in his said disorder, therefore this meeting appoints **William Barker Joseph Tucker** and **Benjamin Taber** to Labour further with him and make Report next Monthly meeting

Queries ans^d Epistle sign^d and friends appointed to Quarterly meeting

The Queries have been Read and answer'd in this Meeting and on Epistle Sign'd and order'd forward to the Quarterly Meeting by our Represen tatives who are **Jame Davis Gideon Howland William Anthony Ju^r** and **Abiel Gifford** and they to report next Monthly meeting.

G Slocum & J Slocum Disowned

Whereas **George Slocum** and **Joshua Slocum** Sons of **Charles Slocum** deceased, having a Birthright amongst by Virtue of their Parents marriage among us, but they having long since removed out of the compass of this meeting without any recommendation to any other or request any, and this Meeting being Informed by the Monthly meeting of **Greenwich** that they have Lived widly from the way of Truth and friends; perticurly being Remarkable for a Light unsteady behavor, and not attending meetings therefore this meeting doth disown the Said **George** and **Joshua Slocum** from a right of membership among us

4th month 1778

At a Monthly Meeting held in **Dartmouth** the 20th of 4th month 1778
The Representatives ᴧare **Benjamin Taber** and **Abiel Gifford**, Present.
William Sanford Ju^r not having read his Paper by reason as tis Said

W Sanford's paper re fered

that his wife not being well it is therefore refered to next monthly meeting on the Same condition as before.

N Lapham request re fered

The matter Respecting **Nicholas Lapham**s Children is refer'd to next monthly meeting, and the Same friends continued in that Service and then to make report

Certificate for J Rotch

A Removable Certificate for our friend **Joseph Rotch** and wife to the Monthly meeting of **Nantucket** was Signed in this meeting by the Clerk

T Russell's paper read

Timothy Russell's ᴧpaper having been read and returned to this meeting is accepted . . . Said paper is as Followeth

Timothy Russell's acknowledg ment

To the Monthly Meeting of friends held in **Aponaganset** on the 15th of 12th mo 1777
Respected friends I some time ago Purchased Some Prise goods which I am now Sorry for, and do condem the Same, hoping for ᴧthe time to come may be more careful of medling with Such goods: therefore I desire that friends may pass by this offence and let me remain under their care as before
From your well wishing friend – – –   **Timothy Russell**

Certificate for D Shep= =hard Ju Signed D Shephrd Senor refer'd

A Removal Certificate for **David Shepard Ju^r** his Wife and two Children the monthly meeting of **Smithfield** was Signed in this meeting
But the friends that were appointed; not having prepared a Certificate for **David Shepard Senior**, they are Still continued for that Service and to make report next monthly meeting

J Cornel received

The Comittee appointed to confer with **James Cornel** on his request to Come under friends care, make a Satisfactory report, therefore he is acceped as a member of this Meeing.

C Hathway
case refer'd

The Committee appointed to Labour with **Caleb Hathway** make Report that they have Treated with him, but have not obtained the desired Effect to their Satisfaction, but yet they desire said matter Continued, which is accordingly refer'd to next monthly meeting and then they to make Report

The report
of Quarter
ly meet
ing Com^te

The friends appointed to attend the Quarterly meeting report they all attended according to appointment, and have produced an Epistle from the Same which was read and well accepted, together with an Epistle from the Meeting of Sufferings which containing much Good Advice, was Recommended to Friends perticarly Notice

B Tucker
Disowned

This Meeting is informed that **Benjam^in Tucker** hath Married out of the Unity of friends. after being previously cautioned. and advised to desist: therefore – – he is hereby disowned from being a Member of this meeting. And **William Mosher** is appointed to inform him thereof and Report to next monthly meeting

M Davil
received

The Woman friends Inform that they have received into Unity **Mary Davil [Davoll]** wife of **John Davil [Davoll]**, which this Meeting concurs with

Time of meet
ings to begin

This Meeting Concludes that all our Meetings Begin at the Eleventh hour for the Ensuing Six months, Except at **Bedford [New Bedford]** and there to begin as usually they have done

This Meeting Collected L2 – 4^s – 7^d ½

5th month
1778

At a Monthly Meeting held in **Dartmouth** the 18th of the 5th month 1778

The Representatives are **Seth Russell** and **Samuel Smith** . . Present

W Sanford
reciv'd

William Sanford Ju^r his paper having been read ^and returned, therefore he is accepepted by this meeting

Certificate for
D Shepherd
Senor

A Removal Certificate for **David Shepard** his Wife and Children under age, dedicated to the Monthly Meeting of **Smithfield** was Signed in this Meeting

W Sanford Ju
his paper

William Sanford Ju^r Paper which he gave in to the meeting is as followeth

To the Monthly Meeting of friends to be holden in **Dartmouth** at **ponagan^set** the 18th of the 8th month 1777

Those Lines Comes to Inform you that I have Purchased Prize goods So called: for which I am Sorry for the Same, and am free to Condemn the Same: and desire friends would pass by my offence, and let me Remain under their care, and I hope to be mor Carful for the futer

From your friend – –   **William Sanford Ju^r**

Hathway's
case refer'd

The Commttee appointed in the case of **Caleb Hathway** not being fuly Satisfied in that matter do therefore request it Still continued. it is therefore Refer^d to next Monthly Meeting, and said Committee yet Continu'd, and desired to make return to Said next Monthly meeting.

B Tucker
not Inform'd

William Mosher not having informed **Benjamin Tucker** of his denial
he is therefore continued for that Service and to report to next Monthly Meeting

Report of Bed
ford meetings

The friends appointed to oversee the meeting at **Bedford** (not being called
upon last Monthly meeting) have now given in their report that they have
attended the Same with hath been kept up deacently and in as good
order as Useally they have been heretofore

Certificates
for N. Howland
& R. Smith
Signed

Removal Certificates for **Naomy Howland Rebecka** ∧Howland her Daughter
with **Rebecca Smith** wife of **Daniel Smith** with their Children except
the youngest; directed to the Monthly meeting of the **ninepartners**
were Signed in this meeting

N. Lapham's
children recevd

This Meeting in Concurrence with the Womens Meeting doth Accept
of **Nicholus Lapham**'s Children as Members of this Meeting

R Allen & wife
Disowned

This meeting is Informed that **Robart Allen** hath married out of the
Unity of friends, after being precautioned by friends: this meeting
therefore doth ~~do~~ hereby deny him from haveing a right of membership
with us: And the Women friends Inform that they have denyed
Easter Allen now wife of **Robart Allen** which this meeting concurs
with, and **Seth Russel** is appointed to inform said **Robart Allen** of his
Denial, and to make report next Monthly Meeting

H Woodman
Disowned

The Women friends Likwise Inform they have denyed **Hannah Woodman**
wife of **Robart Woodman** . which this meeting doth also concur with

J Sowle's Inten
tion of marri=
age

Jonathan Sowle Ju and **Bersheba Russell** declared their Intentions
of taking Each other in Marriage in this meting, and were desired to wait
until the next Monthly meeting for their answer – –
They haveing first obtained Consent of Parents and produced the
Same in Writting to this meeting

Friends ap
pointed to
settle with
Treasurer

Our friends **Samuel Smith** and **Thomas Hicks** are appointed to Settle
account with the Treasurer and make report next Monthly Meeting
This meeting Collected L2 – 19ˢ – 5ᵈ ½

W Anthonys
Bill
order'd to
be paid

William Anthony Juʳ hath given in an account to this meeting
for keeping **Alice Smith** 26 weeks Ending the 28ᵗʰ of the 4ᵗʰ month last
att 4/8ᵈ per week which amounts to L1 – 6ˢ – 4ᵈ Silver money which is
allow'd, and the Treasurer is Ordered to pay the Same In such manner
and in Such currancy as the Overseers of the poor hath Contract and
directed

6ᵗʰ month
1778

At a Monthly Meeting held in **Dartmouth** the 15ᵗʰ of 6ᵗʰ mon 1778
Seth Russell and **Thomas Hicks** are Representatives, both Present
Prince Allen is appointed Clerk for this Day

G Folger and
Sylvanus
Folgers

George Folger proposed his Intention of Marriage with **Rebecca
Slocum** and were desired to wait Till next Monthly meeting for their

proposals of marriage   answer – Also, **Silvanus Folger**, and **Avis Slocum** proposed their Intentions of Marriage, and were desired to wait till next monthly Meeting for their Answer

Adjournd   This Meeting adjourns to next Second Day ₑₙₐ

Mett   This Meeting mett by Adjournment the 22ⁿᵈ of the 6ᵗʰ month 1778 The Representatives being called both Present

B Tucker and R. Allen informd of their denial   **William Mosher** makes report he hath Informed **Benjamin Tucker** of his denial according to appointment; **Seth Russell** also Reports he hath Informed **Robert Allen** of his Denial, according to appointment of last Monthly meeting

C Hathways case referd   The Commitee appointed to Treat with **Caleb Hathway**, Report that they have had a coferrance with him but he gave them but little Satisfaction, do request said matter yet continued which is accordingly and the Same Committee continued in that Service; And **Joseph Gifford Caleb Russell** and **Adam Gifford** are aded to them and to make report next monthly meeting . . . And if in case said **Hathway** Still persists in his disorder, said Comittee is directed to draw up a Testimony against him and bring it to next Monthly meeting

J Sowle's Certificate   **Jonathan Sowl Juʳ** hath produced a Certificate from **Accoakset** meeting Certifying his Clearness respecting Marriage and Convesation

A Lancaster the & D Sands Visit   Our Beloved Friends **Aaron Lancaster** and **David Sands** attended this meeting with their Certificates, the first from the monthly meeting held at the **Oblong** the 18ᵗʰ of the 2ⁿᵈ month 1778. The Latter from the Monthly meeting held at the **Nine Partners** the 22ⁿᵈ of 5ᵗʰ month 1778 Which being read to Satisfaction: Their Visit and Testimony in the Service of the Gospel was well accepted. And **William Anthony Juʳ**

Certificats for Sd friends appointed   and **Samuel Smith** are appointe to draw Certificates for said friends and bring them to the Adjournment of this Meeting

J Sowles answer   **Jonathan Sowle** and **Bersheba Russell** appeared for their answers Which was that they might Proceed to take Each other in marriage in some Conveniant time, between this and next Monthly meeting adviseing with the Friends that this meeting Shall appoint for that purpose who are **Samuel Smith** and **Thomas Hicks** and they to See their marriage Solemnized orderly and make report to next monthly meeting

Settleing accompte Refered   The friends appointed at our Last Monthly meeting to Settle accompts with the Treasuerer not having fulfilled their appointmₑₙₜ they are Continued for that Service and to make report next Monthly Meeting

E Johnson recᵈ   The Women Friends Inform they Received into Membership **Elisabeth Johnson** Wife of **James Johnson**, with their two Daughters wich this Meeting Concurs with

J Roch Certifi=
cate returnd

Joseph Roche having Returned the Certificate that this Meeting gave forth for himself and wife: But his removing at present being obstructed and his Said wife having already removed [tho?] This meeting Signed a Certificate for this Said Wife, and have omitted his own at Present

E Hatheways
Certificate
accepted

Elisabeth Hathway hath produced a removal Certificate for herself and four of her Children Namely **Jonah**, **Lydia**, **Mary**, and **George** which was Read and Accepted, together with a removal Certificate for **Elisabeth Hathway Ju**r Which is also accepted

　　　　　　　　This meeting Collected ʟ4 – 15ˢ – 1ᵈ – in Paper money
　　　　　　　　And　　　　　　　　　0 – 16 – 0 　– in Silver money

adjourn　This Meeting Adjourns to the 24ᵗʰ of this Instant after the meeting ᵒf worship

mett　This Meeting mett by adjournment the 24ᵗʰ of the 6ᵗʰ month 1778

　　　　　　　　The Represtatives being Called both Present

Certificates for
A Lancaster
and D Sands
Signed

Certificates for our friends **Aaron Lancaster** and **David Sands** were Signed in this meeting and Directed to the Monthly meetings where they belong

Representative
appointed to
Quarterly meet-
=ing

　　　　　　　　The Queries were Answered and an Epistle ~~Signed~~ to the Quarterly meeting Signed and Ordered forward to said Quarterly Meeting by the Representatives, Who are **Caleb Russell**, **William Mosher**, **Seth Russe[l]** and **Abiel Gifford**, and they to report next Monthly Meeting

Miniute for
Anna Gifford

Anna Gifford Inform'd this meeting that she hath thought of attending **Sandwich** Quarterly meeting next to be at **Falmouth** and this meeting, after Considering thereof do Concur therewith; Her publick Testimony being approv'd off with us, And the Clerk is order'd to give her a Coppy of this minnute

7ᵗʰ month
1778

At a Monthly Meeting held in **Dartmouth** the 20ᵗʰ of 7ᵗʰ month 1778

　　　　　　　　The Representative are **James Davis** and **Benjamin Taber**, Present

　　　　　　　　Received Certificates for **George Folger Ju**r and **Sylvanus Folger** Setting forth their clearness respecting Marriage

G Folgers &
S Folger's
answers Given

George Folger Jur with **Rebecca Slocum**; And **Sylvanus Folger** with **Avis Slocum** appeared for their Answers: Which was that each Cupple might proceed to take each other in Marriage in Some Convenant time between this and next Monthly Meeting Adviseing with the friends that this meeting Shall appoint who are **William Sanford, William Barker Prince Allen** and **Joseph Barker,** and they to See said Marriage Solemnized orderly and make report next Monthly meeting

Report of
J Sowle's
Marriage

　　　　　　　　One of the friends appointed Last Monthly meeting to oversee the marriage of **Jonathan Sowle Ju**r and **Bershaba Russell** make report that he attendᵉᵈ Said Marriage which was as orderly as Usual the other friend did not attend by Reason he was at the Quarterly Meeting. But **William Anthony Ju**r

made report that he attended in the room of the other said friend: and that
it was accomplished orderly.

accounts Settled with the Trea=surer The committe appointed to Settle accounts With the treasure reports
theay have answered there appointment and there remane in the Stok after all is
Paid that this meeting hath alredy Given order for

viz. in Silver money L1 – 8ˢ – 11ᵈ

in Paper money L3 – 2 – 5

Caleb Hathway Disown'd The Commitee that had the care of that matter Respecting **Caleb
Hathway** report that they have had an oppertunity of conference with him
and he gave them little or no Satisfaction: Therefore, We hereby Disown
the said **Hathway** from being under our Care: And a publick Testimony
being Signed in this meeting against him by the Clerk, who is to ordered
to Read the Same Publickly in our Usual manner and make report thereof
to next Monthly meeting; and **Seth Russell** is ordered to Inform him of
his Denial and report to next monthly meeting

Report from Quarterly Meet-ing. The Representatives ‸to the Quarterly meeting being Called upon, Report they all attended except
Caleb Russell, who hath rendered his reason for not attending which hath been
accepted. And they have produced an Epistle from the said Quarterly
Epistles Receiv'd meeting which was Read: together with Epistles from **London** yearly
meeting, from the General Spring meeting of Ministers and Elders held
at **Philadelphia**, and one from our Last Yearly Meeting all of which
have been read: And as they contain, much good and wholesom advice
Friends are Earnestly desired to observe and deliberately consider the
Same. And as there is a considerable number of those **London** Epistles
they are distributed among friends familys.

Rules and orders Received & Boundries between monthly meetings. Our Said Quarterly Meeting hath Communicated to us Several Rules and
Orders Concluded upon at our Last Yearly Meeting Respecting our discipline
Also the Settlement of the bounderies between **Swanzey** Monthly meeting
and this. And likewise, an alternation of the Boundaries between this
Monthly meeting and **Accoakset**
: all of which the Clerk is ordered to Record in
their proper places

four dollars to be paid P. Gifford The Treasurer is Orderᵈ to pay **Peleg Gifford** four Silver Dollars ~~for~~
or its Equivelent in paper for keeping the Meeting house half a year

This Meeting Collected in Paper money – –   2ᴸ – 16ˢ – 9ᵈ

out of which was paid to **Caleb Rusell** for shoeing ‸friends horses   2 – 3 – 6

Remains in Paper – –   0 – 13 – 3

Collected in Silver money – –   0 – 9 – 4

The Paper respecting the Settlement of the Boundery Lines between
the aforsaid Monthly meetings Is as followeth

To the Quarterly Meeting of Friends ∧next to be held at **East Greenwich** for **Rhod Island**

Settlement of the boun dries Be tween the monthly meetings

We the Committee appointed to Revise and Settle the Bounderies Between **Rhoad Island**, **Swanzey**, **Dartmouth**, and **Accoakset** Monthly monthly meetings, having received the Same; and that there is Some Inhabitants Live between **Swanzey** and **Dartmouth** Monthly meetings. That it is not easy to determine, to what monthly meeting they belong: Therefore, We have concluded that the dividing line Between said Monthly meetings run in the following manner (viz) That all those friends Living in **Freetown** to the Northward of **Fall river** and **Dartmouth** belonging to this Quarterly Meeting: Shall belong to **Swanzey** Monthly meeting

alteraton of bounds

We also with the concurance of **Dartmouth** and **Accoakset** Monthly Meetings make the following alteration in the boundries between said Meetings (viz) Beginning in the Old Line at the Northeast corner ~~of~~ bound of **James Sowl**s Land, from thence a North line till it comes to **F[r]eetown** Line. Nevertheless we Submitt it to the Quarterly meeting
2 month 14th day 1778

         Philip Tripp
         Thomas Ester
         William Anthony Jur
         Theofila Shove Jur

8th month
1778

At a Monthly meeting held in **Dartmouth** the 17th of the 8th month 1778 The Representatives are **Abiel Gifford** and **John Devol** [**Davol**] both Present

Report of G F & S Folger's marriage

The friends appointed to attend the marriages of **George Folger** and **Rebecca Slocum**, and **Sylvanus Folger** and **Avis Slocum**, have made report that they attended said marriages, and that they were orderly Solemnised

Testimony a gainst C Hatha [way] hath been read

Report hath been made that the Testimony against **Caleb Hathway** hath been read as ordered and that **Seth Russell** hath Informed said **Hathway** of his Denial agreeable to appointment

Received a Coppy of the Testimony Given forth by our Last Yearly meeti[ng] against a Pamphlet on Taxation: &c Which hath been Read in this meeting agreeable to the direction of Said yearly meeting
Said Testimony is as followeth

A Testimony Given forth from our yearly Meeting held at **Smithfield** from the 12th in the 16th of the 6th month Inclusive 1778 for **New England**

Testimony of the Yearly meeting against a pamphlet on Taxation

Whereas a Peice in Manuscript upon the Subject of Taxation &c Was written by a Member of our ∧Religious Society, and came under Consideration of our meeting for Suffering, before the Author was known, and some matter contained therein being altogether dissatisfactory to friends, and Inconsistent with our Religious Testimony: Inquiry was made, an[d?] indeavers used

to prevent the publication, or Spreading thereof without the desired Effect
but the Same with Some additions, and alteration, was published, under
the Title of "A Letter from a friend, to Some of his Intimate friends."
Contrary to the good Order of our Society, and the incouragement
received from the author: - And the matter being laid before this meeting
And watily [weightilly] Considered, We are constrained to give forth our Testimony
against the Said Piece, and the Spirit if Conveys to the reader, as tending
to Leaven the minds of friends with the Spirit of the World, Lament
=ably prevalent, and to bring those who pay attention to Religious
Scruples under Suffering and Introducing Discord, and divisions amongst
friends ^as well as containing matter disagreeable to our Practice and testimony
as a people . . . . And also against the manner in which it was published
to the World. being inconsistant with a rule, Long since laid down
and consented to by our Society[25]
Signed in and by order of our said yearly Meeting By **Thomas Latham Jnr** Clerk
~~~~~~~~~~   this time

Coppy

Order to pay
P. Gifford
The Treasurer not havnig paid **Peleg Gifford** the money as ordeed
Last Monthly Meeting; he is therefore still directed to pay the Same
and make report next monthly meeting

Certificate
for J Roch
Signed
A Removal Certificate for **Joseph Rotch** directed to the
Monthly meeting on **Nantucket** was Signed by the Clerk he
having Removed theither.

G Gifford
paper acced
Gideon Gifford hath given in a paper to this meeing Condemning
his buying a Ticket in a Lottery, which this meeting accepts

Few lines
to Swanzey
in behalf of
E Thurston
This meeting hath Signed and Sent a few lines to the monthly
Meeting of **Swanzey**, Informing them that **Edward Thurston Juor**
his wife and their Children are deemed as Members of our Society
and are within the bounds of that meeting as now Settled

Chusing
overseers
refered
A new Choice of Overseers is Refer'd to next Monthly meeting
and those that have Stood as Such the year past are Continued untill
next monthly meeting

R Thrasher
& A Wanton
Disowned
The Women friends inform they have denied **Rebeckah Thrasher**
Wife of **Samul Thrasher** and **Abigail Wanton** wife of **John Wanton**
which this meeting Concurs with

25. The manuscript in question was the work of Timothy Davis (1730–1798), a recorded minister and
member of Rochester Monthly Meeting. Davis argued that it was acceptable for Friends to pay taxes in
time of war, even if they knew that some of the tax revenue would go for military uses. This ultimately led
to a separation that included some Dartmouth Friends. See Hagglund, "Disowned Without Just Cause,"
217–48; and Alice Sue Friday, "The Quaker Origins of New Bedford, 1765–1815" (Ph. D. diss., Boston
University, 1991), 191–375; and above, n. 16.

Certificate for
N Howland
& R Smith
Signed

A Removal Certificate for **Naomy Howland** wife of **Job Howland**
with **Rebecca** her Daughter was Signed in this meeting directed to
the Monthly Meeting at **East Hoosuck**

This Meeting Collected L4 .. 1ˢ .. 9ᵈ – in paper money

Collected   0 .. 9 .. 9   in Silver money

9ᵗʰ month
1778

At a Monthly Meeting held in **Dartmouth** the 21ˢᵗ of 9ᵗʰ moᵗʰ1778
The Representatives being called **Joseph Tucker Juʳ** present
Abraham Howland not present by reason of Sickness

P Gifford
paid

Peleg Gifford hath informed this meeting that the Treasurer hath
paid him the monᵉy as ordered, the Said Treasurer not being
present at this time

Choosing
overseers
refered

A new choice of Overseers is refer'd to next monthly meeting
and the former ones are still Continued in that Service .. and
Abiel Gifford is aded to them

meetings
omitted

This meeting doth Conclud to discontinue all our Weekday meetings
on the Same Week our Quarterly Meetings is to be held in

E Gifford's
Request

Elijah Gifford hath given in a paper to this meeting Requesting
for himself and Children to ~~come~~ be taken under the care of friends therefore
this meeting appoints **Thomas Hicks Nicholas Howland** and **William
Barker** to take an opportunity of Sollid conferrnce with him and
Endeavor to find the motive of his request, and make report next
Monthly meeting

J Allen's
paper
accepted

John Allen hath given ^in a paper to this Meeting Condemning his
being Concernd in a Lottery and Likewise hath verbaly Expressed himself
in this Meeting. Signifying his Sorrow in regard to said matter
Which this meeting accepts for Satisfaction

Queries an
swer'd
Epestle
Signed &
Representa'
appointed

The Queries were answered in this meeting and an Epistle Sign'd
for the Quarterly meeting and order'd forward to said Quarterly meeting
by our Representatives who are **William Barker Caleb Russell** and
Joseph Barker and they to report next Monthly Meeting

E Mosher
Taken
prisoner

This Meeting being inform'd that **Elihu Mosher** being carried
away Prisoner by the Brittish Troops, therefore we appoint **Seth
Russell James Davis** and **Abiel Gifford** to confer with the meeting
of Sufferings in order to procure his relief as they shall think proper[26]

complaint
against
L Mosher

The overseer Inform that **Lamuᵉl Mosher** hath so far gon Contrary to
our Profession, as to drop some bad Expressions in the manner of Swareing
and other thretning Language, and said overseers hath Laboured with him therfor
and he having Condemn'd Said expressions to those that heard them yet declines

26. On September 5, 1778, Major General Charles Grey and a force of 4,000 troops raided the villages
of New Bedford and Fairhaven, where they destroyed storehouses, shipping, and supplies.

to Condemn them Publickly to the Satisfaction of this Meeting therefore we appoint **Benjamin Howland 2ⁿᵈ Benjamin Taber** and **Joseph Tucker Juʳ** to Labour with him as they may think proper and Report next Monthly meeting

certificate for E Mosher

A Certificate for **Elihu Mosher** who was carried away Prisoners was Signed in this meeting directed to the Meeting of Sufferings: Informing them of his being a member of our meeting and Clear in regard to Military matter

This Meeting Collected in Silver money– – L0 – 7ˢ – 3ᵈ

Collected in Paper money– –   2 – 11 – 7

10ᵗʰ month 1778

At a Monthly Meeting held in **Dartmouth** the 19ᵗʰ of the 10ᵗʰ month 1778

The Representatives are **William Barker** and **John Williams** -- Present

Chusing Over-seers refered

A new Choices of Overseers is Still refer'd to next Monthly meeting and those that have been in that Service continued till a new choice

E Gifford's requeˢᵗ Refered

The friends appointed to confer with **Elijah Gifford** on his request, Repent that for want of a Conveanent oppertunity they have not fulfiled their appoint ment, they are therefore continued in said Service, and to make report next monthly meeting

L Mosher's case refered

The friends appointed to treat with **Lamul Mosher** report they have not fulfilled their appointment, one of them being Sick they are therfore continued In said Service, and **Joseph Gifford** is added to them and they to make report next Monthly meeting

Overseers of the poor continued

The time of the appointment of overseers of the poor being Expired they are now again continued in that Service untill a new Choice is made

Friends app-ointed to over see the bury ing ground

This meeting having Concluded to make a new choice of Friends to have the care of our burying Ground. Who Shall be Interred therein that are not members of the Society, and who not – Who are **William Sanford William Barker** and **Joseph Tucker Juʳ** and also **William Mosher Benjamin Rider** and **John Devol** for **Newtown**

N Howland & T Hicks to over see the meet ing house

This meeting also appoints **Nicholas Howland** and **Thomas Hicks** to have the care of our old meeting house and Lands and to keep the fences in repair Round the Same

Trustees to the Deeds appoint ed

This Meeting appoint the following friends as Trustees to take Deeds of this meetings Land the former ones being Some of them Deceased (viz) **William Mosher, Samuel Smith William Anthony Juʳ** and **Joseph tucker Juʳ**

C Russell request Certificate

Charles Russell requests a Removal Certificate to the Monthly meeting at **East Hoosuck**, therefore **Benjamin Smith Juʳ** and **Samuel Smith** are appointed to mak due inquiry into his Circumstances, and draw one for him if they find things clear and bring it to the next Monthly Meeting

Certificate for J Smith Signed

A Removal Certificate for **John Smith** son of **Isaac** deceast was Signed in this Meeting directed to the Monthly meeting at **East Hoosuck** he having removed theither

W Anthony Ju his Bill

William Anthony Juʳ hath given in an acount to this Meeting for keeping **Alice Smith** from the 28ᵗʰ of the fourth month Last to the 28ᵗʰ

ordered to be paid

Instant including 26 weeks at Twenty eigh Shillings per week old Tennor Silver Money and to be paid in Silver or its Equivilent in Paper money which this meeting orders paid accordingly: The amout thereof is ʟ36 – 8ˢ in Silver old Tennor.

Time meetingᵉ begin

This Meeting concluds that all our meetings begin at the Eleventh Hour for the year ensuing except at **Bedford** and that to begin as usually they have done.

B Taber ap pointed Trea surer

Benjamin Taber is appointed Treasurer in the Roome or Sᵗead of our Well beloved friend **Prince Allen** deceased: for the year Ensuing

S Smith and T Hicks to settle ^with heirs of former Treasurer

And **Samuel Smith** and **Thomas Hicks** are appointed to Settle accounts with the Heirs of the former Treasurer deceased, and make Report next Monthly Meeting

This Meeting Collected in Silver – –   0ᴸ – – 5ˢ – – 00ᵈ

Collected in Paper money   2 – – 13 – – 10

11ᵗʰ Mo 1778

At A Monthly Meeting held in **Dartmouth** the 16ᵗʰ of the 11ᵗʰ month 1778 The Representatives are **Caleb Russell** and **Joseph Barker** - - -Present

A New choice of Overseers is again refer'd to next Monthly meeting

E Gifford & children accepted

The Committee appointed to confer with **Elijah Gifford** and family Report, that most of them visited said family (one of said Commitee being detained by Sickness) and found a degree of Satisfaction and Sincerity among them. Therefore this meeting accepts of said **Elijah Gifford** and Children to be under the care of this meeting

The Women friends also inform they have accepted **Deborah Gifford** the wife of the said **Elijah Gifford** which this meeting concurs with

Overseers of the poor apoin[t]ed

Caleb Rusell Giₐ**deon Howland Benjamin Howland 2ⁿᵈ Samuel Smith** and **George Smith** are Chosen Overseers of the poor for the year Ensuing

L Moshers paper accepted

The friends appointed to Treat with **Lamuel Mosher**, gave in their Report, which was in degree Satisfactory, and he hath given in a paper to this meeting Condemning his misconduct, which this meeting accepts provided he cause the Same to be read Publickly as Usual, and return said paper to next Monthly meeting

Settleing with the Treasury continued

The Friend appointed to Settle accounts with the Heirs of the former Treasurer report, that they have not fully accomplished the Same, they are therefore continued in said Service and to make report next monthly meeting

Frinds to revise and correct the miniuts

Samuel Smith Thomas Hicks Benjamin Howland 2ⁿᵈ and **William Anthony Ju**ᵘ are appointed to Revise and Correct this meetings Minnutes in order for them to go on Reᶜcord and to make report next monthly meeting

S Craw mov =ed without Certificate	**Shearman Craw** having removed within the bounds of **accoakset** Meeting Without giving notice thereof to this meeting, We therefore Signed and sent a few lines, to Inform the said meeting at **Accoaket** of his Removal
Certificate for B Rick etson signed	This meeting Sin∧ged a Certificat for **Benjamin Ricketson** son of **William Ricksetson**'s to the Monthly meeting of **East Hoosuck**, as he is a going theither to settle his outward affaires.
J Russell request a Certificate	**John Russell** informes this meeting that he is about to Remove to **East Hoosuck** and desires a Certificate, therefore **Benjamin Smith Ju**ʳ and **Gideon Howland** are appointed to draw one for him if they think Proper, and bring it to next monthly meeting.
Certificate for C Rusel signed	This Meeting hath Signed a ∧Removal Certificate directed to the Monthly Meeting at **East Hoosuck** and **Saratoga**. For **Charles Russell** his wife **Rebecca** and Little daughter **Amie** they having Removed theither to dewell.
A Howland Ju Disowned	This Meeting is Informed that **Abraham Howland Ju**ʳ hath married out of the Unity of friends, after being precautioned by friends: therefore he is disowned from being a member of our Society and from under the care care of this meeting, and **Benjamin Smith Ju**ʳ is appointed to Inform him thereof
Complaint a gainst J Akin	The Overseers Inform that **John Akin** hath appeared in bearing of Arms and hath been Treated with by friends but declines to Condemn the same there-fore **John Williams** and **Joseph Tucker Ju**ʳ to Treat further with him on that account, and also on account of his Neglecting to attend our Meetings and to make report next Monthly meeting

This meeing Collected in Silver money   0ᴸ – 9ˢ – 10ᵈ
Collected in paper money   4 – 5 – 0

12ᵗʰ month 1778	At a Monthly meeting held in **Dartmouth** the 21ˢᵗ of the 12ᵗʰ month 1778 The Representativ are **Caleb Russell** and **Seth** R[smuged] **Huddleston** - Present
Overseers appoiⁿted	We appointed our friends **Abiel Gifford Benjamin Taber Benjamin Smith** 2ⁿᵈ **Seth Huddleston Joseph Barker William Anthony Ju**ʳ and **William Barker** Overseers for the year Ensuing
L. Mosers paper read & accepted	**Lamuel Moshers** Paper having been Red agreeable to the direction of last monthly meeting and returned the ˢᵃᵐᵉ to this meeting. Which is accepted and is as followeth
L. Mosher paper of acknowledg ment	To the Monthly meeting of Friends to be held at **Dartmouth** 16ᵗʰ 11ᵗʰ month 1778 Whereas, some time past I get into a Passion, so far as to drop Some bad Expression in the manner of Swareing: For which I am heartily Sorry and do Condemn, And desire Friends so far to pass it by as to let me Remain under their Care **Lamuel Mosher**
settled with the Treasurry	The Friends appointed to Settle accounts with Heirs of the former Treasurer Report they have fulfilled their appointment, And have settled accounts

down to the 9th month last Inclusive; and remains in the Stock 5ᴸ – 15ˢ – 6ᵈ
in paper money and 1ᴸ – 15ˢ – 10ᵈ in Silver money

Miniuts revisᵈ and corrected The friends appointed to Revise and correct this meetings minutes, report
they have fulfilled said appointment and left them with ∧ᵞᵉ Clerk to be recorded

Certificate for J Russell referd The friends Chosen to draw a Certificate for **John Russell** and to inspect into
his Clearness Report, they have not fulfilled said appointmen in full, they are
therefore Continued in Said Service, and **Abraham Howland** is added
to them, and they to make report next monthly meeting

The Case of John Akin refered The friends appointed to Labour with **John Akins** report they have
not accomplished Said appointment for want of an oppertunity they are
also continued in the Same Service and to make their report to next
Monthly meeting

E Thurstons Certificate Returned back Our Cirtificate in favour of **Edward Thurston** and his family directed
to **Swanzey** monthly meeting being returned back to this meeting again
therefore we appoint **Thomas Hicks Samuel Smith** and **William Anthony Jᵘ**
to consider what be necessary for this meeting to act further, in that
matter and make Report to next monthly meeting

Certificate for E Mosher This meeting hath Signed and sent a Certificate to the monthly meeting
at **Pembrock** for **Eliakim Mosher** a young son of **Joanna Mosher** he being
about to go as an apprentice there

This meeting Collected   5ᴸ – 3ˢ – 7ᵈ in paper money
0 – 13 – 2 ½ in Silver money

money de liver'd to the Treasureʳ There was delivered to the Present Treasurer the Sum of 5ᴸ – 15ˢ – 6ᵈ in
Paper money and 1 – 15 – 6ᵈ in Silver money By the Committee that Settled
accounts ~~wh~~ with the heirs of the former Treasurer

adjourn This meeting Adjourns to the 30th of this Instant after the meeting of
Worship which is to begin at the 11th hour

Mett Met by adjournment the 30th of the 12th month 1778
The Representatives being called **Caleb Russell** present **Seth Huddleston** not present

J Allen request a Certificate **John Allen** informs that he is about to Remove with his family to
Live within the bounds of **Saratoga** or **Hoosuck** Monthly meeting and
Requests a removal Certificate for himself and Children therefore
Abiel Gifford and **John Devol** are appointed to make due Inquiry
into his Circumstances and draw one for them and bring it to next
Monthly meeting if they find things Clear

J Jonsons request **James Johnson** Request to come under the care of this meeting with his
Son **William**: And **William Mosher** and **Thomas Hicks** are appointed to
Take an oppertunity of Solid Conference with him in order to know the
reason of his Request, and make return to next Monthly meeting

Complaint against S Wilcox Ju   The Overseers inform that **Stephen Wilcox Ju**^r hath taken up Armes in or for War: and hath neglected the due attendance of our Meetings for which they have Treated with him but did not give them Satisfaction Therefore this meeting appoint **Caleb Russell** and **Benjamin Howland** to Treat further with him, and to make report to next Monthly meeting

Certificate W Howland   There was Signed in this meeting a Certificate for **William Howland** Certifying his being under the care of this meeting, as he is about going a Voige to Sea

Chusing Visitors refered   It hath been proposed in this meeting to chuse some friends to Joyn or assist the Overseers in Visiting and treating with disorderly members of this meeting, Perticuly those that Neglect the due attendece of our Religious Meeting; But this meeting being small by reason of the Severity of the Season the matter is refer'd to next Monthly meeting

Queries answered   The Queries were Answered. And an Epistle Signed in this meeting to the Quarterly meeting and order'd forward by our Reprsentatives who are

Representatives appointed   **William Mosher Abiel Gifford Samu**^{el} **Smith** and **William Anthony Ju**^r and they to report next monthly meeting

---

1779 1ˢᵗ month   At a Monthly meeting held in **Dartmouth** the 18th of 1st moth 1779 The Representitives are **Benjamin Rider** and **Benjamin Taber** Present

J Akin's case refer'd   **John Akin** being gone to Sea the Committee appointed to Labour with him make report they have not fulfiled their appointment they are still Continued in the Same Service and to make report when they shall have Opportunity to perform the Same

Certificat for J Russell refered   The Committee appointed to draw a Certificate for **John Russell** not having fully accomplished the Same they are ^{there}fore still continued in Said Service and make report next monthly meeting

The case of [E] Thurston refered   The Comittee appoined to consider the matter in regard to **Edward Thurton** J^r and family not Having fully accomplished the Same they are Stil continued for for the Same Service and report next Monthly meeting

Certificacate for J Allen refered   The Committee appointed to draw a Certificate for **John** ∧**Allen** report they have made Some progress in the Said matter but not having accomplished the same they are also continued in said service and to make return next Monthly meeting

[J] Jonsons request refer'd   The friends appointed to confer with **James Jonson** in regard to his request to Come under friends care Report they have had an opportunity of conferren^c with him: and that he gave them a dreegree of Satisfaction yet that matter is also continued and to Said friends in the Same Service untill next Monthly meeting

S Wilcox Ju case refered   The friends appointed to Labour with **Stephen Wilcox Ju**^r Report they have ∧^{not} fulfilled the Same; they are also continued for the Same Service and to make report next Monthly meeting

Return from the Quarterly meeting The friends appointed to attend the Quarterly meeting Report they all attended agreeable to apointment, and have produced an Epistle from the Same together with a number of **London** Printed ∧General Epestils. One of which being Read, with the s^d Quarterly meetings Epistle to good Satisfaction and the Said **London** Epistles distributed among friends and recommended to to be read in their families

Collections called for to Supply yearly meeting Stock It is Recommended by the Quarterly meeting, and also by Writeing from the meeting for Sufferings to Send up as speedily as may be Collections to Supply the yearly meeting Stock: And this meeing concluds to raise the Sum of Twenty pounds for that use

Job Sisson having Produced his Parents consent that he may proceed in marriage with **Ruth Sheppard**

J Sisson's proposal of marriage **Job Sisson** and **Ruth Shepherd** declared their Intentions of taking each other in marriage: and were desired to wait till next Monthly meeting for answer

This meeting Collected in Silver money   . . .   0^L . . 15^s . . 9^d

in paper money   . . . 12 . .   1 . . 4

Order to pay P Gifford four Dollars This meeting orders the Treasurer to pay **Peleg Gifford** four Silver Dollars or the Vallue thereof in Paper currancy, it being for keeping the meeting house half a year . . . Also to pay **William Anthony**'s bill formerly given in and Accepted

Adjournd This meeting Adjourns to the 27th instant after the meeting of Worship

Mett Met by adjournment the 27th day of the 1st month 1779

The Representatives are **Benjamin Rider** and **Benjamin Taber** Present

Friends appointed Visiters Our friends **Joseph Tucker Caleb Russell** and **Thomas Hicks** are appointed to Joyn and Assist the Overseers in Visiting and Labouring with the disorderly members, as mentioned Last Monthly meeting and they are desired to visit and Labour with them in Love in order for their Restoration: and if after they have discharged themselves in that respect Such of said members that continue disorderly: They to bring their Names and their Crimes to the meeting in Order for them to be dealt further with as our discipline requires

Wm Allen req^uest Certificate **William Allen** Son of **Philip** deseased being about to remove within Compas of **Saratoga** Monthly meeting and desires a Certificates therefore **Abiel Gifford** and **John Devol** are appointed to take the needful care in that case and make Return to next monthly meeting

W Hart's paper accept^ed **William Heart** hath given in a paper Signifying his Sorrow for being Concerned in a Lottery which is accepted

O Beard Disowned The Overseers Inform that **Obediah Beard** hath married out of the unity of friends after being Precautioned. Therefore he is Deny'd and disown'd from being a member of our Society, and **Seth Huddelston** is appointed to inform him hereof and make report to next monthly meeting

Friends appointed to take in Subscriptions We appoint of our friends **Jonathan Wilbore [Wilbur] John Williams William Hart Joseph Tucker Ju^r** and **Gideon Howland to** goe forth with Subscriptions that was Signed in this meeting to raise money: as expressed in Said Subscriptions and Pay the money to the Treasurer of this meeting, and make return to next Monthly meeting of the sum so raised

C Russells and W Barkers Bills **Caleb Russell** hath xhibited an account to this meeting for keeping Some Traveling friends horses and Shoeing them to the amount of 8^L – 2^s – 0 which is allow'd: and the Treasurer is ordered to pay the Same: And also to pay **William Barker** four Dollars or the vallue thereof for keeping the meeting house half a year, Some time past: And also 18 shillings for paper for bringing Some Hay for the use of friends, and make return next monthly meeting

2nd Mo 1779 At a Monthly Meeting held in **Dartmouth** the 15th of 2nd month 1779
The Representatives **Peleg Gifford** and **Samuel Smith** Present

Certificate for J Russ A certificate for **John Russell** directed to ∧ Monthly meeting at **East Hoosuck** was Signed in this meeting by the Clerke.

E Thurstone case The friends appointed in the case of **Edward Thurstone Ju^r** have brought a few Lines – being an Indorsment on the former Certificate directed to the Monthly meeting of **Swanzey** : Setting forth of their being members and Recommending them to Sold Meeting

Certificate for J Allen refered The friends appointed to draw a Certificate for **John Allen** report that things not being Settled by reason of Sickness they are therfore continued in Said Service and to report next monthly meeting

J Jonson Received The friends appointed to Confer with **James Johnson** on his request to come under friends care have Made a Satisfactor report; therefore he the Said **James Johnson** and his Son **William** are received into Membership with us.

S Wilcox Ju Disowned The friends appointed to Treat with **Stephen Wilcox Junor** Report they have fulfilled their appointment, but he gave them no Satisfaction therefore he is disowned from being a member of our Society, and the same friends are appointed to draw a Publick Testimony against him, and bring it to next Monthly meeting: And **William Ricketson** is order'd to Inform him of his Denial

M Russel Disowned This meeting is Informed that **Michael Russell** hath married out of the unity of Friends and hath been Treated with on that account by friends both before and after Said Marriage and he gave them no Satisfaction. Therefore he is disowned from being ∧ in Membership with us: And **William Ricketson** is order'd to Inform him of his Denial and make report next monthly meeting

S Craw
Disowned

The overseers inform that **Shearm^{an} Craw** hath removed away in a disoderly manner, without the knowledge or concurrance of this meeting into the Compas of another, and neglects to attend meetings, and they having Treated with him on these accounts but he gave them ˄no Satisfaction therfore he is denyed from being a Member of our Society, and **Seth Huddleston** is orderd to inform him of his denial and report next Monthly meeting

Report of
the Treasurer

The Treasurer reports he has paid all the money as order'd last monthly meeting, Except that to **Peleg Gifford** and that he designed to pay and report next Monthly meeting

Certificate for
[W] Allen

A removal Certificate was Signed in this meeting for **William Allen** Son of **Philip** deceased, dedicated to the monthly meeting of **East Hoosuck**

Berd informed
[JS?] Certficate

Seth Huddleston reports he hath informed **Obediah Beard** of his denial according to appointment

Received a Certificate from **Accoakset** Monthly Meeting ^{for} **Job Sisson** Signifying he is a member of their Society and Clear from any marriage Entanglement

Friends to
collect money
continued

The friends appointed to Collect the money by Subscriptions not haveing fully accomplished, the Same, they are still continued in said Service and to make report to the adjournment of this meeting

BS, JC : JA
Request
Certificates

Benjamin Sawdy, **James Cornwell** and **James Allen** having informed this meetin that they perpose to take a Journey up the Countrey and desires Each of them a Certificate: Therefore, **Thomas Hicks, Elijah Gifford William Mosher** and **John Smith** are appointed to make inquiery into their Clearness and draw Certificates for them if they find them clear and bring them to the adjournment of this meeting.

J Sissons
answer
[is?] given

~~Job Shson~~ **Job Sisson** and **Ruth Shepard** apear'd for their answer Which was that they might prceed to take each other in Marriage in Some conveniant time befor next monthly meeting: adviseing with the Friends that this meeting Shall appoint to See the Said marriag accomplis'd who are **William Sanford** and **William Barker** and they to make report next Monthly meeting

[W] Barke^r Ju
[re]quest a
[Cer]tificate

William Barker Junor being about to go as apprintice: with his brother within the Compass of **East Hoosuck** or **Saratoga** monthly meeting and desiers a Certificate, therefore **Joseph Tucker Ju^r** and **William Sanford** are appointed to take the needful care in that respect, and draw one for him if they think Proper and bring it to the adjournment of this meeting

[W] Russell
[R]equest a
[C]ertificate

William Russell having informed that he hath concluded to remove with in the Compass of **East Hoosuck** or **Saratoga** Monthly meeting, and requests a removel Certi˄ficate therefore **Benjamin Howland 2nd** and **Nicholas Lapham** are appointed to Treat with him on that account: And if they find – things clear then to draw one for him and bring it to next monthly meeting

[C]ertificate for Anne Smith A Removal Certificate for **Anne Smith** wife of **Thomas Smith** and their Children whose names are **Sarah**, **Lloyd**, **Paul** and **Barnabas** was Signed directed to the Monthly meeting at **East Hoosuck** and **Saratoga**

Collected . . . . .   In paper money . . . . . 7 – 10 – 3
In Silver money   0 –   7 – 6

Adjourn This meeting Adjourns to the 24ᵗʰ of this Instant after the meeting of Worship

mett Met by adjournment this 24ᵗʰ of the 2ⁿᵈ month 1779

The Representatives being called both Present

[C]ertificates for [B]S, JC : JA A Certificate for **Benjamin Sawdy** was Signed in this meeting directed to the Monthly meeting at **Saratoga** he being about to Travel theare

Certificates for **James Cornel** and **James Allen** were Signed in this meeting directed to the Monthly meeting at **East Hoosuck** and **Saratoga** they being about to go theither

Certificate for [W] Barker Ju Also A Removal Certificate for **William Barker Juʳ** was Signed in this meeting directed to the Same meetings as above he being a going there to dwell

A Allen's paper refered **Abraham Allen** hath given in to this meeting a Paper Condemning his Being concerned in a Lottery and the meetⁱng not being fully clear to accept the Same

Therefore **Elijah Gifford Thomas Hicks** and **Joseph Tucker Juʳ** are appointed to Examin into the Circumstance of the matter and make return next monthly meeting

Complaint against P Gifford Ju The Overseers Inform that **Peleg Gifford Juʳ** hath appear'd in a War Like manner with his Gun in order to Stand Wach with others of the Militia and also been found with others Shoouting at a Turkey set up for that purpos for which disorderly conduct this meeting doth appoint our friends **William Mosher**, **Samuᵉl Smith** and **Gidᵉon Howland** to Labour with him in order to Shew him his Error and make return next Monthly meeting

W Mosher appointed to draw money for yearly meeting Stock We appoint **William Mosher** to draw the Sum of Twenty Pounds out of the Treasury of this meeting, and pay the Same to the Yearly meeting Treasurer to Supply the yearly meeting Stock: Also take all the money that is Collected by this meetings Commity for the meeting of Sufferings; and pay the Same there, and make report ^ᵗᵒ the next monthly meeting.

Complaint against J Gifford The overseers inform that **Job Gifford** hath Neglected to attend our Religious Meetings after he was Treated with on that account: And also hath set up Selling Spirituous Liquᵒrs, and thereby Suffering unbeᶜᵒᵐⁱⁿᵍ company att his house Therefore this meeting doth appoint **Benjamin Howland 2ⁿᵈ**, **William Barker** and **Jonathan Willbor [Wilbur]** to Labour further with him on these accounts and to make report next monthly meeting

3ʳᵈ Mo 1779   At a Monthly meeting held in **Dartmouth** the 15ᵗʰ of 3ʳᵈ month 1779
The Representatives are **Elijah Gifford** and **Abiel Gifford**, present

A miniut   Received a Coppy of a minute from our meeting of Suffrings held
from meet   the 8ᵗʰ Instant, directing that the Same, with a Testimony from the yearly
ing for Suf
fering &   meeting of **Philadelphia** by adjournment from the 29ᵗʰ of the month to the
Testimony   4ᵗʰ of the 10ᵗʰ month 1777 (which was Read in this meeting) be both Publickly
*from **Philadel***
To be read   Read in all our meetings, which this meeting concurs with and the Clerk
is ordered to Read them accordingly

Certificate   A Removal Certificate for our friends **John Allen** his Wife and Children
J Allen   Directed to the monthly meeting of **East Hoosuck** or **Saratoga** was Signed in this
meeting by the Clerk

Testimony   A Testimony of Denial against **Stephen Wilcox Junor** was signed in
against   this meeting by the Clerk who is ordered to Read it Publickly in the usual
S Wilcox Ju   manner and make report next monthly meeting

also against   And **William Ricketson** reports he hath informed said **Wilcox** of his denial
M Russel   and also **Michel Russell** of his Denial according to appointment
Likewise **Seth Huddleston** informs that he hath informed **Shearman Craw**
of his denial as order'd Last monthly meeting

Order to   Treasurer not having paid **Peleg Gifford** as order'd he is again
pay P G   desired to do the Same and make report to next monthly meeting

Report of   The Friends appointed to attend the marriage of **Job Sisson** and **Ruth**
J Sisson's   **Shepard**, report that they attended said marriage, and saw nothing but
marriage   that it was orderly accomplished

Certificate   A Removal Certificate for **William Russell** directed to **East Hoosuck**
for W Rusel   or **Saratoga** monthly meeting was Signed in this meeting he having gone
there to dwell

The case of   The friends appointed to Treat with **Abraham Allen** report they
A Allen   have Treated with him, but the matter not being Settled it is refered to
refered   next monthly meeting and the Same friends continued in Said Service and
they to make Report next monthly meeting

P Gifford Ju   The Committee apointed to Treat with **Peleg Gifford Juʳ** Report that
case re   they have had conference with him but did not give them full Satisfaction
reffer'd   but request the matter may be continued Longer; Therefore they are continued
to next monthly meeting in the Same Service and then they to make report

W Mosher   **William Mosher** reports he hath fulfilled his appointment in regard to carrying
[?] he hath   the ᵐᵒⁿᵉʸ ᵗᵒ ᵗʰᵉ yearly meetings Treasurer: and also to the meeting of Sufferings and hath
[?] the money   produced a coppy of the minute from the Clerk of the meeting of Sufferings
that they had Received the Sum of 17ᴸ – 17ˢ – 4ᵈ in paper and 12 Shillings in hard
money for the use of the poor come from **Rhoad Island** that are not of our Society

The case of   The Comittee appointed to Treat with **Job Gifford** report they have had a
[J] Gifford   Conference with him and he gave them little or no Satisfaction Nevertheless
refered

the matter being Weightily coⁿsider'd it is refered to next monthly meeting and the
Same Committee Still continued, and if he doth not give them some satisfaction
they then to draw a paper if denial against him and bring it to next monthly meeting

Friends approin ted to attend Swanzey monthly meeting

The few lines of Indorsment directed **Swanzey** monthly meeting and Signed by the
Clerk at our monthly meeting in the first month last was now read, and do appoint
our friends **Thomas Hicks William Anthony Ju^r** and **Samuel Smith** to attend
Said meeting at **Swanzey**, with said Indorsment in order to treat with them on
that account: in behalf of this meeting and endeavor to show them the State
of the Case, and make return to this meeting when they have accomplished the Same

A Howland A Barke & [J] Ricketson [J] Howland requesting Certificates

Abraham Howland son of **Job Howland** desires a removeable Certificate to the
monthly meeting of **East Hoosuck** and **Saratoga** – – And also **Asa Barker** a young
Son of **David Barker** being about to ^go an apprintice to live within the Compas
of **Smithfield** monthly meeting – also **John Ricketson** informs he is about to
go to the **Oblong,** or thereabout in order to purchase a place to live at
Requesting of us a few lines by way of Certificate – and likewise **Jethro Howland**
Son of **Benjⁿ Howland** being about to go to **East Hoosuck** or therebout to
make Some Stay and also desires a Certificate – Therefor this meeting appoints
Samuel Smith Elijah Gifford and **Thomas Hicks** to draw Certificate for them
and Sign them in behalf of this meeting if they shall think proper when they
have duly enquired into their Circumstances and made return to next monthly meeting

	L	s	d
Collected in paper Currency	6	10	3
In Silver Currency	0	13	0

This meeting Adjourns to the 24th instant after the meeting for Worship

Mett by adjournment this 24th of the 3rd month 1779

A Devol and B Gifford Ju Request

Abner Devol and **Benjamin Gifford Ju^r** Each gave in a paper to the
Preparative meeting requesting to come under Friends Care: Therefore we
appoint **William Mosher Abial Gifford** and **Samuel Smith** to take an Opportuni^{ty}
of Solled Conference with them in order to desern the true motive of their
Request and make return next monthly meeting

W Ricketson bill for hay

William Ricketson gave in account to this meeting for c500 of Hay
which is allowed it being 18 Shilling in hard money or its Equi^{ve}lent in
paper and ye Treasurer is ordered to pay the Same.

Complaint a gainst J Shepard J Smith [H] Smith [E] Russell T Howland & I Howland

The Overseers Inform that **John Shepard, John Smith, Henry Smith**
Elijah Russell, Timothy Howland and **Isaac Howland** son of **Benjamin**
have Joyned with others in purchasing and Owning a Vessel that was Taken
in the War, or by way of Violence: yet as it hath been Signified that
Said owners were Ignorant that She was Such a Vessel this meeting therefore
doth appoint **Caleb Russell William Mosher Elijah Gifford Samuel Smith**
and **John Devol** to inquire into the true state of the case, and Circumstances

attending the same and bring in their Judgm't thereupon to our next
monthly meeting

Complaint against [I] Howland

The overseers also Inform that **Isaac Howland** son of **Benjamin** is found
Guilty of the Sin of fornication as appears by the accusation of **Merebah Smith**
and hath also been neglecting in attending meetings and the above said
Committee are appointed to Labour with on that account and draws a Testimony
of denial against him if he do not give them satisfaction, and bring it to next
monthly meeting

Friends appointed to attend the Quarterly Meeting

We appoint our friends **William Mosher Thomas Hicks Joseph Tucker Ju^r**
William Barker and **Gideon Howland** to attend the Quarterly meeting and present
the Epistle which was aproved and Signed in this meeting by the Clerk also the
Answers to the Queries which was read and approved in this meeting and they to
Make report next monthly meeting

4th Mo 1779

At a Monthly meeting held in **Dartmouth** the 19th of 4th month 1779
The Representatives are **Abiel Gifford** – Present

Testimony against S W not read

The Clerk Informs he hath not read the Testimony against **Stephen**
Wilcox as order'd he is therfore desired to perform the same and make
Return next monthly meeting

P Gifford not paid

The Treasurer reports he hath not paid **Peleg Gifford**, he is therefore
ordered to pay and make report when it is paid

The case of A Allen refered

The friends appointed in the case of **Abraham Allen** report they
have been ingaged in the matter but it not being fully Settled to Satisfaction
they are Continued in the same service and to make report next
monthly meeting

a paper of denyal is ordered to be drawn against P Gifford Ju

The Friends continued Last monthly meeting to treat with **Peleg Gifford Ju**
Report they have fulfilled their appointment and he declines to make
Satisfaction and that they think they are clear from any further Labour
with him they are therefore appointed to draw a paper of denial against him
the said **Peleg Gifford Ju^r** And they with **Joseph Gifford** and **William Sanford**
to Inform him thereof and make report next monthly meeting

The case of J Gifford refered

The Committee Continued to Treat with **Job Gifford** report they have had
some late Conference with him, wherein he gave some degree of Satisfaction
they are therefore Still continued in the Said Service and make report next
monthly meeting

Report of Friends appinted to Sign Certificats

The Friends appointed to prepare and Sign Certificates in the behlf of
this meeting report they have performed the same. Except that for **Abraham**
Howland (Son of **Job**) and they are Still continued to draw one for him if
they think proper, and bring it to next monthly meeting

The case of A Devol & B Gifford refered

The friends appointed to Treat with **Abner Devol** and **Benjamin Gifford**
Report they have had Some conference with them and that they gave them some
degree of Satisfaction. the matter is therefor refered to next monthly meeting

and they continued in said Service and then to make report

W Ricketson not paid　　The Treasurer reports he hath not paid **William Ricketson** as ordered he is therefore ordered to pay the Same and make report when he hath paid

The friends appointed to Enquire into and to Judge the matter of the owners of the Vessel said to be taken by War and Violence who have given in the following report which after being read and considered is accepted and is as followeth

[the bottom half of the page is blank]

The case of [I] Howland [r]efered　　The friend appointed to Treat with **Isaac Howland** son of **Benjamin** Report, they have had conference with him, but he did not give the full Satisfaction, yet they did not drauft a Testimony against him they are therefore continued in the Same Service and report next monthly meeting.

Report of friends [a]ppointed to [at]tend Quarterly meeting　　The friends appointed to attend the Quarterly meeting report they all attended Except **Joseph Tucker Jur** and he hath rendered an Excuse for his not attending which is accepted; and they have produced an apistle from the Quarterly meeting which was Read and well accepted.

[Ce]rtificate [requ]ested for [D] Barker　　**David Barker** desires a Certificate for his young Son **Shove Barker** to the monthly meeting at **Swanzey** he being gone there to Live as an aprentice

[J] Cornel re= quest a Certificate　　And also **James Cornwell** being about to Remove within the compass of **East Hoosuck** or **Saratoga** Monthly meeting: and Request a removal Certificate to Said meeting: Therefore **Jonathan Willbor Joseph Tucker Jur** and **Elijah Gifford** are appointed to make inquiry into above said matter and draw Certificates for them if they find things Clear and bring them to next monthly meeting

Report of the meeting at Bedford　　The Term for holding meetings granted to the friends at **Bedford** being Expired the overseers thereof made report that it hath been kept up as Usual and request it continued which is Granted for one month only and **Benjamin Taber Caleb Russell** and **Seth Russell** are appointed to have the oversight thereof and to make report next monthly meeting

	L	s	d
Collected in paper Currency – – –	5	4	9½
Collected in Silver currency – – –	0	9	8

5th Mo 1779　At a Monthly meeting held in **Dartmouth** the 17th of 5th month 1779

The Representatives are **Joseph Barker** and **Benja Rider** Present

The Clerk hath made Report the Testimony of Denial against **Stephen Wilcox Junor** hath been Read according to appointment which is as followeth

Testimony of [D]enyal against [S] Willcox Ju　　Whereas **Stephen Wilcox Jur** having had a Right of membership among Friends, and under the Care of this meeting yet through unwachfulness and disregarding the Principal of Truth, he hath fallen into great Indiffer-=ency of mind, so as most wholly to Neglect attending our Religious – – meetings: He hath also of Late appeared with his Gun in a Warlike

poster: which Conduct of his being Inconsistant with our Peacable Princi-
=ples that we make Profession of, and friends having Laboured with
him in Love on these accounts, but he not adhearing to the advice of
friends herein, We do therefore Give this forth as a publick Testimony
against him the Said **Stephen Wilcox Ju**ʳ disowning him from being a – –
member of our Society, untill he by unfeigned Repentance and acknoleᵈgment
of the Error of his ways, he shall be restored to the way of Truth

Given forth, and Signed in ∧ & on behalf of our Monthly meeting of friends held in
Dartmouth the 15ᵗʰ of 3ᵈ month 1779 by   **William Anthony Ju**ʳ Clerk

The case of
A Allen   The Committee appointed in the Case of **Abraham Allen** make report
refered   that they have still been in the progress of that Service, but it being not
yet fully settled to Satisfaction: It is therefore refered to next Monthly
meeting, and the same friends continued and then they to make report

Complaint   This meeting is Inform'd that **William Bowdish Ju**ʳ hath fallen into
against   the Sin of Fornication; therefore **William Mosher** and **Joseph Tucker Ju**ʳ
W Bowdish Ju are appointed to Treat with him on that account, and to draw a paper
of denial against him if he do not give them Satisfaction and bring
it to the next monthly meeting

Received   The Women Friends Inform that they have received Removal
Certificates Certificates for **Elizabeth Allen** Widdow and **Meriah Hoxcie** both from **Sandwich**
E. Allen & Monthly meeting, which this meeting concurs with
M. Hoxcie

Certificate   The Removal Certificates that were Signed in this meeting Some
Signd for   months past for **John Allen** and his wife and Children and Brother
J. Allen   **William Allen** were now altered, and Signed being now directed
to the **Nine partners** Monthly meeting they being about to remove there

Peleg Gif   **Peleg Gifford Ju**ʳ hath given in a paper to this meeting Signifying
*ford Ju*ʳ   his Sorrow for his offences taken notice of by the meeting which
paper   being considered; the matter is refered to next monthly meeting under
refered   the care of the Same Committee as before, and they to Visit him and
Treat with him again and make report next Monthly meeting

The case of   The Committee continued in the case of **Job Gifford**, report
J Gifford   that he hath dissisted from Selling Spirituous Liquors the matter is
referred   therefore refered to next monthly meeting for a further proof his
Sincerity under the care of said Committy then to make report

Certificate   A Removal Certificate was Signed in this meeting for **Abraham**
for A H   **Howland** (son of **Job**) directed to the monthly meeting of **East Hoosuck** and **Saratoga**

The case of   The Friends appointed to confer with **Abner Devol** and **Benjamin**
A Devol &   **Gifford Ju**ʳ on their request to come under friends care report that
B Gifford   they desire it continued which is accordingly under the care of said
refered   Committee and they to make report next monthly meeting

*I Howland
Disowned*

A Testimony of Denial was Signed in this meeting against **Isaac Howland** (son of **Benja**) and the Clerk is ordered to Read the Same Publickly as Usual and make report next monthly meeting

meetings granted at Bedford

The Overseers of the meeting att **Bedford** report said meeting hath Been kept up orderly as Usual and they request it continued which is Granted So far as for them to hold their said meeting in the Usual manner untill the monthly meeting in the 10ᵗʰ month next and the Same friends to have the Oversight thereof, as had last before and then they to make report

Certificate for S Barker

There was a Certificate Signed in this meeting for **Shove Barker** young Son of **David Barker** to the monthly meeting at **Swanzey** as he is gone there to live as an Apprentice

	L	s	d
Collected in paper Currency	7 –	6 –	2
in Silver Currency	0 –	11 –	8

A Howland and W Anthony Ju gave in their bills for keeping A Smith

Abraham Howland and **William Anthony Juʳ** have Each given in their account for keeping **Alice Smith** Each to the Amount of 3ᴸ – 18ˢ – [?] in Silver money or the Vallue thereof in paper which is for keeping Said **Alice** for the Six months last past next preceeding the 28ᵗʰ of the 4ᵗʰ month last which said accounts are allowed; and the Treasurer is ordered to pay the Same as far as he is Supply'd with money by the meeting

adjourn

This Meeting Adjourns to the 26ᵗʰ Instant after the meeting of Worship

mett

Mett by Adjournment his 26ᵗʰ of the 5ᵗʰ month 1779 The Representatives being called both Present

P Cornel H Smith & J Potter request Certificates

Paul Cornel [Cornell] having removed within the compas of **East Hoosuck** and **Saratoga** Monthly meeting desires a removal Certificate; and **Hezekiah Smith** and **John Potter** having gone to make some Stay within the Compass of the Monthly Meetings of the **Oblong** and **Nine Partners** and Likwise request Certificates. Therefore this meeting appoints **Benjamin Rider William Anthony Juʳ** and **Samuel Smith** to make due inquiry into their Circumstances and clearness of the afore said young men and draw Certificates for them if they think proper and bring them to next Monthly meeting

J Cornel Certificate Refered

The Matter for Signing **James Cornel [Cornell]** and wife Certificate is refered to the next Monthly meeting for the Women friends Concurrence.

Receipt from Yearly meeting

Received a Receipt Signed by the yearly meetings Treasurer that he hath Received the Sum of 19ᴸ – 10ˢ—in paper currency and 10 Shilling in hard money of this meeting for the yearly meeting Stock

Complaint against T Smith (Son of Levi)

The overseers Inform that ~~Levi~~ **Thomas Smith** Son of **Levi** (deceased) hath taken up Armes in order for War and doth reather Justify the Same when they

Treated with him on that account: Therefore **Joseph Tucker Ju^r** and
Benjamin Rider are appointed to Treat further with him on that account
and if he declines to condemn the Same then they to draw a Testimony of
Denial against him and bring it to next monthly meeting

6th month 1779　At a Monthly meeting held in **Dartmouth** the 21st of 6th month 1779
The Representatives are **Caleb Russell** and **Joseph Barker** Present

S Underhill &　Our Beloved Friend **Solomon Underhill** hath attended this meeting in
J Walters Visit　Company with our beloved friend **Joseph Walters** both of whom hath been
Recommended to our Satisfaction from their respective places of aboad[abode]
whose Visit and Services among us have been well accepted.

A Allen's paper　The Committee continued in the case of **Abraham Allen** report that
accepted　he hath given them Satisfaction in regard to his offence: Therefore the
Paper he gave n to this meeting Some months past Condemning the
Same is now accepted for Satisfaction which is as followeth

Such is as　Whereas Some time past I was so unwise as to be concerned in a
follows　Lottry which I find in my Self was wrong, which I do condem and desire
that friends will so far pass it by as to let me remain under your Care

　　　　　　　　　　　　　　　　　　Abraham Allen

The case of　The friends appointed to Treat with **William Bowdish Ju^r** not having
W Bowdish Ju　fulfilled their appointment they are there Continued in said service
refered　and to make report next monthly meeting

J Gifford case　The Committee appointed in the case of **Job Gifford** report that he
Continu'd　yet continues to desist from Selling Spiritiuous Liquors: yet they request
it Still continued. It is therefore according continued their Care and
to report to the meeting when they shall be satisfied therein

A Devol recevd　The Committee appointed in the Case of **Benjamin Gifford Ju^r** and
Abner ~~Devlor~~ **Devol** report that he the S^d **Abner Devol** hath given them
Satisfaction, he is therefore received into Membership with us. But
B Gifford's　the receiving of **Benjamin Gifford** is refer'd under the care of the
case referd　Same friends for a further proof of his Sincerity and they to report
to this meeting when they shall see fit.

I Howland's　The Clerk reports that he hath Read the denial of **Isaac Howland**
betrayal read　agreeable to the appointment of last Monthly meeting, and hath also
informed him of Said Denial – Which is as followeth

I Howland's　Whereas **Isaac Howland** Son of **Benjamin Howland** and **Elizabeth** his
~~Disowned~~　wife having his Education among friends under the care of this
Testimony　meeting, but by disregarding the Testimony of Truth in himself
of Denial　hath fallen into the Sin of fornication as appears by the accusation
of **Meribah Smith** and he no wise clearing himself there from
to friends Satisfaction, but upon Inquiry we have reason to believe
the accusation to be Justly grounded, and friends having Extende

Their Labour of Love with, with him in order for his Recovery
But our Labour not being Effectual. This meeting being concerned
for the Clearing of Truth and friends from the reproach of Such Evil
Conduct do therefore give this forth as a publick Testimony against
him the Said **Isaac Howland** disowning him from being a member
of our Society until by unfeigned Repentance and return from the
Error of his ways he shall be restored to the way of Truth.

Given forth and Signed in and behalf of our monthly meeting held
in **Dartmouth** the 17th day of the 5th month A. D. 1779 by

William Anthony Juͬ Cle[rk]

Certificate
J,Cornel Wife
& children
A removal Certificate for **James Cornel [Cornell]** his Wife and Children
Directed to the Monthly meeting at **East Hoosuck** and **Saratoga**
was signed in this meeting by the Clerk

T Smith (son
of Levi)
Disowned
A Testimony of denial against **Thomas Smith** (son of **Levi**) was
Signed in this meeting and the Clerk is ordered to read the Same
Publickly as Usual, and Make report thereof to our next Monthly
meeting: and **Caleb Russell** is appointed to Inform said **Thomas**
of his denial and make report next Monthly meeting

Collected in paper Currency – £10 – 9ˢ – 10ᵈ

In Silver Currency –   1 – 1 –   8½

adjournd
This meeting Adjourns to the 24ᵗʰ Instant after the meeting of Worship
which is to begin at the 11ᵗʰ hour

Mett
Mett by adjournment the 24ᵗʰ of the 6ᵗʰ month 1779
The Representatives being Called both present

P. Gifford Ju
case continued
The Committee appointed to confer with **Peleg Gifford Ju**ͬ make report
that they have meet and treated with on the account of his
outgoings but he not giving them full Satisfaction the matter is
Refered under the care of said Committee to next monthly meeting
who are then to make report

Certificate
for H.Smith
Certificates were Signed in this meeting for **Hezekiah Smith** and
Paul Cornel [Cornell], the first directed to the Monthly meeting of Oblong or
Nine Partners, the Latter to the monthly meeting of **East Hoosuck** or **Saratoga**

J Potters
case suspe=
=nded
The matter concerning **John Potters** is Suspended by reason things
are not fully Clear therefore **William Anthony Ju**ͬ and **Samuel Smith**
are desired to Inform him of his deficiencies as soon as opportunity
will a low[allow] and they also are to proceed in such measures relative to
to said matter as they may think best and make return to the
meeting when they have accomplished the Same

D. Shepherd
request a
Certificate
Daniel Shppard [Shepherd] desiers a Certificate to **Sandwich** monthly meeting
Setting forth his right of membershiph and Clearness of Marriage Entangle
=ment therefore **William Barker** and **William Sanford** are appointed

to take the nessessary care therein and report next Monthly meeting

B. Sawdy **Benjamin Sawdy** desires a removal Certificate to **East Hoosack** or
request a **Saratoga** monthly meeting; therefore **William Mosher** and **Abiel Gifford**
Certificate are appointed to take the nec[e]ssary care in that affair and make
Report next monthly meeting.

Complaint The Overseers Inform that **Paul Slocum** is accused of the Sin of
against Fornication with **Rhoda Reed** who accuses him of being the father
P Slocum of her Bastard Child, and Said Overseers having Laboured with
him on that account, he nowise Clearing himself from Said accusation
　　　Therefore this meeting doth appoint **Benjamin Howland 2nd** and **Thomas
Hicks** to Treat further with him on that account and if he do not give
them Satisfaction to draw a paper of denial against him and bring it
to next monthly meeting.

Butts receiv^d 　　　The Women Friends inform that they have received **Anna Butts** under
their Care: also they have disowned **Mary Wood** wife of **Abraham Wood**
and **Abigail Howland** Wife of **Isaac Howland** all which this meeting
Concurs with

Certificate for 　　　This Meeting Si[g]ned Certificates for our Friends **David Sands**
D. Sands & **Solomon Underhill** and **Joseph Walter** directed to the monthly meeting
Underhill they belong too Certifying our Unity with their publick Testimony
and Labour whilst amoung us

Queries 　　　The Queries were Answered and an Epistle signed in this meeting
answerd and Ordered forward to the Quarterly meeting by our Representatives
representatives who are **Samuel Smith Abiel Gifford Joseph Tucke [Tucker] Ju^r** and **William
appointed Anthony Ju^r** and they to report next monthly meeting.

7th month 1779 Att a Monthly meeting held in **Dartmouth** the 19th of 7th month 1779
The Representatives are **William Barke [Barker]** and **Abiel Gifford** present.

The case of 　　　The friends appointed to Treat with **William Bowdish Ju^r**. Report
W Bowdish Ju that they have had Conference with him and that he hath given
refered them a good degree of Satisfaction and he hath given in a paper
to this meeting condemning his outgoing; Yet the matter is refered
to next monthly meeting for a further proof of his Sencirity [Sincerity] and the
Said friends to have the oversight of his conduct, and to report next
Monthly meeting

T Smiths 　　　The Clerk reports he hath read the Testimony of denial against
denyal read **Thomas Smith** as directed last monthly meeting, and **Caleb Russell**
Reports he hath informed him thereof according to appointment
which is followeth.

Testimony of 　　　Whereas **Thomas Smith** (son of **Levi Smith** deceased) in the **Town of
denyal against Dartmouth** and **Province of the Massachusets Bay**. Having had his
T Smith

Education among friends, but through unwachfulness and disregard-
=ing the Testimony of Truth in his one heart; have so far deviated
from the peaceable Principle we make profession of as to take up Armes
in order for War, and friends having Laboured with him in Love to
Show him the Error of his way but their Labour of Love not having the
desired affect: Therefore this meeting is concerned to give this forth
as a publick Testimony, denying him the said **Thomas Smith** from
being a Member of our Society, and from under the care of this
meeting: Nevertheless desireing, if be consistant with Divine Wisdom
that he might yet come to a Sight and Sence of the Error of his way
and return to the way of Truth.

Given forth by friends at their Monthly meeting held in **Dartmouth**
The 21st of the 6th month 1779.

Signed in and by order of said meeting by

William Anthony Ju^r Clerk

Certificate for A Removal Certificate for **Benjamin Sawdy** his Wife and their
B Sawdy Wife Children directed to the monthly meeting at **East Hoosuck** or **Saratoga**
and Children was Signed in this meeting they having gone there to dwell

Certificate for A Certificate for **Daniel Shepard** directed to the monthly meeting of
D Shepherd **Sandwich**, Setting forth his clearness in regard to marriage and conversation
was Signed in this meeting by the Clerk

The case of The friends continued in the case of **Peleg Gifford Ju^r** mak report that
W.Bowdn that they not being fully Satisfied therein request it Still continued
continu.d which is accordingly continued to next monthly meeting under the
Care of the Same friends as heretofore and then they to make report

P Slocum The friends appointed to Labour with **Paul Slocom [Slocum]** report that they
Disowned have fulfilled the Same, and that he did not give them Satisfaction
Therefore they have produced a Testimony of denial which was Signed
against him the Said **Paul Slocum**, by the Clerk who is directed to
read the same publickly as Usual and make report to our next monthly
meeting: and **William Barker** is appointed to Inform him there of and
Report next monthly meeting

Report of The Friends appointed to attend the Quarterly Meeting Report
Friends they all attended according to appointment and have produced an Epistle
from Quar from the Same which hath been read and well accepted; together with
terly meet Transscrips of Epistles from **London** and **Philidelphia** which were also
=ing Read and the Seasonable advices therein Communicated to us well receivd

J Akin The friends appointed Some months past to Labour with **John Akin**
Disown.d Report they have fulfild their appointment and that he gave them no
Satisfaction, Therefore He the said **John Akin** is disowned from being in

Membership with us, and **John Williams** is appointed to Inform him of
his denial also to draw a Testimony of his denial against him and bring it to next
monthly meeting

A Mott
Disown.d

The Women Friends Inform that they have deny.d **Anna Mott** wife
of **Jacob Mott** which this meeting concurs with

Certificate
for Lamu
Smith

This meeting hath Signed and Sent a Certificate or Information to the
Committee appointed by the meeting for Suffering, agreeabl to said meeting
Requests concerning **Lamuel Smith** a member of this meeting who is
Taken and carried into **New York** and there remained a Prisoner under
distressed Circumstances by the last account we had from him the
Said **Lamuel**

Certificate
for S Hud
dleston he
being dra=
=ughted as
a soldier
Friends to
asist him

This meeting being Informed that our Friend **Seth Huddleston** is
Draughted [Drafted] as a Soldier and is required to appear att **Ta[u]nton** within a
few days for that purpose. Therefore this meeting thinks proper and
hath given him a Certificate. Setting forth his being a member among us
Also do appoint our friends **Abiel Gifford John Williams** and
William Anthony Jur. To assist him in all things relative thereto
in order for his release, and other things as they in the Wisdom
of Truth Shall think best

This meeting Collected in paper – £7 – 7ˢ – 6ᵈ

Collected in silver –   0 – 12 – 3

---

8 month 1779

Att a Monthly meeting held in **Dartmouth** yᵉ 16ᵗʰ of 8ᵗʰ month 1779
The Representatives are **Abiel Gifford** and **John Devol** present

The case of
W, Bowdish
*Ju*r *refered*

The Committee who had the oversight of the conduct of **William**
Bowdish Jur report, they have seen nothing amiss in him since last
Monthly meeting yet the matter is refered to next monthly meeting
and the Same friends to have the oversight of him and report next
monthly meeting

P Slocums
denial read
he informed

The Clerk reports that the Testimony against **Paul Slocum** hath
been Read as ordered, also **William Barker** reports he is informed as ordered
which Testimony is as followeth

The Testimony
of denial
against
P Slocm

Whereas **Paul Slocum** (son of **Benjamin Slocum** and **Phebe** his wife)
Having had his Education among friends under the care of this meeting
yet by departing from the Testimony of Truth in his own heart hath
so far gone astray as to fall into the reproachful Sin of Fornication
as appears by the accusation of **Rhoda Read**; and friends having
Laboured with him in Love in order to discover to him the Evil
thereof, and to restore him to the way of Truth,

But our Labour of Love not being Effectual to the Satisfaction of this
meeting: Therefore for the Preservation of Truth, and friends from the
Reprach of Such Enormous evils this meeting is concerned to give this

forth as a publick Testimony against him hereby disowning him the
the said **Paul Slocum** from being one of our Society, and from under
the Care of friends: Desiring nevertheless if it be agreeable to divine
Pleasure that he may yet find a place of Repentance and by an unfeined
acknowledgment of the Evil of his way return to the way of Truth

    Given forth and Signed in and on behalf of our monthly meeting
held in **Dartmout** the 19th of the 7th month 1779

                    by **William Anthony Ju**r Clerk

J Akins case
continued he
being gone
from home

    The Friends appointed to Inform **John Akin** of his Denial and
draw a Testimony against him report that it is accomplished by
reason Said **Akin** being gone from home: Therefore the said friends
are desired to accomplish the same as soon as may be and mak report
to this meeting

J Clark request
Certificate

    Jonathan Clark Informs he is about to Remove with his wife and children
within the Compas of **Nine Partners** Monthly meeting and desires a
Certificate therefore **Benjamin Chase** and **Abiel Gifford** are appointed
to Joyne the Women and take the necessary Care therein and draw a Certificate
if they think proper and bring to next monthly meeting

P Gifford Ju case
continued by a
[New?] Comtee

    The Committee in regard to **Peleg Gifford Ju**r Report that they
have fulfiled their appointment and things not appearing fully clear
to accept him, and said Committee being dismist by their request
And **Joseph Tucker Josep [Joseph] Barker** and **Benjamin Rider** are now appointed
to Treat with him the sd **Gifford** and report next monthly meeting.

S Howland
Disowned

    The Women Friends Inform they have Denied **Sarah Howland** now
Wife of **Warren Howland**; And that they have Received into membership
Hannah Willbore which this meeting concurs with

    The Treasuerer Reports he hath paid **William Ricketson** Three dollars
hard money as ordered and also paid **Peleg Gifford** four dollar as ordered
Likewise in hard money

C Howland
returnd his
Certificate to
request another

    Cornelus [Cornelius] Howland having returned to this meeting a Certificate that
he formerly had to goe to Sea: And now again request a Certificate also
to goe to Sea: Therefore **Benjamin Smith Ju**r **Samuel Smith** and
William Anthony Jur are appointed to inspect into the Circumstances
of the Voige [Voyage] that he intends, and draw and Sign Such a Certificate for
him in behalf of this meeting as they may think proper, and make report
thercof to next monthly meeting

order to pay
T Howland

    The Treasurer is ordered to pay **Timothy Howland** five dollars for
keeping the meeting house half a year: or the Value thereof in paper

                    Collected in paper Currency – £4 – 4s – 0d
                    Collected in silver currency –   0 – 14 – 1

9th month 1779   Att a Monthly meeting held in **Dartmouth** the 20th of 9th month 1779

The Representatives are **Joseph Barker** and **John Williams** Present

W Bowdish Ju^r
[?]paper ac
cepted

The friends appointed to have the oversight of **William Bowdish Ju**
make report to Satisfaction, and his paper again Read this meeting
doth conclude to accept of the Same, provided he cause the Same
to be Read publickly at the Close of a publick meeting for Worship
on first day, he being present and return the Same to next
monthly meeting, Said paper is as followeth

W BowdishJu
[?] paper of
acknowlegment

To a Monthly meeting of Friends held at **Dartmouth** 19th of 7th mo 1779
under a due Consideration of my misconduct in time past. I publish
these lines in duty to a Society whome I have reproached, by being
Seduced by the Enemy to Fornication an^d have Contracted marriage
Contrary to the proper order of Friends, and must Confess I have
not been attendant to the Several meetings of friends as becometh
a member of the Society: which exorbetant behavour I acknowleg
as a dishonor to the worthy ~~Societ~~ profession of friends and with
Sorrow unfeigned I condemn whereof I am guilty; and desire
Friends to pass by my offence and yet to number me amongst them

　　　　　　　　From your unfeigned friend **William Bowdish Ju**^r

Benj. Gifford
Junor received

The Friends appointed to confer with **Benjamin Gifford Ju**^r
make a Satisfactory report in regard to his request: Therefore he
is now Received under the care of this meeting as a member of our Society

Certificate
for J Clark
refered

The Friends appointed in regard to **Jonathan Clark**s Certificate
Report they have been in a progress in that matter, but Some of his
affairs, not being fully Settled, the Matter is refered to next
monthly meeting, and the friends continued in said Service and
then they to make report

J Akins
denyal Sign^d
read &he
Informd

The friends appointed to draw a Testimony of denial against
John Akin, have accomplished the Same, which hath been Read and Signed
in this meeting and the Clerk is ordered to read it publickly as usual
and make report thereof to our next monthly meeting, they also report
they have informed him of his denial agreeable to appointment; which
is as followeth

Testimony
of denial
against
J Akin

Whereas **John Akin** having had a Right of membership with us but
hath so far deviated from our Christian profession as to appear withn
Military Company under Armes in order for defence for which he
hath been Laboured with in Love in order to reclame him, but it
not having the desired Effect, and he continuing to Justify the
Practice or reather not to retract it, we think it necessary, for the
Clearing of Truth and friends to give this forth as a publick Testimony
against him.

Nevertheless it is our desire that he may yet be convinced of the
Impropriety of bearing armes under this Gosple Dispensation, and retur[ned]
> Given forth at our Monthly meeting held in **Dartmouth** 20th of 9th mon[th]
> Signed in and on behalf of said meeting by

William Anthony Juᵣ Clerk

Certificate for
C, Howland

The friends appoited to draw and sign a Certificate for **Cornelus Howland**
report they have fulfiled the Same

T Howland
not paid

The Treasurer not having paid **Timothy Howland** as ordered
for want of mony as we understand he is ordered to pay the same
when furnished with money, and make report next monthly meeting

The case of
P Gifford Ju
Continu.d

Two of the friends appointed to Treat with **Peleg Gifford Ju**ᵣ
Report they have Treated with him, but that he did not fully comply
to Condemn his conduct to friends Satistfaction: but in as m[u]ch
as one of Said friends was not there with the other two when they
Treated with him by reason of disappointment, therefore they are
Still continued to Treat with him and if he do not give them Satisfaction
they are ordered to draw a paper of denial against him and
bring to next monthly meeting

A Committee
appointed
on account
of Schools

It being recommended to this meeting, by a Committee of the Quaterly
meeting to appoint a Committee to Confer with them on the weighty
Subject of Erecting Schools for the better Education of our youths
This meeting doth appoint **Thomas Hicks Elijah Gifford Caleb
Russell Caleb Green Joseph Barker William Anthony Ju**ᵣ **John
Devol** and **John Williams** for that Service

J Russell
B Ricketson
Certificates
returned

Certificate that this meeting Some time a goe granted to
John Russell and **Benjamin Ricketson** directed to **East Hoosuck**
Monthly meeting are now returned with Indorsement to Each Setting
forth the orderly conduct of said friends while there, they being now
Returned home

Collected in paper – – £4 –   0ˢ – 0ᵈ

Collicted in Silver – – 00 – 15 – 2

Adjourn

This Meeting Adjourns to the 27th Insant at the Eleventh Hour

Mett

Mett by adjournment the 27th of 9th month 1779
The Representatives being called both Present

[Co]mplaint
against
[S] Russell and
he disowned

This meeting being Informed by the Preparitive meeting and Overseers
That **Stephen Russell** hath Married out of the Unity of Friends after
being previously Cautioned to desist by the Overseers: Therefore the
Said **Stephen Russell** is denied from membership in the Society and
Joseph Barker is appointed to Inform him hereof and make report to
next monthly meeting

[G] Smiths request refered

George Smith having Requested at the Preparitive meeting that his Children might be Received into Membership with us: But he the Said ~~not~~ **George** not apparing at this meeting to Continue his request it is therefore refered to next Monthly Meeting for further Consideration

Complaint against H Howland

The Overseers Inform by way of preparative meeting that **Humphry Howand [Howland]** (son of **Benjamin**) hath been in the practice of going to horse races and Suffering his own beast to run: and he likewise doth very much depart from that plainness of apparrel, and otherwise, that Truth require: after being freequanly [frequently] Spoken to on that acount by friends: Therefore this meeting doth appoint **Caleb Russell Elijah Gifford** and **John Devol** to Labour further with him on those accounts and make report next monthly meeting also to draw a paper of denial against him if he do not make them Satisfaction

Meetings dis continued

This meeting doth hereby discontinue all our weekday meetings within the Compass of this meeting for next week only, they being so near the time of the Quarterly meeting

Epistles Received

Received a Transcript of the Epistle of the last yearly meeting of Friends on **Long Island**,[27] together with one from our last yearly meeting which were both Read and the Seasonable advices therein given well accepted

Queries answerd

The Queries were answered and an Epistle Signed in this meeting

Representatives appointed to Quarterly meeting

and Ordered forward to the ~~to~~ Quarterly meeting by our Representatives Who are **Caleb Russell Joseph Barker William Mosher Samuel Smith Abiel Gifford** and **John Williams,** and they to report next monthly meeting

A Report of a Committee formerly appointed by this meeting to Inspect into the birthright of Children hath been now Read and Considered and being approved is a followeth

Report of the Committee to Inspect Birth rights of Chil dren

Agreeable to appointment We have Considered the matter respecting our members, Who have a proper Birthright: and we find that in or about the year 1763 our monthly meeting came into the Same measure (or narly[nearly] so) in said matter as the yearly meeting did afterwards in the yer 1774 which was then Established as a Rule in the Society: Wherefore we think the Same Rule with us ought to begin in the first month 1763 unto which Rule we refer, as our Rule to be governd by; and we further think that the former Rules and customs of our meeting ought to remain and stand good down to Said dates of the first month 1763 which was as near as we can Collect as followeth (viz) that all Such Children whose parents or even a father only were members, Such Children were deemed members, whe

27. Another variant name for New York Yearly Meeting.

ther Such parent or parents requested for their children or not, or whether Such
parents were members by Birthright or otherwise
Given forth this 12th day of the 3rd month 1777

Prince Allen
Thomas Hicks
Benjamin Smith Ju^r
Samuel Smith
William Anthony Ju^r

10th month
1779

Att a Monthly meeting held in **Dartmouth** the 18th of 10th month 1779
The Representatives are **William Mosher** and **William Gifford** present

W. Bowdish Ju
paper read
and accepted

    William Bowdish Jus Paper having been Read as directed last monthly
meeting is now returned and accepted

Certificate
for J Clark
Wwife and
Children

A Removal Certificate for **Jonathan Clark** and his wife **Susanna** and
their Children was Signed in this meeting by the Clerk directed to
the monthly meeting at the **Nine Partnethers [Nine Partners]** they being about to
remove there: the names of theire Children being entered in Said
Certificate are as followeth **Lydia Philip Elisabeth Jonathan**
and **Ruth**

T Howland
paid

    Treasurer Reports he hath paid **Timothy Howland** as ordered

J Akin de-
nial read

    The Clerk reports he hath Read the paper of denial against
John Akin according to appointment of last monthly meeting

Report of
the Com^{tee}
on the of
Erecting
Schools

The Committee appointed at our last Monthly meeting to Confer
with the Quarterly meetings Committee on the case of Errecting Schools
make Report that they have had a Conference accordingly and that
They have fallen in with the meashurers Recommended by our last
yearly meeting: And said Quarterly meetings Committee have
advised that Each monthly meeting chase a Solid Judicious Committee
to have the Standing oversight of Such Schools, and to See that they be
Erected accordingly: Therefore this meeting doth appoint **Abiel Gifford**
Caleb Russell William Anthony Ju^r John Williams Elijah Gifford Jonathan
Willbour Caleb Green John Devol and **Samuel Smith** for that purpose

S Russell
Informed

    Joseph Barker reports that he hath informed **Stephen Russell** of his
denial agreeable to appointment

Testimony
of denial
Sign,d a
gainst
P GiffordJu

The Committee Continued to Treat with **Peleg Gifford Ju^r** Reports that
he did not give them full Satisfaction: Therefore they have prodced
a paper of denial against him which was Signed; and **Joseph Tucker Ju**
is appointed to Inform him thereof, and that he hath a Right of an appeal,
And Said paper to Lay on file untill the time of appeal is Exipir,^d
and then the Clerk to read the Same Publickly in the Usual manner
and make report to this meeting when he hath performed the Same

Return of Friends from Quarterly meeting — The Friends appointed to attend the Quarterly meeting being
Called upon make report that they all attended agreeable to appointment
And have produced an Eppistle from the Same which hath been Read
and well accepted: And as there is money requested to Suply the
yearly meeting Stock, the matter for raising the Same is refered
to the adjournment of this meeting

Collected in Silver money – 0£ – 10ˢ – 7ᵈ

Collected in paper Curency – 11 – 7 – 0

adjourn — This Meeting Adjourns to the 27ᵗʰ instant after the meeing of Worship

mett — Mett by adjournment the 27ᵗʰ of the 10ᵗʰ month 1779
The representatives being Called both Present

G Smiths request referd — The matter in Regard to **George Smiths** Request concerning his
Children is refered to next monthly meeting

Hum How case referᵈ — The Committee appointed to Labour with **Humphry Howland** having
Proceeded in that Service buh not being fully Clear in the case request
the matter refered which is refered to next monthly meeting and they continued in
that Service, and then they to make report

S. Gifford & S Rusell gave in papers of ackno=legment refered — **Stephen Gifford** and **Stephen Russell** Each gave in a paper to
to this meeting Condemnin their misconduct, and the day being now far
Spent, Said matters are refered to next monthly meeting

[Report?] of the overseers of **Bedford** meeting — The Time Granted for holding meetings at **Bedford** being now Expierd
The Friends that had the Oversight thereof being Called upon make
report that it hath been kept up orderly as usually and Request it
Continued as Usual which is Granted until the 4ᵗʰ month next year-
And **Seth Russell John Williams** and **Benjamin Taber** are appointed
to have the Oversight thereof and to make report at the Experton thereof

Time of meeting begin — This Meeting concluds that all our meetings for the future begin
at the Eleventh hour until otherwise ordered by this meeting Exepting
only that at **Bedford** which is to be held as heretofore

raising money refered — The matter of raising money to Supply the yearly meeting Treasury
is Refered to next monthly meeting

11ᵗʰ month 1779 — Att a Monthly meeting held in **Dartmouth** the 15ᵗʰ of the 11ᵗʰ month 1779
The Representatives are **Benjamin Smith** 2ᵈ and **Thomas Mott** Present

The report of Peleg Gifford being Informed of his denial — **Joseph Tucker** Juʳ not being present to make report concerning his Informing
Peleg Gifford Juʳ of his denial therefore that matter is refered to next Monthly
meeting and then he to make report

Friends appointeᵈ to Visit **G. Smith** on account of his request — **George Smith** having Requested for his Children to be Taken under ~~the~~
Friends Care, Therefore this meeting doth appoint **Benjamin Smith** 2ᵈ and
William Anthony Juʳ to Joyn with the Women friends and Visit the
Family in Soled manner and acquaint themselves of the State thereof
and make report to the next monthly meeting

Report concern H Howland

The friends appointed to Treat with **Humphry Howland** make report that they have Confered with him on the account of his out goings and that he gave Incoragment to refrain therefrom in futer and gave in a paper Condemning the Same Therefore the Same Committee are continued in Said Service and to make report next monthly meeting

Friends appointed in case of Russell and Gifford

This meeting doth appoint **Thomas Hiks [Hicks] Joseph Barker** and **Benjamin Howland 2ᵈ** to treat with **Stephen Russell** and **Stephen Gifford** in regard to their misconduct, which they and each of them gave in a paper to this meeting Signifying their Sorrow for the Same: and **Stephen Russell** Requesting therein to be Restored to Unity with friends again and the Committee to make report to next monthly meeting

N Gifford gave in a paper

Nathaniel Gifford gave in a paper to this meeting condemning his being concernᵈ in a horse race, Therefore this meeting doth appoint **Elijah Gifford** and **Samuel Smith** to confer with him on that account and to report to next monthly meeting

advice from school Comᵗᵉᵉ

This meeting hath Received advice and direction from the Quarterly meetings School Committee in regard to Erecting Schools, which is well accepted & Concluded to be conformed to by this meeting

Rules for requesting Schools

Also received from said Committee Rules for Regulating of Such Schools which are recommended to this meetings, Schools Committee for their notice & observation Five of whom this meeting orders shall or may act in behalf of the whole of them, and they are advised to meet together to act and do what be needful in that matter as often as conveniently as they can or as need may require

Friends appointed to take in subscriptions for yearly meeting stock

This meeting being directed by the Qarterly meeting to raise money by way of Subscription to Supply the yearly meeting Stock, Therefore this meeting doth appoint **Thomas Mott, Henry Smith, Seth Russell, Daniel Gifford, Timothy Howland,** and **Daniel Ricketson** to take in Subscriptions for that purpose and to pay on the money so Subscribed to this meetings Treasurer and make report of the Sum Total to this meeting as Soon as they have acomplished the Same

J Howland proposal of marriage

John Howland and **Reliance Shepherd** declared their Intentions of Takeing each other in Marriage, and were desired to wait till next Monthly meeting for their answer: and Our friends **Caleb Russell** and **John Williams** are appointed to inquire into **John Howlands** Clearness in regard to marriage and make report next monthly meeting

Certificate for A Shepherd

This meeting hath Signed a Removal Certificate for **Anne Shepherd** a young Daughter of **David Shepherd** directed to the monthly meeting of the **Oblong** She being gone there to Live

R G Receivd

The Women Friends Inform they have Received a Removal Certificate for **Rhoda Gifford** Wife of **Stephen Gifford** from the monthly meeting of **Accoakset**

Jean Smith Disown.d

They also Inform they have disowned **Jean Smith** Wife of **David Smith** and this meeting hath Signed a Testimony against her in concurrance with the Womens meeting: and the Clerk of this meeting is directed to Read said Testimony

Pucblickly in the Usual manner and make report to next monthly meeting

This meeting Collected in hand money – 0£ – 14ˢ – 6ᵈ

in paper money – 16 – 15 – 0

Conclud to to mend the fences

This meeting Concluds to meet in General to Erect and mend up the fence s Round this meeting house yard on the 27ᵗʰ Instant If fair weather if not the 29ᵗʰ

adjourn

This meeting Adjourns to the 24ᵗʰ Instant after the meeting of Worship

mett

Mett by adjournment the 24ᵗʰ of the 11ᵗʰ month 1779

The Representatives being Called **Benjamin Smith 2ᵈ** Present **Thomas Mott** not present

C Wood gave in a paper

Chilon Wood gave in a paper Condemning his marrying out of the Unity of Friends therefore we appoint **Elijah Gifford** and **Jonathan Willbor [Wilbur]** to have the

care of that matter: and to Indeavour to discover the Sincerity of the young man in his condemning Said matter and make report next monthly meeting

C Sherman & G Russell gave in papers

Caleb Shearman and **Gilbart Russell** each gave in a paper Condemning their Joyning with companies in a Warlike and Stand Gard (as they call it) Therefore we appoint **William Sanford Joseph Tucker** and **John Williams** to have an oppertunity of soled [solid] conference with them in order to discover their Sincerity in that matter and make report next monthly meeting

J Devol

John Devol Informed that he hath thououghts of going to the **Nine Partners** to Visit his friends and we concuring therewith as he is a

and

member of our meeting and under ~~of~~ our care - And

G Howland going Jorney[ᵍ] Clerk orderd to give copy of minuts

Gedian Howland he is going to **East Hoosuck** and **Nine partners** to Visit his friends and he being a member of this meeting and under our Care therefore the Clerk is ordered to give each of them a Coppy of this minute

A Howland gave in a bill

Abraham Howland gave in a bill for keeping **Alice Smith** to the amount of 1£ - 12ˢ - 7ᵈ hard money and the Treasurer is ordered to said account and make report next monthly meeting

Chusing over seers of yᵉ poor referd

The year being Expired of the Service of the Overseers of the Poor, but a new Choice is refered and Said Overseers continued until next monthly meeting

Friends ap pointed to re vise yᵉ minits

We appoint our Friends **Thomas Hicks Benjamin Smith 2ᵈ John Williams** and **William Anthony Juʳ** To revise and Correct this meetings minnuts in order to go on Record

Also to Settle account with the Treasurer and make report next monthly

W Barker Ju returnd his Certificate

meeting

William Barker Juʳ returned from **East Hoosuck** with his Certificate that went from this meeting which is now accepted

J Barker re turnd his Certificate request a nother

James Barker returned his Certificate from **East Hoosuck** with their Indorsment thereon to Satisfaction, and now request from us a removal one to **Hoosuck** monthly meeting: Therefore we appoint **William Sanford**

and **William Anthony Ju**ʳ to take the Necessary care therein; and draw and Sign one in behalf of this meeting if they think fit and make report next monthly meeting

12ᵗʰ month 1779 Att a Monthly meeting held in **Dartmout** the 20ᵗʰ of 12ᵗʰ month 1779 The Representatives are **Samuel Smith** and **Nicholas Lapham** Present

P G informd of denial   **Joseph Tucker Ju**ʳ reports he hath Informed **Peleg Gifford Ju**ʳ of his Denial according to appointment

G Smith & children accepted **Benjamin Smith 2**ᵈ and **William Anthony Ju**ʳ Reports they have Visited **George Smiths** family on his request for his Children to be received under Friends Care, and that they found good Satisfaction therein, Therefore this meeting doth acccept of said Children to be under the care of this meeting whose names are **Abner, Ruth, Rhobe** and **Willia**

Case of H Howland referᵈ   Part of the Committee appointed to confer with **Humphry Howland** Report that they not having fully accomplished this matter and request it continued Therefore it is refered to next monthly meeting and the Same Committee Still Continued in Said Service and to report next Monthly meeting

Giffords pa per accepted   Part of the Committee appointed to Treat with **Nathaniel Gifford** in regard to his being concern,d in a horse race, make report that he gave them Satisfaction: Therefor this meeting doth Acccept of his paper condemning his Said disorder for Satisfaction

report on J Howlᵈ clearness   The friends appointed to Inquire into Clearness of **John Howland** Report they find nothing hinder to his proceeding in marriage with **Reliance Shepherd**

Smiths denial read   The Clerk reports he hath Read the Testimon of denial against **Jane Smith** according to appointment

Certificate for Sisson   This meeting Signed a removal Certificate for **Ruth Sisson** wife of **Job Sisson** to the monthly meeting of **Accoakset**

J Howlands answer given respecting marri age   **John Howland** and **Reliance Shepherd** appeared for their Answer Which was that they might proceed to take Each other in Marriage in Some Convenient times before next monthly meeting; advising with the friends this meeting Shall appoint to Oversee Said marriage who are **Caleb Russell** and **Benjamin Taber,** and they to make report next monthly meeting

N Giffords pro posal of marri age   **Nathaniel Gifford** and **Mehettebel Trafford** declared their Intentions of Taking Each other in marriage, and were desired to waight till next monthly meeting for their answer: and **Jonathan Willbor** and **Thomas Hicks** are appointed to make inquiery into the young mans Clearness Respecting marriage; and to make report next monthly meeting

A Howland not paid.   The Treasurer not having paid **Abraham Howland** by reason he hath not called for it, he is Still ordered to pay the Same if called for and make report next monthly meeting

J Barker bound in a Journey Clerk ordered to give a coppy of the minute

John Barker having Signified to this meeting of his Intention to take a Journey with his brother **James** into the Government of **New York** and expects to be at Some meetings in them parts, Which this meeting approves of he being a member of our Society and a member of this meeting and the Clerk is directed to give him a Coppy hereof

The case of Caleb Sherman G Russell refered

The Friends appointed to Treat with **Caleb ~~Russell~~ Shearman** and **Gilbart Russell** report they have not fully accomplished the Same (tho mad[e] Some progress therein) therefore the matter is referred to next monthly meeting and the Same friends Continued in Said Service and then to report

D Shepherd req uest a Certificate

Daniel Shepherd request a Removal Cirtificate to the Monthly meeting at **Sandwich**, Therefore **William Sanford** and **William Barker** are appoin =ted to make due inquirey into his Clearness and draw one for him if they find things clear and bring it to next monthly meeting

Request of P Mac comber Wife Children

Philip Maccomber his Wife and Children having requested to come under the care of Friends; Therefore this meeting appoint **Thomas Hicks** and **William Anthony Ju^r** to have a Soled [Solid] Confference with them in Concurence with the Women friends in order to discover the motive of their request and to make report to next monthly meeting

Complaint a gainst J Howland

The Overseers Inform that **James Howland** hath been a Voiage to Sea as Master of a Vessel that Carried Armes for War, and they having Treated with him on that account, he reather Justified himself therein Therefore this meeting doth appoint **Caleb Russell** and **John Williams** to Treat further with him on that account and make report to next Monthly meeting

This meeting hath Collected In hard money – 0£ –   2^s – 6^d

In paper money – 12 – 18 – 0

adjournd

This meeting Adjourns to the 29th Instant after the meeting for Worship

mett

Mett by Adjournment the 29th of the 12th month 1779

The Representatives being called both Present

The case of S Russell & S Gifford Refered

The mater Respecting **Stephen Russell** and **Stephen Gifford** not being accomplished are refered to next monthly meeting and the same friends continue^d in that Service and then they to make report

C Woods paper accepted

The friends appointed to Treat with **Chilon Wood** make report that he gave them a degree of Satisfaction, and his paper condemning his marrying out of the Unity of friends; being again Read, is accepted for Satisfaction

Chusing Overseers of poor referd

The matter of a new Choice of overseers of the poor is refered to next monthly meeting and those of the former choice Continued until a new Coice is made

Revising miniuts Settleing with Trea surer referd

The Committee appointed to Revise and Correct this meetings minutes And to Settle account with the Treasurer not having accomplished the Same they are Still continued to performe the Same and to make report next monthly meeting

Comᵗᵉᵉ
appointed
to Collect
Friends
Books to=
=gether

This meeting understanding that our Books have been much Scattered abroad; therefore this meeting appoints **Thomas Hicks Jonathan Willbor** an **Daniel Ricketson** to Collect said Books together and make out a fair List of them; and also to prepare a Sutible chest to put them in at this meeting house that they may be for the General Service of friends And Said Committee to make report of their Service herein, and also return Said List of the Books to next monthly meeting

Chusing
overseers
refer,d

The time of the former appointment of Overseers being Expired a New Choice is refered to next monthly meeting and they continued in that until then

This meeting Adjouns to the 5ᵗʰ day of next month

Mett by adjournment the 5ᵗʰ day of the 1ˢᵗ month 1780

The Representatives being called **Samuel Smith** present **Nicholas Lapham** not present

Queries
answer,d

Representatives
appointed
to draw
money for
yearly meet
ing

The Queries were answered in this meeting and an Epistle Signed and directed to the Quarterly meeting by our Representatives who are **Samuel Smith**, **Abiel Gifford**, **William Anthony Juʳ** and **Gideon Howland**; And they are directed to draw the Sum of 40£ paper money, and 30 Shillings Silver money out of our Treasury, and pay the Same to the yearly meetings Treasurer to Suply the yearly meetings Stock, and make report next monthly meeting

---

1ˢᵗ month
1780

Att a Monthly meeting held in **Dartmouth** the 17ᵗʰ of 1ˢᵗ month 1780

The Representatives are **William Barker** and **Abraham Howland** present

Request of
P Maccober
refered

The Committee appointed to Confer with **Philip Maccomber** and Family report that they have not fully accomplished Said appointment Therefore the Same friends are Still continued in Said Service and to make report to next monthly meeting

Certificate
for D Shep
herd

A Removal Certificate directed to the monthly meeting of **Sandwich** was Signed in this meeting for **Daniel Shepherd**

Report of
J Howland
marriage

The friends appointed to Oversee the Marriage of **John Howland** and **Reliance Shepherd** report that they attended said marriage and that it orderly Solemnized

The case of
H Howland
refered

The Friends appointed to Treat with **Humphry Howland** report that they have Several times Treated with him on that account and altho in Some respects he gave a degree of Satisfaction, but for a further Proof of his Sincerity Said matter is refered to next monthly meeting and they are then to make report

Cas of
G Russel
Refered

The friends appointed to Treat with **Gilbart Russell** report that that they have not fulfilled their appointment by reason of the difficulty of the weather they are Still continued to perform it & report next monthly meeting

980 · BOOK III: 1762–1785 [1780]

Caleb Shermans paper accepted | But The Same Friends report they have Treated with **Caleb Shearman** who gave them Satisfaction; Therefore his paper Condemning his disorder is now accept =ted Provided he cause the Same to be Read publickly in the Usul maner and Return the Same to next monthly meeting

Howland disown,d | The Friends appointed to Treat with **James Howland** for his disorder make report, they have performed the Same, and that he did not give them Satisfaction; Therefore he is disowned from being a member of our Society, And **John Williams** is appointed to draw a Testimony of denial against him, and also to Inform him thereof and bring it to next Monthly meeting

Huddleston Received | The Women friends Inform that they Received into Membership **Lydia Hudleston [Huddleston]** Wife of **Seth Hudleston [Huddleston]**, which this meeting hath Unity with

E Gifford and H Wilcox disowned | This meeting hath Signed Testimonys of denials against **Elisabeth Gifford** and **Hannah Wilcox**, and the Clerk is ordered to read publickly in the Usual manner, and to make report next monthly meeting

S Gifford pa= =per accepted | The greater part of the Committee appointed to confer with **Stephen Gifford** report that they have performed the Same who gave a good degree of Satisfaction; Therefore his paper which he hath given Condemning his misconduct is accepted provided he cause the Same to be publickly Read as Usual and Return the Same to next monthly meeting

This meeting is informed John Churchmans Journals are ready | This Meeting is Informed by a miniut of the meeting for Sufferings That a Number of **John Churchmans** Journals which they had Engaged are now ready; and advise that Friends would Send up their Subscriptions with their money at two-thirds of a Silver dollar per Book to the next meeting for Sufferings[28] – and our friends **Samuel Smith William Mosher** and **John Williams** to take in Subscriptions and make report to the adjournment of this meeting

This meeing Collected in hard money – 00£ – 15ˢ – 6ᵈ

In paper money – 11 – 12 – 0

adjourn | This Meeting adjourns to the 26ᵗʰ Instant after the meeting for Worship

mett | Mett by adjournment the 26ᵗʰ of the 1ˢᵗ month 1780

The Representatives being called both Present

Report on N Gifford clearness re= garding marri= age | The friends appointed to inquier into the Clearness of **Nathaniel Gifford** Respecting clearness in regard to marriage make report, that they have made inquiry and do not find any thing Sufficient to hinder their proceeding in marriage

28. John Churchman (1705–1775) was a minister from Nottingham Monthly Meeting, Chester County, Pennsylvania, and another leader of the "reform" movement among Friends. See *An Account of the Gospel Labours and Christian Experiences of a Faithful Minister of Jesus Christ, John Churchman, late of Nottingham, in Pennsylvania Deceased; To Which Is Added—a Short Memorial of the Life and Death of a Fellow Labourer in the Church, Our Valuable Friend Joseph White, Late of Bucks County* (Philadelphia: J. Cruikshank, 1779).

The case of
S Russell
referd
The friends appointed to Treat with **Stephen Russell** report they have been with him and had a Conference with him on the account of his disorder and think best the matter be continued, therefore the matter is refered to next monthly meeting and the Same friends continued in Said Service and then then they to make report

N Gifford
answer given
Nathaniel Gifford and **Mehetabel Trafford** appeared for their Answer which was that they might proceed take each other in marriage in Some Convenient time before next monthly meeting advising with the friends this meeting Shall appoint to Oversee the Same who are **Elijah Gifford** and **Jonathan Willbor** and they to make report next monthly meeting

Overseers of
the poor appoin
ted
This Meeting appoints **Elijah Gifford, Gideon Howland, Caleb Green Abraham Howland, Giles Slocum,** and **Thomas Russell** Overseers of the Poor for the year Insuing

Revising minuts
and Settling with
Treasurer
Referd
The Friends appointed to Revise and Correct this meetings minuits and to Settle accounts with the Treasurer reports they have not accomplish the Same they are therefore continued in Said Service and make report next Monthly meeting

Report of money
raised
The friend appointed to raise money by way of Subscription have now made report Return of the Sum total so Collected wich is 108£ – 10ˢ – 6ᵈ In paper and 2£ – 3ˢ – 7ᵈ in hard money which they have delivered to the Treasurer of this meeting

Overseers ap
point
This meeting appoints **Abiel Gifford, Benjamin Smith 2ᵈ, Benjamin Howland 2ᵈ, Seth Huddleston, Caleb Russell,** and **Benjamin Taber** Overseers for the insuing

G Gifford
receiv,d
The Women friends Inform they have received **Grace Gifford** into unity which this meeting Concurs with

Report of
Friend that
attended
Quarterly
Meeting
The friends appointed to attend the Quarterly meeting Report they all attended agreeable to appointment and have produced an Epistle from the Same which hath been Read and well accepted; The Said friends also report they have Sent the money to be conveyed to the yearly meetings Treasurey, which was Sent by them

The chusing
a Comᵗᵉᵉ
on account
of attening
Quarterly
meeting is
referd
The Quarterly meetings by their Epistle have recommended to us to appoint a Committee to Joyne their Committee to confer the matter of Enlarging **Sandwich** Quarterly meetings by Joining part of this Quarter there to; ~~which~~ which this meeting doth refer to next monthly meeting for further Consideration

The report
in regard
of books
The friends appointed in regard to this meetings Books and to procure a box to put them in report they have procured a box and produced the Same to this house, and they have Likewise been in a progress to Collect said Book, but have not fully accomplished the Same, they are therefore Continued in Said Service and make report next monthly meeting

The friend appointed to Treat with **Gilbart Russell** that they have fulfilled their appointment therein and that he gave them a degree of Satisfaction, therefore this meeting doth Except of his paper Condemning his disorder, provided he cause the Same to be read publickly in the usual maner and returne Same to next monthly meeting

The Friend Continued to have the care of **Humphry Howland** report that he hath given them a degree of Satisfaction yet there appearing Somthing in his Habit that friends are not fully with; therefore it is Refered to next monthly meeting under the care of the Same friends as before

These two Last Paragrafts belong to the third month, but were Entered hear through mistake; Therefore they are Re Entered again In their proper place

---

2ⁿᵈ month 1780

Att a Monthly meeting held in **Dartmouth** the 20ᵗʰ of 2ᵈ month 1780

The Representatives are **Joseph Booker** and **Jonathan Willbor** pesent

P Maccomber Received under friends care

The friends Continued to confer with **Philip Maccomber** and Children Report that they have fulfilled the Same who gave them a good Degree of Satisfaction; Therefore this meeting doth accept of him the Said **Philip Maccomber** and his three Sons Namely, **Gardner**, **Barnabus** and **Abraham** to be under the care of this meeting

The case of H Howland refered

The matter respecting **Humphry Howland** is refered to next monthly meeting under the care of the Same friends as before who are then to report

Receiv,d a Certificate for J H

Received a removal Certificate from the monthly meeting of **Swanzey** for **John Howland** who has removed hear the Same Setting forth him to be a member of the Society which is accepted

The case of G Russel refer,d

The friends appointed to Treat with **Gilbart Russell** make report that they have not accomplished the Same by reason of Some Indisposition of body, and Some disappointment; Therefore they are Still continued in Said Service and to make report next monthly meeting

C Shermans paper read & accepted

Caleb Shearman having caused his paper to be read as Expressed last monthly meeting which is accepted for Satisfaction

J Howland denial signd orderd to be read

A paper of Denial against **James Howland** was Signed in this meeting and the Clerk is ordered to read the Same publickly at the Close of a meeting of Worship on first day of the week and to make report thereof next monthly meeting and **John Williams** reports he hath informed Said **Howland** as odered

Testimony against EG & HW. read

The Clerk reports that the Testimony against **Elisabeth Gifford** and **Hannah Wilcok** have been Read as ordered last monthly meeting

Stephen Giffords paper having been read as ordered is now acceted for Satisfaction – and is as followeth

S Giffords paper

To the monthly meeting next to be held at **Ponaganset** on the 18ᵗʰ of the 10ᵗʰ month 1779. Dear friend – Whereas I Some time past have So far departed fom the

Principles of Truth as to fall into the Sin of Fornication as apears by my wifes having a Child So So[o]n after marriage, for which miscondut I and heartily Sorry for and do condemn, desireing God may forgive me, and that friends would so far pass this mine offence by as to let me remain under their Care, From your unfeigned friend　　　　　　　　**Stephen Gifford**

The case of S Russel referd　　The friends appointed in the case of **Stephen Russell** report they have taken the necessary care in that respect, but think best said matter be continued; theref[ore] it is refered to next monthly meeting uder [under] the care of Said friends who are then to make report

Report of S[sic]G marriage　　The Friends appointed to Oversee the marriag of **Nathaniel Gifford** and **Mehetibel Trafford** report they attended the same which was orderly accomplished as far as they could discover

report of friends revise miniuts settle with Treasurer　　The friends appointed to Revise and Correct this meeting miniuts and to Settle account with the Treasurer make report they have fulled the Same and have Left Said miniuts with Clerk to go on record – They also report there remains in the Treasury £97 – 2ˢ – 0 in paper money and 1£ – 2ˢ – 6ᵈ in Silver money

Concerning Sand wich Quarterly meeting refered　　The matter in regard to Enlarging **Sandwich** Quarterly meeting having been under Consideration of this meeting, and divers [diverse] friends Expressed their opinions. It is fered [referred] to next month meeting

Certificate for B Sawdy Wife & Children　　A Removal Certificate for **Benjamin Sawdy** his Wife and Children was Signed in this meeting directed to the monthly meeting at **Saratog,** and **East Hoosuck** a former one having been Granted by this meeting which he hath not Received

G Howlands account for keeping A Smith　　**Gideon Howland** hath given in an account for keeping **Alice Smith** from the 6ᵗʰ of the 6ᵗʰ month to the 28ᵗʰ of the 10ᵗʰ month 1779 being 20 weeks and 5 days at a Silver Dollar pr week or the Vallue thereof, to be paid in Such money as the meetin Collects, amounting in Silver Lawfull money to £6 – 5ˢ – 0ᵈ which this meeting allows and the Treasurer is Ordered to pay the Same and make report next monthly meeting

Hum Russells proposal of marriage　　**Humphr Russell** and **Bethiah Eldrech** (after obtain consent of parents) Declared their Intentions taking each other in marriage and were desired to wait till next monthly meetin for their answer; and **Benjamin Taber** and **Joseph Gifford** are apointed to Inquire into the young mans Clearness and to make report next monthly meeting

Information sent to Sandwich Respecting J Shea rman & Son　　A few lines directed to the monthly meeting of **Sandwich** was Signed in this meeting Informing them that **Joshua Shearman** and his Son **Joshua** had Sometime past removal Certificates from this meeting and by Informa=　=tion had not delivered them

Collecting books continued　　The friends appointed to Collect our Books report they have made Some progress therein; they are Still continued in Said Service and to report next monthly meeting

Complaint against J Bowdish — The Overseers Inform that **James Bowdish** hath married out of the Unity of Friends, and his wife hath had a Child Soon after marriage; Therefore this meeting doth appoint **John Williams** and **Seth Russell** to Treat with him therefor and to make report to next monthly meeting
They also to draw a paper of denial against him if he do not make them Satisfaction

A Ricketson paper — **Abraham Ricketson** hath given in a paper to this meeting Codemning his former misconduct Perticularly Horseracing for which he was Denied; Therefore this meeting doth appoint **Thomas Hicks** and **Samuel Smith** Confer with him on that account and make report next monthly meting

order to pay T Howland — This meeting orders the Treasurer to pay **Timothy Howland** five dollars or the Vallue thereof in paper for keeping the meeting house half a year

This meeting Collected in paper – 13£ – 13^s – 0^d

In Silver – 00 – 15 – 5

3rd month 1780 — Att a Monthly meeting held in **Dartmouth** the 20th 3rd month 1780
The Representatives are **Thomas Hicks** and **Benjamin Rider** present

G Russell paper Excepted — The Committee appointed to Treat with **Gilbart Russell** report that they have fulfilled their appointment therein, and that he gave them a degree of Satisfaction: Therefore this meeting doth except his paper Condemning his misconducts Povided he Cause the Same to be read Publickly in the Usual manner and return the to next monthly meeting

H Howland Case Continued — The friends continued to have the care of **Humphry Howland** report That he hath given them a degree of Satisfaction; ~~Therefore this meeting~~ yet there appearing Something in his habit that friends are not fully Satisfiyd with therefore it is Refered to next monthly meeting under the care of the Same friends as before in order for them to pevail upon him to dissest from wearing such apperal as well as to convince him of the Evil thereof and to make report next monthly meeting

S Russell Receiv.d — The friends appointed to Treat with **Stephe Russell** report that they have had Several conferences with him on the account of his disorder for which he was disowned) who hath given a degree of Satisfaction; Threfore he is Received into membership again

B Slocum receiv.d — The Women friends Inform they have Received a Removel Certificate for **Bethiah Slocum** wife of **Jonathan Slocum**

H Wilbor Certificate — This meeting hath Signed a removal Certificate for **Hannah Willbor** directed to the monthly meeting at the **Ninepartners** She being about to Remove thear

The Clerk reports the Testimony of Denial against **James Howland** hath been read as ordered at our Last monthly meeting; which is as followeth

J Howlands
Testimony
of denial

Whereas **James Howland** having made Profession with us the
People called Quakers, But for want of adhearing to the dictats of best
Wisdom, hath So far deviated from our Christian principles as to tak the
Command of an Armed Vessel – for which he hath been Laboured with
in Love to reclaim him from Such practices; But our endeavors not having
the desired Effect, and he declineing to condemn the Same; We are there
=fore Concerned to give this forth as a Testimony against Such Conduct
Hereby disowning him from being a member of our Society untill he
Shall come to a Sight and Sense of his out goings, and by unfeigned
Repentance return to the way of Truth, which is our Earnest desire
    Signed in and on behalf our Monthly meeting held in
    Dartmouth the 21ˢᵗ of the 2ⁿᵈ month 1780
               by **William Anthony Juʳ** Clerk

Report of
H Russell
Clearness

The Friend appointed to Inquire into the clearness of **Humphry
Russell** report they have made Inquiry and find nothing to hinder his proceding

Answer
given to
H Russell

Humphry Russell and **Bethiah Eldrich** appeared for their answer
which was that they might proced to take each other in marriage
in Some convenient time before next monthly meeting adviseing
with the friends that this meeing Shall appoint to Oversee the Same
who are **Benjamin Taber** and **William Anthony Juʳ** and they to
make report next monthly meeting

The friends appointed to collect this meetings books report they have
been in a progres therein and they not being all collected they are still continued
in Said Service and to make report when they find freedom

Bowdish
disown.d

The friends appointed to Treat with **James Bowdish** report they have
fulfild the Same, but that he did not incline to make friends any Satisfaction
Therefore he is hereby disowned from being a member of our Society, and
Said friends have drafted a Testimony of Denial against said **Bowdish**
which hath been Read and Signed in this in this meeting and the Clerk is
ordered to read the Same publickly as Usual, and report thereof next
monthly meeing – And **John Williams** is appointed to inform said **Bowdish**
of his de[n]ial and make report next monthly meeting

Ricketsons
case continuᵈ

The friends appointed to confer with **Abraham Ricketson** report that
hath gone away and that they have not had oppertunity to Treat with him
therefore they are Sill continued in Said Service and make report when
they have accomplished the Same

T Howland
not paid

The Treasurer reports he hath not paid **Timothy Howland** as ordered
he is therefore directed to do it and make report to next monthly meeting

Certificate
requested for
A Barker

David Barker Requested a Certificate for his Son **Asa Barker** to the month-
=ly meeting at **Sandwich** he being gone there to Live as an apprentice, Therefore

Joseph Gifford and **Joseph Tucker Ju**ᵣ are appointed to take the necessary care in that respect and to draw one for him and bring to next monthly meeting

Certificate requested for E Hathaway

We being Informed that the Widdow **Elisabeth Hathaway** and her family being about to remove from hence to **RhoadIsland** to Live; Therefore **Joseph Barker** and **Samuel Smith** are appointed to take the needful care in that Respit and to draw a removal Certificate for them if they find things clear; (They to Join with the Women friends in Said case) and report to next monthly meeting

Hez Smiths Certificate

There was a Certificate Signed in this meeting by the Cerk for **Hezekiah Smith** directed to the monthly meeting at the **Nine partners**, as he hath thoughts of going there to make Some Stay in his Labour

*Queries answer*ᵈ

The Queries were Answered in this Meeting, and an Epistle Signed directed to the Quarterly meeting by our Representatives **William Mosher, Samuel Smith. Thomas Hicks, William Anthony Ju**ᵣ and **Abiel Gifford** and they to report next monthly meeting

*Representative Quar*ˡʸ*meeting*

G Howland not paid

The Treasurer having not paid **Gideon Howland** he is desired to accomplish It and make report to next monthly meeting

                  Collected in paper – 18£ – 19ˢ – 2ᵈ

                  Collected in Silver –   0   – 11 – 8

---

4 month 1780

Att a Monthly meeting held in **Dartmouth** the 17ᵗʰ of 4ᵗʰ month 1780 The Representatives being caled **John Devol** present **Elijah Gifford** who was appointed at the Preparetive meeting not present

G Russells paper Read

Gilbart Russell caused his paper to be publickly Read and returned to this meeting as ordered Last monthly meeting – Which is as followeth

Which is as follows

To the Preparative and Monthly meeting of Friends to be held at **Dartmouth** the 10ᵗʰ of 11ᵗʰ month 1779

Whereas I Some time past did Inconsiderately go on a Military Gaurd which I now am Sorry for and do Condemn desireing friends to pass it by and let me remain under their Care from your friend **Gilbert Russell**

H Howlands case refered

The matter of **Humphry Howland** is refered to next monthly meeting by reason but one of the Committee being present and the Said Committee then to make report

Report of H Russells marriage

The Friends appointed to See **Humphry Russell** and **Bethiah Eldriedges** Marriage Solemnized report they attended said marriage and Saw nothing but that it was in a degree orderly

J Bowdish paper read

The Clerk Reports that **James Bowdishs** paper of Denial hath been Read as ordered, and **John Williams** report he hath informed Said **Bowdish** of his denial – Which is as followeth

Which is as follows

Whereas **James Bowdish** having had a Right of membership with us the People Called Quakers in **Dartmouth** – But for want of taken heed to the reproof of Instruction in his own heart hath so far gone a Stray as to fore

Be found guilty of the Sin of Fornication as appears by his wifes having a Child Soon after mariage and also neglects the attendance of our religious Meetings: For which offences he having been treated with, but declines to Condemn the Same, to friends Satisfaction. – We therefore give this forth as a Publick Testimony against Such conduct, hereby disowning him the Said **James Bowdish** from being a member of our Society and from under the Care of this meeting – Nevertheless desireing he may come to a Sence of his outgoings and return is our desire

Signed in and on behlf of oure afore Said meeting held in **Dartmouth** this 20th day of 3d mo 1780   By **William Anthony Ju**r Clerk

G Howland
paid
The Treasurer reports he hath paid **Gideon Howland** the money as Ordered Last monthly meeting but he not having paid **Timothy Howland**, therefore he is continued to accomplish the Sane, and to report next monthly meeting

Report of
Representatives
from Quar
terly meetg
The Representatives to the Quarterly meeting Report that they all attended but **Thomas Hicks** who Sent a reasonable excuse and they produced an Epistle from Said Quarterly meeting which was read and well accepted

B Mosher
proposal of
marriage
Barnabus Mosher Jur and **Ruth Anthony** appeared in this meeting and Declared their Intentions of Taking Each other in marriage; and were desired to waite till next monthly meeting for their answer: and **John Devol** and **Abiel Gifford** are appointed to inquire into the young mans clearness Respecting marriag and report next monthly meeting

Advice to
Collect
Friends
Sufferings
Received from the meeting for Suffering Some regulations for taking Friend Sufferings, which we desire the Comitty, appointed in our meeting Some time past for to collect friends Suferings – To observe & comply with

adjournd
This meeting Adjourns till tomorrow after meeting: Which meeting being Called by reason of a Funeral

mett
Mett by adjournment the 18th of 4th month 1780

The Representatives being Called **John Devol** present **Elijah Gifford** not present

Certificate
for A Barker
refered
The Committee appointed to draw a Certificate for the **Asa Barker** not being Present the matter is refered to next monthly meeting and Said friends Continued in the Same Service then they to make report

E Hathaway
Certificate
not accom=
=plished
The friends appointed last monthly meeting to Joine the women friends in Drawing a Removal Certificate for **Elisabeth Hathaway** and famamily not having accomplised the Same by reason the matter was not presented to the Womens meeting Said friends are therefore Still continued in Said Service and to make report to next monthly meeting

The case of
J Sherman
& Son
Inspeted
Whereas **Joshua Shearman** and his Son **Joshua** having some years past Removed from hence into the Compass of **Sandwich** monthly meeting and having removal Certificates: but as we are informed of Late they have not delivered said Certificates to Said meeting: This meeting therefore

appoints our friends **John Williams** and **Caleb Green** to Treat with them the Said **Joshua** and Son on the account of their great neglect, and to Inquire into their conduct Since removed and make report next monthly meeting

A Devol request a Certificate

Abner Devol request a Certificate to the monthly meeting at **Sandwich** Setting forth his clearness respecting marriage: Therefore **Joseph Barker** and **Thomas Hicks** are appointed to take the needful care in that case Respect and bring one to next monthly meeting

L Sherman Disown,d

The Women friend Inform they have denied **Lois Shearman** now wife of **Andrew Sheaman [Shearman]** which this meeting Concurs with

Collected in paper money – £19 – 17ˢ – 0ᵈ

in Silver money – 00 – 5 – 2

5ᵗʰ month 1780

Att a Monthly meeting held in **Dartmouth** the 15ᵗʰ of 5ᵗʰ month 1780 The Representatives are **Abiel Gifford** and **Joseph Tucker Juʳ** present

H.Howland case conti= =nued

The Committee appointed to Treat with **Humphry Howland** not giving in a Satisfactory report from him, not yet fully clear in their ~~appoint~~ Discharge of their appointment they are therefore Continued in Said Service and to make report when they find themselve clear in that matter

T Howland not paid

The Treasurer not having paid **Timothy Howland** as directed last monthly meeting: he is therefore continued for that Sevice and to make report next monthly meeting

B Moshers Clearness

The Friends appointed to Inquire into the clearness of **Barnabus Mosher Juʳ** Report they have taken due care in that respect and find nothing to hinder his proceeding marriage:

Answer to Barnabus Mosher

Barnabus Mosher and **Ruth Anthony** appeared for their answer which was, that they might proceed to take Each Other in marriage in Some Conveniant time before next monthly meeting: adviseing with the friends this meeting Shall appoint to Oversee the Same, who are **Abiel Gifford** and **John Devol** and they to report next monthly meeting

Friends added to collect Suf= ferings

One of the Committee that this meeting appointed to Collect friends Suffering being deceased: our friends **Thomas Hicks, Elijah Gifford** and **Caleb Green** are now added for that Service

A Barkers certificate

A Certificate for **Asa Barker** Son of **David Barker** was Signed in this meeting directed to the monthly meeting at **Sandwich** being gone to live as an apprentice there

The case of J Sherman Seʳ was continued

The friends appointed to Treat **Joshua Shearman** and his son **Joshua** make report tha they have fulfilled their appointment therein; and that **Joshua Shearman senior** doth condemn his not giving his Certificate to the meeting it was directed to and some other of his misconduct; but he being in the unwarrantable practice of the neglect of the due attendance of Religious meetings: Therefore said Committee are continued to treat further with him and to make report next monthly meeting

J Sherman Ju^r disowned

They also report that the young man hath attended Seperate meetings and that he gave them no Satisfaction therein; Therefore this meeting doth disown him from being a member of the Society: and the Said Committee are ordered to draw a Testimony of denial against him and Informe him thereof and bring Said Testimony to next monthly meeting

Cerificate for A Devol

A Certificate for **Abner Devol** directed to **Sandwich** monthly meeting Setting forth his clearness respecting mariage was Signed in this meeting

Certificate for E Hathaway

A Removal Certificate for **Elisabeth Hathaway** and Such of her Children as were members of this meeting directed to the monthly meeting of **RhodIsland** was Signed in this meeting they being gone there to Live

Certificate for L Barker

Also a Removal Certificate for **Lydia Barker** and her four daughters Directed to the monthly meeting at the **Ninepartners** was Signed in this meeting they being about to remove theither

Certificate for M Greene

Also a Removal Certificate for **Martha Greene** directed to the monthly meeting at **East Greenwich**, She having gone to reside there

G Howland give in a bill

Gideon Howland hath given in a Bill for keeping **Alice Smith** from the 28th of the 10th month last to the 28th of the 4th month Including 26 weeks at a Silver Doller per week or its Value in Such money as the meeting Collects together with the addition of two dollars fo keeping her when Sick amounting to the Sum of £8 – 8^s – o^d hards money which this meeting alows and Orders the Treasurer to pay when Suplied with money   Collected in Silver – 1£ – 1^s – 11^d
        Collected in paper – 19£ – 10^s – 10^d

W Mosher and S Smith was [?] two books

Out of which Collection Eight Shillings in Silver was paid to **William Mosher** and **Samuel Smith.** Who have Reimbursted Said Sum to pay for two of **John Churchmans** Journals for this meeting

Request to enquire into said Conversation of D Wilbor

A Paper directed to the monthly meeting at **East Hoosuck** and **Saratoga** Requesting them to Enquire into the Late Conversation of **Deborah Willbor** and make Some return to this meeting. Said paper was Signed in this Meeting, and the Clerk is ordered to take a Coppy thereof ~~and~~ To keep on file

6th month 1780

Att a M^onthly held in **Dartmouth** the 19th of 6th month 1780 The Representatives are **Elijah Gifford Thomas Hicks and Benjamin Smith 2^d** all present

John Lloyds Visit

Our Friend **John Lloyd** attended this meeting with a Certificate from the monthly meeting held at **Gwynedd** in the County of **Philidelphia** Dated the 25th of 4th month 1780 which was Read to Satisfaction and his Visit and Labour in the Service of the Gospel well accepted

Receivd a Certificate for Stephen Buffinton

Received a removal Certificate the monthly meeting of **Swanzey** Bearing date the 5th of the 6th month 1780 For **Stephen Buffinton** his wife **Sarah** and their Children, they having removed here to reside

T Howland paid	The Treasurer reports he hath paid **Timothy Howland** as ordered
Report of Barⁿ Mosher marriage	The Friends appointed to Oversee the marriage of **Barnabus Jᵘ Mosher** and **Ruth Anthony** report they attended Said marriage and did no See but that it was accomplished orderly.
The case of J. Sherman Continued	The friends who were appointed to Treat with **Joshua Shearman Junor** Saw and to draw a Testimony of Denial against **Joshua Shearman Junor** Request that matter may be refer,d to next monthly meeting as they have not had oppertunity to accomplish the Same
Complaint against J Smith and Son John	The Overseers Inform by way of the Preparitive meeting that **Joseph Smith** and his Son **John** and **William Taber** and ^his son **Edward** have been in the practice of attending Such meetings as are held out of the Unity of Friends, and that he the Said **John Smith** hath allowed some of Said meetings ₐ^to be held in his owne house: and Said Overseers and other friends having Laboured with them for their ₐ^sd misconduct but they Still continue to persist in and Justify the Same, and much neglect the attending our meeting. Therefore we appoint our friends **Elijah Gifford, Seth Russell, Thomas Hicks, John Devol, Jonathan Willbor,** and **William Anthony Jur** To Labour further with them and to Endeaver in Love and meekness to convince them of the Evil tendency of Such a practice and to restore them to unity with friends againe: and to make report next monthly meeting
E Hathaway Certificate returned another Sent	The Removal Certificate that was Signed at our Last monthly meeting for **Elizabeth Hathway** and her Children being now returned by reason of Some incorrect ₐ^[?] therein and another was prpared and Signed in this meeting in the Liew thereof
Queries an= swered	The Queries were Read and answers thereto prepared, approved and Signed, and the Epistle to the Quarterly meeting Read, Signed and sent
Representativᵉˢ to the Quarterly meeting	to the Said Quarterly meeting by our Representatives who are **Abiel Gifford William Anthony Ju** and **Caleb Greene** and they to make report next monthly meeting
The Treaty of attending Quarterly meetg referd	This meeting hath been Informed by one of the Committee appointed by our yearly meeting, that they are to Treat with this meeting respecting being aded to **Sandwich** Quarter: And Requesting our attention by a Committee, which is refer.d to next monthly meeting
A Almyˢ Certificate receiv.d	The Women friends informs they have received a removal Certificate for **Ann Almy** from the monthly meeting of **RhodIsland** She having ~~here~~ Removed here to Inhabit
Coppy of the ^minit was Signd for J Lloyd	A Coppy of the minuit respecting the Visit and Service of our Friend **John Lloyd** was taken of and Signed in this meeting by the Clerk: and delivered to him for his use when he may return home to his friends

This meeting Collected in Silver ..　0£ .. 17ˢ .. 3½ᵈ

In – paper .. 23 .. 01 .. 0

7th month
1780

Att a monthly meeting held in **Dartmouth** the 17th of 7th month 1780
The Representatives are **Caleb Russell** and **William Mosher** – present

Report from
Quarterly
meeting

The Representatives to the Quarterly meeting report they all attended
agreeable to appointment and have produced an Epistle from the Same
Which was Read to good acceptance, wherein is Recommended a Subscrip
tion to Supply the yearly meeting Treasury with one handed pounds

[Epi]stles
receiv.d

Coppies of Epistles from our last yearly meeting, a written one from
London of the year 1779 and one from **Pensylvania** of the 9th month last
were all read in this meeting to good Satisfaction

J. Harts Certi
[fi]cate receiv,d

A Removal Certificate for **Jonathan Heart** his wife Experiane and their
child **Martha** was read in this meeting and accepted they being removed
here to Inhabit

The case of
Shearman J
refered

The matter continued respecting **Joshua Shearman** and **Joshua Shear=**
=man Ju**r** not being fully completed, they are Still refer,d to next monthly
meeting, and the same friends as before are continued in that Service
and to report to next monthly meeting

J Smith and
Son John and
[W] Tabor & Son
Edward are
[denied] & each
of them Disowned

The greater part of the friends appointed to Treat with **Joseph Smith**
and Son **John**, and **William Taber** and Son **Edward** make report that
they or the most of them, have accomplished Said Service, and that all and
Each one of them in particular, persisted to Justify their misconduct
in attending Saperate meetings without retracting the same; nor desireing
Friends to wait further with them: Therefor this meeting taking the matter
into Solled [solid?] consideration do conclud to disown the Said **Joseph Smith**,
his son **John**, and **William Taber** and his son **Edward** and said Committee
are appointed to draw a Testimony or Testimonies ∧of denial against them and
Inform them thereof and bring it to next next monthly meeting

Committee
appointed on
account of clar
[ity?] Sandwich
Quarterly
meeting

The matter in regard to appointing a Committee to Treat with the
yearly meetings Committee Respecting inlarging **Sandwich** Quarter was Consi-
=dered: and do appoint our Friends **Samuel Smith Abiels Gifford William
Mosher, Caleb Russell, William Anthony Ju**r**, Thomas Hicks, Elijah Gifford**, and
John Williams, for that Service and to make report when they have accomplished
the Same

*Benj Smith Ju*r*
give in a bill

Benjamin Smith Jur** hath given in an account to this meeting for
keeping **Alice Smith** about 10 weeks in the year 1776, amounting to 18£ old
Tennor which is app∧roved and the Treasurer is ordered to pay the Same
When Supplyed with money by this meeting

[?] Mosher dis=
owned

A Testimony of denial against **Appltin**[?] **Mosher** was Signed in this meeting

Coppy of the
miniut orderd for
Allen

James Allen being about to take a Journey to **East Hoosuck** and **Saratoga**
in order to make Some Stay there: and hath Informed this meeting there
of: and as he is a member of out Societ the Clerk is ordered to give him
a Coppy of this minuit

The Women Friends Inform that **John Slocums** wife and Children having removed to **RhodIsland**, and as there are Several Sons among the children: This meeting doth appoint **Joseph Tucker Ju Joseph Barker** and **Thomas Hicks** to assist and Joine with the Women in making inquir[y] into their Circumstances, and prepare a Certificate for them if they find things clear

And also to draw a Certificate for **David Barker** and Sons who hath Removed into the Compass of the **Ninepartners** monthly meeting, if on Inquiry they may think proper and ∧[bring?] to next monthly meeting.

	£	s	d
Collected in Silver ..	5	10	2
in paper ..	15	18	0

Att a Monthly meeting held in **Dartmouth** the 21ˢᵗ of 8 month 1780
The Representatives are **Elijah Gifford** and **Caleb Green** present

The friends appointed to D∧ᵣaft a Testimony of denial against **Joshua Shearman Juner,** have performed the Same and brought it to this meeting; which was Signed by the Clerk who is ordered to read it publickly in the usual manner and make report next monthly meeting

They also report they have Informed him of ∧ʰⁱˢ Said denial as directed Last monthly meeting: The Said Committee also report they

Have Treated with **Joshua Shearman Senor** and that he did notify them Satisfaction: Therefore he is disowned h'reby from being a member of our Religious Society; and Said Committee are appointed to Inform him hereof and to make report next monthly meeting

Testimonies of denial against **Joseph Smith** and his son **John** and **William Taber** and his wife **Mary**, and their Son **Edward**, and daughter **Patience**, were Signed in this meeting by the Clerk who is ordered to Read them publickly in the Usual manner and make report next monthly meeting; and the Committee who had the care of these matter[s] are desired ∧ᵗᵒ inform them of their denial and make report next monthly meeting

The friends appointed to Joine and assist the women in regard to **Martha Slocum** (wife of (**John Slocum**) and their Childrens Certificate reports the matter is not accomplished; they are therefore continued in said service and to report next monthly meeting

The Same Committee being appointed to draw a Certificate for **David Barker** and sons; who report that things are not fully clear, they are therefore Still continued in the Same Service and to make report next monthly meeting

The Overseers Inform by the way of the preparative meeting that **Eliassib Smith** hath been in practice of attending meetings that are held out of the Unity of our Societ, and hath been laboured with to desist but he still continues to Justify himself therein and hath no desire that friends Should wait any longer for him to Consider of said matter; yet this meeting doth appoint our friends **Joseph Tucker Ju^r** and **John Devol** to labour further with him the said **Eliassib Smith** and if they do not find any Sattisfaction; to draft a Testimony of denial against him and inform him thereof and bring said Testimony to next monthly meeting

Certificate requested for J Gifford   **Abiel Gifford** desires Certificate for his Son **John Gifford** setting forth his Right of membership among us: to the monthly meeting of **Accoakset** he having gone to reside within the Verge of that meeting, with a friend - which is granted by these lines therefore the Clerk is ordered to give him a Coppy of this minuit

B Smith Ju is paid   The Treasurer reports he hath paid **Benjamin Smith 2^d** as orderd last monthly meeting

a Certificate requested for J Smith   This meeting hath been informed that **John Smith** (Son of **Peleg**) is removd to reside within the compass of **East Hoossuck** and **Saratoga** monthly meeting and as he hath a Birth right in the Society, this meeting doth appoint [**Samuel**?] **Smith** and **Benjamin Howland 2^d** to draw a paper to Inform the meeting where he resides, the Circumstances of him the said **John Smith** and make report next monthly meeting

Friends Desired to Meet clear Some land   Friends concluds to meet in general to clear up the land round our Meeting house. Therefore friends are desired to meet Generally the 28th [Insant?] for that purpose if the weather be Suitable if not the first fair day

Collected in Silver . . 1$^£$ . . 1^s . . 7^d

Collected in paper . . 23 . . 9 . . 0

adjournd   This meeting Adjourns to the 30th Insant after the meeting of Worship

mett   Mett by Adjournment this 30th day of the 8th month 1780

The Representatives being called. both present

Friends appointed to Collect money for yearly meeting Stock   As it is Recommended in the Last Epistle from the Quarterly meeting That one hundred pounds Lawful hard money be raised to Supply the yearly meeting Treasury: Therefore this meeting doth appoint our frie[n]d **Caleb Green, James Tucker, George Smith, Jonathan Willbor,** and **Benjamin Gifford Ju^r** to Collect by Subscriptions, Such Somes as frie[n]ds may have freedom to give, and pay the same to this meetings Treasurer And make report to this meeting of the Sum total so Collected [when ready?]

Friends appointed to pro=cure Hay   As there will be Hay wanting at the Quarterly meeting **Nicholas Lapham, William Barker, and Jonathan Willbor** are appointed to procure same on that account.

Order to pay BH   The Treasurer is Orderd to pay **Benjamin Howland the 3^d** five Silver Dollars for keeping the meeting house half a year

[Ce]rtificate for
Ann Gifford

Anne Gifford having desired our Certificate to the Quarterly meeting at Salem. She having it on her mind to Visit that meeting: Therefore one was drafted and Signed in this meeting Setting forth her ~~unt~~ unity and her acceptable publick Testimony

Potter disor-
derly Conduct

Whereas **John Potter** Some time past went up to **the Ninepartners** to make some Stay there: and **William Anthony Ju** and **Samuel Smith** being appointed to inspect into his Circumstances, and finding things not clear was directed by this meeting to inform him of his disorder and to take what other needful can they may think proper in that respect and make report when ready: accordingly they now report: That he the Sa[i]d **John** went away in a disorderly manner with= =out the advice friends, or without the consent of his Gardian, he being under age and he not having yet returned, nor any late account been receiv^d from him: Therefore this meeting doth Still continue said Committee to make further inspection into the conduct of the Said **John Potter** as oppertunity may offer and act therein as they in the leadings of Truth may See meet and make report when they may see fitt

9ᵗʰ month
1780

Att a Monthly meeting held in **Dartmouth** the 18ᵗʰ of 9ᵗʰ month 1780 The Representatives **Benjamin Taber** and **Jonathan Willbor** present

Shermans
denial not recvd

The Clerk reports he have not read the denial of **Joshua Shearman Ju^r** as directed last monthly meeting, he is therefore Still continued to perform it and make report next monthly meeting

and **John Williams** reports that **Joshua Shearman Senior** hath been Informed of his denial as ordered

denial against
Smith & Son
read

The Clerk informs that the denial of **Joseph Smith** and **John Smith** hath been read as directed last monthly meeting and was informed of this denial . . . Which is as folloeth

The Testimony
of denial
against Smith
& Son Jon

Whereas **Joseph Smith,** and his son **John,** having long made pro- =fession with us the people called Quaker and been under the care of this meeting; but have so far departed from the principals we profess as to frequant meetings held out of the unity of our Society and Joine in publi^ck Worship with them that are disowned by us the afore said people; also the Said **John Smith** frequantly aloweth such meetings to beheld in his house and friends having bestoed much Labour in Love to reclame them from such practices that are so contrary to the principels we profess: But our Labour not having the desired effect to friends Satisfaction and they continue to Justify themselves therein; Therefore for the maintaing the princi =pals we profess are concerned to give forth this Testimony against them the said **Joseph Smith** and **John Smith**, hereby disown[n]ing them from being in unity with us, and from under our care, yet if it be agreeable to Divine goodness, that they may be resored to the way of Truth and find mercy, which is our sincer desire

Given forth and Signed ∧in and on behalf of our monthly meeting
held in **Dartmouth** the 21st of 8th month 1780 by **William Anthony Ju** Clerk

Testimony against Tabor & family not recd
The Clerk reports he hath not ∧read the Testimony of denial against **William Tabor** his wife and their children, **Edward** and **Patience** he is desired
to accomplish it and make report next monthly meeting
and the Committee who had the care thereof are desired to Inform them
of their denial and make report next monthly meeting

Certificates for Ba'ke[r] and Slocum not accomplished
The friends appointed to draw a Certificate for **David Barker** and
and also to Joine the Women in drawing a Certificate for **Martha Slocum** and ∧her Children report that neither of them are accomplished
they are therefore continued in said Service and make report
next monthly meeting

E S case refer'd
The Friends appointed to Treat with **Elishib Smith** not havi[ng]
accomplished the Same they are desired to fulfil Said Service and to
report next monthly meeting

a few lines for J Smith Sign,d
John Smith son of **Peleg** deseased having removed to **East Hoosuck**
a few Lines directed to that meeting, Setting forth his having a birth
right in the Society was Signed in this meeting by the Crerk [Clerk]

Treasurer not paid B Howland
The Treasurer reports he hath not paid **Benjamin Howland** 3d for
keeping the meeting house as ordered; he is now ordered to pay the said
Benjamin six dollars and two thirds for keeping house 8 months last part
and make report next monthly meeting

Complaint against A Taber
The Overseers Inform that **Ameziah Taber** (son of **William**) is in the
Practice of attending meetings held out of the Unity of our Society and hath
been Laboured with by said overseers and he reather Justifies himself therein
Therefore we do appoint **John Williams** and **Stephen Buffinton** to Treat
with him the Said **Ameziah**, and if they do not find Satisfaction they are
to draft a Testimony of his denial and inform him thereof, and bring
said Testimony to next monthly meeting

Hump∧hry Shearmans proposal of marriage
Humphry Shearman and **Marcy Lapham** having declared th[e]ir
Intentions of taking Each other in marriag, they are desired to wait till next
monthly meeting for their answer and our friends **Benjᵃmin Smith** 2d and
William Sanford are appointed to Enquire into the young mans Clearness in
Respect to marriag and they to make report to next monthly meeting

Friends appointed to Sell Wood
We appoint our friends **James Tucker, Nicholas Lapham** and **Philip Maccomber** to Joine the overseers of the poor, and Endeavor to Sell wood of
of the meetings ∧Land to pay the Expence of Supporting our poor, if they think proper
when they Inspect the wood and to cut as much as they shall think best for
the meeting, and no more; and make report to this meeting from time to
to time when it is accomplished, with account of the Wood so Cutt

A Comm^tee apointed to Joine the overseers in Visiting Friends

Whereas sometime past this meeting did appoint a Committee of Friends to Joine the overseers in Visiting and Stiring up the neglect member thereof and now Some of Said friends with Some others having accomplis[hed] Said Service; have now made report of doings therein which is well accep[t]ed and ordered to be recorded, which is as followeth

The report of Said Visiting Friend

Whereas some time past Some Friends were appointed to assist the overseers in Treating with Some of our Neglegent members, and some thus appointed with Some other friends having had a concern on their minds to Joine and make General Visit to friends families throug our monthly meeting, for the revival of our antient Discipline in Stirring up the Careless Lukwarm Indolent members to Love and good works: and having Drawings in our minds, not only to the disobedient but those that are Setting their faces Zionwards, in order to encourage and Strengthen one another with desires that the wast places may yet be rebuilt, and by being willing to be Obedient our weak minds ^were Strengthned from time to time Through the many deep Exercies of mind in so weighty a Service and find Peace and Satisfaction therein: which is a Sufficient Reward

And now after having accomplished said Visit which in General was well accepted: yet not without some Exceptions in some particular families

State of Friends

It Remains to give so^me account of the State of Friends in our meeting We Trust there are some that are Labouring to do their days work in the Truth Seems to be Low so that it might be truly said as formerly by whom shall Jacob, or the true Seed arise, which is in our ^[appearing?] but small and much pressed down with the many things that are hurtful, Especially by the Love of money Pride and forgetfulness of God

Dated 18th of 9th month 1780

Freborn Rider   Thomas Hicks
Susanna Smith   Abiel Gifford
Deborah Hicks

Gifford dis-[missed] from be=[ing] overseer

Abiel Gifford Informed the preparitive meeting also this meeting that he desired to be dismest from the place of an overseer ^and friends having weightily considered thereof do dismiss him accor[d]ing to his request, his Service having been well accepted

Collected in pape[r] money – – 3 – – s8 – – 0
Collected in Silver money – – 1 – – 4 – – 7 ½

Adjourn This meeting adjourns to the 27th Ins[t]ant after the meeting of Worship

Mett Mett by adjournment the 27th of the 9th month 1780

The Representatives being called both present

Cornel Sent paper to this [meeting] Which [re]ferred to

Zebulon Cornel having given a paper to this meeting his falling into the Sin of Fornication, with all other of his misconduct and request to be restored under Friends care again and he is removed into the compass of **East Hoosuck**

[the?] Monthly [m]eeting at [E Hoosuk] or [Sara]toga and **Saratoga** monthly meeting and cannot convenienly be treated by us here, this meeting doth appoint our friends **Samuel Smith** and **William Anthony Ju**^{r} to Write to that meeting requesting them in our behalf to Endeavor to discover the Sincerity of him the said **Zebulon Cornel** and Inform us thereof

[?] Hussey a[n]d Woods Visit **Jonathan Hussey** and **Isaac Wood** attended this meeting and each produced a few lines from the meeting at **East Hoosuck** and **Saratoga** setting forth their concurrance with said friends Visits moring[?] us which said lines were Satisfactory and their Visit well accepted

Allens request   **John Allen** (Son of **Jonathan**) hath given in a paper to this meeting requesting to be taken under friends care therefore our friends **William Mosher** and **Abiel Gifford** are appointed to take an oppertunity of Sollid conferrece with the perticioner in order to discover the motive of his request and make report thereof next monthly meeting

[Ap]point Overseer [seer]s refered An additional Choice of Overseers hath been proposed and referred to next monthly meeting for further Consideration

[Qu]eries answerd [Epistle] signd & [rep]resentatives [appo]inted The Queries were answered and an Epistle Signed in this meeting for the Quarterly meeting and Said answers with said Epistle forwarded to said Quarter^{ly} meeting by our Representatives who are **Thomas Hicks**, **Abiel Gifford**, **Elijah Gifford** and **Caleb Russell** and they to make report next monthly meeting

Friends appoint [ted] to Collect the [?] Testi [?]of pub [?] Friends [?] in order [?] who [?]sury   As there have been Several Publick friends latly rem^{o}ved by death from among us, and our discipline requiring that Some Testimony or particular account of such friends be transmitted to the Quarterly and yearly meeting; this meeting doth appoint our Friends **Thomas Hicks, Caleb Russell, William Mosher** and **Abiel Gifford**, to collect the necessary particurlyrs in order; and to d^{r}awft such Testimony or Testimonies, if they ~~think~~ shall think it necessary and make report when they have accomplished the same they to Joine herein with **Samuel Smith** who was formerly appointed for that Service with **Humphry Smith** but the said **Humphry** being dece^{a}ssed the above friends are appointed in his Stead[29]

[10th] month 1780 Att a Monthly meeting held in **Dartmouth** the 16th of 10th month 1780 The Representatives being **Caleb Russell** and **Abiel Gifford** both present

[Choo]sing overseers [cont]inued   The matter of an additional ch^{o}ice of overseers being considered and Several nominated, but said matter is Still continued to next monthly meeting

report of Testi [moni]es of denials   The Clerk reports he hath Read the Testimonies of denials of **Joshua Shearman Ju**^{r} **William Taber** and his Wife and their Son **Edward** and Daughter **Patience** agreeable to appointment, but they not being informed

29. These testimonies or memorials, as they later were called, were often useful sources of biographical information. Unfortunately, Dartmouth Friends did not record them in the minutes. See Erica Canela and Robynne Rogers Healey, "'Our Dear Friend Has Departed This Life': Memorial Testimony Writing in the Long Eighteenth Century," in *Quakerism in the Atlantic World, 1690–1830*, ed. by Robynne Rogers Healey (University Park: Pennsylvania State University Press, 2021), 23–43.

of their denials as we hear off, therefore **Samuel Smith** is desired
to Inform them the Said **Taber**s of their denials and make report next
monthly meeting - Their Said denials are as Followeth

Testimony of Against Sherman Ju^r

Whereas **Joshua Shearman** (Son of **Joshua**) hath had his Education
among Friends, but hath so far departed from the principels profess
of Truth and Unity of Friends as frequently attend meetings held

Out of Unity of our Society neglecting the attendence of our meetings
of Worship and discipline and he not inclining to condemn the same
after ~~of~~ our Labours of Love ∧with him therein - Therefore for the clearing of Truth
and Friends, we are concerned to give forth this as a Testimony
against him the Said **Joshua Shearman Ju**^r as not being a member of our
Society, yet desireing he may be favoured with a Sight of his errors and
out going, and that he may find a return to the way of Truth

Given forth and Signed ∧in and on behalf of our monthly meeting
of Friends held in **Dartmouth** the 21st of 8th month 1780

By **William Anthony Ju**^r Clerk

Testimony against W Taber his Wife Mary and Son & daughter

Whreas **William Taber** and his wife **Mary Taber**, and **Edward Taber**
thir Son, and **Patience Taber** their daughter having all maid profession
with us the people called Quakers and been under the care of this meeting
But hath so far departed from the principles we profess, so as to frequent
meetings held out of the Unity of our Society and Joine in publick Worship
with them who are disowned by us the people afore said, and the said
Patience also app^earing disagreeable in some of her dress and friends having
Laboured much in love to reclame them from such practices but our labour
not having its desired effect to friends Satisfaction, and they continue to Justify
themselves therein: therefore for the maintaining the principles we profess we
are concerned to give this forth as a Testimony against them the said **William
Taber** and **Mary** his wife, and **Edward Taber** and **Patience Taber** their Children
hereby disowning them from being in unity with us and from under the care of
this meeting: yet if it be agreeable to divine goodness, that they may be restored
to the way of Truth and find mercy is our Sincear desires

Given forth and Signed in and on behalf of our monthly meeting
held in **Dartmout[h]** the 21st day of the 8th month 1780

By **William Anthony Ju**^r Clerk

Susanna Smith Clerk

D Barkers Certificate Refered

The friends appointed to draw a Certificate for **David Barker** not finding
things clear, are s[t]ill continued in said service and to make report when
it is fulfilled

E Smith Disowned

The friends appointed to Treat with **Elisabeth Smith** report they have
performed their appointment but that he did not give them any satisfaction

in regard to his misconduct: Therefore they have drafted a Testimony against him; which after being read and considered was Signed in this meeting by the Clerk who is directed to read it in the Usual ˄maner and make report next monthly meeting

The case of A Taber Continued — The friends appointed to Treat with **Amaziah Taber** (Son of **William**) not having accomplisht the same, they are still continued in said service and to make report next monthly meeting

B Howland not paid — The Treasurer reports he hath not paid **Benjamin Howland 3ᵈ** as ordered there not being a sufficiency in stock he is nevertheless ordered to pay the same when he is supplied with money by this meeting and to make report

The case of J Allen refer,d — The Friends appointed to discover the motive of the request of **John Allen** desires that matter refer,d to next monthly meeting which is referred under their case they are then to make report

report of the Repre sentatives — The Representative to the last Quarterly meeting report that they all attended and produced an Epistle from that meeting which was read in this meeting and well accepted

Complaint against C Briggs — The Overseers Inform by the way of the preparative meeting that **Caleb Brigg** has married out of the unity of friends after being precaution by said overseers; therefore the said **David Briggs** ʰᵉʳᵉᵒᶠ is disowed as a member of our Societ and from under our care and **Jonathan Willber [Wilbur]** is appointed to Inform him of the same and report thereof next monthly meeting

I Kelly J Sowl S Barton S Hamond Visited this meeting — Our Friends **Isaac Kelley** from **East Hoosuck: James Sowle Solomon Barton** and **Samuel Hammond** from **Ninepartners** hath attended this meeting with Certificates from the respective monthly meetings they [?]

Which were read in this meeting to Satisfaction, and their Visitt well accepted all which were Indorsed with a few lines and Signed by the Clerke

[?]te of H [Shear]man Clear [?] marriage — The Friends appointed to inquire into clearness of **Humphry Shearman** Report they find nothing materal to hinder his proceeding in marriage

answer to Sherman — **Humphry Shearman** and **Mercy Lapham** appeared for their answer, which was that they might proceed to take Each other in marriage in some convenient time before next monthly meeting adviseing with the friends that this meet-=ing shall appoint to oversee the same who are **William Sanford** and Ben==jamin Smith 2ᵈ and they to make report next monthly meeting

Smith re-[queste]d his [Cer]tificate — **Hezekiah Smith** returned a Certificate which was granted him by this meeting some months past; it being Endorsed at the month meeting of **Ninepartners**

[Certi]ficate for Slocum & [Chi]ldren — A Removal Certificate for **Martha Slocum** and several of her Children whose names are **Benjamin, Martha, John, Pardon, William, Sarah, Thomas, Christopher Elizabeth** and **Mary**; was Signed in this meeting directed to the monthly meeting of **Rhode Island**

Smith disown — A Testimony of denial against **Mary Smith** daughter of **Jonathan Smith** was

Signed in this meeting and the Clerk is directed to read the Same publickly at the close of the meeting of Worship before next monthly meeting and then to make report of the same

Russell
[dis]owned

The Women friends Inform they have denied **Mehetable Russell**, now **Akin** Daughter of **Jacob Russell** deceased which this meeting concurs with

[Free]born Rider
[receiv]es a Certi-
ficate the Clerk
[desi]r,d to
[give] a coppy
to miniut

Our Friend **Freeborn Rider** Informs us that she has a desire to attend the Quarterly meeting next to be held at the **Long Plain** for **Sandwich** and at the old meeting house at **Cushnet** and desired our Certificate; these may inform that she is a Friend in Unity and her Publick Testimony well accepted And the Clerk is desired to give her a Coppy of this minuit

Mosher to
[?] a coppy of
miniut

Our friend **William Mosher** hath Informed this meeting of his Intention to goe to the **Ninepartners** upon business, and hath thought of attending the Quarterly meeting at **Oblong** which this meeting approves, he being a Friend in Unity, and a member of the Select meeting; and the Clerk is directed to give him a Coppy of this minuit to Inform Friends thereof

[E.] Allen & T
Allen to have
[c]oppy of this
[m]iniut

Our friends **Ebenezer Allen** and **Thomas Allen** informes this meting that they intend to go to Visit their friends and Relatives at the **Ninepartners** And at **East Hoosuck** and **Saratoga**; which this meeting approves and the Clerk is desired to give them a Coppy hereof

[Clerk] to give
a [co]ppy of this
[min]uit to
Greenes

Our Friend **Caleb Greene** informs this meeting of his Intention to go to the **Oblong** and **Ninepartners** and hath thoughts of attending the Quarterly meeting at **Oblong** on business which this meeting approves, he being in Unity and a member of this meeting and the Clerk is directed to give him a coppy hereof

Collected in Silver money – –   1$^£$ – –   5^s – – 1^d
Collected in paper money – – 10 – – 10 – – 0

[11th] month
1780

Att a Monthly meeting held in **Dartmouth** the 20th of 11th month 1780
The representatives are **Jonathan Willbor** and **Seth Huddleston** Present

[Chu]sing
overseers
[def]ered

The matter of Chusing Overseers having again been under consideration and Same is Suspended untill the expiration of the time of these that now Stand as Overseers

Tabor his
[wi]fe &
Children
[inf]orm of their
[denial]

Samuel Smith informs he hath Informed ~~Edward~~ ∧William **Tabor**, his wife **Mary** and **Edward Taber** and **Patience Taber** their Son and daughter of their Denial

denial read

The Clerk reports he hath read the Testamony of denial against **Eliashib Smith** according to appointment which is as followeth

[Te]stimony a
[gai]nst
Smith

Whereas **Eliashib Smith** Son of **Joseph Smith** having made Profession with us the People called Quakers; But hath so far departed from the principles we make Profession of as to attend Sepperat meetings that are held out of the Unity of our Society, and Join in publick Worship with them ∧that have been

Disowned by us and Friends having Laboured with him in Love to Show
him his misconduct therein: but their labour of Love not having the desired
Effect, Friends are concerned to give this forth as a publick Testimony
against him the Said **Eliashib Smith**, hereby disowning him ~~the~~ from being
a member of our Society and from under the care of this meeting; yet we
Sincearly desire if it be consistent with divine wisdom that he may be
favoured with a sense of his misconduct and find mercy

  Given forth by friends at their monthly meeting held in **Dartmout[h]**
  the 16th of the 10th month 1780 and Signed in and by order of said meeting

        By **William Anthony Ju**r Clerk

*A Taber
Disowned*
  The friends appointed to Treat with **Amaziah Taber** report they
have fulfilled the Same, but that he did not give them any Satisfaction
therein but Justified his practice; therefore drafted and brought a Testimony
of denial against him, and have Informed him thereof: which was Signed
by the Clerk who is directed to read it publickly at the Close of a first
day meeting for Worship and report the Same to next monthly meeting

*The case of
J Allen
Continu-d*
  The friends appointed to confer with **John Allen** on his request have made
a Satisfactory report, nevertheless said matter is still continued under their
care untill next monthly meeting and then they to make report
The Friends appointed attend

*report of
H Shermans
marriage*
  The Marriage of **Humpry Shearman** and **Mercy Lapham** report they
attended the same and that it was accomplisht in a becoming manner

*C Brigg in
form,d of
his denial*
  Jonathan Willbor reports he hath Informed **Caleb Briggs** of his denial
according to appointment

*M Smith de
nial read*
  The Clerk reports he hath Read the Testimony of denial of **Mary
Smith** daughter of **Jonathan Smith** as appointed

*J Potters
request*
  Joshua Potter hath given in a paper to this meeting Requesting for
himself and several young children Namly **Esther**, **Zilpha**, **Gardner
Phebe Patience** and **Apphia** to be taken under the care of Friends
Therefore this meeting doth appoint **William Mosher Thomas Hicks** and
Thomas Mott: to Joine the women friends, and to take an oppertunity
of a Solled conference with him in order to discover the motive of
his request, also to Inspect the Circumstances and make report next
monthly meeting

*Benj Hath=
way Ju
request*
  And **Benjamin Hathaway Ju**r making the like request and **Seth Russell
Stephen Buffinton** and **James Davis** appointed for the same purposes
as above and they to make report to next monthly meeting

*G Howland
request
to be dism
ist overseer*
  Gideon Howland request to be dismissed from Standing in the plan
of Overseer of the poor which is granted and he dismissed accordingly

G. Howland
bound a
Jorney
Clerk to give
Coppy of min
nuit

Gideon Howland Informs this meeting of his Intention to go to **East Hoosuck** and **Ninepartners**, to do some business and to see his friends which this meeting approves; he being a member of our Society and under the care of this meeting and the Clerk is directed to give him a Coppy of this minuit

Friends ap
-pointed to
take in Sup
scrptions
Griffiths books

Proposals for Reprinting of **John Griffiths** Journals &c was Received from our meeting for Sufferings, Therefore **William Anthony Ju͟r** **Abiel Gifford**, and **John Williams** are appointed to take in Sub-=scriptions for said Journals and make report when they have accomplished the Same[30]

R Barker
proposal of
marriage

Robert Barker and **Ruth Tucker** declared their Intentions of Taking Each other in marriage, and were desired to wait till next monthly meeting for their answer and **Bannabus Mosher** and **John Devol** are appointed to Enquire into the young mans clearness and make report next monthly meeting

Bills given
in

The Several following accounts were given in to this meeting which were examind and allowed [in?] To **Thomas Wilcox** – – – – – – – $3^£ – 15^s – 6^d$

Seth Russell to the glaiser for mend glass	$1 – 13 – 3$
To **Philip Macomber** for Hay – –	$2 – 6 – 6$
To **William Barker** – – – – – – –	$2 – 15 – 10$

All in Lawful hard money – –

And the Treasurer is Ordered to pay the Same he is Supplied with money and make report to this meeting

[Repo]rt and
[requ]est of
[Bedf]ord
meet

The Friends that were appointed to have the oversight of the meeing at **Bedford**, Report that it hath been kept up in a good degree Orderly and s[t]ill request same continued as usual as here͟ofore; which is granted and the same to continue untill some Inconvendiencey attend the same and our friends **Caleb Russell, Benjamin Taber John Williams William Mosher Thomas Hicks Benjamin Smith 2ᵈ Abiel Gifford** and **William Anthony Ju͟r** are appointed to Visit Said meeting when Convenency will slow and to make report to this meeting as frequently as they may see occation

Collected in Silver money – – – $1^£ – 6^s – 8d$
Collected in paper money – – – $1 – 10 – 0$

[12ᵗʰ] month
1780

Att a Monthly meeting held in **Dartmouth** the 18ᵗʰ of 12ᵗʰ month 1780

The Representatives are **Elijah Gifford** and **Joseph Tucker Ju͟r** both present

Tabers dnial
[re]ad

The Clerk reports he hath read the Testimony of denial of **Amaziah Taber**, persuant to appointment Which is as followeth

[Testi]mony
agains͟ Tabor

Whereas **Ammeziah Taber** (son of **William**) having made Profession with us the people called Quakers but hath found in the practice of

30. See note 3 above for the 1779 edition of this journal. It was reprinted in Philadelphia in 1780.

freequenting and Joining with Sepperate meeting hel.ᵈ out of the Unity of our
Societ and we having discharged ourselves in Labours of Love to reclaim him
the Said **Ammeziah** but he still continues to Justify the practice; Therefore
for the clearing of Truth, we give this forth as a Testimony against him
hereby disowning him from being one in Unity with us. Nevertheless it is
our desire that he may come to a sence of his outgoing and return to the
way of Truth

    Given forth at our monthly meeting held in **Dartmouth** the 20ᵗʰ of 11ᵗʰ month 1780
    Signed in and by order of said meeting By **William Anthony Juʳ** Clerk

Allen receiv
[ed un]der our
case

    The Comittee appointed in the case of **John Allen**s Request make the
Like report as at the Last monthly meeting which is Satisfactory Therefore he
the Said **John Allen** is Received under our Care

case of
Potter refer,d

    The Friends appointed in the case of **Joshua Potters** Request report that
they have had a Conference with him in his family and received a degree
of Satisfaction, and the matter is refered to next monthly meeting and Said
friends still continued in said service and to make report next monthly
meeting

case of
Hathaway
[re]fered

    And likewise the Committee appointed in the like case with **Benjamin
Hathway Juʳ** Report that he gave them a good degree of Satisfaction, which
matter is also referred to next monthly meeting and the same friends Conti=
=nued in said service, and then they to make report

[repo]rt of
R Barker
[clear]ness respect
[to m]arriage

    The Friends appointed to inquire into the Clearness of **Robart Barker**
Report they have made inquirry ᴧᵗʰᵉʳᵉⁱⁿ, and find nothing Sufficient to hinder
his proseeding in marriage, agreeable to his proposal

[Comp]laint
against
Ricketson &
Howland

    The Overseers Informed by way of the Preparitive meeting that **John Barker
Benjamin Ricketson** and **William Howland** have Joyned with a considerable
Large Company of young people, and went together under pretence of roast=
=ing and eating of Quawhoggs, and after providing and pertaking of a
considerable Entertainment at the Shore, both of provision and Spiritous
Lickquors, Several of them went to a house and there took very undue
Liberty Even to musick and Dancing: And said Overseers having
Treated with them on that account, but they not giving them Satisfaction
therefore this meeting doth appoint our friends **William Anthony Juʳ
Thomas Hicks** and **Joseph Gifford** to treat farther with them therein and
make report next monthly meeting

[Re]port of
money
[colle]cted for
[supp]ly meet

    The Friends appointed to Collect monᶜy by way of Subscription to Sup-
ply the yearly meeting Treasury make report that they have fulfilled their
appointments and have Collected the Sum of 10ᵉ - 7ˢ - 3 ½ᵈ LM and
Delivered. to this meetings Treasury for the use above said

Answer to R Barkers proposal of marriage

Robart Barker and **Ruth Tucker** appeared for their answer in regard to their proceeding in marriage; Which was, that they might proceed to take Eac[h] other in marriage, in some convenient time before next monthly meeting a[d]= =vising with the friends this meeting Shall appoint to see their said marria[ge] orderly accomplished, who are our friends **Barnabus Mosher** and **John Devol**; and they to make report next monthly meeting

E Smith Disown,d

The Women Friends inform they have disowned **Elisabet Smith** wife of **Joseph Smith**, which this meeting concurs with and the Clerk hath signed a Testimony of denyal against her

Collected in hand money 1ᶠ – 18ˢ – 3½ᵈ

In Paper – – – –   3 – 6 – 00

adjournd   This Meeting Adjourns to the 27ᵗʰ Instant after the meeting of Worship

meet   Mett By adjournment the 27ᵗʰ of the 12ᵗʰ month 1780

The Representatives being called are both Present

Queries answer,d

The Queries were read and answers prepar,d in this meeting and an Epist[le] Signed by the Clerkes which were ordered forward to the Quarterly meeting by

Representa^tives appointed   our Representatives, who are **Abiel Gifford William Anthony Juʳ Caleb Green John William**, and they to Report to the next monthly meeting

Subscripti ons for Schools

Our friends **Samuel Smith, Caleb Green, Jonathan Willbor** and [?] **William Mosher** are appointed to procure and take in Subscriptions for Schools agr[ee?] to a direction from the meeting for Sufferings of the ninth month Last three[?] said friends to make report when ready

B Rider condemnd his reflect =ing Speach

Benjamin Rider appear,d in this meeting and Virblely [verbally] condemned his oppo[?] at the sitting of this meeting and dropt some Expressions by way of reflections on **Benjamin Gifford** which gave friends some uneasiness, But he appearing [as?] above said and condemning the same, friends conclus to accept of his ackn[ow]= =ledgment for Satisfaction

Testimony of E Gidley & her manu scrip Sent up to 2 m

A Copy of a manuscrip Wrote by our beloved Friend **Elisabeth Gidley** d[?] withe Testimony that this meeting formerly gave concerning her was read in this meeting, and Sent up to the Quarterly meeting by our Representatives[31]

1ˢᵗ month 1781

At a Monthly meeting held in **Dartmouth** the 15ᵗʰ of the 1ˢᵗ month 1781

The representatives ^ᵃʳᵉ **John Devol** and **Joseph Tucker Juʳ** Present

The case of J Potter refered

The friends appointed to confer with **Joshua Potter** and his young Children being called upon, report nothing different from that of Last monthly meeting the matter is therefore referred to next monthly meeting under the same care as before and Said friends then to report

B. Hathway Received in unity

Likewise the friends appointed in the Like case with **Benjamin Hathway Ju** make a Satisfactory report, therefore this meeting doth receive him the said **Benjamon Hathway** under our care

31. Presumably Dartmouth Friends thought Elizabeth Gidley's manuscript worthy of publication, but there is no record of it being printed.

Report of
R Barkers
marriage
　　The Friends appointed to oversee the Marriage of **Robert Barker** and **Ru[th]
Tucker** report that they attended the same: and saw nothing but that it was
accomplished orderly

Overseers
appointed
　　Our Friends **Benjamin Smith 2ᵈ**, **Caleb Russell**, **Caleb Green**, **Elijah Giffo[rd]**
Seth Huddlestone and **Joseph Barker**, are appointed Overseers for the year
Ensuing, or till others are chosen, Who are desired diligently to attend to the
Leadings of Truth, therein Endeavour to See that the Testimony thereof be
kept to in the several members thereof according to the discipline of the Church

overseer of
the poor
appointed
　　Our Friends **John Devol, Jonathan Willbor, Philip Maccomber,**
Thomas Mott, Nicholas Lapham, Seth Russell and **Abraham**
Howland, are appointed Overseers of the Poor for the year Ensuing

Sissons
[cer]tificate
　　A Certificate for **Nathaniel Sisson** was produced and read in this Meeting
from the monthly meeting at the **Nine Partners** Seting forth his Clearness respectin[g]
marriage; He hath also produced his mothers Consent for him to proceed in marri-
=age with **Graces Gifford** – – Therefore

Sissons
[prop]osal of
[Ma]rriage
　　Nathaniel Sisson and **Grace Gifford** declared their Intentions of taking Each
other in marriage: and were desired to wait till next monthly meeting for their answer
　　　　　　　　　This meeting collected in Silver　7ᶠ – 11ˢ – 10ᵈ
　　　　　　　　　　　　In Paper　30 – 2 – 00

adjourn　This Meeting adjourns to the 24ᵗʰ instant after the meeting for Worship

mett　Met By adjournment the 24ᵗʰ of the first month 1781
　　The Representatives being called **Joseph Tucker Juʳ** Present **John Devol** not
Present by reason of indisposition of body

[mo]ney paid
to [year]ly
meeting
　　The Representatives from the Quarterly meeting report that the money for the
yearly meetings Treasury was forwarded to the yearly meetings Treasury and
a Receipt produced for the Same

Gifford & Wife
[gave] in a paper
　　Nathaniel Gifford and Wife gave in a paper to the Preparitive meeting Condem-
=ning their falling into the Sin of Fornication, but said paper being mislaid it is
Refered to next monthly meeting

case of
[WH] BR TB
[re]fered
　　The friends appointed to Treat with **William Howland, John Barker** and
Benjamin Ricketson, Request that matter refered to next monthly meeting which
is accordingly

[re]port from
[Qua]rterly
[mee]ting
　　The Representative to the Quarterly meeting report that they all attended, and
have produced an Epistle from said Quarterly meeting which was read in this meet=
=ing to good satisfaction

[C]ertificate
B Shepherd
[req]uested
　　John Shepherd having requested (by way of the Preparitive meeting)
a removal Certificate to **Sandwich** monthly meeting, for his Son **Barnabus**
Shepherd, therefore our friends **William Barker** and **Thomas Russell** are
appointed to Enquire into the young mans conduct, and Clearness in respect
to marriage: and if they find things clear to draw a Certificate and bring
to next monthly meeting

[Jo]nas Slocum [acu]sed of [f]ornication

One of the Overseers Inform (with another Friend) that **Jonas Slocum** hath fallen into the Sin of Fornication, as charged upon him by **Elisabeth Akin**: Therefore, our friends **William Anthony Juʳ Samuel Smith** and **Stephen Buffinton** are appointed to Treat with said **Jonas Slocum** on that matter and make report to next monthly meeting

[A]ltering the [Qua]rterly [mee]ting referd [to] this meet [ing]

Proposals for altering or dividing the Quarterly meeting was Read and Signed in this meeting by the Clerk, in order for a concurrence of the other – – Monthly meetings therein

[cer]tificate D Barker [and] sons to be [?] till af- [-fairs?] settled

A Removal Certificate for **David Barker** and Three Sons Namely **Edward David** and **James**, directed to the **Nine Partners** monthly meeting, was signed in this meeting by the Clerk: and as there are some of his outward affares not fully Settled: the Committee is ordered to keep the same, and not deliver it until his said affairs are settled to satisfaction

---

[2ⁿᵈ] month 1781

At a Monthly Meeting held in **Dartmouth** the 19ᵗʰ of 2 month 1781
The Representatives are **Abiel Gifford** and **Barnabus Mosher** – – Present

[Joshu]a Porter [&] Children [re]ceived [u]nder Friend [car]e

The Friends appointed to consider and confer with **Joshua Potter** and his young Children, on their request to come under friends care: Report that they had an oppertunity of Sollid conference with them, to Satisfaction Therefore, the said **Joshua Potter** and children, namly **Esther, Zilphah Gardner, Phebe, Patience and Apphia** are received under our Care

Potter and [?] receiv,d

The Women Friends Inform they have received **Mary Potter** and **Rhoda Potter** under their Care which this meeting concurs with

[ans]wer to N [Siss]ons prosal [?] marriage

Nathaniel Sisson and **Grace Gifford** appeared for thei answer in regard to proceeding in marriage: Which was, that they might proceed to take Each other in marriage, in Some convenient time before next monthly meeting adviseing with the Friends this meeting Shall appoint

To See Said Marriage orderly accomplished; who are **William Moshe[r]** and **Abiel Gifford** and they to make report next monthly meeting

Friends appointed in the case of N Gifford & wife

Nathaniel Gifford and his Wife,s Paper being produced, and Read in this meeting - therefore, Our Friends **Abiel Gifford** and **William Anthony Juʳ** are appointed to Joyne the Women friends to take an oppertunit of Sollid Conference with them the Said **Nathaniel** and wife in order to discover their Sencerity and Sorrow; and make report next monthly meeting

Certificate fr B Shep= =herd

A Removal Certificate for **Barnabus Shepherd** directed to the monthly mee[ting] of **Sandwich** setting forth his night of membership, and clearness of marriage Entanglements – Were Signed in this meeting

The Case of J Slocum refered

The matter respecting **Jonas Slocum** is refered to next monthly meeting under the care of those friends who were appointed to treat with him they having made Some progress and desires it refer,d which is accordingly refered and they then to make report

Certificate for H B wife of R Bennet

A Certificate was Signed in this meeting directed ^to the monthly meeting Rhod Island in behalf of **Hannah Bennet** Wife of **Robart Bennet** Setting forth her right of membership and Recommending her to the care of that meeting

The case of W H: JB. B R. referd

The Committee having the care of that matter Respecting **William Howlan[d]** **John Barker** and **Benjamin Ricketson** desires it refer,d which is referd under their care, and they to make report next monthly meeting

D Barkers Certificate Deliver,d

The Committee which had the care of **David Barkers** Removal Certificate Report that his afaires were Settled to Satisfaction and the said Certificate deliver,d to him – –

D Wood wife of J W disown,d

The Women Friends Inform that they have denyed **Deborah Wood** wife of **Stephen Wood** which this meeting concurs with

Phebe Sis= =sons request

Phebe Sisson having Requested for her Children to be taken under the care of this meeting, Therefore our Friends **William Mosher** and **Seth Huddlestone** are appointed to Joyn the Women friends in their care and Enquiery in that matter and make report next monthly meeting

Letter in behalf of D Wilbor

This Meeting Received a Letter from the monthly meeting of **Saratoga** Dated 11th of 1st month 1781 Informing that **Deborah Willbor** hath married Out of the Order of friends

W. Gifford desires a Certificate

William Gifford desires a Certificate to the Monthly meeting of **Accokset** Setting forth his Right of membership and clearness respecting marriage Therefore this meeting doth appoint our friends **Joseph Tucker Jur** and **William Wood** to inquire into the young mans Clearness and if they find things Clear to draw a Certificate and bring with them next monthly meeting

J Russell C Barker J Howland G Smith gave in pa pers Conde mning their misconduct

Jonathan Russell, Caleb Barker, Joseph Howland 2d and George Smith 2d Having given in paper Condemning their misconduct in going to an Entertainment Some time past and taking undue Liberty thereat; Therefore our Friends **Thomas Hicks, Joseph Gifford, William Anthony Jur Stephen Buffinton Jonathan Willbor** and **Seth Huddleston**, are appointed to take an oppertunity of Solled Conference with these young men to discover their Sincerity and make report next monthly meeting

Complaint against W[N] Taber

This Meeting is inform,d by the way of Preparitive meeting that **Nicholas Taber** is in the practice of freequenting and Joyning with meetings held out of the Unity of our Society, and after being Laboured with: Declines to Condemn it to friends Satisfaction: Therefore our friends **Benjam[in] Taber Jur** and **Joseph Gifford** are appointed to treat with said **Nicholas** and if he doth not give them Satisfaction, to draw a paper of denial and bring to next monthly meeting

H Smiths Bill

Henry Smith gave in a bill to this meeting for Hay and Carting to the amount of 3£ -- 12s - 0d Which the Treasurer is ordered to pay

Collected in Silver money – 5$^£$ – 6^s – 11^d

Collected in paper money – 8 – 16 – 0

[3rd] month *1781*	At a Monthly Meeting held in **Dartmouth** the 19th of 3rd month 1781 The Representives are **Benjamin Smith 2^d** and **Chilon Wood** . Present
[repo]rt of [Sis]sons *Marriage*	The Friends appointed to see the marriage of **Nathaniel Sisson** and **Grace Gifford** accomplished, report that they attended said marriag and did not see but that it was orderly Consumated
[Ru]th Sowl & *daughters* [r]eceived under [our] care	This Meeting is inform,d by the Women friends that they have ‸received **Ruth** **Sowl** wife of **Joseph Sowl** with her Daughters whose names are **Susanna** **Mary** and **Thankful** which this meeting concurs with
[Dav]id Brooks [Ru]th Coffins *[visi]t*	Our Esteemed Friends **David Brooks** and **Seth Coffin** attended this meeting Producing Certificates, Dated 2nd of 10th month 1780 at **Deep River** **Gilford County North Cor^{r}olina**; which was Read in this meeting with Satis= =faction, and their Visit and Labours of Love, acceptable, Comfortable and Edifying[32]
[John] Formoan [atte]nded this [mee]ting	Our Esteemed Friend **John Forman** also attended this meeting and produce^d a Certificate, Dated at the Monthly meeting at **Gwyneed [Gwynedd]** in the Cou^{n}ty of **Philidelphia** in **Pensylvania** the 30th of 1st month 1781 which was read in this meeting; and his Visit, and Labour of Love, acceptable Comforta^{ble} and Eddifying to us[33]
[Th]omas Scatter [good] also [att]ended this [me]eting	Our ^{esteemed} Friend **Thomas Scattergood** Likwise attended this meeting in Company with our above said friends and his visit and Labour in love were acceptable and Eddifying to us[34]
The case of [N] Gifford & *wife refered*	The Friends apointed to Joine the Women friends in confering with **Nathaniel Gifford** and Wife report that they had an oppertunity with them and that they gave them a degree of Satisfaction, but request the matter may be continued another month which accoringly refered under the same friends as before, together with **Jonathan Willbor** who is added to them and they to make report to next monthly meeting
[The] case of [Sl]ocum refer^d	The friends appointed to treat with **Jonas Slocum** desires it continued another month, which is accordingly and they to make report to next monthly meeting
[Ce]rtificate for [W]illiam *Gifford*	A Certificate was Signed in this meeting for **William Gifford** directed to the Monthly meeting of **Accoakset** Setting forth his right of membership and clearness respecting marriage

32. David Brooks (1737–1814) was a native of Virginia. Seth Coffin had moved to North Carolina from Nantucket in 1773. See Hinshaw, ed., *Encyclopedia*, I, 528, 532, 777.

33. John Forman (ca 1712–1793) was a minister from Gwynedd in what is now Montgomery County, Pennsylvania. See James Hazard, comp., "Gwynedd Monthly Meeting," typescript, 2018, p. 66 (Friends Collection, Earlham College, Richmond, Ind.)

34. Thomas Scattergood (1748–1814) was a native of Burlington, New Jersey. He traveled widely among Friends in North America and also visited the British Isles. See *Memoirs of Thomas Scattergood: Late of Philidelphia, a Minister of the Gospel of Christ* (London: Charles Gilpin, 1845).

Taber dis=
[ow]ned

The Friends appointed to Treat With **Nicholas Taber** ∧report that they had an Oppertunity of Sollid conference with him but that he did not ∧seem disposed to give them any Satisfaction they therefore according to appointment produced a Testimony against him which was Signed ∧in this meeting by the Clerk who is desired to read the Same, at a close of a first day meeting of Worship Some time between this and next monthly meeting and make report to next Monthly monthly meeting

Hathway to
[inform] N Taber
[of] denial

And **Benjamin Hathway** is appointed to Inform said **Nicholas** thereof giving him a Coppy of the Testimony if he desires it, and make report to next Monthly meeting

Jonson desires
Certificate

James Jonson desires a Certificate to **Nantucket** Setting forth his Right of membership, therefore our friends **Samuel Smith** and **Abraham Howland** are appointed to draw one and bring with them to the adjournment of this meeting

Hart & A A
[certifi]cate of
[mar]riage

Seth Hart and **Abigail Anthony** declared their Intentions of Taking Each other in Marriage, and they were desired to waite till next monthly meeting for their answer and our friends **William Mosher**, and **Benjamin Rider** are appointed to inquire into the young mans Clearness Respecting marriage and make report to next monthly meeting

Certificate
*for **Freeborn***
Rider

A Certificate in behalf of **Freeborn Rider** directed to Friends within the Verge of **Sandwich** Quarterly meeting was Signed in this Meeting by the Clerk Setting forth her Right of membership and servi[ce] in the Ministry

Certificate
Grace Sisson

A Certificate was Signed in this Meeting by the Clerk in behalf of **Grace Sisson** setting forth ∧her right of membership; directed to the monthly meeting at the **Nine Partners**

Certificate
receiv,d
for H B
wife of WB

The Women friends Inform that they have Received a removal Certificate from **Swanzey** directed to this meeting for **Hannah Bowdish** Wife of **William Bowdish Junor**

Certificate
receivd for
Abigail Devol

Also one from **Sandwich** monthly meeting to this meeting, For **Abigai[l] Devol** wife of **Abner Devol**, Setting forth their Right of membership

Certificate
for D^avid
Brooks and
J Forman

A Few lines by way of Endorsment were Signed by the Clerk on the Certificates of our Esteemed Friends **David B∧rooks** and **John Forman** Expressing their attending this meeting, and that their Visit and Labours in Gosple Love with us was Eddifying and, Satisfactory

also S Coffin Visit

also that of **Seth Coffins** acceptable visit in Company with the other Friends

Certificate
*for **Thomas***
Scattergood

A Few Lines by way of Certificate directed to the monthly meeting of **Philadelphia northan** district was Signed in this meeting by the Clerk expres =sing **Thomas Scattergoods** attending this meeting, and his acceptable Visit and Labour in Gospel Love

　　　　　　　　　　　Collected in Silver money – 1£ – 15s – 2d

adjournd   This meeting is adjourned to the 28th insant, after the meeting of Worship

mett   This Meeting Mett by adjournment the 28th of 3rd month 1781

The Representatives being called both Present

The case of   The Friends appointed to ~~attend~~ Confer with **Jonathan Russell, Caleb Bar[ker]**
J Russell
& company **Joseph Howland 2nd**, and **George Smith 2d**, and other report, that Some of
refered   the Committee had an Oppertunity of conference with the young men and s[aid]
Committee Desires the matter may be refered ~~to~~ another month, which is accord
=ingly refered under their care and they to make report to next monthly mee[ting]

Certificate   A Certificate in behlf of **James Jonson** Setting forth his right of
for J Jonson Membership directed to the Monthly meeting of **Nantucket** was Signed
in this meeting by the Clerk – –

Joseph Wing   **Joseph Wing** having requested to come under the care of ^Friends of this meeting
desires to Therefore this Meeting appoints our Friends **William Anthony Jur** and
come under
care of friends **Elijah Gifford** to take an Oppertunity of Solled conference with Said
Joseph in order to discover the motive of his request, and make
report thereof to next monthly meeting

Prince Potter   **Prince Potter** having requested for himself and children to come und[er]
request for Friend Care this meeting therefore appoints our friends **William**
himself &
children **Mosher, Jonathan Hart**, and **Benjamin Chase** to Joyn with the Women
Friends Care Friend, and take an opertunity of Solid conference, with Said **Prince**,
and family, in order to discover the motive of the request, and they
also to make report thereof to next monthly meeting

Testimonies   Testimonies concerning our Beloved friends who are deceased viz
of deceased **Adam Mott, Paul Russell** and **Susanna Gifford**, all whom were
Friends
Sent to Quar Publick Friends, were read in this meeting and Signed by the Clerk Coppie[s]
terly meet of which were ordered to be maid out and sent to the Quarterly meeting
ing

The follow=   Two of the Friends appointed to confer with **Swanzey** monthly
ing report meeting, respecting **Edward Thurston Jur** his Wife and Children
made of have made the following Report
E Thurston
& Wife   Whereas **Edward Thurston** ^Ju and his wife **Parnal** having a Right
of membership amoung friends at **Dartmouth** Some year past, and hath
~~and~~ Lived within the bounds of **Swanzey** monthly meeting a number
of years and not requesting a Certificate from **Dartmouth:** and of late Said
Monthly meeting taking the matter under Consideration; and by a Committee
from Each Monthly meeting, whose names are hereunto Subscribed, Enquiery
have been made into their Lives and Conversations, and it not only appears
that they neglect the attendance of Meetings, but fall so much Short of living ~~up~~
up to the Principles of Truth in bringing up their Children and many other
respects: that we think it mo^st for the honnour of Truth to disown him
the Said **Edward Thurston** his wife **Pernal**, and their Children from having
any right of membership among us

William Anthony Ju^r	Eber Chase
Robert Slade	Thomas Hicks
Azariah Shove	Benjamin Buffinton

the 5th of 3rd month 1781

report accept,d

Said report is so far Accepted as to appoint our Friends **Thomas Hicks** and **Thomas Russell** to Treat with them for the afore said disorder; and to make report to next Monthly Meeting

Friends appoint [?] revise & [repo]rt the minui^{ts} [a]nd Settle with Treasurer

Our Friends **Thomas Hicks, Caleb Green William Anthony Ju^r** and **Samuel Smith** are appointed to Revise and Correct this Meetings minutes in order that they may be Recorded – as ~~to~~ well as to record those things to be Recorded from the yearly meeting in Book of Discipline: as also to to Settle Accounts with the Treasurer, and make report next monthly meeting

[rep]ort of Bills [p]aid

The Treasurer reports he hath paid the following Bills as Ordered (viz)

To **Henry Smith** for Hay – – – – 3$^£$ – 12^s – 0^d

To **Philip Macomber** for Hay – – 2 – 6 – 6

To **Gideon Howland** for keeping **Alice Smith** – 8 – 8 – 0

[Gi]deon Howland [gave] in ª Bill for [k]eeping A Smith

Gideon Howland gave in a Bill to this meeting for keeping **Alice Smith** 30 weeks and three days amounting to the Sum of – 9$^£$ – 14^s – 6^d

[H]enry Howland [gave] in a bill for [the] same

Also **Henry Howland** gave in a bill for keeping the Same woman 16 weeks at 9^s/ per week amounting to the Sum of Twenty four Dollers

Both which Bills the Treasurer is ordered to pay when he is Supplied with money for the Same

[Quer]ies answer,d

The Queries have been Read and answers thereto prear,d, Read and approv^{ed} with an Epistle to the Quarterly meeting, all of which were Signed and Sent by

[re]presentatives [app]ointed

our Representatives to the Quarterly meeting who are our friends **William Mosher, Thomas Hicks Samuel Smith** and **Thomas Russell**

4th month 1781

At a Monthly Meeting held in **Dartmouth** the 16th of 4 month 1781 The Representatives are **Stephen Buffinton** and **Philip Maccomber** - Present

case of [N] Gifford and [wif]e refered

The Friends appointed to Joyn the Women friends in a Conference with **Nathaniel Gifford** and Wife report, that as they have not had an Oppertunity of Such a conference Since Last monthly meeting, therefore desires that matter refered, which is accordingly refer,d under their care and they to make report next monthly meeting

[T]he case of [J] Slocum Refered

The friends appointed to Treat with **Jonas Slocum** desiers it refer,d another month, which is accordingly refered under the care of the Same Friends, who are to report next monthly meeting

Taber inform,d his denial

Benjamin Hathway reports that he hath informed **Nicholas Taber** of his denial

denial not [?] Read

The Clerk reports, that he hath not read the Testimony of Said **Nicholas**,s denial as ordered, he is desired therefore to read the Same at the close of a first days meeting for Worship, between this and next monthly meeting, and then make report thereof

Report of S
Harts clearness

The Friends appointed to Inquire into **Seth Harts** clearness refer-
=ing marriage report that they find nothing Sufficient to hinder his
proceeding in marriage

Answer to
Seth Hart,s
proposal
of marriage

Seth Hart and **Abigail Anthony** appearing for their answer
Which was that they proceed to take Each other in Marriage in Som[e]
convenient time between this and next monthly meeting adviseing with
the Friends this meeting shall appoint to See Said marriage accompli[shed]
who are **William Mosher** and **Benjamin Rider**; and they to report to the nex[t]
Monthly meeting

Receiv,d
Freborn Ri
ders Certifi
cate with
Endorment
from Sandwich

A few lines, by way of Endorsment on the Certificate of our esteemed Frie[nd]
Freeborn Rider, (Expressing her attending the Several Settings of the Quarter[ly]
and monthly meetings of **Sandwich** to Satisfaction) was read in this
Meeting – –

Maria Smith
Wife of John
Smith dis=
=owned

A testimony ˄against **Maria Smith** Wife of **John Smith**, was Signed in this
meeting, in concurrence ~~of~~ with the Women friends therein, And the Clerk
is directed to read the Same at the Close of a first days meeting of worship
between this and next monthly meeting, and make report next monthly m[eeting]

The case of
J Wing
Refered

The Friends appointed to take an opertunity of Solid conference
with **Joseph Wing**; reported that they had an oppertunity with him and
that he gave them a good degree of Satisfaction, but that they desire
the matter refered another month, which is accordingly refered to next
Monthly meeting, under the Same Friends care, and they then to make rep[ort]

W Howlands
paper
accepted

This meeting accepts of **William Howlands** paper (which he gave in Some
time past, Condemning his misconduct in Joining with a young company
in mirth and merriment at an Entertainment of roasting and eating
Quahawks) for Satisfaction

The case of
P. Potter
Refered

The Friends appointed to Joine Women friends in a Solid conference
with **Prince Potter** and family report, that they have not had an opper
=tunity with him; and desires the matter refered, which is accordingly referd
to next Monthly meeting under their care, and they then to make report

The case of
E Thurston
refered

The Committee appointed to confer with **Edward Thurston** and family
desires the matter refered, which is according refered under their care to
next monthly meeting and they then to make report

Revising
miniuts &
Settleing
with Treasurd

The Friends appointed to Revise the Minutes and Settle with the
Treasurer desires it Refered another month which is accordingly referd
under their care and they to make report next monthly meeting

Report from
Quarterly
meeting

The Representatives to the last Quarterly meeting Report that they
all attended, and produced an Epistle from Said meeting, which was
Read in this meeting to Satisfaction

Report ᵒᶠ th Comᵗᵉᵉ
on acount
of Bibles

The Committee appointed to take in Subscriptions for Bibles agreeable to
the Recommendation of the Meeting for Sufferings, now report that the

Number of Bibles Subscri =bed for	Several members of this meeting with Some of their Friendly neighbours have Subscribed for 7 folio, 45 large Quarto: 39 large Octavo and 29 Small Octavo Bibles, which are to be Sent for an account and Risk of the Subscribers who are to pay whatever the Cost and charge of the Bibles may be: amounting to the number of 120 in the whole
report accep =ted	The above report is accepted and a Coppy thereof is ordered to be Sent up to the meeting for Sufferings.
The paper B Ricketson and Compa -ny Sent in is accepted	The Paper of **Benjamin Ricketson, Caleb Barker, William Barker Ju John Barker, Joseph Howland 2ᵈ, Jonathan Russell**, and **George Smith 2ᵈ** given in Some time past, Condemning their misconduct in going to an Entertainment, where undue Liberty was taken: which paper is accepted for Satisfaction; Provided the above said young men Cause it to be read Publickly at the close of a first day meeting for Worship before next monthly meeting, they being present: and to make return and and report thereof next monthly meeting
[H] Howland [requ]est a [certi]ficate	**Henry Howland** Request a Removal Certificate for himself a Children, to the Monthly meeting at **Accoakset**, therefore our friends **Benjamin Howland 2ᵈ** and **William Anthony Juʳ** are appointed to take the necessary care therein and bring one to next monthly meeting if they think proper

Collected in Silver – 1[£] – 10^s – 1^d

[5ᵗʰ] month 1781	At a Monthly Meeting of Friends held in **Dartmouth** the 21ˢᵗ of 5 month 1781 The Representatives are **William Barker** and **William Wood** – Present
[c]ase of [N] Gifford & [wi]fe refered	The Friends appointed to Joine the Women Friends in a Conference with **Nathaniel Gifford** and Wife, report, that they have not had oppertunity as desired, therefore desiers it refer,d which is accordingly refered, under the Same friends care; and they to make report next Monthly meeting
case of Slocum refered	The Friends appointed to Treat with **Jonas Slocum** desires that matter refer,d another month, which is accordingly refered under the Care of the Same friends who are to report to the next monthly meeting
[N] Tabers [de]nial read Denial of [M] Smith read	The Clerk reports he hath read the Testimony of denial against **Nicholas Taber**: as also that against **Mariah Smith** wife of **John Smith** as ordered Last Monthly meeting. That against **Nicholas Taber** is as followeth
Testimony of denial against [Ni]cholas Taber	Whereas **Nicholas Taber** hath had his Education amoung us the People called Quakers, but hath so far departed from our Religious Principles as to freequent meetings of Worship which are held out of the Unity of our Society and he being Laboured with to desist there from, and it not having the desired Effect: We are therefore confrained to give this forth as a Publick Testimony against him the Said **Nicholas Taber**, Disowning him from being a member of our ˌreligious Society, and from under our care: but with fervent desires that he may be favoured with a Sight and Sense of the Error of his out going and Experience the incom of Divine regaurd

Given forth at our Monthly meeting held in **Dartmouth** the 19 of 3 month 1781

Signed in and on behalf of s^d meeting by **William Anthony Ju^r** Clerk

[The] report of Seth [Ha]rts marriage

The Friends apointed to see the Marriage of **Seth Hart** and **Abigail Anthony** accomplished, report, that they both attend and did not see but that it was orderly Consumated

[T]he case of [Jo]seph Wing refered

The friends appointed to confer with **Joseph Wing**, reports that they had not the desired oppertunity with him, therefore desire it referd another month, which is accordingly referred under the Same friends Care and they to make report next monthly meeting

[P] Potter his Wife and Children [re]ceived into [u]nity with Friends

The Friends appointed to Joyne the Women friends in a Solid conference with **Prince Potter** and Family report, that they had an Oppertunity of conference wherein they had a good degree of Satisfaction, Therefore this meeting (on their request, and in concurence with the Women friends meeting) Accepts of the Said **Prince Potter** his Wife **Hannah** and all their Children now born, to be under our Care

[Ed]ward Thurston [his] Wife & Children disowned

The Friends appointed to Treat with **Edward Thurston** and family wherein they were Joined by the women friends report that they had an oppertunit of conference with Said **Edward** and family, and that they therein had no Satisfaction; Therefore this meeting doth disown said **Edward** his wife **Parnel**, and their Children, from having any right of membership among us, and from under our care[35]

Clerk to desired to Transmit A Copy herof to Family

And the Clerk is Desired to Transmitt a Coppy of this Minniute to Said Family, and make report next monthly meeting

The paper of Benj^a Rick itson & Compa= =ny hath been read

The Clerk Informs that **Benjamin Ricketson, Caleb Barker William Bark[er] John Barker Joseph Howland 2^d Jonathan Russell** and **George Smith 2^d** have cased [caused] their Paper to be read as directed last monthly meeting and returned said paper which is as Followeth

The paper of acknowledg ment of Benjamin Ricketson and Compa =ny

To the Monthly meeting of Friends to be held the 19th of Second month 1781 Whereas We Some time past Joined a considerable large company in an Entertainment with roasting and eating Quawhoks [Quahogs], whereat were also provided victuals and Spiritous Licquor, and after pertaking of the Same with Mirth and merriment we (with said company) repaired to a house where was musick and dancing, and so far Joined with them, as to remain at the house till the Company disperssed: For which misconduct we are Sorry, and do condemn, desireing Friends may so far pass it By as to let us remain under their care – From your real Friends

           Joseph Howland 2^d   **Benjamin Ricketson**

           Jonathan Russell   **Caleb Barker**

---

35. This is an unusual case, as normally the disownment of parents did not affect the membership of their children.

George Smith 2ᵈ   William Barker Juʳ
John Barker

Certificate for Henry Howland refered The Friends appointed to take the necessary care respecting a Certificate for **Henry Howland** and Children to the Monthly meeting of **Accoakset** report that they have not accomplished one by reason of an objection: therefore it is refered another month under the Same friends care they to make Report next Monthly meeting

W Russell gave in a paper referd to a Comᵗᵉᵉ **William Russell** gave in a paper to this meeting condemning his making a Gameing Instrument – yet in Order to discover his Sincerity in condemning it, This meeting doth appoint Our Friends **Seth Russell, Stephen Buffinton** and **John Williams,** to take an oppertunity of Solid conference with him ~~to~~ Said **William** and make report next monthly meeting

H Howlands paper accepted **Humphry Howland** gave in a paper Some considerable time past condemning his misconduct, in horse:racing and other things – Which is now Accepted for Satisfaction, provoided he causes it to be read publickly at the close of a day meeting of Worship, he being present at the reading thereof, returning and making report of the Same to next monthly meeting

W Howland desires a cop=py of miniut of his mem bership **William Howland** Informes this meeting by the way of the Preparitive Meeting, that he intends to go to **Nantucket** in order to go to Sea from thence if he Should find a voiage agreeable to his mind: he desireing a coppy of a minniute thereon he having a righ of membership among us

This meeting desires he may be under the care of **Nantucket** monthly meeting while there, and the Clerk is desired to give him a coppy thereof

Correcting the miniuts & Set with Treasurer refered The Friends appointed to Settle accounts with the Treasurer and revise the Monthly meeting minutes request it refer,d another month wich is accordingly under their care and they to report next monthly meeting

Report of Wood Sold The Committee appointed to have the care of Selling Wood report that they have Sold Seven Cords at two dollars pʳ Cord, which is Fourteen Dollars and paid the Same to the Treasurer

Collected in Silver money 1£ – 6ˢ – 0ᵈ

adjourn This Meeting is Adjournd to the 30ᵗʰ Instant after the meeting for Worship

mett Mett by adjournment the 30ᵗʰ of the 5ᵗʰ month 1781

The Representatives are **William Barker** and **William Wood** – Present

Complaint against C Sherman This meeting is inform,d by the way of Preparitve meeting that **Caleb Sherman** hath married out of the Unity of friends, & Friends having Treated with him thereon, but it is Refer,d to next monthly meeting for Consideration

J Gifford Jn desires a certificate send to a Comᵗᵉᵉ **Joseph Gifford Junʳ** desires (by the way of Preparitive meeting) a Removal Certificate, for himself and Children, to the Monthly meeting of **Sandwich** as he hath removed within the Verge of that meeting to Live, therefore this Meeting doth appoint **William Barker** and **Stephen Buffinton**

to take the necessary care therein; and if they find things clear to
bring one to next Monthly meeting

S Smith desires
coppy of miniut
[?] member
[ship?]

Stephen Smith son of **Benjamin Smith Ju**ᴿ desireing a coppy of a
Miniute of this Meeting Setting forth his Right of Membership here
directed to the Monthly meeting of **Falmoth** in **Salem Quarter** as he
has gone to do some business there, and the Clerk is directed to give a coppy
hereof; He having a right of membership among us

And this meeting desireing he may be under friends care while there

complaint
against
David Hart
referd to a Com^tee

This meeting is Inform,d by way of the preparative meeting that
David Hart hath removed out of the Verge of this Meeting and not requested
our Certificate, which not being according to good order amoung us therefore our
friends **John
Devoal [Devol]** and **Abiel Gifford** are appointed to treat with him thereon and
make report when ready

Jonathan
Greene desires
a certificate
[trans]mmitted

Jonathan Greene desireing a removal Certificate to the Monthly meeting
of **Greenwich**, Setting forth his right of membership and clearness
respecting marriage he having gone there to reside therefore our friends
Benjamin Tabor and **William Wood** are appointed to take the necessary
care therein, and if they find things clear to bring one to next monthly
Meeting

B Shepherds
Certificate
returned for a
amendment:
an [Endors?]
ment was made
and forwarded
back

Barnabus Shepherds Certificate being returned from the Monthly
Meeting of **Sandwich** with Endorsmnent, informing that Said Certificate
did not metion [mention] his outward afaires being Settled: Enquiry being made
therein and finding things clear therein, an Endorsment was made
thereof on said Certificate and forwarded

M Maxfield
received under
Friends care

The Women Friends Inform that they have received **Mehitable Maxfield**
Wife of **John Maxfield**, under their care; which this meeting concurs with.

B Allen(son of
Philip) requests
some advice

The Overseers Inform that **Benjamin Allen** (son of **Philip Allen** deceasᵈ)
desires the advice of Friends, respecting Some of his Outward affairs
therefore our Friends **Henry Smith**, **Stephen Buffinton**, **Caleb Russell**,
and **Ebenezer Allen**, are appointed to Visit Said **Benjamin** and advise
and assist on those affairs, as Truth may Direct and make report next
Monthly Meeting

6 month
1781

At a Monthly Meeting held in **Dartmouth** the 13ᵗʰ of 6ᵗʰ month 1781
The Representatives are **Caleb Russell Joseph Barker Elijah Gifford** and
Henry Smith Present

Thornton &
Smith and
Carrington
Visit

Our Esteem Friends **James Thornton** from **Abington** & **Samuel
Smith** of **Philadelphia** both of the **Province of Pensylvania** and **Thomas
Carrington** of **New Garden** attended the meeting, Producing Certificates
from the meetings they belong to: and their Visits and Labours in
Gospel Love acceptable Also

W Mufflin *D Cowper &* *G Churchman* *Visit*	Our Esteemed Friends **Warner Mifflin** of **Duce Creek Kent County** in **Delaware**, **David Cowper** of **Haddonfield** in **New Jersey**, and **George Churchman** of **Nottingham , England** producing Certificates from the Monthly meetings they belong to, and their Visits here well accepted[36]
N Gifford *[&] wife*	The friends appointed to Confer with **Nathaniel Gifford Ju**ʳ & wife report that they before that matter continued another month that is according defer.d till next monthly meeting under their care then they to make Report
J. Slocum *case*	The Friends appointed to Treat with and inspect into the Conduct of **Jonas Slocum**, report that they desire that matter continued another month under their care they then to make Report
Joseph Wing *case*	The friends appointed to confer with **Joseph Wing** report that they had an oppertunity of conferrence with him, and that he gave them a degree of Satisfaction, yet desire yᵉ matter continued another month [?] is accordingly under the Same friends care and they to make report next monthly meeting
E Thurston *informd*	The Clerk informed he hath Transmitted a Coppy of the minnuite of Last monthly meeting, to **Edward Thurston** and family respecting their denial, as ordered
objection *against* *Hen. Howland* *Certificate*	The friends appointed to take the necessary care respecting a Removal Certificate for **Henry Howland** and children report that the Same Objections remains as was last monthly meeting therefore the matter is continued under the Same friends care and they to make report When ready
W. Russell *case refer,*ᵈ	The friends appointed to have a Soled conference and inspection into the conduct of **William Russell** in order to discover his Sencerity in condemning his misconduct in making a Gaming Instrument Report: They have had Some conference with him but desires the matter refered another month with an addition of friends therein, Who are **William Mosher** and **William Anthony Ju**ʳ and they together to take the necessary care therein and make report to next monthly meeting

36. James Thornton (1727–1794), a minister and a native of England, emigrated to Pennsylvania in 1750. See *Memorials Concerning Deceased Friends*, 43–49. Samuel Smith (1737–1817) was a minister from Philadelphia. See ibid., 156–62. Thomas Carrington (1721–1781) was a minister from New Garden Monthly Meeting, Chester County, Pennsylvania. See Philadelphia Yearly Meeting Men's Minutes, 1780–1798, p. 44, Philadelphia Yearly Meeting Archives. Warner Mifflin (1745–1798) was a minister from Duck Creek Monthly Meeting, Kent County, Delaware, and an indefatigable opponent of slavery. See Gary B. Nash, *Warner Mifflin: Unflinching Quaker Abolitionist* (Philadelphia: University of Pennsylvania Press, 2017). George Churchman (1730–1814) was an elder in Nottingham Monthly Meeting in Chester County, Pennsylvania, not England, and a close friend of Mifflin. See ibid., 57, 60; and J. Smith Futhey and Gilbert Cope, *History of Chester County, Pennsylvania, with Genealogical and Biographical Sketches* (Philadelphia: Louis H. Everts, 1881), 497. David Cooper (1724–1794) was a minister from Woodbury Monthly Meeting, which was part of Haddonfield Quarterly Meeting. See Philadelphia Yearly Meeting Book of Memorials, 1686–1850, pp. 371–73, Philadelphia Yearly Meeting Archives.

Certificate to be appinted for forreign friends

Our Friends **William Anthony Ju**ʳ and **Samuel Smith** are appointed to draw Certificates for our Friends **James Thornton, Samuel Smith Thomas Carrington Warner Mufftin** [Mifflin] and **George Churchman** who Attended this meeting. – bringing with them Said Certificates to the adjournment of this meeting

adjourn,d

This Meeting is adjourned to the 27ᵗʰ instant after the meeting of Worship of that day

mett

The 27ᵗʰ mett by adjournment The Representatives all present Except **Caleb Russell** who is gone to the yearly meeting at **Nantucket** **Caleb Greene** is appointed Clerk for this time

H Howland paper not read

Humphry Howlands paper not being Read as directed last monthly meeting he not being informed thereof he is now inform,d and dire[cted] to cause the Same to be read and Returned as mentioned last monthly meeting

To Settle with Trea surer

The Friends appointed to Settle accounts with the Treasurer and Revise the monthly meeting minutes Report that they have revised the minutes but have not accomplish,d the rest, therefore the finishing the Same is defered under their care till next monthly meeting and then to make report

C Shearman disorder

Our Friends **William Barker** and **Joseph Tucker Ju**ʳ are appointed to make Enquiry and Treat with **Caleb Shearman** on his marrying out of the Unity of friends: and make report thereof next monthly meeting

J Greene certificate

A Removal Certificate was Signed in this meeting by the Clerk for **Jonathan Greene** directed to the monthly meeting at **Greenwich** Setting forth his Right of membership Clearness respecting marriage and Outward affairs being Settled, he having gone to Said place to reside

B Allen Case

Part of the Committee appointed to Visit **Benjamin Allen** (Son of **Philip** deceased) and advise and assist him in Some of his outward affaires report, that they Visited him and gave him Such advice as they thought necessary but the matter not being fully accomplished His Brother **Jedidiah** being concerned in the matter with him hereto= =fore the Same friends are continued in that Service who are to advise Said **Benjamin** and **Jedidiah** and others of that family concerned therein as they may find necessary and make report next monthly meeting

J Gifford case

The Friends appointed Some considerable time past to treat with **Job Gifford** report that they have Confer,d with him Several times and he hath desisted from his misconduct, and gave Said Friends a good degree of Satisfaction; Therefore Said report is accepted as Satisfactory

Silvia Smith Requesting for her young Son **Benjamin Howland Smith** to be received under Friends care: therefore our friends **Thomas Hicks** and

Philip Maccomber are appointed to take necessary care in the matter and make report next monthly meeting

Certificates for Traveling Friends

Certificates were Signed in this Meeting by the Clerk for our Esteemed Friends **James Thornton** and **Samuel Smith** directed to the Several monthly meetings they belong to: Setting forth their acceptable Visit and Service in the Ministry, and Soled and waitty [weighty] conversation: Certificates were also Signed as above Said for our Friends **Warner Mufflin [Mifflin]**, **Thomas Carrington** and **George Churchman** directed to the Several monthly meetings they belong to Setting forth their acceptable Visit and Service in the Love of the Truth

Queries ans answer.d

The Queries have been Read and answers answers thereto prepared, and after Some amendment, approved and Sent by our Representatives to the Quarterly meeting, with the Epistle, which was Read, approved, And Sign,d by the Clerk

Representatives Quarly meeting

~~The~~ Our Friends **William Barker**, **Caleb Greene**, **Abner Devoal [Devol]**, **Seth Huddleston**, and **Benjamin Gifford Ju**ʳ are appointed to attend our next Quarterly meeting, and make report to our next monthly meeting

7 month 1781

At a Monthly Meeting held in **Dartmouth** the 16ᵗʰ of 7ᵗʰ month 1781 The Representatives are **John Williams** and **Joseph Tucker Ju**ʳ Present

Representatives report

The Representatives to the Quarterly meeting report, that they all attended that meeting, and have produced an Epistle from the Same which was read in this meeting to Satisfaction: And the weighty advice therein Respecting Friends Settleing their outward Estates, and making their Wills whilst in helth, is Recommended to the Solid attention of Each member of this meeting

A Transcrip of the Epistle of the yearly meeting from **London** last year was also produced by the sd Representatives and read in this meeting to Satisfaction

N Gifford & Wife Case

The Friends appointed to Confer with **Nathaniel Gifford** and Wife report, that they had an oppertunity with them and that they gave them Some degree of Satisfaction; yet as they are Slack in attending Religious meetings, and for a further discovery of the Sincerity of Said **Nathaniel** and Wife, in the Condemning their misconduct, the matter is continued under the care and inspection of the Same friends who are to report when ready

J Slocums Case

The Friends appointed to Treat with **Jonas Slocum** and inspect into his conduct report they do not find his fruits Sufficient~~ly demonstrate~~ to demonstrate a State of Sincear Repentance: yet not being out of hopes he may yet return; therefore Said matter is refer.d under the Same friends care and they to make report next monthly meeting

J Wings Case

The Friends appointed to confer with **Joseph Wing** report that

they had an oppertunity of Solid conference with him and that he gave
them Some degree of Satisfaction: yet this meeting concluds to continue
that matter one month longer, and it is accordingly refer.d to next
monthly meeting under the Same friends care and they then to make Report

W Rusell
Case

~~The~~ Friends appointed to have a Solid conference with and inspection into
the conduct of **William Russell**, in order to discover his Sincerity in condem
ning his misconduct in making a Gameing Instrument, report that they
had an oppertunity with him and that he gave them so much Satisfaction
that this meeting concludes to accept of his paper for Satisfaction, provided
he cause Said paper to be read, at the close of one of our publick meetings
for Worship on a first day between this and next monthly meeting and
make return and report of the Same

H Holand
paper not
Read

The Clerk informs by desire of **Humphry Howland** that his paper hath not
been read as directed at last monthly meeting therefore the Clerk is desired
to direct him to cause it to be read as directed last monthly meeting

P. Sissons
Children
Received.

This meeting in concurence with the Womens meeting do conclude
to receive **Phebe Sisson**s Children whose names are **Stephen**, **Ruth**, and
Judith, under our care

Settled with
Treasurer

The Committee appointed to Settle accompts with the Treasurer report
that they have accomplish.d the same, and find in Stock four Shillings
and Eight pence Lawful hard money 0 – 4 – 8 not paid out which
Benjamin Taber is ordered to pay to **Jonathan Willbor**: And the
Meeting: ~~and the~~ in debt for order 9£ – 11^s – 4^d not yet paid
Thereby the meeting in debt 9£ – 6^s – 8^d Lawful hard money

A Ricketson
Request
thro.d out

The Committee appointed in 2nd month 1780 to treat and Confer
with **Abraham Ricketson** on his request to be restored among
Friends and he not apearing to continue his request, this meeting
Concludes to discharge that matter and Said Committee from that Service

Respecting
the books

Part of the Committee appointed in 2nd month 1780 to Collect this
meetings Books report that they have made Some progress therein and they are
therefore continued in that Service and to make report next monthly meeting

J Potter
Case

The Committee appointed in 2nd month 1780 to take the necessary care in the
matter respecting **John Potter** going away in a disorderly manner Report that
they have made Some progress therein and they are yet contintinued in that
Service and to make report when ready

D Hart
Case

The Friends appointed to treat with **David Hart** on his removing out of
the Verge of this meeting without requesting a Certificate Report that they
have treated with him and that he did not give any Satisfaction: Said Committee
also inform that Said **David** is in the practice of attending meetings
held out of the Unity of our Society and that they had Treated with him on

that account, and that Justified himself, therefore, **Seth Russell** and
John Williams are appointed to take an oppertunity of Solid Conference
with him thereon and if he doth not give them Satisfaction to draw a
Testimony of denial against him and inform him thereof and bring said
Testimony with them to next monthly meeting

B. Taber
Dismisd
J Willbor
Treasu
=rer   **Benjamin Taber** having Served this meeting as Tresurer for Some time to
Satisfaction, and requesting to be dismist there from, he is therefore dismissed
and **Jonathan Willbor** is appointed to that Service for the year Ensuing

Collected 2£ – 17ˢ – 4ᵈ

A Nichols
miniute   This meeting Received a Coppy of a miniute from **South Kingstown** in behalf
of **Andrew Nichols 3ʳᵈ**, Son of **Andrew Nichols Juʳ** informing of his Right
of membership and of his removing from that meeting to **Bedford**
to Live with a friend

adjourn.d   This Meeting is adjourned to the ²⁵ᵗʰʰ Instant after the meeting of Worship
of that day

mett   Mett by adjournment the 25ᵗʰ of the 7 month 1781
The Representatives being called **Joseph Tucker Juʳ** present
John Williams not present for which no Excuse was rendered

C Sherman
Case   The Friends appointed to make Enquiry and Treat with **Caleb Sherman**
on his marrying out of the Unity of friends Report that they had an
oppertunity with him and that he gave them no Satisfaction

They also Inform that Said **Caleb** is guilty of fornication as appears by his
wife having a Child Soon after marriage therefore the Same friends are
continued: to Joyn the Women friends in treating with Said **Caleb** and
Wife, if they do not find Sufficient Sattisfaction to draw a Testimony of denial
and bring to next monthly meeting

[Benj?] Allens
case refer,d   **Caleb Russell** in behalf of the Committee appointed to Visit **Benjamin**
Allen (Son of **Phillip** deceased) and the rest of family, report that
they appointed a time and place to meet them, but they not meeting them
as appointed the Committee desires the matter defer,d another month which
is accordingly Referred Under their care till next monthly meeting they
then to make report

Smiths request   The Friends appointed to take the necessary care respecting the request
of **Silvia Smith** for her young Son **Benjamin Howland Smith** to be taken
under Friends care, report that they have taken the necessary care therein
by taking an opertunity of Solid conference with Said **Silvia** thereon, who gave them
a good degree of Satisfaction, Respecting the Religious Education of her Child
therefore this meeting in a Solid consideration thereon concluds to receive Said
Benjamin Howland Smith under our care

minuit for B Howland Smith   **Silvia Smith** Requests a Coppy of a minute of this meetings to the monthly meeting of **Nantucket**, Signifying the right of membership of her Son **Benjamin Howland Smith** (he being this day received into membership with us) he being gone to **Nantucket** to School: therefore the Clerk is desired to forward to Said monthly meeting of **Nantucket**, a Coppy of this minniute

J Jonson Cer= tificate returnd   **James Johnson** hath returned a Certificate which he received from this meeting of the 17th of 3d month 1781 Last directed to the monthly meeting of **Nantucket**; he not making any Stay there

8 month 1781   Att a Monthly Meeting held in **Dartmouth** the 20th of 8th month 1781
The Representatives **Abiel Gifford** and **Jonathan Hart** - Present

Comtee in being joyn.d to Sand= wich Quarter   There being a Committee appointed by the Quarterly meeting to Confer with this meeting on account of **Dartmouth** monthly meeting, being Joyn.d to **Sandwich** Quarter: therefore we appoint our Friends **William Anthony Ju Thomas Hicks Samuel Smith Abiel Gifford William Mosher Seth Russell** and **Henry Smith**, to Confer with Said Committee, with all other friends that hath a desire to meet on that Conference and they to report next monthly meeting

adjournd   This Meeting Adjourns to the 29th Instant after the meeting of Worship

mett   Mett by Adjournment the 29th of the 8th month 1781

J Slocums Case refered   The Friends continued in the Case of **Jonas Slocum** report that they had another conference with him and not being fully Satisfied it is referd to next monthly meeting under the care of the Same friends as before and then they to report

J Wings Case Refer,d   Likewise the Friends appointed in the case of **Joseph Wings** report Still gives a degree of Satisfaction therefore it is refer,d to next monthly meeting and the Same friends to take the care thereof and then to report

W Russells paper read is as Follows   **William Russells** Paper having been Read according to direction and is returned to this meeting. – and is as followeth

To the Monthly meeting of friends to be held in **Dartmouth** 21st of 5th mo 1781 Dear friends, Whereas I Some time past through unwatchfullness did so far depart from the principle of Truth and friends as to make a Gaiming Instru = =ment or Table for the purpose of playing a Sort of Game called Bacgammon Since doing which I have been favoured to See my great error there th with with its concequences, for which Error I am Sincearly Sorry for and do Condemn desireing Friends may pass it by so far as to let me remain under their Care and that I may be so far favoured to dwell So near the divine princi= =ple for the futuer as not to fall into any since Such inormity for the future

                                        William Russell

Consening Books   The Friends appointed to Collect this meetings Books report that they made Some further progress therein but it not being fully accomplished they are continued therein and desired to make report to this meeting when they have fulfilled the Same

David Hart
disown,d

The friends appointed to confer with **David Hart** Report they have fulfilled their appointment and that he did not give them any Satisfaction therefore this meeting disown him from being a member of this meeting and hath Given forth a Testimony of denial against him and the Clerk is [?] to Read the Same publickly or procure it Read in the usal manner and make return next monthly meeting, And **Seth Russell** is desired to inform Said **David Hart** thereof and that he hath a right of an apeal and he to report next monthly meeting

J Williams
excuse rec,d

John Williams hath Render,d a Satisfactory reason for his not attending the adjourment of our Last monthly meeting when being a Representative of the Prepariive meeting

C Shearmans
Case refer,d

The friends appointed in the case of **Caleb Shearman** make report, they have not accomplished their appointment (tho they made Some progress there) they are therefore Continued in that Service as before to make report next monthly meeting

The friends appointed to advise and assist **Benjamin Allen** and his [?] **Jedidiah** & Report that they have had a conference with the Said parties [?] yet thee Committee request Said matter continued, It is therefore Continued to next monthly meeting under the care of Said Committee who are then to make Report

H Howland
paper read

This meeting is Informed that **Humphry Howlands** Paper hath been Read agreeable to the direction of the Monthly meeting: and is as followeth

To the Monthly meeting of friends in **Dartmouth**
Whereas I have inconsiderately resorted to places of horse racing, and co[?] to my mares running runing Several times: I also, with others went and partook of the Entertain of Quaghaugs at the Shoar after which we went to a house and took undue Liberty, even to musick and dancing a[?] misconduct of mine, I am Sorry for, and do hereby Condemn the Same together with the wearing Such apparel as is not approved among friends and I desire friends so far to pass it by my Unwarrantable behavior in these and all other respects as to Suffer me Still to remain under Their Care   From your friend **Humphry Howland**
Dated in **Dartmouth**
the 14th of 2d month 1781

P Beards
deial

The Women Friends Inform they have denied **Phebe Beard** Daughter of **John Beard** which this meeting Concurs with

Trustees for
meeting
house lands

It hath been proposed to make a additional Choice of Trustees to [?] the Title of the meeting house land at **New Town**; therefore **Joseph Tucker Junor Jonathan Hart, Barnabus Mosher Ju** and **William Gifford** are appointed for that Service unto whom a Deed or Deeds are [?] to be made: and to hold Said land for the Use of Friends till others be appointed in their Stead for that Service

G. Howlands Bill — **Gideon Howland** hath given a bill for nursing and tending **Alice Smith** during her Sickness the last Seven months he keep her, over and above the Usal alowence allow,d by the Oveseers of the poor 8 dollars [?]

P Maccomber — **Phillip Maccomber** also gave in an account as allow,d by Said Oversears, for a pair of Shoes 0£ – 9ˢ – 0
which accounts the Treasurer is ordered to pay when Suplyd with money by this meeting

Wood Sold — The friends to Sell our wood report they have Sold 2½ Cords for Five dollars which money Deliverd to the Treasurer

This Meeting Collected – – –   1£ – 4ˢ – 7½ᵈ

adjourn — This meeting adjurns to the 5ᵗʰ day of next month after meeting of Worship on Said day

mett — Mett by adjournment the 5ᵗʰ day of the 9ᵗʰ month 1781
The Representatives being called both present

A Russells prosel of marriage — **Allen Russell** and **Abigail Allen** Declared their Intentions of taking Each other into Marriage (after having Consent of parents) and were desired to wait till next monthly meeting for their Answer
And **William Mosher** and ~~Wood~~ **William Wood** are appointed to make the necessary inspection into the said **Allen Russell**s clearness respecting marriag and conversation and make return to next monthly meeting

Testimony Conserning P Russell — The Testimony concerning **Paul Russell** that this meeting gave forth Some time past, was returned to this meeting, with Some amendment by the direction of the Quarterly meeting, which was Read approved and Signed by the Clerk

9 month 1781 — At a Monthly Meeting held in **Dartmouth** the 17 day of the 9ᵗʰ month 1781
The Representatives are **Stephen Buffinton** and **William Gifford** both present

Comᵗᵉᵉ report on Joining to Sandwich Qurter and — The Committee appointed to confer with a Comittee from the Quarterly meeting on account of this meeting being Joyned to **Sandwich** Quarter: Report that they have fulfil,d their appointment, and think it not best for us to be annexed Thereto at present which report this meeting accept

Sent to Qurly meeting Comᵗᵉᵉ — A Report from this meeting was Signed by the Clerk directed to the Quarterly meetings Committee on the Subject of this meetings being annixed to **Sandwich** Quarter, Signifying, that we think it not best under present Circumstances to be So annexed

J Slocums Case Continu,d — The Friends continued in the case of **Jonas Slocum** desires it continu,d another month, it is accordingly continued under their: and if on their having another opportunity of Solid conference with him, they do not find Satisfaction, that they draw a Testimony of his denial, inform him thereof and bring said Testimony to next monthly meeting

J Wing Recevd — The friends appointed in the case of **Joseph Wing** report that he Still gave them a degree of Satisfaction, and that they think it may now be Safe for

the meeting to receive him under our Care, Wherefore this meeting received
the Said **Joseph Wing** into membership with us and under our Care

The Clerk informs he hath Read the Testimony of **David Hart**s denial
as directed last monthly meeting. Which is as followeth

D Harts Tes=
=timony of
denial

Whereas **David Hart** having had his Education among us the People
Called Quakers, but hath lately removed out of the Verge of this monthly meeting
in disorderly manner; and freequents meetings held out of the Unity
of our Society, and Friends having laboured with him in much love
but it not having the desired Effect

Therefore for the clearing of Truth we are concerned to give this forth as a
Publick Testimony against him the Said **David Hart**, hereby disowning
him from being any longer a member of our Societ. Neverthe it is our
desire that he may come to a Sense of his out going and return to the way
of Truth – Given forth and Signed in our monthly meeting held in
Dartmouth ~~the~~ by adjournment the 26th day of the 8th month 1781 By

William Anthony Jur Clerk

D Hart not
inform.d

Seth Russell informs he did not inform Said **Hart** of his Denial and
Right of appeal which he is yet desired to, and make report thereof to next
monthly meeting

Caleb
Sherman
disowned

The friends appointed in the case of **Caleb Shearman** report that
that they had an oppetunity of Solid conference with him and that
he did not give them any Satisfaction; therefore they produced a
Testimony of his denial which was Read in this meeting and
Signed by the Clerk who is directed to Read the Same
at the close of a first day meeting of Worship between this and
next monthly meeting, And **Joseph Tucker Ju**r is desir,d to inform
Said **Shearman** of his denial and Right of appeal and report to
next monthly meeting

A Russells
Clearness

The Friends appointed to inspect into **Allen Russells** Clearness
Respecting marriage and Conversation, report that they do not find
any thing Sufficient to hinder his proceeding in marriage

A Russells
Answer

Allen Russell and **Abigail Allen** appearing in this meeting for
their answer: Which was that they might proceed to take Each
other in marriage at Some convenient time before next monthly
meeting adviseing with the Friends this meeting Shall appoint to
See Said marriage orderly Solemnized; And **William Mosher** and
William Wood are are appointed to see Said marriage orderly
Solemniz,d and make report next monthly meeting

J Williams
request a
Certificate

John Williams requested (By the way of the Preparitve meeting) a
Certificate to the monthly meeting of **RhodIsland** Setting forth his
clearness resecting marriage, and Conversation, Wherefore our friends

Benjamin Taber and William Anthony Ju^r are appointed to take the
Necessary care in that matter; and if they find things clear, to draw
one and bring with them to next monthly meeting

P Maccober
request a
removal
Certificat

Philip Maccomber Informing by the way of the Preparitive meeting)
That he hath thoughts of moving to the Ninepartners with his family
to Live desireing Friends advice therein, and a removal Certificate for
himself and family if Friends think proper Wherefore Elijah Gifford
Thomas Hicks and Samuel Smith are appointed to take the necessary
Care in that matter and if they things clear to bring a Removal
Certificate with them to next monthly meeting

B Allens
Case
Continu,d

The fiends appointed in the case of Benjamin Allen Jedidiah Allen
and others of their family, Report, that they have had a further
Oppertunity with them, and that as the matter is difficalt they request
it continued another month which accordingly continued and Joseph
Barker is added to them in that case and they are to act therein
as they in the Wisdom of Truth may be directed, and make report to
next monthly meeting

meetings
discontinu=
=ed

This meeting concluds to discontinue all our Week day meetings in
~~the~~ the week of the next Quarterly meeting be held here this yeare
And that our next Preparitive meeting beheld the 26th of this instant

Receiv,d
S Crisps
& M Brooks
Epistles

This meeting having receiv,d from the meeting for Sufferings Forty
of Stephen Crisps Epistles and Forty of Mary Brooks on Silent
waiting at pence Lawfull money per Set: To be paid for by those
members who chuse to have them, therefore our Friends William Mosher
Danniel Ricketson, Henry Smith, Caleb Greene and Timothy ~~Russell~~
Howland are appointed to dispose of sd Books as they See proper and
bring the money if ready to the adjournment of this meeting[37]

Wood Sold

The Committee appointed to Sell wood, report, that they have Sold five
Cords and one Eight at two dollars per Cord is Ten dollars and a Quarter
Which is paid or Sent to the Treasurer – –   3£ – 1 – 6
                                       Collected –   2 – 11 – 3

adjournd

This Meeting adjourns to the 26th Instant after the meeting for Worship

mett

Mett by adjournmet the 26th of the 9th month 1781

37. The Crisp work is probably Stephen Crisp, *An Invitation to Friends, Concerning the Present and Succeeding Times. Being a Faithful Exhortation and Warning to All Friends Who Profess the Truth, to Beware of the Manifold Wiles of the Enemy, and to Stand Armed in the Light of the Lord God of Heaven and Earth, (Against His Assaults,) That So They May Be Read to Answer the Call and Requirings of the Lord*, first published in London in 1666. A new edition was published by James Phillips in London 1780. "Mary Brooks on Silent Worship" is M[ary] B[rook], *Reasons for the Necessity of Silent Waiting, In order to the Solemn Worship of God. To Which Are Added, Several Quotations from Robert Barclay's Apology* (London: Mary Hinde, 1774). Three additional editions had been printed by 1778. See Smith, Catalogue of Friends' Books, 321–22.

The Representatives being called both Present

Queries answerd The Queries have been read and answers thereto ~~prepared and~~ read and approv,d, also an Epistle Signed by the Clerk all which is order,d

The Representatives forward to the Quarterly meeting by our Representatives who are **Elijah Gifford John Devol Samuel Smith** and **Stephen Buffinton** and they To make report next monthly meeting

S Butters mi= niute **Samuel Butter** attended this meeting with a Coppy of a miniute from the monthly meeting of the **Ninepartners** Seting forth his being a Member in unity, which was Indorsed in this meeting

R. Smiths miniute indors,d In concurrence with the Women Friends **Robe Smiths** Certificate from **East Hoosuck** monthly meeting was ndorsed in this meeting

Epistles dis= posed of The friends that had the disposal of **Stephen Crisps** Epistles and **Mary Brooks** on Silent waiting report that they have disposed of them and Sent the money to the mceting for Sufferings

---

10 month 1781 At a Monthly Meeting held in **Dartmouth** the 15ᵗʰ of the 10ᵗʰ month 1781 The Representatives are **Henry Smith** and **Joshua Potter** present

Report of yᵉ Comᵗᵉᵉ from Quarterly meeting The Representatives to the Quarterly Meeting Report that they all attended and produced an Epistle to this meeting: as also a Coppy of an Epistle from the Yearly meeting held in **Philadelphia** for **Pensylvany** and **New Jersey** & c: which Epistles were Read to Satisfaction

Jonas Slocum disowed The friends continued in the Case of **Jonas Slocum** report that they have had a Soled Conference with him but he gave them no Satisfaction they they thereupon produc,d a Testimony of his denial which was Signed by the Clerk who is desired to Read the Same at the Close of of a first day meeting for Worship between this and next monthly meeting Said friends also report that they have Informed said **Slocum** that Friends would proceed to disown him

D Hart informd of his denial **Seth Russell** reports that he hath inform,d **David Hart** of his Denial According to appointment and his right to an appeal

Testimony of denial of Caleb Shear= =man The Clerk reports he hath read the Testimony of denial against – – **Caleb Shearman** according to appointment: and **Joseph Tucker** reports that he hath informed Said **Shearman** of the Same: Which is as follows Whereas **Caleb Shearman** Son of **Philip Shearman**; And **Hannah** his Wife daughter of **Jacob Russell** deceased; Having had a Right of Membership with us the people called Quakers, but through unwach= =fulness and by disregarding the Testimony of Truth in their owne hearts, have so far deviated therefrom, as to fall into the Sin of Fornication, which is Evident by their having a Child Soon after marriage: And Friends having Treated with them in Love

in Order to Shew the Evil of their Transgression, and restore them
to the way of Truth: But their Labour of Love not having the desired
Effect to Friends Satisfaction: Friends are concerned to give this forth
as a Testimony against them the Said **Caleb Shearman** and **Hannah**
his Wife, hereby disowning them from being members of our Society and
from under the Care of this meeting: yet our desire is that they may
become truly Sensible of their Transgression and be restored to the way of
Truth

      Signed in and on behalf of men and womens   By **William Anthony Ju**ᵣ Clerk
monthly meeing held in **Dartmouth** the 17ᵗʰ of 9ᵗʰ mo 1781   **Susanna Smith** Clerk

report of
A Russells
marriage
    The Friends appointed to See the marriage of **Allen Russell** and **Abigail**
Allen orderly Solemniz,d, report that they attended Said marriage and
that they did not discover but that it was Solemniz,d in a good degree Orderly

John Williams
Certificate
not accompli=
=shed
    The Friends to take the necessary care in inquiring into **John**
Williams Clearness and Certificate in **Rhod Island** monthly meeting
~~Settng~~ Setting forth the Same, Report, that they have not accom=
=plished it by reason of Some Obstacle and that therefore they desire another
month with an addition to the Committee it is accordly deferd and
William Mosher John Devol and **Joseph Gifford** are added to them and
They to make report to next monthly meeting

Certificate
for P. Mac
comber his
Wife & Chil
dren
    A Removal Certificate was provided to this meeting for **Philip**
Maccomber his Wife **Susanna** and their Children Whose names are **Edith**
Gardner, Barnabus Abraham, and **Hannah**, directed to the monthly
meeting of **Ninepartners** Setting forth that Said **Maccomber** affairs
were Settled to Satisfaction as far as appears, and that he and his
Wife are Members in Unity as also the Childrens right of membership
which Certificate was Signed by the Clerk

The Case
Ben Allen
Settled
    The friends that had the care of that matter between **Jedidiah** and
Benjamin Allen report that matter is mutually Settled between the
parties concerned

W Sanford
request
a Certificate
    William Sanford Inform.d (by the way of the preparitive meeting) that has
Thoughts going to the **Ninepartners** to See his Relations, also to make Some
Stay there and desireing a few lines from this meeting which this meeting
Concurs with, He being a member in Unity, and the Clerk is desir,d
to give him a Coppy of this Minniute

S Russell
request a
Certificate
    Seth Russell Informing this meeting that he intends a Visit to **Oblong**
and **Ninepartners** to See his Relations, and to attend the Quarterly meeting
at **Oblong** – Requesting a few lines thereon – He being a member in Vnity
and the Clerk is desired to give him a Coppy of this ~~meeting a~~ miniut
And this meeting approves of the Same

Conserning another preparitive meeting

    This Meeting taking into Consideration the advice of the Quarlerty meetings Committee for Visiting the monthly meetings: The Expedency of Setting off another Preparitive meeting in this monthly meeting – wherefore we appoint **Joseph Tucker, Caleb Russell, William Mosher, Benjamin Taber, William Anthony Ju**ᵣ**, Samuel Smith, Thomas Hicks Stephen Buffinton, Joseph Barker, Joseph Gifford, Seth Huddleston, Henry Smith** and **Abiel Gifford** a Committee and to Joine the Women friends and to Take the Same into Solid Consideration and if they find it proper that there Should be one, that they describe its Bounderies and make report thereon to next monthly meeting and any other Concerned friends may Joine the Said Committee therein if they See proper

Collected – 1£ – 19ˢ – 0 ᵈ

---

11 month 1781

At a Monthly Meeting held in **Dartmouth** the 19ᵗʰ of 11ᵗʰ month 1781
The Representatives are **John Devol** and **Henry Smith** Present
    The Clerk informs he hath Read the Testimony of denial of **Jonas Slocum** as directed last monthly meeting; Which is as Follows

Testimony of denial of J Slocum

    Whereas **Jonas Slocum** having had his Education among Friends but through unwachfulness hath So far departed from his Education and our Religious Profession as to fall into the Sin of Fornication as appears by the accusation of **Elisabeth Akin** (that he was the father of her Child) and friends having freequently Treated with him on account of his Crime in order to discover to him the evil thereof But our Labour therein not obtaining the desired end or effect to friends Satisfaction; Therefore, for the clearing our Name, and Truth from the reproch therof, this meeting doth give this forth as a publick Testimony against him and do hereby disown him the Said **Jonas Slocum** from being in membership with us untill by Sincear Repentance he Shall be restored to the way of Truth
    Given forth and Signed in and on behalf of our monthly meeting of Friends held in **Dartmouth** 15ᵗʰ of the 10ᵗʰ month 1781

By **William Anthony Ju**ᵣ Clerk

Report on dividing preparitive meeting

    The Committee appointed to take into Consideration and inspection the Expedency of dividing our Preparitive meeting report that by reason of so many and so great weaknesses prevailing among us pirticurly the want of a true discipline being kept up in friends familyes
    The want of Unity in Some places, and other defects, that it is their opinion that the matter be continued under their care for further Trial" it is accordingly continued under the care of Said Committee who are desired to inspect and Labour to remove those defects and make report to next monthly meeting

Joseph Wing request a few lines from this to **Accoxet** monthly meeting
Setting forth his right of membership and clearness respecting marriage and
Conversation; therefore we appoint **Elijah Gifford** and **Chilion Wood**
to to take the necessary care in that matter and if they find things
Clear to draght a Certificate and bring one to the next monthly meeting

J Allen request
[?]
Certificate

John Allen (Son of **Jonathan**) Request a removal Certificate to the monthly
meeting of **Ninepartners**, as he expects to Remove there with his Parents
to reside therefore **William Gifford** and **Jonathan Hart** are appointed to
take take the necessary care in that matter and if they find things clear
to draught and bring one to next monthly meeting

Howland
[illegible]
[illegible]

Gideon Howland desires a coppy of a Miniut Setting forth his right of mem=
=bership here; directed to the monthly meeting of **East Hoosuck** he being
about to take a Journey there on business, which this meeing approves
he being a member of this meeting, and the Clerk is directed to give him
a Coppy hereof

R[*blot*] Received a Removal Certificate for **David Shepherd** and **David
Shepherd Ju**ᴿ from the monthly meeing **Smithfield** their wives and Children
which Childrens names are **Caleb, deborah, Gideon, Allen, Elisabeth** and
Lydia David Shepherd Junor his Childrens names are **Thomas Reliance**
and **John**

Barker pro-
duce
Certificate

James Barker attended this meeting and produced a Certificate from
the monthly meeting at **East Hoosuck** Setting forth right of
membership and their Unity of his Visiting his relations on which
Certificate was Endorsed his attending this meeting to a degree
of Satisfaction

[?]tin Recd

The Women friends Inform they have admitted **Patient Austin**
Wife of **Joseph Austin**, into membership: which this meeing
Concurs with

[?]ficate

The Committee appointed to ~~the case~~ take the necessary care in
the Case of **John Williams** request for a Certificate to **RhodIsland** monthly meeting, Setting forth his Clearness Respecting
Marriage and Conversation, Report, That they find things
~~so far~~ clear in that case; provided Said **John** would acknowledg
his misconduct (in this meeting) toward a young Woman he
formerly kept Company with: And he appearing in this meeting and
acknowledging and condemning the Same, desiring Friends
to pass it by – And this Meeting accepts the Same for Satisfaction
Whereupon a Certificate was prepared and Signed by the Clerk – –
directed to the Monthly meeting of **RhodIsland** in his behalf Setting
forth his clearness respecting marriag and Conversation

Collected 2£ – 1ˢ – 6ᵈ

12 month
1781   At a Monthly Meeting held in **Dartmouth** the 17ᵗʰ of 12ᵗʰ month 1781

The Representatives **Stephen Buffinton** and **Barnabus Russell** both present

A Certificate in behalf of **Joseph Wing** directed to the monthly meeting at **Accoaxet,** Setting forth his clearness respecting marriag and Conversa= =tion was Signed in this meeting by the Clerk

Allen
Certificate   A Certificate in behalf of **John Allen** (son of **Jonathan**) directed to the monthly meeting of **Ninepartners** Setting forth his being a member of this meeting, Clearness respecting marriage and Settlement of his out= ward affaiers was produced in this meeting and Signed by the Clerk

Queries
Answer.d
Represenᵗ
apointed   The Queries were read in this meeting and answers thereto Read and approved and an Epistle to the next Quarterly meeting prepared and Signed by the Clerk; all which is forwarded to Said Quarterly meeting by our Representatives; Who are **Stephen Buffinton, Benjamin Smith 2ⁿᵈ Samuel Smith William Anthony Juʳ** and **Barnabus Russell** And they to report next monthly meeting

M Wilcox
desires a
few lines   **Micajah Wilcox** Informing this meeting he intends a Visit to **Oblong** to see his Relations, and make Some Stay there; desireing a few lines thereon: this meeting approving of the Same he having a Right of membership amoung us, and the Clerk is directed to give a Coppy of this miniute   Collected – 1£ – 1ˢ – 10ᵈ

adjorn.d   This meeting adjourns to the 26ᵗʰ Instant, after the meeting for Worship

Mett   Mett by Adjournment the 26ᵗʰ of the 12ᵗʰ month 1781

The Representatives being called both present

dividing
preparative
meeting
refer.d   The Committee appointed to inspect into the expedency of dividing our Preparitive meeting and to Remove Some defects amoung us Report that they have made some progress therein and desires said matter continued; it is therefore defer.d to next monthly meeting under their care and then they to make report

Complaint
against
J Johnson   The Overseers inform.d in writing that **James Johnson** had conducted very unbecoming in his Conversation as Set forth in said writeing: There fore we appoint **William Barker, David Shepherd & Henry Smith** to enquire into the case and Labour with said **Johnson** for the above matters as Truth may open the way and report next monthly meeting

This Meeting adjourns to the 6ᵗʰ day of next month after the meeting for Worship

Mett by adjournment the 6ᵗʰ day of the 1ˢᵗ month 1782

The Representatives being called neither of them Present

Comᵗᵉᵉ col
lect friend
Sufferings
report   The Committee appointed Some time [?] to Collect Friends Sufferings made Report. That they have made Such progress therein as to Collect most of them to this time, and the account of them being read in this meeting and approved was directed to be signd by the Clerk and sent up to the meeting for Sufferings and a Coppy thereof Left on file

1st month
1782

Report from
Quarterly
meeting

At a Monthly Meeting held in **Dartmouth** the 21st of 1st month 1782
The Representatives are **Luthan Wood** and **William Gifford** present
	The Representatives to the Quarterly meeting, Report, that they all
attended that meeting, and now produce an Epistle from the Quarterly
meeting – a Transcript of last Yearly meetings: Epistles Coppies of two
miniuts of the meeting for Sufferings, and an Epistle from **New York**
all which were read ~~to~~ in this meeting & well accepted: and by the
Epistle from the Quarterly meeting and **New York**, and one of the miniuts
from the meeting for Sufferings we have a discription of the Sorrowful
Dangers which some members of Society have expos.d them Selves and the
Reproach the Truth may be brought under by them in the pursuite of such
Voyages and business as is therein pointed out – This meeting feeling a

Com^tee appoin
ted on ad
=vioice from
New York
& on Clan
=destine Trade

concern to make enquiry and gaurd & preserve our fellow members from
the Consequences of these things: do appoint **William Anthony Ju^r**
William Wood, John Devol, William Gifford and **James Davis** a Committee
to make the necessary enquiry in the compass of this monthly meeting
Respecting these things and to Labour therein as they in True Wisdom
may be directed and to make report next monthly meeting[38]

on dividing
preparitive
meeting

	The Committee to inspect into the expedency of dividing our Preparative
meeting and to Labour to remove some defects amoung us report that they
have made Some further progress therein & desire said matter Continud it is
refer.d to next monthly meeting under their care they then to make report

[?] case of
J Johnson
continued

	The Friends appointed to enquire into and Labour with **James**
Johnson on his unbecoming Conversation, Report, that they have taken
the necessary care in that matter; And that he acknowledges his mis=
=conduct, and is willing to make Friends Satisfaction, and that they
think it best to be continued under the care of a Committee to see it
fully accomplished; therefore this meeting doth continue the Same
under the care of the Same Friends who are to make report of their progress
therein to next monthly meeting

Collected – £1 – 18s – 4d

adjourn

Mett

This meeting Adjourns to the 30th Instant after the meeting for Worship
	Mett by adjournment the 30th of the 1st month 1782
	The Representatives being called both present

matters refer.d
next month
ly meeting

	There being Several matters advised and recommended from the Yearly
and Quarterly meetings, they are defer.d to the Consideration of next

38. The epistle condemned "Freighting and clearing out Vessels, from different parts of thus
Continent, for particular Ports, under Solemn engagements of the faithful performance thereof, instead
of which they have sometimes under a pretence of being taken, and sometimes without such a Covering,
gone directly to different places, thereby intentionally falsifying that which they had solemnly agreed to."
See Meeting for Sufferings: Minutes, 1775–1793, 1st Mo. 9, 1782, pp. 162–65, New England Yearly Meeting
of Friends Records (MS 902) (Special Collections and University Archives, UMass Amherst Libraries).

monthly meeting, on account of the small number of meembers at
this adjournment

Friends Suffer ings Collected
The Committee appointed to Collect Friends Sufferings, Report that
they have Collected an additional account Since last monthly meeting
which after being read was approved and ordered to be Sent up to the
meeting for Sufferings and a coppy left on file

2ⁿᵈ month 1782
At a Monthly Meeting held in **Dartmouth** the 18ᵗʰ day of 2ⁿᵈ month 1782
The Representatives are **William Barker** and **Abner Devoal [Devol]** both present

William Jack son attended this meeting
Our Esteemed Friend **William Jackson** attended this meeting with a
Certificate from **New Garden** Monthly meeting in **Chester County** in
Pensylvania dated the 10ᵗʰ of 1ˢᵗ month 1781. also a few lines from the
Same monthly meeting dated ~~the 2ⁿᵈ month~~ 3ᵈ of 2ᵈ month 1782
Which were Read in this meeting to Satisfaction and his Visit and
Labour of Love acceptable to us[39]

The Committee appointed Last monthly meeting to make inquiry
and inspection if there be any Such Conduct in any of our members as
describ.d in the Epistle from **New York** to the Quarterly meeting and
in a miniute of the meeting for Sufferings Report – as here annexed
,, To the Monthly meeting to be held the 18ᵗʰ of 2ᵈ month 1782

Comᵗᵉᵉ report on Clandestine Trade
According to apointment; we have met and taken into Cosideration
,, the Contents of the Epistle from **New York** made inquiry among our
,, members and where Suspicion arose have cautiond and advised endea=
,, =voring to Set forth the bad tendency of Such proceedings accordings
,, according to our ability: and as nothing appears openly, conclude
,, best to let the matter rest for the present under friends weighty Conside-
,, ration and inspection

From your friends **James Davis**   **William Wood**
William Anthony Juʳ **John Devoal [Devol]**
                William Gifford

This meeting Concluds to continue Said Committee in the further care
of that matter and make report of their progress therein to next monthly
meeting

Report on divid ing preparative meeting
The Committee to inspect into the expediency of dividing our
Preparitive meeting and to Labour to remove defect amoung us
Report, that they have made some further progress therein and that as
it is a matter that cannot be speedily accomplished desire it continued
it is therefore continued under their further care and progress who are
to make report thereof to next monthly meeting

39. William Jackson (1746–1834) was recorded a minister in 1775. See Memorials concerning Deceased
Friends, 214–26.

J Johnsons case refer.d　　The friends appointed to Labour with **James Johnson** on his unbe=
=coming Conversation and his acknowledging his misconduct there-
=in, Report that they wait to receive an answer from **William Hassey**
at **Nantucket**, whom **James** Said had wronged him and on that ~~accont~~
account desires the matter defer.d. This meeting ~~this~~ defers s^d matter under
the same friends, who are desired to Labor to discover the Sincerity
of **James** condemning his misconduct and they to make report of
their progress thereof next monthly meeting

B Wings Certificate　　**Bennet Wing** Informes this meeting that he intends Marriage with
Rhoda Ricketson Daughter of **William Ricketson** & the said **Bennet**
produceing a Certificate from **Sandwich** monthly meeting Setting forth his
Clearness ~~Setting forth~~ respecting marriage he also hath consent of Parents
in Writeing

Letter from Nantucket behaf G Fol= =ger　　**George Folger** informes this meeting he intends marriage with **Rebeckah**
Shove. And produced a few lines from two Friends of **Nantucket**
monthly meeting Setting forth that they find nothing to hinder his
his having a Certificate on that account, at their next monthly meeting
and that they were appointed by the meeting for that purpose.
Said **George** also produced consent of Parents in writeing

B Wings proposal of marriage　　**Bennet Wing** and **Rhoda Ricketson** appeared in this meeting and
declared their intentions of taking Each other in marriage

G Folgers proposal of marriage　　as also **George Folger** and **Rebeckah Shove** who were desired to wate
till next monthly meeting for their answer

Collected – £2 – 3^s – 10^d

Respecting the Bibles　　This Meeting Receiv^d a Coppy of a miniute of the meeting for Sufferings
containing an extract from an Epistle from **Philidelphia** respecting
the Bibles, Which Friends Subscribed for: Expressing that there is no
way yet opened for procuring them to Satisfaction and this mnniute and extract were
Read in this meeting

adjourned　　This Meeting is adjurn.d till tomorrow at the 11th hour

mett　　Met by adjournment the 19th day of the 2^d month 1782
The Representatives being called both Present.

Respecting being Joind to Sandwich Quarter　　The matter refer.d from last Quarterly meeting to us in regard to our
Endeavouring to remove the Obstacles that renders the unfitness of our being
Annexed to **Sanwich** Quarter: was taken into weighty consideration in this
meeting: and we are very desireous to be in Labour to remove the above
Dificiencies as Truth opens the way: and as there is a large Committee under
appointment by this meeting, in order to remove those defects Complained of
This matter is referd to next monthly meeting under their care

The Women Friends Inform that there is a Difficalt matter Subsisting among

The women Friends desires assistance them and desire the assistance of this meeting: therefore we appoint our Friends **William Wood, James Davis, Benjamin Slocum, Stephen Buffinton Seth Russell, Peleg Gifford, Giles Slocum, Benjamin Chase** and **Abiel Gifford** to advise and assist the Women Friends as Truth opens the way

Concerning frinds books The Committee appointed Some time past to Collect this meetings books report, that they want some addition as there is one assent Therefore we appoint **Joseph Tucker Junor Elijah Gifford** and **Benjamin Howland 2ᵈ** to Joine withe the former Committee and accomplish that matter and to Settle with **Caleb Russell** in behalf of this meeting as said **Caleb** took Some books to dispose of for this meeting

Hannah Smith Bill The Overseers of the poor handed in an account to this meeting from **Hannah Smith** for keeping **Alice Smith** 35 weeks to the amount of £10 – 10ˢ – 0ᵈ Lawful money which being accepted, The Treasurer is ordered to pay the Same when he is suplied with money from this meeting

Certificate for Henry Howland This meeting sign.d a Removal Certificate for **Henry Howland** and **Abigail** his Wife and **Prince** and **Beriah Howland** their young Children directed to the monthly meeting of **Accokset** they being remov.d there to Live

Jeremiah Smith [?] **Jeremiah Smith** attended this meeting with a Coppy of a miniute of the Monthly meeting held at **Saratoga** the 11ᵗʰ of 1ˢᵗ month 1782 which was to Satis =faction, The Said miniut being Endorssed in this meeting to the Same purpose and Signed

3 month 1782 At a Monthly meeting held in **Dartmouth** 18ᵗʰ of 3ʳᵈ month 1782 The Representatives are **William Wood** and **Thomas Russell** both present

Report on Clandes= =tine Trade The Committee to make Enquiry if there be any Such Conduct in any of our members as describd in the Epistle from **New York** to the Quarterly meeting and miniute from the meeting for Sufferings Report, that they have made Some further inspection and find nothing different from their report last monthly meeting that matter is therefore conti= =nued under the care of the Same Friends who are to report of their progress therin to next monthly meeting

[?] on di= viding prpri= ative[?] meeting The Committee to inspect into the expedency of dividing our preparative meeting and to Labour in removing Such defect as they find among us Report: that they hve been in a further progress in those things and that it their Judgmet that they be continued under of a Committee for a yet further Pogress in those weighty matters

report respect ing being Joind [to?] Sandwich Quarter The same Committee having that matter in charge respecting this meeting being annexed to **Sandwich** Quarter as recommended from last Quarterly meeting, Report, – as Follows ~~Whih~~ Which is accepted

„ We of the Committee unto whom the matter was Refer.d respecting „ being annext to **Sandwich** Quarter, having taken Said matter under

,, Consideration, and find those obstacles Still reaining [remaining]which we have
,, been in a Labour to remove, But as that is a work of time, we as a
,, Committee have been unde deep Engagement of mind that this good work
,, may be affected in its proper Season in which exersise we had measurably
,, to witness the owning hand and arm of Divine goodness to be with us
,, to our encouragement; but as yet we do not find the way open to be
,, Joined to **Sandwich** Quarter as those Obstacles are remaining which is
,, cause of pain and Sorrow of heart

    Signed by Order and in behalf of said Committee By   **Samuel Smith**
                                                               Deborah Hicks

Dated this 14ᵗʰ of 3 month 1782
The above said Committee are Continued in Said Service and to report
next monthly meeting

J Johnsons
Case defer.ᵈ
    The Friends appointed to Labour with **James Johnson** on his mis=
conduct; and to discover his Sincerity in condemning the Same report
That ~~that~~ they have made further progress therein, yet they desire the
matter deferd to next monthly meeting, which is accordingly under
their care they then to make report

Received a Cer=
=tificate for
G Folger
    Received a Certificate from the monthly meeting of **Nantucket**
in behalf of **George Folger** Setting forth that he is a member of
Society and Clear of marriage Entangelments thare

Stephen Barker
request a
Certificate
    Stephen Barker requests a Certificate to the Monthly meeting of
Sandwich, Setting forth his Right of membership and Clearness
Respecting marriage: therefore **Benjamin Gifford Juʳ** and **John
Devoal [Devol]** are appointed to take the necesary care of that matter and
if they find things clear to bring a Certificate to next monthly meeting

T Russell desiers
advice in dispos
ing Estate
    At the Request of **Timothy Russell** for advice from this meeting
respecting his disposeing his outward Estate; we appoint our
Friends **Giles Slocum** and **Joseph Barker**, to advise said **Timothy**
therein, and Report to next monthly meeting

George Folger &
[Bennet] Wing
[Received] their
answers respec
ting marriage
    George Folger and **Rebeckah Shove** appearinging in this meeting
for their answer; as also **Bennet Wing** and **Rhoda Ricketson**
which were Each Cupple might proceed to take Each other in –
Marriage at some convenent time between this and next monthly
meeting: adviseing with the Friends therein which this meeting
Shall appoint to See Said marriages Orderly Solemnized and our
Friends **Thomas Russell** and **Jonathan Willbor** are appointed to see
the first cupple and **Joseph Gifford** the last cupples amrriages orderly
Solemnized; and to make report next monthly meeting

                    Collected £1 – 6ˢ – 3ᵈ

adjourns   This meeting is adjourned to the 27th instant after meeting for Worship

mett   Mett by adjournment the 27 of the 3^d month 1782

The Representatives being called both present

addition to the Com^{tee} for S Barker   The Friends appointed (at the first Sitting of their meeting) to take the necessary care on the request of **Stephen Barker** for a Certificate Request an addition to their number in that matter, therefore **Seth Huddelston** and **William Mosher** are added to them

Queries an swered   The Queries were answered in this meeting, and an Epistle Signd to the Quarterly meeting all which are forwarded to the Said

Representa= =tives   Quarterly meeting by our Representatives **James Davis**, **Caleb Greene** Representatives (**in margin**) **William Mosher**, **Chilon Wood** and **Benjamin Chase** and they to report to ~~and they to report~~ next monthly meeting

Orderd to Draw mo ney for year =ly meeting   This meeting directs that the Representatives to the Quaterly meeting Draw the sum of £3 – 12^s – 0 Out of our Treasury and pay the Same to the yearly meeting Treasurer in order to Supply the yearly meeting Stock and report next monthly meeting

Com^{tee} to assist Women fri^d report the matter Se=t =tled   The Friends appointed last monthly meeting to assist the Women Friends in a difficult matter Subsisting in their meeting Report therein, and that matter is Settled as will apear by the records of of the Womens meeting

---

4 month 1782   At a Monthly Meeting held in **Dartmouth** the 15th of 4 month 1782 The Representatives are **John Devol** and **Seth Huddelston** both Present

Return from Q meeting   The Representatives to the Quarterly meeting, Report, that they all attended and produced an Epistle from the meeting which was read in this meeting to Satisfaction: As also the Extracts from our last yearly meeting miniutes

Copies of Epistles Receivd   This meeting Receiv.d 160 Epistles Coppys of the last Epistles from the yearly meeting in **London** : also 160 Coppies of the Representation on behalf of Friends, to the President of Council, and the Assembly of **Pensylvania** One of Each of which were read in this meeting to good Satisfaction

Chusing overseers refer^d   The Choice of overseers being under consideration at this time it is Refer.d to next monthly meeting for further consideration, as also Overseers of Poor who are continued till others are appointed

Report on Clandstine Trade   The Committee to make inquiry, If there be any Such conduct in any of our members, as discribed in an Epistle from **New York** to the Quartly meeting, Report that they have had that matter under ~~can~~ Inspection but do not find any thing different from last report; they are therefore Continued in that Service, and are desired to make diligent and Impartial Inquiry in those things, and make report next monthly meeting

<table>
<tr><td>Report on
clandestine
Trade
dividing
preparitive
meeting</td><td>The Committee to inspect into the expedency of dividing our Preparitive meeting and Indeavor to remove the obstacles which hinders such a division make report that they have been Still further in a labour therein and think it best deferd another month for further progress; it is accordingly defer.d under their care who are then to report</td></tr>
</table>

Report on clandestine Trade dividing preparitive meeting

The Committee to inspect into the expedency of dividing our Preparitive meeting and Indeavor to remove the obstacles which hinders such a division make report that they have been Still further in a labour therein and think it best deferd another month for further progress; it is accordingly defer.d under their care who are then to report

On being annexed to Sandwich Qarter

The same Committee had the matter in charge respecting the Meeting being annexed to **Sandwich** Quarter: and made report of their sence therein Last monthly meeting: which is all that appears needful therein at present

Case of James Johnson

The Friends appointed to Labour with **James Johnson** on his misconduct and Sencerity of Condemning it, Report, that they have not fully accomplished that matter, it is therefore continued under their care and if he doth not make give them Satisfaction, that they draw a Testimony of his denial and bring to next monthly meeting

Certificate for Stephen Barker

The Friends appointed to take the necessary care in the request of **Stephen Barker** for a Certificate to **Sandwich** monthly meeting Seting forth his right of membership and clearness respecting marriage Report that they have taken the necessary care therein and brought a Certificate with them which was read in this meeting and sign.d by Clerk

~~The friends appointed last~~

T Russell case

The Friends appointed last monthly meeting to advise **Timothy Russell** according to his request, in Selling his outward Estate, Report, that they have advised him therein tho' the matter of his disposing his Estate, is droped for the present

George Folger and Bennett Wing marriage

The friends appointed to see **George Folger** and **Rebecca Shoves** and also **Bennett Wing** and **Rhoda Ricketsons** marriages orderly Solemnized make Report that they all attended said marriages and that they were Solemniz.d in Some degree Orderly

money paid to Quarly meeting

The Representatives to the Quarterly meeting inform, that they Receiv.d the money, ordered last monthly meeting, for our monthly meetings Treasurer, to be paid to the yearly meeings Treasurer, and that it was paid to him as directed

Judith Hathaway disown.d

The Women friends inform.d last monthly meeting, that they deny.d **Judith Hathaway** Wife of **Jethro hathaway** 2.d, which tho then omitted being minitted, yet this meeting concurs there with

J Moshers proposal of marriage

Joseph Mosher and **Elisabeth Briggs** Declared their Intentions of marri= =age, and were desired to wait till next monthly meeting for their answer Said **Mosher** having produced a Certificate from **Smithfield** monthly meeting also parents consent

Andrew Nicols Certificate Endors.d

Andrew Nicols the 3.d being about to return to live with his father again within **South Kingston** monthly meeting, this meeting Endorst a

few lines on the back of his Certificate which he brought from said
monthly meeting

Meetings Books Collected　　The Committy appointed Some time past to collect this meetings Books
Now make report, that they have collected them, as by the list on file,
And that they have Settled with **William Mosher** and Rece^d – 0 – 17 – 5 of
of him and £0 – 12^s – 0^d of **Caleb Russel [Russell]** for Books which they Sold belong=
=ing to this meeting Said money is paid to the Treasurer

Jon^a Wilber & Thos Russell to take care of sd Books　　**Jonathan Wilbor** and **Thom^a Russell** are appointed to have the care
of this meetings Books as a fore said and to lend them out to whom they
may see proper, and to see them return.d, and they to remining that Service
till others are appointed when they are to make Report.

[?] make fence　　Friend concluded to to meat tomorrow generally to mend up the
Fence round our meeting house

　　　　　　　　　　　　　　　　Collectted – £1 – 4^s – 4^d

Adjourns　　This Meeting Adjourns to the 24th Instant after the meeting of Worship
mett　　Mett by adjournment the 24 of 4 month 1782
The Representatives being called both Present

Collecting Suffering　　The Committee appointed sometime past to Collect friends Suffering
have not accomplish that part of the business in compleating their
account of Friends Sufferings as to present it to this meeting and
desire the meeting to adjourn

Jos Rotch Certificate　　Received a Removal Certificate from the monthly meeting of
Nantucket, in behalf of **Joseph Rotch**, who hath removed in the
Compass of this meeting to Live

Adjournd　　This Meeting adjourns to the 8th of next month after the meeting for Worship
Mett by adjournment y^e 8th of the 5 month 1782. The Repre=
sentatives are **Seth Huddleston** present and **John Devall [Devol]** not
Present. For which he hath rendered no excuse

[?] account of Sufferings　　The Committee to Collect accounts of Friends Sufferings having
Corrected those accounts that wear [were] returned from the meeting
of Sufferings, which after being Read were approved and
Sent up to the meeting for Sufferings.

5 month 1782　　At a Monthly Meeting held in **Dartmouth** ye 20th of 5th mo 1782
The Representatives are **Jonathan Willbor** and **Prince Potter** present

Overseers refe.rd　　The appointing Overseers being again under consideration
it is refer.d to next monthly meeting; as also Overseers of the poor

To assist Women friends　　On the Women friends requesting the assistance of this meeting
in a dificult case subsisting in their meeting; our friends **Abial
Gifford, James Davis Elijah Gifford, Seth Huddelston Caleb Greene**
are appointed for that purpose, and to report to next monthly
meeting

John Barker request a Certificate

John Barker requests a Certificate to the Monthly Meeting of **Rhod Island:** Setting forth his clearness respecting marriage and conversation: Therefore **Stephen Buffinton** and **Peleg Gifford** are appointed to take the necessary care in that matter and if they find things clear to draw a Certificate and bring to next monthly meeting

on Ellicit Trade

The Committy to make enquiry if there be any Such unwar= rantable conduct in any of our members as described, in an Epistle from **New York** to the mee[ti]ing for Sufferings, – Report, that they have laboured and advised where they have Susspected Such conduct – they are continued in that Service and **Benjamin Taber** is added to them; and they are desired to make further Inspection and labour in those things; and make report next monthly meeting

dividing preparitive meeting

The Committee to Inspect into the Expeedency of dividing our Preparitive meeting, and to endeavour to remove Such obstacles as hinders Such a division: Report that they have continued their labour therein, and that it be refer.d another month; which is accordingly under their care, and they then to make report

James Jon= =son case

The Friends appointed to Labour with **James Johnson** on his misconduct, and to discover his Sincerity in condemning it report that they have laboured further with him; Yet they they are continued in that Service, who are desired to extend their further care in that matter; and if he on their labour with him doth not give them Satisfaction, to draw a Testimony of his denial and bring to next monthly meeting; Informing him thereof: or otherwise to make report accordingly

Jos Mosher answer

Joseph Mosher and **Elisabeth Brigg** appeared in this meeting for their Answer; and their answer was; We do not find any thing to hinder their proceeding in marriage and that they might proceed to take Each other in marriage at some convenient time between this and next monthly meeting – advising with the Friend this meeting Shall appoint to see said marriage Orderly Solemnized Said friends are **Benjamin Smith 2ᵈ** and **William Anthony Juʳ** who are to report next monthly meeting

Wᵐ Sanford minite returnd

William Sanford returned the Coppy of the miniute of this meeting of yᵉ 10ᵗʰ month last: with an Endorsment from the monthly meeting of **Ninepartners**, that he attended that meeting to Satisfaction

Wm Barker   **William Barker** gave in an account of Hay and carting
Hay   for this meeting amounting to £1 – 7ˢ – 6ᵈ. Which the Treasurer
Is directed to pay   Collected – £1 – 3ˢ – 11ᵈ

---

6 Month   At a Monthly Meeting held in **Dartmouth** yᵉ 17ᵗʰ of 6ᵗʰ month 1782
1782   **Jonathan Willbor** is appointed Clerk for this day
Representatives are **Peleg Gifford Joseph Barker Seth Huddleston** and
Benjamin Howland 2ᵈ all present

John Barker   A Certificate for **John Barker,** to the Monthly meeting at **Rhod Island**
Certificate   Setting forth his right of membership and clearness respecting marriage
was Signed in this meeting by the Clerk

L Smith   **Lamuel Smith** informs this meeting that he is about to take a Voyage
request a   to Sea, and he requesting our Certificate, Setting forth his right of member=
Certificate   =ship: therefore we appoint our friend **Joseph Tucker Juʳ Peleg Gifford**
Thomas Russell and **Jonathan Willbor** to inspect the Circumstances of
of the Vessel and Voiage, and if they find things clear, to prepare a
Certificate and bring it to the Adjournment of this meeting if **Lamuel**
doth not want it before, if he doth the Committee may Sign in behalf
of Said meeting

adjourn.d   This Meeting Adjourns to the 24ᵗʰ of this Instant
Mett   Mett by Adjournment this 24ᵗʰ of 6ᵗʰ month 1782
The Representatives are **Peleg Gifford, Joseph Barker, Seth Huddleston**
and **Benjamin Howland 2ᵈ** all present

Chusing over=   The choise of Overseers coming again under the notice of this meeting
=seers refer'd   It is refer'd to next Monthly meeting for a choise of them; as also over=
seers of the poor

Women   The Friends appointed to assist the Women by their request last
Visited   monthly meeting; Report, that they have assisted in the ability affordeᵈ

report on   The Committee to make further enquiry, if there be any Such unwar=
unwarrantable   rentable conduct in any of our members as discribed in an Epistle from
Trading   **New York** to the meeting for Sufferings: Report that they have made
further enquiry, and where such conduct was Suspected, have given
Such advice as they wear [were] enabled to: Yet that matter continued under
their futher care who are to report to next monthly meeting

[?]dividing   The committee to inspect into the expediency of dividing our Prepari=
preparitive   =tive meeting, and labour to remove such Obstacles as hinder such a
meeting   division, Report that they have continued their labour therein; yet desire
the matter continued another month; it is accordingly defer'd under the
care of the Same Committee to next monthly meeting they then to report

Case of James   The Friends appointed in the case of **James Johnson's** misconduct Report
Johnson   that they have not accomplished that matter, as one of the Committee was

Sick, and they request it may be defered, till next monthly meeting under
their care, and **Stephen Buffinton** and **William Sanford** are added to them
who are desired to extend their care in that matter so as to accomplish it
before next monthly meeting and then to make report

Joseph Moshers
marriage

The friends appointed to attend the marriage of **Joseph Mosher**
and **Elisabeth Briggs,** Report that they attended said marriage and
that they did not find but it was in Some good degree orderly Solmenized

Women's
request

The Women friends requesting to this meeting to assist them in
Labouring to remove defects respecting Plainness, and other
defect, Which this meeting taking into serious consideration
do appoint **James Davis Abiel Gifford** and **Caleb Greene** a

A Committee, to Joine the Women in that Service in removing
those defects so prevelent amoung the youth and others and make
Report to next monthly meeting

Elis Mosher
Certificate
Signed

A Removal Certificate in behalf of **Elisabeth Mosher** ~~was~~
Wife of **Joseph Mosher** Setting forth her right of membership directly
to the monthly meeting of **Smithfield** was Signed in this meeting
by the Clerk   Collected – £1 – 9ˢ – 10½ᵈ

Adjornd

This meeting adjourns to the 26ᵗʰ Instant after meeting for Worship

Mett

Mett by adjournment the 26ᵗʰ of 6ᵗʰ month 1782

The Representatives being called are **Peleg Gifford**, **Joseph Barker**
Seth Huddleston, and **Benjamin Howland 2ᵈ** all present

Clerk for
this day

Caleb Greene, being assistant is appointed Clerk for this day.

Laml Smith
Certificate
Sign'd

A Certificate was Signed in this meeting by the Clerk, in behalf of
Lamuel Smith, Setting forth his right of membership directed to whom
it may concern; he being about to take Voyage to Sea.

Complaint
against
Giels Slocum
& Caleb
Anthony

The Overseers Inform (by way of Preparitive meeting) that **Giles**
Slocum Juʳ and **Caleb Anthony** did some time past fall into a
bodily Strife, so far that Some blows were given for which they
have been laboured with by said Overseers, but they did not find them
dispos'd to give friends Satisfaction: Therefore **Daniel Ricketson**
Prince Potter and **Jonathan Willbor** are appointed to take an opper=
=tunity of Solid conference with the young men, and if they do not find
Satisfaction to draw a Testimony of their denial and bring to the next monthly
meeting, and if otherwise to make report accordingly

Request
from Sand=
=wich

This meeting receiving the following request from **Sandwich** monthly meeting
From our Monthly meeting of Friends held at **Rochester** for **Sandwich**
the 1ˢᵗ day of the 6 month 1782

To the monthly meeting of **Dartmouth**
Philip Howland, Having had a right of membership with us and

Served an apprintiship in the verge of your meeting, Since which
we have been informed, he has deviated from our religious principles perticully
in Sailing in a Vessel Armed in a warlike manner – which misconduct
we now desire you will labour with him for, as Truth and our discipline
may direct – with our Salutation of love we conclude your Friends
and Brethren

   Signed in and on behalf of Said meeting by **Richd Delano** Clerk

Committee on Philip Howlands case Whereupon our Friends **Joseph Tucker Ju^r** and **James Davis** are appoint=
=ed to labour with the Said **Philip Howland** on his said misconduct and
if he doth not give them Satisfaction, to prepare a Testimony of his denial
and bring with them to next monthly meeting

Sent up to Quar= =terly Meeting The Queries were read and answers thereto read, and after some
amendment, were approved, and sent up to the Quarterly meeting with
our Epistle which was also read and Signed by the Clerk and Sent
up by our Representatives, who are **Samuel Smith**, **Barnabus Mosher Ju^r**
Micajah Wilcox and **Thomas Russell**, and they to make report next
monthly meeting.

7 month 1782 At a Monthly meeting held in **Dartmouth** y^e 15th of 7th month 1782
The Representatives are **John Devol** & **Chilon Wood** both present

Overseers appointed The Choice of Overseers being refer'd from last monthly meeting to
this where upon **James Davis**, **Joseph Barker**, **Caleb Greene**, **Seth Hud=**
=dleston & **Caleb Russell** are appointed, and a further choice referd to
next monthly meeting

Overseers of Poor The Choice of Overseers of the Poor being also refered to this meeting
Seth Russell, Jonathan Willbor, John Devoal [Devol], Thomas Russell, Barnabus
Russell and **Chilion [Chilon] Wood** for that Service the year ensuing

dividing preparitive meeting The Committe to inspect into the expedency of dividing our Preparitive
meeting, and to labour to remove such obstacles which hinder Such a
division Report, that they have continued their labour therein, yet
desire the matter refer'd another month; it is accordingly defer'd
under the care of the Same Committee to next monthly meeting they then
to make report

[?]portion unwarrentable [Trading] The Committee to make further enquiry and discovery, if there is
any such unwarrantable conduct in any of our members as de=
=scribed in an Epistle from **New York** to the meeting for Sufferings
with a coppy of a minute of that meeting thereon Report, that they
Endeavoured to discharge themselves in that Trust by inspecting,
and where any have been Suspected, to labour with them as way
opened – yet they are continued that Service and to make report
next monthly meeting

James Johnsons case

The friends appointed in the case of **James Johnson**'s misconduct report, that they have not accomplished that matter, and that it might be defer'd till next monthly meeting, it is accordingly defer'd under their care, who are desired to accomplish the same as soon as may be and make report to next monthly meeting

Giles Slocum Ju^r and Caleb Anthony Case

The Friends appointed to treat with **Giles Slocum Ju^r** and **Caleb Anthony** on their falling into a bodily Strife in which blows were given Report, that they have had a Soled conference with the young men who gave them a good degree of Satisfaction, with a paper condemning their said misconduct; Which accepted for Satisfaction, provoided they cause said paper to be read in a publick manner at the close of a first day meeting of Worship before next monthly meeting they being present and make report thereof to that meeting

Collected – £1 – 2^s – 8^d

Adjornd

This meeting adjourns to y^e 24th Instant after the meting of Worship

Mett

Mett by adjournment y^e 24th of 7th month 1782 Reprsent^es both present

*Testimony a= against **Philip Howland** Sign'd & inform.d*

The Friends appointed to labour with **Philip Howland** on his mis= =conduct and if he did not give them Satisfaction to draw a Testimony of his denial, Report, that they had an oppertunity with him and that he did not give them Satisfaction they therefore produced a Testimony of his denial, which was read and after a little alte= =ration Sign'd by the Clerk, who is directed to read the Same publick =ly in our usual manner, and make report to next monthly meeting Said Committee also report that they informed Said **Howland** of the conclusion of this meeting

Return from Quarterly Meeting

The Representatives to the Quarterly meeting report that they all attended said meeting to Satisfaction. and produced an Epistle from the Quarterly meeting, also Transcrips of the following

Epistles Rec^d

Epistles Viz One from our Yearly meeting this year one from the Yearly meeting in **London** last year one from **Pensylvania** last year one from **Westbury** on **Long Island** ~~last~~ this year also Coppy of the Extract from our last yearly meetings minutes all which were read in thi meet to good Satisfaction

Report of Comittee on Plainness

The Committee to Joine the Women in labouring to remove Some defects respecting Plainness, and other defects among us Report, that they have maid Some progress therein, as way hath opened, and that they yet feel the weight of that Service: They are therefore continued therein, and to make report thereof when ready

Chilon Woods request for children **Chilon Wood** requesting his children may be admitted under our Care: **Thomas Hicks** and **John Devol**, are appointed to ~~take the~~ Joine the Women, and to take the necessary care therein and make report to next monthly meeting

8 month 1782 At a Monthly Meeting held in **Dartmouth** yᵉ 19ᵗʰ of 8ᵗʰ month 1782 The Representaives are **Luthan Wood** and **Thomas Mott** both present

chusing overseers refer.ᵈ An additional choice of Overseers being refer'd from Last monthly meeting to this; and some friends being named thereto yet it is refer'd to next monthly meeting

Preparitive meeting The Committee Inspect into the expedency of dividing our Preparitive meeting and to labour to remove Such Obstacles as hinder Such a division Report, that they have continued their Labour and desires the matter defer'd another month under the caare of the Same Committee; it is accordingly defer'd under their care to next monthly meeting they then make report

Contraband Trading The Committee to make further enquiry and discovery, if there is any such unwarrantable conduct in any of our members as discribed in an Epistle from **New York** to the meeting for Sufferings, with a Coppy of the meeting for Sufferings thereon, Report nothing different from last monthly meeting; they are therefore continued in that Service except **James Davis**, who desires to be dismissed therefrom, on account of other Services: he is accoringly dismissed, and **Jonathan Willbor** is appointed therein, who with the others of the Committee, are desired to attend closely to the Service and make report to next monthly meeting

James Johnson The Friends appointed in the case of **James Johnson** Report that they have not accomplished that matter he being absent from home it is therefore continued under their care, who are who are desired to accomplish the Same before next monthly meeting if it may be: and report to Said meeting

Giles Slocum Caleb Anthony The Clerk Informs that **Giles Slocum Juʳ** and **Caleb Anthony** have not caused their paper to be read as directed last monthly meeting by reason of disappointment they are therefore directed to take necessary care in that matter and report to next monthly meeting

The Clerk informs that the Testimony of the denial of **Philip Howland** had

Philip Howland denied been read as directed last monthly meeting which is as followeth Whereas **Philip Howland** of **Dartmouth** having had his Education among Friends, and under our care, but hath so far departed from the peacable profession we make, as to go Several voyages to Sea on board of Vessels Arm'd in a warlike manner, for which condition he hath been laboured with, but he continuing to Justifie the Same

Friends are concerned to give this forth as a publick Testimony
hereby disowning him from being a member of our Society and from a[-]
our care – Nevertheless it is our desire that he may com-to a Sight
and Sense of his outgoing, and a return to the way of Truth

     Given forth at our Monthly Meeting held in **Dartmouth**
by adjournment the 24th of ye 7 month 1782

     Signed in and on bhalf of said meeting by **Wm Anthony Jur** Clerk

report on Chilon Woods request   The Friends appointed to Joine the Women and take the necessary
care in **Chilon Wood**s request, make a Satisfactory report; yet
that matter is refer'd to next monthly meeting under their care
they then to make Report

Russells Bill   **Thomas Russell** hath brought in an account to this meeting for
Some repairs of the meeting house, amounting to £2: 2: 9 which
being examined is approved

[?] Gifford returned   This meeting received a copy of a minute from **Accoaxset**
Monthly meeting of 13th of 7th month last: Signifying that **John Gifford**
son of **Abiel Gifford** has returned to this meeting

friends to rec= eive Subscrip= tions   Our Friends **Micajah Wilcox, Barnabus Mosher Jur, Barnabus
Russell, Gideon Anthony, Caleb Barker, and Elijah Gifford**, are
appointed to receive such Sums as friends may Subscrib in their
freedom, toward supplying the yearly meeting Stock of £50 and report
of the Sum total so Subscribed to next Monthly Meeting

     Collected £1 6s 11d

---

9 month 1782   At a Monthly meeting held in **Dartmouth** ye 16th of 9th month 1782

The Representatives are **Benjamin Taber** & **Thomas Russell, Benjamin
Taber** present; **Thomas Russell** not present, for which no excuse or
Reason being offered

Benj Smith overseer   The additional choice of Overseers being refer'd to this meeting **Benja=
=min Smith 2d** is appointed to that place, in addition to those appointed in
the 7th month last, and a further choice is refer'd to next monthly meeting

dividing Preparitive meeting   The Committee to Inspect into the expedency of dividing our Preparitive
meeting, and to labour to remove such obstacles which hinders such a
division Report, that they have been in a labour therein; but that they
have not got through it to Satisfaction, therefor desires the matter
Continued, they accordingly continued in that Service and to report
when ready

Contraband trading   The Committee to make further ~~ther~~ enquiry, if there be any such
unwarrantable conduct in any of our members as described in an Epistle
from **New York** to the Quarterly meeting; with a coppy of the meeting
for Sufferings thereon; Report nothing different from last monthly

meeting they are therefore continued in that Service and to report
to next monthly meeting

James Johnson　　　The friends appointed in the case of **James Johnson**, Report, that
they have not accomplished that matter, by reason **James** being gone
from home, a great distance; they therefore desire the matter continued
another month, it is accordingly refer'd to next monthly meeting
under the care of the Same friends who are desired to accomplish the
same by that time and make report thereto

Giles Slocum　　　Report hath been made that **Giles Slocum Ju^r** and **Caleb Anthony**'s
Caleb Anthony　　paper was read as directed last monthly meeting

Chilon Woods　　　The friends appointed to Joine the women friends and take the
children Rec^d　necessary in **Chilon Woods** request for his Children make a Satisfactory
report: therefore this meeting concluds to admitt his Children whose
names are **Charles** and **Ruth**, into membership with us and under our care

Mary Wing　　　The women inform that they have received a removal Certificate
Certificate　from **Accoaxet** monthly meeting in behalf of **Mary Wing** wife of **Joseph Wing**

Lydia Bowdish　　　This meeting hath Signed a Certificate or Information to the monthly
Certificate　meeting of the **Oblong**, respecting **Lydia Bowdish**, daughter of **William
Bowdish**, who hath gon there some years past to live

　　　　　　Collected This meeting Collected – 1£ – 13^s – 8½^d

adjourn　　　This meeting adjorns to the 25th of this Instant after meeting of worship

Mett　　　Mett by adjornment ye 25th of 9th month 1782
The Representatives being called both present

Tho Russell　　　**Thomas Russell** render'd Sufficien reason for his not attending
at the first sitting of this meeting which is accepted

Ben Smith 3^d　　　The Overseers inform by the way of the Preparitive meeting that
Benjmin Smith son of **Eleazer** hath taken an oath in common form
before a Majestrate: it is also reported of him that he partakes
of Spiritous Lickquors to excess, that he uses Vulger and profain
Language at times: he also much neglects the attendance of our
Religious meetings, for which misconduct labour hath been bestow=
=ed for his recover, yet we appoint our friends **William Anthony Jr**
and **Thomas Russell** to labour further with him the said **Benjamin**
and if he doth not give them Satisfaction to draw a Testimony of his
denial and bring to next monthly meeting

Freeborn　　　This meeting gave forth a Testimony sign.d by the Clerk concerning
Rider　our Friend **Freeborn Rider** deceased in order to be sent up to
Testimony　the Quarterly meeting a Coppy thereof ordered to be kept on file

yearly meet=　　　The Committee appointed to to raise money by way of Subscription
=ing Stock　to Supply the Yearly meeting Stock report that they raised the Sum

of Eight pounds, which is ordered forward to the Yearly meeting
Treasurer by our Representatives

The queries were answer'd and said answers ordered forward

Sent to Qrtly meeting to the Quarterly meeting by our Representatives who are **Benjmin Taber**, **Jonathan Hart**, **Caleb Green** and **Benjamin Smith** 2ᵈ and they to make report to next monthly meeting

This meeting Adjonnes to yᵉ 6ᵗʰ day of next month after meeting of worship

Adjornd mett Mett by Adjournment yᵉ 6ᵗʰ of yᵉ 10ᵗʰ month 1782

The Representatives being called **Thomas Russell** present **Benjamin Taber** not present; and Sufficient reason being renderd for his absence

This meeting takeing under consideration the disadvantage of

meeting discontinued holding our week day meeting on that week the Quarterly meeting is held here: Therefore do discontinue all our week day meetings in that week which the Quarterly meeting is held the present year: within within the compass of this monthly meeting

There was an account Sign'd in this meeting, to the Quarterly meet=

account to Qarˡʸ meeting =ing and Ordered forward by our Representatives above named

At a Monthly meeting held in **Dartmouth** yᵉ 20ᵗʰ of 10ᵗʰ month 1782

10 month 1782 The Representatives are **Abraham Howland** & **Prince Potter** both present

The additional Choice of Overseers being refer.d to this meeting

Overseers appointed **Benjamin Taber** and **Joseph Tucker Juʳ** were appointted to that place in addition to those who were lately appointed for the year ensuing or till others are appointed in their Stead: And they together are desir.d to Seek for Wisdom to Labour and deal Impartially with all offenders in order that our Testimony may be kept up in the Several braches thereof

The Committee to make inquiry if there are Such unwarrentable and

On contraband Trade in any of our members, as discribed in an Epistle from **New York** to the Quarterly meeting with a Coppy of the meeting for Sufferings there on Report that they have been in a further labour therein: yet they are continued in that Service; and are desired to attend closely to that which will enable them to labour effectually with those in Such practises; and Report to next monthly meeting

The Friends appointed to labour further with **Benjamin Smith** son of

[?] Smith 3ᵈ referd **Eleazer,** on his taking an Oath in common form before a Magestrate and some misconduct, Report that they have had an oppertunity with him, yet desire the matter defer,d for further opportunity: it is accordingly deferd under their care to next monthly meeting they then to make report

The Representatives to the Quarterly meeting that they all attended *return from Quarterly meeting* that meeting, and produced a coppy of an Epistle from that meeting which was read in this meeting to good Satisfaction: they also return.d the Testimony concerning **Freeborn Rider**, and account concerning **Samuel Chase** for Some amendment

Freeborn Rider Testimony The Committee appointed to draw Testimonys concerning deceased friends are desired to make necessary amendment and addition in the Testimony concerning **Freeborn Rider** that was returned from the Quarterly meeting for that purpos: and make report to this meeting

[Ad?]vice of Qurly Meeting on Wills Com^{tee} appointed The Quarterly meeting (in their last Epistles) among other advices advise, that friends be careful to make their Wills without delay as Time waits for none: and some late affecting instances of Sundry Re= =movals death; and others incapiciated to make them, are fresh motives for renued care and attentions in this part of our Discipline. And That each Monthly meeting appoint a Committee, to call upon friend and excite them to a Speedy and active compliance therein: Upon which our Friends **Joseph Gifford, Samuel Smith, William Anthony Ju William Mosher, Giles Slocum**, and **Thomas Hicks** are appointed for that Service, and also to attend to that where friends have little or no Estate, but have children under age, Either provoid Suitable Gardians that the Children may be brought up and Educated among Friends – Said Committee to make report at our monthly meeting next preceeding next Quarterly meeting

The friends appointed in the case of **James Johnson** Report that they have taken the necessary care in that matter and have draughted and produced a Testimony against him: as follows

James Johnson denial Wheareas **James Johnson** hath had a right of Membership amongst us the People called Quakers, but by his departing from the Testimony of Truth, has been assisting in fitting of Vessels concerned in War: Likewise in useing of thretning Language against the People of **Nantucket**, and asserting that **William Hussey** had wronged him and when called upon he could not make it out: he hath also been too neglectful in attending of our Religious meetings: all which misconduct said **James** hath been La= boured with for, but our labour of love not having the desired effect Therefore, for the clearing of Truth and Friends from Such Scandalus conduct, we give this forth as a publick Testimony again said **James Johnson**, denying of him from being one in Unity and from being in membership with us the afore Said people: But with desire he may be so far favoured as to have a Sight and Sence of his mis=

conduct, and return to the way of well doing, and find for forgivness
with the Almighty

    Signed in and on behalf of our Said Monthly meeting
held in **Dartmouth** on the 21ˢᵗ day of the 10ᵗʰ month AD 1782

                By **William Anthony Juʳ** Clerk

Which was Signed in this meeting by the Clerk who is directed
to cause the Same to be read publickly at the close of a first day
Meeting for Worship before next Monthly meeting and Report to
Said meeting, and **William Barker** is appointed to Inform said
James of his denyal and make report to this meeting

meeting discontinu =ed
    This meeting concluds to discontinue all our week day meetings
within the compass of our monthly meeting, in that week the Quar=
=terly meeting may be held here in futer, and that whenever our
Preparitive meeting happens to fall in that week that the same be
held on the 4ᵗʰ day of the next week before

Wᵐ Barker Ju published
    William Barker Juʳ and **Deborah Shearman** Informed this
meeting of their Intentions to take each other in marriage they
are desired to wait till next monthly meeting for their answer
where upon **Peleg Gifford,** and **William Sanford** are desired to take
the nessary care and Enquiry into the said **William**s clearness respect=
=ing marriage, as also his Conversation, and make report next
Monthly meeting

John Shep= =herd Juʳ request
    John Shepherd Juʳ being about to go to **Oblong** to make some
tarry there, desires this meetings concurrence therein, this meeting
takeing it into consideration approves thereof, he having a right
of membership amoung us: and the clerk is directed to give him a
copy of this minute   Collected £1 – 8ˢ – 8ᵈ

Order on Treasurer
    This meeting directs the Treasurer to pay **Thomas Russell**
Twenty four Shillings which he disbursed for Hay, and Report
to this meeting

adjournd
    This meeting Adjorns to the 30ᵗʰ of this Instant after meeting for worship
mett Meet by adjournment yᵉ 30ᵗʰ of the 10ᵗʰ month 1782
The Representatives being called; **Prince Potter** present, **Abraham
Howland** not present for which some Excuse being rendered

11 month 1782
At a Monthly meeting held in **Dartmouth** yᵉ 18ᵗʰ of 11ᵗʰ month 1782
The Representatives are **John Devol** and **Benjamin Rider** both present

Jos Austin certificate
    This meeting Received a Certificate from the Monthly meeting
of **South Kingstown**, in behalf of **Joseph Austin**, Son of **Jeremiah
Austin**, Signifying his right of Membership, and recomending to
the care of this meeting; which is accepted

On contraband
Trade

The Committee to make enquiry if there is any of our members
acting or concerned in any contraband Trade:&:c: Report nothing
different from lasst monthly meeting they are therefore continued
in that Service (except **Benjamin Taber** who is dismissed there from
on account of other Servises) and they are desired to make diligent
enquiry and labour as they see needful and make report to
next monthly meeting

James Johnson
denal read

The Clerk reports the Testimony of Denyal of **James Johnson** hath
been read as directed

denials
drawd

The Friends appointed to draw Testimonies of denial against
John Howland son of **John** deceased, and **Benjamin Allen** son
of **Philip** deceased and inform them thereof, Reported and brought
draughts against each of them and that they have been informed
of their denials – Said Testimonies are a followeth

John How=
lands deni=
al

Whereas **John Howland** son of **John Howland** deceased having
had ~~his~~ a right of Membership among us the people called Quaker
But throug unwachfulness and disregarding the Testimony of
Truth and his own heart have so far deviated there from
as to fall into the Sin of Fornication, which is evident by his
Wifes having a child soon after marriage, also married out of
the unity of Friends: and friends having Treated with him in
love in order to shew him the evil thereof, but not receiving
any real Satisfaction; theref friends are concerned to give this
forth as a Testimony against him, the said **John Howl**and hereby
disowning him from being a member of our Society, yet our desire
is that he may become truly Sensible of his Transgression and be
Restored to the way of Truth

Given forth and Signed in and on behalf of our monthly meeting
held in **Dartmouth** yᵉ 18ᵗʰ of 11ᵗʰ month 1782 by **Wᵐ Anthony Jnʳ** Clerk

Allens
Denial

Whereas **Benjamin Allen** son of **Philip Allen** deceased having
had a right of membership with us the People called Quakers but
unwatchfulness and disregarding the Testimony of Truth in his
own heart have so far departed therefrom, as to fall into the Sin
of Fornication, which is evident by his Wifes having a child
Soon after marriage, also married out of the Unity of friends and
Friends having treated with him in love in order to shew him
tho Evil thereof, but not Receiving any real Satisfaction: Therefore
Friends are concerned to give this forth as a publick Testimony
against him the said **Benjamin Allen** hereby disowning him
from being one in membership of our Society, yet our desire is that

he may become truly Sensible of his Transgression and be resord [restored]
to the way of the truth

Given forth and Signed in, and on behalf of our Monthly meeting
held in **Dartmouth** this 18th of 11th month 1782 by **Wᵐ Anthony Juʳ** Clerk

[?] be read   Which are Signed in this meeting by the Clerk who is directed
to have said Testimonies read publickly at the close of a first
day meeting for Worship, before next monthly meeting, and
make report thereof

Abraham   **Abraham Anthony** son of **Philip** deceased and **Latitia Smith**
Anthonys   Daughter of **Benjamin Smith,** Informed this meeting, of their Intenti=
proposal of   =ons to take Each other in Marriage, said **Abraham** having produced
marriage   a Certificate from **RhodIsland** monthly meeting, Setting forth that
he is a member of that meeting, and clear of marriage intanglement
he also produced consent of parent in writeing; upon which they
were desir'd to waite till next monthly meeting for their Answer

Anne Gifford   A Certificate was Signed in this meeting by the Clerk, in behalf
certificate   of our frind **Anne Gifford,** Setting forth that she is a member in Unity with
us, and that her publick Testimony is acceptable among us: Which
was directed to **Sandwich** monthly meeting, She being about to make
a Visit within the Limmits of that meeting

John Williams   **John Williams** Informs that he hath thoughts of removing to
request advice   **RhodIsland,** desireing Friends advice therein; whereupon we
appoint **Caleb Russell, Benjamin Taber,** and **Caleb Greene** to advise
with him therein, and Report to next monthly meeting

Collected £1 – 11ˢ – 3ᵈ

adjon.d   This meeting adjorns to yᵉ 4th of next month at yᵉ close of meeting for woship
mett   mett by Adjournment yᵉ 4th of 12th month 1782
The Representatives being called both present

Ben Smith 3ᵈ   The Committee appointed in the case of **Benjamin Smith 3ᵈ**
denial   Reports they have had a conference with him but he giving them
sign'd   no Satisfaction; therefore they have produced a draft of a Testi=
=mony of denial against him which was Sign'd by the Clerk
who is desired to read it publickly at the End of a first day meeting
for Worship and make report next montly meeting; and **Thomas**
Russell is appointed to Inform him thereof and make report
next monthly meeting – Said Testimony is as followeth

Ben Smith   Wheras **Benjamin Smith** son of **Eleazer,** having had a right
denial   of membership among us the people called Quaker, but through
unwatchfulness, and disregarding the Testimony of Tuth [Truth] in his
own heart have so far deviated ~~there~~ from our Religious princiles

as to take an Oath in common Form, before a Majestrate, and
much neglects the attendance of our Religious meeting, and friends
Having Treated with him in love, in order to Shew him the Evil
thereof: but not receiving any real Satisfaction, are concerned to
give this forth as a publick Testimony against him the Said **Benjamin
Smith** hereby disowning from being a member of our Society, yet our
desire is that he may become truly Sencible of his misconduct and
be restored to the way of Truth: and by a Sencear acknowledgment
return to the Unity of his Friends again

 Given forth and Signed in and on behlf of our monthly meeting of
Friends hld in **Dartmouth** by adjornment yᵉ 4ᵗʰ of 12ᵗʰ month 1782

By William Anthony Juʳ Clerk

 William Sanford and **Peleg Gifford** report they have made the
Necessary enquiry in regard to **William Barker Junor** and find
nothin Sufficient to hinder his proceeding in marriage: Therefore

Wm Barkers
Answer
 William Barker and **Deborah Shearman** appeard for their
Answer; Which was, they might proceed to take Each other in
Marriage in Some convenient time before next monthly meeting
advising with the friends that this meeting Shall appoint to
oversee Same, who are our friends **William Sanford** and **Peleg
Gifford**, and they to make report next monthly meeting

George Smith 2ᵈ
proposal
of marriage
 George Smith 2ᵈ and **Mary Smith** (daughter of **Humphy**) declared
their Intentions of taking Each other in marriage, and wear
desired to wait till next monthly meeting for their Answer
And our Friends **Chilion Wood** and **William Anthony Juʳ** are
appointed to Enquire into the young mans clearness in respect
to marriage, and conversation, and make report next monthly meeting

Rachel Weaver
Receiv'd
 The Women Friends Inform they have received into membership
Rachel Weaver, which we concur with

Ben Shearman
Bill
 Benjamin Shearman hath given in an accompt for carting
Hay for this meeting amounting to the Sum 18 Shillings which is
accepted, and the Treasuer is ordered to pay the Same, and make
Report next monthly meeting

---

12 month
1782
At a Monthly meeting held in **Dartmouth** yᵉ 16ᵗʰ of 12ᵗʰ month 1782
The Representatives are **Stephen Buffinton** & **Seth Huddleston** both present

On contraband
Trade
 The Committee to make enquiry, if there are any of our
Members acting or concern'd in any contraband Trade &
Report, That they have maide further enquiry and that further
Care therein is necessary, they are therefore continu'd, and desir'd
to have renewed attention to that matter and make report to next
Monthly meeting

Testimonies of denials read

The Clerk Informs that the Testimonies of denials against **John Howland** son of **John** deceas'd, **Benjamin Allen** son of **Philip** deceas[d] and **Benjamin Smith 3**[d], have all been read as directed last monthly meeting

Report on John Williams request

The Friends appointed to advise with **John Williams,** on his intend =ed removal to **RhodIsland**, Report that they had taken a Soled oppertunity with him, and after giving him such advice as appeared necessary gave it as their Sense; That as he had made cosiderable Step towards a Removal by disposing part of his possessions before he asked friends advice he must now proceed as he could conveniently, with his ingage= and the Truth

B Smith 3d not informed

Thomas Russell Informs he hath not inform'd **Benjamin Smith 3**[d] of his denial, as directed, by reason said **Benjamin** was gone to Sea he is therefore desir'd to do the Same as soon as he has an oppertunyty and make report thereof

W[m] *Allens Certificate*

This meeting received, and excepted a Certificate from the monthly meeting of **Nine=Partners**, in behalf **William Allen** son of **Philip** deces[d] Signifying his right of membership, and that he is clear of marriage Engagements

W[m] *Barker married*

The Friends appointed to Oversee the marriage of **William Barker** and **Deborah Shearmans** report, that they attended said marriage and did not discover but that it was In a degree orderly Solmnized

George Smith 2[d] *proposal disap= =proved*

The friends appointed to inspect into the clearness of **George Smith** respecting marriage Report that things are not clear for such a prossodur [procedure?] according to the order establishe among us

James Davis dismist from Overseer

James Davis informs that he finds his mind dismised from the Service of an Overseer, and request a dismission from that place this meeting considering other Servises doth dismiss him from that Service

[A]braham Anthony Answer

Abraham Anthony and **Latitia Smith** appearing for their Answer which was, that they might proceed to take each other in marriage in Some convenient time before next monthly meeting, advising with the friends that this meeting shall appoint to oversee the same who are **Jonathan Willbor** and **William Anthony Ju**[r] and they to make report next monthly meeting

Abiel Gilford dismist from Committee

Abiel Gifford requesting to be dismised from the Committee for dividing the preparitive meeting on account of other Servises this meeting taking the Same into consideration doth dismis him from that Committee

Treasurer's report

The Treasurer Reports he hath paid **Benjamin Shearman** 18 Shillings for carting Hay, as ordered last monthly meeting

Collected – £5 – 8ˢ – 6ᵈ

Adjorned　This meeting adjorns to ye 25th Instant at ye conclusion of meeting of worship

Mett　Mett by adjournment ye 25th of 12th 1782

　　　　　The Representatives being called both prefect

Committee on
Account of
Wills report　The Committee appointed to call on Friends and excite
them to a steady active compliance in making their Will
Report that they have made some progress in that matter
and that they find a great deficiency amoung us on that account
The Committee is therefore continued in that Service; and to make
Report to the monthly meeting next proceeding the Quarterly
meeting in 4th month next

Esther Potters
Certificate　A certificate in behalf of **Esther Potter** daughter of **Joshua Potter**
directed to the monthly meeting of **Accoxset**, Signifying her right
of membership was Signed by the Clerk in concurrence with the
Women friends

Freeborn
Riders
Certificate　Our Testimony concerning **Freeborn Rider** deceas'd, being returned
to this meeting, by the Quarterly meeting, for a Small amendment
the same was done and is again Sent up to the Quarterly meeting

Sent to Quar=
=terly meet
ing　The Queries ware answer'd in this meeting, and an Epistle Sign'd by
the Clerk, and ordered forward to our next Quarterly meeting by our
Representatives, who are **Stephen Buffinton**, **William Mosher**, **Caleb
Greene**, **Chilon Wood**, and **Joseph Tucker**, they to make report
next monthly meeting

Report
concern=
=ing John
Potter　The Friends appointed in the case of **John Potter** some time past to
make inspection into his conduct &c. Now make report that they have
Answer,d their appointment therein: and that he the said **John Potter**
hath fallen into other misconduct particularly, in proceeding in mar=
=riage out of the Unity of Friends, and his wife having a Child son [soon] after
marriage, and they having Treated with him for his Said misconduct
and he did not give them Satisfaction, therefore said Committee are conti=
=nued in said Service and to treat further with him, and if her [he] do not
give them Satisfaction to draw a paper of denial against him and bring
it to next monthly meeting

1 month
1783　At a Monthly meeting held in **Dartmouth** y^e 20th of 1st month 1783
The Representatives are **Seth Huddleston** & **Stephen Gifford** both present

on
Contraband
Trade　The Committee to make enquiry if there are any of our members
acting or concerned in any contraband Trade &c, Report that they
have made but little progress in that matter since last monthly
meeting, and therefore they are continued in that Service, Except
Jonathan Willbor who sent a request to be dismist from that Service
on account of Sickness in his family: he is accordingly dismissed

and **William Mosher** is added to Said Committee, who are desired
to attend diligently to the matter in charge and report to next
Monthly meeting

Ben Smith 3 inform.d   **Thomas Russell** informs he hath inform.d **Benjamin Smith 3ᵈ** of his
Denial as desir'd last monthly meeting

The Friends appointed to oversee the marriage of **Abraham Anthony**
and **Latitia Smith** reports that he with the other friend attended
the marriage – and that it was in Some good degree orderly Solemniz.d

Return from Quar meet =ing Epistles Recᵈ   The Representatives to the Quarterly meeting report, that they
all attended, and produced an Epistle from said meeting, together
with a coppy of a minute, which ware read in this meeting to good
Satisfaction, and the weighty advice in said Epistle friends are
desired to attend to particularly that to Parents and Children
Respecting marriage

Committee to be appointed   The Quarterly meeting directs in a coppy of Said minute to appoint
Some sutible friends to assist the Quarterly meetings Committee
in assisting those who have held Slaves, as well as those that have
been so held:⁴⁰ We defer appointing then to next monthly meeting
that the matter may be further considered

John Potter case   The Friends appointed to treat with **John Potter** on account of
his misconduct particularly in marrying out of the Unity of Friends
&c: Report, that they have had a further oppertunity with him, and
that he gave them some encouragement of Satisfaction; and friends
weightily considering said matter, do refer it to next monthly meeting
under the care of the same friends as before and then they to make
Report

John Williams request   **John Williams** request a Removal Certificate to the Monthly meeting of
RhodIsland for himself and Children; Therefore this meeting
appoints **Benjamin Taber** and **Seth Russell** to take the necessary care
in that respect, and to Joine the women friends therein; and report
their doings in said matter to next monthly meeting

Stephen Barker request   **Stephen Barker** Request a removal Certificate to the monthly
meeting at **Sandwich** he being about to move there to dwell if friends
concur therein: Therefore this meeting appoints **William Wood**
Stephen Buffinton and **Barnabus Mosher Juʳ** to draw a Cirtificate for

---

40. Since the previous discussion of slavery in the minutes, the Massachusetts Supreme Court ruled
in the Quock Walker case in 1781 that slavery was inconsistent with the Massachusetts Constitution.
That decision has often been assumed to mark an effective end to slavery in Massachusetts, but recent
research suggests the process of emancipation in the state both began earlier and continued longer than
has been generally understood. See Gloria Whiting, "Emancipation without Courts or Constitution: The
Case of Revolutionary Massachusetts," *Slavery & Abolition* (Nov. 2020), 41:458–78.

him if on enquiry they find things clear and make report next monthly meeting

Robert Nisbet visit

Our Friend **Robert Nesbit** attended this meeting with his Certifi=
=cate dated **East Hoosuck** yᵉ 12ᵗʰ of yᵉ 12ᵗʰ 1782 read to Satisfaction and his Visit
and Labours of Love of the Gospel were Satisfactory to us and a few
Lines Endorsed on his Certificate Signifying the same

Friend Anthony visit

Our Friend **David Anthony** attended this meeting also in compa
=ny with our afore said friend, with a few lines from the said monthly
meeting of **East Hoosuck**, which was read, and his Visit was to Satis=
=faction and an Enorsment made Signifying the Same

Adjourd

This Meeting Adjourns to the 29ᵗʰ of this Instant at the close of meeting for Worship

mett

Mett by Adjournment the 29ᵗʰ of yᵉ 1ˢᵗ month 1783

Complint against Abraham Gifford

The Overseers inform that **Abraham Gifford** hath kept company somewhat in a private
manner and married with one out of the Unity of Friends and that they
have Treated with him on that account but he did not give them
any real Satisfaction: therefore, we appoint **Thomas Hicks** and
Chilion Wood to labour with said **Abraham** and if he doth not
give them Satisfaction, they are to draw a Testimony of Denial
against him and bring to next monthly meeting; Or report accord=
=ingly when ready

The case of George Smith 2

Whereas, upon the report of the Committee appointed to enquire
into the clearness of **George Smith** 2ᵈ Respecting marriage it apearᵈ
things were not clear: and since which this meeting is inform,ᵈ
he hath proceeding in marriage out of the Order of Friends: therefore
this meeting appoints **Stephen Gifford** and **Nicholas Lapham** to
Inqure into the State of the matter, and Labour with him as they
may see fit; and if they do not find Satisfaction to draw a Testimony
of Denial against him: and they to make reports as soon as the
nature of the case will admitt

Complaint against Caleb Gifford he disown,d

The overseers inform that **Caleb Gifford** hath kept company
with a woman not of our Society, and married out of the Unity of
Friends, after being precausioned by said Overseers: therefore
this meeting disowne the said **Caleb Gifford** as a member amoung
us, and from under our care as a member of our meeting and **William
Barker** is desired to inform him therefore and report to next monthly
meeting

miniute for Gideon Anthony

Gideon Anthony Informs this meeting that he proposes going
to **East Hoosuck** and **Saratoga** and expect to tarry Some time there
on a visit among his relation, with a prospect of doing Some business
there, which this meeting concurs with, he being a member and
the Clerk is desired to give him a coppy of this minute

Address ~~meet~~ *from meet Sufferings*

This meeting Received Seventeen Coppies of an address from the Meeting for Sufferings on the Subject of the Yearly meeting School one of which was read in this meeting to Satisfaction, and they are delivered to those friends who have the care of this meetings Both to be distributed a moung friend as they may find proper[41]

account from Isaac Russel on Alice Smith

The Overseers of the Poor have render,d an account of agreement with **Isaac Russell** for keeping **Alice Smith** one of the por of the meeting for one year the amount being fifty Silver dollars, is directed by the meeting to be paid to the said **Isaac Russell** by the Treasurer whenever there is a Sufficiency in Stock for that purpose

To Settle with Treasur= =er

We appoint **Samuel Smith Joseph Tucker Ju**ʳ and **William Anthony Ju**ʳ to Settle accounts with the Treasurer and revise this meetings minutes in order for their being placed on Record and make Report to next monthly meeting

2 month 1783

At a Monthly meeting held in **Dartmouth** yᵉ 17ᵗʰ of 2ᵈ month 1783 The Representatives are **John Devoal [Devol]** & **Benja**ⁿ **Taber** both present

John Lawton Certificate

Received a Certificate from **RhodIsland** mo meeting in behalf of **John Lawton** son of **Isaac** Signifying his residence in this monthly meeting and his being a member; and clear of marriage Ingagements Was read in this meeting to Satisfaction

Contraband Trade

The Committee to make enquiry if there are any of our members acting or concerned in any contraband Trade, etc: Report, that they have attended somewhat to that matter and made further inquiry therein: Yet they are continued ~~there~~ in that Service and are desired to give more attention thereto, and make report to next monthly meeting

Case of John Potter

The friends appointed to have the care of the matter respecting **John Potter**'s misconduct, in marrying out of the Unity of friends etc desires the matter may be continued another month; it is accordingly defered under their care till next monthly meeting, and **Sthephen Buffinton** is added to them they then to make reports

*Com*ᵗᵉᵉ *on ac= count of Slaves*

According to the minute from the Quarterly meeting to appoint Some Suitable friends to assist their Committee in visiting those who have heretofore held Slaves among us, and those that have been so held we appoint **Thomas Hicks** and **William Mosher** for that Service and to make report to this meeting as soon as the Circumstance of the matter will admitt

Stephen Bark certificate

The friends appointed to take the nessesary care respecting a Removal Cirtificate for **Stephen Barker** Report that they have

41. The school opened in Portsmouth, Rhode Island, in 1784, but closed in 1788. Reopened in Providence in 1819, it continues in existence as the Moses Brown School. See Rayner Wickersham Kelsey, *Centennial History of Moses Brown School 1819–1919* (Providence: Moses Brown School, 1919).

Taken the necessary care therein and have presented a Certificate to
this meeting, directed to the monthly meeting of **Sandwich** Signifying
his right of membership and that his outward affairs was settled to

*Eben Bakers
proposal of
marriage*

to Satisfaction as far as appears; which was Signed by the Clerk

Ebenezer Baker and **Susana Mosher** appeared in this meeting and
declared their Intentions of taking each other in marriage; and they
were desired to wait till next monthly meeting for their Answer said
Ebenezer having produced a Certificate from **Accoxset** monthly meeting
Signifying he was a member and clear of marriage engagements;
and consent of parents in writeing.   Collected 2 – 10 – 1

adjourd   This meeting Adjourns to the 11th hour to morrow

mett Mett by Adjournment the 18th of 2nd month 1783

The Representatives being call,d are **John Devol** & **Benjª Taber** both present

*case of John
Williams
certificate*

The Friends appointed to take the necessary care respecting a
removal Certificate for **John Williams**, having not fully accomplished
that matter, they are therefore continued to have the care of the Same
and report to next monthly meeting

*Abraham
Giffords case*

The friends appointed to have the care of that matter respecting
Abraham Gifford,s misconduct in keeping company and marrying out
of the Unity of Friends Report, that they have taken proper care therein
and that it appears he is guilty of the sin of Fornication, from his
wifes having a child Soon after marriage; Therefore the same friends
are directed to draw a Testimony of denial against him the said
Abraham and inform him thereof and bring said Testimony to next
monthly meeting

*George Smith 2
case*

The Committee appointed to labour with **George Smith** on account
of his disorderly marriage being called upon; inform that they had
not accomplished the Same; and it appearing necessary that there be an
addition to the Committee, we therefore appoint **William Anthony Junor**
to assist said Committee, who are to Joine the Women friends therein and
make report to next monthly meeting

*Caleb Gifford
Informed*

William Barker reports he hath informed **Caleb Gifford** of his denial as
directed last Monthly meeting

*Subscriptions to
[?] forth*

It appearing that there are Several accounts due from this meeting to
a much larger amount than there is money in Stock to discharge the Same
Therefore our friends **Daniel Ricketson Seth Russell Thomas Mott Stephen
Gifford** and **Jonathan Willbor** are appointed to apply to friends without delay
and take in Subscriptions for that purpose and return the Sum so Collected
to the Treasurer and make report of the Sum to next monthly meeting

*Treasury Settled
State there of*

The Committee appointed to Settle accounts with the Treasurer and rcvise
the meetings minutes in order for their being recorded, Report as followeth

We the Subscribers have Settled accounts with the Treasurer this 9th day of
the 2d month 1783 and remains in stock 4£ – 4s – 9d Lawful money and the
meetings debts (as by accounts allowed) are 14 – 5 – 0   **Joseph Tucker Jur**
                                                          William Anthony Jur

The Committee appointed in the 6th month last to Joine the Women Friends
to remove some defects amoung our youths and others respecting plainness and
other defects; make report as followeth

report of Visitors   To the Monthly meeting of Men & Women Friends to be held in **Dartmouth**
The 20th of the first month of 1783

We your Committee of Men and women Friends appointed to unite in our
indeavors to remove some defects amoung our youths and others respecting
Plainness and other defects as Truth might open the way have Sollidly
Considered, and confer,d on that weighty work and service, and in that [?]
which is in the bond of peace; way was opened for a general visit of our mem=
=bers and therein we have endeavored to proceed and labour, and have in
Report of deep wadeings and heavy exercises under A sense of the many weaknesses and
visitors   defects amoung us as a meeting which hinder the groth and spreading of
the pure Seed of Life: and we have to remark with Sorrow, that it was [?]
with Some few: to the almost forsakeing their assembling themselves together
and that also a departure in some of the youths and others from that
Simplicity Truth requires, and which leads to plainness in Conversation
&c. if kept to would be as a call and invitation , not only to those amoung us
but even to those that are without. There were however, some prospects
which were encourageing, and even Some also amoung the youth with
such we were nearly United, greatly desireing their growth and establish
ment in the Truth: and that none may Sit down and be contented in a State of
'ease' and indiffrency, in a concern of the utmost importance, but all may come
up more and more in a lively Zeal for the cause and Testimony of Truth

We have also to remark, that tho our Service was weighty and labourious
yet our Visits Seemed generaly kindly recieved

And as divers others who were not members often happened in families we
visited Such we informed of our freedom to Sit with us if they were desireous
(as was also the case of divers black people) in which we often felt the
gathering Arme to be near; and a measure of that compulsive love extended
which calls even from the high ways and hedges that his house may be filled

For further encouragement we may say that we had to experience
that Unity still continued amoung us throughout the visiting, with
that Peace and Satisfaction which is the Sure Reward of Obedience
Tho' we had many provings and Trials, under an experience and
Sense of our own weakness, and inability to performe any thing to

the Honnour of the great Master, Or Satisfaction to ourselves,
Without his emediate assistance

	Martha Gifford
Abiel Gifford	Sussana Smith
James Davis	Joanna Gifford
Caleb Greene	Martha Chase

The above Report was accepted: and read in this Meeting to Satisfaction

On seting up Publications at our meet =ing house The increasing concern of this meeting on account of the disagree= ableness of having Publications Sett up at our Meeting house which some times disturbs our meeting; reviveing on our minds: We appoint **Thomas Hicks, William Anthony Ju**ʳ and **Stephen Buffinton** to apply to those who have and do Sett up those things so contrary to the tender Scruples of us therein, and inform them of the mind of this meeting on that account, and Report to next monthly meeting

Concerning appointing Elders This Meeting is Inform'd from the Select meeting of Ministers and Elders that there is a want of an adition of Elders, and **Caleb Greene** being nominated for that Service: and this Meeting nominates a Committee to Joine the women friends, who have nominated **Mercy Slocum** to that Service Committees names are **Joseph Barker Benjamin Taber Benjamin Smith 2**ᵈ and **Caleb Russell,** they to Join the Elders in that matter and they to report to next monthly meeting

Isaac Kellys Visit Our frend **Isaac Killey** attended this meeting with a Certificate from yᵉ monthly meeting at **East Hoosuck** held yᵉ 12ᵗʰ month 1782 Setting forth their Unity with his accompanying **Robert Nesbit** on a Religious visit in those parts, whose visit and labour of love being Satisfactory to us, we having Endorssed thereon Setting forth the same

[3?] month 1783 At the monthly meetng held in **Dartmouth** the 17ᵗʰ of 3rd month 1783 The Representatives are **Joseph Tucker Jur** & **Wm Gifford** both present

contraband Trade The committee to make inquiry if there are any of our memebers act= ing or concerned in any contraband Trade & c. Report they have attended to and made further inquiry into that matter yet it appearing nessece ry that friends have deligent attention to it there fore the said committee are continued in that Service, and to make report next monthly meeting

[?] Potter The friends appointed to have the care of the matter respecting **John Potter** misconduct in marrying out the Unity of Friends & C Resport that they have had an oppertunity with him which was Somewhat Satisfactory yet they are continued in that services and further care of that matter and to make report to next monthly meeting

The friends appointed to draw a Testimony of **Abraham Gifford**,s Denial and inform him thereof produced one as follows

Abraham
Gifford
denial

Whereas **Abraham Gifford** having had his Education and Birthright
among friends but he through unwatchfulness and disregarding the
Testimony of truth in his own heart has So far departed therefrom as to
keep Companywith a young woman not a member of our Religious Society
and thereby fell into the Sin of Fornication, and So married out of Unity
which Sin plainly appears by her haveing a child so soon after marriage
and friends having Laboured with him on them accounts but our Labour
not having had the desired Effect to friends Satisfaction: therefore for the
Clearing of Truth and friends from such practices we are concerned to give
this forth as a publick Testimony against the Said **Abraham** disowning him
from being a member of our society

Given forth at our monthly meeting held in **Dartmouth** the 17th of 3rd mo 1783
and Signed by order and in behalf of said meeting By **Wm Anthony Jur Clerk**
who is directed also to read the same publickly at the close of a first day
meeting for worship between this and next monthly meeting and report thereto

in Setting up
Publication

The Friends appointed to apploy to those that set up publications at
our meeting houses, report that they have applied most of them, who
appeared somewhat condescending to friends request in desisting
from that practices: yet the Same Friends are continued to have the
Standing oversight of that matter

In Deviding
Preparitive
Meeting

The committee appointed some time past to consider the expendency
of dividing our preparitive meeting, make the following report
together with the minutes of Said committee; which was read in this
meeting to satisfaction: and the appointing a Committee to Succeed those
to Inspect further into these matters is refered to next monthly meeting

Benj Gidly
Minute

Benjamin Giddley Informs that he proposes to go to **East Hoosuck** and **Saratoga**
to make Some tarry there to do some hand labour this meeting concuring
therewith he having a right of membership, the Clerk is desir'd to give him
a Coppy of his minutes

Eben Baker
answer

Ebenezer Baker and **Susanna Mosher** appeared for their answer
Which was that they might proceed to take each other in marriage
between this and next monthly meeting, they adviseing with
the Friends this meeting shall appoint, who are **Jonathan Host**
Benjamin Rider to see said marriage orderly Solemnized said
friends to make report thereof next monthly meeing

Chilion Wood
request a
Certificate

Chilion Wood informed that he hath an intention of going to
East Hoosuck and **Saratoga** to make Some Stay, desireing our
concurrence: and Certificate, therefore this meeting appoints
William Barker & **Stephen Buffinton** To
To make due Inspection into the matter, and draw a Certificate if they

find things clear and bring it to the adjournment of this meeting

Collected £2 – 1 – 9½

adjournd
This meeting is adjournd to the 26th Instant at the close of the meeting for Worship

mett
Mett by adjournment ye 26th of 3rd month 1783

Representatives are **Joseph Tucker Jnr** and **William Gifford** both present

Clerk ap= =pointed
The Clerk being absent by reason of Sickness **Caleb Greene** is appointed Clerk for this time

John Williams Case
The matter in respect to **John Williams** Certificate not being fully acom= =plished by the Committee it is continued under their care for the Same Service, and they to make report next monthly meeting

George Smith 2 Case
The matter in respect to **George Smith** 2d not being fully accomplished the Committee ~~the~~ Requesting it further continued, it is likewise continued to next monthly meeting, under the same care as before and then they to make report

Elders deferd
The Committee apointed to Joine the Elders in regard to makeing an addition choice of Elders, make report, that they have had Several Soled conferences on the Subject and that it was their united opinion that the said choice be defered some time longer therefore it is continued under their care, who are desired to attend to that Important matter; and to make report to our monthly meeting, next proceeding our Quarter= =ly meeting in the Seventh month next

Chilion Wood Certificate
The friends appointed in the case of **Chilion Wood**'s Certificate have presented a draft, which hath been read, approved and Signd by ye Cerk

Susan Barker Cirificate
The women friends informe that they have received a removal Certi= =ficate from the monthly meeting of **RhodIsland**, for **Susanna Barker** wife of **John Barker**, which this meeting concurs with

Alice Woods Case
The Women friends requesting our assistance in respect to answering a request to them from the womens monthly meeting of **RhodIsland** concerning **Alice Wood**, therefore this meeting appoints **William Barker Joseph Barker** and **Caleb Russell** to Joyn the women therein and they to report to our next monthly meeting

Sent to Quar= terly meeting
The Queries have been read and answers thereto read and after Some amendment were approved also an Epistle to the Quarterly meeting was prepared approved and Signed by the Clerk, and Sent up to the Quarterly meeting by our Representatives, who are **Samuel Smith Caleb Greene James Davis** and **Abiel Gifford**, and they to make report to our next monthly meeting

money Col= =lected
The Committee appointed to Collect money by Subscriptions report that they have Collected the Sum of Nine pounds foure Shillings £9-4-0 and delivered the Same to the Treasurer of this meeting

4 month
1783
At a Monthly meeting held in **Dartmouth** yᵉ 21ˢᵗ of 4ᵗʰ month 1783

The Representatives are **Thomas Mott** and **William Gifford** both present

On Contraband Trade
The Committee to make inquiry, if there are any of our members
are acting or concerned in any contraband Trade &c, Report that
they have had a conference on that matter; and from present Cirdumstances
Request a dismisson from that Service; and this meeting considering
the Same doth dismiss the Said Committee accordingly

Abraᵐ Gifford denial read
The Clerk responds hath the Testimony of denial against **Abraham Gifford** hath been read as directed last monthly meeting

Eben Baker Married
The friends appointed to attend the marriage of **Ebenezer Baker** and **Susanna Mosher**, Report that they attended Said
marriage; and that they did not discover but that it was orderly Solemnized

John Potters Case
The friends appointed to have the care of that matter respect=
ing **John Potter,s** misconduct in marrying out of the Unity of
Friends &c: Report, that they have had another oppertunity with him
in which he gave them some Satisfaction; yet they are continued in
that Service for a further oppertuny with him and to make report
to next monthly meeting

Preparitive meeting
The appointing a Committee to succeed thy former which reported
last monthly meeting – to inspect into the Expediency of dividing our
Preparitive meeting &c; is refered to next monthly meeting

John Williams Case
The friends appointed to have the care respecting **John William**'s Removal Cer=
=tificate, report that they have not accomplished the matter; they are
therefore continued to have the care of it; and if they find things clear to
accomplish the Same and report to next monthly meeting

George Smith 2ᵈ
The Committee appointed to have the care of the matter respecting
George Smith 2ᵈ Report that they have taken some care therein but
request the matter continued; it is accordingly defered under
the Same friends care who are to report next monthly meeting

Alice Woods Case
The friends appointed to assist the Women friends in answering a
request from **RhodIsland** monthly meeting concerning **Alice Wood**
Report they have attended to that matter, but have not accomplished
it they are therefore continued in that Service & to report when Ready

Return from Quarterly meeting
The friends appointed to attend the Quarterly meeting Report they all
attended excep **Abiel Gifford**, who rendered a Sufficient Reason for
for his not attending; also they produced an Epistle from said meet=
=ing which was read to Satisfaction

Report of Visiters on account of Slaves
The friends appointed to Joyn the Quarterly meeting Committee
for Visiting those who have held Slaves: and those who have been so
held, made report in writeing as follows; We the Committee appoint

in the case of Slaves, have to report, that we Joined the Quarterly
meetings Committee, and have Visited those who have held Slaves and
those who have been held in Said State; and have Endeavoured
In Love and tenderness to Impress their minds with a Sense of Religious
duty, and laboured for a proper & Suitable Adjustment of the matter

The 21st of 4th month 1783   **Thomas Hicks**
Said Report is accepted & said friends are dismised   **William Mosher**
from that Service

Weston Smiths The Overseears inform, that **Wesson Smith**, (after being precaussioned)
Case hath Sailled in an Armed Vessel or Letter of Marque, which took a
Vessel by force of Armes: and has Since been laboured with on that
account; but did not Seem in any disposition to give Friends Satisfaction
and has now gone to Sea; therefore this meeting appoints **Benjamin Taber**
and **Caleb Greene** to draw a Testimony of his denial and report to next
monthly meeting

Freelove The Women friends inform that they have received a Certificate from
Gifford **Accoakset**, in behalf of **Freelove Gifford** wife of **William Gifford** which
Certificate this meeting concurs with

Latilia Antho= In concurrence with the Women friends a removal Certificate
ny Certificate was Signed by the Clerk in behalf of **Latitia Anthony** wife of
Abraham Anthony directed to **RhodIsland** monthly meeting

Complaint The overseers inform that **Barker Little** hath removed in the compas of **Accoa=**
against =**set** monthly meeting, without Certificate or advice of Friends: and also
Barker that **Henry Howland** Son of **Henry** hath removed in the compass of the Same
Little & monthly meeting: without Certificates – and that both of them use profane
Henry How= and corrupt Language at times, and much neglect the attendance of
=land Ju^r our Religious meetings: Which said Overseers laboured with them
for but they did not give them Satisfaction: We therefore appoint
Jonathan Hart, **John Devaul [Devol]** and **Thomas Mott** to take a Solled
oppertunity, and labour further with ~~with~~ Said **Barker** and **Henry** on
them accounts; and if they or either of them do not give them Satisfac
tion to bring a Testimony or Testimonies of their denial, and inform
them thereof & Report to next monthly meeting

David Chase The Overseers inform that **David Chase** have countenanced and
misconduct alowed the consumating a marriage in his house, contrary to the order of
Friends and that they treated with him and he Justifies the Same
therefore we appoint **William Anthony Ju^r**, **William Wood** and **William
Mosher**, to Labour with him further on that account, and report to
next monthly meeting

minute for **Seth Russell** informs he intends a Journey to **New Jersey** on business
Seth Russell if friends concur therewith; and this meeting concuring he being a

member in Unity; & the Clerk is desired to give him a coppy of this minuit

Collected £1 – 2 – 6

Adjourns This meeting adjourns to the 30th of this instant at the close of meeting of worship

Mett Mett by adjournment the 30th of 4th month 1783

The Representatives being called are **Thomas Mott** & **Caleb Barker** present

advice from meeting of Suffrings on School The meeting for Sufferings having recommended a renewed engage= =ment to Friends to be in the way of theire duty, in Subscribing for the establishing the yearly meetings Schools and in order therefore that the monthly meetings Should appoint Committees to take in Subscriptions the meeting for Sufferings having furnished us with Printed blanks for Subscriptions for them accordingly – Therefore we appoint **Joseph Tacker Ju** **Thomas Mott** and **Caleb Greene** for that purpose, who are to make Return to the Treasurer of the Yearly meetings School when they have accomplished receiving Subscriptions, and also make report to this meeting of the Sum Total so Subscribed

Ben Gifford Confession **Benjamin Gifford Ju**r hath given in a paper to this meeting condemning his keeping company with a young woman sometime disorderly & Resorting Some times at places unbecoming those under our profession And Several of the overseers who inform that they have treated with **Benjamin** thereon, who gave them a good degree of Satisfaction, and this meeting taking the Same into consideration doth accept of the Same for Satisfaction

Lydia Devaul denied The Women friends inform that they have received a Letter from the monthly meeting of **Oblong**, Signifying they had taken the necessary ~~had taken the necessary~~ care respecting **Lydia Devaul**, formerly **Lydia Bowdish** and had denied her, which this meeting concurs with

John Lawton Certificate Endorst A few Lines was Endorsed on **John Lawton** (son of **Isaac**) Certificate from **RhodIsland**: and Signed by the Clerk Signifying his attending our meeting with his Certificate, and of his conduct being ~~orderly~~ in Some degree Orderly while amoung us he having returned to **RhodIsland**

---

5 Month 1783 At a Monthly meeting held in **Dartmouth** the 19th of 5th month 1783 The Representatives are **Jonathan Willbor** and **Prince Potter** both present

[?] Potters Case The Friends appointed to have the care of the matter respecting **John Potters** misconduct in marrying out of the Unity of friends &c report that they have attended to it, and that **John** gave them a degree of Satisfaction: But that there is some obstruction to the accomplish= =ing the matter, and in order that it may be removed desires it may be defered, it is accordingly defered under their care till next month= =ly meeting they then to make report

[?] Preparative
meeting

The appointing a Committee to Succeed the former in the inspection of the expedency of dividind our prepairitive meeting &c coming again consideration; is thought best to be omitted for the present

John Williams
Case

The friends appointed to have the care respecting **John Williams** Removal Certificate, Report that they have not accomplished it by by reason of some Obstruction which they are desired to endeavor to have removed, that the matter be accomplished and report made to next monthly meeting

Bersheba Wood
Received

The Women friends Inform that they have admitted **Bershaba Wood** Wife of **Chilion Wood** into membership which this meeting concurs with

[?] Smith 2ᵈ
Case

The Committee appointed to have the care of the matter respecting **George Smith 2ᵈ** report that they have not accomplished that matter and therefore desires it continued it is accordingly defered under their care, who are to report to next monthly meeting

The friends appointed to draw a Testimony of **Weston Smiths** denyal; produced one as Follows

Weston Smith
denial

Whereas **Weston Smith** Son of **Levi Smith** deceased hath had his education amoung us the people called Quakers but hath so far departed from the religious and Peacable Principle which we profess as to Sail a Voiage in an Armed Vessel or Letter of Marque which took a Vessel by force of Armes; previous to going Said Voiage he was precausioned by Friends, and hath since been laboured with on that account. but did not Seem disposed to give friends Satisfaction; Therefore for the clearing Truth and Friends from Such unwarrantable conduct; we are concerned to give forth this as a publick Testimony against the same, hereby disowning the Said **Weston Smith** from having a right of membership amoung us the people afore said, untill it shall please God to favor him with a Sight and Sense of his Error, that he may return with Re= =pentance unfeigned, which that he may is our desire

Given forth and Signed in and on behalf of the Monthly meeting of the people afore said held in **Dartmouth** yᵉ 19ᵗʰ of 5ᵗʰ month 1783

By **Wm Anthony Juʳ** Clerk

Which was Signed in this meeting by the Clerk who is desired to cause the Same to be read publickly at the close of a first meeting for worship between this and next monthly meeting and make report to the same and **Caleb Greene** is desir'd to inform **Weston** thereof when he returns and make report to this meeting

Barker little
and Henry
Howlands
Case

The Comittee to Treat further with **Barker Little** and **Henry Howland** (son of **Henry**) on account of their removal without Certificates and other misconduct report that they have not had

an oppertunity with **Barker**, but they had with **Henry** who did not
give them Satisfaction and they have draughted a Testimony of his
denial and informed him thereof the Testimony is as Follows

Henry How=
=land Ju^r
denial

Whereas **Henry Howland Ju^r** Having had his education amongst
Friends, but by unwatchfulness and disregarding the Principle of
Truth in his own heart hath removed out of the Compass of our
meeting without requesting our Certificate; also uses corrupt langu[age?]
and much neglects the attendance ˏof our Religious meetings all which
misconduct friends have laboured with him for, in order to convin[ce?]
him of his Errors, but our Labours of love not having the desired effect
to our Satisfaction: Therefore we are concerned to give this forth as
a Publick Testimony against him the Said **Henry Howland**, disowning
him from being a member of our Society. Nevertheless it is oure desire
that he may have a Sight and Sense of his outgoings and return to the
ways of Truth

 Given forth and Signed by order and in behalf of our monthly meeting
held in **Dartmouth** the 19th day of ye 5th month 1783 By **Wm Anthony Ju^r** Clerk

 Which was Signed by the Clerk who is directed to cause the Same to be red [read]
at the close of a first day meeting between this and next monthly meeting and
make report to the Same ~ and the Committee are continued to have
the necessary care of that of **Barker Little** and report to monthly meeting

Ben Giffords
proposal
of marriag

 Benjamin Gifford and **Rhoda Potter** declared their Intentions of taking
each other in marriage and were desired to wait till next monthly meeting
for their answer ~ and **William Wood** and **William Mosher** are appointed
to make Enquiry into the mans Clearness respecting marriage and conversa=
=tion and report to next monthly meeting

David Chase
deferd

 The Friends appointed to Labour further with **David Chase** on account
of his allowing the accomplishing a marriage in his house out of
the order of Friends, report that they have had an oppertunity
with him, but he did not give them Satisfaction, yet the matter
is defer'd till next monthly meeting for further consideration under
the care of the same friends they then to make report

Gid^[n?] Sanfords
minute

 This meeting is infor^m'd that **Gideon Sanford** has gone to the **Ninepartners**
to make Some Stay with a Friend there, and requests a
few lines from this meeting Signifying his right of membership; this
meeting concuring he having a right of membership, and
the Clerk is desired to give him a Coppy of this minute

       Collected £1 – 0 – 5^d

6th month
1783

At a Monthly meeting held in **Dartmouth** ye 16th of 6th month 1783
The Representatives are **Peleg Gifford Jonathan Willbor** [Wilbur] and **Abiel**

Gifford, Present - And **Caleb Russell** not present as he attends the yearly meeting

Caleb Green
Clerk
 The Clerk not attending this meeting at this time, being gone to the yearly meeting, **Caleb Greene** is therefore appointed Clerk for this time

Chilon Wood
request a
Certificate
 Chⁱlion Wood requesting (in writting) a removal certificate for himself and Children, to **Saratogua** monthly meeting, as he is now gone, and about to remove his family and Settle there. We there= fore appoint our friends **Abraham Howland** and **Jonathan Willbor** to Joyn the Women friends and take the necessary and tim,ˡʸ care of that matter and if they find things clear to draw a Certificate and bring

adjournd to the adjournment of this meeting

The minutes of last monthly meeting not being[?] present this meeting adjourns to the 23ᵈ instant, at the close of a meeting for Worship on Said day

mett The 23ᵈ of 6ᵗʰ month Mett by adjournment; The Representatives Being called, **Peleg Gifford**, **Jonathan Willbor**, **Abiel Gifford** and **Caleb Russell**, all present

[Weston?] Smith
[denial?] read
 The Clerk informs that the Testimonies of the denials of **Weston Smith** and **Henry Howland** (son of **Henry**) have been read as directed last monthly meeting

[John?] Williams
Case
 One of the Committee appointed to have the care respecting **John Williams**'s Certificate report that it is not yet accomplished and desires there may be another friend appointed to assist him therein as the other is absent therefore **Joseph Gifford** is appointed to assist there in, and they to accomplish that matter and report to next monthly meeting

The friends appointed to inspect into the Clearness of **Benjamin Giffords** clearness respecting marriage and conversation report that they find nothing to hinder his proceeding

Ben Giffords
answer
 Benjamin Gifford Juʳ and **Rhoda Potter** appeared in this meeting for their Answer which is they may proceed to take each other in marriage, at some convenient time between this and next monthly meeting, adviseing with the friends this meeting appoints to See the marriag orderly Solemnized who are **William Mosher** and **William Wood** and they to make report to next monthly meeting

[?]annexing
this meeting
[to?]Sandwich
Quarter
 A Committe from the yearly meeting attended this meeting at this time, and among other advices advised that this meeting appoint a Solid Committee to confer with the yearly meetings Committee on the Subject of annexing this meeting to **Sa[n]dwich** Quarter which is Refered to next monthly meeting   Collected £1 – 16ˢ – 2ᵈ

adjourns   This meeting adjourns to the 25th Instant at the close of the meeting of Worship

mett   25th of 6th month Mett by adjournment ~ The Representatives are **Peleg Gifford**, **Jonathan Willbor, Caleb Russell** and **Abiel Gifford** all present

John Potters Case   The friends who had the care of the matter respecting **John Potters** misconduct in marrying out of the unity of Friends report that it is not accomplished and desires ye matter defered another month; it is accordingly defer'd under the same friends care who are desired to accomplish the same before next monthly meeting and make report to the Same

George Smiths Case   One of the Committee (the other not being presen[t] nor reasons sent for his absence) appointe‸d to have the care of the respecting **George Smith the Second** Report it is not accomplished therefore it is defered till next monthly meeting under the Same Friends care they then to make report

Barker Little Case   The Friends appointed to have th[e] care, and treat with **Barker Little** on acount of removing with a Certificate and other misconduct, report that they had an oppertunity with him, tho not fully to Satisfaction, as desired they are therefore continued to have the care of that matter, and make report to next monthly meeting

David Chase Case   The friends appointed to labour further with **David Chase** on account of his allowing the accomplishing a marriage in his house out of the order of Friends, report that they have had another oppertunity with him, but that he did not give them Sattisfaction so fully as desir'd yet the matter is defer'd till next monthly meeting, they then to make report

Phebe Bowdish denied   The Women friends inform they have denied **Phebe Bowdish** daughter of **William Bowdish** which this meetin[g] concurs with

The Women friends inform they have admitted into membership **Mary Wood** wife of **Abraham Wood** which this meeting concurs with

Isaac Smith bad conduct   The overseers inform that **Isaac Smith** son of **Gershem** hath sometimes resort =ed to places whare undue liberty is taken, Such as gameing, musick and Dancing, and Joining therein, and useing profain and unbecomeing language, also keeps company with a young woman not of our Society, and much Neglects the attendance of our Religious meetings

For which misconduct, and disorders the said Overseers have labou[red] with him for, but he did not Condemn the Same to Satisfaction; therefore We appoint **Elijah Gifford** and **John Devaul** [**Davol**] to take a Solid oppertunity and treat with him further thereon, and report to next monthly meeting

Abraham Wood req= uest   **Abraham Wood** hath given in a paper to this meeting condeming his misconduct in prepareing instruments for War; and request to come und[er?] Friends care; and he has now removed within compass of **Saratoga** monthly meeting; therefore we appoint **Benjamin Taber Caleb Green** and **William Anthony Ju**r to take the nessecery care of that matter; and prepare a drau[ght?]

of the State of the Same to Send to that monthly meeting, and bring it to next monthly meeting

overseers of poor The Overseers of the poor desires an addition to their number, therefore We appoint **Jonathan Hart** and **William Gifford** to that Service as an ad= =dition to the former under appointment some time past, and they together are desired to attend to the Service as Truth may require

on account of Elders The Committee to Joine the Elders; in ˄respect of an additional choice of Elders make report, that they have had further attention, and ~~furthe~~ Solid conference on the Subject, and that it is their united opinion, that the said choice be defered Some time longer ~ It is therefore continued under their care and Solid attention and to make report to our monthly meeting next pro- =ceeding [*sic*] the Quarterly meeting in the 10ᵗʰ month next

Sent up to Quarly meeting The Queries were read and answers thereto prepared, and an account to the Quarterly meeting also prepared and Signed by the Clerk which was sent up to said meeting by our friends **William Mosher**, **Caleb Green** and **Thom[as?] Mott** and **Abiel Gifford** who are appointed to attend the Quarterly meeting

David Smith request a Coppy **David Smith** formerly a member of this meeting, requesting a coppy of the Testimony of his denial, this meeting taking the Same into consideration doth commit the [*sic*] to the care of our Representatives to request the advice of the Quarterly mee[t]ing therein Said Representatives to mak[e] report to next monthly meeting

Chilion Wood case One of the friends appointed to have the care of **Chilion Wood**s Certificate report that it is not accomplished, they are therefore continued in care of that matter and to accomplish the Same and report to next monthly meeting

Concerning Posting up publicati= ons The Committee appointed some time past to request of those who are in authority in the Town in respect of Posting up Publications at our meeting houses: having informed some of them thereof; and the Town having Sent a papper to this meeting, by the sa˄ᵢd Committee: which was read in this meeting, wherein they desired this meeting would give Some reasons for the objections: for their so posting up publications – this meeting taking the Same under consideration, do appoint our friends **Stephen Buffinton**, **Thomas Hicks, William Anthony Juʳ, Samu[e]l Smith, Joseph Gifford, Giles Slocum Elijah Gifford, Jonathan Willbor, William Mosher**, and **Caleb Greene** to prepare a draught [draft] an answer to Said Towns request, and bring it to the adjurment [adjournment] of this meeting

adjours This meeting adjourns to the 4ᵗʰ of next month at the 9ᵗʰ hour in the morning

mett Met by adjournment the 4ᵗʰ of yᵉ 7ᵗʰ month 1783 The Representatives called are **Caleb Russell, Peleg Gifford, Abiel Gifford** and **Jonathan Willbor [Wilbur]** all present

A draught prepard & Sent to the Town The Committee appointed to prepar[e] a draught to the Selectmen &c [etc.] as an answer to their Request, prepared one and presented to this meeting which was Sighned [signed] by the Clerke and we appoint **Samuel Smith**, **Joseph Barke[r]** and

William Mosher, to present the Same to the Town, and they to keep a coppy on file and report to next monthly meeting

[7?] month
1783
At a Monthly meeting held in **Dartmouth** yᵉ 21ˢᵗ of 7ᵗʰ month 1783
The Representatives are **Joseph Austin**, **William Wood** and **Timothy Howland** all present

[R?]eturn from [Qu]arterly met [ing] [Ep]istles: &.c: Received
The Representatives appointed last monthly meeting to attend the Quarterly meeting Report, that they all attended, and produced an Epistle from said Quarterly meeting, together with extracts from the Last yearly meeting minutes: as also Transcrip[t]s of our last yearly meetings Epistle, and one from the yearly meeting of **London** last year, one from the yᵉarly meeting of **Philidelphia** this year, and one from the yearly meeting held at **Westberry** for **New York** ~ all which was read in this meeting to Satisfaction
And our Representatives to next Quarterly meeting are to give information to said meeting, of the Circumstances of recording the yearly meetings Extracts which are to be Recorded in our book of Discipline

John Williams Case
The Friends appoin[t]ed to have the care of the matter Respecting **John Williams** Certificate, Report that it is not accomplish, as the obstructions thereto are not removed, and desire it continued, which is accordingly deferd under their care, and they are desireᵈ to accomplish the Same and report to the adjour[n]ment of this meeting

Ben Gifford married
The Friends appointed to see the marriage of **Benjamin Gifford Juʳ** and **Rhoda Potter** orderly Solemniz'd report that they attended said mar==riage, and that it was as far as they discover'd orderly Solemniz'd

on account of annexing this meeting to Sandwich Quarter
The appointing a Committee to confer with ‸that of the yearly meeting, on the Subject of annexing this meeting to **Sandwich** Quarter; coming again ~~under~~ before this meeting; We appoint **William Mosher**, **Stephen Buffin‸ton**, **Thomas Hicks**, **William Anthony Juʳ**, **Benjamin Taber**, **Caleb Russell Joseph Tucker Juʳ** and **Samuel Smith** to that Service who are to report when ready

George Smith 2ᵈ Case
Two of the Comittee (the other being absent) to have the care of the matter respecting **George Smith 2ᵈ** report that they have made some progress therein, but the Womens Committee request it continueᵈ it is accordingly defered under the Same Friends care who are to report to next monthly meeting

Barker Little Case
The friends appointed to Treat further with **Barker Little** respecting his removing without a Certificate and other misconduct report that they have had an oppertunity with him and that he gave them so much incouragement that they desire the matter continued another month, it is accordingly d[e]fer'd under their care till nexᵗ monthly meeting they then to make report

John Potter
The friends appointed to take necessary care of the matter respecting **John Potter**s misconduct in marriing out of the unity of Friends and other miscon

=duct Report that they have laboured with him in order to convince him of error, but have not Received Satisfaction; therefore we disown the said **John Potter** from haveing a right of membership among us; and the Same friends are desired to draw a Testimon[y] of his denial and inform him thereof, and Report to next monthly meeting

David Chase The Friends appointed to labour further with **David Chase** on accoun[t] of his allowing the accomplishing a marriage in his house out of the order of Friends Report that they have laboured further with him in order to convi[n]ce him of his Error: but that he did not give them Satisfaction yet the matter is defered under the Same friends care who are desired to labour with him, not only on that account, but on that of his neglecting the attendance of our Religious meetings and report to next monthly meeting

Eunice Mars Certificate The Women friends inform they have Received a Certificate from **Nantucket** [in?] behalf **Eunice Marshel**, who lives in the compass of this meeting which Certifi[cate?] was read in this meeting to Satisfaction

Sarah Wever Recived The women Friends Inform, that they with the concura[n]ce of this meeting com[ply?] to admit **Sarah Weaver** into membership; which we concur with

to give David Smit a coppy This meeting concluds to give **David Smith** a coppy of the Testimony of his denial and the Clerk is desir'd to give him a Coppy thereof and report to the adjournment of this meeting   Collected £1 – 0 – 6 [½?]

Adjournd This meeting adjourns to the firs[t] 4th day in next month at the close of the meeting for Worship

Mett Mett by adjournment ye 6th of the 8th month 1783

The Representatives being called are **Joseph Austin William Wood** and **Timothy Howland** all present

Certificate for Chilion Wood The Friends appointed to have the care of a Removal Certificate for **Chil**[ion?] **Wood**, and his wife **Barsheba**, and their Children, who are **Charles** and **Ruth** to the monthly me[e]ting at **Sarratoga,** have produced one, Set[t]ing forth their being members, and in a degree of orderly lives and Conversations, which after some amendment was Signed by the Clerk

Isaac Smith disown'd The friends appointed to treat further with **Isaac Smith** son of **Gershem** report that they have discharged themselves in that matter, according to appointment but **Isaac** gave them no Satisfaction, therefore we with the concurence of the Womens meeting do disown the said **Isaac Smith** from having any right of membership among us; and the same friends are desired to draw a Testimony of his denial, and inform him thereof, and report to next monthly meeting

Respecting Abra Woods request The Friends appointed to prepare a draught [draft] of a request to the monthly meeting of **Saratoga** respecting **Abraham Wood**s reque[s]t produced one; which after some amendment, was Signed by the Clerk who is desired to forward the same

John Williams Certificate
    A Removal Certificate in behalf of **John Williams**, and his Children **Obediah**, **Jonathan**, and **Nicholas** Signifying their being members, and that **John**s outward affares was Settled to general Satisfaction directed to **Rhod[e] Island** monthly meeting was Signed by the Clerk

David Smith
    The Clerk informes he hath given **David Smith** a coppy of the Testimony of his denial as directed

To preserve meetings Epistles & papers
    It appearing necessary to this meeting that all the former Epistles and Trans= =scrip[t]s of Epistles be collected, and they, as well as those which may come in future be preserved on File. We therefore appoint **Thomas Hicks**, **Jonathan Willbor [Wilbur] Elijah Gifford** and **Samuel** ˄Smith to take the necessary care of them; and also of all the papers respecting Schools; and where to be recorded, and make report when ready

Report of Com^tee Sent to ye Town
    The Friends appointed to present an answer to the Town, respecting our reasons of objecting publications being Set up at our meeting houses, Report they all attended and presented the Same in consequence of which the Town Voted that all publications Should be hereafter Set up elsew[h]ere

Visitors apointed
    The case of Some negligent members who have and do much neglect the at= =tendence of our Religious meetings, as well as other defects in them and others being renewedly noticd by the meeting, with desire for their Reformation and better attention to these important matters and to clear our Selves toward them as a meeting: therefore we do appoint our friends **Abiel Gifford**, **Thomas Hicks** & **James Davis**, to Joine the Women and Visit all Such, ˄neglect ones and others, as they may find freedom, and as Truth may open the way, and to labour in Love and tenderness to reclaim Such from such unwarrantable practices, and report when ready

Obediah Allen Certificate Endorsed
    Endorsment on the Certificate of **Obediah Allen**, and his wife **Phebe** were Signed by the Clerk; Setting forth their conduct, while their last abode here, ~~droct~~ directed to the monthly meeting of **Saratoga**

[8?] month 1783
At a Monthly meeting held in **Dartmouth** ye 18th of ye 8th month 1783 The Representatives being called are **John Devaul [Davol]**, **Caleb Greene** & **Caleb Barker** all present

[Ge?]org Smith 2^d
    The Committee appointed to have the care of the matter respecting **George Smith** 2^d report that they have had Some furthe[r] care therein but have not accomplished the Same, and request it defer'd it is dfer'd accord =ingly till next monthly meeting they then to make report

[B?]arker Little
    The Friends appointed to treat further with **Barker Little** respect= =ing his removing without a Certificate and other misconduct report that they have attended Somewhat to that matter, but have received no Satisfaction from **Barker**, yet the matter is deferred for their accom= =plishing as by former minute and to make report to next monthly meeting

The Friends appointed to draw a Testimony of denial of **John Potter**
and Inform him thereof Produced a draught [draft] as follows

John Potter   Whereas **John Potter** son of **John Potter** late of **Dartmouth** deceased and
Testimony of **Margret** his wife, Having had a right of membership among Friends, but by
denial departing from the Simplicity of truth, and the dictates therof in his own
mind, have fallen into Several disorders, particurlarly, whilst he was
u˄nder Gaurdianship he absented himself from his Gaurdian, and fell into
Loose company, and kept company with a young woman not of our
Society, and fell into the Sin of Fornication, and contracted marriage
with the said young woman, who had a child soon after said marriage
And friends having laboured with him therefor, but not receiving
satisfaction: Therefore for the clearing of Truth and Friends from
the Imputation of such reproachful conduct this meeting is concerned to
give this forth as a publick Testimony against the same hereby disown=
=ing him the said **John Potter** from being a member of our Religious Society
until by ˄an unfeigned repentance he shall be restored to the way of Truth

Given forth, and Signed in and behalf our monthly meetting held in **Dartmouth**
the 18th day of ye 8th month 1783 ~   **William Anthony Jur** Clerk

                                     Mercy Slocum Clerk for this day
which was read and with the concurrence of the womens meeting was Signed
by the Clerk who is directed to cause the Same to be read publickly at the
close of a first day meeting for Worship before next monthly meeting
and report to the Same; The Same friends report that they informed
John of his denial

Isaac Smiths   The Friends appointed to draw a Testimony of the denial of **Isaac**
Testimony **Smith** (son of **Gershem**) and inform him thereof report that they have
of denial accomp[l]ished the Same, said Testimon[y] is as follows

From our Monthly meeting held ˄at **Dartmouth** ye 18th of 8th month 1783
Whereas **Isaac Smith** (son of **Gershem Smith**) Having had his Education
among Friends, but through unwatchfulness, hath so far departed
from the Truth, and good order of Friends, as to Resort to a place
where was Singing and Dancing, and Joined himself therein, and
useing profain and unbecomeing Language, and neglects the attendance
of our meetings: and also keeps company with a young woman not
a member of our society; all which misconduct he hath been
Laboured with for, and it not havin the desired effect; therefore
Friends for the clearing of Truth, do give this forth as a publick
Testimony against Such Conduct, and disown him from being a
member any longer of our Society, Nevertheless it is our desire that
he may be favoured to come to a Sight and sense of his outgoings and

return to the way of Truth. Signed in and on behalf said meeting By

Wᵐ Anthony Juʳ Clerk

Mercy Slocum Clerk this day

Which with the concurence of the womens meeting was Signed in Each meet[ing?] by the Clerks, and the Clerk is desired to cause the same to be read publickly [at?] the close of a meeting for Worship before next monthly meeting, and report be madᵉ to the Same

David Chase　　The Friends appoint to labour further with **David Chase** on account of his allowing the accomplishment of a marriage in his house out of the order of [friends?] and on account of neglecting the attendance of our Religous meetings Report that they have laboured further with him therefor but he gave them no Satis= =faction: ₍therefore for₎ the clearing of Truth, and Friends from such disorderly conduct We with the Concurrence of the womens meeting do disown the said **David Chase** from having any Right of membership among us: and **John Devaul [Davol]** is desired to informe him thereof and report to next monthly meeting

Complint against Gilbert Russell　　The Overseers inform that **Gilbert Russell** is in the practice of keeping com= =pany with young woman not a member of our Society also appears in apparel far from that Simple plainness that becomes our profession for which they have lab[oured?]

with him but have not received any Satisfaction, therefore we appoint **William Anthony Juʳ Joseph Tucker Jun[i]or**, and **Josep[h] Austin**, to labour further with him

on account of his misconduct, and report to next monthly meeting

Report of School Com= =mittee　　The School Committee laid the following report before this meeting We of the Committee appointed to advise and assist in the Erecting friends Schools, and in the maintainance of the Rules ₍orders₎ established by friends for the Virtious Education of the youth in Such Sᶜʰools, have now to report that we have attended in some measure to that Service; But as these things are but new among us our progress herein hath been but small; Friends not all being fully acquainted, in every respect of the method proposed for the Esta blishing such Schools and some that are acquainted therewith do not Submit themselves thereto divers Schools having been set up without our advice or consent, and several School Teachers have been Implyed [employed] by Friends, who are not members of our Society: Yet notwithstanding these painf[ul?] obstructions we hope and beleive as friends dwell under a Sense of the weight of this Excel= =lent work it will gradually go on from step to stepᵗ as Truth shall lead the way, and by degrees open our eyes to see more clearly the many advantages arising from a Reformation in this Important brach [branch?] of our Discipline We would therefore return this our Report to the monthly meeting, desireing to be dismised from our appointment, that a new appointment may be made; all which is Submitted to your Consideration   **Caleb Russell**

Dated this 28ᵗʰ of yᵉ 5ᵗʰ month 1783   **Abiel Gifford**   **Samuel Smith**

Which is refered to next monthly meeting   **Jonathan Wilbur**   **Wm Anthony Juʳ**

For further consideration

William Russell proposal of marriag
William Russell (son of **Abʳᵃham** deceᵈ) and **Hepzabah Mosher**, declared their Intentions of takeing each other in marriage, he having consent in writeing of his Parent: and they are desired to wait till next monthly meeting for their answer and **Benjamin Chase** and **William Gifford** are appointed to make the necessary enquiry into the young mans clearness in respect to marriage and his conversation; and report to next monthly meeting

money pro= cured for yᵉ School
The Committee to receive Subscriptions for the yearly meetings School report that they have procured the Subscription of £13–13–0 yet they are con= =tinued in that Service and to report when Ready   Collected £0 – 16ˢ – 2

feed to be preserved
This meeting thinks it proper to ₐᵉⁿᵈᵉᵃᵛᵒʳ ᵗᵒ preserve the feed round our meeting house within the yards, against our next Quarterly meeting, therefore we appoint our friends **Joseph Barker Peleg Gifford** and **Jonathan Wilbur** to use their endeavours to preserve said feed for that purpose: also to Procure Hay if needed for said Quarterly meeting

---

[9?] month 1783
At a Monthly Meeting held in **Dartmouth** yᵉ 15ᵗʰ of the 9ᵗʰ month 1783

The Representatives are **Elijah Gifford John Devaul [Davol]** & **Benjᵃ Taber** all present

Ebenezer Chase Juʳ Certificate
Received a removal Certificate from the monthly meeting of **Swanzey** in behalf of **Ebenezer Chase Juʳ** Signifying he was a member of that meet= =ing, and that he had Settled his outward affairs to Satisfaction: and **Abial [Abiel?] Gifford**, **Benjamin Chase**, and **William Gifford** are appointed to Visit said **Ebenezer**, and inspect into his circumstances, and report when ready

Gideon Anthony minute returnᵈ
Gideon Anthony returned a coppy of a minute of this meeting in the first month last, with an Endorsment thereon from **East Hoosuck** Signifying he appeared in a good degree of an orderly life and conversa= =tion and a diligent attender of meetings while there

Answer to Queries
Answers to the Queries were prepared and read in this meeting and some Sutiable remarks made thereon

George Smith 2ᵈ
The Committee appointed to have the care of that matter respecting **George Smith 2ᵈ** and wife report that they have had several oppertunities of Solid conferences with them, and received some degree of Satisfaction yet the matter is defered under the same friend care for further proof of their Sincerity and they to report to nex[t] monthly meeting

John Potter & Isaac Smiths denial been read
The Clerk informs that the Testimonies of Denials of **John Potter** and **Isaac Smith** son of **Gershem** have been read as directed last monˡʸ meeting

David Chase in= formd
John Devaul [Davol] informs that he hath informed **David Chase** of his denial as directed last monthly meeting

Gilbart Russel denied

The Friends appointed to treat further with **Gilbart [Gilbert?] Russell** on acount of his keeping company with a young woman not a member of our Society and other misconduct Report that they have taken an opertunity of Solid conference with him; and he did not object against anything alleig'd [alleged?] against him by our minutes; nor Shew any disposition to Retract therefrom Therefore for the clearing of Truth and Friends from such disorderly conduct, we with the concurence of the womans meeting do disown the said **Gilbart [Gilbert?] Russell** from haveing any right of Membership among us and **Joseph Gifford** is appointed to inform him thereof, and report next monthly meeting

Wᵐ Russell clearness

The Friends appointed to make the necessary enquiry into the Clearness of **William Russell** (son of **Abraham**) respecting marriage and conversation Report that they had taken the necessary care anᵈ that they find nothing Sufficient to hinder his proceeding in marriage

Wᵐ Russells proposal of marriage

William Russell and **Hepzabah Mosher** appeared for their answer which was that they might proceed to take Each other in marriage at some convenient time between this and next monthly meeting, adviseing with the Friend this meeting shall appoint to see said marriage Solemniz'd Who are **Benjamin Chase** and **William Gifford**, and the[y] to report next monthly meeting

The Friends apointed to treat further with **Barker Little** respecting his misconduct, report that they have discharg'd themselves in that matter, and have provided ˰ᵃ draught of a Testimony of his denial as follows

Barker Littles Testimony of denial

Whereas **Barker Little** having had his Education amongst Friends, but through unwatchfulness and disregarding the Prin =ciple of Truth in his own heart have much neglected the attendenᶜᵉ of our Religious meetings, also uses profane language at times, and hath removed out of the Verge of this meeting without a Certificate or advice of Friends and friends having laboured with him The Said **Barker** in order to convince him of his outgoings, But our Labours of Love not having the desired effect to Satisfaction therefore we are concerned to give this forth as a publick Testimony against him the said **Barker Little**, disowning him from being member of meeting, Nevertheless, it is our Sincear desire that he may have a Sigh[t?] and Sence of his outgoings, and with unfeigned Repentance turn to the ways of Truth

Given forth and Signed ˰ⁱⁿ and ˰ᵇʸ Order of ˰ᵒᵘʳ said meeting yᵉ 15ᵗʰ of 9ᵗʰ mo 1783 　By

Wm Anthony Juʳ Clerk

Susanna Smith Clerk

which with the concurrance of the Women was Signed in each meeting by the

Clerks; and the Clerk of this meeting is desir'd to cause the same to be read in the usual, the same friends informed **Barker** of his denial ~

Ruth Sowl &
daughters
Certificate

A Removal Certificate for **Ruth Sowl [Sowle?]**, and her daughters **Susanna Mary** & **Thankful**, directed to the monthly meeting of **Accoaksett** Signifying their right of membership; was Signed by the Clerk

Ephraim
Mosher pro=
p°sal of -
marriage

Ephraim Mosher and **Joanna Mosher** declared their intentions of taking each other in marriage, and were desired to wait till next monthly meeting for their Answer: he having produced a Certificate from **Ninepartners** he Signifying his clearness respecting marriage

Adam Mott
desires
advice

Adam Mott desires the advice of Friends respecting Selling his Interest and removing his family: therefore we appoint **William Gifford Benjamin Chase** and **Prince Potter** to take the necessary care in that matter and they to report to next monthly meeting

To inspect
yᵉ rights of
Joanna Mosher
Children

Joanna Mosher widdow being about to marry we app[o]int **William Anthony Ju[r]** and **Thomas Russell** to inspect into the circumstances of her children that their rights by former marriages be not neglected; and report to next monthly meeting   Collected £1 – 8ˢ – – 9ᵈ

adjournd

This meeting is adjournd to the 24ᵗʰ Instant after the meeting of worship

mett

mett [*erasure*] by adjournment yᵉ 24ᵗʰ of 9ᵗʰ month 1783 Representatives all present

appointing
School Comᵗᵉᵉ
referᵈ

The appointing a School Comᵐittee coming again under consideration and is Refer'd to next monthly mee[t]ing by reason this meeting is so Small

Jane Mosher &
daughter
under
dealing

The Women Friends inform that they have taken **Jane Mosher** and her Daughter ᴧ**delilah** under dealing for their misconduct, by written report of the men and women Overseers, and complaint of others; this meeting doth therefore appoint **Jonathan Wilbur**, **John Devaul [Davol]** and **Joseph Austin** to Joine the women friend in inspecting that matter, and Labour with the offenders; and if they do not find Satisfaction from them or either of them, to draw a Testimony of their denial accordingly, and inform thereof, and bring said Testimony to next monthly meeting

Concerning
Elders

The Committee appointed to inspect into the matter of chusing an addi= tion of Elders, have reported their approbation of **Caleb Greene** and **Mercy Slocum** for that Service; Therefore this meeting doth approve of them, and do appoint ᴧˢᵈ **Caleb Green** and **Mercy Slocum** to the place of Elders accordingly, having the Unity and concurrence of the womens meeting therein

Representatives
to Quarˡʸ
meeting

We appoint our friends **Caleb Russel, Jonathan Wilbor, Abiel Gifford, Caleb Green**, and **Benjamin Smith 2ᵈ** to attend our next Quarterly meeting, as Representatives, and present the answers to the Queries, and also the Epistle, which was Signed in this meeting and rcport ncxt monthly meeting

Complaint
against
Ben Gifford
and wife

The Overseers Inform that **Benjamin Gifford Ju^r** and **Rhoda** his
Wife are guilty of the Sin of Fornication, as by their own Confesion
Said Overseers hath Laboured with them therefor bu[t] received no Satis=
=faction; and said **Benjamin** and wife hath absented themselves and cannot
reasonably be spoke with ^therefore with the concurrence of the womens meeting we disown
them the said **Benjamin** and ^wife **Rhoda** from membership among us; and
Samuel Smith is appointed to draw ^ a Testimony of their denial and
bring to nex monthly meeting, and inform them thereof in writeing when
way is open

Wm Anthony Ju^r
atends a Jor=
[ney?] to
Hoosuck &c

William Anthony Ju^r Clerk of this meeting informs that he intends
a Journey to **Hoosuck** and **Saratoga** to Visit his relations in them parts
as also to attend the Quarterly meetings at **Oblong** and **Ninepartners**
and this meeting concurring with the same, he being a member of
this meeting & **Thomas Hicks** to give him a coppy of this minute and
Sign the same in behalf of this meeting

money to be raisd
for yearly meet
ing Stock

It having been recommended by the yearly meeting that £150 be
raised for the yearly meeting Stock: Therefore we appoint our friend
Gideon Howland, John Devaul, Joseph Austin and **Elijah Gifford**
to receive in Subscriptions made in freedom for that purpos[e], and they
to make report as soon as they have discharg^d themselves therein

Joanna Mosher
reqest a
Certificate

The Women friends inform that **Joanna Mosher** reque[s]t a removal
Certificate to **Ninepartners**: and desires the assistance of men friends
therein, therefore We appoint **William Anthony Ju^r** to Join the
Women, and take the necessary care therein and report to next monthly meeting

---

10 month
1783

At a Monthly meeting held in **Dartmouth** ye 20th of ye 10th month 1783
The Representatives being called are **Joseph Barker Benjamin**
Rider and **Barnabus Russell**, all present

Giden Sanfords
minute returnd

Gideon Sanford returned the coppy of a minute of this meeting
in : 5th month last; with an Endorsment from **Creek** meeting
Signifying he attended their monthly meeting to Satisfaction

George Smith 2^d

The Committe appointed to have the care of that matt^er respecting
George Smith 2^d and wife, report that they have made some progress
therein but desires it may be deferred another month, it is accord-
=ingly deferred under the same friends care till next monthly meeting
they then to make report

Rights of Joan=
=na Mosher
Settled

The friends appointed to inspect into the Circumst^ances of the Rights
of **Joanna Mosher**s children, by former marriage, report that they
have taken the necessary care therein and find thing Settled to
mutual Satisfaction

Gilbart Russell
inform^d of
denial

Joseph Gifford informs that he hath inform'd **Gilbert Russell** of
his denial as directed last monthly meeting

Wm Russell married

The Friends app[o]inted to see **William Russell** and **Hepzibah Mosher**s Marriage orderly Solemniz'd Report that the^y attended thereto and did not find but that it was orderly Solemnized

Barker Little denial read

The Clerk informs that the Testamony of the denial of **Barker Little** hath been read as directed

Report to Adam Motts request

The friend appointed to have the care of the matter respecting **Adam Mott**s request last monthly meeting, Report, that they have taken the necessary care therein, and gave Such advice as they tho^{ught} best; yet they are continued in that Service of advice and care as they shall find necessary and report when Ready

Case of Jane Mosher deferd

The Friends appointed to Joine the Women friends, in inspecting [?] and treating with **Jane Mosher** and her daughter **Delilah** Report that they have not accomplished the same and desire it deferd it is according[ly?] defer under the Same friends care and attention till next monthly meeting, they then to make Report

School Com^{tee} appointed

The School Committee made Report in writeing in the 8th month last and is Recorded in page 496 which is accepted and they dismised from that Service : And we now appoint **Samuel Smith, Jonathan Wilbur William Gifford, Caleb Green, Joseph Austin, Benjamin Howland 2^d** and **Thomas Mott**, a School Committee for the year ensuing who are to proceed in that appointment agreeable to the direction of the yearly me[eting?] [*smudge*] [any?] four of which Committee to Set as a Comm[i]ttee and not less

Elisa: Little Certificate & children

A Removal Certificates fo^r **Elizabeth Little** wife of **Barker Little** and their Children ~ **Lydia Nathan, Charles, Rebeckah, Zerriah** & **Sylvester** and **Susannah Barker** wife of **Ebenezer Barker**; directed to the Monthly meeting at **Accoakset** Setting forth their being members In corrence [*sic*] with the womens meeting were Signed by the Clerk

Rhoda Wing Certificate

A Removal Certificate directed to the monthly meeting of **Sandwich** in behalf of **Rhoda** wife _^^{of} **Benⁿet Wing**, setting forth her being a member in concurence with the women friends was Signed by the Clerk

Ephraim Moshers answer

Ephraim Mosher and **Joanna Mosher** appeared in this meeting for their Answer : Which was that they might proceed to take each other in marriage at some convenient time, between this and next monthly meeting, advising with the friends this meeting shall appoint to see the marriage orderly Solemnized ~ who are **John Devaul [Davol]** a[nd] **Abiel Gifford**, and they are to make report to next monthly meeting

A few Lines was endorsed on the copy of a minute **Obediah Gifford** prod[uced?] from the **Crie^ek [Creek]** monthly meeting Signifying he attended this meeting to Satisfacti^{on}

Collected   £1 – – 9^s – – 3 ½

adjournd

This meeting is adjorned to the 29th instant at the usual time of day

met

29th of ye 10th month, 1783 Mett by adjournment; The Representatives called are **Joseph Barker**, **Benjamin Rider**, and **Barnabus Russell** all present

Caleb Green Clerk The Clerk not being present haveing gone his intended Journey therefore **Caleb Greene** is appointed Clerk for this time

Return from Quarterly meeting The Representatives to the Quarterly meeting, report that they all attended that meeting, and produced an Epistle from the same, which was read in this meeting to Satisfaction; and their ˄request to make some alter= =ation in the Womens apartment, in order to accomidate it for Holding the Quarterly meeting is refer'd to next monthly meeting

A Testimo= =ny of de[n]ial of Ben Gifford and wife A Testimony of Denial of **Benjamin Gifford** and wife **Rhoda** was prepaired as Follows

Whereas **Benjamin Gifford Jur** and **Rhoda** his wife, Having stood as members of our Society, under the care of this meeting, but throug[h] in attention to the dictates Truth, they have fallen into the sin of Fornication as appears by their own Confession and friends having Laboured with ~~em~~ them on that account in order for their restoration and recovery But it not having the desired effect, and instead there of the said **Benjamin** and **Rhoda** suddenly moved themselves away to a distant land where they could not conveniently be further Treated with on that account: Therefore this meeting being concerned for the clearing of Truth s Testimony herein, do disown them the Said **Benjamin Gifford** and **Rhoda** his wife from being members of our Society until by a Sencere Repentance and amendment of Life they may be restored to the way of Truth

Given forth, and Signed in and on behalf of our [*smudge*] monthly meeting of men and women friends held in **Dartmouth** by adjournment the 29th day of the 10th month 1783 By ~   **Caleb Greene** Clerk this tim[e?]

Mercy Slocum Clerk this time

which was read and after some alteration was Signed by the Clerks of Each Meeting; and **Benjamin Chase** is desired to cause the same to be read in the usual manner at **Newtown** and report to next monthly meeting

Chusing over seers refered The choice and appointment of Overseers for the year ensuing is proposed, as the time agreed on since last appointment is expired yet a new choice is defered till next monthly meeting for further consideration

Joanna Mosher Certificate deferd The Women Friends inform that the matter respecting **Joanna Mosher**s Certificate is defered till next monthly under the friends care who was appointed therefor

Giles Russell request ~~to~~ advice **Giles Russell** request the advice friends respecting disposing or Selling his outward Estate, therefore we appoint **Elijah Gifford**,

and **Nicholas Lapham**, and **Timothy Gifford** to advise him therein
as way may open, and report when Ready

11 month
1783

At a Monthly meeting held in **Dartmouth** yᵉ 17ᵗʰ of 11ᵗʰ month 1783

The Representatives are **Joseph Tucker Juʳ**, **Joseph Austin**, and
Seth Huddleston, being called are all present

The Clerk yet being absent **Caleb Greene** is appointed Clerk for
this time

George Smith 2ᵈ

The Committee appointed to have the care of the matter respect=
=ing **George Smith 2ᵈ** and wife Report, that they have had some
encourragement of Satisfaction, yet desire the matter defer'd, it
is accordingly defer'd till next monthly meeting under the same
friends care they then to report

Case of Jane Mosher and her daughter Delilah referᵈ

The Committee in the case of **Jane Mosher** and her daughter
Delilah not having accomplished the same, and request it
continued, it is therefore continued till next monthly meeting
under the care who are to report next monthly meeting

Ephraim Mosher married

The Friend to oversee the marriage of **Ephraim Mosher** and
Joanna Mosher report that they attended the Same, and Saw
nothing but that it was orderly Solemnized

Respecting altering meeting house

The matter respecting alteration of our meeting house for the
better accommodating it for the Quarterly meeting as by their
request; coming under consideration; We appoint **Peleg Gifford**
Giles Slocum, **Gideon Howland**, **Caleb Russell**, **James Tucker**, **John**
Tucker Samuel Smith, **Thomas Hicks**, and **Benjamin Smith 2ᵈ** a
Committee to consider of said alteration, and accomedation and
ₐwhat is necessary to be done therein; and report to next monthly meeting

John Shepherd Ju minute re= =turnd

John Shepherd Juʳ having returned to this meeting with the
Coppy of a minute of this meeting in the 10ᵗʰ month last year Indorsed
by the monthly meeting of the **Oblong** the 13ᵗʰ of last month, Signifying
his orderly behaviour while among them which is accepted to Satisfaction

Benjamin Chase Reports that the Testimony of denial of **Benjamin**
Gifford Juʳ and his wife **Rhoda** had been read according to appointment

Overseers referᵈ

The matter of Chuseing overseers, coming again under consideration
is refered to next monthly

Josiah Wood acknow= =ledgment

Josiah Wood gave in a paper to this meeting condemning his mi[s?]
conduct for which he was denied, therefore this meeting appoints
Elijah Gifford and **Thomas Hicks** to have an oppertunity of Solid
conference with him on that Subject in order to discover his Sincerity
and to report next monthly meeting

Joanna Mo=
sher
Certificate

A Removal Certificate for **Joanna Mosher** directed to the monthly meeting at the **Ninepartners**, Setting forth her being a member of our Society, and that she had Settled her outward affairs to Satis= =faction; was Signed in this meeting in concurence with the Women's meeting

advice from
meeting for
Sufferings
of coppies
given

Received the following advice from the meeting for Sufferings Viz It appearing necessary that some General advice be given respecting what coppies from our Records Such who have hearetofore been members of our Societ[y] may reasonably exspect to be furnished with ~ This meeting gives it as their Sence and Judgment, that it may be adviseable for any monthly meeting to direct their Clerks, on application of any Person heretofore, a member of our Society, or their Survice in friends relations, or others; to give coppies of their denials, marriage Certifi= =cates; of their Births and Deaths, of their Children and Friends, and of any other minute necessary for asserting their Rights on the Same reasonable Terms, as the like coppies are or would be grant~ed to members of our Society

Coppy of a minute of the meeting for Sufferings held at **Dartmouth** the 6th of the 10th month 1783 Extxtracted by **Thomas Arnold** Clerk Which was read and accepted and is to the Satisfaction of this meeting

Daniel &
Alice Wing
Certificate

Received a Certificate from the monthly meeting of **Sandwich** in behalf of **Daniel Wing** a minor, living at **Peleg Slocum**'s, which is accepted: Also in behalf of **Alice Wing** a Girl, which as she is placed out from among Friends; We return the care of her to them; which was Signified by an Endorsment returned on Said Certificate, which was Signed by the Clerk

Abigail
Briggs
request

The Women inform that **Abigail Briggs** hath requested to be admitted under Friends care; We therefore appoint **Jonathan Wilbur** and **Samuel Smith**, to Joine the women friends to take the necessary care therein, and make report to next monthly meeting

Jethro Russell
request

Jethro Russell having requested at the Preparitive and this meeting to be admitted under friends care, we therefore appoint **William Wood** and **Seth Huddlestone** to take a Solid oppertunity with him and family in order he may be rightly Initiated, and make Report to next monthly meeting

Ruth Mott
under
dealing

The Women Inform they have taken **Ruth Mott** under dealing for her misconduct, and have appointed a Comittee to treat with her, which this meeting concurs with; and appoints **William Gifford**, and **Stephen Buffinton** to Joine the women friends therein, and report to next monthly meeting

Collected £1 – 16s – 7 ½d

order on Treasurer

Treasurer is ordered to pay to **Giles Slocum** One pound Ten Shillings for half a Load of Hay he Supplied this ‸meeting with last, and report to this meeting

The Treasurer Reports he hath paid Giles Slocum, as ordered

12 Month 1783

At a Monthly meeting held in **Dartmouth** yᵉ 15ᵗʰ of yᵉ 12ᵗʰ month 1783 The Representatives from the Preparitive meeting are **Benjamin Taber**, **Thomas Mott** and **Stephen Gifford** all Present

Queries approv'd

The Queries were read and Answers thereto read and after Some amendment were approved by this meeting

Overseers appoint

The matter of Chusing Overseers coming again under conside= ration, We therefore appoint **Benjamin Taber**, **Joseph Tucker Juʳ** **Joseph Austin**, **Benjamin Smith 2ᵈ**, **Josep[h] Barker** and **Caleb Russell** to the place of Overseers for the year Ensuing and from that time ‸till others shall be appointed in their Room; who are desir= =ed to attend to their own Gifts therein to see that the cause of Truth be keep to in the Several members of our meeting

Wᵐ Giffords Certificate

Received a Certificate on account of **William Gifford** (son of **Ephraim** deceased) Setting forth his clearness in regard to ~ marriage, and that he is a member of Society, directed to this meeting, from **Accoakset**; also he hath produced consent of his mother therefore

Wᵐ Giffords proposal of marriage

William Gifford and **Hannah Smith** declared their Intentions [of] taking Each other in marriage and were desired to wait till next monthly meeting for their Answer

Gideon Anthonys minute

Gideon Anthony Informed this meeting that he intends to go to **East Hoosuck** or **Saratoga** in order to make some Stay with which meeting doth concur he being a member hereof and the Clerk is deser =ed [desired] to give him a coppy of this minute

Wᵐ Anthony Juʳ return from Hoosuck

William Anthony Juʳ having returned from his Journey at **East Hoosuck** and **Saratoga**, produced a few lines from the monthly meeting there Setting forth his attendance with them to Satisfaction

The Committee appointed to alter or Repair our Meeting House make Report as follows

Report on alter= ing meeting house

We the Committee appointed to alter or Repair our meeting house, and after meeting Several times, have agreed to move the Partition as far Eastward as the Great doore: and to have a passage out the Little Room up Stairs: And that the Same be Effected as Soon as may be; and also that the Womens Chamber be repaired to make it warm, and that the Roof be mended ~ Signed by direction of the Committee by Dated this 10ᵗʰ of 12ᵗʰ month 1783   **Samuel Smith**

Com^{tee} to alter= meeting house   Which is accepted, and in consequence thereof our Friends **Peleg Gifford**, **Philip Trafford**, and **William Anthony Ju^r** are appointed to See said meeting house altered and repaired accordingly and report next monthly meeting

Collected – £1 – 19^s – 3^d

money for yearly meet= ing Stock   The Friends appointed ^{to} Collect money by way ^of Subscription have made Report, that they have Collected the sum of Collected £8 – 13^s – 3^d to Supply the yearly meeting Stock

adjournd   This meeting adjourns to the 24th of this Instant, after meeting of Worsh^{ip}

Mett   Mett by adjournment the 24th of 12th month 1783

The Representatives being called, are **Benjamin Taber Thomas Mott** and **Stephen Gifford** all present

George Smith 2^d   The Committee appointed to have the care of that matter Respecting **George Smith 2^d** and wife Report that they have taken Further care therein and that they had some Satisfaction; Yet the matter for further Satisfaction of this meeting is Defer'd till next monthly meeting under the same friends care, who are then to Report

Jethro Russell   The Friends appointed to have the care of **Jethro Russell**s request Report that they have visited him to some Satisfaction: yet Judge it best to defer the matter some time longer for futher Satisfaction It is accordingly defer'd under the same friends care till next monthly meeting, then to report

Jane Mosher & daughter   The Committee in the care of **Jane Mosher** and daughter **Delilah** desires the matter continued; it is accordingly defer'd till next ~~mon~~ monthly meeting, they then to Report

Josiah Wood   One of the Committee in the case of **Josiah Wood**s Paper Con= =demning his misconduct, for which he was denied, request that matter continued ~ it is accordingly defer^d till next monthly meet[ing?] The committee then to Report

Ruth Mott   The Friends appointed to Joine the Women friends, in treating with **Ruth Mott** ~ Report that the matter is not accomplished it is therfore continued under the same friends care till next monthly meeting they then to make report

Complaint against Francis Allen Ju^r   The Overseers inform that **Francis Allen Jun[i]or** much neglects the attendance of our Religious meetings: and hath attended a marriage out of the Unity of friends, and appears far from that plainness which we profess: for which defects, the said Overseers hath laboured with him, but he did not give them Satisfaction: therefore we appoint our Friends **William Barker** and **William Anthony Ju^r** to labour further with him thereon, and make report to next monthly meeting

Jonathan
Tallman
request

Jonathan Tallman requests by way Preparitive meetings to be ad=
=mitted under our Care, We therefore appoint our Friends **Seth Hud=**
=**dleston** and **Stephen Buffinton** to take a Solid oppertunity with said
Jonathan in order to discover his motive therein and make report to
next monthly meeting

overseers
of poor
referd

The Choice of Overseers of poor (the year being expired since last choice) is refer[d]
to next monthly meeting

Wᵐ Russell
disorder

Received a request and Information by some Friends appointed by **Saratoga**
monthly meetings of the 18ᵗʰ & 19ᵗʰ of last month; Signifying that **William**
Russell removed from thence to **Dartmouth** without Certificate leaving his
outward affairs unsettled to the Satisfaction of Friends: We therefore appoint
Benjamin Howland 2ᵈ & **Nicholas Lapham** to treat with said **William** there[on]
and Report to next monthly meeting

Sent to
Quarterly
meeting

An Epistle to the Quarterly meeting was prepared, and Signed by the
Clerk, and directed to be forwarded by our Representatives, who are
William Anthony Juʳ, **James Davis**, **Caleb Barker**, and **Joseph Austin**,
and they to make report to next monthly meeting

order on
Treasurer
for Noah
Russell

The Committee to provide Hay for th[e] last Quarterly meᵉting past; have
brought **Noah Russell**'s account for one Tun the amount being ~~Twlve~~
Twelve Dollars which the Treasurer is directed to pay, when he hath
money from the meeting and make report to this meeting

To review
minutes
and Settle
with Trea=
=surey

Samuel Smith, **Jonnathan Wilbur Benjamin Howland 2ᵈ** and **George Smith**
are appointed to review and Inspect this meetings minutes of the year
past in order that they may be Recorded, and Settle accounts with the
Treasurer, and make Report to next monthly meeting

[1ˢᵗ?] Month
1784

At a Monthly Meeting held in **Dartmouth** yᵉ 19ᵗʰ of 1ˢᵗ month 1784
The Representatives from the Preparitive meeting are **John Howland**
Joseph ₍Barker₎ and **Prince Potter**, all present.

Josiah Wood

The friends appointed to Treat with **Josiah Wood**, Report that they
have had an oppertunity with him to a degree of Satisfaction; and
he having given in a paper condemning his misconduct; which this
meeting concluds to accept of for Satisfaction, Provided he cause
Said paper to be publickly read at the close of a first day meeting
of Worship, he being present, and return it to next monthly meeting

Alice Wood

This meeting in concurence with the Women friends, hath Signed an
information to **RhodIsland** monthly meeting respecting **Alice Wood**
informing them that we have made enquiry into her conversation
and find nothing ₍Sufficient₎ to hinder her being receiv'd into membership

meeting house

The Friends appointed to repair the Meeting house: &c: Report that
they have made some progress therein, but ₍not₎ accomplis[h]'d fully, they

are therefore continued in said Service, and ˄to report to next monthly meeting

Georg Smith 2
[&?] wife

The friends appointed in the case of **George Smith 2ᵈ** and wife Report that they have had another opertunity of Solid conference with them, and that they gave them so much Satisfaction as that Friends may receive their acknowledment; and this meeting Sol= [id?] weighing the matter and having the concurrence of Women friends, do conclude to accept of their said acknowledgment for Satisfaction Provided they cause Said paper of acknowledgment to be publickly Read at the Close of a first day worship, and they both present and return the Same to next monthly meeting

Francis Allen
Juʳ

The Committee appointed to Treat with **Francis Allen Juʳ** Report that they treated with said offender, and that he gave them no Sa= =tisfaction; therefore this meeting doth Disown him the said **Francis Allen Juʳ** from being any longer a member of our Society

Wᵐ Gifford
proposal
Answer

William Gifford and **Hannah Smith** appeared for their answer Which was that they might proceed to take Each other in marriage in Some convenient tim[e] before next monthly meeting, adviseing with the friends that this meeting Shall appoint to oversee the same who are **Willam Anthony Juʳ** and **Jonathan Wilbur** and they to make Report to next monthly meeting

Jonᵃthan
Talman

The Friends appointed to have a conference with **Jonathan Talman [Tallman]** on his request Report, that they have had a Solid Satisfactory opper= =tunity with him, and think he is in Some degree Sincear in his request

Benjᵃ Gidley

Benjamin Gidley having returned home hath produced a Certificate from the monthly meeting of **Saratoga**, Setting forth his orderly conducᵗ while there, which is to our Satisfaction

Joshua
Maccomber

Joshua Macumber attended this meeting with a coppy of a minute from the monthly meeting at **Saratoga** which was read to Satisfaction and an Indorsement wrote theron Signifying the Same

Collected ~ ~ ~ £1 – 5ˢ – 9ᵈ

adjournd

This meeting adjourns to yᵉ 28ᵗʰ instant after the meeting for worship

mett

Mett by adjournment yᵉ 28ᵗʰ of yᵉ 1ˢᵗ month 1784 The Representatives being called are all present

John Howland is appointed to Inform **Francis Allen Ju** of his denial make report next monthly meeting

Jonathan
Talman

The matter in regard to **Jonathan Talmans [Tallmans]** request coming again under consideration, and Solidly considering thereof, do conclude to grant his request, and do receive him into membership with us, We haveing the concurence of women friends hearin [herein]

Jethro
Russell

The Friends appointed to confer with **Jethro Russell** on his request to be taken under friends care, make Report, that they have had a

Solid oppertunity of Conference with him, which was in degree Satis
=factory, and this meeting taking it under consideration do accept of
him into Membership with us having the womens concurence herein ~

Overseers
of poor
The matter of chuseing Overseers of the poore is referd to the next
Monthly meeting, and the former ones are contin[u]ed to that time

Wᵐ Russell
Saratoga
The friends appointed in regard to ~~Sara~~ the request of **Saratog[a]** month
=ly meeting concerning **William Russell**, Report, they have Treat[ed?]
with him for his mis conduct, and that he gave them some encourage
=ment to endeavour to Satisfy friends at that meeting; but it is
not yet don, therefore said Committee are Still continued to See
that he doth perform according to encouragement given and to
make Report when it Shall be done, or otherwise, when they shall
think friends have waited a Sufficient time therefor ~

Quarterly
meeting
The friends appointed to attend the Quarterly meeting Report
they all attended agreeable to appointment, who have produced an
Epistle from Said meeting, which hath been read to Satisfaction, and
the advices contained therein Refer'd to next monthly meeting for
further consideration

Jane Mosher
& daugh
=ter
The Committee appointed (in conjunction with the womens meet=
=ing) in the case of **Jane Mosher** and her daughter **Delila [Delilah]** make
Report, that they have had Several Solid oppertunities with them and
that the said **Jane** gave them So much Satisfaction they think it may [be?]
Safe to Let the matter drop in regard to her the said **Jane Mosher**
but as to her daughᵉʳ **Delila** She did not give them Satisfaction, ther
=fore they have drafted a Testimonial against said **Delila** which
hath been read, and the said report and denial hath been
accepted, and said Testimony Signed by the Clerk who is directed
to read the Same publickly at the close of a meeting of Worship on a
first ₄day and make report to next monthly meeting

Recept
from year
=ly meeting
Our Representatives to the Quarterly meeting have produced a
Rece[i]pt from the Yearly meetings Treasurer tha[t] he Recᵈ £8 – 13ˢ – 3ᵈ
to Supply the yearly meeting Stock

Seats for
Bˡacks
This meeting being informed that the Black people that attended
Our meeting for Worship have at sometimes ⁿᵒᵗ been ₄Sutiably provided with Seats
Therefore this meeting appoints **Thomas Hicks John Devaul [Davol] Phlip [Philip]**
Trafford William Anthony Juʳ Caleb Russell Joseph Austin and
Abiel Gifford to inspect into that matter and provide Such Seats
as they may think best and inform them thereof and make report
when accomplished

Revise
minutes
The Committee appointed to Revise this meetings minutes report
they have revised said minutes, and directe them to be recorded

and that they have Settled accounts with this Treasurer
And that ther[e] remained in Stock before the date hereof after
all Orders are paid that are alowed the Sum of £9 – 4 – 2
which Sum was then in Stock which was yᵉ 17ᵗʰ of first mo 1784
which was before our last Collection

Phebe Lap=
ham

The women inform that **Phebe Lapham** keeps company with
a man not of our Society, and request our assistance therein there
fore we appoint **Georg[e] Smith** and **William Anthony Ju**ʳ for that
purpose and they to report next monthly meeting

Abraham
*Allen reques*ᵗ

Abraham Allen informs this meeting he has thoughts of disposeing
of his Estate, and desires friends advice therein therefore we
appoint **Giles Slocum** and **Elijah Gifford** to inspect into his Circum
=stances and to advise him as they find best, and report to next
monthly meeting

Deborah
Howland

The women request the assistance of this meeting in regard to
Deborah Howland who hath removed within **Accoakset** monthly
meeting without a Certificate therefore we appoint **John Devaul**
and **Seth Huddlestone** for that purpose and to report their doing
therein next monthly meeting

2 month
1784

At a Monthly meeting held in **Dartmouth** yᵉ 16 of 2ᵈ month 1784
The Representatives from Prepariritive meeting being called are
Barnabus Russell Thomas Mott and **Daniel Ricketson** all present

Josiah Wood

The Clerk informes that **Josiah Wood**s paper hath been read
as directed last monthly meeting and the paper returned to
this meeting, and said **Josiah** receiv'd accordingly

Meeting house

The Friends appointed to repair the meeting house report
that they have not accomplish'd it yet by reason of the Severity of
the weather, they are therefore continued to accomplish the Same
and Report to next monthly meeting

Georg Smith 2
[&?] wife

The Clerk informs that **George Smith 2** and wife ~~may~~? have caused
their paper of acknowlᵉdg[?]ments to be read as directed last monthly
meeting, and the said **George Smith** and wife are readmitted into
membership accordingly

Wᵐ Gifford
married

The friends appointed to attend the marriag of **William Gifford**
and **Hannah Smith**, report that they attended said marriage
and did not see but that it was orderly Solemnized

Fransis
Allen

John Howland informs that he hath informed **Francis Allen Ju**
of his denial, as directed last monthly meeting

Quarterly
meetings
advice

The advices of the Quarterly meeting coming again under the
consideration of this meeting, viz, the Treating weightily and

tenderly which [with?] Such as may be in the practice of Sleeping in meet=
=ing, as also ~~the~~ tenderly advising those who pray ungaurdedly
incline to the practice of deali~~ng~~ in Spiritous Licquor; and that
dealing in them may be discouraged amoung Friends, Therefore
mee[t] ing appoints **Abial Gifford**, **Caleb Greene**, **Thomas Hicks**, **William
Gifford**, **Joseph Austin**, **Jonathan Wilbor**, **John Devaul** and
Seth Huddleston to Treat with the former and advise the latter
agreeable to the Quarterly meetings advice, and the mind of
Truth therein; and make report from time to time as may
be necessary

Deborah Howland   The friends appointed to asist the women in regard to
Deborah Howland who hath removed within **Accoakset**
Monthly meeting without a Certificate and too much neglects the
attendence of our Religious meetings, Report ˄there on that they with the
women have taken a Solid oppertunity with her the said **Deborah**
but that She did not give them any Satisfaction therefore this
meeting doth concur withe the women in dis owning her

mary Wood Certifi= =cate   A Removal Certificate was Signed in this meeting by the Clerk on
concuren[ce] of women friends, for **Mary Wood** wife of **Abraham Wood**
directed to the monthly meeting at **Saratoga** signifying her right
of membership

Chusing Clerk   The further advice of the Quarterly meeting respecting the chuseing
Clerks for our meeting Annualy is refered to next monthly meeting

Overseers of poor   The choice of overseers of the poor being refered to this meeting **Gideon
Howland**, **John Devaul**, **Caleb Barker** **Jonathan Wilbor**, **John Howland
George Smith** and **William Gifford** are appointed for that Service the year
Ensuing

Mary Bowdish   The Women request the assistance of men friends in treating with
Mary Bowdish ~ therefore we appoint **Joseph Barker** and **Seth Huddleston**
to assist the Women, and make report to next monthly meeting

                  Collected – £1 – [*smudge*] 18^s – 5^d ~

Adjorn^d   This meeting adjourns to the 25th instant after the meeting for worship

Mett   Mett by adjournment the 25th of the 2nd month 1784
The Representatives being called were all present

Delila Mosher   The Clerk reports that the Testimony ^{of} denial ~~of~~ against **Delila [Delilah] Mosher**
hath been read as directed last monthly meeting

Abraham Allen   The friends appointed to advise and assist **Abraham Allen** report that
they have not fully accomplished Said matter therefore they are continued
in that Service, and to report next monthly meeting

Anna Marshal

The Women inform they have Received a removal Certificate for **Anna Marshall** from the monthly meeting of **Nantucket** which this meeting concurs with

Dividing Prepariti =ve meeting

It is proposed wheither it may not be best to divide our Preparitive meeting into two distinkt Preparitves meetings, Therefore we appoint our friends **James Davis**, **Thomas Hicks**, **Abiel Gifford**, **Stephen Buffinton**, **Elijah Gifford** and **William Anthony Ju^r**, to Joine the Women friends and take that mat^ter under Consideration; and if they think best to divid[e] said meeting they to prepare Boundris [Boundaries] between Said m^eetings and report to next monthly meeting

Barnabas Russell

Barnabus Russell Informs this meeting that he hath thoughts of going to **Philadelphia** on buisness, and request a minute from this meeting; We concuring with His request; He being a member of this meeting the Clerk is desired to give him a coppy of this minute

Bedford meeting House

The friends at **Bedford** hand,^ed in a Petition for to hav^e a meeting ho^use built there and friends taking the matter under consideration do appoint **Joseph Tucker Ju^r William Gifford Peleg Gifford**, **Benj Smith 2** & **Nichlas Lapham** to take that matter under consideration, & report their Sense & Judgment thereon next monthly meeting

Phebe Lap [=ham]

The Comm^tee appointed to assist the women in that matter respecting **Phebe Lap =ham** desire it Refer'd and it is defer'd to next monthly meeting they then to report

Part of the Com^tee appointed in the matter respecting **Ruth Mott** report they made some progress there^in and Rec^d no Satisfaction and She hath proceeded in marriage out of the unity of friends & the women inform they have disowned her the S^d **Ruth Mott** which this meeting doth concur with

---

[3] Month 1784

At a Monthly meeting held in **Dartmouth** ye 15th of ye 3 month 1784 The Representatives from the Preparitve meeting are **William Barker Seth Russell** and **William Gifford** all present

[repa]ir meeting house

The friend^s appointed to repair the meeting house report that they have proceeded Somewhat further therein, but not having accomplish'd the Same they are continued in that Service and report next monthly meeting

[Saml] Gidley

Two of the Overseers inform that **Samuel Gidley** hath proceed,^ed ,to keep company, and contract marriage with a woman not of our Society, after being precautioned and treated with on that account Therefore this meeting (with with the concure,^nce of the womens meeting) do disown him the said **Samuel Gidley** from being a member of our Society and **Josiah Wood** is desir'd to inform him thereof and to make report next monthly meeting ~

Mary Bowdish

The fr^iends appointed to Joine the women in Treating with **Mary Bowdish**, not having accomplis[h]ed it they are Still continued in said Service and to report next monthly meeting

Abraham Allen The friend appointed to advise with **Abraham Allen** in regard to his disposeing of his Estate, report that they have performed said Service and it was their advice for him so to dispose of his ⸍Sd Estate if a suitable oppertunit[y] Should present which report is acceped by this meeting

Bedford meet [ing?] house The friends appointed in the matter respecting the petition of **Bedford** friends building a Meeting house thear make the follow= =ing Report; which is accepted by this meeting and this meeting doth conclude to refer it to our next Quarterly meeting for their aᵖprobation and assistance if they may think proper

Comᵗᵉᵉ reprt [?] on To the monthly meeting of **Dartmouth** to be held 15ᵗʰ of [4?]ᵗʰ month 1784 according to appointment Some of us attended with a Committee from the Quarterly meeting Respecting friends request at **Bedford** to build a meeting house there: and after concluding ᵘᵖᵒⁿ ~~house~~ ᵗʰᵉ bigness of said house; to be 48 by 36 feet Computeing the cost of 400. We think propper for Friends to come to Subscriptions in order to accom= plish said matter

Joseph Howland	**Benjamin Smith Jur**
Giles Slocum	**Wᵐ Anthony Juʳ**
	Wm Gifford

Collected ~~~ £1 – 5ˢ – 11ᵈ ~

Meeting in Allens neck Some friends in **Allens neck** and other Friends requesting the priviledge of one meeting or more in that neck; this meeting taking the Same under Consideration conclude with the womens ⸍ᵐᵉᵉᵗⁱⁿᵍ concurence to grant said request, and direct that one meeting for Worship be held at **Susanna Allen**s in said **Allens neck** and that on the Sixth -day of this week to begin at the eleventh hour, and our friends **Elijah Gifford, Giles Slocum**, and **Thomas Hicks** are appointed to attend and have the care therof and report to next monthly meeting

Adjourn'd This meeting Adjourns to the 24ᵗʰ Instant aft⸍ᵉʳ the meeting for worship

Mett Mett by adjourment the 24ᵗʰ of yᵉ 3 month 1784

The Reprᵉsentatives from the Preparitve meeting are **William Barker Seth Russell** and **William Gifford** all present

Clerk appoint ed The advice of the Quarterly meeting respecting the Choice of Clerk to be chosen annually being referᵈ from last monthly meeting and considerᵈ

William Anthony Junor is therefore appointed to continue in that Service the years Ensuing.

Phebe Lapham The friends appointed to assist the Women in respect to **Phebe Lapham** Report that it is not accomplished they are therefore cont- =nued in that Service and to report next monthly meeting

Rebecca Rotch   The Women inform they have received a removal Certificate from **Nantucket** monthly meeting in behalf of **Rebecca Rotch** which [this] meeting concur with

on dividing Prepari =tive meeting & boun= daries   The Committee appointed to Join the Women friends, to consider matter of dividing the Preparitive meeting into two distinks Prepar[-]tive meetings, and propose Bounderise between them Report as Follows— We the Committee of men and women Friend appoint by the Monthly meeting for considering the dividing the Preparit[ive] meeting, have Solidly considered and conferd on with Several other friends on that matter, and it is our Sense and Judgment that it is best it should be divided and called north & South preparative meeting and that Line of division be thus viz
Beginning at the Southeast corner of **Jonathan Tucker**s land on the **West Side** of **Clark**s or **Shearman**s Cove, from thence till it goes to the Southward of **John Howland**s house, including said house to the Northward of said line, from thence to the Southeast corner of **James Tucker**s homstead farm, from thence in a direct line to the brook called the half mile Brook where said brooks crosses the Road Northward of **Stephen Buffinton**s, from thence to the South =east corner of the land formerly belonging to **James Shearman** on the West side of the High way and from thence to the Southeast corner of **Zephaniah Eddy**s land in **Accoakset East** line

Bedford 3 mo 5th 1784	Judith Russell	William Anthony Jur
	Mary Smith	Abiel Gifford
	Sarah Howland	James Davis
	Sarah Anthony	Stephen Buffinton

Report accepted Time & place fixed   Which Report is accepted and with the concurence of the Women said Preparitive meeting is divided accordingly, and the denomination of them approved of; and that the **South preparitive** meeting be held as usual at our ~~South~~ old meeting house in **Ponaganset** and the **North Prepa-ritive** meeting be held on fifth day at **Newtown**, and at **Bedford** on Sixth day next proceeding our Monthly meeting, and the time for hold-ing it at Each place be concluded by a Committee for that purpose who are **William Anthony Ju**ʳ **Joseph Tucker Junor** and **Stephen Buffinton** they to Join the Women and to make report next monthly meeting and that first North Preparative meeting beheld at **Newtown** next month

Hannah Tucker Request   And notwithstanding the boundaries are as above said, yet by the request of **Hannah Tucker** and her two daughters **Rebeckea** and **Joanna** they are to Preparitive members of the South Preparitive meeting

To Qurly meeting   The Queries were answered and an account prepared to the Quarterly meeting which was Signed by the Clerk which account and answers were forwarded by our Representatives who are **Samuel Smith John Howland Caleb Greene** and they to report to next monthly meeting

[4] month
1784 At a Monthly meeting of Friends in **Dartmouth** ye 19th of 4th month 1784 The Representatives being called were from the **South Preparitive** meeting **Elijah Gifford** and **Nicholas Lapham,** from the **North Preparitive** meeting **Caleb Russell** and **Seth Huddleston** all present

[Ca]leb Condon Received a removal Certificate on behalf of **Caleb Congdon** from the monthly meeting of **Providence** Setting forth his right of membership and that he is come to learn a Trade within the Compass of this meeting which this meeting accepts

[?] meeting house The Committee appointed to repair the meeting house report that it is not yet fully accomplished therefore they are continued to accom= plish it and make report next monthly meeting – –

[?]Gidley **Josiah Wood** not having made any report of his informing **Samuel Giddley [Gidley]** of his denial therefore he is desired to report next monthly meeting

[R]eport from quarterly meeting Report was made of the Representatives all attended the Quar= =terly meeting except **Caleb Greene,** who sent a reasonable excuse which was accepted and they produced an Epistle from said Quarterly meeting which was read and the contents thereof recommend ed to individles to observe; and as the Quarterly meeting hath Concluded upon the Sum of £5-16s-9d more from **Dartmouth** to Supply the yearly meeting Stock, therefore those friends that had the last Subscriptions for the Supply of the yearly meeting take said Subscriptions and endeavour to raise Said money by Friends Subscribing thereto again and they to report next month= =ly meeting **Joseph Austin** being dismissed by reason of his of his absence **John Howland** is aded in his room

[Re]port of meeting [A]llens neck The friends appointed to have the care and Oversight of the meeting that was appointed in **Allens neck**, report, that they attended said meeting which was conducted orderly and pritty good Satisfaction which report the meeting accepts of

Preparitive [m]eeting The Committee appointed to consider of the holding of the North Preparitve meeting report that said meeting be held one half the time at **Newtown:** and the other half the time at **Bedford** which report this meeting accepts of

Amie Proud Certificate The Women friends inform they have received a remo= =val certificate from the monthly meeting of **Greenwich** on behalf of **Amie Proud.** Which meeting concurs with

Phebe Lapham Disowned The Women friends inform they have disowned **Phebe Lapham,** Now **Phebe Russell** which this meeting concurs with

Bedford meeting house

As the Quarterly meeting hath appointed a Committee to attend this meeting and Confer with us and friends at **Bedford** in request to Building a meeting house att **Bedford** therefore we appoint our friends **Joseph Howland Benjamin Smith 2 William Anthony Jur Giles Slocum** and **William Gifford** as a committee to Join the quarterly meetings Committee in that matter to consider on the bigness of said [house?] and compute the Cost, and to Consider all other matters necess[ary] therein and make report when ready

Giles Slocum Ju

Some of the Overseears inform by way of the Preparive meeting [that?] **Giles Slocum Ju^r** too much neglects the attendence of our Religious meetings and appears at times far from that plainess in habbit [as?] becomes our Profession – Also hath atten[d]ed one mariage and the Entertainment of another, which marriages were out of the Unity of [our?] Society and that they Laboured with him for the above offence[s] but Received no Satisfaction therefore we appoint **Seth Huddleston William Barker** and **Thomas Mott** to Labour further with him for the above said offences and make report to the next monthly meeting

Isaac Russell account

The Overseers of the poor handed in an account from **Isaac Russell** for keeping **Alice Smith** Eleven months, together with her Funeral charges to the amount of £16 – s10 – d0 which this meeting approves of and the Treasurer is ordered to pay the same when he is supply'd with mony and report to this meeting.

Timothy Howland account

The Overseers of the poor handed in an accompt from **Timothy Howland**, for keeping **Hannah Barker** 13 weeks to the amount of £4 –[?] which this meeting accepts and the Treasurer is ordered to pay the same when Supplied with money and report to this meeting

Giles Russell

The Friends appointed some time [prep ?] to advise with **Giles Russell** respect[=?] =ing Selling his Interest, report, that they advised with him therein accord [=?] =ing to their ability, which report is accepted

Collected £1 – 13^s – 6^d

---

5 month 1784

At a Monthly meeting of friends held in **Dartmouth** 19th of 5th month 1784 The Representatives from the **South Preparitve** meeting are **Peleg Gifford** and **Jonathan Willbor [Wilbur]**: from the **North Preparitive** meeting **Joseph Austin** and **Seth Huddleston** all Present

On our meet= ing house

The Committee appointed to repair the meeting house report that they have accomplished said buisness as far as appears nessesary at present

Sam Gidley

Josiah Wood reports that he inform'd **Samuel Gidley** of his denial as ordered

Giles Slo =cum Ju^r

The friends appointed to Treat with **Giles Slocum Ju^r** on account of his disorderly conduct, &c, Report that they have had a Solid

oppertunity, and Labour'd with him but did not receive their desir[']d
Satisfaction, but request that it may be continued for further Labour
they are therefore continued in that Service to Treat further with him
and to make report next monthly meeting —

Barnabas Russell   **Barnbas Russell** having returned from his Jorney to **Philidelphia**
have returned the Coppy of this meetings minute which was made for the
Purpose, to Satisfaction

Philip Allen Jos Hart   **Philip Allen** And **Joseph Hart** hath given in each of them a paper confes [=?]
=sing and condemning their being in the practice of Gameing therefore
this meeting do appoint **Jonathan Willbore [Wilbur]**, **William Anthony Ju**ʳ
and **Caleb Barker**, to inspect into the matter and treat with
them on that account and report next monthly meetin

Mary Bowdish [di]sownd   The W°men friends inform that they have concluded to disown **Mary
Bowdish [Bowditch]** wife of **William Bowdish [Bowditch]** with the concurence
of this
meeting, which we do concur therewith, and have Signed a Testimony
of denial against her the Said **Mary**, Jointly with the women friends
and the Clerk is directed to read the same publickly at the Close of
a first day meeting for Worship before next monthly meeting, and
then to make report

[N]at Gifford wife disownd   The Committe appointed some time past to Treat with **Natha**=
=**niel Gifford** & wife report that they have had Several Solid Confer=
=ences with them, but their Labore not having the desired effect
but that they still continue much remiss in the due attendence of
our meetings and Friends having waited long for their return
and not finding in them that Satisfaction which we desire, do
disown them from being members of our Societ[y], and **William
Anthony Ju**ʳ and **Jonathan Willbor [Wilbur]**, are appointed to draw a Testimo=
=ny of denial against them and bring it to next monthly meeting, and
also to inform them of their denial, and make report thereof
to next monthly meeting

Collected [£]1 – 4^s – 10^d

[A]djourn'd   This meeting adjourns to the Second day of next month after
the meeting for Worship

Mett   Mett by adjournment yᵉ 2ᵈ day of 6ᵗʰ month 1784
The Representatives from the Preparitives meetings being called
are all present

In Joining Sandwich Quarter   Most of the Committee of men and women friends appointed to consi=
=der and confer with the yearly meetings Committee on annexing this
meeting to **Sandwich** Quarter not having an oppertunity with said
yearly meetings Committee, as they did not attend the meeting

as Expected; yet our said Committee have given in the following report

Report of said Committee　We of the Committee appointed the monthly meeting of **Dartmouth** to consider of the matter in regarerd to our being set off to **Sandwich** Quarter, have mett and Solidly considered there up on, our minds being measurably disposed to act therein as best Wisdom shall direct – but we have not as yet discovered any prospect of any ad= =vantage either toward promoting the cause of Truth or General good in Society, Sufficient in our opinion to make the proposed Alteration.

Given forth by your Committee y^e 25th of 5th month 1784

Stephen Buffinton	**Caleb Russell**	**Elisabeth Slocum**
Wm Anthony Ju^r	**Benj^a Taber**	**Mary Smith**
Jospeh Tucker Ju^r	**Thos Hicks**	**Mercy Slocum**
	Sam[?] Smith	

which report is accepted & said Committee is directed to lay the same with a coppy of this minute before said yearly meetings Committee & report to next monthly meeting

Money for yearly meet= =ing Stock　The Friends appointed to receive Subscriptions for the Supplying the yearly meetings Stock Report they have collected £5 – 10^s – [11?]^d and this meeting added thereto makeing the sum £5-s16-d9 as directed by the Quar= =terly meeting which is directed to be forwarded to the yearly meetings Treasurer by **John Howland** and to report next monthly meeting

Account for repareing meeting house　The friends that repaird the meeting house gave in their account of the same to the amount of three pounds Eleven Shillings which the Treasurer is directed to pay when Supplied with money

---

6 month 1784　At a monthly meeting of Friends held in **Dartmouth** ye 21st of 6th month 1784 The Representatives from the **South Preparitive** meeting are **Joseph** [Ta?] and **Nicholas Lapham**; from the **North Preparative** meeting **John De**[?] and **Benjamin Taber** all present

Alice Wood Certifi^{te}　The Women inform they have received a removal Certificate from **RhodIsland** monthly meeting in behalf of **Alice Wood** which was read to Satisfaction

Lydia Arter Rec-　The Women also inform that they with the concurence of this meeti[ng] have admitted **Lydia Arter** into Membership which this meeting units [?]

Samuel Hopkins　Our Friend **Samuel Hopkins** attended this meeting with a Coppy of a Minute of a monthly meeting of **Philidelphia**, att the **Bark**[?] meeting house for Northen districks the 25th of 5th month 1784

John Willis　Also our Friend **John Willis** attended this meeting with his C[erti=] =ficate, dated at **Westbury** on **Long Island** y^e 25th of 5th month 1784

Tiddeman Hull　Also our friend **Tiddeman Hull** attended this meeting with a Coppy of a minute from **Creek** monthly meeting held at **Nine partners** the 21st of 5th month 1784

Jos-Willits   Also our friend **Joseph Willits** [**Willis**?] attended this meeting a Companion to **John Willis** and produced a Coppy of a minute of **Westbury** monthly meeting of the 26th of ye 5th month 1784

All which Certificates and minutes were read in this meeting to [Sa?]

Giles   The friends appointed to Treat with **Giles Slocum Jur** desires that
Slocum   matter defer['?]d another month for a further oppertunity with him
Jur   it is accordingly deferd under the same friends care who are to repo[rt] next monthly meeting

Philip   The friends appointed to Inspect into the matter and treat with
Allen   **Philip Allen** and **Joseph Hart**s condemning their being their being
JosHart   in the practice of gameing with Cards report that they have taken a Solid oppertunity with the young men which was Somewhat Satis= =factory, yet the matter is continued under the Same Friends care in order to discover their Sincerity in condemning that practice and the friends to make report next monthly meeting

The Women inform they have concluded to disown **Mary Bowdish** [**Bowditch**] wife of **William Bowdish** [**Bowditch**] (with this meetings concurence) which we do concur with, and Signed a Testimony of denial against her the said **Mary** Jointly with the women friends, and the Clerk is directed to read the Same publickly at the close of a first day meet= =ing for Worship before next monthly meeting and then to report

The Clerk Informs sd Testimony hath been Read . is as Follows

Mary Bowdi   Whereas **Mary Bowdish** [**Bowditch**], wife of **William Bowdish** [**Bowditch**] having
=sh   made profession with us, and under the care of this meeting but through
Tetimony   unwatchfulness. hath so far departed from the principles Princi[=?]
of denial   ples we profess, as to attend meetings held out of the Unity of Friends for which misconduct She hath been Laboured with in love, but our Labour not having the desired Effect; therefore thinking ourselves Clear from any further Labour with her do disown her the said **Mary Bowdish** [**Bowditch**] from any right of membership with us, and from under the care of this meeting; Nevertheless hopein She may come to a sence of her outgoings and return to the way of peace

Given forth at our Monthly meeting held in **Dartmouth** 17th of 5th mo 1784
Signed in and on behalf of said meeting

By   **Wm Anthony Jur** Clerk
Mercy Slocum Clerk

George Smith 2   **George Smith** and wifes paper of Confession and acknowledgment not
[an]d wife   being recorded in the proper place it is Recorde here and is as Followeth
[ac]knowledg   To the Monthly meting of Friends next to be held at **Dartmouth**
ment   Beloved Friends

With concern and Sorrow of mind, we have to acquaint you that
by departing from the dic[t?]ates and Testimony of Truth in our own
minds, and giving way to the Temtation of the enemy have fall=
=en into the reprachful Sin of Fornication as appears by our
having a Child soon after marriage which occationed us to mar=
=ry out of the Order of Truth: Now these are to Testify to Friends
and publickly to declare to all the world that we are Sencearly Sor=
=ry for our ⁱᵒTransgression and do hereby condemn the Same desire=
forgiveness from the Almighty against whose righteous Law
we have sinned, taking the Shame and reproach to ourselves
desireing hereby to clear Friends and the Testimony they bear
from the Same. and desire friends so far to pass by our offence
that if the occation of the reprach hereby given shall be removed
they would continue us under their care. desireing in future this
Divine protection to be preserved from the Like Transgression

  From you Friends ~~~ **George Smith**

Natⁱ Gifford Dated yᵉ 18ᵗʰ of 4ᵗʰ month 1783 **Mary Smith**
[a]nd wife

  The friends appointed to draw a Testimony of denial of **Nathaniel**
Their testi **Gifford** and wife and inform they thereof report that they have
mony of denial given them a Coppy of the minute of their denial and produced a
Testimony as follows

  Whereas **Nathaniel Gifford** and **Mehitable** his wife having
had a Birthright amoungst Friends and under[?] the care of this
Meeting, but by ~~departing~~ not adhearing to the dictates of Truth in
their own hearts, and giving way To the Temtations of the Enemy
hath fallen into the reproachful sin of Fornication as appears by
their haveing a Child soon after marriage also they appearing
Slack in attending Relⁱgious meetings, altho Friends bestowing
much Labour in love to convince them of the Evil thereof, and
the Incumbent duty of attending Religious meetings but our
Labours not haveing the desired Effect to friend Satisfaction
and they remaining much remiss in attending meetings; therefore
we are concerned to give this forth as a Testimony against
such conduct, hereby disowning them the said **Nathaniel Gifford**
and **Mehitable** his wife from being in membership with us;
yet that they may come to a Sight and Sence of their outgoings and
return to the way of truth is our Sencear desire

  Given forth and Signed in on behalf of our monthly meeting of
Friends held in **Dartmouth** this 21ˢᵗ of 6ᵗʰ month 1784

By **Wᵐ Anthony Juʳ** Clerk

Mercy Slocum Clerk

Which is to Satisfaction, and Signed by the Clerk who is desir'd
to cause the Same to be read at the Close of a first day meeting
before next monthly meᵉting, and report to the Same

yearly meet
ing Comᵗᵉᵉ
Informed

The Committee appointed to Confer with[e?] the yearly meetings
Committee and lay a Coppy of a minute of this meeting before the[m]
Report that they accomplished the Same

Receipt
from year
=ly meeting

John Howland produced a Rece[i]pt from the Yearly meeting
Treasurer for five pounds Sixteen Shillings and nine pence on
account of this meeting for the Yearly mee[t]ings Stock

Queries &
answers to
be compild

The Queries with answers to them from the Preparitive meetings were
read in this meeting, and our friends **Abiel Gifford Samuel Smit[h]**
Jonathan Willbor [Wilbur] and **William Gifford** are appointed to Comp[?]
Said answers. into general ones from this meeting to the Quarterly
meeting, and prepare an account to the Quarterly meeting, and
and bring to the adjournment of this meeting
Collected £2 – 1ˢ – 5ᵈ

adjournᵈ

This meeting is adjournd to the 2ᵈ day of next month at the close
of the meeting for Worship

mett

Mett by adjournment yᵉ 2ᵈ day of yᵉ 7ᵗʰ month 1784
The Representatives being called are all present

answers
compild
Sent to
Quarterly
meeting

The friends appointed to compile the answers to the Queries have
accomplished said buisness, and this meeting approving of the
general Answers, also have Signed an Epistle to the Quarter[ly]
meeting all which are forwarded to said Quarterly meeting
by our Representatives who are **James Davis Caleb Greene** anᵈ
Joseph Austin and they to report next monthly meeting

Abigail
Briggs
Recᵈ

The women inform they have admitted **Abigail Briggs** wife of **Da[?]**
Briggs into membership which this meeting concurs with

John Tuck
ers bill

John Tucker handed in a bill to the amount of £2 – 8ˢ – 0ᵈ
for one Tun of hay for the use of the Quarterly meeting 1782
which this meeting approves of and the Treasurer is directed
to pay the Same when Supplied with money

7 month
1784

At a Monthly meeting held in **Dartmouth** yᵉ 19ᵗʰ of yᵉ 7ᵗʰ month 1784
The Representatives from the **South Preparitive** meeting are **William**
Darker and **Stephen Russell**: from the **North Preparitive** meeting
Joseph Austin and **John Devaul** [Davol], all present

Hugh
Judge

Our Friend **Hugh Judge** attended this meeting with a Certificate
from the Monthly meeting of **Wilmonton** [Wilmington] in the **County of New Castle**

upon **Deleware** dated yᵉ 17ᵗʰ of yᵉ 6ᵗʰ month 1784[42]

Joseph Tatnal

Also our Friend **Joseph Tatnale** attended this meeting as a Companion to the above mentioned friend having the concur= =rence of said monthly meeting at **Wilminton** as expresed in said Certificate whose company anᵈ Certificate were to Satisfaction

Giles Slocum Juʳ

The friends appointed to treat with **Giles Slocum Juʳ** report that they have had further oppertunity with him and he request the matter may be continued another month, it is accordingly con= =tinued under the Same friends care who are to report to next monthly meeting

Jos Hart Philip Allen

The friend appointed to Treat and discover the Sencerity of **Philip Allen** and **Joseph hart** in their condemning their misconduc Report they have taken a further oppertunity with the young men which was some what Satisfactory, yet the matter is defered under those and **William Gifford** and **Elijah Gifford** who arᵉ desired to make a more Conclusionary report to next monthly meeting.

Nat Gifford & [wifes] denial [not] read

The Clerk informs that the Testimony of denial of **Nathani̶** =el Gifford** and wife has not yet been read as directed he is there desired to cause the Same to be read as heretofore directed and make report to Next monthly meeting

Gideon Anthony

Gideon Anthony returned a Coppy of a minute of this meet= =ing in 15ᵗʰ of 12ᵗʰ month last with a few line endorssed there =on from **Saratoga** monthly meeting Signifying he made Some Stay and Stidily attended meetings there

[Re]port from [Qu]arterly [m]eeting

The Friends appointed ~ Report they all attended the Quarterly meeting, and prod[u]ced an Epistle therefrom and Transcrips of the following ~ One frorm **London** last year; One from **Philidelphia** last year;& One from **Westbury** on **Long Island** this year; and that from the Yearly meeting this year, together with the Extracts from the minutes from Said yearly meeting all which was read in this meeting to Satisfaction

Report of Visitors

The Friends appointed to Join the Wome[n] friend in Visiting those who neglect the attendance of our Religious meetings and those otherwise defective make report which is accepted ~~and is~~ as Satisfactory ~ and is as followeth

We your Coᵐmittee appointed to unite in labour in order to Stir up those who are neglegent in the attendance of our Religious meet=

42. Hugh Judge (1749–1834) was a minister who lived several places in Delaware and Pennsylvania before moving to Belmont County, Ohio, where he died. See *Memoir and Journal of Hugh Judge: A Member of the Society of Friends, and Minister of the Gospel; Containing an Account of His Life, Religious Observations, and Travels in the Work of the Ministry* (Philadelphia: J. Richards, 1841).

to a Solid consideration of the dangerous Situation they are in,
that So an amendment herein may be discovered to our Satisfaction
and Comfort. ~ We have vise^ited divers families, and in the
ability ~~we k~~ received have endeavour to discharge our Selves
in which we find peace and Satisfaction And hope it may prove
useful to those visited. ~ from your friends   **Thomas Hicks**

To the Monthly meeting to be	}	**Martha Gifford**	**Abiel Gifford**
=held in **Dartmouth** by ad=	}	**Sarah Gifford**	**James Davis**
Journment – 2^d of 6th mo 1784	}	**Joanna Gifford**	

[T]heodate
Jonson

A certificate was Signed by the Clerk directed to the Monthly
meeting of **Rhod Island** in behalf of **Theodate Jonson** [**Johnson**] daughter of
James Johnson and **Elisabeth** his wife, Signifying she is placed to
to live with a friend there; That she was a member of our Society

[E]pistle refer'd

The Epistle from the Quarterly meeting being againe read and
weighty advices therein noticed; yet a further consideration there=
=of is refer'd to next monthly meeting .

Benj^e Ricketson

The overseers inform by way of the Preparitive meeting that
Benjamin Ricketson have attended a marriag or at an entertain=
=ment for a marriage, that was held out of the Unity of Friends
for which the said Overseers Laboured with him but receiv'd
no Satisfaction, w[h]ere upon we appoint **Peleg Gifford** ₐ^John Howland and **Stephen
Buffinton** to labour further with said **Benj^a** and report to next
monthly meeting

*Jonathan
Slocum*

Jonathan Slocum gave in a paper condemning his misconduct for
which he was disowned, therefore **Elijah Gifford** and **Timothy
Howland** are appointed to take a Solid oppertunity with said
in order to discover his Sencerity, and make report to next
monthly meeting

Collected £1 – 6^s – 1^d

*money paid
for Book*

Out of which the Treasurer has paid **Caleb Green** 13 – 6
For a Blank Book for Records by direction of this meeting ~

*8 month
1784*

At a Monthly Meeting of Fr^iends held in **Dartmouth** ye 16th of 8th month 1784
The Representatives from the **S^outh Preparit[i]ve** meeting are **Stephen Buffinton**
~~Jonathan~~J^r **Caleb Barker**: from the **North Preparitive** meeting are
Caleb Greene and **Jonathan Hart** all Present

*Nat^l Gifford
request*

Nathaniel Gifford requests a Coppy of the Testamony of his denia[l]
which the Clerk is directed to furnish him with and make report [to]
next monthly meeting

*Deb Potter
Rece^d*

The Women inform they have concluded to accept of **Deborah
Potter**s paper condemning her misconduct provided She chuseth it

to be read publickly in the usual manner which this mee[t]ing concur wi[th]

Ruth Bow=
=dish

Ruth Bowdish [**Bowditch**] hath returned her Certificate with an Endorsme[nt] from **Oblong** Monthly meeting Signifying She had attended with it

Giles Slocum
*Ju*ʳ

The friends appointed in the case of **Giles Slocum Ju**ʳ desires the matter continued another month, it is therefore continued under the same friends care then to report to next monthly meeting

*Nat*ˡ *Gif=*
ford deni=
=al read

The Clerk informs that the Testimonʸ of denial of **Nathanial Gifford** and wife, hath been read as directed

Ben Rick=
=etson

The friend appointed to treat with **Benjamin Ricketson** repor[t] that they had an oppertunity with him which was in degree Satisfac[=] =tory and said **Benj**ᵃ gave in a paper to this meeting condemning his misconduct in attending an Entertainment for a marriage out of the unity of friends which is excepted [accepted?] for Satisfaction

Jonathan
Slocum

The friends appointed report they having taken a Solid oppertun[ity] with **Jonathan Slocum** which was in degree Satisfactory; yet the matter is defer'd under the same friends care to next monthly meeting they then to make report

advice from
Quarterly
meeting

The weighty advice from the Quarterly meeting by Epistle being again Considered is recommended to the Solid attention and practice observence of Friends accordingly

Philip Allen
Jos Hart

The friends appoin[t]ed in the case of **Philip Allen** and **Joseph Hart** desires the matter defer'd another month, it is accordingly continud under the Same friends care till next monthly meeting they then to make report

Jonathan
Tucker
disorder

The Overseers inform that **Jonathan Tucker** hath so far departed from the Principles of Truth as to utter or diliver Some vile and profane expres[=] =sions, for which he hath been with but did not condemn it to Satisfaction therefore we appoint **John Howland William Wood John Devaul** [**Davol**] and **William Gifford to** take a Solid oppertunity with said **Jonathan** intreating with him for that and other misconduct and Report to next monthly meeting

[Ca]leb Green
and a Jour
[n]ey

Caleb Greene informs this meeting he intends a Journey to **Ninepart** =ners, and as far as **East Hoosuck** in order to Settle Some buisness and to Visit his relations and expects to visit Some meetings of friends and desires our concurence with a few lines Signif[y]ing the Same we therefore aprove of his proceding he being a friend in unity and an Elder, and the Clerk is desired to Vest him with a Coppy of this minute

[A]braham
Russell

Abraham Russell gave in a paper condemning his misconduct in Joining in an Entertainment for a marriage out of the order of friends

we therefor appoint **David Shepher [Shepherd]** and **Jonathan Hart** to take a Solid
oppertunity with him ∧in order to discover his Sencerity therein and report to
next monthly meeting

                                                            Collected £1 – 9ˢ – 7½ᵈ
Thomas Russell   **Thomas Russell** presented an acᶜompt against this meeting   1 – 2 ½
for Schooling some poor children of this meeting   1 – 10 – 10
amounting to £ 0 – 11ˢ – 4ᵈ which the Treasurer is directed to pay
when in Stock

[9ᵗʰ] month   At a Monthly Meeting held in **Dartmouth** yᵉ 20ᵗʰ of 9ᵗʰ month 1784
1784   The Representatives from the **South Preparitive** meeting are
William Barker and **Jonathan Willbore [Wilbur]** from the North Preparitive
meeting are **David Shepherd** and **Benjamin Chase** all present

[St]ephen   Received a Removal Certificate from **Sandwich** Monthly meet=
Barker   =ing recomending **Stephen Barker**, his wife **Margret** and his Son
[Ce]rtificate   **Samuel** to this meeting as members of Society, and in degree of
Received   Orderly Lives

[Co]ppy of Nat   The Clerk informs he hath Signed and Sent forward (by the hanᵈ
[Gi]fford denial   of **Samuel Gifford**) a coppy of the Testimony of denial of
sent   **Nathaniel Gifford** which he requested

Jonathan   The Committee appointed in the case of **Jonathan Slocum**
Slocum   Report they have made some procedure therein, and request the
matter continued with an aᵈdition to the Committee; therefore
Jonathan Willbor [Wilbur] is added to them for that service, and
they to report next monthly meeting

Philip Allen   Four of the Committy in the case of **Philip Allen** and **Joseph**
Jos hart   **Hart** make Report that they have measurably discharg'd them=
=selves with them and are free friend should receive their paper
of acknowledgment, which this meeting accordingly accepts
for Satisfaction provided they cause said paper to be read
publickly at the Close of a first day meeting for Worship and return
said paper to next monthly meeting

Giles Slocum Juʳ   The friends appointed in the case of **Giles Slocum Juʳ** Report that
they have had another Solid oppertunity with him, and labour'd
to convince him of the hurtful tendency of those practices laid
to his charg, but that he did not give them Satisfaction; yet
Several friends expressing their concern for the continuence
of that matter it is accordingly defer'd under the Same Com=
=mittees care: and concerned friend with the Committee as
they Shall find freedom to take another oppertunity with
Giles and report to next monthly meeting

Elisabeth Sanford Rec^d –   The Women inform they have a^dmitted **Elisabeth Sanford** wife of **Elisha Sanford** into membership with us; which we con= =cur with

Jonathan Tucker   The friends appointed to Treate with **Jonathan Tucker** [of] his misconduct Report that they have ˄^not accomplished said matter for want of oppertunity and desires the matter defer'd it is ˄^accordingly defer'd under their care who are to report to next monthly meeting

Abraham Russell   The Friends appointed ˄^to have a Solid oppertunity with **Abraham Russell** in order to discover his Sencerity in condemning his mis[=] =conduct Report that they have not had Such an oppertunity as he is gone some distance from home they are continued in that Service and to report to next Monthly meeting

Wm How= =lands pro= =posal of mariage   **William Howland** and **Abigail Willbor** [Wilbur] declared their intention of Marriage with Each other and were desir'd to wait untill next monthly meeting for their answer, and **Benjamin Smith 2** and **William Anthony Ju^r** are appointed to inquire into the young ma[ns] clearness respecting ˄^marriag and Conversation and make report to next monthly meeting

Wm Sanford Ju^r   **William Sanford Ju^r** gave in a paper condemning his misconduct in neglecting the attendance of meetings and Sueing **Benjamin Allen** at the Law; where upon **William Wood Peleg Gifford** and **John Howland** are to take a Solid oppertunity with him and inspect into the matter in order to discover his Sencerity and report to next monthly meeting

Collected £1 – 2^s – 1^d

adjourd   This meeting adjourns to the first day of next month after meeting of worship

mett   10th month 1st mett by adjournment

Representatives being called are all present

answer to Queries & Epist =le sent to Qur^t meeting   The Queries with the answers from Each Preparitive meeting were read in this meeting from which general answers were made out and forwarded together with an Epistle to (which was Signed by the Clerk) to the Quaterly meeting by our Representatives who[?] **John Devaul,** [Davol] **Joseph Barker, Benjamin Smith 2** and **John Howland** and they to report next Monthly meeting

James Davis Martha Gifford recomm ended   This Meeting being inform'd that the Select meeting approves of the Publick appearence in the Ministry of **James Davis** and **Martha Gifford,** – And Friends taking the Same into Solid consideration, do conclude with the con[cu]rrence of Womens Meeting to Recommend Said **James Davis** and **Martha Gifford** to the

Select Quarterly meeting as Ministers – and the Clerk is di=
=rected to forward a coppy of this minute to said meeting

Thomas Hicks paper   **Thomas Hicks** gave in a paper condemning his not axpressing himself so Cleᵉarly as might have been ~~for~~ best respecting ₐᵃ reference with **Humphry Smith**, which paper was read, but not being Satisfactory ₐᵂᵉ ᵃᵖⁿᵗ **Peleg Gifford Seth Huddleston** and **John Howland** to inspect into the matter and Treat with **Thomas** thereon and make report to next Monthly meeting

John Howland Son of Benjᵃ   The Overseers gave in a complaint against **John Howland** (son of **Benj**ᵃ) for useing unbecoming and profane Language to **Zebedee Mac= Daniel**, for which they laboured with him but he did not give them Satisfaction. we therefore appoint **George Smith** and **William Wood** to treat further with him the sᵈ **John** and report to next Monthly meeting

Wᵐ Russell Bedford disorder   The Overseers inform by way of Preparit[i]ve meeting that **William Russell** of **Bedford** have fallen into the repr[o]achful Sin of Fornication as appears by his own confession to them and they having discharged themselves towards him therefore we appoint **William Barker** and **John Devaul [Davol]** to Joine the women friends and Treate further with him and if he doth not give them Satis= =faction to draw a Testimony of his denial and make report of the Same to next monthly meeting

Wᵐ Russell [?ter] Creek Certificate   Received a removal Certificate from the Monthly meeting of **Saratoga** dated yᵉ 17ᵗʰ of 6ᵗʰ month last in behalf of **William Russell** Signifying he is ₐᵃ member of our Society and Settled his outward affairs to Satisfaction; which was read to Satisfaction and is accepted in lieu of our Committees report in that case

[10]ᵗʰ month 1784   At a Monthly meeting held in **Dartmouth** yᵉ 18ᵗʰ of 10ᵗʰ month 1784 The Representatives from the **South Preparitve** meeting are **Peleg Gifford** and **George Smith** from the **North preparitive** meeting are **Caleb Russell** and **William Gifford** all Present

[R]eport from [Q]uarterly meeting   The Representatives to the Qarterly meeting report they all at= =tended except **Benjamin Smith 2** who being not well sent his reason for his non attendence which was accepted and said Re= =presentatives have produced an Epistle fr[om] said Qurterlly meeting which hath been read to Satisfaction

[P]hilip Allen [J]oseph Hart   This meeting hath been inform'd that the papers of **Phⁱlip Allen** and **Joseph Hart** hath been ₐʳᵉᵃᵈ according to direction of -last monthly meeting and said papers returned to the meeting which are as follows

Dartmouth yᵉ 15ᵗʰ yᵉ 5ᵗʰ month 1784

*[Ac]knowledg=
ments*
To the Monthly meeting of friends held in **Dartmouth**
Whereas I have practiced at times playing at Cards, which
being contrary to the good Order of Friend; and being in Some
measure convinced of the evil thereof, do hereby heartily con=
=demn my misconduct therein, and desire Friends to pass
by and let me remain under their care, desireing in future
to be preserved from Such practices. from your friend

Philip Allen

Dartmouth 15ᵗʰ of 5 mo 1784

To the Monthly meeting of friends to be held in **Dartmouth**
　　Whereas I have practiced at times playing ᵃᵗ cards which
being contrary to the good Order of friends, and being in
Some measure convinc'd of the evil thereof do hereby heartily
Condemn my misconduct therein ~~therei~~ and desire friends
to pass it by Let me remain under their care, desireing in
future to be preserved from Such practices

From your friend **Joseph Hart**

*Abraham
Russell*
　　The Friends appointed to Treat with **Abraham Russell**
Report that they have fulfild their appointment and that he
gave them a good degree of Satisfaction; therefore said **Abraham**'s
paper condemning his misconduct is accepted for Satisfaction

*Jonathan
Slocum*
　　The friends appointed in the case of **Jonathan Slocum** having
made some progress therein, but not haveing accomplish'd it desir[e]
it continu'd, it therefore is referd to next monthly meeting and
said committee are accordingly continued in said Service and
then they to make report

*Jonathan
Tucker*
　　The friends appointed to treat with **Jonathan Tucker** report
that he being gone from home they have not fulfil'd their ap=
=pointment, they are therefore continued in that Service and to
report to next monthly meeting

*Wᵐ How
=lands
Clereness*
　　The friends appointed to enquire into the clearness of **William
Howland** report they have made inquirey and do not find
any thing to hinder his proceeding in marriage

*William
Sanford Juʳ*
　　The friends appointed in the case of **William Sanford Ju**ʳ report that they
have made some progress therein, and have had him and **Benjamin
Allen** together who have put themselves in some way of Settlement
But they not knowing ~~it~~ that it is fully Settled said friends
are continued in that Service and they to make report to next
monthly meeting

Giles Slocum Ju^r   The friends concerned in the case of **Giles Slocum Ju^r** report that some of them have paid him a Visit, but not being able to make a conclusive report therein, it is continued to next month =ly meeting then they to make report

John How =land son of Benj^a   The Committee in the case of **John Howland** (son of **Benjamin**) Report that have not accomplished that matter by reason he was gone from home they are therefore continued in that Service and to make report when accomplished

William Russell Bedford   The Committee in the case of **William Russell** of **Bedford** report that they haven not had an oppertunity to fulfil their appointment they are therefore continued in that Service and they to make Report next monthly meeting

Thomas Hicks   The Friends appointed ^to inspect into the case of **Thomas Hick** Report that he hath Signed a paper which they think may be accepted for Satisfaction, which said paper having been read [i?] is accepted accordingly; provided he cause the Same to be publick =ly read in the us[u]al manner and returne the same to our next Monthly meeting

Ezra Russell   Received a Certificate from the monthly meeting of **Smithfield** [*carryover line*] Recommending **Ezra Russell** a young man under age to the care of this meeting as a member thereof

William Howland and **Abigail Willbore** [**Wilbur**] appear'd for their answer; which was, that they may proceed to take Each other in marriage Some convenient time before next monthly meeting adviseing with the friends that shall be appointed to oversee the same, who are **William Anthony Ju^r** and **Samuel Smith** and they to make report next monthly meeting

Abraham Wood   We are informd by a letter from **Saratoga** monthly meeting that they have taken the Necessary care in regard to **Abraham Wood**'s acknow= =ledgment, and that they think well of accepting the same Provided it be publish'd where the disorders were comitted and have for that purpose Sent us said paper of acknowledgment and the Clerk is desired to read the Same publickly as usual and make Report to next monthly meeting; and said **Wood** a ~~Cert~~ Removal Certificate, if after enquiry they shall find that his outward affairs are Settled to Satisfaction; and **Seth Russell** is added for the Service

Joseph Willbor [and] wife   **Joseph Willbore** [**Wilbur**] and **Abigail** his wife gave in a paper to this meeting desireing to come under friends care, therefore **Stephen Buffinton** and **Abiel Gifford** are appointed to take

an oppertunity of Sollid Conference with the Petitions in order
to discover the motive of their request they to Join the women
herein, and to report to next monthly meeting

Elizann
Shelden
disown'd

The Women inform that **Elizann** now wife of **Jonathan Shelden**
hath married out of the unity of Friends, and that they have
disowned her, which this meeting concurs with

Joseph Austin
[b?]ound a Jor=
ney

Joseph Austin informes that he intends to take a Journey to
the **Nine=partners** on buisness, and requested our concurence [*carryover line*]
which this meeting taking under consideration do concur there
with he being a member of our Society and the Clerk is desired
to give him a Coppy of this minute

Raisd
money to be
meeting
Stock

Our Quarterly meeting having Proportioned to this meeting
to raise the Sum of Sixteen pounds Lawful money to Supply
the Quarterly and yearly meetings Stock; therefore **Caleb Russell**
Samuel Smith, **William Gifford**, **John Howland**, **Gideon**
Howland, and **Jonathan Willbore** [**Wilbur**] are appointed to pro=
=portion said sum to each Prepari[ti]ve meeting and draw Sub=
=scriptions for that purpose, and make report next monthly
meeting　　　　　　　　　　　Collected £1 – 10^s – 4^d

---

11 month
1784

At a Monthly meeting held in **Dartmouth** y^e 15th of 11th month 1784
The Representatives from the S Preparitve meeting are **Elijah**
Gifford and **Philip Traford**; and those from the North Prepa=
=ritive meeting are **Benjamin Taber** and **Thomas Mott** all present

Jonathan
Slocum

The friends appointed in the case of **Jonathan Slocum** report
that they have been in a progress in that Service but not having
accomplished it to Satisfaction they are therefore continued in
that service and to make report next monthly meeting

Thomas Hicks
acknowledg
ment

Thomas Hicks haveing ret[u]r^{n}ed his paper and report of its
being read agreeable to the direction of last monthly meeting
and is as follow　　　　　To the Monthly meet^{ing} held 18th : 10th m^o 1784
　　　Whereas I did not express my mind so fully and intention
so fully to **Humphry Smith** in respect to leaveing a matter to
Reference, in so clear a means as I might have don[e], ~~which~~
and I beleive would have been best, which ‸[give?] occation for
our Religious Society to be reproachfully Spoken of
which condu^{c}t of mine I am Sorry for and as hereby
condemn　　　　　　　　　　　**Thomas Hicks**

Jonathan
Tucker

The friends appointed in the case of **Jonathan Tucker** make Some
what a favorable report in regard to him, he giving encourrage=
ment of reforming from the evil of his ways, and request said matter

should be continued for Trial of his Sencerity it is accordingly con=
=tinued, and said friends to have the inspection over him and to
Report next monthly meeting

Joseph
Willbor

The friends appointed to confer with **Joseph Willbore** and
Wife, respecting his pertition make a Satisfactory report Report
and that they think it may be safe for to receive them into mem=
=bership, we do therefore with the Joint concurence of the Women
Receive said **Joseph Willbore** and Wife into membership with us

William
Sanford Ju^r

The friends appointed in the case of **William Sanford Ju**^r report
that the matter is not fully Settled to satisfaction, they are therefore
continued to ~~see~~ Endeavour to see that it be accomplish,d agree=
=able to good Order and to make report next monthly meeting

Giles
Slocum
Ju^r

The Friends having the care of the matter in regard to
Giles Slocum Ju^r not making a full and conclusive report in
regard to said matter: it is therefore continued to next monthly
meeting under the same care as heretofore and then they to
make report

William
Russell

The friends appointed in the case of **William Russell** make
Report that the matter is not accomplished by reason that one of
them was unwell, they are therefore continued in the same
service and **Seth Russell** is added in the room of **William Bar**=
=**ker** who is unwell and is dismist and they to report to next monthly meeting

Elizabeth
Wing

The women inform that they have concluded to deny **Elizabeth
Wing** widdow for attending Sepperate meeting not of our Society
and continues therein; which this meeting concurs with

William
Howland
married

The Friends appointed to oversee the marriage of **William
Howland** and **Abigail Willbore** report that they attended the
Same and Saw nothing but that it was accomplished in a
degree Orderly

Eaquel pro=
potion be=
tween Pre
paritives
meeting

The friends appointed to proportion the money to each
Prepariture meeting Report that they have divided the Sum
Equally between them and have drafted Subscriptions in
order to Collect the Same; therefore **Prince Potter**, **Jethro
Russell David Shepherd Ju**^r **Hezekiah Smith Caleb Barker**
and **Timothy Howland** are appointed to take said subscription
and receive the Collections and to pay the same to the Treasurer
and to make return to this meeting of the Sum total so Collected
when they have Collected the Same who are desired to accom=
=plish it as soon as they conveaniently can

Samuel Smith
Clerk

Samuel Smith is chosen Clerk for this day

Collected – £1 – 7^s – 8^d

adjourn'd　　This meeting adjourns to the 24th of this Instant after meeting of worship

mett　Mett by adjournment the 24th of 11th month 1784

　　　　The Representatives being called all present except **Benjᵃ Taber**, who hath Sent an excuse for his absence & is accepted

Abraham Wood　The friends appointed in the case of **Abraham Wood**, not having accomplished that matter, one of them being not well, Request it continued, which is accordingly ~~to~~ defer'd to next monthly meeting under the care of the Same friends as before and then they to make Report

Amie Howland Rec'd　　The women friends inform that they have received **Amie Howland** into membership with us which this meeting concurs with

Tittle of meeting House & Lands　　This meeting taking under consideration the mater in regard to the Tittle of our Meeing House and Lands, do appoint **Caleb Barker John Howland** and **Elijah Gifford** or either three of them with and in addition to the former Trustees to hold said Lands, and do also appoint our friends **Caleb Russell**, **Joseph Barker** and **Jonathan Willbor** to see that Tittles be made Secure in the manner and form that the meeting for Sufferings have agreed and concluded upon and they to make Report next monthly meeting

Hanna Barker　　**Jonathan Willbore** hath handed in an account to this meeting for keeping **Hannah Barker** & for a pair of shoes the amount £5 – 17ˢ – 6ᵈ which being alwed by the Overseers of the poor this meeting approves thereof and orders the Treasurer to pay the Same when Supplied with money

Meetings in Allens Neck　　The friends in **Allens Neck** and there aways have proposed to have some meetings for Worship held at the wddᵒw **Susannah Allens** for the Ensuing Winter Season, which this meeting take =ing under consideration; Our friends **James Davis**, **Abiel Gifford** and **Stephen Buffinton** are appointed to Visit those friends in Said **Neck** either Collectively or Individlily as they think best, and make Report their Sense to next monthly meeting wheither it may be for the prohiotion of the Cause of Truth or not, and if granted, how many meetings shall think best and they to Join the women herein

Benjamin Howland 3 Comprained Of　　The Committee appointed some time past to advise with those who may ugaurdedly incline to the practice of dealing in Spiritous Licqurs; made Report that **Benjamin Howland 3** is in that Practice, and altho' they have treated with him thereon, an advised him to

desist yet he continues therein in Such a manner as is repoch=
=ful to our Society: therefore this meeting appoints **John Howland**
Elijah Gifford, **Philip Trafford** and **Samuel Smith** to labour
further with him the said **Benjamin** in order for his restoration
from such a practice, and they to report to next monthly meeting

School Com^{tee}   The time of the School Committees appointment being
Expired the same are continued for one month Longer
And **George Smith** and **William Wood** are added to them

---

12 month At a Monthly Meeting of Friends held in **Dartmouth** 20th of 12th m^o 1784
1784   The Representatives from the **South Preparitive** are **Giles Slocum**
and **Peleg Gifford** from the **North Preparitive** meeting are **Joshua**
Potter and **Joseph Austin**, all Present

Report   One of the Committee appointed to Joine the Quarterly meeting
concerning
those that Committee in Visiting those that have held and those that have been
have held held as Slaves, Report that they proceeded therein and find
& those that
have been Two cases that remain in an unsettled way which need further care
held Slaves and Labour, which report being accepted, the s^d friend of the
Committee is directed to lay the said case before the Overseers
who are directed to inspect therein, and the Committee is dismissed
from that Service

Jonathan   The Friend appointed in the case of **Jonathan Slocum** requests
Slocum that matter continued, having been in a further labour therin, yet
have not accomplished it; it is continued under the same friends
care who are desired to accomplish their appointment and report
to next monthly meeting

Giles   Two of the friends appointed in the case of **Giles Slocum Ju^r**
Jonathan
Slocum Report that they have had another oppertunity with to discover
the State of his mind but reced no further Satisfaction; and
Friends haveing discharged themselves towards him, do here=
=by disown him from membership with us, and **Elijah Gifford**
is directed to to inform him thereof and report to next monthly meeting

William   The Friends appointed in the case of **William Russell** of **Bedford**
Russell
disown'd Report that they that they have taken a further oppertunity with
him and not receiving Satisfaction drafted a Testimony of
his denial – with which the women concuring, and **Caleb**
Greene is direct to cause the same to be read publickly in the usal
manner at **Bedford**, and inform said **William** thereof and
Report to next monthly meeting

Annis Gid=   The women inform they have concluded to deny **Annis Gidley**
=ley denid which this meeting concurs therewith

Elisabeth
Wing dis
=own'd

The Women produced a Testimony of the denial of **Elisabeth Wing** which being read, was concur'd with and Signd by the Clerk who is directed to cause the Same to be read publickly in the usual manner before next monthly meeing and report to the Same

Abraham
Wood

The Clerk reports that **Abraham Wood**s paper of acknowledg= =ment hath been read as directed

Abraham
Wood
Certificate

A Removal Certificate was Signed by the Clerk in behalf of **Abraham Wood,** directed to the monthly meeting of **Saratoga** Signifying his acknowledgment was accepted and outward affairs Settled to Satisfaction he having moved and Settled there

On Tittle
of Lands

The Committee to see the tittles of our meeting houses and Lands made Secure, &c Report, they gone into that matter and request it Defer'd, they are therefore continued in that Service and to make report next monthly meeting

School Com^{tee}

The [?] School Committee with the addition of those last month are continued in that Service till others are appoint in their Steed

Benjamin
Howland 3

The friends appointed to Treat with **Benjamin Howland 3** respecting his keeping a Tavern &c Report that they have treat= =ed with him accordingly; but he not giving them the desir'd Satisfaction; yet think it best it be continued and he fur= ther treated with; it is accordingly continued under the same friends care who are to report next monthly meeting

on meetings
in allen's
neck

The friends appointed to Visit Friends in **Allen's neck** and consider of their request for holding meetings there, Report that they have Visited Friends there accoring to appointment and think it best for them to have Some meetings ~~there~~ granted to be held there this meeting taking the matter under Consideration do with the concurence of the women grant said request so far as for them to hold meeting as follows; Two first days meeting in each month, that is One on the first day next before, and one on the first day after our Monthly meeting – and midweek meeting on Third days, in each week our mid week meetings are usually held for Worship; Only to be continued till the monthly meeting in the 4th month next; under the care of **Elijah Gifford Timothy Gifford** and **Jonathan Willbore** who are to report to this meeting at the Expiration of said Time

John How=
=land Son of
Benjamin

The Friends appointed to Treat with **John Howland** (son of **Benj^a**) produced a paper from him condemning his misconduct which is accepted Satisfaction provided he cause the same to be read in the usual publick manner, and return it with Report to the Same to next monthly meeting

On Building Bedford meet =ing House   The Committee appointed in the case of Building meeting House at **Bedford** report that they had attended to the matter, and concluded on the Size ~~of~~ to be 48 feet by 36 – and compected the Cost to about £400 and think proper that Friends come to a Subscription for that purpose, Therefore we appoint **Seth Russell**, **John Howland**, **Barnabas** ~~**Howland**~~ **Russell Edmond Maxfield** and **Caleb Russell** Collect by way of Subscriptions such Sums as Friends may give for the Building said house, which said Committee are also to see built accomedated and accomplished as soon as conveaniency & Circumstances will admit and report from time to time of their progress therein
This meeting is adjournd to the 20th of this instant after meeing of worship
Mett by adjournment
The Representatives being called are all present

Jonathan Tucker   The friends appointed in the case of **Jonathan Tucker**, Report that they have had another oppertunity with him which was not much to Satisfaction: yet desire the matter continued; it is accordingly defer'd till next monthly meeting they then to make report

William Sanford Ju^r   The Friends appointed in the case of **William Sanford Ju**^r Report that it not Settled to Satisfaction they are therefore continued to use further endeavours that it be accomplished and **Barnabas Russell** are added to them in that Service, and they to make report next monthly meeting

Collections   The South Preparitive meeting in their account inform they have
Collected and Sent to the Treasurer of this meeting   £0 – 12^s – 5^d
And the North Preparative meeting ~~~~~~~~~~~~   <u>0 – 15 – 8</u>
                               1 – 8 – 1

Ebenezer Mosher   The Overseers inform that **Samuel Mosher** (son of **Ebenezer**) walks so far from the good Order established among Friends as to attend a marriage accomplished out of the Order of Friend and appears far from that Simple plainness we profess, much neglecting the attendance of our Religious meetings for all which he hath been Labour'd with but did not give Satisfaction therein therefore we appoint **Benjamin Howland 2** and **Caleb Green** to treat further with him thereon and Report to next monthly meeting

Sent to Quarterly meeting   The Queries being answer'd in each Preparitive meeting, from which general Answers were prepared and read in this meeting – Also an Epistle prepared for the Quarterly meeting, all which are forwarded to said Quarterly meeting by our Representatives who are **Abiel Gifford**, **James Davis**, **Stephen Buffinton** and **Caleb Greene** and they to report next Monthly meeting

Abiel Gifford
bill for
Hay

Abiel Gifford gave in an account for Hay, and Carting, expended at our last Quarterly meeting to the amount of £3 – 6ˢ – 0 an account whereof was handed to the Quarterly meeting and the Treasurer is Ordered to pay **Abiel Gifford** when Supplied with money

Subscripti=
=ons

The Friends appointed to raise money by Subscriptions Report that they have collected in the South preparitive meeting £5 – 5ˢ – 11ᵈ

North Preparitive meeting 6 – 15 – 3

Total 12 – 1 – 2

To be con=
=tinued

Which they have paid to the Treasurer: and the Prepartives meetings are desired to continue their Subscription till the Sum of 16 pounds be rais,ᵈ

Hannah
Gifford

In concurence of women Friend a removal Certificate was Signed by the Clerk in behalf of **Hannah Gifford** wife of **Wᵐ Gifford** to yᵉ mᵒ meeting of **acoaxset**

Revise
minuets

Samuel Smith Hezekiah Smith Wᵐ Anthony Juʳ & Caleb Russell are ap= =pointed to Settle accounts with the Treasurer and revise the minutes of this meeting in order they may be recorded & report next monthly meeting

Order on
Treasurer

The Treasurer is directed to pay the above sᵈ Sum of £12 – 1ˢ – 2ᵈ and add 12/30 out of the Treasurry there, to the Representative to the Quarterly meeing & report to next monthly meeting: The said Representatives are to Send it to the Quarterly meeting Treasurer and Report of the Same to this meetin

---

1ˢᵗ month
1785

At a Monthly Meeting held in **Dartmouth** yᵉ 17ᵗʰ of 1ˢᵗ month 1785 The meeting being conveaned ,The Representatives named from the Preparitives meetings are from the **South Joseph Tucker Juʳ** and **Timothy Howland: North Joseph Austin** and **Thomas Mott**, who being called are all Present

Jonathan
Slocum

The Friends appointed in the case of **Jonathan Slocum** report that they have not accomplished the same, and desired it continued; it is accordingly continued under the Same friends care who are desired to accomplish the same and report next monthly meeting

Elijah Gifford informs that he hath not acquainted **Giles Slocum Juʳ** of his denial as directed, he is therefore continued in that Service and Report to next monthly meeting

Elizabeth
Wings

The Clerk informs that the Testimony of denial of **Elizabeth Wing** hath been read as directed which is as follows

Testimony
of denial

Whereas **Elisabeth Wing** widdow to **Samuel Wing** ~~deceased~~ Late of **Dartmouth** deceased; Having had her Education and lived in Profession with friends untill now of Late she hath so far departed from our Profession as to attend such meetings as are held out of the Unity of Friends and we having treated with her in love in order for her restoration and return, but She not adhearing to our advice and Counsel given, but still continues

and persist therein and to Justify her said Practice; Therefore
we do publickly disown her the said **Elizabeth Wing** from being
a member of our Religious Society, until by a Sincear return and
and Reformation she Shall be restored to the way of Truth

　　　Given forth and Signed in and on behalf of our monthly meeting of
men and women friends held in **Dartmouth** yᵉ 20ᵗʰ of yᵉ 12 months 1784

　　　　　　　　　　By **Wᵐ Anthony Juʳ** Clerk

　　　　　　　　　Mercy Slocum Clerk

On Tittle of meeting house and Lands　The Committee to inspect and see the Tittles of our meeting
Houses and Lands made Secure &c. Report, that they have made
Some Progress therein, but as it will take some time to compleat
it desires it continued; the Same friends are therefore continued
in that Service and to report when ready

Benjmin How land 3　Part of the Committee in the case of **Benjamin Howland 3ᵈ**
Report that they have had further opperuny with him, But
not receive much Satisfaction; Yet the matter is continued
under the same friends care who are to report next monthly meeting

John Howland son of Benjᵃ paper read　The Clerk Informs that **John Howland** (son of **Benjamin**
hath caused his paper condemning his misconduct to be read
as directed

Jonathan Tucker　The Friends appointed in the case of **Jonathan Tucker**
report that they have not accomplished that matter tho' they
have mad some Inspection therein, and desires it refer'd, it is
accordingly continued under the Same Friends care who are
directed to take a Solid oppertunity with said **Jonathan**
and Report to next monthly meeting

William Sanford　The Friends appointed in the case of **William Sanford Juʳ**
Report they have made further progress therein, but not being
accomplished it is continued under their care who are to report
to next monthly meeting

Return from Quarterly meeting　The Representatives to the Quarterly meeting Report that
they all attended except **Abiel Gifford**, who Sent a Satisfactory
reason of his non attendence, said Representatives produced an
an Epistle from the Quarterly meeting which was read in this
meeting to Satisfaction, and the further consideration of it is
refer'd to next monthly meeting, They also produced a Recept
from the Quarterly meetings Treasurer for £12 – 14ˢ – 0 the money
Sent from this meeting, and that the account of £3 – 6ˢ – 0 was accepted
by the Quarterly meeting expended for Hay

Caleb Green returnd　**Caleb Greene** returned a coppy of a minute of this meeting in the 8ᵗʰ mo
Last, he having returned from his Journey and Visit

Revising minuit not ac compli shed The Friends appointed to Revise this meeting minutes &c not having accomplished it they are continued in that Service and to Report to next monthly meeting

Collected at the South Preparetive meeting the sum of   0 – 7 – 3½

at the North the sum of – _ 0 – 14 – 4 _

Total –   1 – 1 – 1½

Samuel Mosher disown'd The Committee appointed to Treat with **Samuel Mosher** respect= =ing his disorder Report that they had a Solid oppertunity with him, but he gave them no Satisfaction nor no encouragement to Satisfy Friends: therefore with the concurence of the Women friends we hereby disown the said **Samuel Mosher** from being a member of of our Society – and **Caleb Greene** is desired to inform him

William Russell Testimony of denial **Caleb Greene** Informs that the Testimony of the denial of **William Russell** of **Bedford** hath been read, as directed, **William** being pre= sent at the reading thereof – Which is as follows

Whereas **William Russell** (son of **Jonathan Russell** of **Nantucket** having made profession with us the People called **Quakers**; But through in attention to the dictate of Truth, hath so far departed from its chaste Principles which we profess; as to fall into the gross Sin of Fornication, as appears by his own Confession; and Friends having labour'd with him on that account, and he not rendering the desired Satisfaction; – Therefore for the clearing Truth and Friends, from such reproach we are concerned to give forth this as a Public Testimony against him the said **William Russell** conduct hereby disowning, and disallowing him from being a member of our Religious Society, untill he may be favour'd with a Sight and a Sense way of Truth; which is Our Sincear desire

Given forth and Signed in and on behalf of a Monthly meeting of the People afore Said held in **Dartmouth** the 20th of 12th month 1784 By —   **Wm Anthony Jur** Clerk

---

2 Month 1785 At a Monthly meeting held in **Dartmouth** ye 21st of 2ond month 1785 The Representatives from the South Preparitive meeting are **Giles Slocum** and **Stephen Gifford**: From the North, **Seth Russell** and **Seth Huddleston**, who being called are all present

Giles Slocum Jur informed **Elijah Gifford** reports that he hath informed **Giles Slocum Jur** of his denial as directed

Eliakim Mosher's Certificate Received a Certificate from the Monthly meeting of **Pembrock** in behalf of **Eliakim Mosher** signifying that he hath Served out his apprintiship there, and behaved in a good degree Orderly; and clear of marriage Engagements ~ Which is accepted

Jonathan
Slocum
case

The Friends appointed in the case of **Jonathan Slocum** report that they have had Several oppertunities with him; and that he gave them some Satisfaction: yet for further proof of sencerity; the same Friends are continued for that Service; and take such further Steps therein as may appear best; and report to next Monthly meeting

Joseph Austin
returnd

Joseph Austin returned a Coppy of a minute of this meeting he have= =ing returned from his Journey to the **Nine Partners**

Rebecca Rotch
Certificate

A Removal Certificate in behalf of **Rebecca Rotch** Widdow of **Joseph Rotch**, directed to the Northern destrict of **Philidelphia** was read and Signed by the Clerk expressing that she is a member of our Society; and hath Settled her affairs to Satisfaction

Wm Sanford Ju^r
case

The Friends appointed in the case of **William Sanford Ju^r** desires that matter continued it is accoringly defer'd under their care till next Monthly meeting they then to report

Benj^a
Howland 3
case

The Commity in the case of **Benjamin Howland 3^d** report that they have had another Solid oppertunity with him; but not to Satisfaction; yet the same friends are continued to treat further with him thereon and make report to next monthly meeting

Reviseing
Minutes
Settling with
Treasurer

The Friends appointed to revise the minutes and settle accounts with the Treasurer Report that they have accomplished the last minutes and left them with **William Anthony** to Record, and have Settled accompts with the Treasurer, up to the 18th of the first month 1785 and find this Meeting hath given him order to pay out to the amount of £10 – 5 – 8½ more than he is supplied with money to pay as yet; consequently this meeting is in Debt that Sum

Unice Russell
disown'd

The Women inform that they have concluded to deny **Unice = Russel** wife of **William Russell** of **Bedford [New Bedford]** which this meeting concurs with

Saml Mosher
informed

Caleb Greene reports he hath informed **Samuel Mosher** of his denial as directed

Overseers deferd

The year being expir'd of the Service of the overseors, yet a new Choice is defer'd till next monthly meeting at the opening of the buisness therein

Abra Mosher
minute

Abraham Mosher informs he intends a Journey to **Nine partners** with a view of doing some buisness there, which this meeting concurs with, he being a member of this Meeting, and the Clerk is desired to give him a Coppy of this Minute

Abra^m Russell
Certificate
requested

Abraham Russell requestin Certificate from this meeting to the Monthly meeting of the Northern destricts of **Philidelphia** Expressive of his being a member and, clearness respecting marri

And Conversation, Therefore **Benjamin Taber** and **John Howland**
are appointed to take the necessary care therein, and if they find
no Obstacle, they to Report a Certificate to the adjounment of this meeting

Eben Chase request　　　**Ebenezer Chase** desireing a Removal Certificate to the Monthly
meeting of **Swanzey**, he being about to remove there, **Abiel Gifford**
and **William Gifford** are therefore appointed to take the necessary care
therein, and report to next Monthly meeting

Jonathan Tucker's Case　　　The Friends appointed in the case of **Jonathan Tucker**, report that
they have treated further with him on his misconduct, but that he did
not give them Satisfaction: and produced a draught of a Testimony
against him, which with the concurence of the Women Friends was
Signed by the Clerk who is desired to cause the same to be read in the
usal publick manner and report to next Monthly meeting; and the same friends are
desired to inform **Jonathan** thereof ~ Which Testimony is as followes

Jonathan Tucker's Testimony of denial　　　Whereas **Jonathan Tucker** having had his Birth and Education among
us the people called Quakers; but for want of more clostly adhearing
to the dictates of his own Conscience has been guilty of Useing profain
and unbecoming Language; as also frequently, and unnecessaryly resorts
at Taverns & too frequently pertakes of Spiritous Licquors; all which being
inconsistant with our Religious Profession: We having Laboured with
him for the above offences but do not find Satisfaction; therefore we
give this forth as a publick Testimony against his conduct hereby dis=
owning him the Said **Jonathan Tucker** from being a member of our ~~Society~~
Religious Society untill through unfeigned Repentance he shall return
to the ways of Truth which is our Sencear desire.

Given forth and Signed in and on behalf of our Monthly meeting of friends
held in **Dartmouth** yᵉ 21ˢᵗ of yᵉ 2ⁿᵈ month 1785

By **William Anthony Juʳ** Clerk

Money raisd for Stock　　　The North Preparitive meeting informs that they have raised the
Remainder of their propotion of money for Yearly meeting and Quarterly
meeting: and paid the Same to the Treasurer of this meeting

To sell wood　　　This meeting concludes to make Sale of some of the wood standing
on this meetings Land; at the discression of **Samuel Smith**, **Giles Slocum**
Thomas Hicks, and **Gideon Howland**, who are appointed for that Service
and they to make report of their proceedings therein from time to time

money collected　　　The Preparitive meetings in their account inform they have Collcted
and Sent up to the Treasurer viz from the South ~~~　0 – 15ˢ – 0
from the North ~~~　0 – 18 – 11

Adjournd　　　This meeting is adjournd to the 9ᵗʰ Instant after the meeting for Worship

Mett 3 month 9 mett by adjournment ~ The Representatives being called

Giles Slocum and **Stephen Gifford** present; **Seth Huddlestone** and **Seth Russell** not present, nor any reason sent of their absence

Abraham Russell's Certificate One of the Friends appointed to take the necessary care for **Abraham Russell**s request for a Certificate report that they have made the necessary enquiry therein and find no Sufficient obstacle to granting his request and therefore produced a Certificate, which after some alteration was Signed by the Clerk

Report concerning Wood sold Part of the Committee to make Sale of wood report that it is their oppinion that a considerable Quantity may yet be disposed of, tho they have Sold one hundred Cords to **Josiah Wood** at four Shillings & Six pence per Cord Handing

And that if Friends would assist in getting a Quantity to the Land=
=ing it may be Sold to more advantage, therefore said Committee are desired to draught & Promote Subscriptions for Friends to cut and Cart as much as they Shall be free to; in order to defray the charge of this meeting and bring said Subscriptions to next monthly meeting

3ᵈ mᵒof 1785 At a Monthly meeting held in **Dartmouth** 21ˢᵗ of 3ᵈ mᵒ 1785
The Representatives from the Preparative Meetings are from
the South ~ **Philip Trafford** & **Elijah Gifford**
        North ~ **Benjᵃ Butter** & **Jonathan Hart**
who being called are all present

choice of overseers The choice of overseers being refer'd from last Mᵒ meet-
ing to this: **Benjamin Taber Joseph Austin Joseph Tucker junʳ Elijah Gifford William Gifford Jonathan Hart**
Are appointed for that service for the year ensuing or till others may be appointed in their stead

Jonᵃ Slocum's case defer'd The friends appointed in the case of **Jonathan Slocum** report; that they have not all had oppertunity so as to accomplish that matter & desire it continued, it is accordingly deferd under their care & they to make report ~~accord~~ to next monthly meeting.

Eben. Chace's certificᵉ defer'd The committee appointed in the case of **Ebenezer Chase** report that they have not accomplished sᵈ business therefore they are continued in Sᵈ service & to report the next Monthly meeting

Jonᵃ Tucker's Denial read The Clerk informs that the Testimony of the Denial of **Jonathan Tucker** hath been read as directed & the committee report that **Jonathan** hath been inform'd thereof.

Benj. Howland's case defer'd The comittee in the case of **Benjamin Howland** 3ᵈ report that he hath given them so much encourage-
ment that they desire the matter continued, which

is accordingly defer'd under the same Friends
care who are to report to next Monthly meeting

Denial
W. Russell's
Wife
In concurrence with the Women's meeting, a Testimo-
ny of the denial of **Eunice Russell**, wife of **William
Russell** of **Bedford** , was sign'd by our Clerk

Ann Jessop
visit
Our Friend **Ann Jessop** attended this Meeting
with her Certificates from **New Garden** Monthly
meeting and Quarterly meeting of the 8th month last
which were read in this Meeting to satisfaction &
her visit and labours of Love were also to satisfaction[43]

S. Huddlest
on's
excuse
Seth Huddleston gave the reasons of his nonattend-
ance of the Adjournment of last Monthly meeting
of the 8th month last, which were satisfactory.

The South Prepar.e meeting in their account inform they have collected and handed to the Treasurer
of this Meeting   16 – 2
The North Preparative Meeting   13 – 5
Total   1 – 9 – 7

Queries
answer'd
The Queries were read with the Answers from
the Preparative Meetings, and **Samuel Smith** &
Jonathan Wilbur, are appointed to compile sd answers
into general ones and bring to the Adjournment of this
Meeting, with an account to this Meeting, with an
Account to the Quarterly meeting –

E Mosher's
Certificate
sign'd
A Removal Certificate was sign'd by the Clerk
in behalf of **Eliakim Mosher,** to the Monthly meeting of **Nine partners** expressing his right of membership and membership and clearness respecting marriage.

J & Rebecca
Russell's
children rec.d
With the Concurrence of the Women, this
Meeting admits into Friend's care, **Jethro**
and **Rebecca Russell**'s Children by their re-
quest of their Parents, the Children's names are
Martha, **Mary** and **Howland**.

Adjourn'd
This Meeting is adjourn'd to the 2d of
next month at the 11th hour

Met
4th month 2d Met by adjourment
The Overseers being called are all present

43. Ann (Matthews) Floyd Jessop (1738–1822) was a minister from New Garden Monthly Meeting
in Guilford County, North Carolina. See Paula Stahls Jordan and Kathy Warden Manning, *Women of
Guilford County, North Carolina: A Study of Women's Contributions, 1740–1979* (Greensboro: Greensboro
Printing Company, 1979), 23–24.

Caleb Greene app.ᵈ Clerk

The Year of the service of the Clerk being expir'd and **William Anthony junʳ** having serv'd
this Meeting as Clerk for some years to satisfaction: therefore **Caleb Greene** is appointed Clerk
for the year ensuing, or 'till another be appointed
in his place.

Wᵐ Sandford junʳ Case con-tinu'd

The Friends appointed in the Case of **William Sandford junʳ** report, that it is not accomplish'd
and desire it continu'd, it is accordingly defer'd under the same Friends care, 'till next Monthly meeting, they then to report.

A Propos.ˡ to Q.ˡʸ meeting respecting answerᵍ Queries

A Proposal from this Meeting in concurrence with the Women, was forwarded to the
Quarterly meeting: that it be recommended to
the Yearly meeting, whether the answering the
Queries once a year only, would not be more useful, than every Quarter, or at least, that some
of the Principal ones only be answer'd at each Quarter
One of the Friends appointed to compile the
Answers to the Queries and prepare an Account
to the Quarterly meeting reports, that he with

Represᵗⁱᵛˢ to Qʸ meetᵍ

the other Friend, took the necessary care therein and
produc'd said Answers, which were read in this
Meeting together with the Account or Epistle to
the Quarterly meeting, after adding what appear'd
to be necessary, were sign'd by the Clerk and forwarded by the Representatives appointed to attend
the Quarterly meeting who are **James Davis**,
Caleb Greene & **Elijah Gifford**, who are to make report to next Monthly meeting.

An addi tional mi nute point ing out the service of the overseers

As the service of the Overseers is not
pointed out to them, in any manner particular
in the Minute of their appointment, the following is concluded to be a necessary addition for
that purpose, viz, They are desired to meet together frequently by themselves, in as retired a manner as may be, and endeavour to center down to their
own Gifts and Measures in order to get under a due
Sense of the Weight of the Work assigned them; and
under this Engagement of mind to keep up a careful

Watch and Inspection over themselves and the several
Members of this Meeting to see that the Cause
and Testimony of Truth be kept up and maintain-
ed and where any shall appear faulty or defective
or walk disorderly, tenderly to treat and Labour with
them, in order to discover to them the Evil of their
ways; but if such cannot be reclaimed and
they appear manifestly Guilty of the Matter in
charge, that then Information in Writing be
brought to the Meeting of the State of the
Fact and Circumstances attending it and they
are particularly desired to watch and guard
against, and discourage, that backbiting,
slandering spirit so prevalent among us, making report to this Meeting of the progress
of their Service from Time to Time.

    The Committee to sell Wood, produc'd a

Subscrip^n for cutting & carting Wood — Draught of Subscriptions for Cutting and
Carting which was read and sign'd by the
Clerk, and they are to proceed therein when it
may appear best.

    The Overseers inform that **Richd Lapham**
son of **Nicholas**, hath far departed from that
simple Plainness that we profess in several

R Lapham disorder — respects, particularly in tying his hair with
a Riband [ribbon], for which he hath been labour'd
with by said Overseers but he not giving them
satisfaction – therefore **Philip Trafford** and
William Anthony jun^r are appointed to take
a solid opportunity and treat with him
further thereon, and report to next Monthly meeting

5th month 1785 — At a Monthly meeting held in **Dartm^t**
the 16th of the 5 month 1785
The Representatives from the South Prepar.^{e}
Meeting are **Benjamin Howland 2^d** and **George
Smith**, from the North, **Prince Potter** and
Seth Russell, who being called are all present.

    The Committee in the Case of **Jonathan**

Jon^a Slo cum's case dis miss'd — **Slocum**, report, that they have made further progress therein; yet the obstacles for the accomplish
ment thereof are not remov'd to satisfaction, &

that it is their judgment it should be dismiss'd
from this Meeting and Friends taking the same
into Consideration do dismiss the same accordingly
and the same Friends are desir'd to inform him
of the reasons thereof.

A Removal Certificate was sign'd by the Clerk
Certificate sign'd for Eben Chace directed to the Monthly meeting of **Swansey** in
behalf of **Ebenezer Chace**, signifying he is a mem-
ber and settled his outward affairs to satisfaction

The Friends appointed to treat with **Rich^d
Lapham** on his Misconduct, report that they
R.Lapham have not both had opportunity with him, it is
therefore defer'd under their Care, with **Caleb Greene**
'till next Monthly meeting, they then to make report.

In Concurrence with the Women, a Testimony of
Testim Denial of Abig. Cornel signd the Denial of **Abigail Cornel [Cornell]** wife of **Elihu Cornel**
was read and sign'd by the Clerk, and **Wm Anthony Ju^r**
is appointed to read the same, in the usual
public manner and report to next monthly meeting.

The Friends appointed in the Case of **W^m
Wm Sandford case defer'd Sandford jun^r** report that they have attended thereto, but not accomplish'd it to satisfaction; it is
therefore continued under the same Friends
Care, who are to report to next M^o meeting.

The Committee in the Case of **Benj^a Howland
3^d** report, that some further opportunity with him
B. Howland 3^d case defer'd and that he signified he should continue in his
Practice, yet at the Desire of some Friends, the
matter is continu'd under the same friends care, as
heretofore, who are desir'd to labour further with him
and report to next M^o meeting.

The Friends appointed to enquire into **James
Report James Allen's clearness respecting Marriage Allen**'s clearness and conversation respecting Marriage, report, that they find nothing sufficient
to hinder such a Procedure

The Friends appointed to take the necessa-
S. Buffinton's Certific^e defer'd ry Care for a removal Certificate for **Stephen
Buffinton** and Family, report, that they have
not yet accomplish'd it, they are therefore continued
to accomplish it and report to next M^o meeting

James Allen and **Sarah Howland jun^r** appear'd

for their answer, which is, that we find nothing
sufficient to prevent their proceeding to take each
other in Marriage, at some convenient time be-
between this and next monthly meeting, advising
with the Friends this Meeting appoints to see said
Marriage orderly solemniz'd, who are **Wm Anthony J^r**
and **Elijah Gifford**, who are to report to next M^o
meeting.

The Friends appointed to take a solid opportunity with **Obadiah Beard**, report, that they had

O. Beard readmitted such an opportunity, in which they found a good
Degree of satisfaction: - he is therefore, with the concurrence of the Women, readmitted into Membership with
us, and **Wm Anthony Junr** is appointed to inform
him thereof.

The Treasurer having remov'd some distance, **Ca-**

C. Barker Treasurer **leb Barker** is appointed for that service, for the year
ensuing, or 'till some other may be appointed in his

Com^tee to settle acco^t with former Treas^r Stead, and **Wm Anthony Junr** and **Samuel Smith**
are appointed to settle Accounts with the former Trea-
surer and report to next M^o meeting.

The Overseers inform that **Job Deval** son of
John, thro' unwatchfulness and giving way to a

Compl^t ag^st Job Deval vain and Wanton mind, getting into loose and
unprofitable Company, by which he hath so far depart-
ed from our chaste Principles, as to fall into or come
under the scandalous Report of being guilty of the
reproachful Sin of Fornication, by the Declara-
tion of **Sarah Russell** daughter of **Elisha**, he the
said **Job** having been labour'd with thereon, but he
denying said Crime, therefore **Joseph Gifford**, **Samuel
Smith** & **Caleb Russell** are appointed to enquire into the State of the Case and labour there
in as way may open and Report to next M^o Meeting.

Received a removal Certificate from
the Monthly meeting of **Acoaxet** in behalf of
Zephaniah Edy his Wife **Anna** and their
Children Namely **John**, **Job**, **Mary** & **Sarah**
signifying they are Members, and that their
outward affairs are settled to pretty good satis-

faction which is accepted, they have removed and
settled among us.

The Overseers inform that it appears to

Philip Allen them that **Philip Allen** and **Joseph Hart**, are
&
Jos. Hart guilty of the unwarrantable practice of gaming
at Cards, for which they labour'd with them, but
they condemning it not – therefore **Wᵐ Anthony**
Junʳ Wᵐ Gifford & **John Deval** are appointed
to treat further with them thereon, and report
to next Mᵒ meeting

Addition **James Davis Joseph Austin & Caleb**
to Trustees **Greene** are appointed as an Addition to the
for holding
Titles to Trustees for receiving & holding our Tittles to
Meeting house our Meeting house Lands.

Collection The Sᵒ Preparᵃ Meeting in their account
they have Collected & paid to the former Treasʳ   10
The North d̲ᵒ collected and handed to
the Present Treasrʳ   1 –   – 3
Total   £1 – 10 – 3

6 mᵒ At a Monthly meeting held in **Dartmouth**
1785 the 20ᵗʰ of the 6ᵗʰ month 1785
The Representatives from the South Preparᵃ meeting are **Thoˢ**
Russell and **Joseph Wilbur** from the North, **Bar-**
nabas Russell and **Seth Huddlestone** all present.

Received a removal Certificate from the month

Wᵐ Tripp ly Meeting of **Acoaxet**, recommending **Wᵐ Tripp**
Certificate and Wife **Elizabeth** to our Care, with their Chil-
from 'Coaxet dren, namely **Othniel**, **Maria**, **Lydia** & **Elizabeth**,
they having removed within the Compass of this Meet-
ing to Live, which is accepted.

The Friends appointed to treat further with
Richᵈ Lapham, report that he going to Sea

R. Lapham depriv'd them of an Opportunity of treating with
case defer'd him thereon, it is therefore defer'd under the same
Friends Care 'till next mᵒ Meeting, they then to report.

Testⁱ **Wᵐ Anthony Junʳ** reports that he hath
Ab. Cornel's read the Testimony of Denial of **Abigˡ Cornel [Cornell]**
Denial
read Wife of **Elihu Cornel** according to the Direction
of last Mᵒ Meeting.

The Friends appointed in the Case of **W^m**

Conclusion of Wm Sand-ford jun^r Case **Sandford Junr** report that the Matter between him and **Benjamin Allen** is settled by Arbitration this Meeting therefore concludes to accept of his Paper condemning his Misconduct, for Satisfaction

B Howlands case contin.^d Part of the Committee in the Case of **Benj Howland 3^d**, report, they have had with other friends a solid Opportunity with him, and that he desir'd it may be continu'd, it is accordingly defer'd under the same Friends care 'till next M^o meeting – they then to make report

W. Anthony j^r Report **Willm Anthony jun^r** reported that he inform'd **Obadiah Beard** of his readmittance into Membership as desir'd last M^o meeting

Report of Committee J Allen's Mar-riage One of the Friends appointed in the oversight of the Marriage of **James Allen** and **Sarah Howland**, reports that he attended said Marriage and according to his sense, it was solemnized in a degree orderly – and that **Elijah Gifford**, the other Friend, could not attend by reason of sickness.

Hart & Allen The Committee in the Case of **Joseph Hart** and **Philip Allen**, desire that matter continu'd 'till next M^o meeting; which is according defer'd under their Care, they then to report

Nanny Gifford's proposal to visit Q^y Meeting Sandwich **Nanny Gifford** informs that she has it on her Mind to attend the Quarterly meeting of **Sandwich**, next to be held at **Nantucket** desiring Friends Concurrence therewith, and this Meeting taking it under Consideration, do approve thereof, she being a Member in Unity and her Publick Testimony approv'd among us, and the Clerk is desir'd to furnish her with a Copy of this Minute.

T. Akin gives in paper **Thomas Akin** gave in a Paper condemning misconduct in going into Company, where were music and Dancing and there drinking so as to unfi[?] him for business: – whereupon we appoint our friends **David Shepherd**, **Caleb Greene** and **Jno Howland**, to take a solid Opportunity with him, and make

inspection, in order to discover his Sincerity, and report to next M⁰ meeting

B. Allen (son of Philip) gives in Paper

Benjᵃ Allen (Son of **Philip** deceas'd) gave
in a Paper condemning his falling into the reproachful Sin of Fornication and Marrying out of the
Unity of Friends, **Thomas Russell** & **Thomas Hicks** are
appointed to take a solid Opportunity with said **Benjᵃ** in
order to discover his Sincerity & report to next M⁰ meeting

Queries answerd

The Queries were read with the Answers
from each Preparᵉ Meeting, and **James Davis**, **Wᵐ
Anthony junʳ**, & **Samuel Smith**, are appointed to
compile said Answers from this Meeting, prepare
an Account to the Quarterly meeting, and bring to
the Adjournment of this Meeting

The South Preparᵃ in their Acct
inform, that they have collected & sent
to the Treasurer.

	11	10 ½
North Preparᵃ Meeting	13	6
£1	4	[?]

Adjᵈ

This Meeting adjourns to the 1ˢᵗ Day of [?]
month at the close of the meeting of Worship.

Met

7ᵗʰ month 1ˢᵗ Met according to Adjournment.
The Representatives being called are all present
except **Seth Huddlestone**, who sent a satisfactory reason in Writing of his Absence.

S. Buffintun's Certificate refer'd

The friends appointed in the Case of
Stephen Buffintun's Certificate, report, that the
Matter is not fully accomplished, they are therefore continued in said service & to report to next
monthly meeting.

Comtᵉᵉ report settling with former Treasurer

One of the Comtᵉᵉ to settle accounts with
the former Treasurer, made report in writing;
"hath he settled sᵈ acctˢ to the 23ᵈ of 6ᵗʰ month last,
and that it appears, that the former Accounts
allowed by this Meeting, amount to ʟ3-10ˢ-9½ᵈ
more, than he was supplied with Mony to pay",
and the present Treasurer is desir'd to pay
the same, as soon as supplied with sufficiency of money.

One of the Committee appointed in the Case of

Job Deval informs, that they have not all had

Job Deval's case defer'd opportunity with him, tho' they have made some progress therein and therefore desire the Matter defer'd: it is accordingly continued under the same friends care 'till next Monthly meeting, they then to report.

Advice from Meet⁶ for Sufferings Received Advice from the Meeting for Sufferings dated the 8ᵗʰ of the 6ᵗʰ month last, wherein they desire, that one of the first Class of Poor, ([?] any in the Monthly meeting) may be sent to the yearly meetings School: this Meeting taking it into consideration, do commit the care and oversight thereof to the Overseers of the Poor and School Committee, who are to Report next Mᵒ meeting

F. Rotch remov'd without Certificate It appearing to this Meeting, that **Francis Rotch** remov'd from this Meeting without Certificate, and resides or is often within the Compass of **Providence** Mᵒ meeting, **Caleb Greene** & **Joseph Austin**, are therefore appointed, to write to said Meeting; what may appear to them necessary and report to next Monthly meeting.

Represen tatives Accoᵗ to the Quarterly Meeting The Friends appointed to compile the Answers to the Queries, have presented them, with an Account to the Quarterly meeting, which after being read are appeared and signed by the Clerk and sent forward to the Quarterly meeting by our Representatives, who are our friends **Thomas Hicks**, **Jonathan Hart**, & **Benjᵃ Chace**, and they to make report to next Monthly meeting.

Infor- mation from Nantucket mᵒ meeting respecting Shubˡ Bunker Jʳ This Meeting is informed by writing from **Nantucket** Mᵒ meeting that **Shubael Bunker Junior** hath resided for sometime, within the Compass of this Meeting, and hath had no Certificate, desiring us to take some care in that respect, and if it appears best, that he have one, that we acquaint them thereof, we thereof appoint **Caleb Russell** and **Barnabas Russell** to take the necessary care therein and make report to next Monthly meeting.

WOMEN'S MEETING, 1699–1782

1

Friends Fellowship must be in ye Spirit and all
Friends must know one another in the Spirit & Power of God.

1 In all ye Meetings of ye County two or three being gathered from ye to go to ye
Generall Meetings for to give notice one to another if there be any that walk
not in the Truth, & have been convinced, & gone from the Truth, & so dishonour-
ed God; ye some may be ordered from the Meetings to go & exhort such &
bring in to ye next Generall Meetings what they say.

2 If any yt Profess ye Truth follow pleasures, drunkenness, gamings, or is not
faithfull in their dealings, nor honest nor just but runs into debt, & so brings
a scandall upon the Truth; Friends may give notice to the Generall Meeting
if there be any such, & some may be ordered to go & exhort ym & bring in their
Answer next Generall Meeting.

3 And if any goes disorderly to get her in Marriage, contrary to ye Practise
of the Holy men of God, & Assemblies of the righteous in all ages; Who declared
it in ye Assemblies of the righteous wn they took one another (all things being
clear)& they booth being free from any other; & wn they do go together, & take one
another, let there not less than a douzen Friends & Relations present, according
to yr former order, having first acquainted the Mens Meeting, & they having
clearness & unity wth ym & it may be Recorded in a book, according to the Word
& Commandment of ye Lord, & if any walk contrary to ye order of Truth herein,
let some be ordered to speak to ym, & give notice thereof to ye next Generall Meeting.

4 And all ye be Widdows wch have Children, & do Intend to marry; Let Query be
made what she hath done for her Children: if there be no Will made, let such
part of her late Husbands Estate be set out for ye Children as is equall, and
according to Truth: & what they can do more afterwards let ym do also. & where
there is a will made let those Legacies, & Portions be improv'd, & secured before
Marriage for the Children of ye deceased, wth what more they can do for them;
& when these things are done let them be Recorded in a Book at ye next Generall
Meeting.

5 And also all Wisdoms in yo severall Meetings, let ym be taken notice of, & informed, & encouraged in their outward business, that there may be no hindrance
in their Inward growth; & so carefully looked after, that they may be nourished,
& cherished, & so preserved in ye Truth that love may be encreased. & if they
have many Children to put out Apprentices, or Servants that may be a
burden to ym to bring up, let Friends take care to ease ym by putting ym forth as
may be meet; let all these things be looked into by every Meeting; & notice there
of given to the next Generall Meeting. & ye some Ordered to see yt all things
are done according to Truth & Righteousness.

6 And such as Marry by the Priests of Baal who are the rough hands of Esau
& fists of Wickedness, & bloody hands; Who have had their hands in the blood
of our Brethren, & who is the cause of all this Banishment of our Brethren,
& have spoiled so many of our Goods, casting into Prison, & keeps many
hundreds at this day, all such as go to ym for wives, or Husbands must come to
Judgment, & Condemnation of ye Spirit wch led them to Baal, & ye Baals
Priests also, or else Friends that keep their Habitations must write against their
& Baal both: for from Genesis to the Revelations you do never read of any Priest
Marryed Peoble; But it is Gods Ordinance, & whom God joyns together let no m

[1]Friends Fellowship must be in yᵉ Spirit and all
Friends must know one another in the Spirit & Power of God.

1 In all yᵉ Meetings of yᵉ County two or three being gathered from yᵐ to go to yᵉ
Generall Meetings for to give notice one to another if there be any that walk
not in the Truth, & have been convinced, & gone from the Truth, & so dishonour
=ed God: yᵗ some may be ordered from the Meetings to go & exhort such &
bring in to yᵉ next Generall Meetings what they Say.

2 If any yᵗ Profess yᵉ Truth follow pleasures, drunkenness, gamings, or is not
faithfull in their dealings, nor honest nor just but runs into debt, & so brings
a scandall upon the Truth, Friends may give notice to the Generall Meeting
if there be any Such; & Some may be ordered to go & exhort yᵐ & bring in their
Answer next Generall Meeting.

3 And if any goes disorderly to get her in Marriage, contrary to yᵉ Pract[ices]
of the Holy men of God, & Assemblies of the righteous in all ages; Who declares
it in yᵉ Assemblies of the righteous w[he]ⁿ· they took one another (all things being
clear) & they booth being free from any other; & wⁿ they do go together, & take one
another, let there not less than a douzen Friends & Relations present, according
to yoʳ former order, having first acquainted the Mens Meeting & they having
clearness & unity wᵗʰ yᵐ & it may be Recorded in a book; according to the Word
& Commandment of yᵉ Lord, & If any walk contrary to yᵉ order of Truth herein,
let some be ordered to speak to yᵐ & give notice thereof to yᵉ next Generall Meeting.

4 And all yᵗ be Widdows wᶜʰ have Children, & do Intend to marry; Let Query be
made what she hath done for her Children: If there be no Will made, let such
part of her late Husbands Estate be set out for yᵉ Children as is equall, and
according to Truth: & what they can do more afterwards let yᵐ do also & where
there is a will made Let those Legacies, & Portions be improv'd, & secured before
Marriage for the Children of yᵉ deceased wᵗʰ what more they can do for them
& when these things are done let them be Recorded in a Book at yᵉ nex Generall
Meeting.

5 And also all Widdows in yoʳ severall Meetings, let yᵐ be taken notice of & infor[m]
=ed & encouraged in their outward business, that there may be no hindrance
in their Inward growth; & so carefully looked after that there may be nourished
& cherished & so preserved in yᵉ Truth that love may be encreased; & If they
have many Children to put out Apprentices, or Servants that may be a
burden to yᵐ to bring up, let Friends take care to ease yᵐ by putting yᵐ forth as
may be meet: let all these things be looked into by every Meeting; & notice there
of given to the next Generall Meeting. & yⁿ [then] some ordered to see yᵗ all things
are done according to Truth & Righteousness.

1. The author and source for this section are not included in the minute book, but it is a combination
of two epistles by George Fox, composed in 1668 and 1669. See *A Collection of Many Select and Christian
Epistles, Letters and Testimonies, Written on Sundry Occasions, by That Ancient, Eminent, Faithful Friend
and Minister of Jesus Christ, George Fox* (London: T. Sowle, 1698), 274-300.

6 And such as Marry by the Priests of Baal who are the rough hands of Esau,
   & fists of Wickedness, & bloody hands; Who have had their hands in the blows
   of our Brethren, & who is the cause of all this Banishment of our Brethren,
   & have spoiled so many of our Goods; casting into Prison, & keeps many
   hundreds at this day; all such as go $_\wedge$unto y^m for wives or Husbands must come to
   Judgment, & Condemnation of y^t Spirit wch leds them to Baal, & of Baals
   Priests also: Or else Friends that keep their Habitations must write against these
   & Baal both; for from Genesis to the Revelations you do never read of any Priest
   marryed People: But it is God's Ordinance, & whom God joyns together let no m[an?]
   put asunder, & they took one another in the Assemblies of the Righteous w^n
   all things were clear: Therefore let all these things be enquired into, & broug[ht]
   to the Generall Meeting; & from thence some ordered to go to them; & to return
   what they say to the next Meeting: & all these before they, or any of them be left
   as Heathens, or written against, let y^m be three or four times gone to, that they
   may have Gospel Order so y^t if it be possible they may come to y^t which at
   first did Convince y^m to condemn their unrighteous doings: so y^t they might
   not leave a hoof in Egypt.

7 And also all such as wear their hats w^n Friends Pray; & are gotten into the old
   rotten Principles of the Ranters; who set up the wearing thereof in opposition
   to the Power of God, & y^m y^t uphold it is for Condemnation by it: & ye Power
   of God is gone over it; & y^m who ranted from the Truth, & have stopt many
   who were coming into it, y^t ye very world can say you are in confusion, &
   divided & gone from your first Principle; who said you were of one Heart,
   & one mind, & one Soul, And therefore y^t Spirit must be cut off by the Sword
   of the Spirit of y^e Lord, y^t they may come to y^t wch at first did Convince y^m, &
   notice must be given to y^e Generall Meeting of all these things; & from thence
   some must be ordered to exhort y^m y^t be in such things to come to y^e first Prin=
   ciple y^e did at first Convince y^m, y^t they may come out of such things; &
   Friends must stand in y^e Noble Seed of God to Judge y^e World, & all y^e fallen
   Angels.

8 And in all Your Meetings let notice be given to y^e Generall Meeting of all
   y^e Poor: And w^n you have heard y^t there is many more Poor belonging to one
   Meeting y^n [than] to another; & y^t Meeting is thereby burdened, & Oppressed let the rest
   of the Meetings help & Assist y^m, so y^t they may ease one another, & help to
   bear one anothers burdens, & so fulfill the Law of Christ, & so see y^t there be
   nothing lacking according to the Apostles Words (mark nothing lacking)
   y^n all is well: for ye Jew Outward tho; they were as the stars of Heaven, & as
   the Sand of the sea, Yet there was not to be a beggar among y^m according to ye Law
   of God; & Amongst the Christians in ye first Age there was a Mans Meeting set up
   at Jerusalem to see y^t nothing was lacking; wch was ye Gospel Order according to
   the Law of Jesus; & this continued so long as they lived in ye Spirit, Life, & Power
   of God, But when ye Apostacy came in, & ye true Church fled into ye Wilderness,
   who was to Continue there 1260 dayes, & the Witnesses Prophesyed in Sackcloth 1260

dayes; & yᵉ Beast was Worshipped just so long 1260 dayes; & yⁿ [then] all things went
out of order, & every thing was wanting in the time they worshipped yᵉ Dragon
& yᵉ Beast & wᵗʰ yᵐ yᵉ false Prophet, Who shall be cast into the lake of fire
And the true Church came up out of yᵉ Wilderness; & yᵉ Manchild wᶜʰ was ~
caught up into Heaven came down again to Rule the Nations wᵗʰ a Rod of
Iron; & yᵉ Marriage of yᵉ Lamb is come; & the Lamb & yᵉ [sᵗˢ?]ᵗˢ Shall have yᵉ
Victory; & the Everlasting Gospel shall be Preached again as was among yᵉ
Apostles, & yᵉ Gospel Order shall be set up as was among yᵐ; & a Mans
Meeting as was at the first Conversion to see yᵗ nothing be lacking in yᵉ
Church, yⁿ all is well, so there is not to be a beggar now among yᵉ Christians
according to yᵉ Law of Jesus as there was not to be any among the Jews
according to the Law of God.

9 And also all the men yᵗ hunt after Women, from Woman to Woman, & also
Women whose Affections run sometimes after one man, & sometimes after another,
& so hold one another in Affection, & so draw out the affections one of another, &
after a while leave one another, & go to others, & do yᵉ same thing; & this doing
makes more like Sodom yⁿ Saints, & is not of Gods ₐ[making?] or joyning where they are not
to be parted, for marriage is Gods ordinance, & Gods command, one to another,
& in yᵗ they feel the Power of the Lord.

10 And notice to be taken of all evill Speakers, Backbiters, Slanderers, & foolish
talkers, & Idle Jesters, for these things corrupt good manners, & is not according
to yᵉ Saints, & Holy ones; whose words are season'd with salt, Ministring
Grace to yᵉ Hearers.

11 And all Such who are Tale-Carriers, & Railers, whose work is to Some Dissention,
are to be reproved, & admonished: for such do not bring People into the unity
of yᵉ Spirit, but by such doings they lose their own Contion [sic]. ~ ~ ~

12 And such as go up & down to cheat, by their borrowing & getting money of
Friends in by places, & have Cheated severall; all such are to be stopt & Judged

13 And If there happen any difference between Friend & Friend of any matters,
If it Cannot before the Generall Meeting Let half a dozen Friends from yᵉ Gene=
=rall Meeting be ordered to put a speedy end thereto, yᵗ Justice may Speedily
be done, yᵗ no difference may rest or remaine among any. And let all your
Generall Meetings be once ₐⁱⁿ everie quarter of a Year, & to be appointed at such
places as may be most Convenient for the most of Friends to Meet in: that yᵉ
house may be cleansed of all that is contrary to purity, virtue, light, life &
Spirit, so yᵗ Friends may not be one anothers sorrow; & troubles; but one
anothers Joy, & Crown in the Lord.

14 And all Friends, See that yᵒʳ Children be trained up in the fear of yᵉ Lord,
In Soberness, & Holiness, Righteousness, & Temperance, & meekness, & Gentleness,
& loveliness, & modesty in their Apparrel & Carriages, & so to exhort your
Children, & Families in yᵉ truth, yᵗ yᵉ Lord may be Glorified in yᵒʳ Familics
& teach your Children wⁿ they are young, & they will Remember it wⁿ they

are old, according to Solomon, so y^t your Children May be a blessing to
you & not a Curse. ~

15 And y^t Friends to buy Convenient burying Places, as Abraham did who
bought a place to bury his dead, & would not bury among the Egyptians, and
Canaanites, & Jacob was brought out of Egypt & Joseph; & they were buryed
in their Grandfathers, & Great Grandfathers burying place; & so Friends
buy Burying Places for y^{or} Meetings; & to keep out of y^e Spirit of y^e Sodomites
& Egyptians & Canaanites, wch corrupt y^e Earth; & let them be decently &
well fenced, y^t you Condemn y^e World of all things.

16 And also y^t Friends buy a Convenient Book for y^e Registring of Births, Marri=
=ages, & Burials, as y^e Holy Men of God of Old did, as you may read, y^t every
one may be ready to give a Testimony, & Certificate If need Require, and any
be called thereunto. ~

17 And also all y^t all y^e Sufferings of Friends of all kind of Sufferings in all y^e
County be gathered up & put together, & Sent to the Generall Meeting, & so sent
to London, y^t nothing of y^e Memorial of y^e blood, & Cruel Sufferings of y^e Bre=
=thren be lost; wch shall stand as a Testimony against the Murdering Spirit of
this World, & be to y^e Praise of the Everlasting Power of the Lord in the
Ages to come, who supported & upheld y^m in such hardships, & Cruelties, who is
God over all blessed for evermore amen. ~

18 And Enquiry to be made concerning all such as do pay Tythes, wch makes void the
Testimony & Sufferings of all our Brethren who have Suffered many of y^m to
death; by which many Widdows & Fatherless have been made; & wch is contrary
to ye Doctrine of ye Apostles, & ye Doctrine of ye Martyrs; & likewise contrary to y^e
Doctrine of the Righteous in this present Age; All such are to be enquired into.
& exhorted. let Query be made concerning all Prisoners that are poor, y^t
they may be relieved, & so encouraged in their sufferings: & also y^t care be
taken for their wives, & Families, that they do not suffer for want of
supply of Outward things: & let enquiry be made how many Prisoners there
are in all your severall Counties; that diligent enquiry be made into all these
things at every Monthly Meeting, & at every Quarterly Meeting; & to take
diligent care accordingly.

Dear Friends be diligent, & let it be your business to serve ye Lord & his
Truth, & to keep up your Mens Meetings Monthly two or three out of every
Meeting, to Meet together in Some co[n]venient place in ye middle of y^{or} County
for to see how all your Meetings is, y^t there be nothing lacking among y^m:
So y^t all may be kept as a Family, & nothing be lacking. y^n all is well, For at
the first Conversion of the Christians at Jerusalem, there was a Mans Meeting
chosen out of ye People. Men y^t were Faithfull, fearing God, & hating Covetouness
& full of ye Holy Ghost; & these men were to see y^t ye Widdows, the Fatherless,
the Poor, & any that was in necessity did not want; & If nothing was
wanting y^n all was well, as you may read in the Acts. And so the Chu[r]ch were

Ruled by Cou[n]sell six hundred years after Christ till ye Pope got up, & ye false
Church, & since the true order of ye true Church hath been lost Whilst the true
Church hath been in ye Wilderness, & the false Church hath gotten up, But
now ye true Church is coming out of ye Wilderness, & ye Everlasting Gospel
is Preached again as it was in the Apostles dayes In ye first Conversion,
So that People do now come to ye first Conversion, & so to ye same Order, so you
that know the Power of ye Lord God keep up y^{or} Meetings in ye Power of ye Lord,
& in his wisdome, & see y^t nothing be lacking y^n all is well, & If all of you y^t
belong to the Meeting Should be Imprisoned y^n keep to y^{or} Meeting in ye Prison.
If that y^{ou} should be kept So close in Prison as y^t y^{ou} should not know ye Conditions
of all ye Meetings, y^n whom you think fit you may speak to to keep up y^e
Meetings, & never let the deceit get advantage of you: for in these Meetings
you do come into ye Practice of ye pure Religion, wch is to visit, cherish &
preserve &c. And he that disobeys this pure Religion disobeys ye Lord.

[2]To the Men and Womens Monthly and
Quarterly Meetings

1 Dear Friends: If there be any difference amongst friends, or betwixt
Friend & Friend let them speak to one another, & If they will not hear
let y^m take two or three of the Meeting they belong to & they may end it
If they can, & If they cannot end it y^n it may be laid before the Monthly
Meeting; & If it cannot be ended there y^n it may be brought to ye Quarterly
Meeting; & there let it be put to half a dozen Friends, & they may go out & End
it y^t they may keep their Meetings Civil, or y^m y^t be at difference may chuse
three Friends, & Friends may chuse three more to y^m, & let y^m stand to their
Judgment; for there is few that loves quietness & peace will have their Names
brought to a Monthly or Quarterly Meeting: to have their Names sounded
over the Country y^t there is strife, but will rather endeavour to end it
amongst y^m selves at their common Meetings, before y^t they come to y^e
monthly Meetings.

2 And y^t no one accuse any one either in Monthly or Quarterly Meetings
publickly, except they have spoken to y^m by themselves first, & by two or three before.

3 Now concerning Marriages, no man ought to speak to a young Woman concerning
marriage before y^t he hath spoken to her Father & Mother and have their consent
& If she have no Father or Mother, but Guardians, & Trustees, then they must
speak to y^m if she be under Age y^t they may have their consent, & so proceed
accordingly; as Abrahams Servant did concerning Isaacs Wife. And you are
to see y^t all Widdows make provision for their Children before they be Marryed
to another, according $_\wedge$^{to} truth & Righteousness.

4 And you are to see that every Man & Woman be free from all Intanglements with
either Woman or Man before y^t they be Married & If they have been engaged
you must have a Certificate under the hands of y^e Person y^t they have been entangled

2. This section also comes from the Fox epistles referenced in note 1.

with; so y^t all things may be done in peace, & unity & Righteousness according to
ye Truth that is in every Man, & Woman, & if ye young Man or young Womans
Relations be of the World they must have their consent, & a Certificate from y^m.
And if ye Man or Woman comes from beyond Sea. or out of another County,
Y^e must have a Certificate from the Men & Womens Meeting there. how they have
lived, & wheither they be free from all other Persons by any engagement,
Covenant of Contra^{c}t concerning Marriage, & if they are not clear they must
Answer y^t, & cleared by Certificate under their hands before they proceed any farther.

5 And if any man should defile a Woman he must Marry her If she be a beg
gar, & he have never so many hundreds. for he must fulfill the Law of God, so y^e
Law of God commands it that he must Marry her, & Condemn his Action.
& clear Gods Truth. But no such Marriage where the bed is defiled we bring
into our Men & Womens Meetings; but four or five Friends (If such a thing hap
=pens) draw up a Certificate, & they set their hands to it that they will live faith
fully together as Man & Wife & fulfill the Law of God. And this I write If
ever such a thing should happen, But I Hope y^t Friends will be careful, & keep
in the fear of y^e Lord, that they may have esteeme of y^e Lords Truth & their
own bodies, & ye honourable Marriage where the bed is undefiled.

6 And all true Marriages must be layd first before the Womens Meetings; y^t If
there be any thing concerning y^e Woman they may deal with it, & never let it go so
far as the Men: & when things are clear, then three or four Women may go
along with y^e Man & y^e Woman to y^e Mens Meeting, & give in their Testimo=
=ny concerning y^m to y^e Mens Meeting, & so y^n you may enter into your books that
they have appeared such a day of y^e month; & year. And y^n two men Friends of the
Mens Meeting, & two Women Friends of y^e Womens Meeting may enquire
betwixt y^t & y^e next Monthly Meeting If any have ought to say concerning the
Couple y^t are not clear, & If there be any that hath any thing against them
they may come & speak to those two Men & Women concerning of them, & so they
may meet together and make an end of it before y^e next Monthly Meeting. & so
not to trouble the Meeting wth any weakness that may appear, & if they have ended i[t]
and there be nothing against it, y^n the four Friends may give in their Tes
=timony of y^m to y^e Men & Womens Monthly Meeting, And so when they do
take ^{one} another they may appoint a Meeting on purpose, & they may let their
Relations, & as many of the World as they $_\wedge$^{will} know of it. so if any thing be upon
any Friend to declare of the duty of Marriages they may do as they are moved
And y^n the Man & y^e Woman may stand up & declare how that they take one
another in the Presence of God, & in the presence of his People according to the
Law and Ordinance of God, & according to the Practise of the Holy Men &
Women of God as it is written in the scriptures of Truth to live faithfully together
as Husband & Wife so long as they live &c. And they must have a Certificate ready
drawn up, with ye day of ye Month & Year, & ye place, & there subscribe to it at that
time; & as many Friends & as many of ye World as will, may set their hands to it,
as at many Marriages they do: And the Certificate is to be read in the Present

Meeting when they take one another publickly among all yᵉ People, & this
is the way & order of our Marriages, for we do marry none, But it is Gods
Joyning, but we are witnesses; & then it is Recorded in a Book, & this is accord
ing to yᵉ Practise of yᵉ Holy Men of God.

7 Now concerning your Mont[h]ly Men & Womens Meetings, & your Quarterly Men &
Womens Meetings; First as concerning your Monthly Men & Womens Meetings
all yᵉ Fait[h]full Men & Women are to make up the Mens Meeting & yᵉ Womens
Meeting, & let yᵐ yᵗ are not faithfull let yᵐ be admonished in the Lords Power to
live in Truth, modesty, & soberness, & so as they walk they may come to your
Men & Womens Meetings, & yᵉ Men to Meet in one Room, & yᵉ Women in another,
& so to wait upon yᵉ Lord; for all things must be done in his Power & Name &
there is many things yᵗ ˄ⁱˢ propper for Women to look into both in their Families,
& concerning of Women wᶜʰ is not so propper for yᵉ Men, which Modesty in Wo=
=men cannot so well speak of before Men as they can do among their Sex: & Wo=
=men are more in their Families, & have more of yᵉ tuition of their Children, &
Servants yⁿ yᵉ men; they being alwayes among yᵐ; either for the making of them,
or yᵉ marring of yᵐ: and they are to be trained up in yᵉ New Covent, as yᵉ Jews
trained up theirs in yᵉ Old. And many Women are of more capacity yⁿ others are,
& so they must Instruct, & inform yᵉ rest wⁿ they are met together concerning
Ordering of their Children & Families, & that they may prevent many things wᶜʰ
their Children may run into; & they know what will do in a Family, & stir up all
to diligence, & serving the Lord: & what the Women cannot do they may three of four
of yᵐ go from their Meeting to yᵉ Mens, & lay it before yᵐ which is more propper
for them: And what is more propper for yᵉ Women yⁿ yᵉ men yᵉ men may three or
four of yᵐ go & lay it before the Women; so that they may be helps meet together
in the resturation, in Truth & Righteo˄ᵘˢness as man & Woman was before they fell.

8 And If poor Friends have many Children to set fort[h] to Apprentices or Servants,
If yᵉ Women cannot do it the Men may help yᵐ: & If they cannot find Masters
for them, & do it in their Monthly Meetings, they may do it at their Quarterly
Meetings, & place yᵐ amongst Friends yᵗ they may be preserved in yᵉ Truth; & so
they may come in time to teach their Brethren yᵉ same Trades, And help
their Father & their Mother in their Old Age. ~
Now concerning yᵒʳ Quarterly Meetings yᵗ is made up of your Monthly Meet
ings you should speak in your Monthly Meetings who goes to yᵉ Quarterly
Meetings, so that one or two of every particular Meeting may go to yᵉ Quarter=
=ly Meeting, for they that do go to yᵉ Quarterly Meeting must be substantiall
Friends that can give a Testimony of your sufferings, & how things is amongst
you in every particular Meeting; so yᵗ none yᵗ is raw or weak yᵗ is not able
to give a Testimony of yᵉ affairs of yᵉ Church, & Truth may go to yᵉ Quarterly
Meetings, But may be nursed up in you Montly Meetings fit for yᵉ Lords service,
So yᵗ two may go one time from every Particular Meeting, & two another time;
or as it is ordered in your Monthly Meetings; so yᵗ some may go from all yᵒʳ
meetings, that make up of your Montly Meetings, for yᵉ Quarterly Meetings

should be made up of weighty seasoned, & Substantiall Friends that understand
the business of yᵉ Church; for no unruly, unseasoned Persons, should come there,
nor Indeed in yᵉ Monthly Meetings, but who are Simple, seasoned & honest, for
such should be admonished. And If there be any difference come to yᵉ Quarterly
Meetings; either of Men or Women, or Monthly Meetings, after you have
heard yᵐ one by one (& let but one speak at a time never) & to know of them
whether they will stand to yᵒʳ Judgment, & If they will, let half a dozen Friends
go out of yᵉ Meeting & make a finall end of it, for If they will not stand to your
Judgment they are not fit to bring it theither. And if any one should speak or
tattle any thing out of your Monthly, or Quarterly Meetings to yᵉ blemishing or
defaming any Person, or yᵉ meeting, Such are to be brought to Judgment &
Condemnation, for it breaks yᵉ Priviledge, & order of your Heavenly societie in
yᵒʳ Meetings, so yᵗ all may be kept, & preserved in yᵉ Power of yᵉ Lord, & in his Spirit
in Love, & unity. And therefore keep your Meetings Solid & Sober & yᵉ Authority
of your Men & Womens Meetings be in yᵉ Power of God: for every heir of yᵉ Power
has right to yᵉ Authority: & in it keep yᵉ King of Kings, of Lord of Lords, peace in
his Church, & much more I could write of these things, but this at present. & so yᵉ Lord
give you Wisdome that by it you may be Ordered to his Glory. And yᵗ every one
may have a care of Gods Glory his name, & Truth, & yᵗ in his power they do see
yᵗ all do walk as becomes his Glorious Gospel, wᶜʰ hath brought life and Immorta=
=lity to Light in you which will preserve you in Life & Immortality over the
Devil that hath darkend you, & before he was, so that nothing may get betwixt
your souls, & minds, & yᵉ Lord God, yᵗ he may be Gloryfied in you all, & throug[h]
you all, & over you all, Blessed for ever Amen.

G. F. [George Fox]

1   ³My dear Friends
Live all in the Power of yᵉ Lord, & in his Truth, Light, & Life, yᵗ in it you may
all with one heart, Soul, & Mind keep Dominion, & in yᵉ Light Life, & Truth &
Power of God do true Judgment, Justice, & Truth, Righteousness, & Equity,
in all your Mens, & Womens Meetings, wᵗʰout favour, & affections to Relations,
Kindr[e]d, or Acquaintance, or any respect of Persons; for yᵗ If you do not so, let
Judgment come upon you from God to put you down from your places, before
it will If you do not; for yᵉ Power, & Light, & Life, & yᵉ Truth respects not any, but
Justice, Truth, Righteousness, & Equity.

2   Let Mercy overshade the Judgment seat, and let mercy be mixt with
Judgment.

3   Take heed of a foolish pity. If you be not diligent against all Prophaneness
Sin, & Iniquity, & uncleanness, & loosness & debauchery, & yᵗ which dishonoureth
God, yⁿ let all those things come upon you wᶜʰ you should be a stop of, & subdue, &
Keep down with Righteousness, & yᵉ Truth, & yᵉ Power of God, If not be sure
they will If you do not.

3. This comes from a 1669 epistle by Fox. See ibid., 174-75.

4 And in all your Men & Womens Meetings Let all things be done in Love w^{ch}
doth Edifie y^e body, & let nothing be done with strife & vain glory; but keep in
the unity of y^e Spirit which is the bond of peace, & let all things be done in the Wise=
dome of God which is pure & gentle from above, above the Eartly which is below,
sensuall, & Develish. And take heed of hurting any concerning Marriage If the
thing be right) through any Earthly reasoning, lest they do worse,

5 And so all be diligent for the Lord God, & his Truth upon the Earth, & y^e
Inheritance of a Life that hath no end; that you may Live in y^e Seed which is Bles=
=sed for ever.

6 And stop all reports & try y^m, for thou shalt not raise a false report upon my
People saith the Lord.

7 And be diligent in all your meetings to enquire to see to y^e setting forth Appren
=tices, all Fatherless, & poor Friends Children; & y^t all the Poor Widdows be careful=
=ly looked after y^t nothing may be lacking among, y^n all will be well.

8 And y^t all to see the Testimony of Jesus be kept up in all things concerning
his worship, his Way, his Religion, his Church his Testimony against the
World, their works are evil; & Against Oaths, & against the hireling Priests,
for his Doctrine is freely you have received, freely give: & Christs Church needs
not to be mended by men; for he doth mend it himself without Money: & keep
your Testimony against all ye filthy rags of ye World; & for your fine Linnen
the Righteousness of Christ Jesus, And keep y^or Testimony for your liberty in
Christ Jesus, & stand fast in it against all ye false Liberties in Old Adam, &
your Libertie   in   the Spirit of God, and in ye Gospel of Christ Jesus,
against all false and loose Liberties in the flesh: And train up all your Children
in the fear of the Lord, & in his New Covenant (and to keep the sabbath in Christ)
as the Jewes did their Children & Sevants; in the Old Covenant, & so do you
admonish y^or Children, & Servants, & let no man live to himself, but in y^e love
that seek no her own. ~

9 And have an Eye over them y^t comes to Spy out your Libertie in Christ, & will re=
port out of your Meetings things to make advantage and to the defameing of
Persons.

10 And let every one seek the good of another and their welfare in the Truth.

11 And let one make their Conditions every ones, & not their Conditions theirs,
& this keeps in a Father, or Mother to condiscend to a Child; & all live in the seed w^{ch}
hath ye blessings, & ye Wisdome by that you may Order all things to Gods glory over
the Evill seed that is out of ye Truth.

Friends keep to the Antient Principles of Truth.

1 First be at a word in all your callings & dealings without Oppression.

2 To the Sound Language thou to every one.

3 Your Testimony against the Worlds Fashions.

4 Your Testimony against the Priests, & Their Tythes, & maintenance.

5 Against the Old masshouses, & their repairing.

6 Against the worlds Joyning in Marriage, & ye Priests, & to stand up for Gods Joyning.

7 Against Swearing, & the Worlds manners, & fashions.

8 And against all looseness, & pleasure, & Prophaneness whatsoever.

9 And against all the Worlds Wayes, & Worships, & Religions, & to stand up for Gods.

10 And to see that every one that hath done wrong to any one y^t they do restore.

11 And y^t all differences be made up speedily.

12 And that all bad things be Judged speedily, that they do not fly abroad to Corrupt Peoples minds.

13 And that all reports be stopped to ye defaming of any one.

    This is to be read in Friends Meetings as often as they have occasion.

      that people may hear, & fear the Lord.

                                G. F.

[4]Friends, The Law of Love must be kept among all the Saints in Light, which law of love is not provoked; & this Law of love slayes the enmity, & bars all things, & endures all things, & hopes all things; & this Law of love must be kept among all the Children of God, wherein the unity is preserved, & all is preserved by the Law of love in the Love of God, & the Law of Faith must be kept by all the Faithful ones, & amongst them, in the faith of Gods Elect is the Law of faith among the Elect before the foundation of the World was; wch Law of Faith keeps y^m in victory, wth faith gaives Victory & Access to God, & purifies the heart, by wch faith they are saved; wch faith gives victory over that which seperates from God, in wch faith they all please God: And in this Law of faith they have all authority, & victory & unity: and so the Law of Faith keeps ever y^t wch displeases God, & makes People impure, & corrupts them, or brings y^m to destruction, and so by this Faith they are saved & purified, & please God, wch is the Gift of God; & Christ the author of it; & therefore keep this Law of Faith, the Just lives by his Faith, for the Just has ye Law of faith to pass Sentence on y^t wch would not have him have the Victory. but keeps him bondage. all the spiritual have the Law of the Spirit, by which Law of the Spirit they have Authority, & a power to Mortifie sin, & evil, & Crucifie the Deeds of y^e body; and have authority by the Lords Spirit to put off the Old man wth his Deeds; & have Power & authority from the Lords spirit to Crucifie y^e Affections, and the Lusts of y^e Flesh; & by the Law of the Spirit they have authority & Power to judge all Chambering & wantonness, evil speak==ings, & evil words, & evil Communications, & all manner of evil words, & works that proceeds from the evil Spirit out of the Truth, & together with the Works of the flesh, as wrath, Malice, Envy, Theft, Murder, Fornication, By the Law of the Spirit there is a power & authority given to pass sentence, & Judge all these works together wth the Spirit from whence they came. And so by the Law of the Spirit of Life y^t is in Christ Jesus, ye Saints have power, and authority to Jud[g]e the Law

---

4. According to Quaker scholar Lewis Benson, a manuscript of this epistle is in the Library of the Religious Sciety of Friends in London. See Lewis Benson, "Notes on George Fox," typescript, 1981, p. 967 (Friends Collection).

of Sin, & the man of sin from whence it came; & to Judge the Law of death with
the Law of Life, & the Power of death the Devil from whence the Law of death
came, which Law of Life was before death & his Law was, & has power over him
and his Law, and the Saints sit on the head of him, freemen by the Law of Life &
Law of the Spirit that's in Christ Jesus, that was before sin was & his Law death
was, & his Law So the Saints have the Law of Love, yᵉ Law of faith yᵉ Law of
the Spirit, yᵉ Law of Life. In Victory atop Enmity, In Life atop of Death,
in the Spirit atop of Sin, the Law of sin is in Old Adam, in transgression, &
disobedience, & amongst his sons, & daughters in disobedience, & transgression
of Gods Spirit. & such has the Law of sin from the man of Sin, & the Law
of death from the Prince of Death. yᵉ God of the World that lies in wickedness
& the Law of Sin & Death they plead for till they go to the grave, & so plead for yᵉ
prince of Death, & darkness, & the God of their world yᵗ lies in Wickedness as long as
they live, but the Law of Life, & the Law of the Spirit, yᵉ Law of Faith yᵉ Saints
have in Christ Jesus the 2ᵈ Adam, Who is Author of the Law of Love, & yᵉ Law of
Faith which the Saints are to keep & walk in, wᶜʰ they have from Christ, Who never
transgressed, neither was there any guile found in his mouth; & Christ, Who bruiseth
the head to the Serpent. Who is the head of the Law of Sin & death it self, & the Law
in the members. And so in Christ Live. Who bruiseth this; who was, & is the Saints
Life & will be to all Eternity, Who is first, & last, yᵉ Amen.

G. F.

⁵Dear Friends My love in the Lord to you all among whom I have Laboured,
and my desires are the God of all peace, & his Son of Peace may fill all yᵒʳ Hearts
with his Love, & Peace, & Wisdome, & Knowledge in all things to do his Heavenly
glorious Will, in that you will know his Sons doctrine, & as you know it obey it,
& my desires are in the Lord yᵗ you may all walk worth of your Vocation, and
of him that hath called you to holyness & Righteousness, & to peace; so yᵗ his peace
may flow as River, & Righteousness run down as a stream to the gladding of
the City of God, yᵉ walls of wᶜʰ is power, & Salvation, & Light, & Life. And now
my Friends first all yoʳ Meetings keep in the Name of Jesus, in whom you have
all Salvation, wᶜʰ is above every name under yᵉ whole Heaven, in whom there is
no Salvation.
And also all yoʳ Men & Womens Meetings every where keep in the Power of yᵉ Lord
Jesus Christ his Gospel, by which he hath brought Life & Immortality to Light in
you, yᵗ yoᵘ may see over him that hath darkned you, & before he was, wᶜʰ Power will
preserve you in Life & in Immortality: So yᵗ now you may all Labor in the Gosp[el]
the Power of God, in his Glorious Power, & Comfortable Gospel; & Joyfully ser=
=ving the Lord in his Gospel of Peace, through which Gospel you have peace with
God: so that in this Gospel the Power of God there can nothing come betwixt you &
God: Here is your Everlasting Order, not of Man, nor by Man: so that all the faith[=]

---

5. This is entitled "An Epistle to be read in the Men and Womens Meetings," dated 1677, in *Collection
of Many Select and Christian Epistles,* 409-11

=full Men & Women May in the Lords power be stirred up in their Inheritances
of the Same Gospel, & to labour in it, helps Meet in the resturation, as Man &
Woman before they fell. In the Garden of God all are to work in his righteousness,
in his Image, in his Power, in his Garden to subdue the Earth, & to keep the dominion
in his power in the resturation as Man & Woman did in the Image of God before
they fell; & whosoever would hinder you in this Work. it is the same serpents Spirit
that Led Adam & Eve into the fall from the work of God; which now would keep
you in the fall to do his work, & Command, & not the Lords, & therefore over y^t
keep your dominion, Authority, & Inheritance in the Resturation in the power
of God, in which every one of you must give an account to God, & therefore
be diligent in the Lords power, Light, Life, & Spirit in which you all see your services
to God; so y^t he may be glorifyed among you all, & in you all; & over you all his
glory may shine.

And all ye Men & Women in yor Men & Womens Meetings be diligent, Labouring
in the Light, Life, & the power of God the Gospel in ye Garden, & Church of
God; so y^t Righteousness may flow down amongst you, Truth, & Godliness,
Purity, Vertue & Holyness over all that is contrary; & that ye weight, & care
of Gods Glory, and his honour, & his pure holy name, & his Truth, Religion, &
Worship you may all stand up for against that wch would in any wise cause it
to be evil spoken of by ill walkers. & talkers. & let all things you do be done in
love; & condescend one unto another in the Power of the Lord, & in his Truth;
and in it have es.teem one of another, And let all things be done among you
without any strife, for it's love that edifies the body, & knits it together,
& unites it to Christ the Heavenly & holy head.

And Now you Women tho you have been under the reproach because
Eve was first in transgression, but the promise was that the seed of the
Woman should bruise the Serpents head y^t led her first in transgression,
and the Man also: & this promise of God is fulfilled: A Virgin should have a Child,
and they should call his name Emmanuel God wth us again; for Man & Woman
was drove from God out of Paradise, & the Serpent became their head & God of y^e
World; but Christ is come according to the promise of God, & his Prophets who
was born of a Virgin, & therefore saith Mary my spirit hath rejoyced in God my
Saviour, my soul doth Magnifie the Lord for he hath regard to the Low estate of
his handmaid for behold from hence forth all Generations shall call me blessed,
Now here comes the reproach to be taken off from Women who were first in trans=
=gression, & wch are not suffered to speak in the Church: But here Mary did speak &
believe that wch was spoken to her: And also the reproach & transgression taken off
of men that believe in the Seed Christ Jesus; who bruiseth the head of y^e Serpent y^t has
brought Man & Woman into his Image, & his Works, wch Christ destroyes him & his
works, & renews Man & Woman up into the Image of God as they were in before
they fell, & into the Power to have dominion to work in his Garden to subdue
the Earth &c, so that all are now to Labour in the Garden of God y^t are in the
power & Image of God brought by Christ Jesus y^t bruises the serpents head, y^t has been

head in them all: so that Christ Jesus may be head in all Men & Women, & every Man
& Woman may act from him their holy head, Life & Salvation, & keep his heavenly
peace in his Church. And every Living member believing in the Light wch is the Life in
Christ, & so grafted into him ye fountain of Life, water of Life, & do feel the Living springs,
& the Rivers Springing up in y^m To Eternal Life, wch are the Living Stones, y^e Spiritual
Household, of wch Christ is both head, Rock & Foundation & Christ is called y^e Green
tree, which green tree never withers, in whom they are Grafted by belief in y^e Light,
which is y^e Life in him, from whom they all receive their Heavenly Living nou=
=rishment, through wch every graft is nourished, y^n it comes to bud, & bring forth
fruit to y^e praise of the Eternal God, now every one of these living believers are
Members of y^e Living Church in God wch Christ is y^e head of, & every member in y^e
Church hath an Office; & so every member is serviceable in the body in his office.
w^thin the Light wch is over darkness, & was before it was; within the Life over
death, & before it was; & in the Power of God which was before the power of y^e
serpent was; & so they are in this Light. Life & power to execute their Office: I say
within this divine Light, Life, & Power, & Spirit of God for Gods glory. In Truth,
Purity, Virtue, Holyness, & Righteousness they are to stand up for Gods glory,
& the Honour of his Son, & receive him who hath all power in Heaven & Earth
given to him; & all that receive him he gives them power to become the Sons &
Daughters of God; y^n in his Power all are to act, & walk, & serve God in their
Generation, & in it to serve their generation, yea & in the New Creation in
Righteousness, & Holyness, & stand up in his power for his Glory, & in his Power
Righteousness, & Holyness y^t Christ brings unto them, & renues in y^m, & so into y^e
resturation, y^t they may Labour in ye Church & Garden of God in his Power to
his Everlasting Praise & Glory Amen.

G. F.

And all Friends stand fast in the Libertie wherewith Christ hath made you
free, & in the Libertie in the faith which Christ Jesus is the Author, & finiser
of; which Faith purifieth your hearts, & is the Victory, in which you have access
to God; the mysterie of which is held in a pure conscience, in which Faith it hath
its true Ribertie [sic]. And keep in the Liberty of the Everlasting Glorious Gospel of
Peace which is not of Man nor by Man but from heaven; wch Gospel bringeth
& hath brought Life, & Immortality to Light & will preserve you in Life, and in
Immortality over him that hath darkened you: & in this Gospel you have an Ever=
=lasting Liberty, & Peace & in the Truth wch maketh you free from him y^t is out of
Truth, this free state all are to keep in, & also in y^e pure holy spirit of God, & Christ,
y^t doth mortifie all y^t is to be mortified, & Circumcised; & doth Baptize you into
one body: In this Holy Spirit you are to walk, which leadeth you into all Truth,
in which is your Unity, & Fellowship, & giveth liberty from y^t which hath grie[v=?]
=ed it & vexed, & quenched it, & so in the Liberty, & Fellowship, & Unity if y^e Holy,
Pure Peaceable Spirit; & in y^e Unity & Liberty of it you are all to dwell.
which is the Bond of the Prince of Princes Peace.

G. F.

⁶A Paper given forth from Friends of yᵉ half year
Meeting in Dublin.

Dear Friends It being Known to us yᵗ yᵉ antient of dayes is come to bring things
in yᵉ Antient Order yᵗ yᵉ searcher of all hearts is come to search throughly,
yᵗ yᵉ Rock of Ages is appeared for People to build thereon, that yᵉ comelyness,
& beauty of him is now seen whose face hath been ^more marred yⁿ yᵉ face of any Man
whose glorious brightness hath enlightned our understanding; by which Candle
of yᵉ Lord we see yᵉ state of yᵉ Sons & Daughters of Men, & how yᵉ Enemy of
mankind goeth about seeking whom he may devour: & entangle again wᵗʰ yᵉ glory
and beauty of this world; & setting before Men & Women yᵉ comlyness & decency
of the severall fashions & Customes of yᵉ World, as also the delight & pleasures wᶜʰ
may be had there in, by which we see many are ensnared by looking out at
those things & not keep constantly upon their watch Tower, whereby they might
see all the snares, & baits the Enemy of their Souls loads in the broad way, & Crooked
by pathes for their hurt & destruction, & therefore yᵉ Lord hath put it into our
Hearts to be Willing, & to beseech all to be willing to come out, & lay aside all
those dead things. which doth not become the Sons & Daughters Servants &
Handmaids of yᵉ Living God. after yᵗ so gloriously in life & Power he hath
appeared unto yᵐ & we desire yᵗ in all Men & Womens Meetings faithfull
Men & Women be Chosen as have not entᵉred into any of these things, but
are come out, & kept out of yᵐ all since they were Convinced of the Living Truth of
God: Or such as now wᵗʰ a ready & willing mind in yᵉ dread & fear of yᵉ Lord God
Almighty will come out of yᵐ all to yᵉ end yᵗ they wᵗʰout delay in yᵉ meek &
melting Spirit of yᵉ Lord wᵗʰ much tenderness may visit all those yᵗ have -
entred, or keep in yᵉ Worlds fashions in their Apparrel, Household stuff, or
otherwise: or in selling those things wᶜʰ yᵉ faithful People of God cannot Law=
fully use, or wear, & to exhort yᵐ to come out of yᵐ all, & If any are not willing,
& do not come out of those things after they be twice or thrice exhorted, yⁿ those
yᵗ exhorted yᵐ to acquaint the Men & Womens Meetings with it to whom they
do belong, to yᵉ end they may be had before the Meeting to answer for their so doing
yᵗ the glory & Honour of yᵉ Lord may be over all in us to our Comfort & Consolation–

This Paper was subscribed by sixty one Men & Women Friends.

⁷Concerning hasty Marriage.

In case the wife dye, now for yᵉ Husband to take another Wife, or yᵉ Widdow
another man wᵗʰin five or six Months or more yᵉ sober part of yᵉ World would
cry out shame against yᵐ for such unclean Practices: & be ready to say with Chasti=
=ty, Temperance, or Moderation do they manifest more yⁿ some of us who Marry
in so short a time, for it is oft-times the Practice of yᵉ People yᵉ World so to do,
in so much as it is become a common Proverb among yᵐselve by reason of yᵉ hasty
Marriage to say, such a Man Married such a Woman (it being within yᵉ year)

6. A Half-Yearly Meeting was established for Ireland in 1670. It became Dublin Yearly Meeting in 1797.
See Braithwaite, *Second Period of Quakerism*, 261; Rufus M. Jones, *The Later Periods of Quakerism* (2
vols., London: Macmillan, 1921), 111).

7. This is not found in Fox's known published works.

before his wife was scarse cold in her grave, If I say he or she Marry within ye twelve
month; But such Kind of Marriages doth not shew forth your Chastity, & Prudence,
& Moderation; whereas we should shew it beyond the World, both Widdowers & Widdows
that we have power over our selves, & over our affections; & so y^t we are loose by y^e
Power of God to God; & so to keep every way a Dominion, whereby you will Judge y^e
World in these things Namely for their too much forwardness Intemperance & want
of Chastity: & therefore be not too hasty to marry, but shew forth yor moderation and
Chastity in your Orderly Marrying.

G. F.

[8]If a man find a Maid y^t is not betrothed, & take her, & lye with her, y^n ye Man y^t
Lay with her shall give to ye Maids Father fifty shekels of silver, & she shall be his
wife because he humbled her, he cannot put her away, all his Life: Deut: 22.18.19. &
this was ye Command of God in his Law wch y^e Apostle saith in y^e 7th of y^e Rom:
is Spiritual, Holy, just & Good: & we establish y^e Law Rom: 3:31. Now for any
to profess y^e Gospel whose works & actions be below y^e Law they are Judged both
by Law & Gospel: & so by y^e Law of God he must Marry her tho this Marriage is not hono=
=rable. ~

G. F.

An Epistle from Stephen Crisp To be read in y^e Womens Meetings of Friends[9]
Friends In that Love that springs from the Root of Life, which hath brought forth many
Living Branches, doth my Salutation reach unto you, In which we have our Refresh=
=ments, & Incouragements in the Work of God, in this our Generation: & the more
your Minds are gathered into y^t Living Root Christ Jesus, the Everlasting Head
of all Living Members, both Male & female, the more Incouragements you will feel
in your service to God. And therefore, Dear Friends, though you be weak in yourselves
yet in him is strength; & when ye Lack Wisdome, wait upon him, & he will Replenish you,
and fill you with his Heavenly Counsel, to your soul's Refreshment. ~
And my Friends, above all things, live in y^e Fear of God, & in love & Tenderness one to=
=wards another; & Let not the Enemy that lies in wait to destroy, Break the Band
of your Peace; for while ye keep the peace of God unbroken, ye can communicate
one to another of the Gifts & Grace of God, & so will daily feel a being the better one
for another, which will beget a Dearness & Esteem in you towards one another. & in
y^t Dearness & Tenderness meet together about the Lords work Seeking with one Consent
to Exalt the Name of the Lord, & to honour it above your own Merits; & let none
seek Exaltation, but know this, that the Humblest & most self=denying, is highliest
honoured of God, & fittest to do him service; & they that are most long Suffering
& Patient, are most like to Christ the Head; & in such his Vertue will shine,
& so make it self known. ~
And. Friends, have a care in your Meetings, to give due honour unto every
Member in the Body, remembering none are useless, but stir up one another to

8. This is not found in Fox's known published works.
9. Stephen Crisp (1628-1692) was an English Quaker minister. This epistle to women Friends in
Ipswich, England, is found in *The Christian Experiences, Gospel Labours and Writings, of That Ancient
Servant of Christ, Stephen Crisp* (Philadelphia: Benjamin and Thomas Kite, 1822), 293-95.

their Proper Service in yᵉ house of God, & let not the foot be troubled that it is not a hand, nor the hand that is not an Eye, but every one give thanks, that by the Grace of God you are what you are; & be Faithful in your place & Service yᵗ ye may witness a Growth. & in your Meeting together, wait to feel the Rising if yᵉ Life, & opening of yᵉ Wisdom of God in one another, & let that speak and propound things needful & necessary for your Welfare, & yᵉ Welfare of yᵉ Church: And in th[e] Wisdom chuse out two of you Meeting, to commit the trust & Charge of the Contributio[ns] that are among you unto; & let them keep a Booke, in which your Charity and good works may be Recorded, for the Comfort & Example of them yᵗ follow afte[r] Also chuse out one of each particular Meeting, & Lay it upon yᵐ in yᵉ Lord, to take care in their Respective Meeting on your behalf.

1 That no Woman Young nor old. in their Respective Meetings, walk disorderly or Wantonly, but yᵗ they be Admonished & Counselled speedily.

2 That no Necessities that may fall upon any who are worthy, may be neglected or disregarded, nor delayed, until a Meeting, but they may be forthwith Comforted. that so the Enemy who lies in wait to tempt the Poor in the hour of their distress, may be prevented.

3 That no Maids carry themselves unseemly toward their Mistresses, nor Mistresses toward their Servants: but if such things should happen, let the Matter be take[n] up & ended, & not to part asunder with evil in their Minds one toward another; for yᵗ will spread & hurt others.

4 That all Women Professing Truth, & having Children, may bring yᵐ up in yᵉ fea[r] of God; & yᵗ they use no Uncomely, Rash nor Passionate Words unto yᵐ, for yᵗ sows an Evil seed in the Children, which may come up & dishonour God in yᵉ ne[xt?] Generation.

5 That no Women-Friends may speak evil of one another, nor fall out wᵗʰ one another, nor carry evil in their Minds one against another; nor bear Tales ab[out?] to beget others in Evil, & into partyship but yᵗ all such things may be speedily suppress'd & borne down in the Power & Judgment of God.
And let that Woman-Friend give Account to yᵉ Meeting, of such as will not receive admonition, yᵗ some other friends may take the care of such a Matter upon them, & endeavour to break through the hardiness, In yᵉ Wisdome & Love of God.
And if yᵗ Woman-Friend have laid out Money, let yᵉ Meeting order yᵉ two friend[s] who keep yᵉ Collection, to reimburse her; yᵗ so every one may be encouraged in yᵗ work of yᵉ Lord & ye may, as wᵗʰ one shoulder, bear the Lord's burden in this d[ay?] of Travail, & also yᵉ burdens of yᵉ weak, Who sometimes are neither strong enough,[nor?] wise enough to bear their own Burdens; & afterward, they may grow up to be sens[ible?] of yᵒʳ Tenderness, & to bless you in the Name of yᵉ Lord.
So, my Dear Friends, feel my love, & live in yᵗ from whence it springs, & yᵉ God of Love & Life, Bless, Prosper & keep you in his Fear to the End, to be Fellow-helpers with the Lord in his Work, Comfort & Refreshment to your Brethren, and to lea[d?] a Holy, Innocent, Upright, Testimony & Example to yᵉ Generations yᵗ shall [follow ?]
     I rest your Friend in yᵉ Truth.

                                     S. C.

[10]Concerning Marriage in the Kindred

We do grant it was there, & after the Law to keep up their Tribes, & their Lands by Lott (if y^t ye deceased had not Children, they were to Raise up seed to their dead B[ro] ther) but Christ is come y^t raises up the Seed of his dead Brethren, Who redeems out of the Tribes & Earth: For Jew & Gentile all are one without Christ & with in, & (by the Law [of] God & Gospel) to Marry in the kindred was forbidden: for it was ye Custome of ye Heath[ens?] ye Canaanites, & Egyptians. as you may read in Levit:18. And therefore ye Lord commands to Keep his Statutes, & Judgments, & live in y^m, for he was their Lord who Orders, & Governs all his People, & Commands y^t they shall not approach to any that ₐwas near of kin to him: & y^t he was not to Marry the Sister ye daughter of ye Father, Nor ye Daughter of ye Mother wheith[er] she was born at home or abroad, nor the Sons Daughter, nor thy Daughters Daughter y^t is the Cousen; nor were they to Marry wth their Fathers Wives Daughter begotten by their Father, for she was his Sister they were not to Marry with all, for she was a near Kinswoman, Thou shalt not take to Wife thy Aunt; thou shalt not marry Daughter in Law nor thy brothers wife, neither shalt thou Marry a Woman & her Daughter, neither shalt thou Marry thy Sons Daughter, or her Daughters, or her Daughter. therefore we do utterly deny all Marriages to any kindred, to any Cousen, we cannot give Liberty to admit it, John Baptist who saw Christ Reproved Herod for Marrying his Kinswoman. Therefo^{re} Friends live in ye spirit that reproves these things.

And further if any Friend Intends to Marry a Young Woman or Maid let y^m speak to her Father & Mother first if in case they go to their house upon Such an Account about Marriage & not to draw out the Maids affections first, & y^n afterwards to speak to ye Father & Mother, that's the Practice of the Worst of Men in the World, & not the Civil, men in ye World: for if they go upon such an Account to marry a Mans Daughter they will go & speak wth ye Father & Mother first before they proceed in ye thing wth ye Daughter, For Abraham when he sent to take a wife for his Son Isaac, his Servant, Eleazar did his Massage unto Bethuel (before he would eat or drink with them) concern ing ye Marriage & y^n they called the Maid, & speak to her about it, & she Consented, & they said it was of ye Lord, & they could not gain say it. So y^t If you should Meddle with ye young woman first, & draw her Affections, & after speak to her Father, & Mother, this brings the Father & Mother into Sorrow & Trouble, & cannot tell many times what to do fearing least their Daughter should be spoiled, and that brings con-fusion, & is for Judgment as is the worst of Mens Practice, & so I say is for Condemnation

G. F.

[11]All Friends keep in the tender Life of the Lamb over y^t Unruly Puffed up, & swelling Spirit whose work is for strife, contention & division; drawing into looseness & false Liberty under a pretence of Conscience, & dangerous to y^e spoiling of youth, & they y^t do encou= =rage y^m will be guilty of their destruction; & set up a sturdy will instead of Conscience

10. This is not found in Fox's known published works.

11. This epistle was directed to Friends at Hertford in England in 1678. See *A Journal or Historical Account of the Life, Travels, Sufferings, Christian Experiences, and Labour of Love in the Work of the Ministry of That Ancient, Eminent, and Faithful Servant of Jesus Christ, George Fox* (Philadelphia: Marcus T. C. Gould, 1831), II, 223.

in their Rage, & Passion; which will both quench the Universal Spirit in themselves & in every Man & Woman; & so y^t Spirit Shall not have the Libertie in y^{m}selves nor in others; & so hath shut up the Kingdome of Heaven in y^m selves, & also in others: & so a loose Spirit under a pretence of Libertie of Conscience, or a Stubborn Will Making a Profession of the Words of Truth in a forme without Power; all loosness & Villany will be sheltered & covered under this Pretence which is for Eternal Judgment for y^t doth dishonour God: And therefore keep to ye tender Spirit of God in all Humility, & in it you may know y^t you are all Members of one another In the Spirit. & not in ye Flesh; So here is no man Ruling over the Woman as Adam did over Eve in the fall, but Christ ye Spiritul man among, & over his Spiritual Members which is Edified in ye heavenly Love y^t is shed in their Hearts from God where all strife ceases.
11th 5 Month 1678   G. F.

[12]Dear Friends to whom is my Love in ye Heavenly seed in whom all nations, is blessed: oh there fore keep ˄all in this Seed in wch you are blessed; & in wch Abraham, & all ye Faithfull was blest with out y^e Deeds of y^e Law, & so y^e Promise was, & is with y^e Seed, & now wth y^e Law of y^e first Covenant, & in this Seed all Nations & ye are blessed which bruiseth y^e head of y^e seed which broug[h]t the curse, & Seperated between Man & God; this is the
    Seed wch Reco[n]
=ciles you to God, & this is y^e Seed in which you are blessed both in Temporals, & Spirituals, through wch you have an Inheritance y^t cannot be defiled among y^e Sanctified; neither can any defiled thing enter into It's possession; for all defilement is out of this Seed, this is that wch leavens up into ye New lump, & bruiseth the head of ye Wicked Seed y^t Leavens into ye Old Lump, upon whom the sun of Righteoness goes down, & sets, but never goes down, nor sets to y^m that walk in ye Seed in which all nations are blessed, by wch seed they are brought up to God, wch puts down y^t Seed wch Seperated betwixt y^m & God, so y^t there comes to be nothing betwixt y^m & God, & so now all my dear Friends my desire is that you may all be valiant in this Heavenly Seed for God & his Truth upon y^e Earth, & spread it abroad answering y^t of God in all, y^t wth it y^e Minds of People may be turned towards y^e Lord, y^t he may come to be known & served, & Worshiped; & y^t ye may all be y^e Salt of y^e earth to make y^e unsea= =soned Savoury. And in y^e Name of **Jesus** keep yor Meetings who are gathered into it in whose name you have Salvation, & he in the Midst of you, Whose Name is above every Name under the Whole Heaven; & so you have a Prophet, a Bishop, Shepherd, & Priest & Counsellor above all Counsellors, & Priests, Bishops, Prophets, & Shepherds under y^e Whole Heaven to exercise his Offices among you in your Meetings y^t is gathered in his Name; & so Christs Mee[t]= =ing & gathering is above all y^e Meetings & gatherings under y^e Whole Heaven: & so his Body his Church & he y^e Head of it is above all bodies, & Churches, & heads under y^e Whole Heaven; & So y^e Faith wch Christ is y^e Author of, & y^e Worship wch he hath set up, & his Fellowship in his Gospel is above all Historical Faiths, & ye Faiths wch Man hath made together wth their Worships & Fellowships under ye Whole Heaven. And now dear Friends keep your Men & Womens Meetings in ye Power of God y^e

12. This epistle dated 7th Mo., 26, 1678, is found in *Collection of Many Select and Christian Epistles*, 414-16.

Gospel the Authority of y^m wch brings Life, And Immortality to Lighten you. & this
Gospel ye Power of God will preserve you in Life. & Immortality wch hath brough[t]
it to Light in you. y^t ye may see over him y^t hath darkened you from Life & Immo[r-]
-tality (y^t would throw down your Men & Womens Meetings) in ye power of God
ye Gospel; & darken again from this Life & Immortality wch ye Gospel hath brought to
Light, & Will preserve you in Life & Immortality, as your Faith stands in ye Power of God
ye Gospel: in wch every one sees your Work & service for God, & ever Heir of ye Power
of God ye Gospel hath right to this Authority wch is not of Man, nor by Man; wch Gospel
ye Power of God is Everlasting an Everlasting Order & Everlasting Fellowship, & in
Gospel is Everlasting Joy, Comfort, & Peace, & will outlast all those Joyes, Comforts,
& Peace that will have an end, & also that Spirit y^t opposes its Order, & the Glorious
Fellowship. Peace & Comfort in it: And now my Dear Friends my desire is y^t you may
keep in ye Unity of ye Spirit. That Baptizes you all into ‸^one Body. wch Christ is ye Heavenly
Spiritual Head of. So y^t you may See, & Witness to your Spirituall, & Heavenly Head,
& so all drink into Spirit: wch all People upon the Earth is not Like to drink into one
Spirit while they grieve, quench, & Rebell against it nor to be Baptized into one Body, & to
keep the Unity of ye Spirit wch is the Bond of y^e King of Kings, & Lord of Lords
Peace; wch is y^e duty of all true Christians to keep, wch are Inwardly united to Christ.
And so with my Love in y^e Everlasting Seed.

G. F.

[13]Friends; There is a Summer Religion y^t is up, & Flourisheth while y^e Sun Shineth, & whil_e
they have y^e Club, y^e staff & y^e Bag; but w^n y^e Winter & y^e Storm & Tempest cometh
they fly under the hils, & Mountains, & Trees to cover & shelter y^mselves (but this is n[?]
Y^e Nature of y^e Sheep of Christ,) in their Bestiall Religion, whose flight is in y^e Wind
whom the Powers do Seperate from their Religion, Worship Church (as they call it) their D[?]_is
But y^e Nature of y^e Sheep is not so; the Sheep will get a top of y^e highest hill & mountain, & set
their backs & Tails against the Storm, Weather, & Tempest, & bleat for one another: &
the Dogs are abroad among y^e sheep they will run all together, but they y^t are not y^e Sheep_in him
Will scatter, & be scattered w^n any thing feareth y^m; But part the Sheep asunder, & they will_e[?]
all On heaps again; & will keep together. & neither Storm, Tempest, nor Winter, nor Pow[er?]
nor Principalities, can Seperate y^m from the Love of God wch they have in Christ Jesu[s]
their shepherd; & so Christs sheep beareth fruit in y^e winter, & Tempest. & hath neither
bag, staff, nor Club, but is in the Vine bearing fruit; sitting atop on ye Highest
hill & Mountain, with their backs against ye weather.

G. F.

[14]To ye Quarterly Men & Womens Meetings wch are Gathered.
in the Name & Power of Jesus.

Christ ye Second Adam who is both Head & Husband of his Church, &
Redeemer, & Purchaser, & Saviour, & Sanctifier, & Reconciler of his Sons & Daughter
to God: I say his Presence (to wit) Christ, feel among you to exercise his Propheticall

---

13. From 1661, See ibid., 164-65.
14. Dated 1681 in *Journal of . . . George Fox*, 240-41.

Office in opening of you wth his Light, Grace, Truth, Power & Spirit, & Exercise his
Office as he is a Bishop to oversee you with his Light, Grace, Power. & Spirit, tha[t]
you do not go astray from God.

And as Christ is a Shepherd, feel, see, & hear him Exercising y^t Office who
has laid down his life for his sheep, & feed y^m in his Living Pastures of Life, & makes y^m
to drink of his Living Eternal Springs, & Let him Rule & Govern in your Hearts as he is
a King, y^t his Heavenly & Spiritual Government all may live under true Subjec[t]
of his Righteous Peaceable Kingdome that stands in Righteousness, & Power &
Joy in the Holy Ghost, over Satan & his Power, & ye Unclean Unholy Ghost,
& all unrighteousness.

So all you Subjects of Christs Kingdome of Peace & If y^t you want Wisdome,
or knowledge, or Life, or Salvation, Christ is the Treasure, feel him ye Treasure
among you; And every one among you as he has Received Christ walk in him. in
whom you have all Peace, Who bruises ye head of ye Serpent that is ye Author of a[?]
strife, destractions, & Confusion, yea you have Peace wth God & one wth another
tho the trouble be from ye World, & ye Worlds Spirit: & Therfore My dear Fri[ends]
& Brethren Love one another wth ye Love y^t is of God shed in your Hearts, y^t yo[u]
may bear the Marks of Christs Disciples; & y^t Christ be in you & you in him
so y^t God Almighty may be Glorified among you: And w^t ever ye do let it to be do[ne]
in ye Name of Jesus; To ye Praise of God ye Father keeping the Holy Spirit of God
wch was before the Unholy Spirit was; wch holy spirit is your bond of Peace yea y^e
Holy King of Kings & Lord of Lords Peace, & In this Holy Pure spirit is your
Eternal Unity & Eternal Fellowship: In which Spirit of Truth you do serve &
Worship ye God of ye Truth. Who is God over all Blessed forever Amen. & so ye Lord
Guide you all wth his Word of Patience. Word of Life, Power, & Wisdome in all your
Actions, Lives & Conversations & Meetings to Gods Glory. So with my Love
to you all in ye Lord Jesus Christ by whom all things were made, Who is God
over all first & last.

4th Month 1681.   G. F.

[15]G F^s Testimony at a Yearly Meeting in London
3^d Month 1681

To Friends; Blessed be ye Name of the Lord who hath been ye Preserver of his Peopl[e]
to this day, in wch the great Love of God to Mankind hath been made manifes[t]
For Christ said God so Loved the World that he gave his only begotten Son
Y^t [That] whosoever Believeth in him should not Perish, but have Everlasting
Life Joh. 3.16.

Now my Friends y^t this you may mind; Man was drove from God when
he had disobeyed him; & all are in ye Corrupt state while man is drove from God:
But now God so Loved ye World y^t he gave his only begotten Son; His Begotten;
not ye Begotten of Adam in the Fall, Son, nor Daughter, but his Begotten;
For God did not take a Son, or Daughter of Adam, but his Own Son, his only

15. This is not found in Fox's known published works.

Begotten: Now w^n [when] his Son came who Received him? Who had Faith in him? For it's said w^n the Son of Man cometh shall he find Faith in ye Eart[h].

For ye Son of God ye Beloved is ye Author & Finisher of Faith to the Sons & Daughters of Men; Men may make Faiths, & Creeds, but what are they all good for? So now ever Man y^t hath ye true Faith must have it from God; & his Son Christ Jesus; & not from the Sons & Daughters of *Adam* in ye fall. & Transgression.

For God so Loved ye World y^t he gave his Only Begotten Son into ye World, The first born of every Creature; he gave his Son, who by ye Grace of God tasted Death for every Man to be a Propitiation for our Sins, He did not take a Son or Daughter of Adam in y^e Fall y^t they should be a Sacrif[i]ce for y^e Sins of y^e World, but Gods Son; Here was a Promise y^e Seed of the Woman shall bruise y^e Serpents Head. Here is another Promise w[^{ht}?] his Name should be: Immanuel $_\wedge$^{God} with us

So Now Friends Man being drove from God y^e Seed of y^e Woman bruises the Head of y^e Serpent y^t so Man may come back again to God; And therefore every Man & Woman must feel this Emmanuel (God wth us) in y^m for it's not Professing y^e Saints Words, & Painting their Sepulchres as y^e Scribes, & Pharisees did. So now Friends, Man & Woman being drove from God, every Man & every Woman must feel this Emmanuel, if you feel God in you or with you; the Promises are yea & Amen in Christ ye Seed forever; ye Prophets Prophesied of him, & ye Tipes & Figures, & Shadows did Tipify him forth who is ye Substance that hath appeared ye second time without Sin unto Salvation.

The Pharisees & Priests could tell by ye Scriptures where Christ should be Born, but who did Receive him, this Emmanuel? Men all Confess y^t wee have been drove from God, & all Dyed in Adam, they have put on Adam by Death: Here Death & Destruction may talk of ye Fame of God, & Christ Jesus; we by Nature are ye Children of Wrath as Well as others saith ye Apostle; But before People come to be grounded & Established in ye Truth, & Light of Christ **Jesus** they must be turned Inward, & Baptized by one Spirit into one Body.

But now being all dead in Adam, & Batized into his unclean Ghost, this foul Spirit out of Truth, & Plunged into the Death of Adam in transgression in Sin, & Unrighteousness, & all Ungodliness; Here was the Plunging into ye foul unclean Spirit; w^n Adam went from God, & his Holy spirit he dyed, & all dyed in him

Now come to ye Second Adam ye Lord of Glory who was not begotten by the Will of Man, he is a Baptizer: wth w^t: by the Holy Ghost; Now this foul unclean Ghost hath brought all miserie & Darkness, Malice, Envy, & wrath into Man, & by it they are plunged into it.

Now ye second Adam is come; he shall Baptize you wth Fire & ye Holy Ghost to burn up ye Chaff, wch must be burned out of every Man & Woman if ever they come to God; for all having been Baptized into Adam in ye Fall, they must know a Renewing, & a Baptizing again by Christ, before they come into y^e Paradise of God again where this Chaff is cleansed out of y^e Heart.

Here is one Lord, one Faith. one Baptisme. All dead in Adam they must know
a Baptism again: Many may go into Outward Water, but they must come to this Bap=
=tism to be plunged wth this Spirit, this Holy Ghost to have their Corruptions burned up,
& Plunged down by him y^t Gathers y^e wheat into y^e Garner, & burns up y^e Chaff wth
unquenchable Fire. this must be plunged down, & burned up before Man comes to God.

So now my Friends, they that have been Baptized into y^e Death of Adam
in Transgression have put him on; they have not put on Christ: But they y^t are
Batized into y^e Death of Christ have put him on, & put off y^e Old Man, & are Renew=
=ed in their Minds to God again, so every Man & Woman must know this
Baptism of Christ, and as the Apostle did say to some ye are all Baptized into
one Body by one Spirit: So now this Holy pure Spirit of God y^t doth plunge
down Sin & Iniquity, this pure Spirit is y^t which was in Man before y^e foul Spirit
got into Man & Woman by Transgression, the Pure Spirit of God was before y^t was;
And this pure Spirit brings & Unites all into ₍one₎ Spirituall Body wch the Spiritual
man is ye Head of; Who is ye first-born of every Creature; He is not that Son y^t was
Born by ye Will of Man, but by ye Will of God; So y^t No Son or Daughter of Adam
in ye Fall can be Head of the true Church, but he that was ye first begotten of
God, Who tasted Death for every Man, this must People know, & every man feel in
their own Particulars by his Grace & Truth If they will come to Life & Salvation
by Jesus Christ, who is ye Head & Saviour of his Church.

So now Man being drove from God, ye Emmanuel God wth us Christ Jesus
is come into his Temple: There was Figures, Types, & Shaddows in ye time of
the Law, & Severall things did Tipe forth, y^t ye Substance was to come wch is now
come: Therefore Said ye Apostle it pleased ye Father to Reveal his Son; ye Son of God;
not of Old Adam, Reveal his Son in me, y^n he did Preach Emmanuel ₍God₎ with us:
& y^t ye believers were ye Temple of God: The Faith of Gods Elect was known
in Christ; & here is no Life out of this Faith in Christ, but in him is enjoyment of
Peace; Here is ye Comfort of Christ Jesus, ye Emmanuel God with us; here is the seed of
ye Woman y^t bruises ye Head of ye Serpent: so as it was said ye Gospel was preached
to Abraham, saying in thy Seed shall all nations of ye Earth be blessed. So now y^e
Gospel was Preached to Adam, Abraham, Isaac, & Jacob; it is in ye Seed Christ.

And so Friends all People must come into this Seed y^t are blessed, & standing
& Living in this seed here is Glory to God in ye Highest, here is ye standing Rock
ye Rock of Ages, & standing foundation. He that bruises ye Serpents Head is come,
who is ye Foundation, & Rock of all true Believers in ye Light, ye Light in Christ
ye seed to build on, so bruises the Head of all other false Foundations, all y^t wch must
have an end, y^t had a Beginning among men; all their Formallities must have an
end, ye Substance is come; here is ye Foundation, yea ye Heavenly & Holy Foundation,
a Foundation not of Man, but of ye Heavenly Man: not of ye Sons & Daughters of
Old Adam, but ye Son of God. In thy Seed shall all Nations be blessed; & no nation
can be in ye Blessing except in the Seed, O ye Everlasting Love of God to all Mankind:
Here the pure God hath his Glory, & Praise, & Honour over all in his Pure Seed Blessed for
ever: & here is ye Emmanuel God wth Man; here is stability & Settlement upon this Rock

this Seed y^t bruises ye head of ye Serpent (y^t leads from God) in which all Nations are blessed, Thee out of this seed to talk of ye Prophets, Talk of ye Figures & Shaddows y^t Tipe forth ye Seed thou hast not ye Blessing: So here in ye Seed Christ Jesus in ye Gospel shall all Nations be blessed; So all Nations Must come into this Seed in wch ye Living God hath his Praise, his Living Praise, his Living Honour, who is over all in his Heavenly Power.

There is a setled established state, being built on him ye Emmanuel God with us, by whom Man is Reconciled to God: So every man know & feel him your Possession, in whom all ye Promised Figures, Tipes & Shaddows end, in him ye Substance, here is comfort of the Promises enjoying ye Substance, & here Praises arise to ye Everlasting God thorow Christ, & to him y^t was, & is to come, ye second Adam ye Lord from Heaven: So now my friends this Answers to that of ye Apostles in their Dayes, w^t [what] they saw & enjoyed: But now as People come again to this Light & Life, Grace & Truth, & ye Seed Christ Jesus from whence ye same comes: So they come to enjoy him again as ye Apostle saith, E[x]amine your selves, prove your own selves. know you not your own selves, how y^t Jesus Christ is in you except you be Reprobates; the Apostle here would not have People to live in a Profession of God & Christ in Ungodliness. but enjoy & Possess Christ; & to examine y^m selves wheither they are Reprobates, or not, but w^t is a Reprobate? one y^t is Wandred & dr.^{i}ven from God & Christ out of ye Way of Truth, one y^t talks, & has not ye Possession, a Reprobate: There fore ye Apostle would have all to be true Christians, & to have Christ in them Christ in you the Hope of Glory, as Christ was in him.

Therefore all Christians are to come to Try & Examine wheither Christ be in y^m yea or Nay: w^t they Dye unto, & w^t they Live unto, Who it is y^t makes y^m alive again; So he being in y^m y^e Emmanuel God with us, here is no Repro= =bation; Examine your selves: If Christ be not in you. y^n [then] you are Reprobates, the Apostle would have y^m sound Christians, Possessors of Life & not Professors only: & therefore he bid y^m Examine y^m selves, this is y^e day Wherein all must come to Examination, or how can they Preach Christ If he be not Revaled in y^m: for saith y^e Apostle w^n it pleased y^e Father to Reve$_\wedge$al his Son in me consulted not &c. And so he that had y^e Son of God, & knoweth him to be Revealed in him hath Life Everlasting; this must all know & feel in their own particulars He y^t doth Inherit him hath Peace, So now my Friends as People come out of y^e Apostacie into y^e Possession of this Heavenly Seed. Christ Jesus; If you have him you have Life Eternal, you have Peace with God, y^e Emmanuel who Reconciles you to God again; & here you all come to Eat of y^e Living bread y^t comes down from Hea= =ven & drink of y^e Living Waters, here is a Living Well comes to be Opened. O Blessing & Praises to y^e King of Sion, him y^t Lives & Reigns forever; So now Friends here is a Rock known; & we can say w^t Rock is like our Rock who bruises y^e Head of y^e Serpent; All must come to him y^t is over all false Foundations to him y^t brings Man again $_\wedge$into y^e Image of God to build on Christ y^e sure Foundation; So here People come all to Witness to be Baptized into him & put him on; & to know y^e true Baptism y^t plunges down y^e false Spirit, & his works as y^e Apostle saith we are all Baptized by one Spirit into one body, & here we all drink into one pure Spirit; yᵉ Holy Spirit of God; drink in it here is unity.

To drink in this one pure Spirit wᶜʰ is over yᵉ foul Spirit, or else how can it Baptize Man, or Plunge down Corruption if it be not above yᵉ foul Spirit? So drink in this Pure Holy Spirit, here is yᵉ Pure standing Fellow= ship; meet here, Feed here, drink here; many may come to sights, & Talk of these things, but Few come to be possessors of this Pure Spirituall standing. Baptism [?] yᵗ Baptizeth into one Body, & to know Christ who was not Begotten by yᵉ Will of Man but of God; Who came from yᵉ bosome of yᵉ Father to be the Head of yᵉ Church: Now yᵐ yᵗ drink here will not drink of yᵉ Whores Cup will not drink of any Profession of Leligion [sic] set up without yᵉ pure Spirit of God, Because their drinking is in yᵉ Spirit: Now here is a Fello‸ʷship & perfect Unity in yᵉ Heart & Spirit wᶜʰ is yᵉ Bond of Peace unites to God & one unto another in an intire Fellowship wᶜʰ will stand wⁿ all yᵉ Fellowships in yᵉ world are gone, this unites & makes us known one unto another in yᵗ wᶜʰ is Everlasting; not only in this World but in yᵗ wᶜʰ is to come; so this pure Spirit Baptizes into one Body this Spirit brings in Life, & Love, & Peace, & strength, & fills all wᵗʰ good things; Yᵉ foul Spirit hath No room in Man here drinking in this Holy pure Spirit.

So now Friends here in this one pure Spirit is yᵉ Unity of yᵉ Church in God yᵗ Christ is yᵉ Head of, O blessed be God for ever: You Read of the Circumcision in yᵉ Old Covenaⁿt to be Outward; & yᵉ Men were to be Circum =cised before they did eat of yᵉ Sacrifices: for the Uncircumcised were to go down into the Pit; this was in yᵉ Old Testament; But Now in the New- =Testament yᵉ Circumcision is in yᵉ Spirit yᵗ cuts off yᵉ Body of Death & Sin in the Flesh wᶜʰ hath got up into Man & Woman by Transgression; This all must come to Witness yᵉ Circumcision in yᵉ Spirit before they come to feed on yᵉ Sacrifice Christ Jesus yᵉ Bread yᵗ comes down from Heaven.

You must consider yᵗ Father Adam & Mother Eve had not a Body of sin & Death before they went from God, But when they hearkened to yᵉ Serpent they fell from yᵉ Image of God; Therefore there must be a Circumcision in [?] yᵉ Spirit to put off yᵉ Body of Sin & Death wᶜʰ hath got into Man & Woman by Transgression before they come to Feed on yᵉ Heavenly Sacrifice Christ the Heavenly Spiritual Offering; for If they do not come to this Circumcision with yᵉ pure Spirit they cannot come to feed on yᵉ Heavenly Bread; for he yᵗ is heavenly must be fed on by this Holy Heavenly Spirit; So every Man & Woman must know this Heavenly Circumcision, who is yᵉ Circumciser & Baptizer: yᵉ second Adam yᵉ Heavenly Man, he Will baptize & Circumcise you he is yᵉ Substance, this Heavenly Man; Every Mans Eye must be to him in yᵉ light & Life, Grace, & Truth yᵗ comes from him.

The Light wᶜʰ is yᵉ Life in Christ hath been often talked of, & called Naturall, but this is a Mistake; for it is said in yᵉ beginning was yᵉ Word, & in yᵉ Word was Life; so it was Life in yᵉ Word before any Naturall Created Lights were, & before man was made, or Conscience either, yᵉ Life in yᵉ Word was before Old Adam; So they y^t call it Naturall Created Light, or Conscience, are mistaken, Now this Light in Christ wch is ye Light in Man we have not from any of ye Sons, & Daughters of Old Adam; from whom y^n [?] from ye second Adam whose name is called ye Word of God, by whom all things was made; So now every Man y^t comes to be a Believer in ye Light, ye Life, in ye Word Christ; comes to be Grafted into Christ Jesus; here ye Root bears ye branches; these be living Members, & make up a Spiritual Household, So this Light, & Life comes not from Old Adam, or any of his Sons & Daughters, but from ye Second Adam ye Lord from Heaven, therefore they y^t say to ye Contrary, & give ye Light other Names know not what they say; But they who are come into this Light ye Life in ye Word they are established upon Christ who is ye first & Last, & will be to all Eternity, Glory to God for ever: This Light was before all Naturall Lights were (& this Word was before all false words were) This was y^t wch Christ taught to believe in, and they y^t did Believe were setled & Established in Christ; For Gods Love was so great to Mankind y^t he sent his Son a Light into ye World y^t whosoever believes in him should not perish but have Everlasting Life; He y^t believeth not is Condemned already: By one Mans Disobedience Condemnation came upon all. He y^t comes out must believe; He y^t believeth cometh out of Condemnation: Therefore now I say this Light ye Life in Christ keeps every Mans Eye to him from whom they Receive Power, & from whom they Receive his Law, they come to be a Subject under, his Government; here comes every one in their own Hearts to have a Testimony to y^e Light, y^e Second Adam y^e Lord From Heaven, he y^t never transgressed nor Sinned, nor never fell, So y^n he in you, & you in him; here is y^e Generall, Universal Love of God to all man= kind; therefore the Gospel hath & must be Preached to all Nations; for they y^t have Received this Gospel of y^e Son of God have received him, but you may say y^e Apostle calls it his Gospel, yes, he Received it, & was Heir of y^e Everlasting Gospel by y^t wch came from God, & Christ came by none of Adams Sons: So this Order of ye Gospel ye Power of God is not from Old Adam, for this brings under ye Government of Christ, & this Power of God keeps Man clean, & Preserves him, being stronger y^n ye Power of ye Devil: So all Mankind hath a Visitation of ye Gospel of Life & Salvation sounded to their Souls; but it is only y^m y^t Receive it & Obey it y^t have ye Comfort of it for they that are established in ye Gospel are established in ye Power of God, Then this Gospel is their stability; So Glory to God for ever, this Gospel is from Heaven & not from Man, the Enemy cannot come into it every Man & Woman wth this Gospel wch hath brought Life & Immortality to Light they will see Christ, & come under his Government. Power & Wing y^t will preserve, & he will gather y^m as a hen gathers her Chickens under wings to keep y^m from ye Vermin: Now Christ preserves from under ye Power of Darkness ye Devil y^t is ye great devourer of Mankind; & so here under his Power & wing we can say thy Kingdome is an Everlasting Kingdom, it is established in his Power, So stability is in ye Gospel the Power of God.

So now Friends two things are in my mind: first God poured out of his spirit upon all Flesh in ye New Covenant. But in ye Old Covenant God poured forth his Spirit on ye House of Israel & Judah; & they that were in ye Spirit of God y^n saw this day of ye New Covenant: & y^t God would poure of his Spirit upon all Flesh.

So now all Flesh must come to this Spirit of God, & know this Spirit to be poured upon y^m; this was general & ye other particular, he will pour of his Spirit upon all Flesh, so all Flesh must come to this Spirit if they will worship God. this Spirit doth not come from Adam, nor none of his Sons & Daughters, but from God. God Almighty must have ye eye, or Ear in his Spirit, so all come to this Spirit here is ye Comfort & Joy; this is that wch is not of Man; So this Holy Spirit makes all Subject, & settles y^m upon Christ & God, let Waves & Persecutions, & w^t ever come, here in this stand to be Preachers, & Possessors of this, they know in it their End even Everlasting Life

So now here you may see the Love of God to Mankind y^t he would not have y^m to Perish, but to have Everlasting Life in Christ Jesus, but some will say how shall I come to know & have this good Spirit? you must leave ye bad Spirit y^t leads into all badness, Wickedness, & all manner of Evill, but this Pure, Holy Spirit leads into all manner of Vertue, & all y^t is good, there is a distinction one from y^e other; as y^e Apostle saith y^e Fruit of y^e good Spirit is love &c.

So now Friends none to vex & quench, or give y^e Spirit of God; for the Apos= tle saw some in his day going from y^e Light Spirit & Gospel, y^e Power of God, & went into y^e Apostasie; therefore come again to y^e Spirit & Truth y^t leads out of the Apostasie, & so come to Christ; for as y^e Law was given by Moses in y^e Old Testament, so Grace & Truth came by Jesus Christ in ye New; In ye Old Testament they had their Offerings of ye Blood of Bulls, Goats, Rams, & Tythes, Swearing Temple, & all those Outward things: : But in ye New Testament ye Lamb Christ Jesus Offered up himself for all; & Said freely you have received freely give: Swear not at all; & hath abolished those Outward things; so there is a distinction between ye Old Covenant & ye New.

Now as there was a going into ye Apostasie from ye Light, & Grace, & Truth, & Spirit of God in ye Inward parts, So there must be a coming again to ye Grace & Truth y^t is come by Jesus ye Second Adam, & not by ye first Adam if they come out of ye Apostasie; so every Man & Woman must come to this Grace which must be their Teacher; every man come to Jesus from whom they have it; look to him y^t keeps your Eyes, Ears, & Hearts up to himself: But some will say this a Common Grace, a natural Grace, & such Talk.

How can this be a Com^{m}on or Natural Grace? The Grace of God y^t brings Salvation hath appeared unto all Mankind: The Grace & favour of God to all Mankind; If all men do not Receive this Grace how can they come into ye Favour of God? If this be a Naturall & Common Grace y^n they are in ye Naturall Estats, & ye Naturall Man perceives not the things of God; Nay y^t is a Speciall Grace y^t brings Salvation, this is y^t wch turns every Man & Womans eye to Jesus y^t Receives it ye Second Adam ye Lord from Heaven to his Light, Grace, & Truth from Death, & Darkness, y^t thereby in him all may be setled, & grow in Grace, yea from Grace to Grace, & may encrease; So here in this & by this all is kept in ye sence & feeling of ye Love of God wch ye Grace, Truth, Spirit, & Power y^t comes from Jesus Christ, & so

comes from God; This keeps every Mans Eye out of old Adam: keeps out of all Carnall
Worships, Religions, & Fellowships & keeps up to him y^t is Worshipped in ye Spirit
& Truth; & in ye true Worship y^t ye Devil is out of; This is ye standing pure
path; here doth every Man & Woman by ye Grace, Truth, & Spirit, keep their Eye
to Jesus, so to God through him; by this comes every Man & Woman to know
Christ Jesus their Rock & Foundation, & come to be established, & setled on him y^e
Rock over all other Foundations in ye World: So now Friends ye Love of God,
his blessing is come for every Man & Woman y^t Receives it comes to know him
to Reigne in his Grace & Truth, Light, & Life, & Gospel wch is ye Power of God;
every Man & Woman in it Eye him, & he in you dwelling in you, & you in him, such
are sound Christians in Substance & in deed; & therefore prove your selves as y^e
Apostle saith know you not your own selves how y^t Jesus Christ is in you except
you be Reprobates; & If he be in you here is ye substance of ye Tipes, Figures, &
Shadows: Here is a setled Rest, & Sabbath in Christ Jesus for all his Believers in
his Light: O Glory to God for ever.

    For saith ye Apostle look unto Jesus ye Author & Finisher of your Faith,
So now Friends he being ye Author & Finisher of your Faith every Man & Woman
must Receive it from him, & not from Old Adam nor none of his Sons, & Daughters
O let him come into your Hearts y^t came from y^e bosome of y^e Father let him have
Room: w^t Room had he formerly but in y^e Manger among y^e Outward Professing
Jews; let him have Room in your Hearts; For he has but a little Room in y^e Profes=
=sors without Possession, who will not receive his Light, for he hath no Room in y^t
Proud Lifty mind, therefore let him have y^e Reign in you; If he be not in you w^t
is all talk of Religion good for? for If Christ be not wth in, Man is Seperate
from God, from y^e Emmanuel God wth us; & in y^t Estate Man doth not Witness
Peace wth God; but If Christ be known wth in here will be no Reprobate, but
stability; he being wth in, y^t bruises ye Head of ye Serpent.

    Therefore to him y^t is ye God of all Power I shall commit & commend you,
& to ye Word of his Grace to establish you upon Christ Jesus & Therefore every Man
& Woman come to know y^t you have Received his Faith, his Spirit, his Grace his Life,
his Light, & Truth growing up in Christ from whence this comes y^t bruises ye Head
of ye Serpent & Destroys him & his Works; who is above all, Glory to God for ever;
He was & he is & will be to all Eternity: He is a Prophet to open to his People; A.
Bishop to Oversee you: a Priest to sanctifie; a King to Rule & Reign in your heart
by Faith, exercising his Offices among you; so y^t you may all come to sit down in
him in the Heavenly Places in Christ Jesus: If you want Life, Salvation, Wisdome,
Righteousness, Peace, he is ye Treasure, So come to ye Treasure; he was a Priest,
& Prophet, & he is, & will be forevermore to all his believers in his Light; And as
every one has Received Christ Jesus so to Walk in him; tis not talking only but
walking in Christ Jesus; not only to talk of the Light but walk in it, many may
talk of Grace & Truth, but walk in unrighteousness, & unholyness. God is Righteous,
& Holy, who will Judge such; to whom I leave you, & y^t People may Live to God
& Receive ye good things, & blessings that come from God through Jesus Christ, Let

your eye be to him from whom you Receive Life, from whom you Receive Grace,
& Faith, Who is your Redeemer, by which Grace, & Faith your Hearts come to be
purified from dead Works to serve ye Living God; This is he wch Destroyes ye Devil
& his Works; In this Faith ye Holy men of God did believe in wch they pleased God,
Whereas tis said Heb.11. They all Dyed in ye Faith, not Receiving ye Promises;
So they all Dyed in y^t wch came from God; they Dyed in y^t wch Pleased God; & in
y^t wch they had access to him, & in which is ye Unity in ye Faith of Gods Elect,
wch leads out of all ye bad wayes of old Adam; This is ye Faith y^t Jesus Christ
is ye Author, & Finisher of ye Second Adam: this brings People to an Inward
Intire Life, out of all y^t wch will fade away to a Holy Faith, a Holy Life, into
a pure, divine, precious Unity, & so to have access to ye Pure Holy God: in wch you
have life, & salvation, & in wch Faith you Please God.

    So God hath ye Glory who is over all from Everlasting to Everlasting
        blessed for evermore

                                      G. F.

[16]G F^s Prayer
Dear Friends & Brethren: as I was at Prayer in my Chamber upon ye 23:12th Month
1678. & making Interecssion [sic] to ye Lord for Friends his People, y^t ye Lord would be
pleased to preserve them from this Rough, & Foul Spirit y^t was risen up: & ye Lord did
Answer me in my Prayer y^t this Spirit was Risen up for ye Tryall of his People In ye Life,
& Light, & Power, & Grace, & Truth, & I saw more y^n can be Expressed in Words: for it was
Risen to try y^m, & y^t they might keep in ye Power of ye Lord, as in their Habitations:
And so w^n ye Lord hath tried his People, & their Singleness to him, & When this Spirit
hath spent its strength, & gone ye Way of all y^t has Risen before it y^n they may see
how all things work together for good to y^m y^t Love God: And therefore stand fast in y^e
Liberty wherewith Christ hath made you free in his Light, Grace, & Truth, & Power, &
Spirit, & Faith, to Christ, from whence it comes: Christ yor Rock, & Foundation y^t
cannot be shaken, & in whom is this Election, Life, & Salvation so y^t all may stand
to Christ their Lord & Master to be Ordered by him with his Glorious Gospel wch is
not of Man but from Heaven.

    For I saw all Friends as If they were bedewed from Heaven, & they
sate as in a Valley, & wet wth ye dew of Life, & ye other hard dead Spirit was
floating atop wth Words of Truth; wch Spirit is for ye Triall of his People, of their
standing singly in ye Life to god upon their own Foundation. And so as I was at Prayer y^e
    Lord
Answered me that this Spirit of J S & J W, & their company was Raised up for ye Triall of
Friends their standing to God for it was High, & Friends was low in ye Power &
Spirit of God & wet with his dew, & sate in ye Valley, & will Rise w^n their High
will Fall, & therefore Friends are to stand to God.

                                        G. F.

---

    16. A printed version of this prayer is found in *A Vision concerning the Mischievous Separation among Friends in Old England* (Philadelphia: William Bradford), 1692, 3-4.

The Truth is above all, & Will stand over all yᵐ yᵗ hate it, who Labour in
vain against it, & will bring their Old house on their own Head in great
Trouble, & in their Winter, & cold Weather, when that their house is down,
& their Religion is Frozen, & their Rivers dried up, & their husks gone, &
yᵉ Swine begin to cry about their Plantations, & yᵉ Vermine run up & down
their Old Rubbish, & their sparks & Candles ₐare gone out, & hail, & storm lighteth
upon yᵉ head of yᵉ Wicked, yⁿ Woe be to Gog & Magog who hath no covering.
In christ you have Peace, In yᵉ world you have trouble, In Christ you have Peace,
In yᵉ World you have trouble, No Peace wᵗʰ God but in yᵉ Light, No Peace wᵗʰ God but
in yᵉ Covenant of Light, wᵗʰ out is Trouble Amen.

G. F.

Dear Friends be faithfull in yᵉ Service of God, & mind yᵉ Lords business; be diligent,
& bring yᵉ Power of yᵉ Lord over all those yᵗ have gain said it; and all you yᵗ be
faithful go to visit yᵐ all yᵗ have been Convinced from house to house, that if it
be possible you may not leave a hoof in Egypt: And so every one go seek yᵉ Lost
sheep: & bring him home on your back to yᵉ fold, & there will be more Joy of yᵗ
one sheep yⁿ of yᵉ ninety nine in yᵉ fold.

G. F.

[17]You may Read this in your Monthly, Quarterly, & Yearly Meetings.
from our Womens County Meeting in **Lancashire** to be
dispersed abroad among yᵉ Womens Meetings every where
Dear Sisters. In yᵉ blessed unity in yᵉ Spirit of Grace, our Souls salute you
who are Sanctified in Christ Jesus, & called to be Saints, who are of yᵉ true &
Royal Offspring of Christ Jesus, who is yᵉ Root & Offspring of David, & who
is yᵉ Resurrection & yᵉ Life of all yᵉ Saints in Light.

To you yᵗ [that] are of yᵉ true seed of yᵉ Promise of God in yᵉ beginning yᵗ was to
bruise yᵉ Serpents Head, & wᶜʰ is fulfilled in Christ Jesus, of wᶜʰ we are made pertakers,
wᶜʰ is yᵉ Seed yᵉ Promise is to, wᶜʰ yᵉ Apostle spoke of & said God sent forth his
Son made of a Woman, made under yᵉ Law to Redeem yᵐ yᵗ were under the Law
yᵗ we might Receive yᵉ Adoption &c. Gal. 4.4.

To you all every where, where this may come is this written yᵗ in this
blessed Seed wᶜʰ hath yᵉ Promise of yᵉ Eternal God annexed yᵗ he should bruise
yᵉ Serpents Head, & yᵗ in this Seed you all Live & dwell in yᵉ sensible feeling
thereof; in wᶜʰ Seed all Nations of yᵉ Earth is blessed.

That so we may be all Helps Meet for God in yᵉ Restoration, & Co=heirs
wᵗʰ Christ Jesus, who hath purchased us wᵗʰ his precious blood, & hath washed us,
& Loved us, who is no Respecter of Persons: but hath a care, & regard unto all; yᵉ
weak as well as the strong. yᵗ he may have yᵉ Glory of his own Work, who treadeth
yᵉ Wine-press alone.

And yᵗ every particular of us may be ready & willing to answer wᵗ [what] yᵉ Lord
Requires of us in our several places, & Conditions.

17. The exhortatory opening of this section suggests that it came as an admonition from London
Yearly Meeting.

For as many of us as are Baptized into Christ have put on Christ; for we are all ye Children of God by Faith in Christ Jesus; where there is neither Male nor Female &c, but we are all one in Christ Jesus.

And so being in Christ Jesus we are all Abrahams Seed & Heirs according to y^e Promise: not of y^e Bond-woman but of the free Jerusalem from above, wch is y^e Mother if us all.

And so here is our Possession, & Inheritance; y^t every Faithful Mem= =ber of us may claim a Right unto, & an Interest in: y^t all the Powers of Darkness, nor all the Enmity of y^e Old Serpent (whose Head is coming to be bruised) can never Seperate us from, tho he may twine, & twist, & Rage, & Storm y^t his Power shuld be taken from him, but all to no purpose: for y^e Word of ye Eternal God y^t endureth for ever stands upon his Head that the Seed of the Woman should bruise the Serpents Head.

And this is fulfilled, & fulfilling in this ye Day of ye Lords Power, & of the Restoration, & Redemption of his Seed, & Body wch is his Church; wch is coming out of the Wilderness leaning on her beloved; wch is coming in his Power & Great Glory, tho in the Clouds; and every Eye y^t is open sees him; & every Ear y^t is unstopped hears him, & every understanding, & Heart y^t is Enlightened & opened, is Converted, & healed in this Glorious Day, Praise to ye Highest.

So here is the Blessed Image of ye Living God Restored again, in wch he made y^m Male, & Female in the beginning; & in this his own Image. God Blessed y^m both, & said unto y^m Increase & Multiply, & Replenish y^e Earth & subdue it, & have dominion over y^e Fish of y^e Sea, & have dominion over y^e Fowls of y^e Air, And have dominion over y^e Beasts, & over y^e Cattell, & over y^e Earth: & over ever creep= =ing thing upon y^e Face of y^e Earth. & in this Dominion & Power y^e Lord God is esta= blishing his own seed in y^e Male, & in y^e Female over y^e Head of y^e Serpent, & over his Seed, & Power.

And he makes no difference in the Seed between the Male & y^e Female, as Christ saith Matth. 19.4.6. y^t he y^t made y^m in y^e beginning made y^m Male & Female; they were both in y^e work of God in ye Beginning; & so in ye Restoration.

But it is ye Work of ye Old Serpent to put y^m out of ye Work of God as he did, in ye Beginning, Tempt y^m to Sin & transgression, & Disobedience; so he would still keep y^m there, & make a difference, & keep a Superiority, one over another, y^t Christ ye Head should not Rule in Male & Female, & so keep y^m in Bondage, & in slavery, & in difference, & dissension one wth another, & y^n they are fit for his Tentations.

But ye Lord God is coming to destroy this Tongue of ye Egyptian Sea, & to smite it in ye Seven Strams thereof; as in Isai. 11.15. And to make all as a Plain before him: & he will level down, & lay low all the loftiness of Man, & ye Harctiness of Men shall be made low, So y^t ye Lord alone will be exalted in his own Seed & Power in Male & Female in this his day. Isai. 2.17.

And therefore all dearly beloved Friends & Sisters, let us every one be bold, & Valiant, & Faithful, & diligent for y^e Lords everlasting Truth upon y^e Earth in our Day, & Generation: y^t as good stewards we may give a good account unto God of his mani=

fold Graces, y^t we have Received, & do receive of him & from him daily.

And y^t as we have a Cloud of Witnesses y^t is gone before us wch y^e Scriptures of Truth Testifie of that hath Born Witness to his Eternall Truth, & hath been made partakers of the Divine. Blessings, favours, & Graces of Almighty God.

And so God is the same to us in our age & Generation as he was to y^m in their day & Age; we being Taught & led, & Guided by ye same Eternal Spirit as they were wch proceeds from ye Father & ye Son.

So let none be weary, nor faint in their minds, but let all be given up faithfully to ye Leading & Guiding of ye good Spirit of ye Living God: y^t by it every one may know freedome & Rede^{m}ption from ye Bondage of Corruption: wch Spirit ye Lord is Powring forth in these last dayes upon Sons & Daughters, Servants & Handmaidens, so y^t ye General Universal Love of Almighty God is descending, & pouring upon all Flesh in this his Day of Grace, even as he did w^n [when] he bid y^m wait at Jerusalem to Receive Power from on high w^n they were all gather together in an upper Room: & continued wth one Accord, Praying & Making Supplication wth ye Women, & Mary ye Mother of Jesus, & wth his Brethren. Act.1.14.

And ye Holy Ghost was poured upon y^m so plentifully y^t ye Multitude were all amazed, but Peter stood up to witness ye fulfulling of w^t was spoken by ye Prophet Joel, y^t God would pour out of his Spirit upon all Flesh: & your Sons & Daughters shall Prophesie, & on my Servants, & on my Handmaids will I pour out of my Spirit in those dayes, & they shall Prophesie Acts 2.17.19. Here Peter bears witness to ye same Truth & pouring forth .of ye same Spirit in y^t day wch we are Living Witnesses of in this our Day Praises to ye Lord for ever.

So all Dear Friends, & Sisters, make full proof of ye Gift of God y^t is in you & neglect it not in this your day & Generation, but y^t you may be helps meet in the Restoration, & Resurrection of y^e body of Christ wch is his Church, & y^t every one may know their place, & calling therein as y^e Godly Women under y^e Law did.

For all y^t were wise in Heart put their hand to y^e work about y^e Taber= =nacle & all the Women whose Hearts stirred y^m up in wisdome had their several place to work in about y^e Tabernacle as well as y^e Men; for all y^e Congregation of y^e Children of Israel, every one both Men & Women, whose Spirit was made willing they brought y^e Lords Offering to y^e Work of y^e Tabernacle as yo may Read in Exodus [35.?] 25.26.

And likewise Miriam ye Prophetess y^e Sister of Aaron took a Timbrel in her hand & all the Women went out after her in Triumph, & singing Praises to y^e Lord who by his mighty Power had overthrown Pharaoh and his host in the Red Sea. Exod. 15.20.21.

And there was an assembly of Women wch Assembled at y^e door of y^e Taber= -nacle of y^e Congregation. Exod. 38.8.

And likewise Hannah w^n she had weaned her Son Samuel took him & went up to y^e House of y^e Lord, & took wth her three Bullocks, one Ephah, & a Bottle of wine & slew one Bullock, & brought the Child to Eli & offered him up to y^e Lord, & sayd, for this Child, I have prayed, & ye Lord hath given me my portion which I asked of him.

as you may see 1Samu. 24.25.26.27. And this Child Samuel did Minister unto yᵉ
Lord before Eli yᵉ Priest.

And Hannah Prayed: & O yᵉ Gracious words, & Prayer that proceeded out
of her mouth by yᵉ Powerful demonstration of yᵉ Eternal Spirit, & yᵉ Power of Almighty God, in her! 1 Sam 2.1 to 11. wᶜʰ all yᵉ Adversaries & Gain sayers against Womens
Meetings is not able to gain say. nor resist.

Therefore let all mouths be stopped wᶜʰ would limit the Spirit of yᵉ Lord
God in Male, or Female wᶜʰ he hath not limitted. But yᵉ Lord hath regard unto & takes
notice of yᵉ Women, & despises yᵐ not.

And you may Read in Isaiah 32. Where yᵉ Kingdome of Christ Jesus is
Prophesied of, Behold a King shall Reign in Righteousness, & Princes shall Rule in
Judgment; & yᵉ Eyes of yᵐ yᵗ see shall not be dimm, & yᵉ Ears of yᵐ yᵗ Hear shall hear=
ken, & the Heart also of the Rash shall understand knowledge, and yᵉ Tongue of the
Stammerer shall be ready to speak plainly.

Here is yᵉ Glorious Work of yᵉ Lord Prophesied of; & here yᵉ Lord calls.
Rise up yᵉ Women yᵗ are at ease, hear my voice ye careless Daughters, give ear to my
Speech, many dayes & years shall ye be troubled, ye careless Women, for yᵉ Vintage
shall fail, yᵉ gathering shall not come: Tremble ye Women yᵗ are at ease; be troubled
ye careless ones: strip ye & make ye bare; gird sackcloth upon your Loyns; they shall
lament for yᵉ teats, for yᵉ Pleasant Fields, & for yᵉ Fruitful Vines (see here what a
Requiring, or Ariel charge yᵉ Lord layes upon yᵉ Women) until yᵉ Spirit be poured
upon us from on high; & yᵉ Wilderness be a fruit field; & yᵉ work of Righteousness
shall be peace, & yᵉ effect of Righteousness quietness, & assurance for ever. Here yᵉ Lord
had a care & regard to yᵉ Women as well as yᵉ Men and have a Blessing, & a Mer=
-cie in store for yᵐ.

And also in Jeremiah 9ᵗʰ Chapt. throughout where yᵉ Lord brought destruc-
-tion, & wo & misery upon yᵉ Jews, & yᵉ destruction of Jerusalem, because they had for=
=saken yᵉ Law of yᵉ Lord. wᶜʰ he had set before yᵐ, & disobeyed his Voice, & walked
not therein, I will scatter yᵐ among yᵉ Heathen saith yᵉ Lord; & I will send a sword
amongst yᵐ till I have consumed yᵐ.

More over thus saith yᵉ Lord call for yᵉ mourning Womon yᵗ they
may come; for a Voice of Mourning is heard out of Zion; yet hear yᵉ Word of yᵉ
Lord O Ye Women, & let your Ear Receive the Word of his Month; & Teach your
Daughter. Waiting, & every one her Neig[h]bour Lamentation for Death is come up
into our Windows, & is entred into our Palaces, to cut off yᵉ Children from wᵗʰ out, & yᵉ
young from yᵉ Streets; speak thus saith yᵉ Lord yᵉ Carcases of Men shall fall as Dung
upon yᵉ Open field, & as yᵉ handful after the Harvest Man, & none shall gather yᵐ·

Here yᵉ Women had yᵉ Word of yᵉ Lord to speak to yᵉ Men; & here yᵉ Lord
makes use, & had a Service for yᵉ Women yᵗ they should Speak his Word from his mouth
in this dreadful & terrible day.

And also thus saith yᵉ Lord, let not yᵉ Wise Men Glory in his Wisdome,
neither let yᵉ mighty Man Glory in his Might, nor let yᵉ Rich man Glory in his
Riches; but let him yᵗ glorieth Glory in this yᵗ he understandeth & knoweth me yᵗ I am

yᵉ Lord wᶜʰ exerciseth Loving Kindness, Judgment & Righteousness in yᵉ Earth, for in these things I do delight saith yᵉ Lord.

Here yᵉ Lord clearly manifesteth yᵗ he delights in yᵉ knowledge of himself, & of his Righteousness, & Judgment, & Loving kindness, & this he hath a Regard unto both in Man & in Woman, & not in Wise, nor mighty, nor Rich Men.

And In Micah 2.9.10. The Lord saith yᵉ Women of my People have yᵉ cast out from their Pleasant Houses, & from their Children have yᵉ taken away my Glory; rise yᵉ and depart, for this is not your Rest because it is polluted; it shall destroy you even wᵗʰ a sore destruction. &c.

And Christ Jesus in yᵉ days of his Flesh had a dear & tender care, & Re -gard unto Woman, who Received many Gracious blessings, & favours from him; he de- spised not yᵉ Woman of Canaan wⁿ she came unto him for her Daughter yᵗ was vexed wᵗʰ a Devil wⁿ she Worshipped him; & said Lord help me – And wⁿ he saw her Faith he said Woman great is thy Faith, as in Mat.15.

And also yᵉ Woman of Samaria in John 4. Christ Jesus directed her to yᵉ gift of God, & told her whosoever drinketh of yᵉ Water yᵗ he giveth should never thirst but yᵉ water yᵗ he did give should be in her a Well springing up to Eternal Life. So he Reasoned & spoke wᵗʰ her so long till he opened her understanding so yᵗ she perceived yᵗ he was a Prophet.

But Jesus saith unto her Woman believe me (so here you may see yᵉ mind of Christ was yᵗ yᵉ Woman should Believe his Doctrine yᵗ he yⁿ spoke unto her) yᵉ Hour cometh wⁿ yᵉ shall neither in this mountain, nor yet at Jerusalem Worship yᵉ Father; but yᵉ Hour cometh & now is wⁿ yᵉ true worshipers shall wor- ship yᵉ Father in Spirit & in Truth; God is a Spirit, & they yᵗ worship him must Worship him in Spirit & in Truth. &c.

The Woman said unto him, I know yᵗ Messias commeth yᵗ is called Christ; Wⁿ he cometh he will tell us all things – **Jesus** saith unto her I yᵗ speak unto thee am hee.

See wᵗ Love, & plainness he manifested unto this Woman not despising her weakness, nor under valueing her, but he spoke yᵉ plain Everlasting Truth unto her; & set up yᵗ Worship in his own Spirit unto her there; wᶜʰ Remains, & will remain for ever: glorious Praises to his Holy Name for evermore.

And all those Women yᵗ he healed. As Peters Wifes Mother wᶜʰ he healed of a fever; & yᵉ Woman yᵗ had an Issue of Blood; & certain Women yᵗ had been healed of Evil Spirits: & Infirmities; Mary Called Magdalene; out of whom he had cast out Seven Devils; & Joanna yᵉ Wife of Chusa Herods Steward; and Susannah, & many others wᶜʰ ministered unto him of their Substance.

And yᵉ Woman yᵗ had yᵉ Alablaster Box. of Precious Oyntment wash- ed his feet & wiped yᵐ wᵗʰ yᵉ hair of her Head; all these wᵗʰ many more Lament him (as yᵉ Scriptures mention) yᵗ had received precious favours, & blessings from him they all Lamented him as they led him away to be Crucified, & all yᵉ People, & Women Followed him, & bewailed him as they led him away; But Jesus turned unto yᵐ & said, Daughters of Jerusalem weep not for me, but weep for your selves, &

your Children. And yᵉ Women yᵗ followed him from Galilee followed after, & beheld yᵉ Sepulcʰre, & how his body was layd; & they Returned, & prepared spices, & Oyntments; & they Rested yᵉ Sabbaoth, as you may see in Luke 23 Chap.

And upon yᵉ first day of yᵉ Week very early in yᵉ Morning they came unto yᵉ Sepulchre (to wit yᵉ Women) bringing their Spices wᶜʰ they had Prepared, & certain others wᵗʰ yᵐ, & they found yᵉ stone rolled away from yᵉ Sepulchre; & they entred in & found not yᵉ body of yᵉ Lord Jesus.

And it came to pass as they were much perplexed, behold Two Men stood by yᵐ in shining Garments: & as they were afraid, & bowed down their faces to yᵉ Earth they said unto yᵐ, why seek ye yᵗ Living among yᵉ Dead ? He is not here, but is Risen — Remember how he spake unto you wⁿ he was yet in Galilee saying yᵉ Son of Man must be delivered into yᵉ Hands of Sin =ful Men, & be Crucified, & yᵉ third day Rise again, & they Remembred his Words; & Returned from yᵉ Sepulchre, & told all these things unto yᵉ Eleven, & to all yᵉ Rest; It was Mary Magdalene, & Joanna, & Mary yᵉ Mother of James, & other Women yᵗ were wᵗʰ yᵐ wᶜʰ told these things unto yᵉ Apostles, & their words seemed unto yᵐ as [?]ole Tales, & they believed yᵐ not as you may see in Luke 2.4. & Mark 15.40.41. & Matth. 27.35. & Matth. 28.5 So these Women were yᵉ first Preachers of yᵉ Resurrecti= =on of Jesus.

And Jesus himself spoke wᵗʰ Mary before he was ascended unto his Father & said unto her go unto my Brethren; & say unto yᵐ I ascend to my Father & your Father, & to my God, & your God.

And Mary Magdalene came & told yᵉ disciples yᵗ she had seen yᵉ Lord, & yᵗ he had spoken these things unto her.

So here yᵉ Lord Jesus Christ sends his first Message of his Resurrec= =tion by Women unto his own Disciples, & they were faithful unto him, & did his Message, & yet they could hardly be Believed.

And Paul & Silas wᶜʰ was sent forth by yᵉ Apostles, & Elders, & Brethren of yᵉ Church wᵗʰ yᵉ Decrees yᵗ were Ordained of yᵉ Apostles & Elders at Jerusalem for yᵉ Churches to keep; & so were yᵉ Churches established in yᵉ Faith, & Increased in Number daily. &c

And this same Paul & Silas who had yᵉ Decrees went to yᵉ place where Prayer was wont to be made, & sate down & spoke to yᵉ Women which Resorted as in Acts. 16.

So these yᵗ were chosen Men of yᵉ Apostles & Elders, & yᵉ Whole Church wⁿ they were assembled together, who had their Letters & Decrees for yᵉ Churches to Keep; & as they went through the Cities they deliverd yᵉ Decrees, so established yᵉ Churches in yᵉ Faith: And tho yᵉ Holy Ghost Suffered yᵐ not to Preach at Asia nor Bithinia, yet they went among yᵉ Women as well as yᵉ Men

So we having a Cloud of Witnesses of yᵉ Order of yᵉ Gospel, & of yᵉ good Works, & Charitable practises wᶜʰ is Multiplyed in the Scriptures, & yᵉ Practise of yᵉ Saints in Light in yᵉ Primitives times, Women as well as Men yᵗ is gone before us, we may be encouraged in yᵉ Lords name, Power & Spirit to follow their Example, & Practises.

And having ye same Rule wch is in Christ Jesus where neither Circum
cision, nor uncircumcision availeth but a New Creature; & as many as walk according
to & in this Rule, Peace be unto y^m, & Mercy upon ye Israel of God.

And as y^t Apostle saith let us Press forward towards ye mark for ye price of y^e
high calling of God in Christ Jesus.

And let us therefore as many as be perfect be thus minded, & if in any
thing we be otherwise minded, God shall Revoal even this unto us; Nevertheless
where unto we have already attained let us walk by ye same Rule, & mind ye same thing.

And let us come into our practise, & into our possession of our portions,
& Inheritances y^t we have Received from ye Lord.

And let us Stand Faithfull & True witnesses for him in our day again^st
all deceit & Wickedness.

And let us meet together & kept our Womens Meeting in ye Name &
Power, & Fear of ye Lord Jesus whose Servants, & Handmaids we are, & in ye good
Order of ye Gospel Meet.

1   And first for ye Women of every Monthly Meeting where ye Mens
Monthly Meeting is established; Let ye Women likewise of every Monthly Meeting
Meet together to wait upon ye Lord, & hearken w^t ye Lord will say unto y^m, & to know
his mind & Will, & be ready to obey & Answer him in every Motion of his Eternal Spirit,
and Power.

2   And also to make enquiry into all your several Particular Meetings
that belongs to your Monthly Meeting if they be any y^t walks disorderly (as doth
not to become ye Gospel) or lightly, or wantonly, or y^t is not of a good Report, y^n to
send to y^m as you are Ordered by y^e Power of God in y^e Meeting wch is y^e Authority
of it, to Admonish & exhort y^m, & to bring y^m to Judge & Condemn w^t hath been
by y^m done or Acted contrary to y^e Truth.

3   And If any transgression or action y^t hath been done among Wo=
men, or Maids y^t hath done any thing y^t hath been more Publick, & y^t hath got into
y^e Word; or y^t hath been a Publick offence amongst Friends; y^n let y^m bring in a Paper
of Condemnation to be Published as far as y^e offence hath gone, & y^n to be Recorded in a
Booke.

4   And if there be any that goes out to Marry wth ye Priests, or Joyneth in
Marriage wth ye World, & doth not obey ye Order of ye Gospel as it is established among
Friends; Then for ye Womens Monthly Meeting to send to y^m to Reprove y^m, & to bear
their Testimony against their acting contrary to ye Truth, & If they come to
Repentance, & sorrow for their offence, & have a desire to come amongst Friends
again, before they can be Received they must bring in a Paper of Condemnation, &
Repentance, and Judgment of their action, wch must be Recorded in Friends Book.
And also carry a coppy of y^t Paper to ye Priest y^t Married y^m, & Judge, & Condemn, & deny
y^t Action before him, or any of ye World before whom it hath come.

And Dear Sisters it is a Duty Incumbent upon us to look into our
Families, & to prevent our Children of Runing into ye World for Husbands or for
Wives, & so to ye Priests: for you know before ye Womens Meetings were set up many
have done so wch brought dishonour both to God, & upon his Truth, & People.

Therefore it is our Duty & care to prevent such things in yᵉ Power &
Wisdome of God; & to see yᵗ our Children are trained up in yᵉ Fear of God in yᵉ
New Covenant: for yᵉ Jews were to train their Children up in yᵉ Old: For you
know yᵗ we are much in our Families amongst our Children, Maids, & Servants,
& may see more into their Inclinations yⁿ yᵉ Men : And so see yᵗ none Indulge any to
Loosness & Evil, but Restrain it. For you see wᵗ became of Old **Eli**, & his Family
for not Restraining his Children.

5　　　And also all Friends yᵗ keep in yᵉ Power of God & in Faithfull Obedience
to yᵉ Truth yᵗ according to yᵉ Order of yᵉ Gospel yᵗ is Established, yᵗ they bring
their Marriage twice to yᵉ Womens Meeting & twice to yᵉ Mens.

And also all Friends in their Womens Monthly & Particular Meetings yᵗ

The first time they are come to yᵉ Womens Meeting yᵗ yᵉ Women of yᵉ Meeting
do examine both yᵉ Man yᵉ Woman yᵗ they be clear & free from all other Persons,
& that they have their Parents, & Friends, & Relations Consent.

And yᵉ enquiry be made of their cleernesss in each Particular Meeting wᶜʰ
they belong to before their next appearance in yᵉ Womens Meeting.

And If nothing be found but yᵗ they come in cleerness to yᵉ Next Monthly
Meeting yⁿ they proceed according to yᵉ Order of yᵉ Gospel, & Perfect their Marriage in
yᵉ Meeting of Friends, as Friends wᶜʰ they belong to sees it convenient.

But If any thing be found yᵗ they are not cleer but yᵗ others layes challenge
or charge to yᵐ either by promise or otherwise. That yⁿ they do not proceed till they
have given satisfaction both to yᵉ Party's & Friends concerning yᵗ matter according to yᵉ
Order of yᵉ Gospel; And yᵗ If any thing be amiss concerning yᵉ Woman yᵗ yᵉ Woman
Examine it, & look into it, wᶜʰ may not be so proper f [*sic*] yᵉ Men.

6　　　And likewise yᵉ Women of yᵉ Monthly Meetings take care & oversight of
all yᵉ Women yᵗ belongs to their several Particular Meetings yᵗ they bring in their
Testimonies for yᵉ Lord, & his Truth against Tythes, & Hireling Priests once every
Year; since yᵉ Priest claims & challenges a Tythe wᶜʰ belongs to Women to pay as well as
Men, not only for Widdows, but for yᵐ yᵗ have Husbands: as Pigs & Geese, Hens, & Eggs,
Hemp, & Flax, Wooll & Lambs, all wᶜʰ Women may have a hand in.

So it concerns yᵉ Womens Meetings to look strictly through every Parti=
cular Meeting yᵗ every Woman bring their Testimony against Tythes, & yᵗ those
Testimonies be Recorded in yᵉ Quarterly, or half years book once every Year.

7　　　And yᵗ every Monthly Meeting give timely Notice to every Particular
Meeting yᵗ they make ready their Testimonies against Tythes to be brought in at
their Qurterly or half years Meeting as aforesaid. That so all Hearts, & Consciences may
be kept cleer, clean, & sweet to our Precious High Priest of our Profession Christ Jesus.
who is yᵉ Author of our Faith yᵗ becomes us; who Is Holy, & Harmless, & undefiled, &
Seperate from Sinners, Who is made higher yⁿ yᵉ Heavens (Christ Jesus) Who is yᵉ Mi=
nister of yᵉ Sanctuary, & of yᵉ True Tabernacle which God hath Pitched, & not Man;
He is our Everlasting High Priest forever. And so in him we deny all other
Priests both in the time of yᵉ Law & Since yᵗ takes Tithes.

8　　　And also all Friends in their Womens Monthly & Particular Meetings yᵗ
they take speciall care for the Poor & for all those yᵗ stand in need, yᵗ there be no want,
nor suffering for outward things amongst the People of God, for yᵉ Earth is yᵉ Lords,

& y^e fulness of it, & his People is his Portion, & y^e Lot of his Inheritance, & he gives freely & Liberally unto all & upbraids none.

So it Concerns all y^t Fear y^e Lord y^t he hath endued wth an Outward Substance y^t they be free, & Liberal in their Hearts to any y^t stand in need, but espe= cially as y^e Apostle saith to y^e Houshold of Faith.

And so let care be taken for y^e Poor, & Widdows y^t hath young Children y^t they be Relieved & helped till they be able, & fit to be put out Apprentices, or Servants.

And all y^e sick, & weak, & Infirm, or Aged, and Widdows, & fatherless y^t they be looked after, & helped, & Relieved in every Particular Meeting either wth Clothes, or Maintenance, or w^t they stand in need of; So y^t in all things ye Lord may be Glorified, & Honoured; so y^t there be no want, nor Suffering in ye House of God, who loves a cheerfull giver.

9   Also let care be taken y^t every Particular Womens Monethly Meeting have a Book to set down, & Record their businesses & Passages in y^t is done or agreed upon in every Monthly Meeting, or any Service y^t any y^t any [sic] is to go upon; let y^t Book be Read ye Next Monthly Meeting, & see y^t ye business be performed according to what was Ordered.

And also y^t ye Collections be set down in ye Book; & ye Receipts & Disbursments of every Particular Meeting be set down in their Booke & Read at their Womens Monthly Meeting; y^t every Particular Meeting may see & know how their Collections are Disbursed.

And y^t Some Honest Faithful Woman or Women Friends y^t can Read & write keep ye Book & Receive ye Collections; & give a just & true Accont in ye Book of ye Disbursments of y^m according as ye Meeting shall Order, wch must be Read every monthly Meeting; & so give notice w^t is in ye Stock, & w^n it is near out, to give notice y^t it may be supplied.

10   And Likewise y^t there be a General Book in every County for their Quarterly or half years Womens Meeting.

And y^t there come & appear at ye Quarterly Meeting, some (or as many as can conveniently) of every Monthly & Particular Meeting of their Whole County; & y^t Enquiry be made at ye Quarterly Meeting, or Half years Meeting whether there be some of every Montly Meeting; & one or more of every Particular Meeting.

And y^t ye Quarterly Meeting set down ye name of every Particular Meeting in ye Book y^t is wthin, or Pertains to ye Whole County.

And y^t at every Quarterly Meeting they call over every Monthly, & Particular Meeting to see y^t some of every Meeting be there.

And y^t they bring in every Particular Womans Testimony against Tythes. From every Particular Meeting of cleerness of their Meetings from all ye things before Mentioned; & y^t they do all walk & act as becomes ye Gospel.

And y^t every Particular Meetings Testimonies be Recorded as ye Meetings stand severally in y^e Quarterly Booke.

And y^t all other businesses as is there presented or done y^t day may be Recorded in y^t Book.

And so here in y^e Power & y^e Spirit of y^e Lord God Women come to be

Co-heirs; & Fellow Labourers in yᵉ Gospel as it was in yᵉ Apostles dayes; Who Intrea-
=ted ₐʰⁱˢ true Yoke-Fellow to help those Women yᵗ Laboured wᵗʰ him in yᵉ Gospel. Philip. 4:3.

And in his first Epistle to Timothy 5.3. he Exhorted yᵗ Elder Woman yᵗ they
should be as Mothers, & yᵉ Younger as Sisters wᵗʰ all Purity.

And in Titus. 2.3 The Aged Women likewise yᵗ they be as becometh
Holyness, & Teachers of Good things; And yᵗ they Teach yᵉ Younger Women to be sober,
to Love their Husbands, to Love their Children, to be discreet, Chast keepers at home;
Good, Obedient to their own husbands yᵗ yᵉ Word of God be not Blasphemed.

So here was Womens Meetings, & Womens Teachings of one another, so yᵗ
this is no New thing, as some raw, unseasoned Spirits would seem to make it.

So dear Sisters in yᵉ everlasting Truth, we do conclude in yᵉ Apostles
Words to his Brethren in Phil. 4.8.9. wᵗsoever things are true, wᵗsoever things are Ho=
=nest. wᵗsoever things are just: wᵗ soever things are Pure; wᵗsoever things are Lovely;
wᵗsoever things are of Good Report; If there be any virtue, If there be any Praise
think on these things wᶜʰ ye have both Learned, & Received, & heard, & seen in me,
& do yᵐ, & yᵉ God of Peace shall be wᵗʰ you Amen.

And tho we be looked upon as yᵉ Weaker Vessels yet yᵉ strong & Powerful
God whose strength is made manifest, & Perfect in Weakness, he can make us good,
& valiant, & bold souldiers of Jesus Christ; if he Arm us wᵗʰ his Armour of Light.
& give unto us yᵉ sword of his Eternal Spirit; wᶜʰ is yᵉ Word of yᵉ Eternall God, &
cover our Hearts wᵗʰ yᵉ Breastplate of Righteousness, & Crown us wᵗʰ yᵉ Helment
of Salvation & give unto us yᵉ holy shield of Faith; wᵗʰ wᶜʰ we can quench all yᵉ
fiery darts of Satan, & shooe our feet wᵗʰ yᵉ preparation of yᵉ Gospel of Peace, &
set our feet upon yᵉ Mountains, so yᵗ we stand there, & publish glad tidings of great
Joy, & say unto Sion thy God Reigneth; & if he bring us to his banquetting house, &
Spread his banner over us wᶜʰ is Love, there we can stand our ground, & fight our
Lords Battles boldly & valiantly under our Lords Banner, & in our Lords Armor; He
who Respects no Persons, but chuseth yᵉ weak things of yᵉ World, & yᵉ Foolis
things of yᵉ World to confound yᵉ Wise; our sufficiency is of him; & His Armor
& strength is in him: And all yᵉ great strength yᵗ is in Men if they want this
Armor they can do nothing for God; nor he will have none of their service in yᵉ
state, who will have no Flesh to Glory in his presence: Our Gloryₐⁱⁿᵍ in him is, wh[ich?]
doth not, nor will not despise, nor contemn yᵉ weak. And so to him be all Glory
& Power, & Dominion forever & ever Amen.

This is given forth for Information, Instruction & direction yᵗ in yᵉ
blessed unity of yᵉ Spirit of Grace all Friends may be, & Live in yᵉ Practise
of yᵉ Holy Order of the Gospel.

Signed by 96 Women Friends

From yᵉ Generall Womens Meeting
4ᵗʰ Month 1677.

[blank page]

the womens meetings in **Dartmouth** began at **Peleg Slocom**s hous
the · 26 of the 4 month · i699

the · 23 · of the 5 · [illegible] Month ^1699 was our womens meeting held in Dartmoth
at this meeting **John Hedly [Headley]** and **Mary Slocom [Slocum]** laid their intention of
marriage before the meeting the meeting chose two women freinds
Hannah Tucker and **Ruth Tucker** to see after the young womans clear
=ness against the next monthly meeting
at this meeting **Ruth Smith** undertook to sweep the meeting hous
a year at this meeting it was agreed that the meeting at **Mehetable [Mehitable]**
Russells shall be the 4 day of the next week after the womens meeting

the 26 of the · 6 month i699

was our womens meeting held in **Dartmouth** at this meeting **John**
Hedly [Headley] and **Mary Slocom [Slocum]** came the second time to receiue their an
=swer enquiry being made acording to the order of truth ˄and they [illegible]
being clear haue [have] the consent of the meeting to proseed in marriage

the 18 of the 7 month · i699

was our womens meeting held in **Dartmouth**

the 16 of the · 8 · month · i699

was our womens meeting held in **Dartmouth**

the · 13 of the · 9 month · i699

was our womens meeting held in **Dartmouth** agreed of at this meet
=ing that that[?] weekly meeting that was at **peleg Slocum**s the · 4 day before
the monthly meeting · shall be at **Stephen Wilcock**s **[Wilcox]** · one fourth day before
the monthly meeting and one fourth day before the monthly. at **James**
Trips **[Tripps]**. and the rest of the fourth day meetings. at the meeting Hous

the 11 of the io month i699

was our womens meeting held in **Dartmouth**. it was ordered by this meet
ing that their shall be a colection the next monthly meeting

the 8 · of the · 11 · month i699

was our womens meeting held in **Dartmouth** at this meeting **Mary Slocum**
was chose to keep the mony colected by the meeting. colected by this meeting
and deliuered to **Mary Slocum**   0-i5-2
it was ordered by this meeting that their shall be a colection once a quarter

the 5 · of the 12 month i699

was our womens meeting held in **Dartmouth**. at this meeting **John Lapkam [Lapham]**
and **Mary Russell** laid their intentions of marriage before the meeting. the
meeting chose two women freinds **Ruth Tucker** and **Hannah Tucker** to
~~see after the~~ inquire conserning the young womans clearness from all others
against the next monthly meeting

the · 4 · of the first · month i700

was our womens meeting held in **Dartmouth** where **John Lapkam [Lapham]** and

Mary Russell ˄came the secund time to receiue their answer enquiry being made acording to the order of truth. and they being clear of al others haue the consent of the meeting to proseed in marriage

---

the i of the 2 month i700

was our womens meeting Ð held in **Dartmouth**. colected by this meeting 0-15-0

taken out of the stock for the use of freinds   0-12-0

---

the · 29 of the · 2 month 1700

was our womens meeting held in **Dartmouth**

---

the · 27 · of the · 3 month · 1700

was our womens meeting held in **Dartmouth**

---

the 24 of the 4 month · 1700

was our womens meeting held in **Dartmouth** colected by this meeting   0-12-0

---

the · 22 · of the 5 month · 1700

was our womens meeting held in **Da[r]tmouth** taken out of the stock at this meeting
for the use of freinds   0-12-0

at this meeting **Ruth Smith** [n?]undertook the sweeping of the meeting hous for a year

---

the ᴈi9 · of the · 6 · month · I700

was our womens meeting held in Dartmouth

---

the · 16 of the · 7 · month i700 ·

was our womens held in **Dartmouth** colected by this meeting   0-16-1

---

the i4 of the · 8 · month i700

was our womens meeting held in Dartmouth

---

the· 11 of the · 9 · month · I700

was our womens meeting held in **Dartmouth** taken out of the stock at
this meeting for the use of freinds   1-4-0

---

the · 9 · of the · 10 month i700

was our womens meeting held in **Dartmouth** colected by this meeting   0-11-0

---

the · 6 · of the · 11 · month · I700

was our womens meeting held in **Dartmouth**. where **Abraham booth** and
abigaill howland laid their intentions of marriage before the meeting
the meeting chose two women freinds **Mary Slocum** and **Ruth Tucker** to
inquire after the young womans clearness, from all others against the next monthly meeting
taken out of the stock at this meeting for the use of freinds   0-17-0

---

the 3 · of the · 12 · month 1700

was our womens meeting held in **Dartmouth** where **Abraham booth**
and **abigaill howland**. came the second time to receiue their answer inquiry
being made acording to the order of truth and they being clear from all
others have the consent of the meeting to proseed in mariage

---

the · 3 · of the i month · 1700i[*sic*]

was our women meeting held in **Dartmouth** colected by this meeting   0-13-3 taken out of the stock for the use of freinds   0-9-0

the · 31 of the · i month · 17001

was our womens meeting held in **Dartmouth** agreed of at this meeting that the
first days and weekly meetings shall begin at the eleuenth hour. and that the
meetings that were at **Sephen Wilcok**s [**Stephen Wilcox**] and **James Trips** [**Tripp**s]
Shall be kept at the meeting hous

the · 28· of the · 2 · month i7001

was our womens meeting ~~m~~ held in **Dartmouth** agreed of at this meeting that the
fourth day meeting at **James Trip**s [**Tripp**s] shall remain there once in two months.

the · 26 · of the · 3 · month 17001

was our womens meeting held in **Dartmouth** colected by this meeting   0-15-2
~~to~~ at this meeting two women freinds were Chose to giue [give] an acount to the yearly
Meeting at **Roadisland** of any business that may consern the meeting

the 25 of the · 4 · month i7001

was our womens meeting held in **Dartmouth**

the 2i of the · 5 · month i7001

was our womens meeting held in **Dartmouth**. taken out of the stock ≠ at this
meeting for the use of freinds   0-8-9
at this meeting **hannah brigs** [**Briggs**] · undertook the sweeping. the meeting hous
for a year

the i8 · of the · 6 · month i7001

was our womens meeting held in **Dartmouth** colected by this meeting — 0-16-[8]

the i5 of the · 7 · month i7001

was our womens meeting held in **Dartmouth**

the i3 of the 8 month i7001

was our womens meeting held in **Dartmouth** taken out of the stock at this
meeting for the use of freinds   i-14-6

the · 10 · of the · 9 · month i7001

was our womens meeting held in **Dartmouth** colected by this meeting -0-9-0
at this meeting **Mary Slocom** [**Slocum**] and **Ruth Tucker** were chose for the disburs=
ment of monys out of the stock for the use of freinds as they shall see ocation

the · 8 · of the · 10 · month i7001

was our womens meeting held in **Dartmouth**

the 5 · of the · 11 · month i7001

was our womens meeting held in **Dartmouth**

the · 2 · of the · 12 · month i7001

was our womens meeting held in **Dartmouth** colected by this meeting   -0-5-
taken out of the stock for the use of freinds   0-8-1

the · 2 · of the · i · month i7002

was our womens meeting held in **Dartmouth**

the · 30 · of the · i · month i7002

was our womens meeting held in **Dartmouth**

---

the 27 of the · 2 · month i7002

was our womens meeting held in **Dartmouth** ~~at the meeting hous~~
colected by this meeting　　　　　　　　　　　　　　　　　　　　　0-12-1

---

the 25 · of the · 3 · month i7002

was our womens meeting held in **Dartmouth** at this meeting two women
freinds **Ruth Tucker** and **Hannah Tucker** were chose for the yearly meeting at
roadisland to giue acount of any business that may consern the meeting

---

the 22 · of the · 4 · month i7002

was our womens meeting held in **Dartmouth** · at this meeting **Casander Mott** and
abigail wood were chose to make inquiry conserning **James Trip**s [**Tripps**] clearness
upon the acount of mariage. against the next monthly meeting

---

the · 20 of the · 5 month i702

was our womens meeting held in **Dartmouth** colected by this meeting　　　0-16-?
taken out of the stock at this meeting for the use of freinds　　　　　　　0-8-0

---

the 17 of the 6 month i702

was our womens meeting held in **Dartmouth** at this meeting **Mary Smith**
undertook the sweeping of the meeting hous for a year

---

the i4 of the · 7 month 1702

was our womens meeting held in **Dartmouth**

---

the · i2 · of the · 8 · month 1702

was our womens meeting held in ^**Dartmouth** colected by this meeting　　0-12-2
taken out of the stock at this meeting for the use of freinds　　　　　　 ~~0~~ i-4-0

---

the · 9 of the 9 · month i702

was our womens meeting held in **Dartmouth** at this meeting **Ralph Chapman** and
Deliverance Slocom [**Slocum**] laid their ~~int~~ intentions of mariage before the meeting the chose
two women freinds **Ruth Tucker** and **Hannah Tucker** to inquire conserning the young
womans Clearness from all others against the next monthly meeting

---

the · 7 · of the · io · month i702

was our womens meeting held in **Dartmouth**. at this meeting **Ralph Chapman** and
Deliverance Slocom [**Slocum**] Came the Second time to receiue their answer. inquiry being made
acording to the order of truth. and they being clear of all others have the consent
of the meeting to proseed in mariage

---

the · 4 · of the · 11 · month i702

was our womens meeting held in **Dartmouth**. colected by this meeting　　　0-9-8

---

the i · of the i2 · month i702

was our womens meeting held in **Dartmouth** where **Nathaniell Chase** and **Abigaill Share
man** [**Abigail Sherman**] laid their intentions of mariage before the meeting. the meeting
　　chose two women
freinds **Mary Slocom** [**Slocum**] and **hannah tucker** to inquire after the young womans clearness

from all others against the next monthly meeting taken out of the stock at this meeting for the use of freinds   i-0-0

the · i · of the i · month i703

was our womens meeting held in **Dartmouth**. where **Nathaniell Chase** and **Abigaill Share man [Sherman]** came the second time to receiue their answer inquiry being made acording to the order of truth. and they being clear of all others haue the consent of the meeting to proseed in marriage taken out of the stock at this meeting for the use of freinds   0-10-0

the · 29 · of the · i · month i703

was our womens meeting held in **Dartmouth** colected by this meeting   0-10-3

the · 26 · of the · 2 · month i703

was our womens meeting ~~of freinds~~ held in **Dartmouth** it was ordered at this meeting that the meetings the other side **cocset** riuer [river] shall be at **William Wood**s the next first day come week. after the monthly meeting. and one first day come week. after the monthly meeting at **James Trips [Tripps]** till furder order

the · 24 of the · 3 month i703

was our womens meeting held in **Dartmouth** at this meeting two women freinds **Mary ~~m~~ Slocom [Slocum]** and **Ruth Tucker** were chose to giue acount to the yearly meeting at **road island** of any business that may consern this meeting. at this meeting. it was ordered that the next men and womens monthly meetings of business. shall be at the meeting hous

the · 2i · of the · 4 month i703

was our womens meeting held in **Dartmouth** where **Joseph Russell** and **Mary Tucker** laid their intentions of marriage before the meeting. the meeting chose two women freinds **Mary Slocom [Slocum]** and **Ruth Tucker** to see after the young womans clearness, from all others against the next

monthly meeting. colected by this meeting   0i-i4-2

the · 19 of the 5 · month 1703

was our womens meeting ~~of~~ held in **Dartmouth** where **Joseph Russell** and **Mary Tucker** the second time to receiue their answer. inquiry being made acording to the order of truth and they being clear from all ~~of~~ others haue the consent of the meeting to proseed in marriage

the · 16 · of the · 6 · month i703

was our womens meeting held in **Dartmouth**. taken out of the stock at this meeting for the use of freinds   i-0-0
at this meeting **Mary Smith** undertook the sweeping of ^the meeting hous

the i3 · of the · 7 month i703

was our womens meeting held in **Dartmouth** colected by this meeting   0-16-[?]

the · 11 · of the 8 month i703

was our womens meeting held in **Dartmouth** taken out of the stock for the use freinds   0-8-[?]

the · 8 · of the · 9 · month i703

was our womens meeting held in **Dartmouth**. at this meeting **william born [Bourne]** and **hannah Sharman [Sherman]** laid their intentions of marriage before the meeting. the Meet=

ing Chose two women freinds **Ruhamah Smith** and **hannah Tucker** to see after
the young womans clearness from all others. against. the next. monthly meeting

---

the · 6 · of the · 10 month i703

was our womens meeting held in **Dartmouth** where **william born [Bourne]** and **hannah
Sharman [Sherman]** came the second time to receiue their answer enquiry being made
 acording to
the order of truth, and they being clear from all others haue the consent of the
meeting to proseed in marriage. colected by this meeting   0-9-8
it was ordered at this meeting. that the meetings the other side **Cocset** river shall be one
first day at **William Woods**. and one first day at **James Trips [Tripps]** and the fourth day of
the week at **Stephen Wilcocks [Wilcox]** till furder order

---

the · 3 of the · 11 · month i703

was our womens meeting held in **Dartmouth**

---

the · 31 · of the · 11 · month i703

was our womens meeting held in **Dartmouth**

---

the 28 · of the i2 month i703

was our womens meeting held in **Dartmouth** colected by this meeting   0-10-[?]
taken out of the stock at this meeting for the use of freinds   1-0-[?]

---

the · 27 · of the i month i704

was our womens meeting held in **Dartmouth** where **John Russell** and **Rebekah
Riketson [Rebecca Ricketson]** laid their intentions of marriage before the meeting the
 meeting chose two
women freinds **Ruth Tucker** and **Rachell Allin [Allen]** to enquire after the young womans clear
ness f[r]om all others against the next monthly meeting. at this meeting **Ruhamah Smith** and
Hannah Sole [Soule, Sowle] were chose to enquire after **Heniry [Henry] Tucker**s clearness
 on the acount of
marriage against the next monthly meeting

---

the 21 · of the · 2 · month i704

was our womens meeting held in **Dartmouth** where **John Russell** and **Rebecah
Riketson [Ricketson]** came the second time to receiue their answer enquirie being made
 acording to the
orde of truth and they being clear of all others haue the consent of the meeting to proseed
in marriage = taken out of the stock at this meeting for the use of freinds   0-18-[?]

---

the · 22 of the 3 month i704

was our womens meeting held in **Dartmouth**, at this meeting two women freinds
Mary Slocom [Slocum] and **Ruth Tucker** were chose to giue an acount to the yearly meeting at
Roadisland of any business that may consern the meeting colected by this meeting   0-12-[?]

---

the · i9 · of the 4 month 1704

was our womens meeting held in **Dartmouth**

---

the · i7 · of the 5 month i704

was our womens meeting held in **Dartmouth**. at this meeting two women freinds
Mary Slocom [Slocum] and **Rose howland**. were chose to take notise of any diferance

or disorderly walking of any of the woman freinds. that belong to this meeting. and

bring it to the monthly meeting if their be ocation for it at this meeting. **eliashib Smith**

and **Dinah allin** [**Allen**] and **Benjamine allin** [**Allen**] and **Deborah Russell** laid their intentions of marria[ge]

before this meeting. the meeting chose two women freinds **Mary Slocom** [**Slocum**] and
Ruth Tucker to

enquire after the young womens clearness from all others against the next monthly meeting.

the · 2i · of the · 6 · month i704

was our womens meeting held in **Dartmouth.** where **eliashib Smith** and **Dinah allin**
[**Allen**]

and **Benjamine allin** [**Allen**] and **Deborah Russell** came the second time to receive their
answer

enquiry being made acording to the order of truth. and they being clear of all others

haue the consent of the meeting to proseed in marriage. at this meeting two women

freinds ~~were cho~~ **Ruth Tucker** and **Ruth Smith**. were chose for the yearly meeting at

Sallim [**Salem** ?] and **Ruhamah Smith** and **Rose Howlland** [**Howland**] for the quarterly
meeting at **roddisla[nd]**

to give an acount of any business that may consern the meeting. at this meeting **hezekiah
Smi[th]**

wife took the sweeping of the meeting hous for a year. colected by this meeting   0-17-1

taken out of the stock at this meeting for the use of freinds   1-0-0

the · 18 · of the · 7 · month i704

was our womens meeting held in **Dartmouth**

the 16. of the 8 month i704

was our womens meeting held in **Dartmouth**

the. 20. of the · 9 · month i704

was our womens meeting held in **Dartmouth**. at this meeting two women freinds **Mary
Slocom** [**Slocum**]

and **Ruth Tucker** were chose for the quarterly at **Roadisland** [**Rhode Island**] to give an
acount of any

business that may consern the meeting. colected by this meeting   0-i7-io

taken out of the stock at this meeting for the use of freinds   1 - 1 - 8

the. 18 of the · 10 · month i704

was our womens meeting held in **Dartmouth**

the 15 · of the · 11 · month i704

was our womens meeting held in **Dartmouth** where **James Burrill** and **Mehetabell**
[**Mehitable**] **Russell**

laid their intentions of marriage before the meeting. the meeting Chose two womcn frcinds

Mary Slocom [**Slocum**] and **Hannah Tucker** to enquire after the womans clearness from
all others against

the next monthly meeting. at this meeting **Ruth Tucker** and **Rose Howland** were chose
at next

business that may consern the meeting

the 19 of the 12 month i704

was our womens meeting held in **Dartmouth.** where **James Burrill** and **Mehetabell [Mehitable] Russell**

Came the Second time to receive their answer enquirie being made acording to the order of truth

and they being clear of all others haue the consent of the meeting to proseed in marriage

at this meeting **peter Eston [Easton]** and **Content Slocom [Slocum]** laid their intentions of marriage before the

Meeting the meeting Chose two women freinds **Rachel allin [Allen]** and **Hannah Sole [Soule, Sowle]** to see after the

young womans clearness from all others against the next monthly meeting. at this meeting **Mary Slocom [Slocum]** was ‸chose for the quarterly meeting at **Roadisland.** and **Mary Slocom [Slocum]** and **Ruth Tucker**

for the yearly meeting at **Sandwich.** taken out of the stock at this meeting for the use of freinds   1-0-0

the i9 of the i · month i705

was our womens meeting held in **Dartmouth** where **Peter Eston [Easton]** and **Content Slocom [Slocum]**

Came the second time to receive their answer. enquiry being made acording to the order of truth - and they being clear from all others haue the consent of the meeting to proseed in marriage

the i5 · of the · 2 month i705

was our womens meeting held in **Dartmouth**

the ‸2i of the · 3 · month i705

was our womens meeting held in **Datmouth** colected by this meeting — — 0-0̶12-0

at this meeting two women freinds **Mary Slocom [Slocum]** and **Ruth Tucker** were chose for the quarter=

=ly meeting at **roadisland** to giue an acount of any business that may consern the meeting. at this meeting **Ruhamah Smith** and **Ruth Tucker** ‸were chose for the ouersight of this meeting

the i8 of the 4 month i705

was our womens meeting held in **Dartmouth.** it was ordered at the yearly meeting at **roadisland** · 1705 · that their shall be a meeting called on purpose for marriages

The i6 of the 5 month i705

was our womens meeting held in **Dartmouth.** At this meeting **Ruhamah Smith** and **Rachell allin [Allen]** were chose to see after **Jacobs Mott**s Clearness upon the acount of marriage. taken out

of the stock for the use of freinds at this meeting   0-3-2

the 20 of the · 6 · month i705

was our womens meeting held in **Dartmouth.** where **edward perry** and **eliphell [Eliphal] Smith**

laid their intentions of mariage before the meeting. the meeting chose two women freinds **Mary Slocom [Slocum]** and **Hannah Tucker** to enquire after the young womans clear

=ness from all others against the next monthly meeting. at this meeting two women

freinds - **Mary Slocom [Slocum]** and **Ruth Tucker** were chose for the quarterly meeting at **roadisland**. for any business that may consern the meeting. colected by this meeting - 0-16-8
taken out of the stock at this meeting for the use of freinds   i-0-0

the 17 of the · 7 · month i705

was our womens meeting held in **Dartmouth**. where **edward perry** and **eliphell [Eliphal] Smith** came
the second time to receive their answer. enquiry being made acording to the order of truth
and they being clear of all others haue the consent of the meeting to proseed in marriage
at this meeting two women freinds **Ruth Smith** and **Rose Howland** were chose for the
yearly meeting at **Situate**.

the i5 of the ⁸ ~~9~~ month i705

was our womens meeting held in **Dartmouth** at this meeting **Rachell Allin [Allen]** was
chose to be one to see after the disbursments of mony out of the stock with the women
that were chose before

the i9 of the 9 [blot] month i705

was our womens meeting held in **Dartmouth**. at this meeting two women freinds **Mary
Slocom [Slocum]** and **hannah Tucker** were chose for the quarterly meeting at **roadisland** at
this meeting two women freinds ~~were ch~~ **Ruth Tucker** and **hannah Cadman** were chose
to goe to **Elizebeth Macumbor [Elizabeth Macumber]** to enquire ˄the reason of her absenting
from ~~the~~ freinds meetings
the acounts of the monys record and the acount ballanced: colected by this meetingi 0-8-8

the i7. of the 10 month 1705

was our womens meeting held in **Dartmouth** at this meeting two women freinds **Mary
Slocom [Slocum]**
and **Rachell allin [Allen]** were chose to goe the second [?] time to **elizebeth Macumbor
[Elizabeth Macomber]** to discours her about[?]
her absenting her self from the meetings of freind

the 2i of the · 11 month i705

was our womens meeting held in **Dartmouth** at this meeting two women freinds **Ruth
Tuck[er]**
and **Rachell allin** were chose to goe to **Deborah Gifford** to discours her - about sum
reports they
had heard of her

the i8 of the i2 month i705

was our womens meeting held in **Dartmouth** at this meeting two women freinds
Ruth Tucker and **Rachell allin [Allen]** were chose for the quarterly meeting at **roadisland**
for
any business that may consern the meeting – and **Ruth Smith** and **Rose howland** for
the yearly meeting at **Sandwich** colected by this meeting   0-12-6

the i8 of the i month i706

was our womens meeting held in **Dartmouth**. taken out of the stock ˄at this meeting for the use
of freinds   i-0-0

the i5 of the 2 month i706

was our womens meeting held in **Dartmouth**

---

the 20 of the 3 month i706

was our womens meeting held in **Dartmouth**. colected by this meeting   0-9-2

at this meeting two women freinds **Ruth Smith** and **Rachell allin** [**Allen**] were chose for the quarterly

meeting at **roadisland** and **Ruth Tucker** and **hannah Tucker** for the yearly meeting at **roadisland**

for any business that may consern the meeting at this meeting **Mary Slocom** [**Slocum**] and **hannah Sole** [**Soule, Sowle**]

were chose to uisit [visit] **Catharine hudlstone** [**Huddleston**] and to know the reason of her not coming to meeting

at this meeting **Rachell allin** [**Allen**] and **hasadiah Russell** were chose to goe to **Mary brigs** [**Briggs**] the

younger about her marrying without her mothers consent, and conterary to the order of freinds

at this meeting these following lines were read

these are to the monthly meeting of women freinds in **Dartmouth**

whereas I have commited a trespass against the lord and against the truth in commiting of sin which I have been condemned for in my self and am sorry for it and desire the Lord to give me true repentance and forgiveness for the same. and I doe desire freinds to pass by ~~the same~~ my transgression

given under my   **Sarah Sherman**

hand the 20 of

the 3 month i706   the   younger

---

the i7 of the 4 month i706 · was our womens meeting held in **Dartmouth**

~~was our mon~~

---

the i5 of the 5 month 1706 · was our womens meeting held in **Dartmouth**

---

the i9 of the 6 month i706

was our womens meeting held in **Dartmouth** at this meeting **Mary Slocom** [**Slocum**] was chose for

the yearly meeting at **Salim** colected by this meeting   0-i3-3

taken out of the stock at this meeting for the use of freinds   i-5-6

from this meeting **Judah Smith** undertakes for a year the tending of the meeting hous

---

the i5 of the 7 month i706

was our womens meeting held in **Dartmouth**. at this meeting two women freinds, **Ruth Smith** and **eliphell Slocom** [**Slocum**] were chose for the quarterly meeting at **roadisland**

---

the 2i of the 8 month i706

was our womens meeting held in **Dartmouth**

---

the 18 of the 9 month i706

was our womens meeting held in **Dartmouth** colected by this meeting   0-i6-8

taken out of the stock at this meeting for the use of freinds   0-6-6

at this meeting **Ruhamah Smith** and **Ruth Tucker** were chose to see after the disorderly
walking of any that belong to this meeting

---

the i6 of the 10 month i706

was our womens meeting held in **Dartmouth** at this meeting two women freinds **Mary** ~~Slu~~
Slocom and **Rachell allin [Allen]** were chose for the quarterly meeting at **Roadisland**

---

the 20 of the 11 month i706
was our womens meeting held in **Dartmouth**

---

the i7 of the i2 month i706

was our womens meeting held in **Dartmouth** colected at this meeting   0-10-7
taken out of the stock at this meeting for the use of freinds   0-12-"
at this meeting two women freinds **mary Slocom** and **hannah Sole [Sowle]** were chose to
goe to **Deborah**
Gifford about her not coming to meeting. at this meeting two women freinds **Ruth Tucker** and
Rachell allin [Allen] were chose to take notice if any women or woman should come to
this our womans
meeting that is not of us to enquire there business. and if they have none to desire their absence
at this meeting two women freinds **hannah Tucker** and **elizebeth Russell** were chose to goe to
Hezekiah Smiths wife about her not coming to meeting

---

the i7 of the 1 month i707

was our womens meeting held in **Dartmouth** at this meeting a woman freind **Hannah**
Tucker was chose for the yearly meeting at **Sandwitch** and two women freinds **Mary Slocom**
and **Ruth Tucker** for the quarterly meeting at **roadisland** at this meeting two women freinds
Rahamah Smith and **Ruth Tucker** were chose to see after the disorderly walking of any that
belong to this meeting

---

the 2i of the 2 month i707

was our womens meeting held in **Dartmouth** at this meeting two women freinds **Rachell**
allin [Allen]
and **Hasadiah Russell** were chose to goe to **Deborah Gifford** about her not coming to meeting

---

the i9 of the 3 month i707

was our womens meeting held in **Dartmouth** at this meeting two women freinds **Mary**
Slocom and **Hannah Tucker** were chose for the ~~quarterly~~ ∧yearly meeting at **roadisland**
colected by this meeting   0-i0-0

---

the 23 of the 4 month i707

was our womens meeting held in **Dartmouth** at this meeting **Ruth Smith** was chose for
the quarterly meeting at **roadisland** taken out of the stock at this meeting for the use of
freinds   i-0-0

---

the 2i of the 5 month i707

was our womens meeting held in **Dartmouth** at this meeting two women freinds **Mary Slocom**
and **Rachell allin [Allen]** were chose to goe to **Meribah Slocom** about her proseedings
conserning
marriage contrary to her parents minds and the order of freinds

the i8 of the 6 month i707

was our womens meeting held in **Dartmouth** where **Isaak barker** and **eliz^ebeth Slocom** [**Elizabeth Slocum**] laid their intentions of marriage before this meeting the meeting chose
two women freinds ˏ^{Ruth Tucker}
and **Rachell allin** to see after the young womans clearness from all others against the next
monthly meeting. colected by this meeting   0-14-4
taken out for the stock at this meeting for the use of freinds   0-13-0

the i5 of the 7 month 1707

was our womens meeting held in **Dartmouth**

the 20 of the 8 month i707

was our womens meeting held in **Dartmouth** where **Isaak barker** and **elizebeth Slocom**
came the second time to receiue there answer enquiry being made acording to the order of truth
and they being clear haue the coⁿsent of the meeting to proseed in mariage

the i7 of the 9 month i707

was our womens meeting held in **Dartmouth** colected by this meeting   0-6-1

the i5 of the io month i707

was our womens meeting held in **Dartmouth** at this meeting two women freinds
Ruth Smith and **Hannah Tucker** were chose for the quarterly meeting at **roadisland**

the i9 of the 11 month i707

was our womens meeting held in **Dartmouth** at this meeting two women freinds **Ruth Tucker**
and **Hannah Tucker** were chose to goe to **Hannah Jenny** [**Jenney**] to labour with her about
her praying publickly in meetings

the i6 of the 12 month i707

was our womens meeting held in **Dartmouth**. colected by this meeting   0-15-1
taken out of the stock at this meeting for the use of freinds   0-15-6
at this meeting the two women freinds returned **hannah Jenny**s [**Jenney**s] answer conserning
her praying publickly in meetings. which was that she should doe so no more. except the lord
required it of her. at this meeting two women freinds **Ruth Tucker** and **Rachell Allin** [**Allen**]
were chose to viset freinds at **Sepecan**

the i5 of the i month i708

was our womens meeting held in **Dartmouth**. at this meeting two women freinds
Ruth Smith and **hannah Tucker** chose for the quarterly meeting at **roadisland**
at this meeting two women freinds **Ruth Tucker** and **Rachell allin** [**Allen**] were chose overseers
for this meeting. at this meeting two women freinds **Mary Slocom** [**Slocum**] and **Hannah Tucker**
were chose visitors to goe with them to visit freinds famillys

the i9 of th · 2 · month i708

was our womens meeting held in **Dartmouth**. at and wheras formerly there has been
that were chose of publick freinds for visitors upon consideration find an ill conveniency
in it. have from this meeting apointed **Ruth Tucker** and **hannah Tucker** and **Rachell**
allin [**Allen**] and it is ordered that they shall be in the performance of this service. it is
likewise suspected that after a genarall viset. of both men and women that these

women give an acount to the womens meeting. ensuing before the quarterly meeting
how they find things.

---

the i7 of the 3 month i708

was our womens meeting held in **Dartmouth**. at this meeting two women freinds
hannah Tucker and **Ruth Tucker** were chose for the, ᵞᵉᵃʳˡʸ q̶u̶a̶r̶t̶e̶r̶l̶y̶ meeting at **roadisland**
colected by this meeting   0-17-0
taken out of the stock at this meeting for the use of freinds   0-5-0

---

the 2i of the 4 month i708

was our womens meeting held in **Dartmouth** at this meeting two women freinds
hannah Tucker and **abigaill allin [Abigail Allen]** were chose for the quartely meeting at
roadisland

---

the i9 of the 5 month i708
was our womens meeting held in **Dartmouth**

---

the i6 of the 6 month i708

was our womens meeting held in **Dartmouth** at this meeting **Samuell howland**
and **Mary Meriho [Merrihew]** and **Georg thomas** and **Martha Tucker** and **william
Rickison [Ricketson]**
and **Meriba Slocom [Meribah Slocum]** laid their intentions of marriage before the meeting the meeting
chose two women freinds to se[e] after the womens clearness from all others against
the next monthly meeting Colected by this meeting   0-i6-2
taken out of the stock at this meeting for the use of freinds   i-0-0

---

the 20 · of the 7 month i708

was our womens meeting held in **Dartmouth** where **Samuell Howland** and g̶e̶o̶r̶g̶
T̶h̶o̶m̶a̶s̶ **Mary Meriho [Merrihew]** and **georg [George] Thomas** and **Martha Tuker
[Tucker]** and **William Rickison [Ricketson]**
and **Meriba Slocom [Meribah Slocum]** came the second time to receive there answer
enquiry being made
acording to the order of truth and they being clear of all others have the consent of
the meeting to proseed in marriage at this meeting six women freinds were chose to
see the marriages performed acording to the order of freinds at this meeting two women
freinds **Ruth Tucker** and **Ruth Smith** were chose for the quarterly meeting at **roadisland**

---

this meeting was a journd from the i8 of the 8 of month to the i day of the 9 month
1708. at this meeting it, ʷᵃˢ ordered that there should be a p̶a̶p̶?̶?̶ preparitive meeting
the fourth day of the week before the monthly meeting
taken out of the stock at this meeting for the use of freinds   0-12-8

---

the i5 · of the · 9 month i708

was our womens meeting held in **Dartmouth** colected at this meeting   0-8-9
at this meeting two women freinds **Ruth Tucker** and **Mary lapham** were chose to goe to
abigaill Howland to know the reason of her not coming to lay her intention of marriage
before the meeting

the 20 of the 10 month i708

was our womens meeting held in **Dartmouth**. at this meeting the two women freinds make return of **abigaill howland**s answer which was that the fault was not hers that she had not come [*blot*] at this meeting two women freinds **Ruth Tucker** and **Rose howland** were chose for the quarterly meeting at **roadisland**

no womens meeting of business in the · 11 · month i708 by reason of the violentness of the wether

the 2i · of the · i2 · month i708

was our womens meeting held in **Dartmouth**. colected by this meeting   0-i7-1
taken out of the stock at this meeting for the use of freinds   0-10-0

the · 2i · of the i · month i709

was our womens meeting held in **Darmouth** at this meeting **Charls dyer** [**Charles Dyer**] and **Mary**
lapham laid their intentions of marriage before the meeting the meeting chose two women freinds **Hannah Tucker** and **Rose Howland** to enquire after the young womans clearness from all others against the next monthly meeting at this meeting two women freinds **Mary Slocom** [**Slocum**] and **Ruth Smith** were chose for the quarterly meeting at **roadisland**

the i8 of the · 2 · month i709

was our womens meeting held in **Dartmouth**. **Charls** [**Charles**] **dyer** and **Mary lapham** coming for their answer is referd till the next monthly meeting: this meeting chose two women freinds **elizebeth** [**Elizabeth**] **Russell** and **Mary lapham** to goe to **Hannah Jenny** [**Jenney**] to desire
her to forbear speaking or praying or singing publickly in meetings

the i5 of the 3 month i709

was our womens meeting held in **Dartmouth**. colected by this month   0-i5-8

the 20 · of the · 4 · month i709

was our womens meeting held in **Dartmouth** at this meeting three women freinds **Ruth Tucker** and **Hannah Tucker** and **Rachell allin** [**Allen**] were chose for the viseting freinds familys. at his meeting two women freinds. **Hannah Tucker** and **Rose Howland** were chose for the quarterly meeting at **roadisland**

the i8 of the 5 · month i709

was our womens meeting held in **Dartmouth** at this meeting the two women freinds make return from the quarterly meeting at **roadisland**. no business for this meeting

the i5 · of the · 6 · month i709

was our womens meeting held in **Dartmouth** at this meeting **Charls dyer** and **Mary lapham**. came the second time to receive their answer. enquiry being made acording to the order of truth. and they being clear of all others have the consent of the meeting to proseed in mariage. the meeting chose two women freinds to see this marriage performed acording to the order of freinds: colected by this meeting   0-i3-6

the i9 - of the 7 month i709 ·

was our womens meeting held in **Dartmouth**. at this meeting two women freinds **Ruth Smith** and **Rachell allin** [**Allen**] were chose for the quarterly meeting at **roadisland**

the i7 of the 8 month i709

was our womens meeting held in **Dartmouth**. at this meeting **James Russell** and **Rebeckah Howland** laid their intentions of marriage before the meeting the meeting chuse two women freinds to enquire after the young womans clearness from all others against the next monthly meeting. at this meeting the two women freinds make return from the quaterly meeting. no business for this meeting. only to desire that these quiries may be observed. quiery for the monthly meeting to query of the represenives of weekly Meeting. how doe freinds keep their chilldren to the plain language of truth doe freinds attend weekly meetings with their children and servants.

---

the · 2i · of the 9 · month i709

was our womens meeting held in **Dartmouth** at this meeting **James Russell** and **Rebeckah Howland** came the second time to receive their answer. enquiry being made acording to the order of truth. and they being clear of all others have the consent of the meeting to proseed in marriage - colected by this meeting   0-i2-10
taken out of the stock at this meeting for the use of freinds   0-i2-10

---

the   of the · 10 month i709

was our womens meeting held in **Dartmouth**. at this meeting **John Green** and **Mary allin** [**Allen**] laid their intentions of marriage before the meeting. the meeting chose two women freinds **Mary Slocam** [**Slocum**] and **Hannah Tucker** to enquire after the young womans clearness, from all others against the next monthly meeting. at this meeting two women freinds **Mary Slocom** [**Slocum**] and **Hannah Tucker**. were chose for the quarterly meeting at **roadisland**

---

the i6 of the 11 month i709

was our womens meeting held in **Dartmouth** at this meeting **John Green** and **Mary allin** [**Allen**] came the second time to receiue their answer. enquiry being made acording to the order, of truth and they being clear of all others. have the consent of the meeting to proseed in mariage. at this meeting **Jabes barker** [**Jabez Barker**] and **Rebeckah Russell** laid their intentions of marriage before the meeting. the meeting chose two women freinds **rose howland** and **hannah Sole** [**Soule, Sowle**] to see after the young womans clearness against the next monthly meeting. taken out of the Stock at this meeting for the use of friend   i-0-0

---

the 29 of the i2 month i709

was our womens meeting ~~of~~ held in **Dartmouth**. colected by this meeting   0-18-3

---

the 27 of the i month i7010

was our womens meeting held in **Dartmouth**. at this meeting **Jabes barker** [**Jabez Barker**] and **Rebekah Russell** came the second time to receive their answer. enquiry be- ing made acording to the order of truth and they being clear of all others haue [have] the consent of the meeting to proseed in mariage. two women freinds **Hannah Tucker** and **hannah Sole** [**Soule, Sowle**] were chose to see the marage orderly consumated at this meeting **Joseph Chase** and **Abigaill Tucker** laid their intentions of mariage before the meeting. this meeting chose two women freinds[18] **Mary; Slocum & Ruth; Tucker**

---

18. The handwriting changes here; written vertically in the left margin opposite above text are the words "**Ruth Tucker** writes."

to see into yᵉ young womans clearness. our visiters brings in their account to this meeting; this meeting chose **Ruth**; **Tucker** to draw up an Epistle to Send to yᵉ Quarterly meeting two women friends **Rachel**; **Allen & Ruth**; **Tucker & Mary**; **Lapham** are chose to speake wᵗʰ **Abigaill**; **Howland**: concerning her going to marry out of yᵉ good order of friends; **R. T.** is chose to be helpfull to write for yᵉ Meeting

The 17ᵗʰ day of yᵉ 2ᵗʰ mᵗʰ in yᵉ year 1710; ~

was our womens meeting held in **dartmouth**: inquiry being made whether **Jabez: Barker** & **Rebekah**; [Rebecca] **Russell** had solemnized their marriage in yᵉ good order of Truth; yᵉ Answer was yes; that matter concerning **Joseph**; **Chase** & **Abigail**; **Tucker** comming for their Answer is refered to next monthly meeting; yᵉ women frds [friends] yᵗ were chose to attend yᵉ Quarterly Meeting but one of yᵐ [them] went by reason of sicknesse; no business from yᵉ Quarterly meeting to this meeting; yᵉ ~women yᵗ were chose to speake wᵗʰ **Abigaill**; **Howland** conserning her going to marry out of good order of frds did speake wᵗʰ her & she gives no satisfaction; ~ ~ ~

The 15ᵗʰ of 3ᵈ mᵒ in yᵉ year 1710 ~ ~

Was our womens meeting held at **dartmouth**; collected by this meeting 9ˢ-8ᵈ ~ ~ ~ **Joseph: Chase** & **Abigaill Tucker** coming for their Answer is refered to yᵉ next: monthly~ meeting; three women frds were chose with yᵉ men to End yᵉ business concerning **Abigail**; **Howland**s marrying out of yᵉ order of frds & they agree yᵗ a paper of Condemnation ~ ~ Shall goe against her;

The 19ᵗʰ of yᵉ 4ᵗʰ mᵒ in yᵉ year 1710 ~ ~ ~~ ~ ~

Was our womens meeting held in **dartmouth** where **Joseph: Chase** & **Abigaill Tucker** came for their Answer concerning their taking Each other in marriage; inquirey being made & we find nothing to yᵉ contrary but yᵗ yᵉ may proceed in marriage According to yᵉ good order of Truth established amongst frds the women frds **mary: Slocum** & **Ruth**; **Tu[cker]** are Chosen to see yᵉ marriage orderly consumated; yᵉ two women frds yᵗ were Chose to Attend yᵉ Quarterly Meeting gives an accompt yᵗ yᵉ desire of yᵉ Quarterly meeting is yᵗ our collection may be Every mᵒ; it is agreed at this meeting. yᵉ monthly collect[ion] shall begin at our next Quarterly meeting it is yᵉ order of yᵉ yearly meeting at **Rhoad Island** yᵗ all intentions of marriages Shall be brought first to yᵉ prepar[ative] meeting before yᵉ monthly meeting; this meeting chose two women frds **mary**; **Sloc[um]** and **Hannah Tucker** to attend yᵉ Quarterly meeting; at this meeting our frd **Ruth; smith** being about to travail unto **pensilvania** to visit her Children & friends there; desires a Sertificate from this meeting upon yᵗ account which was granted her ~ ~

The 17ᵗʰ of yᵉ 5ᵗʰ mᵒ 1710

Was our womens meeting held in **Dartmouth** at this meeting we received an Epistle ~ from yᵉ Quarterly meeting of women frds held in **Newport** on **Rhoad Island** yᵉ 14ᵗʰ of 5ᵗʰ month in yᵉ year 1710 which was kindly Excepted []: ~ ~ ~ ~ ~ ~ ~ ~ ~ ~

The 22ᵗʰ of yᵉ 6ᵗʰ month in yᵉ year 1710: ~ ~ ~ ~ ~ ~ ~ ~

Was our womens meeting held in **Dartmouth** Collected by this meeting 3ˢ[?]:11ᵈ:16ˢ taken out of yᵉ stock yᵉ use of frds; accompt being given into this meeting concerni= =ng **Joseph**; **Chase** & **Abigail**; **Tucker**s Marriage yᵗ it was orderly consumated; ~ ~ ~

The 18th of y^e 7th month in y^e year 1710; ~ ~ ~ ~ ~ ~ ~ ~ ~ ~ ~ ~
was our womens meeting held in **Dartmouth** Collected by this meeting 6s ~ ~ ~
this meeting made choyce of **Elizabeth**; **Summers** & **sarah**; **Davis** for visiters to ~ ~ ~
visit frds families at **Rochester**; this meeting chose two women frds to attend y^e
Quarterly meeting: **Ruth**; **Tucker** & **Rachel**; **Allen**; this meeting is ajourned untill
ye 4th day before ye Quarterly Meeting: no account brought into this meeting by y^e
Visiters by reason of sicknesse; this meeting Chose **Mary**; **Lapham** to draw up an
Epistle to send to ye Quarterly Meeting; ~ ~

The 16th of ye 8th m^o 1710 ~ ~ ~
Was our womens meeting held in **Dartmouth** collected by this meeting 5^s no ~ ~ ~
Account of any businesse from ye Quarterly meeting to this meeting: ~ ~ ~ ~ ~ ~

The 20th of ye 9th month 1710; ~ ~ ~ ~ ~ ~ ~ ~ ~
Was our womens meeting held in **Dartmouth** collected by this meeting; 7^s:11^d ~ ~ ~

The 18th of ye 10th month · 1710 ~ ~ ~ ~ ~ ~ ~ ~
Was our womens meeting held in **Dartmouth** collected by this meeting 12^s:4^d this ~
meeting chose two women frds. **Hannah**; **Tucker**; & **Mary**; **Layton** [**Lawton**?] to attend y^e
Quarterly meeting; this meeting Chose **hannah** · **Tucker** & **Ruth Tucker** to draw up
an Epistle to send to y^e Quarterly meeting: ~The 15th day of y^e 11th month 1710; ~
Was our womens meeting held in **Dartmouth** Collected by this meeting: 3^s=8^d; taken
out of y^e stock 21^s; y^e women frds y^t were chose to attend y^e Quarterly meeting went
And they bring no account of any businesse to this meeting;/The 19th of y^e 12th m^o <u>1710</u>
Was our womens meeting held at **Dartmouth** Collected by this meeting 4^s;10^d ~ ~

The 26th of y^e first month <u>1710</u>: ~ ~ ~ ~
Was our womens meeting held in **Dartmouth** Collected by this meeting; 9^s ~
taken out of ye stock for ye use of frds at this meeting 11^s: at this meeting ~
ye visiters brings in their account of visiting frds families this meeting chose two ~
women frds **Rachell**; **Allen** & **Ruth**; **Tucker** to attend y^e Quarterly meeting
this meeting chose **Ruth: Tucker** & **Hannah: Tucker** to draw up an Epistle
to send y^e Quarterly meeting; ~

The 16th of y^e 2th m^o 1711 ~ ~ ~ ~ ~ ~ ~
Was our womens meeting held in **Dartmouth** collected by this meeting, 9^s=2^d at this ~
y^e two women frds makes their return from y^e Quarterly meeting of no businesse to this
meeting; this meeting chose **Ruth: Tucker** & **Rachel Allen** to speake wth **Deborah**; **smith**
about her going to marry out of y^e order of frds this meeting chose three women frds
Hann[ah] cker Ruth Tucker & **Judeth Howland** to speak wth **Abigail**; **allen** about ye abusing
of her servant: ~ ~ ~ ~ ~ ~ ~ ~ ~ ~ ~ ~ ~ ~ ~

The 21th of ye 3^d m^o 1711 · ~ ~ ~ ~ ~ ~ ~
Was our womens meeting held in **Dartmouth**; collected by this meeting 7^s:6^d ~ye three women
frds y^t were chose to speake wth **Abigaill**; **Allen**; & **David: Akin** her accuser face to face he not
to be had at y^t time; they speaking wth her conserning the cruel whipping her negro ser-
van[t] She signifying her consenting to it or rather incouraging of it; this meeting Chose
three women frds **Hannah: Tucker**; **Rachell**; **Allen** & **Ruth Tucker** wth three men frds to

draw up her condemnation this meeting by ajournment yᵉ 30ᵗʰ day of yᵉ 3ᵈ mᵒ; Draws up yᵉ ~
aboue sᵈ **Abigaill Allen**s condemnation & orders it to be read before yᵉ next monthly ₍meeting
yᵉ two women friends yᵗ were chose to speake wᵗʰ **Deborah: smith** concerning her going
to marry out of yᵉ good order of frds brings in this account from her yᵗ her frds has not been
so carefull in advising her in time to yᵉ contrary; ~ ~ ~ ~ ~ ~ ~ ~ ~ ~ ~ ~ ~ ~ ~

The 18ᵗʰ of yᵉ 4ᵗʰ m̱ᵒ yeare 1711 -

Was our womens meeting held in **dartmouth** Collected by this meeting 2ˢ:10ᵈ ~ ~
Hannah; Tucker & Mary; Layton [Lawton?] are chose are for to attend yᵉ Quarterly meet-
ing. held at **Newport** on **Rhoad Island** yᵉ 14ᵗʰ day of yᵉ 7ᵗʰ mᵒ; **Hannah; Tucker & Ruth;
Tucke[r]** are chose to draw up an Epistle to send to yᵉ Quarterly meeting **Mary; slocum
& Rachel; Allen & Hasadiah; Russell** are chose to look over yᵉ monthly meeting book &
Collection ₍& ballan[ce] the accompts ~ ~

The 16ᵗʰ of yᵉ 5ᵗʰ mᵒ 1711

Was our womens meeting held in **dartmouth** Collected by this meeting 8ˢ:8ᵈ taken out
Of yᵉ stock at this meeting for yᵉ use of frds 1ᶠ ~ ~ ~ ~ ~ ~ ~ ~ ~ ~ ~ ~ ~ ~ ~

The 20ᵗʰ of yᵉ 6ᵗʰ mᵒ 1711 ~

Was our womens meeting held in **dartmouth** Collected by this Meeting 10ˢ ~ taken ~
out of yᵉ stock at this meeting for yᵉ use of frds 9ˢ=9ᵈ at this meeting yᵉ women
yᵗ were appointed to Look over yᵉ accompts; brings into this meeting yᵉ accompts are
ballanced & there is in yᵉ stock 3ᶠ=12ˢ=4ᵈ it was agreed upon at this meeting yᵗ ~
there should be an accompt taken of yᵉ Collection & disburstments of money once
yearˡy frds yᵗ were chose by yᵉ Last preparitive meeting to goe to **Susanna; Allen** to
know whether yᵉ report is true of her being wᵗʰ child yᵉ frds appointed ~~makes~~
brings into this meeting they have been wᵗʰ her & she nows yᵗ she is wᵗʰ child
And takes all yᵉ blame & shame to her self clears her parents; This meeting finding
an necessity to draw up a condemnation against her for it wᶜʰ being read & signed here -
is ordered to be read Publickly on a first day of yᵉ weeke at this meeting house by ~
William; Soule [Sowle] and make Returne to next monthly meeting ~ ~ ~ ~ ~ ~ ~ ~ ~

The 17ᵗʰ day of yᵉ 7ᵗʰ mᵒ 1711 ~ ~ ~ ~

Was our womens meeting held in **dartmouth** Collected by this meeting ?5ˢ at this ~
Meeting **Ruth; Tucker** was chose to keep yᵉ Collection of yᵉ monthly meeting ~
taken out of yᵉ stock at this meeting for yᵉ use of friends 1ᶠ:12ˢ: This meeting is
ajournd till yᵉ 5ᵗʰ day of yᵉ 8ᵗʰ mᵒ 1711 at this meeting our visiters brings in accompt
they have visited frds families & for yᵉ most part were Kindly Excepted; & where
any thing was amiss & spoken to there seems to be a Spiritt of Condecention ~
Signifying yᵗ they would indeavour it should be soe no more: **Ruth; Smith** ~
& **Mary; Layton** were chose to attend yᵉ Quarterly meeting; **Hannah; Tucker**
And **Ruth; Tucker** were chose to draw up an Epistle to send to yᵉ Quarterly
Meeting:

The 15ᵗʰ of yᵉ 8ᵗʰ mᵒ 1711 ~ ~ ~ ~

Was our womens meeting held in **Dartmouth** Collected by this meeting 5ˢ; taken out
of yᵉ stock for yᵉ use of frds 5ˢ: **Rachel; Allen & Ruth; Tucker** is chose to speake

wth **Sarah; Gifford** to know how She stands in her testimonie concerning her ~ Childrens marrying out of y^{e} order of frds; ~ ~ ~ ~ ~

The 19th day of y^{e} 9th m^{o} 1711
was our womens meeting held in **Dartmouth** Collected by this meeting 5^{s} ~

The 17th day of 10th m^{o} 1711; ~ ~ ~
was our womens Meeting held in **Dartmouth** Collected by this meeting 3^{s}=7^{d} Taken out of y^{e} stock for y^{e} use of frds 1[?]: our visiters signifies y^{t} they have not visited frds families this Quarter; **Hannah; Tucker** & **Ruth Tucker** are ~ Chose to attend y^{e} Quarterly meeting. **Ruth; Tucker** was chose to draw up an Epistle to send to y^{e} Quarterly meeting: ~ ~ ~ ~ ~

The 21th day of ye 11th m^{o} 1711 ~
Was our womens meeting held in **dartmouth** Collected by this meeting 5^{s}.6^{d} Y^{e} women frds y^{t} were chose to attend ye Quarterly meeting did not goe nor send by reason of ye hardnesse of ye weather

---

The 18th of ye 12th m^{o} 1711
was our womens meeting held in **Dartmouth** Collected by this meeting 9^{s}:5^{d}

The 17th day of ye 1th m^{o} 1712 ~
was our womens meeting held in **Dartmouth** Collected by this meeting 6^{s} at this meeting our visiters gives accompt y^{t} things in ye generall are pretty well this Meeting makes choyce of **Hannah; Tuckor** [**Tucker**] & **Mary; Layton** to attend ye Quarterly meeting At this meeting it was agread upon y^{t} ye Paper of ye condemnation should goe forth against **Deborah Smith** for marrying out of y^{e} order of frds not withstanding frds care & advice has been to y^{e} contrary; her condemnation is signed & ordered to be read on y^{e} first day of y^{e} week;

The 21th of y^{e} 2th moth 1712 ~ was our womens meeting
held in **dartmouth** Collected by this meeting 8^{s}=7^{d} y^{e} women y^{t} were chose to attend y^{e} the Quarterly meeting but one of y^{m} [them] went She brings no accompt of any businesse for this meeting;

The 19th of y^{e} 3^{d} m$^{o\ th}$ 1712 ~ ~ ~
was our womens meeting held in **dartmouth** collected by this 7^{s}: 6^{d} ~ ~

The 23^{d} day of y^{e} 4th m^{o} 1712 ~ ~ ~ ~
Was our womens meeting held in **dartmouth** collected by this meeting 12^{s} ·10^{d} Taken out of y^{e} stock. for keeping y^{e} meeting house 2$^{£}$ taken out of y^{e} stock for y^{e} use of frds 1$^{£}$ 2^{s} 6^{d} this me^{e}ting chose two women frds **mary; slocum** And **Rachel: Allen** to attend y^{e} Quarterly meeting:

The 21st day of y^{e} 5th
month 1712, was our womens meeting held in **Dartmouth** collected by this ~ meeting 2^{s} ~ y^{e} women y^{t} were chose to attend y^{e} Quarterly meeting did not goe by reason of sickness; 5^{s} disbursted for ye use of frds; ~ ~ ~ ~ ~ ~

The 18th day of ye 6th m^{o} 1712
was our Womens meeting held in **Dartmouth** collected by this meeting 8^{s}

Our aged friend **sarah; Allen** desires a Sertificate having some intention to Leave
this meeting **Hannah: Tucker. & Ruth; Tucker** are Appointed to draw up
a Sertificate against yᵉ next monthly meeting ~ The 15ᵗʰ day of yᵉ 7ᵗʰ mº 1712
was our womens meeting held in **dartmouth** Collected by this meeting 8ˢ ~
disbursted for yᵉ use of frds 14ˢ; our visiters brings in an accompt to this meeting
That they have visited frds families & in yᵉ generall things pretty well ~ ~
Some things not well we have taken care further conserning it: **Rachell Allen**
And **Ruth; Tucker** are chose to attend yᵉ Quarterlie meeting: ~ ~ ~ ~ ~ ~

The 20ᵗʰ of yᵉ 8ᵗʰ mº 1712 ~

Was our womens meeting held in **Dartmouth** collected by this meeting 3ˢ:3ᵈ
at this meeting **mary: Dyre [Dyer]** desires a Sertificate She intends to goe with her
Husband to **Providence** to settle: frds has taken care yᵗ it may be done
against next monthly meeting.

The 17ᵗʰ day of yᵉ 9ᵗʰ mº 1712

was our womens meeting held in **Dartmouth** Collected by this meeting 5ˢ:10[?]ᵈ
disbursted for yᵉ use of frds 18ˢ: **Mary: Dyres [Dyers]** sertificate is not drawn for
Some consideration at this meeting frds finding nothing to hinder has
Chose two frds **Hannah;Tucker & Ruth;Tucker** to draw a Sertificate ~
Against next monthly meeting ~ The 15ᵗʰ day of yᵉ 10ᵗʰ mᵒᵗʰ 1712
Was our womens meeting held in **dartmouth** Collected by this meeting 9ˢ 4ᵈ
Our visiters Signifies they have not visited frds families this Quarter: two
frds are chose to attend yᵉ Quarterly meeting **Hannah: Tucker & Rachel: Allen**
Ruth Smith is chose to be helpfull to make up yᵉ accompts wᵗʰ **Ruth; Tuck[er]**
Accompts ballanced; & there is in yᵉ stock two pound two shillings & six pe[ⁿᶜᵉ]
Ruth; Tucker is chose to draw up an epistle to send to yᵉ Quarterly meeting

The 19ᵗʰ day of yᵉ 11ᵗʰ mº 1712 ~ ~ ~

was our womens meeting held in **dartmouth** Collected by this meeting 7ˢ:3[ᵈ]
the women yᵗ were chose to attend yᵉ Quarterlie meeting did not goe by
Reason of some Hinderances yᵗ could not be avoided we have no
Accompt from yᵉ Quarterly meeting to this meeting; 7ˢ:3ᵈ disbursted for yᵉ use of frds

The 16ᵗʰ day of yᵉ 12ᵗʰ 1712

was our womens meeting held in **Dartmouth** Collected by this meeting 3ˢ:10ᵈ

The 16 of th i mo 1713

Was our monthly meeting of women frinds held in **dartmouth**
Collected by this meeting 7ˢ five pence 43 disbusted for the
youce of frinds **mary Slocom [Slocum] hannah tucker** are chose to atend
thay quarterly meeting this meeting is agurned tel thay 3 day of
the 2 mo: our visitars gives acount to this meeting that thay
haue visited frinds families and for the most part find things
prety wall; **hannah tucker** and **Ruth tucker** are chos to draw
up an acount to send to the quartarly meeting ₐAbigail Allins [Allen] condemnation whare as i haue
ben consenting to the beting of my negro saruent beyound what

I now think was convenent being ty ed by his hands and stript
for which i have ben consarned in my self and in much trobel
for it and do on i was of my wach at that time and so hard
ness of hart got in which if i had kept to the Spirit of truth
had not consented as above sade: for the clering of truth and
the testimony thare of i give thes lines de[s]ireing that the
lord might pas it by and that i migh come into younity
with the Lords peepel again. **abygel allen** [**Abigail Allen**]

[lower half of page is blank]

The 20 of yᵉ 2 moᵗʰ 1713
Was our Monthly Meeting of Women Friend Held att **Dartmouth**
Colected by This Meeting 7ˢ The Frᵈ That ware Chose to Attend The Q[illegible]
Meeting Brings no Account of any Bisness.

The 18 of yᵉ 3 moᵗʰ 1713
Was our Monthly Meeting of Women Friends Held att **Dartmouth**
Colected by This Meeting 9ˢ 2ᵈ Disbusted for the use of Frᵈ 30ˢ

The 22 of yᵉ 4 moᵗʰ
Was Our Monthly Meeting of Women Friends Held att **Dartmouth**
Colected by This Meeting 7ˢ 2ᵈ Att This Meeting were Chose **Elizabeth
Trip** [**Tripp**] & **Ruth Smith** to Attend yᵉ Quarterly Meetting

---

The 20 of yᵉ 5 moᵗʰ 1713
Was our Monthly Meeting of Women Frᵈ Held att **Dartmouth**
Colected by This Meeting 7ˢ 8ᵈ

The 17 of yᵉ 6 moᵗʰ 1713
Was our Monthly Meeting of Women Friends Held att **Dartmouth**
Colected by This Meeting 7ˢ 4ᵈ

The 21 of yᵉ 7 moᵗʰ 1713
Was our Monthly Meeting of Women Friends Held att **Dartmouth**
Colected by This Meeting 7ˢ 6ᵈ **Rochester** The Weekly Meeting of Women
Frᵈ gives an Account That Things are Pretty well among Them. **Hannah
Tucker** & **Rachel Allin** [**Allen**] are Chose to Attend The Quarterly Meetting This
Meeting is Ajorned tell yᵉ Youths Meeting.

The 20 of yᵉ 8 moᵗʰ 1713
Was our Monthly Meeting of Women Friends Held att **Dartmouth**
Colected by This Meeting 1ˢ 9ᵈ

The 16 of yᵉ 9 moᵗʰ 1713
Was our Monthly Meeting of Women Friends Held att **Dartmouth**
Colected att This Meeting 2ˢ: Disbusted for the use of frᵈ 20ˢ

The 21 of yᵉ 10 moᵗʰ 1713
Was our Monthly Meeting of Women Friends Held att **Dartmouth**

Colected att This Meeting 3ˢ 3ᵈ **Edward Wing** & **Desire Smith** Lead [Laid] Their
Intention of Mariage before This Meeting **Hannah Tucker** & **Marye
Smith** are Chose to Inquire into the Young Womans Clearness. **Hannah
Tucker** & **Mary Smith** are Chose to Attend yᵉ Quarterly Meeting **Ruth Tuc-
-ker** is Chose to draw up an Account to send to yᵉ Quarterly Meeting.

The 18 of yᵉ 11 moᵗʰ 1713/4

Was our Monthly Meetting of Women Friends Held att **Dartmouth**
Colected att This Meeting 6ˢ 6ᵈ Dusbusted out of yᵉ Stock 5ˢ att This Meetting
Edward Wing & **Desire Smith** Came for Their answer Inquiare being Made
Friends finds nothing but That They may Procede in Mariᵃge According to the
good order Procribed among Them.

The 15 of yᵉ 12 moᵗʰ 1713/14

Was our Monthly Meetting of Women Friends Held att **Dartmouth**
Colected att This Meeting 5ˢ 7ᵈ **Ruth Tucker** & **Mary Slocom [Slocum]** are Chosen to Take
an Account of yᵉ Colection and yᵉ Disbustments. The Accounts are Ballanced and There
Remaines in yᵉ Stock 2ˡ 3ˢ 6ᵈ

The 15 of yᵉ 1 moᵗʰ 1714

Was our Monthly Meetting of Women Friends Held att **Dartmouth**
Colected att This Meeting 4ˢ 6ᵈ **Rochester** Weekly Meeting brings in Their
Account that Their visiters hath visited Frᵈ familis and find Things in Prety
good order This Meeting is Ajorned tell yᵉ 4ᵈ before yᵉ Quarterly Meeting our
Visiters brings in Their Account to this Meetting held by Ajornement brings
That They have visited frᵈ families and find good Satisfaction. **Ruth Tucker
Mary Slocom [Slocum]** are Chose to Attend yᵉ Quarterly Meeting Dasbusted 20ˢ on [Truthˢ?]
Account **Ruth Tucker** is Chose to draw up an Account to Send to yᵉ Quarterly
Meeting

The 19 of yᵉ 2 moᵗʰ 1714

Was our Monthly Meetting of Women Friend Held att **Dartmouth**
Colected att This Meeting 5ˢ The Women That were Chose to Attend yᵉ Quarterly
Meetting was not Their

The 17ᵗʰ of yᵉ 3 moᵗʰ 17414

Was our Monthly Meetting of Women Friends Held att **Dartmouth**
Colected att This Meeting 9ˢ 1ᵈ

The 21ᵈ of yᵉ 4 moᵗʰ 1714

Was Our Monthly Meetting of Women Friends Held att **Dartmouth**
Colected att this Meeting 12ˢ 6ᵈ Dasbusted 12ˢ 8ᵈ **Mary Slocom [Slocum] Rachel Allin
[Allen]** Are Chosen to Attend yᵉ Quarterly Meetting **Ruth Tucker** is Chosen is to draw up ~
an Account to send to yᵉ Quarterly Meetting.

The 19ᵗʰ ᵈ of yᵉ 5 moᵗʰ 1714

Was Our Monthly Meetting of Women Friends Held att **Dartmouth**
Colected att this Meeting 8ˢ 1ᵈ Frᵈ That were chose to Attend yᵉ Quarterly Meetti[ng]
Brought an Epesle which was Read and kindly Received

The 16^d of ye 6 moth 1714

Was Our Monthly Meetting of Women Friends Held att **Dartmouth**
Colected att This Meetting 4^s 6^d

The 20th ^{d} of ye 7 moth 1714

Was Our Monthly Meetting of Women Friends Held att **Dartmouth**
Colected att this Meetting 5^s 1^d + 10^s Dasbusted **Ruth Smith** is Chose to Attend
ye Quarterly Meetting our Visiters hath Visited fr^{ds} families & was kindly Rece
ved with good satisfaction and find Things prety well as fare as they see

The 18^d of ye 8 moth 1714

Was Our Monthly Meetting of Women Friends Held att **Dartmouth**
Colected att This Meetting 2^s:5^d Dasbusted 15^s ye Fr^d That were Chose to Attend
The Quarterly Meetting did not go by Reason of Sickness

The 15^d of ye 9 moth 1714

Was Our Monthly Meetting of Women Friends Held att **Dartmouth**
Colected att this Meetting 3^s:6^d Taken out of ye Stock 4^s

The 20^d of ye 10 moth 1714

Was Our Monthly Meetting of Women Friends Held att **Dartmouth**
Colected at this Meetting 8^s 5^d Desbusted 40^s 6^d for The Use of Friends
Hannah Tucker Mary Slocom [Slocum] are Appointed to Attend ye Quarterly
Meetting **Hannah Born [Bourne]** that was being Mar[ri]ed out of ye good Order of Truth
Friends hath sined [signed] a paper of Condemnation against her.

The 24^d of ye 11 moth 1714/15

Was our Monthly Meetting of Women Friends Held att **Dartmouth**
Colected att This Meetting 4^s 11^d Desbusted 6^s one of ye Fr^{ds} That was chose did
Attend ye Quarterly Meetting and brings an Account of no Bisness **Ezieiah [Hezekiah] Smi**
ths Daughter **Mary** her Mariing out of the Order of Friends is left to ye Judg
ment of ye Men and we shall joyn with Them in what they due [do]

The 21^d of ye 12 moth 1714/15

Was our Monthly Meetting of Women Friends Held att **Dartmouth**
Colected att This Meetting 13^s:1^d **Nickleas [Nicholas] Davis & Mary Sommers [Summers]**
hath lead Their Intention of Mariage before This Meetting This Meetting hath Chose
Mary Smith & Sarah Wing to Inquire into The Young Womans Clearness
Hannah Tucker & Ruth Tucker are Chose to balance ye Accounts.

The 28^d of ye 1 moth 1715

Was our Monthly Meetting of Women Friends Held att **Dartmouth**
Colected att this Meetting 5^s 7^d **Nickleas [Nicholas] Davis & Mary Sommers [Summers]**
Came for th[eir] Answer This Meetting finds nothing to hender Them but That they may
Proc[e]de in Mariage According to ye good order of Truth **Benjeman Born [Benjamin**
Bourne] and **Hannah Wing** Lead Their Intention of Mariage before this Meetting **Ruth**
Tucker & Meheatable [Mehitable] Wing are Chose to Inquire into ye Young Womans
Clearness **Mary Laton [Lawton, Layton] & Ruth Tucker** are Chose to Attend ye Quarterly
Meettinge **Rochester**s Weekly Meeting gives an Account That they have Visited Friends

families & are Incoriaged in it **Ruth Tucker** is Chose to draw up an Account to
send to yᵉ Quarterly Meetting

The 18ᵈ of yᵉ 2 moᵗʰ <u>1715</u>

Was Our Monthly Meetting of Women Friends Held att **Dartmouth**
Colected att This Meetting 4ˢ 7ᵈ **Benjeman Born** [**Benjamin Bourne**] & **Hannah Wing** Came
for Their Answer This Meeting finds nothing bat that These may Procede
In Their Mariage According to yᵉ good order of Truth yᵉ Frᵈˢ That were Chose
did Attend yᵉ Quarterly Meetting Brings no bisness to This Meeting

The 16 of yᵉ 3 moᵗʰ <u>1715</u>

Was our Monthly Meetting of Women Friends Held att **Dartmouth**
Colected at This Meetting 7ˢ 6ᵈ

The 20ᵈ of yᵉ 4 moᵗʰ <u>1715</u>

Was our Monthly Meetting of Women Friends Held att **Dartmouth**
Colected at this Meetting 4ˢ 10ᵈ Taken out of yᵉ Stock 6ˢ **Ruth Smith**, **Mary**
Laton [**Layton**] are Chose to Attend yᵉ Quarterly Meetting

The 18ᵈ of yᵉ 5 moᵗʰ <u>1715</u>

Was our Monthly Meetting of Women Friends Held att **Dartmouth**
Colected at This Meetting 4ˢ 6ᵈ one of yᵉ Frᵈˢ That were Chose did Attend
The Quarterly Meetting and brings no Bisness to this Meeting.

The 15ᵈ of yᵉ 6 moᵗʰ <u>1715</u>

Was our Monthly Meetting of Women Friends Held at **Dartmouth**
Colected at this Meetting 5ˢ 9ᵈ Accounts Balanced and Their Remaines
In yᵉ Stock £1:16ˢ

The 19ᵈ of yᵉ 7 moᵗʰ <u>1715</u>

Was our Monthly Meetting of Women Friends Held at **Dartmouth**
Colected at This Meetting 7ˢ 5ᵈ **Rochester**s Weekly Meetting gives an Account
That they have Visited Frᵈˢ families and in some families They find Thing[s]
~~are~~ Indeforant well, This Meeting is ajorned tell yᵉ 4 day before yᵉ Quarterly M
The Visiteres brings in Their Account to This Meeting held by Ajornment.
The 12 day of yᵉ 8 moᵗʰ That they have Visited Frᵈˢ families and find Things are
among Some in good Order **Rachel Allin** [**Allen**] & **Mary Laton** [**Lawton**, **Layton**] are
Chosen to Attend yᵉ Quarterly Meetting **Ruth Tucker** are Chose to draw up an
Account to Send to yᵉ Quarterly Meetting

The 17 of yᵉ 8 moᵗʰ <u>1715</u>

Was Our Monthly Meetting of Women Friends Held att **Dartmouth**
Colected at This Meetting 5ˢ 2ᵈ **Jeames** [**James**] **Barker** & **Elizabeth Tucker** Lead
Their Intention of Mariage before This Meeting **Mary Slocom** [**Slocum**] and
Rachel Allin [**Allen**] is Chose to Inquire in to The Young Womans Clearness
The Frᵈˢ That were Chose did Attend yᵉ Quarterly Meetting and brings
no Bisness to This Meeting.

The 21 day of yᵉ 9 moᵗʰ <u>1715</u>

Was Our Monthly Meetting of Women Friends Held att **Dartmouth**

Colected by This Meetting 9ˢ **Jeames [James] Barker** & **Elizabeth Tucker** Came
for Their Answer This Meeting finds nothing but that they may Procede
In Mariage According to yᵉ good Order of Truth.

The 19ᵈ of yᵉ 10 moᵗʰ 1715

Was Our Monthly Meetting of Women Friends Held att **Dartmouth**
Colected by This Meetting 6ˢ 1ᵈ Desbusted for The use of Frᵈˢ £1:9:6
Hannah Tucker & **Mary Laton [Lawton, Layton]** are Chose to Attend yᵉ Quarterly
Meetting **Ruth Tucker** is Chose to draw up an Account to Send to yᵉ
Quarterly Meetting.

The 23ᵈ of yᵉ 11 moᵗʰ 1715/16

Was Oour Monthly Meetting of Women Friends Held att **Dartmouth**
Colected at this Meetting 6ˢ The Frᵈˢ That were Chose did Attend the
Quarterly Meetting and brings no Bisness to this Meetting.

The 20ᵈ of yᵉ 12 moᵗʰ 1715/16

Was Our Monthly Meetting of Women Friends Held att **Dartmouth**
Colected at This Meetting 6ˢ 7ᵈ

The 19ᵈ of yᵉ 1 moᵗʰ 1716

Was Our Monthly Meetting of Women Friends Held att **Dartmouth**
Colected at This Meetting 6ˢ 7ᵈ **Hannah Tucker** and **Mary Laton [Layton]** is Chose
to Attend yᵉ Quarterly Meetting Desbusted for yᵉ use of Frᵈˢ 20ˢ **Ruth Tucker**
is Chose to draw up an Account to Send to yᵉ Quarterly Meetting.

The 16ᵈ of yᵉ 2 moᵗʰ 1716

Was Our Monthly Meetting of Women Friends Held att **Dartmouth**
Colected at This Meetting 4ˢ We Received an Epestle from yᵉ Quarterly ~
Meetting.

The 21ᵈ of yᵉ 3 moᵗʰ 1716

Was Our Monthly Meetting of Women Friends Held att **Dartmouth**
Colected att This Meetting 11ˢ 6ᵈ

The 18 of yᵉ 4 moᵗʰ 1716

Was Our Monthly Meetting of Women Friends Held att **Dartmouth**
Colected att This Meetting 8ˢ 5ᵈ

The 16 of yᵉ 5 moᵗʰ 1716

Was Our Monthly Meetting of Women Friends Held att **Dartmouth**
Colected at This Meetting 7ˢ 6ᵈ Desbusted for yᵉ use of Friends 7ˢ 6

The 21 of yᵉ 6 moᵗʰ 1716

Was Our Monthly Meetting of Women Friends Held att **Dartmouth**
Colected at This Meetting 7ˢ 6ᵈ Desbusted for yᵉ use of Friends 7ˢ 6ᵈ **Eleazar
Slocom [Slocum]** & **Deborah Smith** lead Their Intention of Mariage before this
Meetting **Hannah Sole [Soule, Sowle]** & **Mary Smith** ₍were chose₎ to make Inquiery Into the
Young Womans Clearness

The 17 of yᵉ 7 moᵗʰ 1716

Was Our Monthly Meeting of Women Friends Held att **Dartmouth** Colected
att this Meeting 6ˢ 6ᵈ **Eleazar Slocom [Slocum] [&] Deborah Smith** Came for Their Answer
Inquiery being Made Nothing appeares but that they may procede In
Mariage According to yᵉ good order of Truth

The 15ᵈ of yᵉ 8 moᵗʰ 1716

Was Our Monthly Meeting of Women Friends Held att **Dartmouth**
Colected at this Meeting 3ˢ 6ᵈ one of The Friends That were Chose did Attend
The Quarterly Meetting and no Besness offers to This Meetting

The 19 of yᵉ 9 moᵗʰ 1716

Was Our Monthly Meetting of Women Friends Held att **Dartmouth**
Colected at This Meetting 8ˢ 2ᵈ.

The 17ᵈ of yᵉ 10 moᵗʰ 1716

Was Our Monthly Meetting of Women Friends Held att **Dartmouth**
Colected at this Meeting 6ˢ 9ᵈ **Mary Slocom [Slocum] & Mary Lawton** are Chose
to Attend yᵉ Quarterly Meeting **Ruth Smith & Ruth Tucker** are Chose
to Ballance yᵉ Accounts **Hannah Tucker** is Chose to keep the Stock That
Belongs to This Meeting Desbusted 15ˢ 5ᵈ for yᵉ use of Frᵈˢ ye Accounts Bal
lanced and Their is in yᵉ Stock £1 15 6.

The 21ᵈ of yᵉ 11 moᵗʰ 1716/17

Was Our Monthly Meetting of Women Friends Held at **Dartmouth**
Colected at This Meeting 8ˢ 6ᵈ The Friends That were Chose did Attend
The Quarterly Meeting and Brought an Epestle which was Read and
kindly Received

The 18ᵈ of yᵉ 12 moᵗʰ 1716/17

Was Our Monthly Meetting of Women Friends Held at **Dartmouth**
Colected at This Meeting 1ˢ 10ᵈ.

The 18ᵈ of yᵉ first moᵗʰ 1717

Was Our Monthly Meetting of Women Friends Held at **Dartmouth**
Colected at This Meeting 2ˢ 2ᵈ **Hannah Tucker & Mary Lawton** is Chose
to Attend yᵉ Quarterly Meetting This Meeting is Ajorned tell yᵉ Youths
Meeting it being yᵉ six day before yᵉ Quarterly Meetting.

The 15 of yᵉ Siesond [Second] moᵗʰ 1717

Was our Monthly Meetting of Women Friends Held at **Dartmouth**
Colected at this Meeting 4ˢ 2ᵈ The Friends that were Chose to attend the
Quarterly Meeting did attend it and brings no Besness to this Meetting

The 20ᵈ of yᵉ 3 moᵗʰ 1717

Was Our Monthly Meetting of Women Friends Held at **Dartmouth**
Colected at this Meeting 13ˢ 11ᵈ Taken out of yᵉ Stock for yᵉ use of Friends 5ˢ 6ᵈ
This as an Account from **Rochesters** preperative Meeting That **Benjeman
Clevan [Benjamin Cleveland] Sarah Davis Juner** is Married Contrary to the good order
of truth altho Friends has Laboured much with them about it The Parents of yᵉ Young

Woman is not found so Clear In there Testimoney against it as Friends Could
a Desired **Hannah Tucker** & **Hepsabeth Hadaway** [Hathaway] are Chose to Discorce
y Them Concerning it

The 24 of yᵉ 4 moᵗʰ 1717
Was our Monthly Meeting of Women Friends Held at **Dartmouth**
Colected at this Meeting 7ˢ.11ᵈ **Edward Wing** & Sarah Tucker Lead [Laid] Their
Intention of Mariage before this Meeting **Mary Slocom [Slocum]** & **Hannah
Sole [Soule, Sowle]** are Chose to Inquire into yᵉ Young Womans Clearness

The 15ᵈ of yᵉ 5 moᵗʰ 1717
Was our Monthly Meeting of Woman Friends Held at **Dartmouth**
Colected at This Meeting 6ˢ 9ᵈ **Edward Wing** [&] **Sarah Tucker** Came for
Their Answer Friends finds nothing against Them but that they may Pro
cede in Mariage According to The good Order of Friends 2ˢ 6ᵈ Taken out of
The Stock for yᵉ use of Friends.

The 19 of yᵉ 6 mᵒ 1717
Was Our Monthly Meeting of Women Friends Held at **Dartmouth**
Colected at This Meeting 11ˢ 6ᵈ The Women That were Chose to Speak wit[h]
Sarah Davis Concerning her daughter and She Signefies to This Meeting
That She has keept her Self Clear and been very much   Concerned for
Their wrong Procdings

The 16 of yᵉ 7ᵐᵒ 1717
Was Our Monthly Meeting of Women Friends Held at **Dartmouth**
Colected at This Meeting 7ˢ 10ᵈ **Rochester** Friends gives an Account That they
have visited Friends families and find Things prety well This Meeting is
Ajorned tell yᵉ Youths Meeting which is before The Quarterly Meeting This
Meeting held by ajornment yᵉ 4ᵈ of yᵉ 8ᵐᵒ our visiters gives an Account that
They have visited Friends families and find Things in prety good order as far
as they See **Mary Layton [Lawton]** is Chose to Attend yᵉ Quarterly Meeting **Ruth Tucker**
is Chose to draw up an Account to send to/this Meeting

the 16 of the 7ᵐᵒ 1777 [sic]

The 21 of yᵉ 8 mᵒ 1717
Was Our Monthly Meeting of Woman Friends Held at **Dartmouth**
Colected at This Meeting 5ˢ 3ᵈ **Daniel Godard [Goddard]** & **Mary Tripp** Lead Their
Intention of Mariage before This Meeting **Mary Slocom [Slocum]** & **Hannah
Cadman** are Chose to Inquire Into yᵉ Young Womans Clearness Taken out
of yᵉ Stock for The use of Friends 5ˢ 7ᵈ Friends That were Chose [?] did attend
The Quarterly Meeting and brings no Bisness

The 18 of yᵉ 9 moᵗʰ 1717
Was Our Monthly Meeting of Women Friends Held at **Dartmouth**
Colected at This Meeting 7ˢ 2ᵈ **Daniel Godard [Goddard]** & **Mary Tripp** Came for Their

Answer and Friends finds nothing but that They may Procede in Mariage Ac
cording to The good Order of Friends **Isaac Howland** [&] **Hannah Allin [Allen]** Lead
Their Intention of Mariage before This Meeting **Mary Slocom [Slocum]** & **Hannah
Tucker** are Chose to Inquire Into yᵉ Young Womans Clearness

The 16ᵈ of yᵉ 10ᵗʰ mᵒ <u>1717</u>

Was our Monthly Meeting of Woman Friends Held at **Dartmouth**
Colected at This Meeting 5ˢ **Isaac Howland** & **Hannah Allin [Allen]** Came for
Their Answer and Friends has Given Them leave to Mary Taken out of yᵉ Stock
30ˢ for yᵉ use of Friends **Mary Lawton** & **Mary Russel [Russell]** are Chose to Attend The Quar
terly Meetting **Ruth Tucker** is Chose to draw up an Account to Send to the Meeting

The 20 of yᵉ 11 mᵒ <u>1717</u>/18

Was our Monthly Meetting of Women Friends Held at **Dartmouth**
Colected at This Meeting 1ˢ This Meeting Received an Eppestle from yᵉ Quarterly
Meetting which was Read and kindly Excepted

The 17 of yᵉ 12 mᵒ <u>1717</u>/18

Was our Monthly Meetting Held at **Dartmouth** Colected at This Meeting 8ˢ
William Sole [Soule, Sowle] & **Rachel Allin [Allen]** Lead their Intention of Mariage before
this Meeting **Daniel Shepard [Shepherd?]** [&] **Mary Sherman** Lead Their Intention of
Mariag **Hannah Tucker Elizabeth Russel [Russell]** are Chose to Inquire Into the Young
Womens Clearness.

The 17 of yᵉ 1 moᵗʰ <u>1718</u>

Was our Monthly Meetting Held at **Dartmouth** Colected at This Meeting 9ˢ
William Sole [Soule, Sowle] & **Rachel Allin [Allen]** Came for Their Answer and Friends
Gave Them Leave to Mary According to yᵉ good order of Friends **Rochester** Women
Friends gives
an Account to This Meetting and it is Ajorned tell yᵉ Youths Meeting

The 21 of yᵉ 2 moᵗʰ <u>1718</u>

Was our Monthly Meetting of Women Friends Held at **Dartmouth**
Colected at This Meeting 5ˢ 1ᵈ **Daniel Shepard Mary Sherman** Came for
Their Answer and Friends finds nothing but that they may Procede in Mariage
According to the good Order of Friends.

The 23 of yᵉ 3 mᵒ <u>1718</u>

Was our Monthly Meetting of Women Friends Held at **Dartmouth**
Colected at this Meeting 5ˢ-7ᵈ

The 23 of yᵉ 4 moᵗʰ <u>1718</u>

Was Our Monthly Meetting of Women Friends Held at **Dartmouth**
Colected at this Meeting 7ˢ-9ᵈ **Mary Lawton Hannah Tucker** are Chose to
Attend The Quarterly Meetting our Visiters gives an Account That They have
Visited Friends families and find Things much as They have been of leate
Disbusted for yᵉ use of Friends 7ˢ 2ᵈ

The 21 of yᵉ 5 moᵗʰ <u>1718</u>

Was Our Monthly Meetting of Womaen Friends Held at **Dartmouth**

Colected at This Meeting 9ˢ 8ᵈ **Ruth Tucker Ruth Smith Hannah Tucker**
are Chose to Ballance yᵉ Accounts

The 18 of yᵉ 6 moᵗʰ 1718

Was Our Monthly Meeting of Women Friends Held at **Dartmouth**
Colected at This Meeting 12ˢ Received an Epestle from yᵉ Quarterly Meeting
which was Read and kindly Excepted The Accounts Ballanced and their is in
The Stock £6=2:6

The 15 of yᵉ 7 mº 1718

Was our Monthly Meeting of Women Friends Held at **Dartmouth**
Colected at This Meeting 6ˢ=7ᵈ **Joseph Mosher Mehittable [Mehitable] Smith** Lead
Their Intention of Mariage before This Meeting **Mary Slocom [Slocum] Mary
Smith** are Chose to Inquire into the Young Womans Clearness **Mary Lawton
Mary Smith** are Chose to attend the Quarterly Meeting

The 20 of yᵉ 8 mo+ 1718

Was our Monthly Meeting of Women Friends Held at **Dartmouth**
Colected at This Meeting 2ˢ 11ᵈ **Joseph Mosher Mehettable [Mehitable] Smith** Came for
Their Answer and Friends gave Them leave to Mary According to the good Order of
Truth The Friends brings no Account of bisness from yᵉ Quarterly Meeting
Disbusted for The use of Friends £1 8ˢ

The 17ᵈ of yᵉ 9 mº 1718

Was Our Monthly Meeting of Women Friends Held at **Dartmouth**
Colected at This Meeting 4ˢ **Adam Mott Abthyer Hadaway [Apphia Hathaway]** Lead
Their Intention of Mariage before This Meeting **Hannah Tucker Mary Lappam [Lapham]**
are Chose to make Inquire Concerning yᵉ Young Womas Clearness.

The 15 of yᵉ 10 moᵗʰ 1718

Was Our Monthly Meeting of Women Friends Held at **Dartmouth**
Colected at this Meeting 4ˢ 6ᵈ **Adam Mott Abthyer Hadaway [Apphia Hathaway]** Came
for Their Answer Friends finds nothing but that they may Procede In Mariage according
to yᵉ good Order of Truth disbusted for yᵉ use of friends 4ˢ **Mary Lawton Marye
Rusel [Mary Russell]** are Chose to Attend yᵉ Quarterly Meeting

The 19 of yᵉ 11 moᵗʰ 1718/19

Was Oor Monthly Meeting of Women friends Held at **Dartmouth**
Colected at This Meeting 1ˢ 6ᵈ we have no Account from yᵉ Quarterly Meeting

The 16 of yᵉ 12 moᵗʰ 1718/19

Was Our Monthly Meeting of Women friends Held at **Dartmouth**
Colected at This Meeting 6ˢ 5ᵈ **Phineas Chase Desiare [Desire] Wing** Lead Their
Intention of Mariage before This Meeting **Elizabeth Wing** with **Mehittable [Mehitable]
Wing** are Chose to make Inquire Into the Young Womans Clearness This Meeting
hath Received an Account from **Rochester** Weekly Meeting w gives an account
That They have Visited Friends families and find Things in prety good Order

The 16 of yᵉ 1 moᵗʰ 1719

Was Our Monthly Meeting of Women friends Held at **Dartmouth**
Colected at This Meeting 8ˢ 1ᵈ yᵉ Visiters gives an Account that they have visi
ted friends families and find Things pretty well **Mary Slocom [Slocum] Hannah Tucker**
are Chose to Attend yᵉ Quarterly Meeting **Ruth Tucker** is Chose to draw up an
Account to sind to that Meeting £1-16 disbusted for yᵉ use of Friends

The 20 of yᵉ 2 mᵒ 1719

Was Our Monthly Meeting of Women Friends Held at **Dartmouth**
Colected at this Meeting 7ˢ 3ᵈ Taken out of the Stock 7ˢ for yᵉ use of Friends
The friends that were Chose to Attend yᵉ Quarterly Meeting brings an Acc
ount That Their is a Woman Chose out of every Weekly Meetting to Attend
The Q Yearly Meetting

The 18 of yᵉ 3 mᵒ 1719

Was Our Monthly Meetting of Women friends Held at **Dartmouth**
Colected at this Meeting 9ˢ 3ᵈ £ 2 disbusted for a Woman that has
Met with a Loss by fire **Rachel Allin [Allen] Dinah Smith** are Chose
to discorce **Dorcace [Dorcas] Earl** Concerning her Daughter **Deborah** Marying
In the way of yᵉ World.

The 22 of yᵉ 4 moᵗʰ 1719

Was Our Monthly Meetting of Women friends Held at **Dartmouth**
Colected 4ˢ 8ᵈ **Phineas Chase Desire Wing** Came for Their Answer friends finds
Nothing to hinder Them but that they may Procede According to the good
Order of Truth This Meeting is Ajorned tell yᵉ Youth Meeting This
Meeting held by Ajornment gives Testimoney against **Ruth Lawton**
for her out going in haveing a Child with out being Maried **Mary Slocom [Slocum]**
Mary Smith are Chose to Attend the Quarterly Meeting **Ruth Tucker**
is Chose to write to the Meeting.

The 20 of yᵉ 5 moᵗʰ 1719

Was our Monthly Meeting of Women Friends Held at **Dartmouth**
Colected at this Metting 3ˢ 6ᵈ Disbusted for yᵉ use of Friends 8ˢ **Ruth**
Lawtons Condemnation is Signed and to be read at **Coket** Meeting House

The 17 of yᵉ 6 mᵒ 1719

Was Our Monthly Meeting of Women Friends Held at **Dartmouth**
Colected at this Meeting 6ˢ This Meeting Received an Eppestle
from yᵉ Yearly and Quarterly Meeting at **Newport** and was Read &
kindly Received £ 2:10 Disbusted for the use of Friends

The 21 of yᵉ 7 mᵒ 1719

Was Our Monthly Meetting of Women Friends Held at **Dartmouth**
Colected at This Meeting 6ˢ Receved an Account from **Rochester** that They
have Receved an Account from yᵉ visiters That hath visited Friends and find
Things for yᵉ most part pretty well visiters of this Meeting gives word that they
find thing in pretty good Order as fure as they See **Hannah Tucker Ruth**

Smith are Chose to attend yᵉ Quarterly Meeting

The 19 of 8 yᵉ moᵗ <u>1719</u>

Was Our Monthly Meeting of Women Friends Held at **Dartmouth**
Colected at This Meeting 3ˢ 5ᵈ **Rachel Allin [Allen] Ruth Tucker** is Chose to go
to **Alice Antone** to discorce her Consirning her Marying out of the Order
of Friends **Rachel Allin [Allen] Abigal Allin [Abigail Allen]** Con is Chose to take **Lyddy
How land** to due for yᵉ Same fault

The 16 of yᵉ 9 m⁰ <u>1719</u>

Was Our Monthly Meeting of Women Friends Held at **Dartmouth**
Colected at this Meeting 3ˢ 6ᵈ **John Summers Preast Davis** Lead [Laid]
Their Intention ᵒᶠ Mariage before this Meeting **Martha Wing** and
Elizabeth Wing are Chose to Inquire into the Young Womans Clearness

The 25 of yᵉ 10 m⁰ <u>1719</u>

Was Our Monthly Meeting of Women Friends Held at **Dartmouth**
Colected at this Meeting 11ˢ 10ᵈ **John Summers Preast Davis** Came for
Their answer and Their is nothing found but that they may Procede
In Mariage According to the good Order of Truth Disbusted for the
use of friends 11ˢ **Mary Lawton Mary Smith** are Chose to Attend yᵉ Quarterly
Meeting **Ruth Tucker**

The 18 of yᵉ 11 mo<u>th</u> <u>1719</u>/20

Was Our Monthly Meeting of Women Friends Held at **Dartmouth**
Colected at This Meeting 5ˢ 6ᵈ Desbusted for yᵉ use of Friends £2[?] 10

The 15 of yᵉ 12 m⁰ <u>1719</u>/20

Was Our Monthly Meeting of Women friends Held at **Dartmouth**
Colected at this Meeting 3ˢ **Ruth Smith Hannah Tucker Ruth Tucker**
are Chose to Ballance yᵉ Accounts Disbusted for The use of Friends 5ˢ 6ᵈ

The 28 of yᵉ 1 m⁰ <u>1720</u>

Was Our Monthly Meeting of Women friends Held at **Dartmouth**
Colected at this Meeting 8ˢ 11ᵈ visiters gives an Account that they have
Visited friends families and find Things prety well **Mary Slocom [Slocum] Hannah
Tucker** are Chose to Attend yᵉ Quarterly Meeting **Abigal Allin [Abigail Allen] Phebe
Tucker** are Chose to discorc **Sarah Wing** for her out goings **Ruth Tucker** is Chose
to write to the Quarterly Meeting

The 18 of yᵉ 2 m⁰ <u>1720</u>

Was Our Monthly Meeting of Women friends Held at **Dartmouth**
Colected at this Meeting 8ˢ 3ᵈ **Brier Godard [Goddard] Ann Smith** Lead Their
Intention of Mariage before this Meeting **Ruth Smith Phebe Tucker**
are Chose to Inquire Into the Young Womans Clearncss The Friends that
were Chose to yᵉ Quarterly Meeting brings an Account that yᵉ Meeting
hath Taken it in to Consideration Concerning yᵉ Chusing of visiters and
Refered to yᵉ Yearly Meeting. The Friends brings in their Accout Concer
ning Their discorse with **Sarah Wing** and She Signifies to them that

The Report is True for ~~The~~ which They have Sined [Signed] a paper to be Read
against her

The 16 of yᵉ 3 mᵒ <u>1720</u>

Was Our Monthly Meeting of Women Friends Held at **Dartmouth**
Colected at this Meeting 5ˢ 5ᵈ **Rachel Allin [Allen] Ruth Tucker** ~~Alliee [Alice]~~
~~Tripp~~ is Chose to discorce **Alice Tripp** Concerning a paper that was
Sent in to the Meetting be She and her Husband

The 20 of yᵉ 4 mᵒ <u>1720</u>

Was Our Meeting of Women Friends Held at **Dartmouth**
Colected at this Meeting 7ˢ 2ᵈ **Brier Godard [Goddard] Ann Smith** Came for
Answer friends finds nothing but that they may Procede In Mariage
According to the good Order of Truth **Mary Slocom [Slocum] Mary Smith** are
Chose to Attend yᵉ Quarterly Meeting.

The 18 of yᵉ 5 mᵒ <u>1720</u>

Was Our Monthly Meeting of Women Friends Held at **Dartmouth**
Colected at this Meeting 11ˢ 11ᵈ Received an Epestle from yᵉ Yearly
Meeting which was Read and kindly Excepted It is Con[c]luded by yᵉ Year
ly Meeting that yᵉ Monthly Meettings Shall Chuse Their visiters once
a Year Disbusted 20ˢ for yᵉ use of Friends

The 15 of yᵉ 6 mᵒ <u>1720</u>

Was Our Monthly Meeting of Women Friends Held at **Dartmouth.**
Colected at this Meeting 8ˢ 6ᵈ **John Waiker [Walker] Sarah Summers** Lead
Their Intention of Mariage before this Meeting **Mehettable Wing**
Doritie Wing are Chose to make Inquire Into the Young Womens Clear
ness this Meetting Chuses **Rachel Allin [Allen] Hannah Tucke[r] Marye**
Smith Hannah Cadmon [Cadman] visitors The Accounts are balanced and thei[rI
is In the Stock £1:12s

The 19 of yᵉ 7 mᵒ <u>1720</u>

Was Our Monthly Meeting of Women friends Held at **Dartmouth**
Colected at this Meeting 7ˢ 11ᵈ **Rachel Allin [Allen]** is Chose to keep the Stock **Mary**
Slocom [Slocum] Mary Lawton is Chose to Attend the Quarterly Meeting

The 17 of yᵉ 8 mᵒ <u>1720</u>

Was Our Monthly Meeting of Women Friends Held at **Dartmouth**
Colected at this Meeting 5[?]ˢ **John Su Waker [Walker] Sarah Summers** Came
for Their Answer friends finds nothing but that they may Procede in Ma
riage According to the good Order of Truth **Samuel Wing Dorite Clivens [Dorothy**
Clifton] Lead Their Intention of Mariage before this Meeting **Martha Wing Bashabe**
Barler [Bathsheba Barker?] are Chose to Inquire Into yᵉ Young Womans Cle arness

The 21 of yᵉ 9 mᵒ <u>1720</u>

Was Our Monthly Meeting of Women Friends Held at **Dartmouth**
Colected at this Meeting 7ˢ **Benjeman Russel [Benjamin Russell] Abigal Howland**
Lead Their Intention of Mariage before this Meeting **Joseph Tucker**

Mary Howland also Lead Their Intention **Phebe Tucker Jeane [Jean, Jeanne] Smith**
are Chose to make Inquiere Into ʸᵉ Young Womens Clearness

The 19 of yᵉ 10 mᵒ 1720

Was Our Monthly Meetting of Women Friends Held at **Dartmouth**
Colected at this Meetting 7ˢ 1ᵈ **Samuel Wing Dorite Cliven [Dorothy Clifton]** Came for
Their Answer friends finds nothing to hinder Them but that they may Pro
cede In Mariage in the good order of Truth **Benjeman Russel [Benjamin Russell] Abigal
Howland** and **Joseph Tucker Mary Howland** Came for their Answer This
Meetting gives leave to ᵗʰᵉᵐ Mary in the good Order of truth Disbusted for ~
the use of friends £1:1 **Ruth Tucker** is Chose to   yᵉ Sende to yᵉ Quart
terly Meetting

The 16 of 11 mᵒ 1720/21

Was Our Monthly Meetting of Women friends Held at **Dartmouth**
Colected at this Meetting 6ˢ **Daniel Weeden Joanna Slocom [Slocum]** Lead Their
Intention of Mariage before this Meetting **Hannah Tucker Phebe Tucker**
are Chose to Inquire into yᵉ Young Womans Clearness. This Meetting hath
Sinned [Signed] a paper against **Sarah Akines [Akin]** for Mariing against friends Con
cent

The 20 of 12 mᵒ 1720/21

Was Our Monthly Meetting of Women friends Held at **Dartmouth**
Colected at This Meetting 8ˢ **Daniel Weeden Joanna Slocom [Slocum]** Came for Their
answer Friends finds Nonthing to Hinder Them gives Leave to Mare in the good Order of
Truth Desbusted for yᵉ use of Friends £1=15

The 27 of 1 mᵒ 1721

Was Our Monthly Meetting of Women Friends Held at **Dartmouth**
Colected at This Meetting 8ˢ. Receved an Account from **Rochester** Weekly Meett
ing That they have Visited Friends families and for the most part find things wel[l]
This Meetting is Ajorned tell yᵉ Youths Meetting. yᵉ 4ᵈ of 2 mᵒ yᵉ Meetting held[?]
by Ajornment our Visiters gives an Account they have Visited friends families
and finds among Some Things in good Order but Others not so well as Could be desired
but friends are in the Labour to Regulate and bring into order. **Hannah Tucker
Phebe Tucker** are Chose to Attend yᵉ Quarterly Meetting **Ruth Tucker** is
Chose to write to yᵉ Meetting

The 17 of yᵉ 2 mᵒ 1721

Was Our Monthly Meetting of Women friends Held at **Dartmouth**
Colected by This Meetting 3ˢ 6ᵈ The friends brings no Account of Besness from
yᵉ Quarterly Meetting.

The 15 of yᵉ 3 mᵒ 1721

Was Our Monthly Meetting of Women friends Held at **Dartmouth**
Colected by This Meetting 6ˢ 3ᵈ Desbusted 6ˢ 4ᵈ

The 19 of yᵉ 4 mᵒ 1721

Was Our Monthly Meetting of Women friends Held at **Dartmouth**

Colected by This Meeting 7ˢ **Thomas Bordain [Borden] Mary Gifford** Lead Their In
tention of Mariage before this Meetting **Mary Slocom [Slocum] Hannah Tucker**
are Chose to mak Inquiere Into the Young Womans Clearness £1 4 Desbusted
for yᵉ use of Friends **Mary Slocom [Slocum] Hannah Tucker** are Chose to Attend the
Quarterly Meeting.

The 17 of yᵉ 5 mᵒ 1721

Was Our Monthly Meeting of Women friends Held at **Dartmouth**
Colected at this Meeting 5ˢ 6ᵈ **Thomas Bordain [Borden] Mary Gifford** Came for their
Answer friends finds nothing to Hinder them gives Leave to Take Each
Other In the good Order of Truth

The 21 of yᵉ 6 mᵒ 1721

Was Our Monthly Meeting of Women friends Held at **Dartmouth**
Colected at This Meetting 4ˢ 6ᵈ

The 18 of yᵉ 7 mᵒ 1721

Was Our Monthly Meeting of Women Friends Held at **Dartmouth**
Colected at this Meeting 10ˢ Desbusted for the use of Friends 13ˢ 6ᵈ Receivd
on Account from **Rochester** Weekly Meetting that they have visited friends
families and finde things prety well This meeting Chuses visiters for this Y
ear **Hannah Cudmon [Cadman] Hannah Tucker Mary Smith Phebe Tucker Mary
Smith Mary Rusel [Russell]** are Chose to Attend yᵉ Quarterly Meeting **Ruth Tucker** is
Chose to R write to yᵉ Quarterly Meeting.

The 23 of yᵉ 8 mᵒ 1721

Was Our Monthly Meeting of Women Friends Held at **Dartmouth**
Colected at this Meeting 4ˢ

The 20 of yᵉ 9 mᵒ 1721

Was Our Monthly Meeting of Women friends Held at **Dartmouth**
Colected at this meeting 9ˢ 6ᵈ

The 18 of yᵉ 10 mᵒ 1721

Was Our Monthly Meeting of Women friends Held at **Dartmouth**
Colected at this Meeting 6ˢ **Abraham Tucker Elizabeth Rusel [Russell]** Lead
Their Intention of Mariage **Mary Rusel [Russell] Mary Smith** are Chose to ma
ke Inquiere Into the Young Womans Clearness **Mary Lawton Phebe Tucker**
are Chose to Attend yᵉ Quarterly Meeting **Ruth Tucker** is Chose to draw
up an Account to send to y Meeting **Hannah Tucker Mary Rusel [Russell]** are Chose
to Speak with **Mary Howland** about her Marging out of yᵉ order of Truth

The 15 of 11 mᵒ 1721/22

Was Our Monthly Meetting of Women friends Held At **Dartmouth**
Colected at this Meeting 3ˢ 6ᵈ **Abraham Tucker Elizabeth Rusel [Russell]** Came
for Their Answer friends finds nothing to hinder Gives Them Leave to Procede
In Mariage According to the good Order of Truth yᵉ friends that were Chose to
Talke with **Marye [Mary] Howland** ‸ˢᵃᵉˢ ˢʰᵉ gives them no Satisfaction.

The 19 of yᵉ 12 mᵒ 1721/22

Was Our Monthly Meetting of Women friends Held at **Dartmouth**
Colected at this Meeting 14ˢ 11ᵈ It is a Concluded **Mary Howland**s Condemnation
Shall be Signed and Read in yᵉ Next Meeting

The 26 of yᵉ 1 mᵒ 1722

Was Our Monthly Meetting of Women friends Held at **Dartmouth**
Colected at this Meeting 5ˢ The Visiters gives an Account that they have visited
friends families and for the most part find things prety well **Mary Slocom [Slocum]**
Hannah Tucker are Chose to Attend the Quarterly Meetting **Ruth Tucker** is
Chose to write to the Meeting

The 23 of yᵉ 2 mᵒ 1722

Was Our Monthly Meetting of Women friends Held at **Dartmouth**
Colected at this Meeting 4ˢ 10ᵈ **Isacc Wood Mary Potter** Lead Their Intention
of Mariage before this Meeting **Hannah Cadman Phebe Tucker** are Chose
to See Into the Young Womans Clearness

The 21 of yᵉ 3 mᵒ 1722

Was Our Monthly Meetting of Women Friends Held at **Dartmouth**
Colected at this Meeting 6ˢ 6ᵈ **Isaac Wood Mary Potter** Came for Their Ans
wer friends finds Nothing to Hinder Them gives Leave to Mare In the good
Order of friends **Seth Rusel [Russell] Hannah Allin [Allen]** Lead Their Intention of
Mariage before This Meeting **Mary Rusel [Russell] Phebe Tucker** are Chose to Make
Inquiere Into the Young Womans Clearness Desbusted for yᵉ use of Friends 1ˢ6 ᵈ [?]

The 18 of yᵉ 4 mᵒ 1722

Was Our Monthly Meetting of Women Friends Held at **Dartmouth**
Colected at this Meeting 6ˢ 5ᵈ **Seth Rusel [Russell] Hannah Allin [Allen]** Came for Their
Answer friends find Nothing to hinder Gives Leave That they may Procede
In Mariage In the good Order of Truth

The 16 of yᵉ 5 mᵒ 1722

Was Our Monthly Meetting of Women Friends Held at **Dartmouth**
Colected at this Meeting 7ˢ 9ᵈ **Jeames [James] Sherman Grisel Merihue [Grizzel
Merihew]** Lead Their Intention of Mariage before This Meeting **Mary Laton [Lawton]**
Phebe Tucker are Chose to make Inquiere Into yᵉ Young Womans Clearness Received an
Epestle from
Rhoadisland [Rhode Island] Yearly Meeting which was Read and kindly Excepted.

The 20 of yᵉ 6 mᵒ 1722

Was Our Monthly Meetting of Women Friends Held at **Dartmouth**
Colected at this Meeting 5ˢ 7ᵈ **Jeames [James] Sherman Grisel Mrihue [Grizzel Merihew]**
Came for Their Answer friends finds nothing to hinder gives them leave to Mare **Rachel Al**
lin [Allen] Ruth Smith Ruth Tucker is Chose to Balance yᵉ Accounts Desbusted for the
use of Friends £1· 2ˢ.

The 17 of yᵉ 7 mᵒ 1722

Was Our Monthly Meetting of Women friends Held at **Dartmouth**

Colected at this Meeting 7ˢ 9ᵈ **Benjeman Wing Content Tucker** Lead Their
Intention of Mariage before this Meeting **Mary Slocom [Slocum] Mary Rusel [Russell]** Are
Chose to Inquire Into the Young Womans Clearness **Mary Lawton Hope Merihue [Merihew]**
are Appointed to Attend yᵉ Quarterly Meetting Desbusted 9ˢ 9ᵈ for yᵉ use of Friends

The 15 of yᵉ 8 mᵒ <u>1722</u>

Was Our Monthly Meetting of Women friends Held at **Dartmouth**
Colected at this Meetting 3ˢ 9ᵈ **Benjeman [Benjamin] Wing Content Tucker** Came for Their
Answer friends finds nothing to Hinder gives them Leave to Mare [Marry] In the Good
Order of Truth **John Lawton Patience Cerby [Kirby]** Lead their Intention of
Mariage before this Meetting **Hope Merihue [Merihew] Mary Lappam [Lapham]** are
Chose to Make Inquiere Into the Young Womans Clearness visiters Chose for this Year
are **Hannah Tucker Phebe Tucker Mary Rusel [Russell] Hannah Cadman.**

The 19 of yᵉ 9 mᵒ <u>1722</u>

Was Our Monthly Meetting of Woman Friends Held at **Dartmouth**
Colected at this Meetting 6ˢ **John Lawton Patience Cerby [Kirby]** Came for their answer
friends finds Nothing to Hinder gives them Leave to Mare In the good Order of
Truth The Accounts Ballanced and their is in the Stock £2 9 10.

The 17 of yᵉ 10 mᵒ <u>1722</u>

Was Our Monthly Meetting of Women Friends Held at **Dartmouth**
Colected at this Meetting 8ˢ Desbusted for yᵉ use of Friends £2 15 **Mary Slocom [Slocum]**
Rebecca Slocom [Slocum] are Chose to Attend yᵉ Quarterly Meetting **Ruth Tucker** is Cho
se to write to the Quarterly Meetting

The 21 of 11 mᵒ <u>1722</u>/23

Was Our Monthly Meetting of Women Friends Held at **Dartmouth**
Colected at this Meetting 5ˢ Received an Epestle from yᵉ Quarterly Meetting
which was Read and kindly Excepted

The 18 of yᵉ 12 mᵒ <u>1722</u>/23

Was Our Monthly Meetting of Woman Friends Held at **Dartmouth**
Colected at this Meetting 3ˢ 1ᵈ

The 15 of yᵉ 1 mᵒ <u>1723</u>

Was Our Monthly Meetting of Women friends Held at **Dartmouth**
Colected at this Meetting 7ˢ 10ᵈ **Hannah Tucker Mary Rusel [Russell]** are Chose to Attend
The Quarterly Meetting visiters gives an Account that they have visited friends
families and find good Satisfaction in it **Ruth Tucker** is Chose to write to the
Meetting.

The 15 of yᵉ 2-mᵒ <u>1723</u>

Was Our Monthly Meetting of Women friends Held at **Dartmouth**
Colected at this Meetting 3ˢ 10ᵈ

The 20 of yᵉ 3 mᵒ <u>1723</u>

Was Our Monthly Meetting of Women friends Held at **Dartmouth**
Colected at this Meetting 3ˢ 4ᵈ Hearing an Accout that **Elizabeth Tripp**

yᵉ Wife of **Joseph Tripp** has a mind to be in unity with friends haveing for
Some Time past been desowned for Mareing out of the Order of Friends This
Meeting Chuses Two friends **Mary Lawton Hannah Cudman** [**Cadman**] to discorce
with her and Return her Answer to yᵉ Next Monthly Meeting.

The 22 of yᵉ 4 mº 1723

Was our Monthly Meeting of Women Friends held in **Dartmouth**
Collected at this Meeting 9ˢᵈ 1ᵈ **Mary Slocum** and **Mary Smith** are Chosen
to Attend the Quarterly Meeting to be holden at **Rhoadisland** 14ˢ ==
Disbusted for the Vse [use] of friends

The 15 of yᵉ 5 mº 1723

Was Our Monthly Meeting of Women Friends held in **Dartmouth**
Collected. by this Meeting 5ˢ 2ᵈ this Meeting Recieved an Epistle from
Rhoadisland Yearly Meeting Which Was Read and Cindly Excepted

The 19 of yᵉ 6 mº 1723

Was our Monthly Meeting of Women friends held in **Dartmouth**
Collected by this Meeting: 8ˢ 1ᵈ Disbusted by this 20ˢ

The 16 of yᵉ 7 mº 1723

Was our Monthly Meeting of Women friends held in **Dartmouth**
Collected by this Meeting 6ˢ 1ᵈ **Phebe Tucker** and **Mary Laton** [**Lawton**] are Chosen
to attend the Quarterly Meeting to be holden at **PorthMouth** [**Portsmouth**] on **Rhoad** [**Rhode**]
Island Ruth Tucker Is Chosen to Righ [write] to the Quarterly Meeting 20ˢ
Disbusted for the Vse fo [*sic*] friends

The 21 of the 8 mº 1723

Was our Monthly Meeting of Women friends held at **Dartmouth**
Where **Samuel Howland** and **Sarah Soul** [**Soule, Sowle**] Laid their Intentions of Marriage and
Ware Desired to Wait for their Answer untill our Next Collected by this
Meeting 5ˢ and 5ˢ Disbusted for the Use of friends

The 18 of yᵉ 9 mº 1723

Was our Monthly Meeting of Women friends Held at **Dartmouth**
Collected By this Meeting 5ˢ 6ᵈ at this Meeting **Samuel Howland** and
Sarah Soul [**Soule, Sowle**] Came for their answer. this Meeting finding Nothing to Heⁿder
them giving them Leave that they Might Marry in the good order of truth

The 16 of yᵉ 10 mº 1723

Was our Monthly Meeting of Women friends Held at **Dartmouth**
Collected by this Meeting 5ˢ 6ᵈ Visiters Chose for this year **Hannah**
Tucker Phebe Tucker Hannah Cadman Hannah Tucker and **Mary Laph[am]**
are Chosen to attend the Querterly Meeting to be Held at **Newport** on
Rhoadisland

The 20 of yᵉ 11 mº 1723/4

Was our Month.ˡʸ Meeting of Women friends Held at **Dartmouth**
No Business presented

The 17 of ye 12 m^o 1723/4

Was our Monthly Meeting of Women Friends Held at **Dartmouth**
Collected by this meeting 5^s 3^d **phebe Tucker** is Chosen to Keep the Stock

The 16 of ye 1 m^o 1724

Was our Monthly Meeting of Women friends Held at **Dartmouth**
Collected by this Meeting 8^s 3^d this Meeting is Aiurned [Adjourned] Untill the
3^{dy} of ye 2 m^o Next: this Meeting Being Met According to Aiurmend
Barnabas Howland and **Rebecah Lapham** Have Laid their intentions
of Marriage Before this Meeting Were Desired to Wait for their
answer Untill our Next **Phebe Tucker** and **Mary Smith** are Chosen
to Make inquire into the young Womans Clearness **Elisabeth**
Tripp and **Phebe Tucker** are Chosen to Attend the Quarterly Meeting to
be held at **porth Mouth** [**Portsmouth**] the 10 of ye 2 m^o 1724 **Ruth Tucker** Is Chose
To Draw Up an Account to the Same

The 20 of the 2 m^o 1724

Was our Monthly Meeting of Women friends held in **Dartmouth**
Collected by this meeting 4^s 19^d **Barnabas Howland** and **Rebecah Lapham**
Came for their Answer the Meeting Finding Nothing to hender give them leave
to Marry in the good order of truth y^e friends that Was Chose to attend the
quarterly meeting Brings No account to this Meeting of any Business

The 18 of y^e 3 m^o 1724

Was our Monthly Meeting of Women friends held in **Dartmouth**
Collected by this Meeting 4^s 3^d ==

The 22 of y^e 4 m^o 1724

Was our Monthly Meeting of Women friends held in **dartmouth**
at this Meeting **Amos Taber** and **Elizabeth Lapham** laid their Inten
tions of Marriage and they are Desired to Wait untill our Next for
their Answer this Meeting Makes Choice of **Mary Russel** [**Russell**] and **Phebe Tucker**
to Make inquire into the young Womans Clearness this Meeting Makes
Choice of **Mary Slocum** and **Hope Mariho** [**Merihew**] to Attend the quarterly Meeting to be
held at **Newport** on **Rhoad Island Ruth Tucker** Is Chose to Draw up an
account to the Same: 3^s Disbusted for the Vse of friends

The 20 of y^e 5 m^o 1724

Was our Month Meeting of Women friends held in **Dartmouth**
Amos Taber and **Elizabeth Lapham** Came for their Answer friends finde No
thing to hender. give them Leave to Marry in the good order of truth =
Collected By this meeting 6^s 1^d this meeting Recieved an Epistle from
Rhoad Island yearly Meeting Which was Read and Cindly Excepted
friends that Was chose to Attend the quarterly Meeting brings No account of
any business to this Meeting

The 17 of y^e 6 m^o 1724

Was our Monthly Meeting of Women friends held in **dartmouth**

Jonathan Wood and Peace Davis Laid their Intention of Marriage and
they Were Desired to Wait Untill our Next for their answer and Phebe
Tucker and Mary Lapham are Chose to make inquire into the young Womans
Clearness Thomas Smith and Sarah Russel [Russell] Laid their intention of Marriage
before this Meeting and they are desired to Wait Untill our Next for their
answer. Also Nathan Jene [Jenney] and Prisciller Taber Laid their Intentions of
Marriage before this Meeting and they Were Desired to Wait Untill our
Next for their answer and Mary Russel [Russell] and Jeen [Jean] Smith are Chose to Make
Inquire into the young Womens Clearness Collected at this Meeting 8ˢ 3ᵈ
Disbusted for the Use of friends 34ˢ Shillings

The 24 of the 7ᵗʰ month 1724
Was our monthly meeting of women friends held in
Dartmouth Jonathan Wood and Peace Davis Came for their answer
this Meeting finding nothing to hinder gives them Leave to marry in the
good order ₐᵒᶠ truth and also Nathan Gene [Jenne] and Pricilla Taber Came to this meeting
for their ₐᵃⁿˢʷᵉʳ and friends finding all thing Clear Gives them Leave to marry in the
order of truth and also At this meeting Simeon Gifford and Susanna Jenkins
Laid their intentions of taking each other in marriage and Was desired
to wait til the next monthly meeting for their answer and ~~frien~~ there
was friends Chose to se[e] into ~~their~~ Clearness of the young woman
Phebe Tucker and Mary Laton [Lawton] are Chose to attend yᵉ Quarterly meeting to be
held at Portsmouth yᵉ 16 of yᵉ 8ᵗʰ month next
There was Collected at this meeting 6 Shilling and three pence

The 19ᵗʰ of yᵉ 8ᵗʰ month 1724 Was our monthly meeting of Women friends held
at Dartmouth Collected by this meeting 3ˢ and 8ᵈ
at this meeting Thoˢ Smith and Sarah Russel [Russell] Came to this meetin[g] for their
answer and nothing appearing to hinder they had their answer and Leave
to marry One: of yᵉ friends that was Chose to attend the Quar[ter]ly meeting Last
did attend and bring no account of any business

The 16ᵗʰ of yᵉ 9ᵗʰ month 1724 Was our monthly meeting of Women friends
held in Dartmouth: Collected at this meeting 0-07ˢ=00 and taken out of the
Stock for yᵉ use of friend 1-10=00 At this Meeting Abigal Ricketson
Gave in a Paper of Cᵒⁿᵈᵉᵐⁿᵃᵗⁱᵒⁿ ~~acknowledgemen~~ of her out going in Marrying Contrary
to the Order of friends Which was accepted and She is under yᵉ Care of friends again

The 21ˢᵗ of yᵉ 10ᵗʰ mo: 1724 Was our monthly meeting of Women friends held in
Dartmouth Collected by this meeting six shillings & 8 pence
at this meeting Jedediah Wood and Keziah Summers Laid their intention of
Marriage Mary Russel [Russell] and Phebe Tucker are Chose to make inquiry into
the young womans Clearness and to make return to the Next monthly meetᵢₙg
David Irish and Jenevereth Summers Laid their intention of marriage
and there was 2 friends chose to make inquiry concerning the young womans
Clearnes and make return to the next monthly meeting

this Meeting Makes Choice of **Mary Laton [Lawton]** and **Phebe Tucker** to attend yᵉ
the Quarterly meeting next to be held at **NewPort** on **Rhoad Island**
Ruth Tucker and **Phebe Tucker** are Chose to Draw up an Epistle to Send to the
Quarterly meeting. **Dinah Smith** and **Phebe Tucker** Chose to ballance the
accounts of this meeting

The 18ᵗʰ day of the 11ᵗʰ month 1724/25 Was our monthly meeting of Women friends
held in **Dartmouth David Irish** and **Jenevereth Summers** Came for their answer
and friends finding nothing to hinder ~~they~~ Gave them Leave to Marry in the Good
Order of truth At this meeting **Nicholas Davis** and **Hannah Wood** Laid their in
=tention of Marriage and Were desired to Wait until the next for their answer
And **Mary Lapham** and **Rebecca Ruseel [Russell]** were Chosen to make inquiery into
the young womans Clearness in that affair – and make return to our next
monthly meeting The accounts ballanced and Remains in yᵉ stock 1=01=05

The 15ᵗʰ of yᵉ 12ᵗʰ month 1724/25 was our monthly meeting of Women friends
held in **Dartmouth** there was Collected by this meeting 0-6=07 and taken out
of yᵉ Stock for yᵉ use of friends 10 Shillings at this meeet,ⁱⁿᵍ **Jedediah Wood** and **Keziah
Summers** Came for their answer and this meeting finding nothing to hinder
Gives them Leave to Marry in the Good order of truth and also **Nicholas Davis**
and **Hannah Wood** Came to this meeting for their answer and the meeting
finding nothing to hinder Gives them Leave to marry in yᵉ Good order
Of truth and the visiters Chose for this year are
Mehetabel Burril [Burrell] and **Rose Howland**

The 15ᵗʰ day of yᵉ first month 1725 Was our monthly meeting of women friends held
in **Dartmouth.** Collected by this meeting 4 Shillings and 8 pence
and this meeting is ajourned until the youths meeting next insuing
This meeting held by ajournment being meet our visiters ‸ᵍᵃᵛᵉ an accoun that they
have visited friends families and for the most part find things pretty well
this meeting makes choice of **Hannah Tucker** and **Phebe tucker** to attend the Quarterly
Meting next to be held at **Portsmouth** on **Rhoad Island** and **Ruth Tucker** is chosen
to Write an Epistle to the Quarterly meeting.

The 19ᵗʰ the 2ᵈ month 1725 Was our monthly meeting of Women friends held in
Dartmouth Collected by this meeting six Shillings At this meeting **Simeon
Gifford** and **Susanna Jenkins** Came for their answer and nothing appearing
to hinder they had their answer that they might proceed to take each other in mar
=riage in the Good order of truth: yᵉ friends that were chose to attend yᵉ Quarterly
Meeting have attended it and there is no account of any business fro yᵉ Quarterly
Meeting to this meeting this meeting received an Epistle from **Elisabeth Webb**
Which was Read and kindly accepted

The 17ᵗʰ of yᵉ 3ᵈ month 1725 Was our monthly meeting of Women friends held
in **Dartmouth** there was Collected by this Meeting 0-03=07 and two friends
Were Chose to Speak with **Contet Howland** Concerning her Going to Marry out
of yᵉ order of friends her answer to them was that it Cannot now be helped

The 21 of yᵉ 4ᵗʰ month 1725 Was our monthly Meeting of Women friends
held in **Dartmouth** Collected by this meeting o=12=03 **Marry Laton [Lawton]** and
Hope Merihöo [Merrihew] are chosen to attend yᵉ Quarterly meeting next to be held at
New Port on **Rhoad Island** yᵉ 9ᵗʰ of yᵉ 5ᵗʰ ₍month₎ next **Phebe Tucker** and **Mehatabel
Burril [Burrell]** are Chose with the men friends to Draw up **Content Briggs**es
Condemnation there was 1-03=06 Disbusted out of yᵉ Stock for yᵉ use of friends

The 19ᵗʰ of yᵉ 5ᵗʰ Month 1725 Was our monthly meeting of Women friends held
in **Dartmouth** Collected by this meeting o-4=01 taken out of yᵉ Stock for yᵉ use
of friends 0-06=00 this meeting Received an Epistle from **Rhoad Island** yearly
Meeting which Was Read and kindly accepted this meeting hath Signed **Content
Briggs** her Condemnation for her Disorderly Marrying

The 16ᵗʰ day of yᵉ 6ᵗʰ month 1725 Was our monthly meeting of Women friends held
In **Dartmouth** There was Collected at this meeting o-07=05

The 20ᵗʰ day of yᵉ 7ᵗʰ month 1725 Was our monthly meeting of women friends held in
Dartmouth Collected by this meeting o-06=07 This meeting makes Choice of
Mary Russell and **Mary Smith** to attend yᵉ Quarterly meeting to be held at
Portsmouth the 8ᵗʰ of the 8ᵗʰ month next

The 18ᵗʰ of yᵉ 8ᵗʰ month 1725 Was our monthly meeting of Women friends
held in **Dartmouth** Collected by this meeting o-02-02

The 15ᵗʰ day of yᵉ 9ᵗʰ month 1725 Was our monthly meeting of Women friends
held in **Dartmouth** Collected by this meeting o-03=06 Disbusted out of yᵉ Stock for
the use of friends twenty Shillings

The 20ᵗʰ of yᵉ 10 month 1725/26 Was our monthly meeting of Women friends held
in **Dartmouth** Collected by this meeting o-07=01 Disbusted out of yᵉ Stock for yᵉ
keeping the meeting house 1-10=00 **Marry Laton [Lawton]** and **Hope Merrihoo [Merrihew]**
are Chose to attend the Quarterly meeting next to be held at **New Port** on
Rhoad Island Phebe Tucker and **Ruth Tucker** are Chosen to write an
Epistle to yᵉ Quarterly meeting **Hannah Tucker** and **Ruth Tucker** are
chose to ballance the accounts of this meeting

The 17ᵗʰ of the 11ᵗʰ month 1725/26 Was our monthly meeting of Women friends held in **Dartmouth**
Collected by this meeting o-5=9 At this meeting **John Lapham** and **Desire Howland**
Laid their intention of marriage **Phebe Tucker** and **Mary Smith** are chose to see
after the young Womans Clearness and bring in their account to the next monthly
Meeting the friend that were chosen to attend the quarterly meeting Did attend it
but bring no account of any Business to this meeting

The 21 day of yᵉ 12 month 1725 Was our monthly meeting of Women friends held
in **Dartmouth** At this meeting **John Lapham** and **Desire Howland** Came for their
answer and friends finding nothing to hinder Gave them Leave to Marry
At this meeting **George Smith** and **Elisebeth Allen** laid their intention of
Marriage and are desired to wat until yᵉ next monthly meeting for their
Answer **Mary Russell** and **Phebe Tucker** are chosen to make inquiry Con
=Cerning the young Woman Clearness and make return to the next month

=ly meeting There was Collected by this meeting – 0-04=10
the accounts of this meeting are ballanced and remains in y^e Stock 0-10=[?]
Hannah Tucker and **Mary Russel** [**Russell**] and **Phebe Tucker** are chosen
visiters for the year Insuing

The 21 day of the first month 1726 was our monthly meeting of women friends
held in **Dartmouth** at this meeting **George Smith** and **Elisabeth Allen** Came
for their answer and friends finding nothing to Hinder gave them leave to
Marry in ye Good order of truth
John Tibbits and **Sarah Soule** [**Sowle**] laid their intention of taking each other in
marriage 2 friends are chose to make inquiry into the young womans clearness
this meeting is adjourned until ye youths meeting next Insuing

This meeting being mett according to adjournment our visiters gives an
account to this meeting that they have visited the families of friends and in
a General Way find things Indeferent well
and 2 friends are Chosen to attend y^e Quarterly meeting at **Portsmouth**
the 8th of y^e 2$^{\underline{d}}$ month Insuing **Ruth Tucker** is chosen to Draw up the accou$_{nts}$
of this meeting to the Quarterly Meeting and there was 5 shillings
Collected at this meeting

The 18th of y^e 2^d month 1726 Was our monthly meeting of Women friends
Held in **Dartmouth**: Collected by this meeting nine shillings & 3 pence
At this meeti$_{ng}$ **John Tibbits** and **Sarah Soule** [**Sowle**] Came for their Answer
and friends finding nothing to Hinder Gave them Leave to Marry in y^e Good
Order of friends: **John Russell** and **Joanna Tucker** have laid their Intentions
of Marriage before this meeting and two friends are Chose to make Inquiry
Into ye Young Womens Clearness the friends that Were Chosen to attend
the Quarterly Meeting have attended it and bring no account of any
business to this meeting there was Disbusted for the use of friends
twenty shillings

The 16th of y^e 3^d mo 1726 Was our monthly meeting of women friends
held in **Dartmouth** Collected at this meeting 6 shillings and 3 pence
at this meeti$_\wedge$ng **John Russell** and **Joanna Tucker** Came for their answer
and this meeting finding nothing to hinder them gives them Leave to marry
In y^e Good order of truth

The 20th of y^e 4th month 1726 Was our monthly meeting of Women friends
held in **Dartmouth** Collected by this meeting nine shillings & six pence
and disbusted for y^e use of friends 4 Shillings and nine pence
This meeting Received an Epistle from **Rhoad Island** yearly meeting of Women
friends Which was Read and kindly accepted This meeting hath chosen 2 Women
frie[n]ds to attend the Quarterly meeting next to be held at **New Port**

The 18 of the 5 month $_\wedge$1726 was our monthly meeting of women friends held in **Dartmouth**
Collected by this meeting ~~18~~ eight Shillings and 4 pence

The 15th of ye 6 month 1726 Was our monthly meeting of Women friends held
in **Dartmouth** Collected at this meeting 8 Shillings and 4 pence
there was 10 Shillings Disbusted for ye use of friends

The 19 of ye 7th month 1726 Was our monthly meeting of Women friends held
in **Dartmouth** Collected at this meeting 5 shillings & 2ds
At this meeting **Seth Kelle** [**Kelley?**] and **Mehetabel Wing** laid their Intention of mar~riage~
and two f̶r̶i̶e̶ Women friends are Chose to make Enquiry into ye young
Womans Clearness and Give an account to ye next monthly meeting how they
find things And this meeting hath Chosen 2 women friends to attend the
Quarterly meeting next to be held at **Portsmouth** ye 14th of the 8 month next
and **Ruth Tucker** is Chose to Draw up an account to the Same

The 17 of the 8 month n̶e̶ 1726 Was our monthly meeting of women friends
held in **Dartmouth** Collected by this meeting 2 Shillings and 6 pence
Disbusted for the use of friends 11 Shillings and 10 pence
the friends that Laid their intentions ye Last monthly meeting Doth not
appear by reason of sickness

The 21 of ye 9 month 1726 Was our monthly meeting of Women friends
held in **Dartmouth:** At this meeting **Seth Kelle** [**Kelley?**] and **Mehetabel Wing**
Came for their answer and nothing appearing to hinder friends gave
them Leave to Marry in the good order of truth
Collected by this meeting 11 Shillings and 8d and taken out of ye Stock
for keeping the meeting house one pound ten Shillings

The 19 of ye 10 month 1726 Was our monthly meeting of Women friends held
in **Dartmouth** Collected by this meeting 3 Shillings and 2 pence
T̶h̶e̶ ̶w̶ two women friends were Chosen to attend ye Quarterly
Meeting next to be held at **New Port** on **Rhoad Island** ye 13th of the 11
month next **Ruth Tucker** is Chose to Write to ye Quarterly meeting

The 16 of the 11 month 1726 Was our monthly monthly [*sic*] meeting of
Women friends held in **Dartmouth** Collected by this meeting 5s 10d
At this meeting **Archipas Hart** and **Sarah Clifton** laid their Intentions
of Marriage this meeting Chuses 2 Women friends to inquire into the
Young Womans Clearness and make return to ye next monthly meet~ing~

The 20 of the 12 1727 Was our monthly meeting of Women friends held
in **Dartmouth** Collected by this meeting 5 shillings & 2 pence
At this meeting **Archipas Hart** and **Sarah Clifton** Came for their
Answer and friends finding nothing to hinder gives them leave to marry
I̶n̶d̶ in the good order of truth and there was Disbusted for the use of
friends 5 Shillings and two women friends are Chosen with the men
to Draw up **Alice Sisson**s Condemnation for her disorderly marriage
and other faults and this meeting is adjourned until the 28 of the
fir[s]t month next

This meeting of women friends held by adjournment yᵉ 23 of the 1 month
1727 Collected by this meeting 5ˢ 2ᵈ
two Women friends are Chose to attend yᵉ Quarterly next to be held
At **Portsmouth** on **Rhoad Island** the 19 of yᵉ 2 month 1727
Ruth Tucker is Chose to Send in an account to yᵉ Quarterly meeting
Our Vissiters gives an account to this meeting that they have visited
friends families in this Village and in a Generall way find things pretty well

The 17ᵗʰ day of yᵉ 2 month 1727 Was our monthly meeting of Women friends
Held in **Dartmouth:** Collected by this meeting 7ˢ 2ᵈ
one of the friends that was Chose to attend yᵉ Quarterly meeting did attend it
and brings no account of any bisiness to this meeting
This meetⁱⁿᵍ Chuses **Ruth Tucker** and **Phebe Tucker** to ballance the accounts
of this ⁱⁿᵍ meeting **Mary Russell** and **Phebe Tucker** are Chosen to Speak with
Sarah Taber now **Merihoo [Merrihew]** Concerning her wrong Doings
Disbusted for the use of friends Seaven Shillings

The 15 of the 3 month 1727 Was our monthly Meeting of Women friends
held in **Dartmouth** Collected by this meeting 5ˢ 2ᵈ

The 19 of the 4ᵗʰ month 1727 Was our monthly meeting of Women friends
held in **Dartmouth** At this Meeting **Thomas Akin** and **Abigal Allen**
Laid their Intentions of taking each other in marriage and this meeting
Desires them to wait until yᵉ next monthly meeting for their answer
and there was two friends Chose to make Enquiery into the young Womans
Clearness and there was two friends Chose to attend yᵉ Quarterly
Meeting next to be held at **New Port** on **Rhoad Island**
Collected at this meeting 7ˢ 2ᵈ and Disbusted for yᵉ use of friends 5ˢ

The 17 of the 5 mon 1727 Was our monthly meeting of Women friends
held in **Dartmouth** Collected by this meeting 5ˢ 8ᵈ
At this meeti[ng] **Thomas Akin** and **Abigal Allen** Came for their answer
And this meeting finding nothing to hinder Gives them Leave to take
Each other in marriage in the Good order of friends
At this Meeting **John Wing** and **Mary Tucker** laid their Intention
of Marriage two Women friends are Chosen to make Enquiry into
the young Womans Clearness 2 Shilling was Disbusted for yᵉ use of friends

The 21 of yᵉ 6 month 1727 Was our monthly meeting of Women friends
Held in **Dartmouth** Collected at this meeting 7ˢ 5ᵈ
and 4ˢ and 6ᵈ disbusted for the use of friends At this meeting **John
Wing** and **Mary Tucker** Came for their answer and this meeting gives
them Leave to take each other in marriage according to yᵉ good
Order of friends This meeting Received an Epistle from **Rhoad Island**
yearly meeting of Women friends Which was Read and kindly accepted
the accounts of this meeting ballanced and there is in yᵉ Stock 1ᶠ=05ˢ=2ᵈ.

The 18 of the 7 month 1727 Was our monthly meeting of Women

friends held in **Dartmouth** Collected by this meeting 0-7ˢ-6ᵈ
this meeting Coses [*sic*] two ˄ᵂᵒᵐᵉⁿ friends to attend the quarterly meeting next
to be held at **Portsmouth** on **Rhoad Island** the 13 of the 8 month Insuing
Hannah Tucker and **Phebe Tucker** are Chose Visiters for this year
and **Ruth Tucker** is Chose to Draw up an account to Send from this
Meeting to yᵉ Quarterly meeting

The 16 of the 8 month 1727 Was our monthly meeting of Women friends held
in **Dartmouth** Collected by this meeting 4 Shillings and 2 pence
The friends that were Chose to attend yᵉ Quarterly meeting one of them did
attend it No account of business from the Quarterly meeting

The 20 of the 9 month 1727 Was our monthly meeting of Women friends
held in **Dartmouth** Collected by this meeting Six Shillings and ten pence

The 18 of the 10 month 1727 Was our monthly meeting of Women friends
held in **Dartmouth** Collected by this meeting 5ˢ
two women friend was Chose to attend yᵉ Quarterly meeting next to be
held at **New Port** on **Rhoad Island**

The 15 Day of yᵉ 11 month 1717 [*sic*] Was our monthly meeting of Women friends held
in **Dartmouth** Collected by this meeting 2 Shillings & 8 pence
The friends that were Chose to attend yᵉ Quarterly meeting one of them
did attend it and brings no account of any business to this meeting

The 19 of the 12 month 1728 [*sic*] Was our monthly meeting of Women
friends held in **Dartmouth** Collected by this meeting 7ˢ 8ᵈ

The 20 of yᵉ 1 month 1728 was our monthly meeting of women friends
held in **Dartmouth** Collected by this meeting Seaven Shillings ———
two women friends are Chosen to Attend yᵉ Quarterly meeting to be held at
Portsmouth on **Rhoad Island** in yᵉ Second month next
Ruth Tucker and **Phebe Tucker** are Chose to Draw up an account
and Send it to yᵉ Quarterly meeting

The 15 of the 2 month 1728 was our monthly meeting of Women
friends held in **Dartmouth** Collected at this meeting 6 Shillings & 2ᵈˢ
and Disbusted for the use of ˄ᶠʳⁱᵉⁿᵈˢ 8 Shillings and 4 pence
The friends that were Chose to attend yᵉ Quarterly meeting did attend it
and bring no account of any business to this meeting

The 20 of the 3 month 1728 Was our monthly meeting of Women
friends held in **Dartmouth** Collected by this meeting Six Shilling & 3ᵈˢ
Disbusted for yᵉ use of friends 8 Shillings & 4ᵈˢ

The 24 day of yᵉ 4 month 1728 Was our monthly meeting of Women
friends held in **Dartmouth** Collected at this meeting 14ˢ 01
taken out of yᵉ Stock for yᵉ use of friends nine Shillings

The 15 of the 5 month 1728 Was our monthly meeting of Women
friends held in **Dartmouth** Collected by this meeting 4ˢ 6ᵈ

This meeti[ng] Received an Epistle from **Rhoad Island** yearly meeting
of Women friends Which was read and kindly accepted
And this meeting makes Choice of **Mary Laton [Lawton]** and **Ruth Tucker**
to go and Discource with **Hannah Howland jun**ʳ Concernin her
Going to marry one that is not under yᵉ Care of friends

The 19 of the 6 month 1728 Was our monthly meeting of Women friends
Held in **Dartmouth** Collected by this meeting 10ˢ
forty Shillings six pence was Disbusted for the use of friends
Ruth Tucker and **Phebe Tucker** are Chosen to ballance the accounts
belonnging to this meeting The friends that we Chose to Speak with
Hannah Howland Junʳ did Speak with her and Shee gave them no
Sattisfaction that Should marry in yᵉ Good order of truth
the accounts Ballanced and and there is in the Stock 2ᵉ 13ˢ 06ᵈˢ

The 16 of the 7 month 1728 Was our monthly meeting of Women friends
held in **Dartmouth** Collected by this meeting Seaven Shillings & two pence
two Women friend are chose to attend yᵉ Quarterly meeting
to be held at **Portsmouth** on **Rhoad Island** on the Second 6 day of yᵉ 8
Month 1728 **Ruth Tucker** is chose to Send an account from this meeting
to yᵉ Quarterly meeting: and this meeting is adjourned until the first
Sixth day in the eighth month next
At this meeting held by adjournment the visiters gives an account
that they have visited friends families and their visits were accepted
in love

The 21 of the 8 month 1728 Was our monthly meeting of Women
friends held in **Dartmouth**: At this meeting **Abram Russell** and
Dinah Allen laid their Intentions of Marriage
two Women friends are Chose to See after yᵉ young womans clearness
The friends that wer chose to attend yᵉ Quarterly meeting did attend
it and bring no account of any business to this meeting
there was Collected by this meeting: 7ˢ 1ᵈ

The 18 of yᵉ 9 month 1728 Was our monthly meeting of Women
friends held in **Dartmouth** Collected by this meeting 10ˢ 11ᵈ
Disbusted for the use of friends 9 Shillings
At this meeting **Abram Russell** and **Dinah Allen** Came for their
answer and yᵉ meeting finding nothing to hinder them gives
them Leave to marry in the good order of truth
Edward Wing and **Patience Ellis** laid their intention of marriage
before this meeting and at this meeting **James Russell** and **Mary
Howland** laid their Intention of marriage **Marry lapham** and
Mary Russell are appointed to enquire into the young womans
Clearness and **Rebecca Russell** and **Rebecca Barker** were
appointed to see into **Patience Ellices [Ellis]** Clearness

The 16 of the 10 month 1728 Was our monthly meeting of Women friends
held in **Dartmouth** Collected at this meeting 2ˢ 6ᵈ
forty and fower Shillings was Disbusted for keeping the meeting
house At this meeting **James Russell** and **Mary Howland** were
permitted to take each other in marriag in the good order of truth
Edward Wing and **Patience Eliss [Ellis]** Came for their answer to this meeting
this meeting gives them Leave to take each other in marriage in
the order of truth: **Ruth Tucker** and **Phebe Tucker** are Chose
to Send an account in writeing from this meeting to yᵉ Quarterly
Meeting

The 20 day of yᵉ 11 month 178 [*sic*] Was our monthly meeting of Women friends
held in **Dartmouth** Collected by this meeting 7ˢ 2ᵈ

The 17 of the 12 month 1729 [*sic*] Was our monthly meeting of Women friends held
in **Dartmouth** and there was Collected by this meeting Six Shillings

---

The 17 of the 1 month 1729 Was our monthly monthly [*sic*] meeting of Women
friends held in **Dartmouth** Collected by this meeting 6 Shillings & 4 pence
our visiters gives account to this meeting that they have visited the most
part of friends families and their visits ~~for~~ in a general way were kindly
accepted but in Some families not so but were Rather reflected upon
Hannah Tucker and **Phebe Tucker** are Chose to attend yᵉ Quarterly
meeting ₍next₎ to be held at **Portsmouth** on **Rhoad [Rhode] Island** and **Ruth Tucker** and
Phebe Tucker are Chose to Draw up an account from this meeting
to yᵉ Quarterly meeting

The 21 day of the 2 month 1729 Was our monthly meeting of Women
friends Held in **Dartmouth** Collected by this meeting 5ˢ 8ᵈ
there was Disbusted at this meeting ~~for the use of friends~~
for the use of friends 5ˢ – — The friends that were Chose to
attend the Quarterly meeting did attend it and brings no account
of any business to this meeting

The 19 day of the 3 month 1729 Was our monthly meeting of Women
friends held in **Dartmouth** Collected by this meeti nine Shillings
At this meeting **Nicholas Davies [Davis]** hath laid their Intention of marri₍age₎
and this meeting Chuses **Mary Lapham** and **Mary Russell** to make
inquiry into yᵉ young womans Clearness

The 23 of yᵉ 4ᵗʰ month 1729 Was our monthly meeting of Women
friends held in **Dartmouth** Collected by this meeting 9ˢ 5ᵈ
Nicholas Davis and **Ruth Tucker** Came for their answer and friends
finding nothing to object against it gave the leave to take
each other in marriage in the good order of truth
and **Mary Trafford** Sent in a paper of her out goings which was
read in this meeting and accepted

The 21 of the 5 month 1729 Was our monthly meeting of Women
friends held in **Dartmouth** Collected by this meeting 9^s 11^s
forty three Shillings and six pence Disbusted at this meeting for
the use of friends
an Epistle from **Rhoad Island** yearly meeting was Read at this
meeting and and kindly accepted

The 18 of the 6 month 1729 Was our monthly meeting of Women
friends held in **Dartmouth** Collected at this meeting 11^s 6^d
~~9 Shillings and eleaven pence~~ eleaven Shillings and six pence
Disbusted for the use of friends 2^s 6^d

The 20 of ye 8 month 1729 Was our monthly meeting of Women
friends held in **Dartmouth** there was Collected by this meeting 4 Shillings

The 17th of ye 9th month 1729 Was our monthly meeting of Women
friends held in **Dartmouth** At this meeting **Benjamin Taber** and
Susanna Lewis laid their Intention of taking each other in marriage
and there was 2 women friends Chose to make Inquiry into the
young Womans Clearness and Give in an account to the next
Monthly meeting: Collected by this meeting 9 Shillings and one penny
and Disbusted for the use of friends 18 Shillings
Ruth Tucker and **Phebe Tucker** are Chose to ballance ye accounts of this
Meeting

The 15th of ye 10th month 1729 Was our monthly meeting of Women
friends held in **Dartmouth** The friends that laid their Intentions of
Marriage ~~bef~~ at the last monthly meeting doth not appear by
Reason of sickness
At this meeting **Ebenezer Shearman** and **Wait Barker** laid
their Intention of Marriage and there was two friends Chose
to Make Inquiry into the young Womans Clearness
At this meeting **Thomas Lapham** and **Abigal Willbor** [**Wilbur**] laid their
Intention of marriage and two women friends more are chose
to Inquire into ye young Womans Clearness
Collected by this meeting 9 Shillings and 11 pence
and 2 friends are Chose to attend ye Quarterly meeting next
to be held at **New Port** on **Rhoad Island** and **Ruth Tucker** is
Chose to Draw an account to the Quarterly meeting
and there was 40 Shillings Disbusted for keeping ye meeting house
The accounts of this meeting Ballanced and Remaines in the Stock 8^s

The 19th Day of ye 11th month 1729 Was our monthly meeting
of Women friends held In **Dartmouth Ebenezer Shearman** and
Wait Barker Came to this meeting for their answer and the
meeting finding nothing to hinder Gave them Leave to marry
In the Good order of truth

And at this meeting **Thos Lapham** and **Abigal Willber** [**Wilbur**] Came
for their Answer and they were Permitted to take each other
In Marriage: At this meeting **Benjamin Taber** and **Susanna
Lewis** Came for their answer and friends finding nothing
to hinder Gave the Leave to marry in the Good or[der] of truth

The 16 day of the 12 month 1729 Was our monthly meeting
of women Friends held in **Dartmouth David Joy** and
Mary Taber Came to lay their intention of marriage
before this meeting. Collected at this meeting 10^s 8^d
Mary Russell and **Sarah Taber** were Chose to Inquire
Into the young womans Clearness

The 16 of the 1 month 1729 Was our monthly meeting of
Women Friends held in **Dartmouth** where **Moses Shearman**
and **Meribeh Wood** laid their Intentions of Marriage before
this meeting **Phebe Tucker** and **Mary Russell** was Chose to See
into the young Womans Clearness
Gedeon [**Gideon**] **Gifford** and **Elizabeth Allen** laid ther intentions of
marriage before this meeting and **Mary Howland** and **Mary
Lapham** were appointed to Inquire into the young Womans
Clearness Collected at this meeting 8^s 0^d
Mary Pennell and **Mary Lewes** [**Lewis**] their Certificates as read at
this meeting and Kindly received With their visits of Love
And this meeting is adjourned till ye first sixth day in next
Month to the youths meeting

The of [*sic*] the 2 month 1730 was our monthly meeting
held by adjournment **Phebe Tucker** and **Mary Russell**
Were chose to attend the Quarterly meeting
and **Ruth Tucker** is Chose to write to the Quarterly meeting

The 20 of the 2^d month 1730 Was our monthly Meeting
of Women Friends held In **Dartmouth David Joy** and
Mary Taber Came for their answer and friends finding
them Clear gave them Leave to proceed in marriage
according to the good order of Friends
Moses Shearman and **Meribeh Wood** Came for their answer
and Friends finding them Clear gave them their answer
that they might proceed to take Each other in marriage
in the Good order of Friends **Gideon Gifford** and **Elizabeth
Allen** Came for their answer and finding nothing to hinder
they had their Answer that they might proceed to take each
other in the Good order of Friends
Collected at this meeting 12^s 7^d The Friends Chose to attend
the Quarterly meeting have attended it as ordered

The 18 of the 3ᵈ month 1730 Was our monthly meeting of
Women Friends held In **Dartmouth Isaac Smith** and **Mary
Willcox [Wilcox]** laid their intention of marriage before this meeting
and **Phebe Tucker** and **Elizabeth Barker** were chose to
Inquire into the young Womans Clearness
Collected at this meeeting 7ˢ 8ᵈ **Rebekah Russell** and **Rachel
Allen** are appointed to Discource with **Audre [Audrey] Gifford**
about her Intangling herselfe With marriage Contrary
to her Fathers Consent

The 28 of the 4 month 1730. Was our monthly meeting
of Women Friends held in **Dartmouth** where **Isaac Smith**
and **Mary Willcox [Wilcox]** Came for their answer and friends
having made Inquiry Could find nothing to Object gave
them leave that they might take each other in marriage
and **Joseph Burden [Borden]** and **Abigail Russell** laid their inten
=tions of marriage before this meeting And we received
an Epistle from the yearly meeting of Women Friends
at **Rhoad Island** which Was read at this meeting And
Received in much love Collected at this meeting 6ˢ 8ᵈ
Mary Lapham and **Mary Howland** Was Chose to Inquire
Into the young Womans Clearness

The 20 of the 5ᵗʰ month 1730 Was our monthly meeting
of women Friends held in **Dartmouth** Where
Joseph Borden and **Abigail Russell** Came for their
answer And friends having made Inquiry Conc[e]rning
their Clerness And finding them Clear gave them leave
to take each other in marriage According to the Good
order of Friends Collected at this meeting 8ˢ 1ᵈ

The 17ᵗʰ of the 6ᵗʰ month 1730 Was our monthly meeting
of Women Friends held In **Dartmouth**
Collected at this meeting 10ˢ 2ᵈ Taken out of the Stock
for the use of Friend 2£-16-00

The 21 of the 7 month 1730 Was our monthly Meeting
of Women Friends held In **Dartmouth**
Collected at this meeting 11ˢ 6ᵈ **Phebe Tucker** And
Mary Lawton are Chose to Attend the Quarterly
Meeting And **Ruth Tucker** is Chose to Write to the
Quarterly meeting.

The 19 of the 8 month 1730 Was our monthly
meeting of women Friends held in **Dartmouth**
Butler Wing and **Bathsheba Cliffton [Clifton]** did lay their
Intention of marriage before this meeting and were

desired to wait till the next monthly meeting
for their answer Collected at this meeting 3ˢ 10ᵈ
18ˢ 10ᵈ taken out of the Stock for the use of Friends
Ruth Davis and **Elizabeth Hillier [Hiller]** were Chose to
Inquire Into the young Womans Clearness

The 15 day of the 9 month 1730 Was our monthly
meeting of women Friends held In **Dartmouth**
Butler Wing and **Bathsheba Clifton** Came for their
answer And Friends having made Inquiry Concerning her
Clearness Could find nothing to hinder Gave them leave
to take each other in marriage according to the good
order of Friends Collected at this meeting 4ˢ 6ᵈ

The 21 day of the 10 month 1730 Was our monthly
Meeting of women Friends held In **Dartmouth** Where
Stephen Wing and **Margrate [Margaret] Clifton** laid their Intenti$_{\text{ons}}$
of Marriag **Elizabeth Hilliar [Hiller]** and **Ruth Davis**
were Chose to Inquire into the young womans Clearness.
at this meeting **Stephen Willcock [Wilcox]** and **Mary Thomas**
laid their intention of marriag and **Phebe Tucker**
and **Mary Howland** are appointed to make Inquiry
into the young Womans Clearness. Collected at this
Meeting 6ˢ 2ᵈ And there was 30 shillings Disbusted out
of the Stock for keeping the meeting House **Mary
Lawton** And ~~Mary Laph~~ **Rebecca Barker** are appointed
to attend the Quarterly Meeeting And **Ruth Tucker** and
Phebe Tucker are Chose to write to yᵉ Quarterly meeting

The 18 day of the 11 month 1730 Was our monthly
meeting of Women Friends held In **Dartmouth**
Stephen Wing and **Margrit [Margaret] Clifton** Came for their
their answer and Friends finding things Clear gave them
Leave to tak Each other in marriage according to
the good order of Friends And **Stephen Willcock [Wilcox]** and
Mary Thomas Came for their answer and Friends
having made Inquiry and finding nothing to hinder
gave them leave to take each other in marriage
according to the good order of Friends **Richard Smith**
and **Dorothy Potter** did lay their Intentions of marriage
before this meeting and Were desired to wait till the
next monthly meeting for their answer
Collected at this meeting 6ˢ 9ᵈ And **Phebe Tucker**
And **Rebecca Russell** were Chose to Inquire Into the
young womans Clearness

The 15 of yᵉ 12 month [*sic*] was our montly meeting of women
Friends at **Dartmouth** where **Richard Smith** and **Dorothy Potter**
Came for their answer and Friends finding nothing to Hinder
gave the Leave to take each other In marriage according to the
Good order of Friends and **Elishib [Eliashib] Smith** and **Audera [Audrey] Gifford** laid
their Intentions of marriage before this meeting and
Humphry Smith and **Mary Wilcox** laid their Inteⁿtions of
marriage before this meeting **Nathaniel Kirby** and **Abigail Russell**
Laid their Intentions of marriage before this meeting **Mary Russll [Russell]**
and **Rebecca Russell** were Chose to Inquire Into **Audera Gifford**s
Clearness and **Elizabeth Barker** and **Rebecca Slocum** were Chose
To Inquire Into **Mary Wilcox**s is Clearness and **Deborah Allen** and
Mary Howland were Chose to Inquire Into **Abigail Russell**s Clearness
Collected at this meeting 5ˢ 3ᵈ this meeting Chose **Ruth Tucker**
and **Phebe Tucker** to Ballance the Book

The 15 of the 1 month 1730 was our monthly meeting of women
Friends Held at **Dartmouth** where **Elishib [Eliashib] Smith** and **Audera [Audrey] Gifford**
Came for their answer and Friends having made Inquiry Gave them
leave to Take each other In marriage **Humphry Smith** and **Mary Wilcox**
Came for their answer and Friends having made Inquiry Could
find nothing to hinder gave them leave to take each other in marriage
According to the good Order of Truth **Nathaniel Kerby [Kirby]** and **Abigail Russell**
Came for their answer and Friends having made Inquiry Could find
Nothing to hinder gave them leave to Take each other In marriage —
According to the Good order of friends Collected at this meeting 8ˢ 6ᵈ
This ~~motlogg~~ monthly meeting is adjourned to youths meeting

---

[bottom third of page is blank]

The 17 of the 3 month [sic] was our monthly meeting of women Friends
held at **Dartmouth** Collected by this meeting 8ˢ 1ᵈ the account ballant
and There Remains 2ᶠ-1ˢ-4ᵈ ~~the~~ in the Stock

The 22 of the 4 month 1731 was our monthly meeting of women Friends
held at **Dartmouth** where our Dear Friends **Ruth Jones** and **Sarah
Moul**s Certificate was Read at this meeting and received ~~with~~ in
Abundance of Love and unity Collected at this meeting 10ˢ 10ᵈ
ᶠ1-3ˢ-4ᵈ Disbursted For the use of friends

The 17 day of the 5 month 1731 Was our monthly meeting
of women Friends held In **Dartmouth** Collected at this meeting
7ˢ:8ᵈ At this meeting there was an Epistle read from the yearly
Meeting ᴀ ᵃᵗ ᴿʰᵒᵈ ᴵˢˡᵃⁿᵈ and Received in much love
Mary Russell and **Sarah Taber** ar Chosen Visitters for **Cushnot**
And **Ruth Tucker** and **Phebe Tucker** are Chosen for **Ponagansett**
and **Hannah Cadmon [Cadman]** and **Peace Wood** for **Coaksett**

And **Content Wing** and **Rebecca Slocum** are Chose to Talk
With **Mary Ricketson** Concerning her marrying out of
the unity of friends

The 16 of the 6 month 1731 Was our monthly meeting
of Women Friends held In **Dartmouth** ~~Where Anthony Arnold~~
~~And Sarah Fish did lay their Intentions~~
Collected at this meeting for the use of friends 8ˢ:1ᵈ

The 20ᵗʰ of the 7ᵗʰ month 1731 Was our monthly meeting
of Women Friends held In **Dartmouth** Wher **Anthony Arnold**
and **Sarah Fish** Laid their Intention of marriage before
this meeting There was Collected at this meeting 7ˢ
Phebe Tucker and **Mary Russell** are Chose to attend the
Quarterly meeting

The 18ᵗʰ day of the 8ᵗʰ month 1731 Was our monthly meeting
of women Friends held In **Dartmouth** at this meeting
Anthony Arnold and **Sarah Fish** Came for their answer
And finding nothing to hinder they had their answer that
they might proceed to take Each other in marriage in an
Orderly way And **Seth Hilliar [Hiller]** and **Dorcus Davis** Laid their
Intentions of marriage before this meeting And **Hannah
Cadman** and **Experience Wing** are appointed to Inquire
Concerning the young Womans Clearness

The 15 of the 9 month 1731 Was our monthly meeting of
Women ~~held~~ Friends held In **Dartmouth** at this meeting
Seth Hilliar [Hiller] and **Dorcas Davis** Came for their Answer
the meeting finding nothing to hinder them gave them leave
To Proceed In marriage In the good order of Friends at this
meeting **John Russell** and **Patience Tucker** laid their
Intentions of marriage they are Desired to Wait ttil next
monthly meeting for their answer **Rebecca Barker** and
Mary Howland are Chose To make Inquiry Concerning
The young womans Clearness Collected by this meeting 6ˢ 1ᵈ

The 20 of ye 10 month 1731 was our monthly meeting of Women
friends held at **Dartmouth** where **John Russell** and
Patience Tucker Came for their answer and Friends having
made Inquiry Concerning her Clearness Could find nothing to
hinder Gave them Leave to take each other In marriage according
to the good order of Friends **Timothy Ricketson** and **Bathsheba
Wilbor [Wilbur]** Laid their Intentions of marriage before this meeting
Rebecca Russell and **Mary Lapham** Is Chose to Inquire Into yᵉ young
womans Clearness **Mary Slocum** and **Rebecca Slocum** Is Chose
to Attend the Quarterly meeting **Ruth Tucker** is Chose to

write to the Quarterly meeting Collected at this meeting 8ˢ 9ᵈ

The 17 of the 11 month 1731 was our monthly meetings of women
Friends held In **Dartmouth** Collected by this meeting 4ˢ-1ᵈ- 10ˢ-disbuˢ[ᵗ]ed
for keeping the meeting house **Timothy Ricketson** and — — —
Bathsheba Wilber [**Wilbur**] Came for their Answer to this meeting Inquiring
being made finding nothing to hinder their proceeding to
marry in the good order of truth

The 21 of the 12 month 1731/2 was our monthly meeting of
Women Friends Held at **Dartmouth** 14ˢ[?] Disbursted for the
use of Friends. at this meeting **Thomas Youen** [**Yewin**?] and
Abigail Wood laid their Intentions of marriage Collected
at this meeting 5ˢ 6ᵈ **Rebecca Russell** and **Mary Lapham**
Is Chose to Inquire Into the young womans Clearness

The 27 of the 1 month 1732 - was Oour monthly meeting of women
Friends held at **Dartmouth** by adjournment where **Thomas
Youen** [**Yewin**?] & **Abigail Wood** Came for their answer and friends
finding nothing to Hinder gave them Leave to take each
other in marriage according to truth
and **John Borden** and **Hannah Russell** Laid their Intentions of
marriage before this meeting **Mary Russell** & **Rebecca Slocum**
Is Chose to Inquire Into the young womans Clearness
Phebe Tucker & **Mary Russell** is Chose to atend the
Quarterly meeting Collected at this meeting 4ˢ 8ᵈ

The 17 of the 2 month 1732 was our monthly meetings of women held
Friends held at **Dartmouth** where **John Borden** and **Hannah Russell**
Came for their answer and Friends finding nothing to Hinder
gave them leave to take each other in marriage In the good order of
Truth the Friends that was Chose to attend the Quarterly meeting
did attend it **Phebe Tucker** & **Rebecca Slocum** is Chose to
Attend the yearly meeting - Collected at this meeting 5ˢ

The 15 of the 3 month 1732 was our monthly meeting of wo
woman Friends held at **Dartmouth** Collected at this meeting 2ˢ

The 19 of the 4 month 1732 was our monthly meeting of women
friends held at **Dartmouth** this meeting Received an epistle
from **Rhodeisland** yearly meeting which was Read and received
In Love Collected at this meeting 3ˢ · 4· 6ˢ · Shillings taken out
of the Stock for the Book posting Boock

The 17 of the 5 month 1732 was our monthly meeting of woman
held at **Dartmouth** collected 8ˢ · 8ᵈ · Taken out of the Stock for the use
of Friends. Collected at this meeting 6ˢ 5ᵈ

The 21 of the 6 month 1732 was our monthly meeting of woman friends

held at **Dartmouth** Collected at this meeting 6ˢ · 3ᵈ · 5ˢ Disbursted
for the use of Friends **Phebe Tucker** and **Rebecca Slocum** is Chose visiters
for **Ponigansit Mary Russell** and **Sarah Tabor [Taber]** is Chose **Cushnot**
Hannah Cadmon [Cadman] and **Kezia Wood** is Chose for **Coaxit**

The 18 of the 7 month 1732 was our monthly meeting of woman —
friends held at **Dartmouth Mary Slocum** and **Phebe Tucker** Is Chose
by this meeting to attend the Quarterly meeting **Ruth Tucker** is
Chose to write to the Quarterly meeting Collected at this meeting 5ˢ 4ᵈ
this meeting is adjourned to the Youths meeting which is to be Held the
first Sixth day in next month

The 26 of the 8 month 1732 was our monthly meeting of woman friends
Held at **Dartmouth** where **William Sanford** and **Rebecca Howland** laid their
Intentions of marriage and **Mary Howland** and **Mary Lapham** were
Chose to Inquire Into the young womans Clearness Collected at
this meeting 3ˢ 8ᵈ.

The 21 of the 9 month 1732 was our monthly meeting of woman friends
held at **Dartmouth** where **William Sanford** and **Rebecca Howland** Came
for their answer and Friends finding nothing to hinder gave them leave
to take each other In marriage according to the good order of Truth

The 18 of the 10 month 1732 Was our monthly meeting of
Women Friends held In **Dartmouth** Where **Richard Craw** and
Joanna Shearman [Sherman] Laid their Intentions of marriage
Mary Lapham And **Rebeca Barker** Is Chose to Inquire into
the young womans Clearness and **William Willcox [Wilcox]** and **Dorothy**
Allen Laid their intentions of Marriage And **Rebecca** ~~Bark~~ₑᵣ
Russell and **Elisabeth Barker** are Chose to Inquire Into the
young Womans Clearness **Phebe Tucker** and **Rebecca Slocum**
are Chose to attend the Quarterly meeting and **Ruth Tucker**
Is Chose Write to the Same

The 15 of the 11 month 1732/3 was our monthly meeting of
women Friends held at **Dartmouth** where **Richard Craw** and **Joanna**
Shearman [Sherman] Came for their answer and Friends finding nothing to
Hinder gave them leave to Proceed In marriage In the good order of truth
and **William Wilcox** and **Dorothy Allin [Allen]** Came for their answer and Friends
finding nothⁿg to hinder gave them leave to Proceed In marriage and
Icabod Kirby and **Rachel Allen** Laid their Intentions of marriage
Mary Russell and **Jane Smith** was Chose to Inquire Into the young
womans Clearness 40ˢ Taken out of the Stock for ~~the~~ keeping the
Meeting house. Collected at this meeting **Peter Allen**s and **Content Smith**
~~Condiemndation~~ Condemnnation was read at this meeting one of the
friends that was Chose to attend the Quarterly meeting did attend it and
no business to this meeting

The 19 day of the 12 month 1722/3 Was our monthly meeting
of Women Friends Held In **Dartmouth Ichabod Kerby [Kirby]**
and **Rachel Allen** Came for their answer and Friends
finding nothing to Hinder gave them their Answer
that they might proceed to take each other in marriage
In the Good order of Truth Collected at this meeting
7ˢ 5ᵈ The two Friends that were Chosen to ₍settle the₎ accompts
Have Ballanced the Book and there remains in the
Stoack 1ᶠ-7ˢ-6ᵈ

The 26 day of the 1 month 1733 Was Our monthly
Meeting of women Friends held In **Dartmouth** by
adjournment Where **Edward Wing** and **Rebecca Slocum**
Laid their Intentions of taking each other in marriage
And **Mary Lapham** and **Rebecca Russell** is Chose to
Inquire into the young Womans Clearness **Phebe Tucker**
And **Mary Howland** is Chose to attend the ~~monthly~~ Qᵘᵃʳᵗᵉʳˡʸ Meeting
To be held at **Portstmouth** [*sic*] yᵉ 13ᵗʰ of the 2 month
And **Ruth Tucker** is Chose to write to yᵉ Quarterly meeting
Collected at this meeting 5ˢ-2ᵈ

The 16 of the 2ᵈ month 1733 Was our monthly meeting of
Women Friends held In **Dartmouth** Collected at this meeting
4ˢ-8ᵈ **Edward Wing** and **Rebecca Slocum** Could not have
their answer this monthly meeting by reason of things
not being Settled In her business

The 21 of the 3ᵐ Was our monthly meeting of Women
Friends held In **Dartmouth** Collected at this meeting 3ˢ 10ᵈ
£1[?] · 10ˢ taken out of the Stock for the use of Friends

the 18ᵗʰ of yᵉ 4 month 1733 Was our monthly meeting of Women
friends held In **Dartmouth** where **Edward Wing** and **Rebecca Slocum** Came
for their answer and finding nothing to hinder gave them their answer
that they might proceed to marry In the good order of Friends
Collected at this meeting 7ˢ 10ᵈ Disbursted for the use of Friends 5ˢ:1ᵈ

The 16 of the 5 month 1733 was our Monthly meeting of woman
Friends held at **Dartmouth** 13ˢ 3ᵈ Disbursted for the use of friends
Collected at this meeting 8ˢ 11ᵈ

The 20 of the 6 month 1733 was our monthly meeting of woman friends
Held in **Dartmouth** Collected by this meeting 4ˢ 2ᵈ.
this meeting is adjourned till this Day 2 weeks the 3 Day of the 7 month 1733
was our meeting held by adjournmnt no business presented to this meeting

The 17 Day of the 7 month 1733 was our monthly meeting of women friend
Held In **Dartmouth** Collected by this meeting 5ˢ
Joseph Benson and **Experience Barlow** laid their Intentions of marriage

Elisabeth Hilliar [Hiller] and Abigail Youen [Yewin?] are Chose to see Into the young womans
Clearness and Epistle from Rhode Island yearly meeting was read and Kindly
excepted Mary Russell Peace Wood are Chose to attend the Quarterly
meeting to be held at Portsmouth in Rhode Island
Mary Russell and Sarah Taber Chose Visiters for Cushnet
Hannah Cadmon [Cadman] and Peace Wood Chose for Coaxet Ruth Tucker Chose
to write to the Quarterly meeting

The 15 day of the 8 month 1733· was our monthly meeting of
women friends held at Dartmouth where Joseph Benson and
Experience Barlow came for there answer the meeting finding
nothing to hinder gave them leave to proceed in the good order of truth
Collected by this meeting 5ˢ Mary Lapham and Mary Tucker

The 19 Day of 9 month 1733 was our monthly meeting of woman
friends held in Dartmouth Collected by this meeting five Shillings ¹ᵈ

The 17 day of the 10 month 1733 was our monthly meeting of women
friends held in Dartmouth Collected by this meeting 2ˢ-6ᵈ
At this meeting Henry Hedly [Headley] and Rachel Shearman [Sherman] hath
laid their Intentions of marriage they were desired to wait for their
answer till next monthly meeting Mary Russell and
Rebecca Russell are Chose to See Into the young womans Clearness
Mary Lapham and Phebe Tucker are Chose to attend the
Quarterly meeting to be held at Newport on Rhode Island Ruth
Tucker is Chose to write to the Quarterly meeting there Is account
brought into this meeting that there Is a poor woman that wants
help Friends has Concluded to take Care about It

The 21 day of the 11 month 1733· was our montly meeting of women
friends held in Dartmouth where Henry Hedly [Headley] and Rachal
Shearman [Rachel Sherman] Came for their answer friends finding nothing to hinder
them gave them leave to take each other in marriage in the good
order of friends truth: Collected at this meeting £4 5ˢ for
Deborah Landers which was disbursted the Same Day

The 18- Day of the 12- month 1733 was our monthly meting — —
of woman friends held in Dartmouth Collected at this meeting 3ˢ
Benjamin Wing and Mary Hillier [Hiller] laid their Intentions of
of [sic] marriage Ruth Davis and Abigail Youen [Ewen] were Chose to
Inquire Into the young womans Clearness

The 20 of the 1 month 1734 Was our Monthly meeting of
Woman Friends held in Dartmouth by adjournment the friend that
laid their Intentions of marriage Came for their answer this meeting
finding nothing to hinder gave them leave take each other In Marriage
according to the good order of Truth Collected by this meeting 9ˢ 9ᵈ
Ruth Tucker Is Chose to write to the Quarterly meeting to be held at

Portsmouth Phebe Tucker and **Mary Tucker** are Chose to attend the
Quarterly meeting at **Portsmouth Ruth Tucker** and **Phebe Tucker**
Are Chose to ballance the accounts of this meeting three ^{shillings} Disbursted
for the use of friends

The 15 of the 2 month 1734 was our monthly meeting of women friends
held In **Dartmouth** Collected at this meeting [*blot*] Twenty Shillings - -
for **Deborah Landers**: 4ˢ 6ᵈ Collected for the Stock accounts ballanced
and there remains In the Stock 2£-3ˢ-2ᵈ.

The 20 day of the 3 month 1734 was our monthly meeting of women
Friends held in **Dartmouth** Collected by this meeting 4ˢ-3ᵈ
The friends that was was [*sic*] Chose to Speake with **Susanna Smith** and
She Saith tis too Late.

The 24 of the 4 month 1734 was our monthly meeting
of women Friends held in **Dartmouth** Where **Mary
Lapham** and **Lydia Soule** [**Sowle**] was Chose to Discource
Alice Sm [**Smith**] Concerning her having a bastard Child
Collected at this meeting 5ˢ 5ᵈ
and Disbusted for keeping the meeting House 20 shillings

The 15ᵗʰ of the 5ᵗʰ month 1734 Was our monthly meeting
of Women Friends held in **Dartmouth** Where **James
Green** and **Hannah Tucker** laid their Intentions of
Marriage **Phebe Tucker** and **Rebeckah Russell** are Chose
to See Into the young Womans Clearness
And at this meeting **William Lake** and **Joanna Bulter** [**Butler**]
Laid their Intentions of marriage and **Mary Russell** and
Mary Lapham are Chose to Enquire into the young Womans
Clearness. We received An Epistle from the yearly Meeting
Which was read And kindly Accepted
Collected by this meeting 4ˢ 7ᵈ

The 19ᵗʰ of the 6 month 1734 Was our monthly meeting
of women Friends held in **Dartmouth** Where **James Green**
and **Hannah Tucker** Came for their Answer And Friends
finding Nothing to hinder Gave them leave to proceed In marriag
According to the Good order of Truth and **William Lake** and
Joanna Butler Came for their answer
and this meeting Permits theme to Proceed In marriage
according to the good order Established amongst us
Collected by this meeting 4ˢ 8ᵈ

The 16 of the 7 month 1734 Was our monthly meeting of
Women Friends held in **Dartmouth** Collected att this meeting 3ˢ 6ᵈ
This meeting appoints **Mary Russell** and **Rebeckah Russell**
to attend the Quarterly meeting ~~Collected by this~~

And **Ruth Tucker** is Chose to write to the Quarterly meeting

The 21 of the 8th month 1734 Was our monthly Meeting of
Women Friends held In **Dartmouth** At this meeting **Beriah
Goddard** and **Unice West** Laid their intentions of marriage
And this meeting appoints **Mary Russell** and **Mary Lapham**
to make Enquiry Into the young Womans Clearness
At this meeting **James Cornell** And **Abigail Tripp** laid their
Intentions of marriage And **Peace Wood** and **Rebeckah Russell**
are Chose to Enquire Into the young Womans Clearness
and **Joseph Merihew [Merrihew]** and **Edeth Whitely** laid their Intentions of
Marriage before this meeting And **Phebe Tucker** and **Rebekah
Bark͜er** are Chose to Enquire Into the young Womans Clearness
There was Collected at this meeting 4s 6d
taken out of ye Stock for the use of friends 6s and 11 pence

The 18 day of ye 9th month 1734 Was our month meeting of
Women Friends held In **Dartmouth** The young Friends that
Laid their Intentions of marriage the Last monthly Meeting
Came for their answers And Friends finding nothing to hinder
Gave them leave to marry In the good [order] of Friends
At this Meeting **Henry Chase** and **Mary Tripp** Laid their
Intentions of marriage before this meeting **Peace Wood** and
Keziah Wood are appointed to Enquire into the young
Womans Clearness and make return to the next monthly
Meeting Collected at this meeting 6s 1d

The 16 of the 10th month 1734 Was our monthly meeting of
Women Friends held In **Dartmouth** Where **Henry Chase**
And **Mary Tripp** Came for their Answer and finding nothing
to hinder the had their answer that they might proceed to take each
other In marriage according to the Good order of Friends
And at this meeting **Rufus Green** and **Martha Russell** Laid their
Intentions of marriage And were Desired to Wait till the next
Monthly Meeting for their Answer And **Rebecca Russell** and **Phebe
Tucker** are appointed to Enquire Into the young Womans Clearness
Collected for **Deborah Landers** 3 pounds

The 20th of the 11th month 1734 Was our monthly meeting of Women
Friend held In **Dartmouth** at this meeting **Rufus Green** and **Martha
Russell** Came for their answer and Friend finding things Clear
Gave them leave to marry according to good order.

The 17th of the 12th month 1734 Was our monthly
Meeting of Women Friends held In **Dartmouth**
Collected at this meeting 9 Shillings & 4 pence

The 17th of the first month 1735 Was our monthly Meeting of

Women Friends held In **Dartmouth** Ther was 20 Shillings ~~taken~~
~~out of the Stock~~ Collected at this meeting
Taken out of the stock for **Deborah Landers** 3 Pounds 10 Shillings
Our visitters brings their account that the[y] have visited
Friends families And find for the most part things pretty Well
Lydia Soule [Sowle] and **Mary Hull** are Chose to attend the Quarterly
Meeting **Ruth Tucker** and **Mary** are Chose to Write to the
Quarterly meeting

The 21 of the 2 month 1735 Was our monthly Meeting
of Women Friends held In **Dartmouth** Collected by this ~
meeting 9ˢ-1ᵈ **Phebe Tucker** and **Ruth Tucker** are Chose to
ballance the accounts this meetings accounts ballanced and nothing
remains in the Stock 7ˢ due to them thatt Keeps the Stock

The 19ᵗʰ of the 3 month 1735 was our monthly meeting of women
friends held in **Dartmouth** Collected by this meeting 7ˢ **Phebe Tucker**
and **Elizabeth Barker** are Chose to Discorse **Meribah Shearman** [Sherman]
Concerning the Scandelous reports that are abroad Concernning her

The 23 Day of the 4 month 1735 was our monthly meeting of
women friends held In **Dartmouth** Collected by this meeting 14ˢ 1ᵈ
for **Deborah Landers** 4ˢ 2ᵈ Collected for the use of friends **Sarah Taber**
and **Rebecca Barker** are Chose to attend the Quarterly meeting
to be held at **portsmouth** In **Rhode Island** the business about
Meribah Shearman [Sherman] Is referred to next monthly meeting

The 21 day of the 5 month 1735 was our monthly meeting of
women friends held In **Dartmouth** Collected by this meeting £1 5ˢ
8ᵈ Disbursted for the use of friends 5ˢ 6ᵈ **Meribah Shearman** [Sherman] desires
would waait till next meeting for answer at this meeting paid for
Deborah Landers 1ᶠ and 2ᵈ

The 18 of the 6 month 1735 was our monthly meeting of women
fr[i]ends held in **Dartmouth** Collected by this meeting 15ˢ 4ᵈ at this
meeting **Meribah Shearman** [Sherman] Sent In a paper Condemning her
Out goings

The 15 day of the 7 month 1735 Was our monthly meeting of
women Friends held In **Dartmouth** Collected by this meeting 12ˢ 9ᵈ
Disbursted for the use of Friends 9ˢ 3ᵈ - 2ˢ 6ᵈ More Collected at
this meeting **Mary Lapham** and **Phebe Tucker** are Chose to
To [sic] attend the Quarterly meeting to be held at **Portsmouth** on
Rhode Island Ruth Tucker Is Chose to write to the Quarterly
meeting 17ˢ 6ᵈ Taken out of the Stock for **Deborah Landers**

The 20 Day of the 8 month 1735 Was our Monthly meeting of
women friends held In **Dartmouth** Collected by this meeting 4ˢ 6ᵈ
the friends that Ware Chose to attend the Quarterly were not there we

here no account of any business from them to this meeting
Meribeth Shearmans Paper was read on a first day and excepted

The 17 day of the 09 month 1735 wa[s] our monthly meeting of women
friends held In **Dartmouth** Collected by this meeting 10^s - **Hannah Cadma**^{n}
and **Kezia Wood** are Chose Visiters for this year for **Coaxet Sarah Taber**
and **Mary Russell** are Chose visiters for **Acushnet** this year
Mary Lapham and **Sarah Gifford** are Chose Visiters for this meeting
this year

The 15 da of the 10 month 1735 was our monthly meeting of women
friends held in **Dartmouth** where **Luke Hart** and **Mary Huddlestone** [**Huttleston**]
laid their Intentions of marriage **phebe Tucker** and **Hannah Tucker**
are Chose to make Inquiry Concerning the young womans Clearness
Collected by this meeting 4^s 3^d - 1^s 3^d More 2^d taken out of the Stock
Ruth Tucker is Chose to write to the Quarterly meeting

The 19 Day of the 11 month was our 1736 monthly meeting of women friends held
In **Dartmouth** Collected by this meeting £1 2^s which was disburst^{ed}
for **Deborah Landers** at this meeting **Luke Hart** and **Mary
Huddlestone** [**Huttleston**] Came for their answer friends finding nothing to
hinder them gave them leave to take each other in marriage
according to the good order of truth

The 16 of the 12 month ^{1736} Was our monthly meeting of women friends
held In **Dartmouth** where **Nicolas** [**Nicholas**] **Howland** and **Zaruiah Russell**
laid their Intention of marriage **Mary Lapham** and **Hannah Tucker**
are Chose to Inquire Into the young womans Clearness

The 15 Day of 1 month 1736 was our monthly meeting of woman
friends held In **Dartmouth** Collected at this meeting 5^s the friends
that laid their Intentions of marriage last monthly meeting came
for their answer Inquiry being made nothing appearing to hinder
them Friends Gave them leave to take each other In marriage
according to the good order of Truth this meeting Is Adjourned to
the youths meeting next ensuing

At this monthly meeting held by adjournment on the
2^d of the 2^d month 1736 our Visitters gives an account
that they have Visited Friends Families In a Pretty
General In this Vilage and in **Cushnot** And find things
for the most part pretty Well as far as they Saw
Mary Lapham and —— are Chose to attend the
Quarterly meeting And **Ruth Tucker** is Chose to write
to the Quarterly meeting

The 19th Day of the 2 month 1736 was our monthly
Meeting of women Friends held In **Dartmouth**
Where **Joseph Brownell** and **Leah Lawton** laid their

intentions of marriage and were Desired to wait till
the next monthly meeting for their answer **Phebe Tucker**
and **Rebecca Russell** are Chose to Inquire Into the young
Clearness Collected by this meeting 11ˢ - **Ruth Tucker** and
Phebe Tucker are Chose to ballance the accounts of this meeting

The 17 – of the 3 month 1736 Was our monthly meeting of
women friends held In **Dartmouth** Collected at this meeting
10ˢ-3ᵈ at ~~thhi~~ this meeting **Joseph Brownell** and **Leah Lawton**
Came for their answer this meeting finding nothing to hinder
them gave them leave to take each other In marriage
accounts ballanced there is in the Stock – £2-8ˢ

The 21 of the 4 month 1736 - Was our monthly meeting of
Women Friends held In **Dartmouth** where ~~Je~~ **William Bowdish** [**Bowditch**]
and **Mary Hart** laide their Intentions of marriage Collected
at this meeting 12ˢ-£1-10ˢ Disbursted for keeping the
meeting howse – 4ˢ more disbursted for the use of friends
Hannah Tucker and **Apphia Mott** are Chose to Inquire
Into the young womans Clearness

The 19 of the 5 month 1736 was our monthly meeting
of women Friends held in **Dartmouth** Collected by this
meeting 8ˢ-3ᵈ the friends that laid their Intention of marriage
last monthly meeting Came for their answer friends
finding nothing to hinder gave them leave to take each
other in marriage according to the good order of truth: This
meeting Received an Apistle [Epistle] from the yearly meeting
which was read and kindly Excepted [Accepted]

The 20 of the 6 month 1736 Was our monthly meeting
of women Friends held In **Dartmouth** And **Peace Wood**
and **Susanna Gifford** Were Chose to attend the Quarterly
Meeting And the visitters of **Coxet** have visitted Friends
Families and Were Seemingly well accepted
And where they found things not agreable they gave
advise that it might be better
and there was 8 shillings and 10 pence Disbusted out
of the Stock ~~for a poor Woman~~ The use of Friends.
And **Ruth Tucker** Is Chose to write to the Quarterly Meeting

The 18 of the 7 month 1736 Was our monthly meeting
of women Friends held In **Dartmouth** Wher **Recompen[se]**
Kerby [**Kirby**] and **Rebekah Cornell** Laid their intentions of
marriage and **Rebekah Russell** and **Sarah Gifford** are
appointed to See Into the young Womans Clearness
Collected at this meeting 5ˢ-10ᵈ and **Elizabeth Barker** and

Mary Tucker are Chose to talk with **Meribeh Shearman**
Concerning her going to marry out of the order of Friends

The 16 of the 8 month 1736 Was our monthly meeting
of Women Friends held in **Dartmouth**
Collected at this meeting 7ˢ-10ᵈ

The 15 of the 9 month 1736 Was our monthly
Meeting of Women Friends Held In **Dartmouth**
Where **Recompence [Recompense] Kerby [Kirby]** and **Rebekah Cornell**
Came for their answer and friends finding nothing
to hinder Gave them leave to take each other in marriage
according to the Good Order of Friends
Collected at this meeting 10ˢ

The 20 day of the 10 month 1736 Was our monthly meet
ing of Women friends held In **Dartmouth** where **Job —
Howland** and **Naomy Chase** laid their Intentions of marriage —
they were desired to wait for their answer till next monthly meeting
Rebecca Russell and **Rebecca Barker** are Chose to make Inquiʳᵉy
Into Concerning the young womans Clearness: **Phebe Tucker**
and **Rebecca Russell** are Chose to attend the Quarterly meeting
Collected by this meeting 8ˢ-6ᵈ disbursted for keeping the meeting
house twenty Shillings

The 17 day of the 11 month ∧1736 was our Monthly meeting of women
friends held In **Dartmouth** Collected at this meeting 5ˢ – **Job —
Howland** and **Naomy Chase** came for their answer friends finding
nothing to hinder their answer was they might take each other in
marriage In the good order of Truth at this meeting **Joseph Tripp**
and **Abigail Wait** laid their Intentions of marriage they were
Desired to wait till next monthly Meeting for their answer
Sarah Gifford and **Lydia Allen** Chose to make enquiry into the
young womans Clearness And **Daniel Russell** and **Ruth
Howland** Laid their Intentions of Marriage before this
Meeting and were desired to wait till the next monthly
Meeting for their answer And **Mary Russell** and **Elizabeth
Barker** are Chose to Enquire into the young Womans
Clearness and make return to the next monthly
Meeting The Friends that Were Chose visiters last year
are Chose to Serve again one year longer
and **Apphia Mott** is Chose to assist our aged Friend
Ruth Tucker in wighting or to write In her absence

The 21 of the 12 month 1736 Was ∧ᵒᵘʳ monthly meeting of
Women Friends held In **Dartmouth** Where **Joseph Tripp**
and **Abigail Wait** Came for their Answer and Enquiry

being made And Friends finding nothing to hinder them
gave them Leave to take Each other In marriage accord
ing to the Good order of Friends also **Daniel Russell** and
Ruth Howland Came for their answer and this meeting
finding nothing to hinder them Gave leave that they
Might preceed to take Each othe In Marriage
According to the Abovesd Good order
Collected at this meeting 7 shillings And 9 pence

The 21 of the 1 month 1737 Was our monthly Meeting
of Women Friends held In **Dartmouth** Collected 9^s : 3^d
Ruth Tucker And **Apphia Mott** are Chose to write
to the Quarterly meeting Our visitters gives an account
to this meeting that they have visited Friends families
In a General Way And in Some Families found things
pretty well And In others not So well Where they Laboured
With them in love for an amendment

The 18 day of the 2 month 1737 Was our monthly
meeting of Women Friends held in **Dartmouth**
Collected at this meeting 5 Shillings And 10 pence
one of the Friends that was Chose to attend it but brought
no account from the Quarterly meeting

The 16 day of the 3 month 1737 Was our monthly
meeting of Women Friends held in **Dartmouth** Where
David Stafford And **Lydia Davel** [**Davol**] Laid their intentions
of marriage And Were desired to wait till the next
monthly meeting for their answer and **Keziah Wood**
and **Sarah Gifford** ar Chose to make Enquiry Concerning
the young Womans Clearness

The 20 of the 4 month 1737 Was our monthly Meeting
of Women Friends held In **Dartmouth**
David Stafford and **Lydia Davel** [**Davol**] Waits till the next
Monthly meeting for their answer

The 18 Day ~~the~~ of the 5 month ‚1737 was our monthly meeting of women
friends held In **Dartmouth** where **David Stafford** and **Lydia Davel** [**Davol**]
Came for their answer Inquiry being made friends finding
nothing hinder them gave them leave to take each other In
marriage according to the good order of Truth Collected by this
meeting 6^s - this meeting Received an epistele from the yearly
meeting which was read and kindly Excepted

The 15 day of the 6 month 1737 Was our monthly meeting of women
friends held In **Dartmouth** Collected by this meeting 4^s-10^d this
meeting Chose **Ruth Tucker** and **Phebe Tucker** to ballance the

accounts of this meeting we have ballanced the accounts and there
remains In the stock £3-1ˢ-7ᵈ

The 19 day of the 7 month 1737 was our monthly meeting of
women frinds held In **Dartmouth** Where **Benjamin Wing** and
Experience Benson laid their Intentions of marriage the[y] were desired
to wait till next montly meeting for their answer **Ruth Davis** and
Margrⁱᵗ Wing are Chose to make Inquiry Concerning the young womans
Clearness Collected at this meeting 5ˢ **Phebe Tucker** and **Sarah
Gifford** are Chose attend the Quarterly meeting **Ruth Tucker**
and **Apphia Mott** are Chose to write to the Quarterly meeting

The 17 Da of the 8 month 1737 was our monthly meeting of women
friends held In **Dartmouth** Where **Benjamin Wing** and
Experience Benson came for their answer and friend finding
nothing to hinder them gave them leave to take each other In marriage
according to the good order of Truth
Also **Joseph Smith** and **Elizabeth Davis** laid their Intentions of
marriage before this meeting they were Desired to wait till next month
ly meeting for their answer **Mary Lapham** and **Mary Russell** were
Chose to make Inquiry Concerning the young womans Clearness Collected
at this meeting 4ˢ-9ᵈ taken out of the Stock for the use of Friends £1-10ˢ

The 21 day of the 9 month 1737 was our monthly meeting of women friends
held In **Dartmouth** Where **Joseph Smith** and **Elisabeth Davis** Came for their
answer and friends finding nothing to hinder them gave them leave to take
other In marriage according to the good order of Truth
also **Joseph Barker** and **Rebekah Smith** laid their intentions
of marriage before this meeting and were desired to wait till
the next monthly meeting for their answer
Rebekah Russell and **Elizabeth Barker** are Chose to enquire
Concerning the young Womans Clearness
Collected at this meeting for the use friends 0£-11ˢ-08ᵈ

The 20 of the 10 month 1737 Was our monthly meeting
of Women Friends held in **Dartmouth**. **Joseph Barker** and
Rebekah ~~Barker~~ **Smith** Came for their answer and
nothing appearing to hinder they had their answer that they
might proceed to marry in the good order of Friends
And **Seth Shearman** and **Ruth Lapham** laid their intention
of marriage before this meeting and were desired to wait
till the next monthly meeting for their answer
Also **Seth Shearman** and **Ruth Lapham** laid their Intentions
of marriage before the abovesd meeting they were desired to wait
untill the next monthly meeting for their answer **Mary Tucker**
and **Rebecca Barker** are Chose to make Inquiry Concerning
the young womans Clearness

Reuben Davel [Davol] and **Mary Ricketson** laid their Intentions of
marriage before this meeting they were Desired to wait for their
answer till next monthly meeting **Sarah Gifford** and **Joanna
Russell** are Chose to make Inquiry Concerning the young
Womans Clearness Collected at this meeting the sum 3£-4ᵈ-6
taken out of the Stock for keeping the meeting house £1
Susanna Gifford and **Apphia Mott** are ᵃᵖᵖᵒʸⁿᵗᵉᵈ Chose to attend the Quarterly
meeting **Ruth Tucker** and **Apphia Mott** are Chose to write to the
Quarterly meeting

The 16 day of the 11 month 1737 was our monthly meeting of women
Friends held In **Dartmouth** where **Reuben Davel** [Davol] and ~~Ma~~
Mary Ricketson came for their answer and after due Inquiry made
Concerning the young womans Clearness and finding nothing to hinder
their answer was they might proceed in marriage between this and
and [sic] the next monthly meeting according to the good order of Truth
Also **Seth Shearman** and **Ruth Lapham** Received the Same answer
that they might proceed In marriage between this and the next monthly
meeting according to the good order Established among Friends
Benjamin Russell and **Hannah Allen** laid their Intentions of marriage
before this meeting they were Desired to wait till the next monthly
meeting for their answer **Mary Lapham** and **Apphia Mott** are Chose
to make Inquiry ~~chose to~~ Concerning the young womans Clearness

The 20ᵈᵃʸ of th 12 month 1737 was our monthly meeting of women
friends held In **Dartmouth** where **Benjamin Russell** and **Hannah Allen**
Came for their answer and an Enquiry having been made Concer
ning yᵉ young womans Clerness and nothin being found to hinder
they had their answer that they might proceed to take each other
In marriage in Some Convenient time between this and the
Next monthly meeting according to good order
and ther was Collected at this meeting 8ˢ-8ᵈ
and **Sarah Gifford** and **Audre Smith** are Chose Visitters for
Ponagansett and **Mary Russell** and **Sarah Taber** for **Cushnot**
And **Hannah Cadman** and **Keziah Wood** for **Coaksett**

At our monthly meeting of Women friends held In
Dartmouth ₐᵗʰᵉ 20 day of ye [1?] month 1737/8 where **Jacob Shearman** and **Margrit Prance** [Prince]
Signified their Intentions of marriage and were desired to
wait till the next monthly meeting for their Answer and
Mary Lapham and **Rebekah Russell** are appointed to make
enquiry Into the young Womans Clearness and Conversation
and make return to yᵉ next monthly meeting
There was Collected at this meeting 5ˢ-6ᵈ
Ruth Tucker and **Apphia Mott** are appointed to Write to the
Quarterly meeting, and this meeting is adjourned till the

First [6̶2̶] day in the 2ᵈ month next

At our monthly meeting of Women friends held in **Dartmouth**
on the 17ᵗʰ of the 2 month 1738 **Jacob Shearman** and **Margrit Prance [Prince]**
Came and Desired their answer and due Enquiry having been made
Concerning the young Womans Clearness and nothing appearing
to hinder they had their answer that they might proceed in marri
-age In some Convenient time between this and the next monthly
meeting Observing good order in the accomplishment thereof
Collected at this meeting 0ᶠ-9ˢ-4ᵈ And **Patienc[e] Wood** the Wife
of **William Wood** remains under dealing and this meeting
hath Chose **Phebe Tucker** and **Mary Tucker** to go and talk
further with her

At our monthly meeting of Women friends held In **Dartmou**ₜₕ
on the 15ᵗʰ of the 3 month 1738 **John Allen** and **Margrate Soule**
Laid their Intentions of Marriage befor this meeting and were desiᵣₑd
to Wait till the next monthly meeting for their answer and
Rebekah Barker and **Joanna Russell** are appointed to Enquire
Into the young Womans Clearness and Conversation and make
return to the next monthly meeting
And **Joseph Havens** and **Rebekah Russell** did lay their Intentions
of marriage before this meeting And were also desired to Wait
till the next monthly meeting for their answer and **Rebekah
Russell** and **Eunice Goddard** are appointed to make Enquiry into
the young Womans Clearness and Conversation and make
return to the next monthly meeting
There Was Collected at this meeting 6ˢ-8ᵈ

At our monthly meeting of Women Friends held In **Dartmouth**
on the 19 day of the 4 month 1738 **John Allen** and **Margrate
Soule** Came for their answer and nothing appearing to hinder
they had their answer that they might proceed to take each other
In marriage in Some Convenient time between this and the
next monthly meeting observing our good order in the
Accomplishment thereof: Also **Joseph Havens** and **Rebeckah
Russell**s Answer was that they might proceed In marriage
as abovesᵈ And **Mary Russell** and **Apphia Mott** are appointed
to attend the Quarterly Meeting And to write to yᵉ Same

At our monthly meeting of Women Friends held In **Dart**ₘₒᵤₜₕ
on the 17 of yᵉ 5 month 1738 We received an Epistle
from the Ɋ yearly meeting at **New Port** which was read and
kindly accepted There was Collected at this meeting 0-5-0
and **Abgail Ricketson** remain yet under Dealing
And **Patience Wood** hath made Sattisfaction for her
out goings

At our monthly meeting of Women Friends held in **Dartmouth**
The 21 Day of the 6 month 1738: Collected at this meeting 0-5-3
And **Ruth Tucker** and **Phebe Tucke[r]** are Chose to ballance the
accompts of this meeting

At our monthly meeting of Women Friends held In **Dartmouth**
on the 18th of the 7 month 1738 And **William Ricketson** and
Hannah Russell laid their Intention of taking Each other in
Marriage before this meeting And were desired to Wa[i]t till the
next monthly meeting for their answer and **Rebeckah Russell**
and **Apphia Mott** are appointed to make Enquiry into the young
Womans Clearness and Conversation and make return to the
next monthly meeting and **Grizzel Shearman** and **Abigail
Jenkins** are Chose to attend the Quarterly meeting
all the acounts ballanced and remains In the Stock 3-17-4

At our monthly meeting of Women Friends held In **Dart
mouth** on ———————————
Collected at this meeting 7s-6d Disbusted at this 2 pounds for a
perticular Friend And **Ruth Tucker** and **Apphia Mott** ar
Chose to Write to the Quarterly meeting

At our monthly meeting of Women Friends held in
Dartmouth on the 16th of the 8 month 1738 **William
Ricketson** Came for their answer And Finding nothing
to hinder them they had their answer that they might proceed
to take each other In marriage in Some Convenient time
between this and the next monthly meeting Observing good
order in the performance thereof
Collected at this meeting 0-7-7

At our monthly meeting of Women Friends held In
Dartmouth on the 20th day of the 9 month 1738
Collected at this meeting 0£-9s-0d And disbusted out of the Stock
for the use of Friends ——— 0£-6s-6d

At our monthly meeting of Women Friends held In
Dartmouth on the 18th of the 10 month 1739 [sic]
There was Collected at this meeting 0-3s-0d
Taken out of the Stock out of the Stock [sic] for keeping the
meeting House one pound. **Susanna Gifford** and **Joanna Mott**
are appointed to attend the Quarterly meeting
And **Ruth Tucker** and **Apphia Mott** are appointed to Draw
an Epistle to the Quarterly meeting

At our monthly meeting of Women Friends held at our meeting
House in **Dartmouth** on the 15th day of the 11 month 1738
Stephen Peckham and **Keturah Arthur** Signified their Intentions

of marriage at this meeting and were desired to wait till the next
Monthly meeting for their answer We have had an account
of her Clearness and Conversation from **Nantucket**
There was Collected at this meeting 0£-4s-0d

At our monthly meeting of Women Friends Held at our
Meeting House In **Dartmouth** on the 19th Day of ye 12 month 1738
Stephen Peckham and **Keturah Arthur** Came to this meeting
For their Answer And there being nothing found to hinder
their answer was that they might proceed to take Each
other in Marriage in Some Convenient time between
this and the next monthly meeting observing Our Good
Order in the accomplishing of it
No business presented from the Quarterly Meeting
And this meeting mad Choice of **Hannah Cadman** and
Peace Wood visitters for **Coaksett Vil[l]age** and for **Ponggansitt**
Mary Lapham Sarah Gifford and **Audre Smith**
And **Mary Russell** and **Sarah Taber** for **Cushnot**
There was Collected at this meeting 0£-3s-0d

At our monthly Meeting of Women Friends held at our
meeting House in **Dartmouth** on the 19th day of the first month
1739 there was Collected at this meeting 0£-3s-6d
And this meeting is adjourned until the first sixth day in
the 2d month next

At our monthly meeting of Women Friends held by adjourn_{mentpeleg}
on the 6 day of the 2 month 1739 **Lydia Soule** and
Meribeh [Meribah] Slocum are appointed to attend the Quarterly
Meeting: And **Ruth Tucker** and **Apphia Mott** are appointed
to ~~attend~~ Draw an Epistle to the Quarterly meeting next
and **Dorcas Shepherd** is added to the Visitters for this year
And **Phebe Tucker** is under Dealing Concerning the matter
about **Ruth Slocum**

At our monthly meeting of Women Friends held In
Dartmouth on the 16 day of the 2d month 1739 **Robert Hall**
And **Isabel Shearman** did lay their intentions of marriage
before this meeting and Were desired to wait till the next
Monthly meeting for their answer and **Mary Lapham** and
Mary Russell are appointed to make Enquiry into the
young Womans Clearness and Conversation And make
return to the next monthly meeting
And **John Potter** and **Hannah Barker** laid their inten
=tion of marriage before this meeting and were Desired as
aforesd and **Susanna Gifford** and **Mary Tucker** are appoin

=ted to See Into the young Womans Clearness and make return
as aforesd Collected at this meeting 0£-10s-9d
Taken out of the Stock for the use of Friends 1-10-0
And **Phebe Tucker** hath not made full Sattisfaction as yet
And **Mary Tucker** is Chose to keep ye Collection mony

At a monthly meeting of Women Friends held at
our meeting House in **Dartmouth** on the 21 of the 3 mo
1739 **Robert Hall** and **Isabel Shearman** and **John
Potter** and **Hannah Barker** Came for their answers
And nothing Appearing to hinder they had their answers
that they might proceed to marry in Some Convenient
time between this and the next monthly meeting
observing the Good order of Friends In the accomplishing
thereof Collected at at [sic] this meeting 0£-6s-5d

At our monthly meeting of Women Friends held at
our meeting House in **Dartmouth** the 18th Day of the 4 mo
1739. **Abraham Stafford** and **Ruth Wood** laid their
their [sic] intentions of marriage before this meeting and
were desired to wait til ye next monthly meeting for
their answer And **Elizabeth Barker** and **Peace Wood**
are Chose to make Enquiry Concerning the young wo-
=mans Clearness and Conversation and make return
to the next monthly meeting

At a monthly meeting of Women Friends held
at our meeting House in **Dartmouth** on the 16 day
of the 5 month 1739 Collected at this meeting 0-10-0
and **Experience Wing** is Chosen visitter for **Rochester**

At our monthly meeting of Women Friends held
at our meeting House in **Dartmouth** on the 20 of the
6 month 1739 **Abraham Stafford** and **Ruth Wood** Came and
desired their answer and nothing appearing to hinder
their answer was that they might proceed to take each
Other in marriage in the good order Established amongst
Friends in some Convenient time between this and the
next monthly meeting and **Audere Smith** and **Apphia
Mott** are appointed to ballance the accompts of this
meeting which they have done and remains
In the Stock 2£-1s-9d

At our monthly meeting of Women Friends held at our
Meeting House in **Dartmouth** on the 17 day of the 7 month 1739
William Russell and **Elisabeth Willber** [**Wilbur**] laid their intentions
of marriage before this meeting and were desired to wait til

the next monthly meeting for their answer and **Mary
Russell** and **Rebeckah Russell** are appointed to make Enquirry
Into the young Womans Clearness and Conversation and
make return to the next monthly meeting
And **Joseph Taber** and **Mary Tinkham** also laid their intention
of marriage and were desired to wait accordingly And **Mary
Russell** and **Ruth Davis** were Chose to Enquire into the young
Womans Clearness as aforesd
Collected at this meeting 0-5-6 and **Audre Smith** and
Apphia Mott are Chose to Draw up an Epistle to the
Quarterly meeting next

At a monthly meeting of Woman Friends held at our
Meeting House in **Dartmouth** on the 15 day of the 8 month
1739 **William Russell** and **Elizabeth Willber** [**Wilbur**] appeared at
this meeting and Signified the Continuation of their intention
as did also **Joseph Taber** and **Mary Tinkham** and things
appearing Clear they had their answers that they might
proceed to mar[r]y in good order in Some Convenient time
between this and the next monthly meeting
Collected for the use of friend 0-5^s-9^d
We received an Episle from **Rode Island** which was read
and kindly accepted

At a monthly meeting of Friends held at our meet
ing House in **Dartmouth** on the 19 day of y^e 9 month 1739
Collected at this meeting for the use of Friends 0$^£$-4^s-6^d
Taken out of the Stock 0$^£$-11^s-10^d

At our monthly meeting of women Friends held in **Dartmouth**
The 17th of y^e 10th month 1739. Collected for the youce of friends 1$^£$=4^s=1^d
Mary Russell and **Peace Wood** are Chose to attend the Quarte[r]ly meeting
Ruth Tucker and **Apphia Mott** are appoynted to Draw an Epissel to the
Quarterly meeting next Ensuing this meeting is aiurned until the first
adjourn^d 6 Day in the next month

At our monthly meeting of Women friends held in **Dartmouth** y^e 21th of y^e 11th mo 17$_{39}$
Peleg Where **Peleg Cornell** and **mary Russell** Laid their intention of marri[a]g[e] they were
Cornel
proposal To wait until the next monthly meeting for their answer **Rebeckah Russell** and
Rebeckah Barker was Chose to make inquiry Concearning the young woman Clear
ness and Conversation and make their Return to the next monthly meeting
Eliz: Wing **Mary Lapham** and **Susannah Gifford** wear [were] Chose to talke with **Elizabeth wing**
Meriba And **meribah Gifford** Conserning their out Goings Collected att this meeting: 4^s[?] =6^d
Gifford Taken out of the Stock for the youce of Friends: £1–5^s–0^d

---

Peleg At our monthly meeting of Women Friends held in **Dartmouth** y^e 18th day of 12mo 17$_{39}$
Cornel
answer Wher[e] **Peleg Cornell** and **mary Russell** Boath appeared Signified the Continuation

of their intention of marri[a]ge and their answer was that they might Proceed

David Smith and **Jean Brown** Laid their intention of marrige Before this meeting

David Smith proposal They wear Desired to wait until the next monthly meeting for their answer

Mary Russell and **Elizabeth Barker** wear Chose to make inquire Conserning

The yo[u]ng woman Clearness and Conversation and make their Return to the next

Monthly meeting Collected for the youce of friends £0=4ˢ=0ᵈ

At our monthly meeting of women friends held in **Dartmouth**: yᵉ 17 of yᵉ 1ᵗʰ mo 1740

David Smith answer Where **David Smith** and **Jean Brown** boath appeared Before this meeting

and Signified the Continuation of their intention of marri[a]ge and their

George Allen proposal Answer was they might Proceed **George Allen** and **Rachel Smith** Laid

Their intention of marriage Before this meeting & they were Desired

To wait until the next monthly meeting for their answer **Rebeckah**

Russell and **Apphia mott** are to make inquirey Concerning the young

Woman Clearness and make their Return to the next monthly meeting

Col[l]ected for the youce of friends: £0=6ˢ=1ᵈ–0[ᵗ?] this meeting is a iourned [adjourned] until

The first Sixth ᵈᵃʸ in the next month **Peace wood** and **Susannah Gifford**

Are appointed to attend the Quarte[r]ly meeting **Ruth Tucker** and **Apphia**

Mott are to Draw up an Epistel to the Quarely meeting next ~~

George Allen answer At our mont[h]ly meeting of women friends held in **Dartmouth** yᵉ 21 of yᵉ 2ᵗʰ mo 1740

George Allen and **Rachel Smith** Both appeared and Signified the Continuation

of their intention of marrige and their answer was they might proceed

Wᵐ Hart proposal **William Hart** and **mary Shepard** [Shepherd] Laid their intention of marrige Before this

Meeting they were desired to wait until the next monthly meeting for

Their answer **mary Lapham** and **Joanna Russell** are to make inquirey

Concerning the yong woman Clearness and Conversation and make their

Return to the next monthly meeting Collected at this meeting the –

Sum of 8ˢ=9ᵈ no Business from the Quarte[r]ly meeting

At our monthly meeting of women friends held in **Dartmouth** yᵉ 20 of yᵉ 3ᵗʰ mo 1740

Wᵐ Hart answer Where **William Hart** and **Mary Shephard** [Shepherd] Boath appearing Before this

Meeting and signified the Continuation of their intention of marriage and

Jos Tripp answer Their answer was that they might Proceed **Joseph Tripp** and **Judah – –**

Mosher Laid their intention of marrige Before this meeting they wear

proposal To wait until the next monthly meeting for their answer **Elizabeth**

Barker and **Grizzel Sʰᵉrman** are Chose to make Enquire [inquiry] Concerning the

yo[u]ng woman Clearness and Conversation and make their Return to the

Phebe Tucker Next monthly meeting Collected at this meeting–1ˢ=6ᵈ- **Phebe Tucker** hath made

Friends Satisfaction

At our monthly meeting of women holden in **Dartmouth** yᵉ 23 of yᵉ 4ᵗʰ mo 1740

Jos: Tripp aⁿswer **Joseph Tripp** and **Judah mosher** Boath appearing Before this meeting and

signified the Continuation of their intention of marriage and their answer was

They might Proceed according to the Good order Established among friends

Friends have maid Choyce of **mary Gifford** and **Keziah Wood** to visit friends

Families at **acokset** this year Collected for the youce of friends the Sum of: 14^s=0^d
Lyda taber and **Mary Russell** are appointed to visit friends families in
Poniganset this year **Keziah Wood** and **Abig[a]il Ginkins** are Appointed to
Attend the Quarte[r]ly meeting next Ensuing **Ruth Tucker** and **Apphia mott**
Are to draw an Epistel to the Quarterly meeting

Dan Russell proposal

At our monthly meeting of women friends held in **Dartmouth** ye 21 of ye 5 ^{mo} 174^0
Where **Daniel Russell** and **Edea Howland** Laid their intention of marrage
They ware [were] Desired to wait until the next monthly meeting for their
Answers **mary Lapham** and **Apphia mott** were Chosen to make Enquire
Concerning the yong woman Clearness and Conversation and make
Epistle Rec^d Their Return unto the next monthly meeting: we Recevid an Epistle
From friends at **Newport** which was Re[a]d and the Love therein [ministered?]
Kindly accepted:

Dan: Russell

At our monthly meeting of women friends held in **Dartmouth** ye 15 of ye 6th mo 1740
Where **Daniel Russel[l]** and **Edea Howland** Both appeared Before this meeting
And Signified the Continuation of their intention of marrige and their answer
was they might Proceed in marrage Betwixt this and the next monthly
Meeting observing Good orders Collected for the youce of friends: £0–7^s–2^d

Nat Bowdish proposal

At our monthly meeting of women friends held in **Dartmouth** ye 15 of ye 7th mo 1740
Nathaniel Bowdash [Bowdish] and **Francies Lapham** Laid their intention of marrage
Before this meeting they ware Desired to wait unt[i]l the next monthly
Meeting for their answer **Rebeckah Barker** and **Elizabeth Barker**
Are Chose to make inquire Concerning the yong woman Clearness and
make their Return to the next monthly meeting Collected for the youce
of friends: =3^s= 10^d **Audrey Smith** and **Apphia mott** and **mary Tucker** are
Chose to Ballance the accompts of this meeting **Susannah Gifford** and
Joanna mott are Appoynted to attend the Quarte[r]ly meeting next
Insuing and **Apphia mott** to write to the Quartely meeting **Mary Lapham**
Elizabeth Barker and **Susannah Gifford** are Appoynted Visitors ^{for} **Ponaganset**
Villige this year: all accounts Ballanced and hear Remains in the Stock: £3=15^s=6^d

Nat^l Bowdish answer

At our monthly meeting of women friends held in **Dartmouth** y^e 20th of y^e 8th mo 1740
Nathaniel Bowdash [Bowdish] and **Franses Lapham** Came for their answer and there
Being Nothing found to hender them their Answer was they might Proceed
Betwean this and the next monthly meeting According to Good orders Established
Among friend Collected for the youce [use] of friends: 5^s=0^d

At our monthly meeting of women friends held in **Dartmouth** y^e 17th of y^e 9th mo 1740
Collected for the youce of friends: 2^s=4^d

At our monthly meeting of women friends held in **Dartmouth** y^e 15th of y^e 10th mo 1740
No Collection this meeting: Taken out of the Stock one Pound: towards keeping
The meeting house: **mary Lapham** and **Susannah Gifford** are Chose to attend
The Quarte[r]ly meeting **Ruth Tucker** and **Apphia Mott** are Appointed to draw
An Epistle to the Quarterly meeting Next insuing

At our monthly meeting of women friends held in **Dartmouth** yᵉ 19ᵗʰ of yᵉ 11ᵗʰ mo 1740
Collected for the youce of friends: – – – – – – – – – £0=11ˢ=11ᵈ

Dan Howland proposal

At our monthly meeting of women friends held in **Dartmouth** yᵉ 25ᵗʰ of yᵉ 12ᵗʰ mo 174⁰
Where **Daniel Howland** and **mary Slocom [Slocum]** Laid their intention of marr[i]age
They ware to wait for their answer until the next monthly meeting
Rebeckah Russell and **Rebeckah Barker** were to make inquire [inquiry] Concerning
The yo[u]ng woman Clearnᵉss and Conveʳsation and make their Return to the Next
Monthly meeting: no Collection this meeting

Dan Howland answer

At our monthly meeting of women friends held in **Dartmouth** yᵉ 16ᵗʰ of yᵉ 1ᵗʰ mo 1741
Where **Daniel Howland** and **mary Slocome [Slocum]** Boath Appeard at this meeting and
Signified the Continuation of their intention of marrage and their answer
was they might Proceed betwixt this and the next monthly meeting observing
Good orders: Collected for the youce of friends: 7ˢ- 8ᵈ= This meeting is a iourned
[adjourned]
until the first Six[th] day in next month **Ruth Tucker** and **Apphia Mott**
Are appoynted to Draw an Epistle to the Quarte[r]ly meeting Next

Wᵐ Gifford proposal

At our monthly meeting of women friends held in **Dartmouth** yᵉ 20ᵗʰ of yᵉ 2ᵗʰ mo 1741
William Gifford and **Elizabeth Tripp** Laid their intention of marrage they
were Desired to wait until the next monthly meeting for their answer
Rebeckah Russell and **Peace Wood** are Appointed to make inquirey Concerning
the yo[u]ng woman Clearness and Conversation and make their Return to the next
monthly meeting: Collected for the youce of friends – – – – £0– 5ˢ– 0ᵈ

Wᵐ Gifford answer

At our monthly meeting of women friend held in **Dartmouth** yᵉ 27ᵗʰ of yᵉ 3ᵗʰ mo 174¹
Where **William Gifford** and **Elizabeth Tripp** Both Appeared at this meeting
And Signified the Continuation of their intention of marrage and their - - -
Answer was they might Proceed Betwix[t] this and the next monthly meeting
Observing Good orders: No Collection this meeting

Visitors

At our monthly meeting of women friends held in **Dartmouth** by an a iurnment
[adjournment]
the 22ᵗʰ of yᵉ 4ᵗʰ mo 1741: Collected for the youce of friends: – – – – – – 5ˢ=2ᵈ
This meeting hath maid Choice of **Keziah Wood** and **mary Gifford** to visit
Friends famelies in **Acokset** this year: **mary Russell** and **Grizzel Sherman**
Are Appointed to attend the Quarte[r]ly meeting next ensuing **Ruth Tucker**
and **Apphia mott** are Appointed to write an Epistle to the Qu[a]rte[r]ly meeting: ᵉⁿˣᵗ

Eliphel Harper Recᵈ

At our monthly meeting of women friends held in **Dartmouth** yᵉ 20ᵗʰ of yᵉ 5ᵗʰ mo 1741
Collected for the youce of friends – – – – – £0=2ˢ=0ᵈ
This meeting Received an Epistle from **Newport** yearly meeting which
Was Re[a]d and Kindley Accepted: **Eliphel Harper** Certificate was Re[a]d in
This meeting and well accepted and She taken under the Cear [care] of the meeting
Eliphel Harper Certificate Came from **Sandwich** monthly meeting:
Taken out of the Stock one Pound ten Shillings

At our monthly meeting of women friends held in **Dartmouth** y^e 17th of y^e 6 mo $\underline{1741}$
No Collection this meeting

At our monthly meeting of women friends held in **Dartmouth** y^e 21th of 7 ^{mo}
1741: Collected for the youce of friends:= 10^s=0^d:
Grizzel Sherman and **Elizabeth Gidley** are Appoynted to attend the
Quarte[r]ly meeting **Ruth Tucker** and **Apphia mott** are Chose to write
To the Quartely meeting Next Ensuing: **Audrey Smith** and **mary**
Tucker and **Apphia Mott** are Chose to Balance the accoumpts [accounts]
of the Above Said meeting: this meeting is a iourned [adjourned] until the first Sixt[h]
Day in Next month

At our monthly meeting of women friends held in **Dartmouth** y^e 19th of y^e 8th mo 1741

The 11th day of y^e 9th mo 1741: All Accounts Ballanced and hear [here] - - –
Remains in the Stock - £3=14^s=7^d

John Gifford proposal

At our monthly meeting of women friends Held in **Dartmouth**
The 16th day of y^e 9th mo 1741 where **John Gifford** and **Bershaba Lapham**
Both Appeared and Signified their inte^{n}tion of marr[i]age they wear [were]
Desired to wait until the Next monthly meeting for their answer
Rebeckah Russell and **Apphia mott** are Appointed to make inquire [inquiry]
Concerning the yo[u]ng woman Clearness and make their Return to the Next
Monthly meeting: Collected for the youce of friends = - - - - 5^s–0^d

John Gifford answer

At our monthly meeting of women Friends held in **Dartmouth** the 21th day
of y^e 10th mo 1741: where **John Gifford** and **Bershaba Lapham** Both Appear[e]d
And Signified the Continuation of their intention of marr[i]age and their
Answer was they might Proceed Betwixt this and the Next monthly
meeting observing Good orders: Collected for the youce of friends = 10^s=9^d= -
Taken out of the Stock: £1=10^s=0^d towards payment for Keeping the meeting
house: **Susannah Gifford** and **Peace Wood** are Appointed to Attend the
Qu[a]rte[r]ly meeting Next insuing at **Rhod island**: **Ruth Tucker** and **Apphia**
Mott are Appointed to Draw up an Epistle to the Qurtely meeting Next

Silas Kirby proposal

At our monthly meeting of women friends held in **dartmouth** ye 18th of ye 11th mo
1741 whear **Silas Kirby** and **Elizabeth Russell** Signified their
intention of marrage they were desired to wait until the next monthly
Meeting for their answer: **mary Lapham** and **Grizzel Sherman** wery [were] Chose
To make inquire Concerning the yong woman Cl[e]arness and Conversation and
Make their Return to the Next monthly meeting: No Collection this meeting

Frances Allen proposal

At our mont[h]ly meeting of women friends held in **Dartmouth** the 15th of ye 12th mo
1741 whery [where] **Frances Allen** and **Rebeckah Tucker** Came and Signified
Their intention of mar[ri]age: they were to wait for their answer until
The Next monthly meeting: Two friends were Chose to inquire into
the yong woman Clearness and make their Return to the Next monthly
meeting: No Collection this meeting

At our monthly meeting of women Friends held in **Dartmouth** the 15th of ye 1th month

Silas Kirby answer

1742: where **Silas Kirby** and **Elizabeth Russel[l]** Both Appeared and Signified the Contin[u]ation of their intention of marrige and their Answer was They might Proceed in marrage Betwixt this and the Next monthly meeting

Francis Allen answer

According to Good orders: also **Francis Allen** and **Rebeckah Tucker** Came and Desired their Answer and friends finding Nothing to hender them their [answer?] was they might proceed in marrage Betwix this and the Next monthly meeting observing Good orders: Collected for the youce of Friends - - - - 6s–3d

Phebe Tucker and **Sarah Gifford** are Appointed to Attend the Qua[r]te[r]ly meeting

Elizabeth Barker and **mary Tucker** are Chose to Talk with **marebah howland** For her out Goings: **Ruth Tucker** and **Apphia Mott** are Appointed to write to The Qu[a]rte[r]ly meeting

---

At our monthly meeting of women friends held in **Dartmouth** ye 19th of ye 2th mo 1742 No Collection this meeting: No Business Presented for the Qurtely meeting

---

At our monthl[y] meeting of women friends held in **Dartmouth** the 17th of ye 3th mo 174₂ Collected for the youce [use] of friends - - - - 3s=9d

---

At our monthly meeting of women friends held in **Dartmouth** ye 21th of ye 4th mo 1742 Collected for the youce friends: 15s=9d= **Peace Wood** and **Mary Gifford** are Appointed to attend the Qurtely meeting Next insuing **Ruth Tucker** and **Apphia mott** are Appointed to draw an Epistle to the Quertely meeting

---

At our monthly meeting of women friend held in **Dartmouth** ye 19th of ye 5th mo 1742 Collected for the youce of friends: 4s=3d: Taken out of the Stock: 15s=9[d?]: for the youce of friends: more taken out of the Stock towards Payment for Keeping the meeting house: =£2=0s=0d

---

At our monthly of women friends held in **Dartmouth** ye 16th of ye 6th mo 1742 Collected for the youce of friends: =7s=8d= this meeting makes Choice of

Visitors

Peace Wood and **Abig[a]il Cornel** [**Cornell**] to visit friends Famelies at **acokset** the year insuing

---

At our monthly meeting of women friends held in **Dartmouth** ye 20th of ye 7th mo 1742: Collected for the youce of Friends – - - - - – - – - 12s=6d–

Elizabeth Gidley and **Sarah Gifford** are Appointed to Attend the Qu[a]rte[r]ly Meeting Next insuing: **Grizzel Sherman** and **mary Tucker** are Chose To talke with **Eliphel Harper** Concerning her Clearness on her Removeal

Eliphel Harper

Ruth Tucker and **Apphia Mott** are Appointed to Daraw an Epistle to the Qurtely meeting

---

At our monthl[y] meeting of women friends held in **Dartmouth** 18th day of ye 8th mo 1742 No Business Pr[e]sented from the Qurtely = meeting **Audrey Smith Mary Tucker Apphia Mott** are to Balance the accounts of this meeting No Collection this meeting: **Elizabeth Gidley** and **Susannah Gifford** are Appointed to talk with **Joanna Howland**

Joanna Howland

Concerning her out Goings

The 8th day of the 9th mo 1742: all accompts Balanced and hear [here]
Remains in the Stock= £2=14S=9d

At our Monthly Meeting of women friends held in **Dartmouth**
The 15th of ye 9th mo 1742: No Collection this Meeting

At our Monthly Meeting of women friends held in **Dartmouth** ye 20th
of 10th mo 1742: Collected for the youce [use] of friends: 4S=6d:
Two pounds taken out of the Stock for Keeping the meeting house
3 Shillings more taken out of the Stock: this meeting Hath maid [made]
Choice of **Peace Wood** and **mary Willcox** and **Sarah Gifford** to Talk with
Leah Brownell for a miss step which She hath taken: **Phebe Tucker** and
Sarah Gifford are Appointed to attend the Quertaly Meeting Next insuing
Ruth Tucker and **Apphia Mott** are to Draw an Epistle to the Same

At our Monthly meeting of women held in **Dartmouth** the 17th of
the 11th mo 1742: hear [here] was Collected for the youce of friends: 10S–0d-

Visiters This meeting maid Choice of **Lyda Taber** and **Mary Russel [Russell]** for to visit friends
Friends families in **Cushnet** this year: this meeting maid Choice of

Alice
Slocum **Audrey Smith** and **Elizabeth Gidley** to Talke with **Ealce Slocom [Alice Slocum]** for
Her out Goings: **Peace Wood** and **Mary Gifford** are Appointed to go with

Nat: Kirby
& wife the men to talke with **Nathaniel Kerby [Kirby]** and his Wife

At our Monthly Meeting of women friend held in **Dartmouth** the 21th day
of the 12th mo 1742: hear was Collected for the youce of friends: £3-0S-6d=

Mary
Wood & this Meeting Chose **Mary Gifford** and **Abig[a]il Cornal [Cornell]** to talk with **Mary**
Sarah Giff= **Wood**: **Mary Russel[l]** and **Elizabeth Barker** are Chose to talke with **Sarah**
=ford **Gifford**

At our Monthly Meeting of Women friends held in **Dartmouth** ye 21 of ye 1th mo 1743

Peleg whear **Peleg Gifford** and **Abig[a]il Shephard [Shepherd]** Laid their intention of marr[i]age
Gifford they ~~Friends~~ Were Desired to wait for their answer until the Next
proposal Monthly meeting: **Hannah Tucker** and **Apphia Mott** were Appointed
to make inquire Concerning the yo[u]ng woman Clearness and Conversation and
make Return to the Next monthly meeting: **Rebeckah Barker** and **Apphia**
Mott are Appointed to attend the Qu[a]rte[r]ly meeting Next insuing: **Ruth Tuck[er]**
and **Apphia Mott** are to Draw an Epistle to the Sam[e] no Collection this
meeting: **Hannah Cadman** and **Susannah Cornal [Cornell]** are Appointed to See into
mary Devile [Davol] Conv[e]rsation

At our Montht[y] Meeting of Women Friends held in
Dartmouth ye 18th of ye 2th mo 1743: where **Peleg Gifford** and **Abig[a]il**

Peleg
Gifford **Shephard [Shepherd]** Boath appear[e]d and Signified the Continuation of their
answer intention of marri[a]ge: and their answer Was they might Proceed
Betwix[t] this and the Next monthly meeting observing Good orders
Collected for the youce of friends: 12S–0d=

Sarah **Sarah Gifford** hath maid friends Satisfaction for the uneasiness
Gifford
made Which She hath Caused among friend Concerning the marr[i]age of
satisfaction her daughter

At our Monthly Meeting of Women friends held in **Dartmouth**
The 15th of ye 3th mo 1743: No Collection this meeting

At our Monthly meeting of women friends held in **Dartmouth**

Furreign
Friends
Visit

The 20th of ye 4th mo 1743: **Kezia Benson** and **Hocks**[?] have visited our
Meeting and their visits wear kindly accepted: Collected for the youce

Bethiah
Wady
Recd

of friends: 6s–8d: **Bethia Wady**s Certificate was Read and well accepted:
Sarah Gifford and **Kezia wood** are Appointed to attend the Qu[a]rte[r]ly ~~~
meeting: **Apphia Mott** is Appointed to draw an Epistle to the Qurtely ~~~
meeting Next insuing

At our monthly meeting of women friends held in **Dartmouth** the

Alice
Bunting
Ann
Gant
Visit

15th of ye 5th mo 1743: here was Collected for the youce of friends: 8s–3d
Ealse Bunting and **Ann Gant**: have visited our meeting and their visits
were Kindly Excepted: and our meeting had good unity with their Certificate
The Epistle from **Newport** yearly meeting was Read and well accepted ~
No Business Presented from the Qurtely meeting

At our monthly meeting of women friends held in **Dartmouth**: ye 15th of

Visitors

the 6th mo 1743: Collected for the youce of friends: 5s=0d= this meeting maid [choice?] of
Peace wood and **Abig[a]il Cornal [Cornell]** to visit friends families in **Acokset**
vilige this year: **mary Lapham Susannah Gifford** and **Elizabeth Barker**
and **Sarah Gifford** are Chose to visit friends families in **Poniganset [Apponagansett]** ~~
vilige this year insuing

At our monthly meeting of Women friend held in **Dartmouth** ye 19 of ye 7th [mo]
1743: Collected for the youce of friends: 6s=6d: **Robard Mosher** and **Sarah**

Robart
Mosher
proposal

Laton [Lawton] Both Appeared at this meeting and Signified their intention of marr[ia]ge
they were Desired to weait for their answer until the Next monthly
Meeting: **Peace Wood** and **Sarah Gifford** are Appointed to make inquire - - – -
Concerning the yong woman Clearness and Conversation and make Return to
the Next monthly meeting: **Audra Smith** and **Mary Wilcox** are appointed to
Attend the Qurtely meeting: **Ruth Tucker** and **Apphia Mott** are to Draw
an Epistle to the Same: taken out of the Stock for the youce of
Friends - - 6s=8d=

At our monthly meeting of Women friends held in **Dartmouth** ye 17th of ye 8th mo

Robart
Mosher
answer

1743: where **Robard Mosher** and **Sarah Laton [Lawton]** Boath appeard and Signified
the Contin[u]ation of their intention of marrage: and friends finding Nothing to
Hender them: their answer Was they might Proceed Betwix this and the
Next monthly meeting observing Good orders Collected for the youce of friends
:6s=6d=: taken out of the Stock: 9s=10d= this meeting Chose **Audr[e]y Smith Mary**
tucker Apphia mott to balance the accounts of this meeting

The 16th of the 9th mo 1743: all Accounts Balanced and here
Remains in the Stock - - -£3–1s–2d-

At our monthly meeting of women friends held in **Dartmouth**

Daniel Wood proposal ye 21th ye 9th mo 1743: where **Daniel Wood** and **mary wady** Boath
Appeared and Signified their intention pf marri[a]ge: they were desired
to wait for their answer until the Next monthly meeting: **Rebeckah
Russel [Russell]** and **Mary Russel[l]** are to make inquirey concerning the yo[u]ng woman
Clearness and Conversation and make their Return to the Next monthly
meeting; Collected for the youce [use] of friends: =5s=0d:

At our monthly meeting of women friends held in **Dartmouth** by
Daniel Wood answer a iorment [adjournment] ye 6th of ye 10th mo 1743: where **Daniel Wood** and **mary wady** Boath
Appeard and signified the Continuation of their intention of marr[i]age
and friends finding nothing to hender them their answer was they might
Proceed in marrage Betwix[t] this and the Next monthly meeting observeing
Good orders: taken out of the Stock: 2£ to wards Keeping the meeting
house: **Mary Lapham** and **Susannah Gifford** are Appointed to attend the
Qu[a]rte[r]ly meeting Next insuing: No Collection this meeting: **Ruth tucker**
and **Apphia mott** are Chose to Draw an Epistle to the Qurtely meeting

At our Monthly meeting of Women friends held in **Dartmouth** y 16th of ye 11th [mo]
1743: No Collection this meeting nor no Business Presented from the
Qurtely meeting

At our monthly Meeting of women friends held in **Dartmouth**
Daniel Gifford proposal ye 20th of ye 12th mo 1743\4: where **Daniel Gifford** and **Ann Howland** Both
Appeared att this meeting and signified their intention of marr[i]age
they were Desired to wait for their answer until the Next monthly
meeting: **Phebe Tucker** and **mary Russel[l]** are to make inquire [inquiry]
Concerning the yong Woman Clearness and make their Return to the
Next monthly meeting: Collected for the youce of friends: =3s–8d~

At our monthly meeting of women friends held in **Dartmouth** ye 19th of y[e] 1th mo
Dan Gifford Answer 1744: **Daniel Gifford** and **Ann Holand [Howland]** Both appear[e]d at this meeting
and Signified the Continuation of their intention of marrage: and
friends finding nothing to hender them: their answer was they
mig[h]t proceed in marr[ia]ge Betwix this and the Next monthly meeting
observeing Good orders= Collected for the youce of friends – – – – 15s–4d
Thomas Smith proposal **Thomas Smith** and **Exsperence Chace** Laid their intention of marr[i]age
Before this meeting: they were Desired to wait for their answer until
John Parks proposal the Next monthly meeting: also **John Parke** and **Sarah Gifford** Both
appe[a]red at this meeting and Signified their intention of marrage they were
Were to wait for their answer until the Next monthly meeting ~ ~
The friends that went out with them are to make inquire Concerning the
yo[u]ng womens Clearness and Conversation and make their Return to the Next
monthly meeting: **Phebe tucker** and **Apphia Mott** are appointed to attend the
Qu[a]rte[r]ly meeting: **Ruth Tucker** and **Apphia Mottt** are to write to the
Qurtely meeting Next insuing

At our monthly meeting of women friends held in **Dartmouth** ye 16 of

Tho Smith and John Parks answer

yᵉ 2ᵗʰ mo 1744: No Collection this meeting **Thomas Smith** and **Exsperance Chace**
John Parke and **Sarah Gifford** all Appe[a]red att this meeting and Signified - -
the Continuation of their intention of marr[i]age: and friends finding
Nothing to hender them their answer was that they might Proceed
in marr[i]ag[e]: Betwean this and the Next monthly meeting observing Good orders:
Nothing of Business Pr[e]sented from the Qurtely meeting: taken out of the
Stock: £1=10ˢ–0ᵈ

At our monthly meeting of women friends held in **Dartmouth** yᵉ 21ᵗʰ of yᵉ 3ᵗʰ mo
1744: Collected for the youce of friends =6ˢ=0ᵈ
Bethiah walker Certificate was Read and She Rece[i]ved und[er] the Cear [care] of our
Meeting

At our monthly meeting of women friends held in **Dartmouth** yᵉ 18ᵗʰ of yᵉ 4 ᵐᵒ
1744 Collected for the youce of friends =6ˢ=7ᵈ: **Susannah Gifford** and **Deborah**
Hunt are Appointed to attend the Qurtely meeting: this meeting maid Choyce
Visitors of **Mary Gifford** and **hannah Mosher** to visit friends famᶦleys in **acokset** this
year insuing: **Ruth Tucker** and **Apphia Mott** are Appointed to write to the
Qurtely meeting

At our monthly meeting of women friends held in **Dartmouth** yᵉ 16ᵗʰ of yᵉ 5ᵗʰ mo 1744
This meeting Rece[i]ved an Epistle from the **Newport** yearley meeting which was
Re[a]d and kindly accepted: No Collection this meeting: **mary tucker** and **Apphia**
Mott are Appointed to give an account to the monthly meeting at
Marcy Fish **Rhod island** Concerning **mercy fish**: Co[n]versation wher She Resided among us

At our monthly meeting of women friends held in **Dartmouth** yᵉ 20ᵗʰ of yᵉ 6ᵗʰ mo
Barna Mosher proposal 1744: **Barabas [Barnabas] mosher** and **Bethiah Walker** Laid their intention
of marrage and friends Desired them to wait for their answer until the
Next monthly meeting: **mary Russel[l]** and **Apphia Mott** are to make
inquire Concerning the yong woman Clearness and Conversation and make
Return to the Next monthly meeting: Collected for the yoce of friends =5ˢ=6ᵈ

At our monthly meeting of Women friends held in **Dartmouth** yᵉ 17ᵗʰ of
Barna Mosher ~~proposal~~ answer The 7ᵗʰ mo 1744: **Barnabas Mosher** and **Bethia walker** Boath appeared and
Signified the Continuation of their intention of marr[i]age and friends finding
Nothing to hender them their answer was they might Proceed in marr[i]ag[e]
Betwean this and the Next monthly meeting observing Good orders
Robart Kirby proposal **Robard [Robert] Kirby** and **Abig[a]il Allen** Laid their intention of marrage Before this
meeting: they were to wait for their answer until the Next monthly
meeting: **Susannah Gifford** and **Deborah Slocom [Slocum]** are Appointed to make inquire
Concerning the yo[u]ng woman Clearniss and Conversation and make their Return
to the Next monthly meeting: No Collection this meeting: **Peace wood** and
Mary Potter are Chose to attend the Qu[a]rte[r]ly meeting Next insuing:
Ruth Tucker and **Apphia Mott** are to darw [draw] an Epistle to the same
this meeting is Aiouned [Adjourned] until the first Six[th] Day in Next month

At our monthly meeting of women friends held in **Dartmouth** yᵉ 15ᵗʰ of yᵉ 8ᵗʰ mo

*John Mac
-cumber
proposal*

1744: Collected for the youce of friends: $7^s=9^d=$ **John macombar [Macomber]** and **Desire**
[?] **Poter [Potter]** Laid their intention of marr[i]ag[e] Before this meeting they
were Desired to wait for their answer until the Next monthly meeting
Keziah wood and **hannah Mosher** are Chose to make inqurey Concerning
the yong woman Clearness and Conversation and make their Re^{t}urn to the
Next monthly meeting No Business Presented from the Qurtely meeting

*Robart
Kirby
answer*

*John Ma
comber
answer*

*Phebe
Russel*

At our monthly meeting of Women friends held in **Dartmouth** ye 19th of
the 9th mo 1744: where **Robard Kirby** and **Abig[a]il Allen** Boath
appeared and Signified the Continuation of their intention of marr[i]age
and friends finding Nothing that hendred them their answer was they
might proceed in marr[i]age Betwix[t] this and the Next monthly meeting
observing Good orders: also **John macomber** and **Desire Potter** Both
Appearing at this meeting and Required their a^{n}swer and friends finding
Nothing to hender them their answer was they might Proceed in marrage
Betwix this and the Next monthly meeting observing Good orders:
taken out of the Stock 2$^£$: No Collected^{ion} this meeting: **mary Tucker**
Apphia Mott audrey Smith are Appointed to Ballanced the accounts of our
meeting: **Audrey Smith** and **mary tucker** are Appointed to talk with
Phebe Russel [Russell]

The 11th of y^e 10th mo 1744: all accounts Ballanced and here Remains in
the Stock: $£0-1^s-9^d$

*John
Wood &
Samuel
Sawdy
proposel*

At our monthly meeting of women friends held in **Dartmouth** y^e 17th of
the 10th mo 1744 **John wood** and **Hannah Wing Samuel Sawdy** and **Pern=
nel mott** Laid their intention of marr[i]age Before this meeting they were
Desired to wait for their answer until the Next monthly meeting
Rebeckah Russel [Russell] and **mary Russel[l]** are Chose to make inquire Concerning
the yo[u]ng womans Clearness and Conversation and make their Return to the
Next monthly meeting: **Apphia mott** and **Keziah Wood** are appointed
to attend the Qu[a]rte[r]ly meeting Next insuing: **Ruth tucker** and **Apphia
Mott** are to Draw an Epistle to the S[a]me: Collected for the youce of friends $=10^s=1^d$

*Samuel
Sawdy
answer*

At our monthly meeting of Women friends held in **Dartmouth** y^e 21th of y^e
11 month 1744 **Samuel Sawday [Sawdy]** and **Pernal Mott** Boath appear[e]d at this
meeting and Signified the Continuation of their intention of marr[i]ag[e]:
and friends finding Nothing that hendred: their answer was they might Proceed
in marr[i]age Beteixt [betwixt] this and the Next monthly meeting observ[i]ng Good
orders No of Business Presented from the Qurtely meeting
Collected for the yo^{u}ce of friends$= 2^s=11^d=$

*John
Wood
answer*

At our monthly meeting of women held in **Dartmouth** y^e 18th of y^e 12th mo 1744
John Wood and **hannah Wing** Boath appear[e]d at this meeting and
Signified the Continuation of the[i]r intention of marrage: and friends finding
Nothing to hender: their answer was they might Proceed in marrage Betwix[t]
this and the Next monthly meeting observing Good orders :
Col[l]ected this meeting $=13^s=8^d=$: taken out of the Stock: $=17^s=6^d=$

At our monthly meeting of Women friends held in **Dartmouth** yᵉ 18ᵗʰ of
the 1ᵗʰ mo 1745: **Phebe Tucker** and **Elizabeth Smith** are Chose to talke with
David Shermans Daughter: **Phebe Tucker** and **Susannah Gifford** are to attend
the Qurtely meeting Next insuing: **Ruth Tucker** and **Apphia mott** are
to Draw an Epistle to the Sam[e]: Collected =4ˢ=7ᵈ=

At our monthly meeting of women friends held in **Dartmouth** yᵉ 15ᵗʰ of yᵉ 2ᵐᵒ
1745: No Business Presents from the Qurtely meeting: Collected =3ˢ=3ᵈ ==

At our monthly meeting of women firiends [*sic*] held in **Dartmouth** yᵉ 20ᵗʰ of 3ᵗʰ mo
1745: Collected this meeting =8ˢ=1ᵈ=0ᵗ: this meeting maid [made] Choyce of

Visitors **Mehetebell Mosher** and **Sarah Parks** to visit friends families the year
insuing: in **Ponaganset** vil[l]age

At our monthly meeting of women friends held in **dartmouth** yᵉ 24ᵗʰ of
the 4ᵗʰ mo: 1745 where **Beriah Godard** [Goddard] and **Susannah Sison** [Sisson] both Appeard at

Beriah this meeting and signified their in tention of marr[i]age they ware [were]
Goddard desired to wait for their Answer until the Next monthly meeting
propos **Phebe Tucker** and **Experents Smith** are to make inquire Concerning
the yong woman Clearness and make their Return to the next monthly meeting

Epistle Our meeting Recevid an Epistle from **Newport** yearly meeting which
Recᵈ Was Read and well accepted; Collected this meeting – – 10ˢ-2ᵈ: Audr[e]y Smith and
Sarah Parke are Chose to attend the insuing Qu[a]rte[r]ly meeting; **Ruth Tucker**
and **Apphia Mott** are to Draw an Epistle to the Quartely meeting ~ ~ ~ ~

At our monthly meeting of women friends held in **Dartmouth** yᵉ 15ᵗʰ of yᵉ 5ᵗʰ mo 1745
Nothing of Business presented from the Quartely meeting; taken out of the Stock
12 Shil[l]ings for the youce [use] of friends; **Beriah Godard** [Goddard] and **Susannah**
  Sisson Boath

Beriah Appear[e]d at this meeting and Signified the Continuation of their intention of mar[ri]ag[e]
Goddard and friends finding Nothing that hendred: their answer was that they might
answer Proceed Betwix[t] this and the Next monthly meeting observing Good orders
Collected for the youce of friends =6ˢ=0ᵈ

At our monthly meeting of women friends held in **Dartmouth** yᵉ 19ᵗʰ of 6ᵗʰ mo
Philip 1745: **Philip Allen** and **Susannah Allen** Boath appeard at this meeting
Allen and Signified ~~Sign~~ their intention of marrage: they wear Desired to wait for
proposal their answer until the Next monthly meeting: **Phebe Tucker** and **Rebeck[ah]**
Russel [Russell] are appointed to make in Quire Concerning the yo[u]ng woman Clearness
and Conversation and make their Return to the Next monthly meeting
Collected this meeting – – 9ˢ–0ᵈ

Sarah this meeting Recevid **Sarah Parke** Certificate on her Return Back to
Parke her native Land which Read was well Accepted; this meeting maid Choice
Certifi of **Mary Gifford** and **Hannah mosher** to visit friends families in **A**
Visitors **Cokset** this year insuing

At our monthly meeting of women friends held in **Dartmouth:** yᵉ 16ᵗʰ of

Philip
Allen
answer

the 7th mo 1745: **Philip Allen** and **Susannah allen** Boath appeared att
this meeting and Signified the Continuation of their intention of marrage
and their Being Nothing found that hendred their answer was that they
might proceed in marrage Betwix this and the Next monthly meeting
observing Good orders; Collected this meeting – -3s–10d **Peace wood** and **Elizabeth**
Gidley are Appointed to attend the Qurtely meeting next insuing
Ruth Tucker and **Apphia Mott** are to write the Quartely meeting ~

Othniel
Tripp &
Lamuel
Sisson
proposal

At our monthly meeting of Women friends held in **Dartmouth** ye 21th of the
8th month 1745: where **othinial tripp** and **Abiga[i]l Ginkins** also **Lemuel Sison [Sisson]**
and **Deborah Wing** all appeared at this meeting and Signified their intention
of marrag: they were Desired to wait for their answer until the Next
monthly meeting: **Phebe Tucker** and **Elizabeth Barker** are Chose to make ~
inquire Concerning the yong womans Clearness and Conversation: and make
Return to the Next monthly meeting: no Business Presented from the Quartely
meeting No Collection this meeting: **Audrey Smith Mary Tucker** and **Apphia**
mott are to Balance the Accompts
the 16 day of ye 9 mo[n]th accounts Ballanced }
and hear [here] Remains in the Stock –£2=15s–0d }

Othniel
Tripp &
Lamuel
Sisson
answer

At our monthly meeting of women friends held in **Dartmouth** ye 18th of ye 9th mo 1745
Where **othinial tripp** and **Abig[a]il Ginkins** also **Lemuel Sisson** and **Deborah wing** all
Appeared at this meeting and Signified the Continuation of their intention of marr[i]age
and friends finding Nothing to hender their answer was they might Proceed in marrage
Betwix this and the Next monthly meeting observeing Good orders
Collected at this meeting for the youce of friends =11s=0d **Mary Russel[l]** and **Sarah Taber**
are Chose to visit friends families in **Cuishnit** vilige this year insuing:

John
Howland
proposal

At our monthly meeting of women friends held in **Dartmouth** ye 16th of ye 10th mo 1745
John Howland and **Deborah Shephard [Shepherd]** Boath appeared at this meeting and signified
their intention of marrag they were desired to wait for their answer until
the Next monthly meeting: **Elizabeth Barker** and **Deborah Slocom [Slocum]** are appointed
to make inquirey Concerning the yong woman Clearness and Conversation and
make their Return to the Next monthly meeting: **Peace Wood** and **Deborah**
Brown are appointed to attend the insuing Quarterly meeting: **Apphia Mott**
is to Draw an Epistle to same No Collection this meeting

John
Howland
answer

Wm Gifford
& Natl
Mosher
proposal

At our monthly meeting of women friends held in **Dartmouth** ye 20th of ye 11mo
1745: **John Howland** and **Deborah Shephard [Shepherd]** Boath appeared at this meeting and
Signified the Continuation of their intention of marrage and friends finding
Nothing that hendred their answer was they might Proceed in marrage betwix this
and the next monthly meeting observing Good orders: **William Gifford** and **Patience**
Russel [Russell]; also **Nathaniel Mosher** and **Ruth Mott** appeared at this meeting and
Signified their intention of marrage: **Phebe Tucker** and **Rebeckah Russel[l]** are appointed
to make inquiry Concerning the yong women Clearness and Conversation and make
their Return to the next monthly meeting: no Business Presented from the

Quartely meeting Collected this meeting =11ˢ=5ᵈ taken out of the Stock 2ᶜ towards towards keeping the meeting house: we received an Epistle from **London** which was Read and Kindly Accepted

---

*Wᵐ Gifford
Natˡ Mo-
sher answer*

*John
Wanton
proposal*

At our monthly meeting of women friends held in **Dartmouth** yᵉ 17ᵗʰ of yᵉ 12ᵗʰ mo 1745\⁶: **William Gifford** and **Patience Russel[l]** also **Nathaniel mosher** and **Ruth Mott** all appeared at this meeting and Signified the Continuation of their intention of marrage and friends finding nothing that hendred: their answer was they might Proced in marrage: Betwix this and the Next monthly meeting according to the Good orders Established among friends: **John Wanton** and **Meraby Slocom [Slocum]**: Laid their intention of marrage Befor this meeting: they were desired to wait for their answer until the Next monthly meeting **Rebeckah Barker** and **Elizabeth Barker** are appointed to ~~see~~ make inqurey Concerning our friends Clearness and Conversation and make Return to the Next monthly meeting Collected this meeting =10ˢ=10ᵈ= taken out of the Stock =ᶜ1-8ˢ=0ᵈ: **Peace Wood** and **Abigil Cornal [Cornell]** are Chose to talke with **John Latons [Lawton]** too Daughters for their out Gouings:

---

*Josiah
Akin
proposal*

At our monthly meeting of Women friends held in **Dartmouth** yᵉ 17ᵗʰ of yᵉ 1ᵗʰ mo: 1746- **Phebe Tucker** and **mary wilcox** are appointed to attend the – – Quarte[r]ly meeting Next insuing= **Apphia Mott** is to draw an Epistle to the same this meeting is a iourned [adjourned] until the first Six[th] day in next month: No Collection this meeting: the two friends have Brought in their accounts Concerning **John Latons [Lawton]** two Daughters; At the a iournment of our monthly meeting **Josiah Akins** and **Judeth Hudleston [Huttleston]**: Laid their intention of marr[i]age: they were Desired to Wait for their answer until the Next monthly meeting: **Phebe Tucker** – and **Rhoda Wing** are appointed to make inquire Concerning the yo[u]ng woman Clearness and ~~Concerning~~ Conversation and make their Return to the Next monthly meeting

---

*John
Wanton
and
Josiah
Akin
answer*

*Isaac
Gifford
proposal*

At our monthly meeting of women friends held in **Dartmouth** yᵉ 21ᵗʰ of 2ᵗʰ mo 1746: **John Wonton [Wanton]** and **meribah Slocom [Slocum]** and **Josiah Aken [Akin]** and **Judeth Hudlestone [Huttleston]**: all appeared at this meeting and signified the Continuation of their intention of marrage: and their Being Nothing found to hender them – – their answer was they might Proceed in marrag Betwix this and the Next – – monthly meeting: observing Good orders: **Isaac Gifford** and **mary Cornal [Cornell]** Laid their intention of marrage Before this meeting they were Desired to wait for their answer until the next monthly meeting: **Phebe Tucker** and **Rebeckah ––– Russel [Russell]** are appointed to make inquire Concerning the yong woman Clearness and Conversation and make their Return to the Next monthly meeting: ~ Collected this meeting: =5ˢ=4ᵈ

---

*Isaac
Gifford
answer*

At our monthly meeting of women friends held in **Dartmouth** yᵉ 19ᵗʰ of yᵉ 3ᵗʰ mo 1746 **Isaac Gifford** and **mary Cornal [Cornell]** Boath appeared at this meeting and Signified their Continuation of their intention of marrage: and after dew [due] Consideration made[?]

Concerning the yong woman Clearness: and Nothing appearing to hender their
answer was they might Proceed in marrage Betwix this and the Next month
ly meeting: observing Good orders: No Collection this meeting

---

Ann
Gifford
Certificate
rec^d

At our monthly meeting of women friends held in **Dartmouth** y^e 23th of y^e 4th mont[h]
1746: we Receivd **Ann Gifford**s Certif[i]cate and well accepted it: **Pernalipy [Penelope] Allen** and
Keziah Wood are appointed to atend the Quartely meeting; Collected this meeting
5^s=8^d= **Apphia Mott** is appointed to Draw an Epistle to the insuing
Quartely meeting:

At our monthly meeting of women friends held in **Dartmouth** y^e 21th of y^e 5th mo 1746
this meeting Receved an Epistle from friends at **Rhoad Island** which we well
accepted: No Business Presented from the Quartely meeting: Collected this meeting: 8^s/7^d

---

Nat
Howland
and
Elish[a]
Coggeshall
proposal

Visitor

At our monthly meeting of women friends held in **Dartmouth** ye 17th of ye 6th mo 1746 ~
Nathaniel Howland and **Joanna Howland** also **Elisha Coxsil [Coggeshall]** and **Elizabeth
Russel [Russell]**
Laid their intention of marrage: they were desired to wait for their answer until
the Next monthly meeting: **Phebe Tucker** and **Joanna Russel**[l] are appointed to make
inquirey Concerning the yong woman Clearness and Conversation and make their
Return to the Next monthly meeting: this meeting appoints **Abig[a]il Tripp** visiter
this year at **acoxset**: no Collection this meeting

---

answer
[to?] friends
proposals

[John?] Law
ton
proposal

At our monthly meeting of woman friends held in **Dartmouth** ye 15th of ye 7th mo 1746
the[?] friends that Laid their intention of marr[i]^age Last monthly meeting all ap[p]eared at this
meeting: and Signified the Continuation of their intention of marrage and after inquirey
Being maid and they appeared: Clear from all ot^hers: their answer was they might
Proceed in marrage Betwix[t] this and the Next monthly meeting observing Good orders
John Laton [Lawton] and **Rebeckah allen** Laid their intention of mar[ri]age Before this
meeting they
were desired to wait for their answer until the Next monthly meeting: **marah Russel**[l]
and **Rebeckah Barker** are to make inquirey Concerning the yong woman Clearness and
Conversation and make their Return to the Next monthly meeting: **Phebe Tucker**
and **Apphia Mott** are appointed to attend the Qu^arte[r]ly meeting and **Apphia mott** is Chose to
Draw an Epistle to the Same: **Hannah mosher** and **Ab[i]gial Tripp** are appointed to talke with
Lyda macombar upon her Request: No Collection this meeting: **Phebe Tucker** and **Elizabeth
Barker** are appointed to make inquirey Concerning **meribah Slocom**s Conversation when
She Resided among us: and also her others [*sic*] affa[i]rs

John
Lawton
proposal
[sic]

At our monthly meeting of women friends held in **Dartmouth** ye 20th of ye 8th mo 1746 ~
John Laton [Lawton] and **Rebekah Allen** Boath appeard at this meeting and Signified the
Continuation
of their intention of marrage: and after inquire Being maid and She appearing Clear from
all others
their answer was they might Proceed in marrage Betwean this and the Next monthly
observing Good orders: no Business Presented from the Quartely meeting: **Audrah Smith**
Mary Tucker and **Apphia mott** are appointed to Balance the account of this meeting – –

No Collection made this meeting

Wm Barker proposal

At our monthly meetᵢng of women friends held in Dartmouth yᵉ 17th of yᵉ 9th mo 1746 ~ **William Barker** and **Hannah wood** Boath appeared at this meeting and Signified their in tention of marriage: they were Desired to wait until the Next monthly meeting: for their answer: **Rebeckah Russel[l]** and **mary Potter** are appointed to make inquirey Concerning the yong woman Clearness and Conversation and make their Return to the Next monthly meeting: Collected this meeting =8ˢ=10ᵈ ~ the 9 day of yᵉ 10th mo: 1746 all Accounts Balanced and here Remains in the Stock: £2=8ˢ=0[?]ᵈ

Wm Barker answer

Jonathan Sisson proposal

At our monthly meeting of women friends held in **Dartmouth** yᵉ 15th of yᵉ 10th mo: 1746 **william Barker** and **Hannah wood** appeared at this meeting and Signified the ~ Continuation of their intention of marr[ia]ge and they appearing Clear from all ot[h]ers their answer was they might Proceed in marrage Betwean this and the Next monthly meeting observing Good orders: **Jonathan Sisˢon** and **Hannah Howland**: Laid their intention of marriage: Before this meeting they were Desired to wait for their answer until the Next monthly meeting: **Phebe Tucker** and **Rebeckah Barker** are appointed to make inquirey Concerning the yong woman Clearness and Conversation and make their Return to the Next monthly meeting: **mary Lapham** and **mary Potter** are appointed to attend the Quartely meeting: **Apphia Mott** is [to draw?] the Epistle to the Qurtely meeting Taken out of the Stock £2=0ˢ=0 towards keeping the meeting house: no Collection this meeting

Jonathan Sisson answer

At our monthly meeting of Women friends held in **Dartmouth** yᵉ 19th of yᵉ 11th mo 1746~ **Jonathan Sisson** and **Hannah Howland**: appeared at this meeting and Signified the Continuation of their intention of marrage: and they appearing Clear from all others their answer was they might Proceed in marrage Betwix this and the Next monthly meeting: observing Good orders: no Business Presented from the Quartely meeting ~~~ No Collection this meeting

Joshua Lapham and Richard Gifford proposals

At our monthly meeting of women friends held in **Dartmouth** yᵉ 16th of yᵉ 12th mo 1746: **Joshua Lapham** and **Hannah Shirman [Sherman] Richard Gifford** and **Elizabeth Cornal [Cornell]** all Signified their intention of marr[i]ag[e]: they were Desired to for their answer until the Next monthly meeting: **Rebeckah Barker** and **Dorkis [Dorcas] Shephard** are appointed to make inquirey Concerning the yo[u]ng womans Clearness and Conversation and make their Return to the Next monthly meeting no Collection this meeting

aforesd friends answer

Appia Mott Clerk

At our monthly meeting of women friends held in **Dartmouth** yᵉ 16th of 1th mo 1747 the friends that Laid their intention Last monthly meeting all appear[e]d at this meeting and Signified the Continuation of their intention of marrag: and they appearing Clear from all others their answer was they might Proceed in marrage Betwix[t] this and the Next monthly meeting observing Good orders: Collected this meeting =12ˢ=4ᵈ – – **Apphia Mott** is Chose Clarke [Clerk] of the womens meeting: **Grizel Shirman [Sherman]** and **Elizabeth Gidley** are appointed to attend the Quarte[r]ly meeting: and **Apphia Mott** is to Draw an

Meribah Wanton
Mary Gifford
Certificat[e]

Epistle to the Same: this meeting is a iorned [adjourned] until the first 6 day in Next month **meribah wanton** and **mary Gifford** each of them Desired a Certificate on their Removel which our meeting Granted

---

James
Tucker
Job Antho[n]y
John Wa[l]
=ker prop
posal

At our monthly meeting of women friends held in **Dartmouth** ye 20th of ye 2 mo 1747: where appeard **Jeames [James] Tucker** and **Ruth Tucker Job antoney [Anthony]** and **Sarah Wing John Walker** and **margrit mosher** who Signified their intention of marrage: they were desired to wait for their answer until the Next monthly meeting: **Rebeckah Barker** and **Elizabeth Barker** and **Sarah Gifford** are appointed to make inquirey Concerning the yong womens Clearness and Conversation and make their Returns to the Next monthly meeting: Collected this meeting: =6s=0d

---

aforesd
friends
answer

At our monthly meeting of Women friends held in **Dartmouth** ye 18th of ye 3th mo where all the friends that Laid there intention of marrage Last monthly meeting appeared at this: and Signified the Continuation of their intention of marrage and they appearing Clear from all others: their answer was they might Proceed in marrage Betwean this and the Next monthly meeting observing Good orders --- No Collection this meeting:

At our monthly meeting of women friends in **Dartmouth** ye 15th of ye 4th mo 1747 appointed to attend the Qurtely meeting: **Phebe Tucker apphia mott** and **apphia mott** is to draw an Epistle to the Same: no Collection this meeting: this meeting is a iorned until the 22 of ye 5 mo[n]th **Wait allen**s Certificate was Re[a]d in this meeting and well accepted: taken out of the Stock: £2=0s=0d=

At our monthly meeting of women friends held in **Dartmouth** ye 20th of ye 5th mo 1747 this meeting Received an Epistle from the yearly meeting: which was Re[a]d and Kindly accepted Collected this meeting for the youce [use] of friend =9s=8d

---

Han[n]ah
Sisson

At our monthly meeting of women friends held in **Dartmouth** ye 17th of ye 6th mo 1747 this meeting appointed **mary Tucker** and **apphia mott** to talke with **hannah Sisson** for a miss step which She hath taken: no Collection this meeting

---

Francis
Barker
David
Gifford
proposal

At our monthly meeting of Women friends held in **Dartmouth** ye 21th of the 7 mo[n]th 1747: **Frances Barker** and **Sarah Howland**: **David Gifford** and **Deborah hart** appeared at this meeting and Signified their intention of marraig: they were desired to Wait for their answer until the Next monthly meeting: **Apphia mott** and **abig[a]il wing** are appointed to make inquirey Concerning the yong woman Clearness and Conversation and make their Return to the Next monthly meeting: Collected this meeting =11s=8d ~ **Grizel Sherman** and **Hannah mosher** are appointed to attend the Quarterly meeting and **Apphia mott** is to draw an Epistle to the Same

---

above sd
friends
Answer

At our monthly meetin of women friends held in **Dartmouth** ye 19th of ye 8th mo 1747: the friends that Laid their intention of marraig Last monthly meeting all appeared at this and Signified the Continuatio[n] of th[e]ir intention of marrag and they appearing Clear from all others their answer [was?] they might proceed in marr[i]age Betwix this and the Next monthly meeting observing Good orders: No Collection this meeting

At our monthly meeting of women friends held in **Dartmouth** yᵉ 16ᵗʰ of yᵉ 9ᵗʰ mo 1747
audrey Smith mary Tucker Apphia Mott are to Balance the accounts of this

Hulda meeting; **Hulda Tripp** is Denied at this meeting for her Disorderly Pr[o]ceeding
Tripp
disownᵈ No Collection this meeting; ~ the 19ᵗʰ of yᵉ 10ᵗʰ mo 1747
all accounts Balanced and here Remains in the Stock =ᶠo=7ˢ=8ᵈ

At our monthly meeting of women friends held in **Dartmouth** yᵉ 21ᵗʰ of yᵉ 10ᵗʰ mo
Benjamin 1747; **Benjamin Howland** and **Ann Brigs [Briggs]** Boath appeared at this meeting and
Howland
proposal Signified their intention of marrage they were desired wait for their answer until
the Next monthly meeting: **Elizabeth Barker** and **Experents [Experience] Smith**: are
   appointed to
make inquirey Concerning the yong womans Clearness and Conversation and make
their Return to the next monthly meeting: appointed to attend the Quartely
Meeting: **mary Lapham** and **Apphia mott** and **apphia mott** is to draw an Epistle to
the Same: Collected at this meeting = 10ˢ–0ᵈ

At our monthly meeting of women friends held in **Dartmouth** yᵉ 17ᵗʰ of yᵉ 11ᵗʰ mo
Jos:Brownel 1747: Appeared **Joseph Brounal [Brownell]** and **Hannah Boudash [Bowdish]**: **Paul
Paul Russel **Russel [Russell]** and **Elizabetʰ**
Wᵐ Sisson
proposal **Boudash [Bowdish]**: **William Sisson** and **Lyda Potter**: all Laid their intention of marriage
Before this meeting: they were Desired to wait for their answer until the Next=
monthly meeting: **Exsperents Smith** and **Hannah Tuckah [Tucker]** are appointed to make
inquirey Concerning the yong womens Clearness and Conversation and make Return
Ben Howlan[d] to the next monthly meeting: **Benjamin Howland** and **Ann Brigs [Briggs]** Received ~~there~~
answer their answer at this meeting: no Collection this meeting

afore sᵈ At our monthly meeting of women friends held in **Dartmouth** yᵉ 21ᵗʰ of 12ᵗʰ mo
friends 1747: the friends that Laid their intention Last monthly meeting all appeard
answer at this meeting and Signified the Continuation of their intention of marrage – –
and they appearing Clear from all others: their answer was they might pʳoceed
in marrag Betwean this and the next monthly meeting: observing Good orders– –
Jacob **Jacob mott** and **anne west** Laid their intention of marrage Before this meeting
Mott
proposal they were Desired to wait for their answer until the next monthly meeting
mary Russel [Russell] and **Hephzibah Hissey [Hussey]** are appointed to make inquirey
   Concerning
the yong woman Clearness and Conversation and make their Return to the
Next monthly meeting: Collected this meeting––––15ˢ=6ᵈ

1 month At our monthly meeting of women friends held in **Dartmouth** yᵉ 21ᵗʰ of yᵉ 1ˢᵗ Mo
Jacob Mott 1748: **Jacob mott** and **Anna west** appear[e]d at this meeting and Signified the
answer Continuation of their intention of marr[i]age: and they appeard Clear
from all others: their answer was they might Proceed in marrag Betwix[t]
this and the Next monthly meeting observing Good orders:
Sam How= **Samuel Howland** and **Ruth Devile [Davol]**: **Beⁿjamin allen** and **Elifal Slocom [Slocum]**
=land
Ben Allen **Jonathan Smith** and **Silviah [Sylvia] Howland**: all Laid their intentions of marrag
Jonathan
Smith Before this meeting: they were Desired to wait for their answer until
proposal the next monthly meeting: **Hannah Tucker** and **Patience Russel [Russell]** are

appointed to make inquirey Concerning the yo[u]ng womens Clearness and
Conve[r]sation and make their Returns to the Next monthly meeting
Phebe Tucker and **Patience Russel[l]** are appointed to attend the Quarte[r]ly meeting
Apphia mott is to Draw an Epistle to the Same: Collected this meeting £0=19s=4d

answer to friends proposal

At our monthly meeting of women friends held in **Dartmouth** ye 18th of the
2th mo 1748: where all the friends that Laid their intention Last monthly
meeting: appeared at this meeting: and Signified the Continuation of
their intention of marraig: and they appearing [clear?] from all others: their
answer was they might Proceed in marraig Betwix this and the next
monthly meeting observing Good orders: Collected at this meeting= 7s=2d

At our monthly meeting of women friends held in **Dartmouth** ye 16th of
the 3th mo 1748: No Collection this meeting

At our monthly meeting of women friends held in **Dartmouth** ye 20th of
ye 4th mo 1748: **Apphia mott** and **Rebeckah Barker**: are appointed to
attend the Quarterly meeting: and **apphia mott** is to draw an Epistle
to the Same: no Collection this meeting

At our monthly meeting of women friends held in **Dartmouth** ye 18th of ye 5th mo
1748: where we Receivid an Epistle from the yearly meeting at ~~Rho~~ **Rhod
island** which was re[a]d and well accepted: Collected at this meeting =9s=6d

Giles & Peleg Slocom proposal

At our monthly meeting of women friends held in **Dartmouth**
ye 15th of ye 6th mo 1748: appeared **Giles Slocom [Slocum]** and **Silvia Russel [Russell]**: **Peleg
Slocom [Slocum]** and **Elizabeth Brown** and Laid their intention of marrag: **Hannah
Tucker** and **Patience Russel[l]** are appointed to make inquirey Concerning
the yong womans Clearness and Conversation and make their Returns to the
Next monthly meeting: no Collection this meeting: this meeting makes
Choice of **Hannah mosher** and **Abig[a]il Tripp** to visit friends families
at **acokset** this year

Answer to friends proposals

At our monthly meeting of women friends held in **Dartmouth** ye 19th of ye 7 mo
1748: the friends that Laid their intention of marrage Last monthly meeting
all Came for their answer: and they appearing Clear from all others their
answer was they might Proceed in marraig Betwix this and the Next
monthly meeting observing Good orders: **Robard Barker** and **Johanna Russel [Russell]**
Walter Easton and **meriba Rickson [Ricketson]**: laid their intention of marraig Before this
meeting they were to wait for their answer until the Next monthly meeting

Clearnes

Phebe Tucker and **Rebeckah Russel** are to make inquirey Concerning the yong woman[n]s
and make their Returns to the Next monthly meeting – –

Wm How= =land & Wm Bennit proposal

William Howland and **Rebeckah Peckham**: **William Bennet** and **Hannah Taber**
Laid their intention of marraig: Before this meeting; they were as above ord to wait for
their answer until the Next monthly meeting: **Mary Russel [Russell]** and **Phebe Tucker**
are appointed to make inquirey Concerning the yong womens Clearness and Conversation
and their Returns to the Next monthly meeting: **Hannah Mosher** and **Patient Russel[l]**
are appointed to attend the Quartely meeting: this meeting appoints **Susannah Gifford**

and **Deb°rah Slocom** [**Slocum**]: to talke with **Mehetabell Allen** for her out Going: no
   Collection
this meeting

*answer
to friends
proposals*

At our monthly meeting of Women friend held in **Dartmouth** yᵉ 17ᵗʰ of yᵉ 8ᵗʰ mo 1748
all the friend that Laid their intention of marraig Before the Last monthly meeting
Came for their answer and they appearing Clear from all others their answer was
that they might Proceed in marraig Betwean this and the Next monthly meeting
observing Good orders: Collected at this meeting= 9ˢ=8ᵈ

At our monthly meeting of women friends held in **Dartmouth** yᵉ 21ᵗʰ of yᵉ 9ᵗʰ mo 1748~
audrah Smith marah Tucker and **Apphia mott** are appointed to Ballance the
accounts of this meeting: no Collection this meeting
the 18ᵗʰ day of yᵉ 9 mo 1748: all accounts Ballanced and here Remains in the Stock= ₤3=18ˢ=10ᵈ

At our monthly meeting of women friends held in **Dartmouth** yᵉ 19ᵗʰ of 10ᵗʰ mo
1748: Appointed to attend the Quartely meeting: **Marah Lapham** and
Apphia Mott: apphia mott is to Draw an Epistle to the Same: Collected this
meeting: 7 Shil[l]ings: Disbusted ₤3–0ˢ–0ᵈ

At our monthly meeting of women friends held in **Dartmouth** yᵉ 16ᵗʰ of 11ᵗʰ mo 1748
No Collection this meeting

At our monthly meeting of women friends held in **Dartmouth** yᵉ 20ᵗʰ of yᵉ 12 m°
1748: where **Increas[e] Allen** and **Hannah Springner** Laid their intention of
marraig: Before this meeting: they are Desired to Wait for their answer
until the Next monthly meeting: **Rebeckah Barker** and **Hannah Tucker**
are appointed to make inquirey Concerning the yong womans Clearness and Conveʳˢᵃᵗⁱᵒⁿ
and make their Returns to the Next monthly meeting: no Collection this
meeting

At our monthly meeting of women friends held in **Dartmouth** yᵉ 20ᵗʰ of yᵉ 1ᵗʰ mo 1749
the friends that Laid their intention of marraig Before the Last monthly meeting
Came for their answer: and they appearing Clear from all others their answer
was that they might Proceed in marraig Betwix this and the Next monthly
meeting: observing Good orders: **Be[n]jamin Shaw** and **Elizabeth Potter** Laid their
intention of marraig: Before this meeting they Were Desired to wait for
their answer unt[i]l the Next monthly meeting: **Rebeckah Russel[l]** and
Abig[a]il Cornail [**Cornell**] are appointed to make inquirey Concerning the yong woman
Clearness and Conversation and make their Returns to the Next monthly
meeting: Collected at this meeting= 15ˢ=6ᵈ

At our monthly meeting of Women friends held in **Dartmouth** yᵉ 17ᵗʰ of yᵉ 2ᵗʰ mo 1749
the friends that Laid their intention of marraig Before the Last monthly meeting
Boath appeard at this meeting for their answer and they appearing Clear from
all others: their answer was that they might Proceed in marraig Betwean this
and the Next monthly meeting: observing Good orders Established among friends
No Collection this meeting

At our monthly meeting of Women friends held in **Dartmouth** yᵉ 15ᵗʰ of yᵉ 3ᵗʰ mo
1749: No Collection this meeting

At our monthly meeting of Women friends held in **Dartmouth** yᵉ 19ᵗʰ of yᵉ 4ᵗʰ mo: 1749
We Receved an Epistle from the yearly meeting Which was Red and well accepted
Appointed to attend the Quartely meeting **Apphia Mott** and **Keziah Wood** and
to write an Epistle to the same: No Collection this meeting

At our monthly meeting of Women friends held in **Dartmouth** yᵉ 17ᵗʰ of yᵉ 5ᵗʰ mo 1749
Collected at this meeting =5ˢ=6ᵈ= **Mehetabell Mosher** and **Mary Tucker** are
appointed to talke with **Lusannah Russel [Russell]** for her Disorderly walkeing

---

At our monthly meeting of Women friends held in **Dartmouth** yᵉ 21ᵗʰ of yᵉ 6ᵗʰ mo 1749
this meeting appoints **Marah Potter** and **Abigil Tripp** to make inquirey into
the Conversation of **Alce Tripp**: Collected at this meeting —— 15ˢ-0ᵈ

At our monthly meetin of Women friends held in **Dartmouth** yᵉ 18ᵗʰ of yᵉ 7ᵐᵒ
1749: **Charles Slocom [Slocum]** and **Sarah Allen Philip Devile [Davol]** and **Elizabeth Sherman**
all Laid their intention of marraig: Before this meeting they were desired to
Wait for there answer until the Next monthly meeting: **Penalipay Allen** ~
and **Deborah Slocom** are appointed to make inquirey Concerning the yong womens
Clearness and Conversation and make their Returns to the Next monthly meeting
Appointed to attend the insuing Quartely meeting: **Marah Potter** and
Abigil Tripp this meeting appoints **Apphia Mott** to write a Certificate
for **Alce Tripp** on her Removeal and Bring to the Next monthly meeting
No Collection this meeting.

At our monthly meeting of Women friends held in **Dartmouth** yᵉ 16ᵗʰ of yᵉ 8ᵗʰ mo 1749
the friends that Laid their intention of marraig Last monthly meeting all
Came for their answer and they appearing Clear from all others· their answer
was they maght Proceed in marrag Betwix this and the Next monthly meeting
observing Good orders: disbusted =2ˢ=6ᵈ: Collected at this meeting =s9=6ᵈ

At our monthly meeting of Women friends held in **Dartmouth** yᵉ 20ᵗʰ of yᵉ 9ᵗʰ mo
1749. where **Francis Allen** and **Marah Ridenton [Mary Wrightington]** Boath appeared and
Signified their intention of marraig Before this meeting they Were
Desired to wait for their answer until the Next monthly meeting —
Elizabeth Barker and **Apphia mott** are appointed to make inquirey
Concerning the yong Womans Clearness and Conversation and make their
Returns to the next monthly meeting. **Audra Smith Apphia Mott** and
Mary Tucker are to Ballance the accounts of this meeting. taken out of
the Stock 2£ no Collection this meeting

The 14 of the 10ᵗʰ month 1749 all accounts Ballanced and here Remains
in the Stock £1-13ˢ-10ᵈ

At our monthly meeting of Women friend held in **Dartmouth** yᵉ 18 of yᵉ 10 mo 1749
Frances Allen and **Mary Ridenton [Wrightington]** appeared and signified the Continuation
    of their
intention of marraig and they appearing Clear from all others. their answer Was they might

Proceed in marraig. Betwix this and the Next monthly meeting observeing Good orders
Appointed to attend the Quartely **Mary Lapham** and **Phebe Tucker: Apphia Mott** is
Appoind to Daraw an Epistle to the Same, no Collection this meeting

At our monthly meeting of Women friends held in **Dartmouth** yᵉ 15ᵗʰ of yᵉ 11ᵗʰ mo 1749
Where **Joshua Cornail [Cornell]** and **Lusannah Gifford** Boath appeard and Signified their
    intention
of marraig. they Were Desird to wait for their answer until the next monthly
meeting **Keziah Wood** and **Susannah Cornal [Cornell]** are appointed to make inquirey
    Concerning
the yong womans Clearness and Conversation and make their Returns to the Next monthly
meeting. No Collection this meeting

At our monthly meeting of Women friends held in **Dartmouth** yᵉ 19ᵗʰ of yᵉ 12ᵗʰ mo 1749~
where **Joshua Cornail [Cornell]** and **Lusannah Gifford** Came for their answer and they
    appearing
Clear from all others their answer was they might proceed in marraig Betwean this
and the next monthly meeting observing Good orders. **Job Gifford** and **Martha Wilcox**
Isaac Killey [Kelley]: and **Judith Sherman** Laid their intention of marraig Before this meeting
they were desired to wait for their answer until the next monthly meeting. **Rebeckah**
Barker and **Patience Russel [Russell]** are appointed to make inquirey Concerning the
    yong women's ———
Clearness and Conversation and make their Returns to the Next monthly meeting
No Collection this meeting. **Mary Lapham** and **Patience Russel [Russell]** are appointed
    to talke with
Abigail Slocom [Slocum] and **Elizabeth Smith** for their out Goings

At our monthly meeting of Women friends held in **Dartmouth** yᵉ 19ᵗʰ of yᵉ 1ᵗʰ mo 1750 ~
the friends that Laid their intention of marraig the last monthly meeting
all appeard at this and Signified the Continuation of their intention of marrag
and they appearing Clear from all others, their answer was they might Proceed
in marraig. Betwix this and the Next monthly meeting observing Good orders
Barnabass Howland and **Pernaliphe Allen** Laid their intention of marraig
Before this meeting. they were desired to wait for their answe until the Next
monthly meeting: **Rebeckah Russel [Russell]** and **Ruth Sherman** are appointed to make
inquirey into our friends Clearness and make their Returns to the next monthly
meeting. **Apphia Mott** is appointed to write to the Quarterly. no Collection

At our monthly meeting of Women friends held in **Dartmouth** yᵉ 16 of yᵉ 2 mo 175⁰
The friends that Laid ~~thier~~ their intention of marraig Before the Last monthly
meeting all appeard at this meeting. and signified the Continuation of their
intention of marraig and they appearing Clear from all others their answer
was they might Proceed in marraig. Betwix this and the Next monthly meeting
observing Good orders Collected at this meeting =9ˢ-0ᵈ- this meeting appoints
Hannah mosher and **Abigail Tripp** to talke with **Rebeckah Kerby [Kirby]** for her
Disorderly Proceeding

At our monthly meeting of Women friends held in **Dartmouth** y^e 21 of y^e 3 mo 1750
Collected =5^s-6^d= taken out of the Stock for the youce of friends £1-10^s-0^d

At our monthly meeting of Women Friends held in **Dartmouth** y^e 18th of
the 4th m^o 1750 **Apphia mott** and **Keziah Wood** are appointed to attend the
Quarterly meeting. **Apphia Mott** is to Draw an Epistle to the same
Collected at this meeting – – – – – – – – – – – – – – – £0-6^s-0^d

At our monthly meeting of Women friends held in **Dartmouth** ye 16 of
the 5 m^o 1750. We Received the Epistle from **Newport** yearly meeting
We kindly accepted: our worthy friends **Ann Sohalfield [Scholfield]** and **Lydia mendanhal**
have visited our meeting which Visit we kindly accepted and our meeting
hath Good unity with their Certificates[19] Collected at this meeting =18^s=8^d

At our monthly meeting of Women friends held in **Dartmouth** ^{by an aiournment} y^e 29 of y^e 6 m^o 1750
Samuel Howland and **Elizabeth Butler** Boath appeared and signified their intention
of marraig. they were Desired to wait for their answer until the next monthly
Meeting: **Mary Russel [Russell]** and **Apphia Mott** are appointed to make inquirey Concerning
the yong womans Clearness and Conversation and make their Returns to the next
monthly meeting

At our monthly meeting of Women friend held in **Dartmouth** ye 17 of ye 7 m^o 1750
Samuel Howland and **Elizabeth Butler** Boath appeared and Signified the Continuation
of their intention of marraig. and they appearing Clear from all others their
answer was they might Proceed in marraig Betwean this and the Next monthly
meeting observing Good orders. **Philip Antoney [Anthony]** and **Mary Godard [Goddard]**.
    John Wing and
Jemima Shephard John Sisson and **Sibbel Hudelstone [Sybil Huttleston]** all Laid their
    intention
of marraig Before this meeting they were Desired to wait for their answer
until the next monthly meeting, **Rebeckah Russel [Russell]** and **Ma^{r}y Smith** are appointed
to make inquirey Concerning the yong womens Clearness and Conversation and make
their Returns to the next monthly meeting. Appointed to attend the Quartely
meeting. **Phebe Tucker** and **Hannah mosher.** no Collection this meeting

At our monthly meeting of Women friend held in **Dartmouth** ye 15 of ye 8 m^o 1750
all the friends that Laid their intention of marraig the Last monthly meeting
Appeard and Signified the Continuation of their intention of marraig and
they appearing Clear from all others their answer was they might
Proceed in marraig. Betwean this and the next monthly meeting observ[in]g
Good orders. no Collection this meeting

At our monthly meeting of Women friends held in **Dartmouth** ye 19 of ye 9 ^{mo}
1750. **Nicolas [Nicholas] Howland** and **mary Sisson** Laid their intention of marraig
Before this meeting they were desired to wait for their answer until
the next monthly meeting **Exsperients Smith** and **Rebekah Barker** are

19. Ann Scholfield was a minister from Pennsylvania. Lydia Mendenhall was apparently her companion. See Larson, *Daughters of Light*, 330.

appointed to make inquirey Concerning the yong womans Clearness and
Conversation and make their Returns to the next monthly meeting
Audra Smith mary Tucker and **Apphia mott** are appointed to Balance
the accounts of this meeting. no Collection this meeting
Pernelipa [Penelope] Howland and **Susannah Gifford** are to talke with **Ann
Almey [Almy]** for her out Goings.) all accounts Ballanced and here Remains
in the Stock – – – – – – – – – £2-3ˢ-0ᵈ

At our monthly meeting of Woman friends held in **dartmouth** yᵉ 17ᵗʰ of yᵉ 10ᵗʰ mᵒ
1750 **Nicholas Howland** and **mary Sisson** Came for their answer and they
appearing Clear from all others their anser was they might Proceed in marraig
Betwean this and the next monthly meeting observing Good orders. no Collection ~

At our monthly meeting of Women friends held in **Dartmouth** yᵉ 21 of yᵉ 11ᵗʰ mo 1750
James Haden [Haydon] and **Deborah Brown. John Russel [Russell]** and **Catherrine
 [Catherine] Williams** all ~
Laid their intention of marraig Before this meeting. they were desired to wait
for their answer until the next monthly meeting **Exsperents Smith** and
Hephzibah Hussey are appointed to make inquirey Concerning the yong womenes
Clearness and Conversation and make their Returns to the next monthly meeting. Collected
at this meeting –19ˢ-6ᵈ

At our monthly meeting of Women friends held in **Dartmouth** yᵉ 16 of yᵉ 12 mo 1750
James Haden [Haydon] and **Deborah Brown** Came and Signified the Continuation of their
intention of ~~their~~ marraig and they appearid Clear from all others their answer
was they might Proceed in marraig Betwean this and the next monthly meeting
observing Good orders. no Collection this meeting

At our monthly meeting of Women friends held in **Dartmouth** yᵉ 18 of yᵉ 1 mᵒ
1751. appointed to attend the Quartely meeting **Grizel Sherman** and
Apphia Mott. this meeting is a iorned [adjourned] until the first Six day in next
month. this meeting appoints **Keziah Wood** and **Abigial Tripp** to make inquirey
Conversation of **hannah Ginin** and her daughters. Collected at this meeting
s14-5ᵈ

At our monthly meeting of women friends held in **Dartmouth** yᵉ 15 of the 2 mo
1752 [*sic*] **John Russel [Russell]** and **Catherine Williams** Came and Signified the
Continuation of their intention of marraig and they appearing Clear from
all others their answer was they might proceed in marraig Betwean this
and the Next monthly meeting observing Good orders. **Stoks [Stokes] Potter** and
Rebekah Shaw Laid their intention of marraig Before this meeting they were
Desired to wait until the Next monthly meeting **Phebe Tucker** and ~~illegible~~
Hannah Tucker were appointed to make inquirey Concerning the yong woman
Clearness and Conversation and make their Returns to the Next monthly
meeting no Collection this meeting

At our monthly meeting of Women friends held in **Dartmouth** yᵉ 21 of
yᵉ 3 mo 1751. **Job Cornal [Cornell]** and **mary Davis** Laid their intention of marraig

Before this meeting. they were desired to wait for their answer until
the next monthly meeting **Exsperents Smith** and **Ruth Shirman [Sherman]** are
Appointed to make inquirey Concerning the yong womans Clearness and
Conversation and make their Returns to the next monthly meeting
Collected at this meeting -2ˢ-6ᵈ.

At our monthly meeting of Women friend held in **Dartmouth** yᵉ 24 of yᵉ 4 mo
1751 **Job Corlal [Cornell]** and **mary davis** Signified the Continuation of their intention of
marraig and they appearing Clear from all others their anser was they
might Proceed in marraig Betwix this and the next monthly meeting
observing Good orders Collected at this meeting -14ˢ-10ᵈ taken out of the Stock
£6-18ˢ-10ᵈ our worthy friends **Jean Elis [Ellis]** and and [*sic*] **Rebekah Harvi [Rebecca
Harvey]** hve visited our meeting[20]
and their testimonyes were well accepted. **Deborah Slocom [Slocum]** and **Patience
Russel [Russell]** are
appointed to attend the Quarterly meeting **Apphia mott** is to draw an Epistle to the Same

---

At our Monthly Meeting of Women Friends held in **Dartmouth** yᵉ 15 of
the 5 m⁰ 1751 **Thomas Hix [Hicks]** and **Elizabeth Hammon [Hammond]** Laid their intention of marraig
they were desired to wait for their answer until the next monthly meeting
Sarah Taber and **Exsprents Smith** are appointed to mak inquirey Concerning
our friends Clearnes and Conversation and make their Return, to the next monthly
meeting. **Beniamin Slocom [Benjamin Slocum]** and **Phebe Wing** Laid their intention of
marraig before
this meeting they were desired to wait for their answer until the Next
monthly meeting **Elizabeth Barker** and **Rebekah Barker** are appointed to make
inquirey the yong womans Clearnes and Conversation and make their Returns to the
Next monthly meeting this meeting appoints **Experints Smith** and **Hannah Tucker**
to make inquⁱrey into the Conversation of **Daborah Haden [Deborah Haydon]** No Collection this
meeting.

At our monthly meeting of Women Friends held in **Dartmouth** yᵉ 19 of yᵉ 6 mo
1751 the friends that Laid their intention of marraig Before the Last monthly
meeting all appeard at this meeting and Signified the Continuation of their
intention of marraig and appearing nothing that hendred their answer
& was that they Proceed in marraig Between this and the —
Next monthly meeting observing Good orders **Joseph Mosher** and **Joanna
Mott** Laid their intention of marraig Before this meeting they were desired
for their answer until the Next monthly meeting **Rebekah Barker** and —
Pernalipa [Penelope] Howland are appointed to make inquirey Concerning the yong womans
Clearness and Conversation and make their Returns to the Next monthly
meeting No Collection at this meeting

---

20. Jean or Jane (Hughes) Ellis (1683-1772), a native of Wales, was a member of Exeter Monthly Meeting
in Bcrks County, Pennsylvania. See Willard Heiss, ed., *Quaker Biographical Sketches of Ministers and
Elders, and Other Concerned Members of the Yearly Meeting of Philadelphia* (Indianapolis: N.p.,1972), 309.

At our monthly meeting of Women Friends held in **Dartmouth** yᵉ 16 of yᵉ 7 mᵒ
1751 **Joseph Mosher** and **Joanna mott** Came and Signified the Continuaton
of their intention of marraig and they appearing Clear from all others
their answer Was they might Proceed in marraig Betwix this and
the Next monthly meeting observing Good orders. **Jonathan Barney** and
Hannah Russel [Russell] Laid their intention of marraig Before this meeting
they were Desired to wait for their answer until the next monthly
Patience Russel [Russell] and **Ruth Sherman** are appointed to make inquirey
Concerning the yong womans Clearnes and Conversation and make their
Returns to the Next monthly meeting. appointed to attend the Quartely
Meeting **Deborah Slocom** and **Pernatipy [Penelope] Howland** and **Apphia Mott** is

to draw an Epistle to the Same. Collected this meeting=9ˢ-0ᵈ
At our monthly meeting of Women Friends held in **Dartmouth** yᵉ 21 of yᵉ
8 mᵒ 1750 [*sic*]. **Jonathan Barney** and **Hannah Russel [Russell]** Boath appared at this
meeting and Signified the Continuation of their intention of marraig
and there appearing nothing that hendred their answer was thᵉy might
Proced in marraig Betwix this and the Next monthly meeting observᶦⁿᵍ
Good orders. **Audrey Smith Apphia mott** and **mary Tucker** are appointed
to Ballance the accounts of this meeting No collection this meeting
taken out of the Stock £2=2ˢ-0ᵈ) The 2ᵗʰ of the 9 month in yᵉ 1751
all accounts Ballanced and the meeting is in Debt) 3£-15ˢ-6ᵈ

At our monthly meeting of Women Friends held in **Dartmouth** yᵉ 18 of yᵉ 9 mᵒ
1751 **Beniamim Smith** and **Susannah Wood** Signified their intention of marrg
Before this meeting they were Desired to wait for their anser until the
Next monthly meeting **Grizel Sherman** and **Experents Smith** are appointed
to make inquirey Concerning the yong Womans Clearnes and Conversation and
make their Returns to the Next monthly meeting
Collected at this meeting = 18ˢ=6ᵈ) this meeting hath maid Choyce of
Ruth Sherman to Keep the Collected money

At our Monthly meeting of Women friends held in **Dartmouth** yᵉ 16ᵗʰ of yᵉ 10ᵗʰ mo
1751 **Beniamin Smith** and **Susannah Wood** Booth appeared and Signified the
Continuation of their intention of marraig. and they appearing clear
from all others their answer Was they might Proceed in marraig Betwix
this and the Next monthly meeting observing good orders. No Collection
this meeting

At our monthly meeting of Women friends held in **Dartmouth** yᵉ 20 of yᵉ 11ᵐᵒ
1751. No Collection this meeting

At our monthly meeting of Women friends held in **Dartmouth** yᵉ 17 of yᵉ 12 moᵒ
1751/2 **William Tripp** and **Lyda Sherman** Laid their intention of marraig
Before this meeting they were desired to wait for their answer until
the Next monthly meeting **Mary Smith** and **Jean Smith** are to make inquirʸ
Concerning the yong Womans Clearnes and Conversation and make their

Returns to the Next monthly meeting. No Collection this meeting

At our monthly meeting of Women friends held in **Dartmouth** yᵉ 16 of yᵉ 3 mᵒ
1752. **William Tripp** and **Lyda Sherman** Boath appeard and Signified the
Continuation of their intention of marraig and they apparing Clear
from all others their answer was that they might Proceed in
marraig Betwean this and the Next monthly meeting observing Good
orders Established among friends. **Isaac Cornal** [**Cornell**] and **Prissilla Mosher**
Laid their intention of marraig Before this meeting they were
desired to wait for their anser until the Next monthly meeting
Hannah Tucker and **Pernalipa Howland** are appointed to make
inquirey Concerning the yong womans Clearness and Conversation
and make their Returns to the Next monthly meeting. appointed
to attend the Quartely meeting, **Apphia mott** and **Keziah wood.**
Apphia Mott is to draw an Epistle Same. Collected at this meeting
£1=6ˢ-2ᵈ

At our monthly meeting of Women Friends held in **Dartmouth** yᵉ 22ᵗʰ
of yᵉ 4 mᵒ 1752. **Isaac Cornal** [**Cornell**] and **Prissilla Mosher** Boath appeared
at this meeting and Signified the Continuation of their intention
of marraig. and they appearing Clear from all others their anser
was that they might proceed in marraig Betwean this and the
Next monthly meeting observing Good orders.
No Collection at this meeting

Yᵉ 19ᵗʰ of yᵉ 5ᵗʰ Mᵒ 1752

At our monthly meeting of Women friends held in **Dartmouth**
Collected at this meeting 00£-09ˢ=60ᵈ

Yᵉ 22ᵗʰ of yᵉ 6ᵗʰ Mᵒ 1752

Was our monthly meeting of Women friends held in **Dartmouth**
Kezia Wood & **Jean Smith** is appointed to attend the Quarterly
meeting and **Apphia Mott** is to draw an Epistle to the Same **Lydia**
Allen and **Penelope Howland** are appointed to make Enquiery
intᵒ the Conversation of **Bethsheba Ricketson** no Collection this Meeting

Yᵉ 20ᵗʰ of Yᵉ 7ᵗʰ Mᵒ 1752

Was our monthly meeting of Women friends held in **Dartmouth**
nothing of business presented from the Quarterly meeting Collected
at this meeting 1£-1ˢ-0ᵈ

Yᵉ 17ᵗʰ of yᵉ 8ᵗʰ Mᵒ 1752

Was our monthly meeting of Women friends held in **Dartmouth**
Where **John Wood** and **Jerusha Taber** both Appeared & Signified
their Intention of Marriage they were desired to Wait for their
answer untill the Next Monthly meeting **Kezia Wood** and **Ruth Sherman**
are to make Inquiery Concerning the Young Womans Clearness
and Conversation and make their Return to the Next Monthly

meeting taken out of the Stock to Ballance the old accompt 3$^£$=15^s=00^d
No Collection this meeting

Y^e 16th of Y^e 10th M^o 1752

Was our monthly meeting of Women friends held in **Dartmouth**
Where **John Wood** and **Jerusha Taber** both appeared and Signified
the continuation of their Intention of Marriage and they appearing
clear from all others their Answer Was that they might proceed
in marriage between this and the Next monthly meeting observing
Good order. **Philip Tripp** and **Sarah Wood** Laid their Intention
of marriage before this meeting they were Desired to wait for
their answer untill the Next monthly Meeting **Sarah Mosher**
and **Hephsibeh Hussey** are appointed to make Enquiery Concerning
the Young Womans Clearness and Conversation and make their Return
to the Next Monthly Meeting.
Elisabeth Barker and **Hephzibeh Hussey** are appointed to
make Enquiery into the Conversation of **Deborah Hayden**
and make their Return to the Next Monthly Meeting
Collected at this meeting 0$^£$=6^s=0^d

Y^e 20th of y^e 11th M^o 1752

Was our Monthly meeting of women friends held in **Dartmouth**
Where **Philip Tripp** and **Sarah Wood** received their answer — —
Prins Howland and **Deborah Slocum** Laid their Intention of marri-
age before this meeting they were Desired to wait for their answer
untill the Next monthly meeting. **Elisabeth Barker** and **Lydia
Allen** are to make Enquiery into the young Womans Clearness and Conversa-
-tion and make their Return to the Next monthly Meeting **Mary Wing**s
Certificate was read at this meeting. No Collection at this meeting.

Y^e 18th of Y^e 12th M^o 1752

Was our monthly meeting of Women friends held in **Dartmouth**
Where **Prince Howland Deborah Slocum** Received their answer.
John Russell and **Deborah Hunt** Laid their Intention of Marriage
Before this Meeting they were Desired to Wait for their answer untill
the Next Monthly Meeting **Hannah Tucker** and **Penelope Howland**
are appointed to make Enquiery into the friends Clearness & Conversation
and make Return to the Next monthly meeting; **Thomas Hathaway**
and **Lois Taber** Laid their Intention of Marriage before this Meeting they are Desired to wait for an answer untill the Next monthly
meeting **Kezia Wood** and **Mary Smith** are to make Enquiery
into the young Womans Clearness and Conversation and make their
Return to the Next monthly meeting; ~ **Susannah Russell**s
Certificate was read at this Meeting and Gave Satisfaction.
Collected at this meeting, 1$^£$=1^s=0^d appointed to attend the Quarterly
meeting **Mary potter** & **Elisabeth Gidley, Apphia Mott** is to

draw an Epistle to the Same

Y^e 13th of y^e 1st M^o 1753

Was our monthly meeting of Women friends held in **Dartmouth** ~
where **John Russell** and **Deborah Hunt Thamas Hathaway**
and **Lois Taber** all appeared and Signified the Continuation of their
Intention of Marriage and they appearing Clear from all others
their answer was that they might proceed in Marriage between
this & Next Monthly meeting according to Good order Established
among friends: **Apphia Mott Ruth Shearman** [Sherman] **Hephzibeh
Hussey** are to Ballance the Accompts of this meeting; No Collection
at this meeting

Y^e 19th of Y^e 2^d M^o 1753

Was our monthly meeting of Women friends held in **Dartmouth**
Collected at this meeting 00$^£$-11^s-8^d

Y^e 6th of Y^e 3^d M^o 1753

accounts Ballanced and here Remains in the Stock 2$^£$-17^s

Y^e 19th of Y^e 3^d M^o 1753

Was our monthly meeting of women friends held in **Dartmouth** ~
2 pounds taken out of the Stock for Recording of the Books;
appointed to attend the Quarterly meeting **Deborah Russell
Apphia Mott** and **Apphia Mott** is to write an Epistle to the
Same[21] Collected at this meeting 01$^£$-3^s-0^d

Y^e 16th of Y^e 4th M^o 1753

Was our monthly meeting of Women friends held in **Dartmouth**
Where **Benjamin Russell** & **Anna Smith** Laid their Intention
of marriage they were Desired to wait for their answer untill
the Next monthly meeting; **Experence Smith Hannah Tucker**
are appointed to make Enquiery into the Young Womans Clearness
and Conversation and make their Return to the Next monthly
meeting No Collection at this meeting

Y^e 21st of Y^e 5th ^{mo} 1753

Was our monthly meeting of women friends held in **Dartmouth**
Where **Benjamin Russell** and **anna Smith** Came & Received their
Answer **Josiah Wood** and **Hannah Tucker** Laid their Intention
of marriage before this Meeting they were Desired to wait for their
answer untill the Next monthly meeting **Experence Smith** and
Zerviah Howland are appointed to make Enquiery Concerning the
Young womans Clearness and make their return to the Next monthly
meeting, no Collection at this meeting

---

21. Epistles were usually directed from superior to inferior bodies. An epistle to the quarterly meeting
from a monthly meeting was unusual.

Y^e 18th of Y^e 6th M^o 1753

Was our monthly meeting of women friends held in **Dartmouth**
Where **Josiah Wood** and **Hannah Tucker** both appeared and
Signified the Continuation of their Intention of Marriage and they
appearing clear of all others their Answer was that they might
proceed in marriage between this & Next monthly meeting observing
Good orders; **John Taber** & **Sarah Walker** Laid their Intention of
Marriage before this meeting they were desired to wait for their answer
untill the Next Monthly meeting; **Sarah Taber Rebekeh Barker**
are appointed to make Enquiery into the friends Clearness & Conversation
and make their return to the Next monthly Meeting: We received
an Epistle from the Yearly Meeting at **Newport** which was read and
well accepted: Collected at this meeting 00$^£$-16^s=6^d
appointed to attend the Quarterly meeting **Phebe Tucker Hannah
mosher**: **Apphia Mott** is to draw an Epistle to the Same

Y^e 16th of Y^e 7th M^o 1753

Was our Monthly meeting of women friends held in **Dartmouth**
where **John ~~Walker~~ Taber** & **Sarah Walker** both appeared
and signified The Continuation of their Intention of Marriage and they appearing Clear from all others their answer was that they might pro=
ceed in marriage Between this and Next monthly meeting observing
Good orders; No business presented from the Quarterly meeting.
 Collected at this meeting 00$^£$=12^s=4^d

Y^e 20th of Y^e 8th M^o 1753

Was our monthly meeting of women friends held in **Dartmouth**
taken out of the Stock for the use of friends 01$^£$-8^s=0^d
No Collection at this meeting

Ye 16th of ye 9th Mo 1753

Was our monthly meeting of women friends held in **Dartmouth**
Where **Daniel Wing** and **Lydia Shephard** [**Shepherd**] Laid their intention of
Marriage before this Meeting they were Desired to wait for their answer untill the Next monthly Meeting. **Patience Russell** & **Ruth Shearman** [**Sherman**] are to make Enquiery Concerning the Young Womans Clearness
& Conversation & make their return to the Next monthly meeting.
Collected at this meeting 01$^£$=00^s=8^d
appointed to attend the Quarterly meeting **Deborah Russell
Hannah Tucker Alice Anthony Apphia Mott** is to draw
an Epistle to the same **Kezia Wood** and **Abigail Tripp** are appointed
to talk with **Rachel Howland** for her out Goings

Y^e 15th of y^e 10th M^o 1753

Was our monthly meeting of Women friends held in **Dartmouth**
Where **Daniel Wing** and **Lydia Shepherd** both appeared & Signified
the Continuation of their Intention of marriage and they appearing

Clear of all others their answer was that they might proceed in
Marriage between this and the Next monthly meeting observing Good
Orders: **Solomon Hoxie** and **Jemimah Shearman [Sherman]** Laid their Intention of marriage before this meeting they were desired to wait for
their Answer untill the Next monthly meeting; **Elisabeth Barker**
Hannah Tucker are appointed to make Enquiery Concerning
the Young Womans Clearness and Conversation and make their return
to the Next monthly Meeting. no business presented from the Quarterly meeting nor no Collection at this meeting

Y^e 16th of Y^e 11th m^o 1753

Was our monthly meeting of Women friends in **Dartmouth**
No Collection at this meeting

Y^e 19th of ye 12th M^o 1753

Was our monthly meeting of women friends held in **Dartmouth**
Where **Solomon Hoxie** & **Jemima Shearman [Sherman]** Came for their answer and
they Appearing Clear from all others their Answer was that they
might proceed in Marriage Between this and the Next monthly meeting
observing Good orders. **Thomas Davis** and **Hannah Wood Isaac Wood**
and **Ruth Barker** all Laid their Intention of marriage before
This meeting they were Desired to wait for their answer untill
the Next monthly meeting **Abigail Kerby [Kirby]** and **Ruth Shearman [Sherman]**
are appointed to make Enquiery Concerning the Young Womans
Clearness and Conversation and make their Return to the Next
monthly meeting; no friends Appointed to Attend the Quarterly
Meeting: **Apphia Mott** is appointed to draw an Epistle to the Ensuing
Quarterly meeting; Collected at this meeting 00$^£$=18^s=6^d

Y^e 25th of y^e 1st m^o 1754

Was our monthly meeting of women friends held in **Dartmouth**
Where **Isaac Wood** and **Ruth Barker** both Appeared and Signified
the Continuation of their Intention of Marriage and they appearing
Clear from all others their answer was that they might proceed in
Marriage between this & the Next monthly meeting observing
Good orders. No business presented from the Quarterly meeting.
Collected at this meeting 00$^£$=16^s=0^d

Y^e 17th of y^e 2^d M^o 1754

Was our monthly meeting of women friends held in **Dartmouth**
Where **John Gidley** & **Susannah Tripp Phillip [Philip] Trafford** & **Naomey**
Allen all Laid their Intention of marriage before this Meeting
they Were Desired to wait for their answer untill the Next monthly
Meeting. **Suvla Howland** and **Ruth Shearman [Sherman]** were appointed to make
Enquiery Womens Clearness & Conversation and make their Returns
to the Next monthly meeting. no Collection at this meeting

Y^e 18th of ye 3^d m^o 1754

Was our monthly meeting of Women friends held in **Dartmouth**
Where **Phillip [Philip] Trafford** and **Neomey Allen John Gidley** and
Susannah Tripp all appeared at this meeting and Signified
the Continuation of their Intention of marriage and they appearing
Clear of all others their answer was that they might proceed in
marriage between this and the Next monthly meeting, observing
Good orders: **Jacob Taber** & **Lydia Howland** Laid their Intention
of marriage before this meeting they were Desired to wait for their answer
untill the Next monthly meeting; **Rebekah Barker** and **Kezia**
Wood are appointed to make Enquiery Concerning the Young Womans
Clearness & Conversation and make their Return to the Next monthly
meeting **Elisabeth Gidley** & **Jean Smith** are appointed to attend the
Quarterly meeting. **Apphia Mott Ruth Shearman** & **Hephzibeh**
Hussey are appointed to Ballance the Accompts of this Meeting.
Collected at this meeting 0$^£$=11^s=3^d
taken out of the Stock for Recording of the Books 02$^£$=10^s

Y^e 9th day of Y^e 4th m^o 1754

all accompts balanced & here Remains in the Stock 01$^£$=07^s=0^d

Y^e 15th of y^e 4th M^o 1754

Was our Monthly meeting of women friends held in **Dartmouth** ~
Where **Jacob Taber** and **Lydia Howland Thomas Davis** and
Hannah Wood all Received their Answers that they might proceed
in Marriage between this and the Next monthly meeting according
to Good orders. no Collection at this meeting

Y^e 20th of Y^e 5th M^o 1754

Was our monthly meeting of Women friends held in **Dartmouth**
Phebe Tucker Deborah Russell are appointed to talk with **Elisabeth**
Gidley for her Disorderly proceeding. Collected at this meeting 3^s=6^d

Y^e 24th of y^e 6th M^o 1754

Was our monthly meeting of Women friends held in **Dartmouth**
Appointed to attend the Quarterly meeting **Phebe Tucker Deborah**
Slocum Patience Russell. Apphia Mott is to Draw an Epistle to the
Same no Collection at this meeting We received an Epistle from the
Quarterly meeting which was well Accepted

Y^e 15th of Y^e 7th M^o 1754

Was our monthly meeting of Women friends held in **Dartmouth**
Kezia Wood and **Abigail Tripp** are appointed to talk with **Lydia**
Kerby [Kirby] for her Disorderly Proceeding, Collected at this meeting 01$^£$=5^s=6^d
This Meeting hath made Choise of **Elisabeth Barker** & **Hannah Tucker**
To talk with **Levinah Howland** for her out Goings
Experence [Experience] Smith and **Hephzebeh Hussey** are appointed to talk with

Hannah Briggs Concerning her marrying from among friends: it is the mind of this meeting that Hannah Mosher and Abigail Tripp Should talk with Lydia Cornwell Concerning her marrying

Yᵉ 19ᵗʰ of Yᵉ 8ᵗʰ Mᵒ 1754

Was our monthly meeting of women friends held in Dartmouth Elisabeth Barker Deborah Slocum & Patience Russell are appointed to talk with Grizzel Shearman [Sherman] Concerning the uneasiness which She caused in the monthly Meeting. no collection at this meeting

Yᵉ 16ᵗʰ of Yᵉ 9ᵗʰ Mᵒ 1754

Was our monthly meeting of Women friends held in Dartmouth Grizzell Sherman hath made Satisfaction for the uneasiness which She Caused in this meeting: appointed to Attend the Quarterly meeting Hannah Mosher Patience Russell. Collected at this meeting 00ᶜ=04ˢ=06ᵈ Apphia Mott is appointed to Draw an Epistle to the Ensuing Quarterly meeting; Apphia Mott is appointed to Draw up the Deniel of Lydia Cornwell and bring to the Next monthly meeting She Refusing to take up with friends advice

The 21ˢᵗ of Yᵉ 10ᵗʰ Mᵒ 1754

Was our monthly Meeting of women friends held in Dartmouth Elisabeth Gidley hath made friends Satisfaction Concerning her Marrying: Lydia Cornwell was Denied at this meeting for her disorderly Marrying: Elisabeth Gidley and Deborah Slocum are appointed to talk with Neomy Trafford Anna Ricketson & Ruth Anthony for their Disorderly proceeding; no Collection at this meeting

The 18ᵗʰ of Yᵉ 11ᵗʰ Mᵒ 1754

Was our monthly meeting of women friends held in Dartmouth Where Ruth Shearman [Sherman] and Alice Anthony Were appointed to make Enquiery into the Conversation of Judah Killey [Kelley] and make return to the Next monthly meeting: no Collection at this meeting

The 16ᵗʰ of Yᵉ 12ᵗʰ Mᵒ 1754

Was our monthly meeting of women friends held in Dartmouth Wher Benjamin Wing and Bethsheba Potter Laid their Intention of marriage before this meeting; they were Desired to wait for their Answer untill the Next monthly meeting: Abigail Kerby [Kirby] and Ruth Shearman [Sherman] are appointed to make Enquiery Concerning the Young Womans Clearness & Conversation and make their return to the Next monthly meeting Hannah Briggs hath made friends Satisfaction for her Disorder in marrying Apphia Mott and Kezia Wood are to attend the Quarterly meeting, and Apphia Mott is to ~~attend~~ Draw an Epistle to the Same: Taken out of the Stock for LS two pound three shillings; This meeting hath made choice of Susannah Gifford & Hannah Tucker to talk with Rebekah Slocum for her Disorders: Apphia Mott is to write a

Certificate for **Judith Killey** [**Kelley**]; Collected at this meeting 01ᶠ=06ˢ=10ᴰ

The 20ᵗʰ of Yᵉ 1ˢᵗ Mᵒ 1755

Was our monthly meeting of women friends held in **Dartmouth**
Where **Benjamin Wing** and **Bethsheba Potter** both appeared and
Signified the Continuation of their Intention of marriage & they appeard
Clear from all others their answer was that they might proceed in
Marriage Between this ˏ& the Next monthly meeting observing Good
Orders: **Walter Cornwell** and **Ruth Wood** laid their Intention of
marriage before this meeting th[e]y were Desired to wait for their
Answer untill the Next Monthly meeting **Elisabeth Gidley Patience
Gifford** are appointed to make Enquiery concerning the young
Womans Clearness & Conversation and make their Return to the Next
monthly meeting: no Collection at this meeting

The 17ᵗʰ of Yᵉ 2ᵈ Mᵒ 1755

Was our monthly meeting of women friends held in **Dartmouth**
Where **Walter Cornwell** and **Ruth Wood** both appeared and Signified the Continuation of their Intention of Marriage and they appearing Clear from all
others their answer was that they might proceed in marriage between this
and the Next monthly meeting Observing Good orders: Collected at this Meeting 00ᶠ=13ˢ=6ᵈ

The 17ᵗʰ of Yᵉ 3ᵈ Mᵒ 1755

Was our monthly Meeting of women friends held in **Dartmouth**
Elizabeth Gidley Patience Russell are appointed to talk with **Silvia
Wilcocx** [**Wilcox**] Concerning her Disorder ~~m~~marrying; this meeting hath made
Choise of **hannah Tucker** & **Hephzibeh Hussey** to purge our monthly
meeting of Disorderly persons for time to come: **Apphia Mott Hephzibeh Hussey Ruth Shearman** [**Sherman**] are appointed to Settle the accompts of this
meeting no Collection at this meeting **Sarah Howland** Desires to Come
under the Care of friends

The 21ˢᵗ of Yᵉ 4ᵗʰ Mᵒ 1755

Was our monthly meeting of women friends held in **Dartmouth**
No business presented from the ~~monthly~~ Quarterly meeting Except appointing friends to attend the Yearly meeting & the friends that are appointed
are **Hannah Tucker Patience Russell**; this meeting Chose **Susannah
Gifford** and **Deborah Slocum** to talk with **Deborah Wilber** [**Wilbur**] about her concern
no Collection at this meeting

The 14ᵗʰ of Yᵉ 5ᵗʰ Mᵒ 1755

All accompts Ballanced and here Remains in the Stock 02ᶠ-19ˢ-10ᵈ

The 19ᵗʰ of Yᵉ 5ᵗʰ Mᵒ 1755

Was our monthly meeting of women friends held in **Dartmouth**
Where **Thomas Cornwell** and **mary Russell** Laid their intention of
marriage they were Desired to wait for their answer until the Next

monthly meeting **Experance Smith** and **Deborah Slocum** are appointed
to make Enquiery Concerning our friends Clearness & Conversation and
make their Return to the Next monthly meeting. **Sarah Howland** is
taken under the Care of friends according to her Desire Collected at this
meeting 1$^£$=5^s=9^d

The 23$^{\underline{d}}$ of Y$^{\underline{e}}$ 6$^{\underline{th}}$ M$^{\underline{o}}$ 1755

Was our monthly meeting of women friends held in **Dartmouth**
by Ajournment where **Thomas Cornwell** and **mary Russell**
both Appeared and Signified the Continuation of Intention of marriage
and there appearing nothing that might hinder their answer was
that they might proceed in marriage between this & the Next monthly
meeting observing Good orders
Appointed to Attend the Quarterly meeting **Elisabeth Barker**
Sarah Mosher: no Collection at this meeting

The 21$^{\underline{st}}$ of Y$^{\underline{e}}$ 7$^{\underline{th}}$ M$^{\underline{o}}$ 1755

Was our monthly meeting of women friends held in **Dartmouth**
No business presents from the Quarterly meeting: Collected at this
meeting 15^s=4^d this meeting appointed **Susannah Gifford Hannah**
Tucker Hephzibeh Hussey to talk with **Wath Allen** for her Disorders
This meeting hath made choice of **Bethiah Macomber** and **Abigail**
Tripp to visits friends families at **Acoaxet** the Year Ensuing

The 18$^{\underline{th}}$ of Y$^{\underline{e}}$ 8$^{\underline{th}}$ M$^{\underline{o}}$ 1755

Was our monthly meeting of women friends held in **Dartmouth**
Where **Timothy Gifford** and **Martha Tucker** laid their Intention of
marriage they were Desired to wait for their answer untill the Next
Monthly Meeting **Deborah Slocum** and **Patience Russell** are appointed to make Enquery Concerning the Young Womans Clearness & Conversation and make their Return to the Next monthly meeting no Collection
at this meeting

The 15$^{\underline{th}}$ of Y$^{\underline{e}}$ 9$^{\underline{th}}$ M$^{\underline{o}}$ 1755

Was our monthly meeting of women friends held in **Dartmouth**
Where **Timothy Gifford** and **Martha Tucker** both appeared and
Signified the Continuation of their Intention of marriage and they
appearing Clear from all others their answer was that they might
proceed in marriage between this and the Next monthly meeting
according to Good orders Established among friends: Appointed to attend
the Quarterly meeting **Penelope Howland Alice Anthony, Apphia**
Mott is appointed to Draw an Epistle to the Ensuing Quarterly meeting
Collected at this meeting 00^c=5^s=0^d

The 15$^{\underline{th}}$ of Y$^{\underline{e}}$ 10$^{\underline{th}}$ M$^{\underline{o}}$ 1755

Was our monthly meeting of women friends held in **Dartmouth**
Susannah Gifford and **Hannah Tucker** have talked with

Elisabeth Sanford for her Disorderly Proceedings but She concluded to
proceed in marriage contrary to the Good orders of friends

The 17th of Ye 11th Mo 1755

Was our monthly meeting of women friends held in **Dartmouth**
Collected at this meeting 00ᶜ-11ˢ-6ᵈ

The 17th of Ye 12th Mo 1755

Was our monthly meeting of women friends held in **Dartmouth**
the friends appointed to attend the Quarterly Meeting are **Hannah Tucker Hope
Briggs Apphia Mott** is to Draw an Epistle to the Same. no Collection at this meet

The 19th of Ye 1st Mo 1756

Was our monthly meeting of women friends held in **Dartmouth**
Elisabeth Gidley mary Cornwell are chose to talk with **Abigail Wing Silvia
Willcocx [Wilcox]** Acknowledgment was accepted **Hannah Hammond** was denied at this
    meeting
for marrying out of the orders of friends **Rebekah Slocum** Remains under dealing
Still no collection at this meeting

The 16th of Ye 2d Mo 1756

Was our monthly meeting of women friends held in **Dartmouth**
Alice Earl is taken under the ciar [care] of this meeting Collected at this meeting 00ᶜ-13ˢ=00ᵈ

The 15th of Ye 3d Mo 1756

Was our monthly meeting of women friends held in **Dartmouth**
Gershom Smith & **Phebe White** both appeared at this meeting and Signified
their Intention of marriage they were Desired to wait for their answer
untill the next monthly meeting **Abigail Tripp** & **Hannah Mosher** are
appointed to make Enquiery Concerning the Young Womans Clearness & Conversation
and make their return to the next monthly meeting: **Elisabeth Gidley Hope Briggs
Hannah Shearman [Sherman]** are appointed to attend the Quarterly meeting. **Apphia Mott**
is to Draw an Epistle to the same: no Collection at this meeting

The 19th of Ye 4th Mo 1756

Was our monthly meeting of women friends held in **Dartmouth**
Where **Gershom Smith** & **Phebe White** both appeared at this meeting and
Signified their Continuation of their Intention of marriage nothing appeared but
that they were clear from all others their answer was they might proceed in
marriage between this & the Next monthly meeting According to Good orders
Samuel Wing and **Elisabeth Barker Deliverance Smith** and **Hannah Smith
Abiel Mackember [Macomber]** & **Rest Devil [Davol]** all laid their Intention of marriage
    before this
meeting they were Desired to wait for their answer untill the next monthly meeting
the friends appointed to make Enquiery Concerning the Young womens Clearness and
Conversation are **Hope Briggs Ruth Shearman [Sherman] Abigail Tripp** & **Hannah Mosher**
no Collection at this meeting

Y^{e} 14th of Y^{e} 4th M^{o} 1756

all accompts Ballanced and here Remains in the Stock 05$^{£}$-16^{s}-04^{d}

The 17th of Y^{e} 5th [mo] 1756

Was our monthly meeting of women friends held in **Dartmouth**
where **Samuel Wing** and **Elisabeth Barker**: **Deliverance Smith** & **Hannah
Smith** ~ **Abiel Macomber** & **Rest Devil [Davol]** all came for their answer and they
appearing clear from all others their answer was they might proceed in
marriage between this and the Next monthly meeting according to Good orders:
Francis Tripp and **Content Griffin** Laid their Intention of marriage before this
meeting they were Desired to wait for their answer untill the Next monthly
meeting – **Phebe Smith** and **Ruth Shearman [Sherman]** are to make Enquiery into
the Young womans Clearness & Conversation: no Collection at this meeting

---

The 21st of Y^{e} 6th M^{o} 1756

Was our monthly meeting of women friends held in **Dartmouth**
where **Francis Tripp** and **Content Griffin** both appeared and Signified
the Cont͵inuation of their Intention of marriage and they appearing Clear from ~
all others their answer was that they might proceed in marriage between ~
this and the next monthly observing Good orders: **Christopher Devil [Davol]** and
Mehetable Allen laid their Intention of marriage before this meeting: they
were Desired to wait for their answer untill the Next monthly meeting;
Kezia Wood Patience Russell are appointed to make Enquiery Concerning the
Young womans Clearness & Conversation: and make their return to the Next monthly
Meeting. We received an Epistle from the Yearly meeting of **Newport** which ~
was read and well accepted. **Apphia Mott Kezia Wood** are appointed to attend
the Quarterly meeting; no Collection at this meeting. **Apphia Mott** is appointed to
Draw an Epistle to the Ensuing Quarterly meeting

The 19th of Y^{e} 7th M^{o} 1756

Was our monthly meeting of women friends held in **Dartmouth** ~
Where **Christopher Devil [Davol]** and **Mehetabel Allen** both appeared at this meeting
and Signified the Continuation of their Intention of marriage and there appearing
nothing that might hinder their answer was that they might proceed in
marriage between this & the Next monthly meeting observing Good orders Established
Among friends: **Mary Chase** wife of **Samuel Chase** is received under the Care of this
meeting Collected at this meeting 00$^{£}$=12^{s}-07^{d} **Hannah Hathaway** is received under
the care of this meeting

The 16th of Y^{e} 8th m^{o} 1756

Was our monthly meeting of women friends held in **Dartmouth** ~
Wait Wood hath made friends Satisfaction for her Disorderly proceeding
Deborah Wilber [Wilbur] is taken under the care of this meeting. this meeting hath
made choice of **Ruth Tucker** to keep the Collected money. no Collection at this
meeting.

The 21$\underline{st}$ of Y$\underline{e}$ 9$\underline{th}$ m$\underline{o}$ 1756

Was our monthly meeting of women friends held in **Dartmouth** ~
Where **Jedediah Allen** and **Eunice Wood** laid their Intention of marriage they
were desired to wait for their answer untill the Next monthly meeting.
Experience Smith and **Patience Gifford** are appointed to make Enquiery concerning
the Young womans Clearness and Conversation. and make their return to the
Next monthly meeting appointed to attend the Quarterly meeting **Phebe
Tucker Deborah Russell: Patience Russell & Apphia Mott** is to draw an Epistle
to the Same Quarterly meeting   Collected at this meeting -06-0

The 18$\underline{th}$ of Y$\underline{e}$ 10$\underline{th}$ m$\underline{o}$ 1756

Was our monthly meeting of women friends held in **Dartmouth** ~
no business presented from the Quarterly meeting. [illegible] **mary Cornwell** and
Elisabeth Gidley are appointed to talk with **Abigail White** for her Disorders
no Collection at this meeting

The 15$\underline{th}$ of Y$\underline{e}$ 11$\underline{th}$ m$\underline{o}$ 1756

Was our monthly meeting of women friends held in **Dartmouth** ~
where appeared **Jedediah Allen** and **Eunice Wood** and Signified the Continuation
of their Intention of marriage and they appearing Clear from all others their
answer was that they might proceed in Marriage between this and the Next ~
monthly meeting according to the Good orders Established among friends.
**Edward Wing Mehetabel Russell William Anthony, Sarah Shearman [Sherman]
Jacob Russell Phebe Willcocx [Wilcox]** Laid their Intention of marriage before this meeting
they were Desired to wait for their answer untill the Next monthly meeting
the friends appointed to Enquire into their Clearness & Conversation is as followeth ~
Penelope Howland Hannah Tucker Hope Briggs Patience Wait [Waite] is Received under
the Care of this meeting Collected at this meeting £01-6-4
taken out of the Stock for the Use of friends £05-0-0

The 29$\underline{th}$ of Y$\underline{e}$ 12$\underline{th}$ M$\underline{o}$ 1756

Was our Monthly meeting of women friends held in **Dartmouth** ~
by ajournment. the friends that Laid their Intention of marriage before the
Last monthly meeting all Came for their answer and there appearing
nothing to hinder them their answer was that they might proceed in marriage
between this and the Next monthly meeting according to the Good orders Established
Among friends. Collected at this meeting £00-17^s-4^d
Apphia Mott is Appointed to write the Epistle to the Quarterly meeting: no friends
appointed to attend the Quarterly meeting

The 16$\underline{th}$ of Y$\underline{e}$ 1$\underline{st}$ M$\underline{o}$ 1757

Was our monthly meeting of women friends held in **Dartmouth** ~
no business Presented from the Quarterly meeting. no collection

The 21$\underline{st}$ of Y$\underline{e}$ 2$\underline{d}$ m$\underline{o}$ 1757

Was our monthly meeting of women friends held in **Dartmouth** ~
Collected at this meeting 01$^£$-8-6

The 21st of Y^e 3^d m^o 1757

Was our monthly meeting of women friends held in **Dartmouth** ~

Where **Elisabeth Sandford [Sanford]** made friends Satisfaction for her Disorderly proceedings Appointed to attend the Quarterly meeting **Hannah Tucker Elisabeth Gidley**
Apphia Mott is to Draw the Epistle to the Quarterly meeting, no Collection at
this meeting

The 18th of Y^e 4th M^o 1757

Was our monthly meeting of women friends held in **Dartmouth** ~

Collected at this meeting for the Use of friends 01$^£$-00-0

Y^e 14th of Y^e 5th M^o 1757

all accompts Ballanced and here Remains in the Stock 05$^£$=16^s=7^d

---

The 16th of Y^e 5th M^o 1757

Was our monthly meeting of women friends held in **Dartmouth** ~

no Collection at this meeting

The 20th of Y^e 6th M^o 1757

Was our monthly meeting of women friends held in **Dartmouth** ~

Where we Received an Epistle from **Newport** Yearly meeting which was well
accepted, **Patience Easty** Certificate was read and friends had unity with it: also **Sarah**
Cornwell Certificate was Read and friends accepted it and She is taken under the Care
of this meeting appointed to attend the Quarterly meeting **Phebe Tucker Elisabeth**
Barker Hannah Mosher Kezia Wood Apphia Mott is appointed to Draw an
Epistle to the Ensuing Quarterly meeting no Collection at this meeting

---

The 18th of Y^e 7th m^o 1757

Was our monthly Meeting of women friends held in **Dartmouth** ~

no business Presented from the Quarterly meeting **Kezia Wood**s Certificate
was Read and well accepted on her Return from visiting friends at **Sand-**
wich Collected at this meeting 00$^£$=05=00

The 15th of Y^e 8th M^o 1757

Was our monthly meeting of women friends held in **Dartmouth** ~

Hannah Dennis hath made friends Satisfaction for her Disorderly proceeding
in marrying out of the orders of friends. no Collection at this meeting

---

The 19th of Y^e 9th M^o 1757

Was our monthly meeting of women friends held in **Dartmouth** ~

Appointed to attend the Quarterly meeting **Phebe Tucker Elisabeth Slocum**
no Collection at this meeting. **Apphia Mott** is appointed to Draw an ~
Epistle to the Ensuing Quarterly Meeting

The 17th of Y^e 10th m^o 1757

Was our monthly meeting of women friends held in **Dartmouth** ~

Where **Henry Howland** and **Abigail Godward [Goddard]** both appeared at this meeting
and Signified their Intention of marriage, they were Desired to wait for their answer
untill the Next monthly meeting, **Soviah Howland Patience Russell** were to make

Enquiery into the Young womans Clearness & Conversation and make their Returns
to the Next monthly meeting **Peace Wood** hath ₍made₎ friends Satisfaction for the uneasiness
which She Caused among friends. no Collection at this meeting

---

The 21st of Y^e 11th m^o 1757

Was Our monthly meeting of women friends held in **Dartmouth** ~
Collected at this meeting oo=18=o taken out the Stock for the use of friends 04$^£$=08^s

---

The 19th of Y^e 12th M^o 1757

Was Our Monthly meeting of women friends held in **Dartmouth** ~
where **Henry Howland** and **Abigail Godhard [Goddard]** both appeared & Signified
the Continuation of their Intention of Marriage and they appearing Clare
from all others their answer was they might proceed in marriage between
this and the Next monthly meeting According to Good orders among friends
Benjamin Shearman [Sherman] and **Elisabeth Lapham** Laid their Intention of marriage
before this meeting they were Desired to wait for their answer untill the Next
monthly meeting **Patience Russell Hope Briggs** were appointed to make Enquiery
into the Young womans Clearness & Conversation and make their Returns to the
Next monthly meeting appointed to attend the ~~monthly~~ ₍Quarterly₎ meeting **Hope Briggs**
Alice Anthony. Apphia Mott is to Draw an Epistle to the Same – no Collection
at this meeting

The 17th of Y^e 1st m^o 1758

Was our monthly Meeting of women friends held in **Dartmouth** ~
where **Benjamin Shearman [Sherman]** & **Elisabeth Lapham** both appeared & Signified
the Continuation of their Intention of marriage and there appearing nothing
to hinder them their answer was that they might proceed in Marriage
Between this and the Next monthly meeting observing Good orders
Thomas Hix [Hicks] and **Deborah Smith** Laid their Intention of marriage before this meeting
they were Desired to wait for their answer untill the Next monthly meeting **Zerviah**
Howland & **Robe Russell** are appointed to make Enquiery Concerning the Young
womans Clearness & Conversation and make their Returns to the Next monthly
meeting no Collection at this meeting

The 20th of Y^e 2^d M^o 1758

Was our Monthly meeting of womens friends in **Dartmouth** ~
where **Thomas Hix [Hicks]** and **Deborah Smith** both appeared at this meeting and
Signified the Continuation of their Intention of marriage and there appearing
nothing to hinder their answer was that they might proceed in marriage
between this and the Next monthly meeting according to Good orders
Abraham Sherman and **Mary Howland Benjamin Butlar [Butler]** and **Easther**
Kemtom [Esther Kempton] Israel Wood and **Hannah Tripp** all Laid their Intention of
Marriage before this meeting, they were Desired to wait for their
answer untill the Next monthly meeting **Kezia Wood Alice Anthony**
are appointed to make Enquery into their Clearness & conversation
and make their Returns to the Next monthly meeting Collected at this
meeting 01$^£$-4^s-0^d

The 19th of Ye 3d Mo 1758

Was our monthly meeting of women friends held in **Dartmouth** ~
Where all the friends appeared that Laid their Intention of marriage
before the Last monthly meeting and Signified the Continuation of their
Intention of marriage and they appearing Clear from all others their
answer was that they might proceed in marriage between this & the Next
Monthly meeting according to Good orders Established among friends
Appointed to attend the Quarterly meeting **Apphia Moot [Mott] Hannah Tucker**
Patience Russell Apphia Mott is to Draw an Epistle to the Ensuing Quarter
ly meeting, no Collection

The 17th of ye Ye 4th Mo 1758

Was our monthly meeting of women friends held in **Dartmouth** ~
no business presented at the Quarterly Meeting **Apphia Mott Hannah**
Tucker Ruth Tucker are appointed to Ballance the accompt of this meeting
Nothing Collected at this meeting

The 14th of Ye 5th Mo 1758

all accompts Balanced and here Remains in the Stock 03£-8s-7d

The 16th of Ye 5th Mo 1758

Was our monthly meeting of women friends held in **Dartmouth** ~
where **Edward Thuston [Thurston]** and **Pernal Sawdy Joseph Soal [Soule, Sowle]** & **Dinah-Tripp** laid their Intention of marriage before this meeting they were
Desired to wait for their answer untill the Next monthly meeting
Kezia Wood Hannah Mosher are appointed to make Enquiery into
the Young womens Clearness & Conversation and make their Returns to
the Next monthly meeting Collected at this meeting 00£~12s~06d

The 19th of Ye 6th Mo 1758

Was our Monthly meeting of women friends held in **Dartmouth**
where **Edward Thuston** & **Pernal Sawdey Joseph Sowl [Soule]** and **Dinah Tripp** all
all [sic] appeared at this meeting and signified the Continuation of their Intention
of marriage and they appearing Clear from all others their answer was they
might proceed in marriage between this & the Next monthly meeting according
to the Good orders Established among friends. Appointed to attend the Quarterly
meeting **Kezia Wood Alice Anthony Apphia Mott** is to Draw an Epistle to
the Ensuing Quarterly meeting no Collection at this meeting we received an Epistle
from the Yearly meeting of women friends at **Newport** which was read and kindly accepted.

The 17th of Ye 7th Mo 1758

Was Our Monthly meeting of women friends held in **Dartmouth**
No business presenting from the Quarterly Neither was there any Collection at this
meeting **Elisabeth Barker Susannah Russell** are appointed to talk with **Mary Wood**
for her out Goings.

The 21[?]th of Ye 8th Mo 1758

Was our Monthly meeting of women friends held in **Dartmouth**

Where **Thomas Cook** and **Susannah Cornweel [Cornell]** Laid their Intention of marriage
before this meeting they were Desired to wait for their answer untill the Next
monthly meeting, **Kezia Wood** and **Patience Russell** are appointed to make
Enquiery into the friends Clearness and Conversation and make Return to the Next
monthly meeting **Mary Davis**es Certificate was Receiv^d at this meeting, no Collection
at this meeting

The 18th of Y^e 9th M^o 1758

Was our monthly meeting of women friends held in **Dartmouth**
at this meeting **Meriah [smudge] Hammond** is taken under the Care of friends
**William tripp Meriah Hammond David Russell Susannah Sowl [Soule] Levi Smith
Silvia Allen** all Laid their Intention of Marriage before this meeting, they
were Desired to wait for their answer untill the Next monthly meeting;
Kezia Wood & Penelope Howland are to make Enquiery Concerning the Young
womens Clearness & Conversation and make their Returns to the Next monthly
meeting, appointed to attend the Quarterly meeting **Elisabeth Gidly [Gidley]**, **Hannah
Tucker**, **Apphia Mott** is appointed to write the Epistle to the Quarterly meeting
Collected at this meeting o$^£$-11^s-9^d att the ajournment of this meeting
Thomas Cook and **Susannah Cornwell [Cornell]** came & Receiv^d their answer

The 16th of Y^e 10th m^o 1758

Was our monthly meeting of women friends held in **Dartmouth**
Where **William Tripp Meriah Hammond David Russell** ~~Sush~~ **Susannah Sowl [Soule]** -
Levi Smith Silvia Allen all appeared at this meeting, and Signified the
Continuation of their Intention of marriage and they appearing Clear from
all others their answer was they might proceed in marriage between this &
the Next monthly meeting according to the Good orders Established among
friends **Phillip Shearman [Sherman]** and **mary Russell** Laid their Intention of marriage
before this meeting they were Desired to wait for their answer untill the Next
monthly meeting, **Alice Anthony Patience Russell** are appointed to make Enqui-
-ery into the young womans Clearness & Conversation & make return to the
Next monthly meeting. No collection at this meeting

The 20th of Y^e 11th m^o 1758

Was our monthly meeting of women friends held in **Dartmouth**
Where **Phillip Shearman & mary Russell** bothe appeared at this meeting
and Signified the Continuation of their Intention of marriage and there
appearing nothing to hinder their answer was they might proceed in marriage
between this & the Next monthly meeting according to the Good orders
Established among friends. Collected at this meeting o$^£$-06^s-0^d

The 18th of Y^e 12th m^o 1758

Was our monthly meeting of women friends held in **Dartmouth**
the friends appointed to attend the Quarterly meeting are **Hannah Tucker**
Alice Anthony and **Apphia Mott** is appointed to write the Epistle to the
Quarterly meeting. no Collection at this meeting **Rhoda Allen** hath made

friends Satisfaction for her out Goings

The 15th of Y^e 1st m^o 1759

Was Our monthly meeting of women friends held in **Dartmouth**
Where **Barnabas Earl** & **Pernal Chase** Laid their Intention of marriage
they were Desired to wait for their answer untill the Next monthly meeting
Kezia Wood Elisabeth Smith are appointed to make Enquiery Concerning
the womans Clearness & Conversation and make their return to the Next
monthly meeting no Collection

The 17th of Y^e 2^d m^o 1759

Was our monthly meeting of women friends held in **Dartmouth**
Where **Barnabas Earl** & **Pernal Chase** both appeared and Signified the
Continuation of their Intention of marriage and they appearing nothing to
hinder their answer was that they might Proceed in marriage between this
and the Next monthly meeting according to Good orders Established among
friends **Seth Russell** & **mary Mosher** Laid their Intention of Marriage before
this meeting they were Desired to wait for their answer untill the Next month
ly meeting **Apphia Mott Kezia Wood** are appointed to make Enquiery Concer
ning the young womans Clearness & Conversation & make their return to
the Next monthly meeting No Collection

The 19th of Y^e 3^d m^o 1759

Was our monthly meeting of women friends held in **Dartmouth**
Where **Seth Russell** and **Mary Mosher** both Appeared & Signified the
Continuation of their Intention of marriage & there appearing Nothing
to hinder their answer was they might proceed in Marriage between this
and the Next monthly meeting observing Good orders the friends appointed
to attend the Quarterly meeting is **Hannah Mosher Ruth Tucker Ruth
Mosher** Collected at this meeting 0$^£$-3^s-0^d
Deborah Slocum Susannah Allen Elisabeth Slocum are appointed
to make Enquery Concerning **Deborah Wilber**s request to visit **Oblong**
Apphia Mott is to Draw an Epistle to the Quarterly meeting

The 16th of Y^e 4th m^o 1759

Was our monthly meeting of women friends held in **Dartmouth**
No business Presented from the Quarterly meeting **Apphia Mott Elisabeth** [?]
Ruth Tucker is appointed to ballance the accompts of this meeting, No Collection
at this meeting

The 15th of Y^e 5th m^o 1759 all accompts Ballanced and here Remains
in the Stock 03$^£$-13^s-10^d

The 21st of Y^e 5th m^o 1759

Was our monthly meeting of women friends held in **Dartmouth**
this meeting hath Chose **Peace Wood** and **Sarah Mosher** visiters for **acoaxet**
the year Ensuing, no Collection at this meeting

The 18th of Ye 6th mo 1759

Was our monthly meeting of women friends held in **Dartmouth**
Where we Received an Epistle from the Yearly meeting of **Newport** which was
read and well accepted the friends Appointed to attend the Quarterly meeting are
Hannah Tucker Alice Anthony Apphia Mott is to Draw an Epistle to Ensuing
Quarterly meeting no Collection this meeting is ajourned untill the first Sixth Day
in Next month

The 16th of Ye 7th mo 1759

Was our monthly meeting of women friends held in **Dartmouth**
Mary Manchesters request is Granted and She remains under the notis [notice] of friends
Peace Layton [Lawton] is Denied at this meeting for marrying out of the orders of friends
Rebekah Burden [Borden] is Denied for her Disorderly marrying, Collected at this meeting 3s-9d
Easther Butler hath made friends Satisfaction for her out Goings

---

The 20th of Ye 8th mo 1759

Was our monthly meeting of women friends held in **Dartmouth**
Nicolas Howland and his wifes acknowledgment is accepted at this meeting **Leah
Merrihew [Merihew]** is taken under the care of friends according to her request collected at this
meeting 00£-5s-0

The 17th of Ye 9th mo 1759

Was our monthly meeting of women friends held in **Dartmouth**
Where **Timothy Davis** & **Hephzibeh Hathaway** Laid their Intention of marriage
they were Desired to wait for their answer untill the Next monthly meeting **Hannah
Tucker Susannah Russell** are appointed to make Enquiery Concerning the young womans
Clearness & Conversation and make their return to the Next monthly meeting, no
Collection at this meeting the friends appointed to attend the Quarterly meeting is
Hannah Tucker Sarah Gifford Apphia Mott is to Draw an Epistle to the
Ensuing Quarterly meeting **Susannah Cook** and **mary manchester** Certificate
are both Signed at this meeting

The 15th of Ye 10th mo 1759

Was our monthly meeting of women friends held in **Dartmouth**
Where **Timothy Davis** and **Hephzibeh Hathaway** both appeared and
Signified the Continuation of their Intention of marriage and after Enquiery they
appearing Clear from all others respecting marriage their answer was they
might proceed in marriage between this & the Next monthly meeting according
to Good orders Established among friends; **Apphia Mott** & **Elisabeth Smith**
is appointed to Draw a Certificate for **Mehetable Wing** no Collection

---

The 19th of Ye 11th mo 1759

Was our monthly meeting of women friends held in **Dartmouth**
Elisabeth Tripp hath made friends Satisfaction for her marrying out of
the Good orders of friends Collected at this meeting   0£-04s-02d

---

The 17th of Ye 12th mo 1759

Was our monthly meeting of women friends held in **Dartmouth**

this meeting appoints **Abigail Tripp** & **Hannah Mosher** to talk with **Bridg-et Allen** Concerning her Disorderly proceedings no friends Appears to attend the Quarterly meeting, **Apphia Mott** is appointed to Draw an Epistle to the Ensuing Quarterly meeting Collected at this meeting 0ᴸ-5ˢ-0ᵈ

The 21ˢᵗ of Yᵉ 1ˢᵗ mᵒ 1760

Was Our monthly meeting of women friends held in **Dartmouth**
No business Presents from the Quarterly meeting
Collected at this meeting .   00ᴸ-11ˢ-00ᵈ

The 16ᵗʰ of Yᵉ 2ᵈ mᵒ 1760

Was our monthly meeting of women friends held in **Dartmouth**
No Collection at this meeting

The 17ᵗʰ of Yᵉ 3ᵈ mᵒ 1760

Was our monthly meeting of women friends held in **Dartmouth**
the friends appointed to attend the Quarterly meeting is **Peace Wood**
and **Sarah Mosher Apphia Mott** & **Elisabeth Smith** is appoint
-ed to Draw an Epistle for the Ensuing Quarterly meeting, this meeting
made Choise of **Hannah Mosher** and **Mary Cornwell** [**Cornell**] to talk with **Mary Kirby** for her Disorderly Proceeding; No Collection at this Meeting

The 21ˢᵗ of Yᵉ 4ᵗʰ mᵒ 1760

Was our monthly meeting of women friends held in **Dartmouth**
No business Presented from the Quarterly meeting; **Apphia Mott**
Elisabeth Smith & **Ruth Tucker** are to Settle the meeting accompts
No Collection at this Meeting
Yᵉ 12ᵗʰ of Yᵉ 5ᵗʰ mᵒ 1760 All accompts Ballanced and
here Remains in the Stock   ᴸ5-3ˢ-00ᵈ

The 19ᵗʰ of Yᵉ 5ᵗʰ mᵒ 1760

Was our monthly meeting of women friends held in **Dartmouth**
Where ~~Abigail~~ **Samuel Shove** & **Abigail Anthony** Laid their Intention
of Marriage they were Desired to wait for their answer untill
the Next monthly meeting **Hope Briggs Kezia Wood** are
Chose to make Enquiery Concerning the young womans Clearness
and Conversation and make returns to the Next monthly
meeting Collected at this meeting   00ᴸ-6-3

The 23ᵈ of Yᵉ 6ᵗʰ mᵒ 1760

Was our monthly meeting of women friends held in **Dartmouth**
where **Samuel Shove** & **Abigail Anthony** both appeared and
Signified the Continuation of their Intention of marriage they appearing
Clear from all others their answer was they might proceed in marr
iage between this and the Next monthly meeting, according to the
Good order Established among friends **Benjamin Russell** and **Elisabeth Slocum** Laid their Intention of marriage before this meeting they were
Desired to wait for their answer untill the Next monthly meeting

Hope Briggs Kezia Wood are appointed to make Enquiery Concerning
the young womans Clearness and Conversation and make returns to
the Next monthly our worthy friends **Ann Gant Mercy Redmon**[?]
and **Comfort Hoeg Mary Rowch** [**Rotch**] their Certificates were Read to
Satisfaction **Peace Deval** [**Davol**] is taken under the Care of friends
Lydia Mackember [**Macomber**] and **Sarah Mosher** are Chose to visit friends
families in **acoaxet** this year Ensuing **Deborah Slocum Hope Briggs**
and **Sarah Mosher** are appointed to attend the Quarterly meeting
no Collection at this meeting **Elisabeth Smith** is appointed to Draw
an Epistle to the Ensuing Quarterly meeting

The 21st of Y^e 7th m^o 1760

Was Our monthly meeting of women friends held in **Dartmouth**
where Divers Epistles were read to Satisfaction and the Love there
in mentioned kindly accepted **Benjamin Russell** and **Elisabeth**
Slocum both appeared at this meeting and Signified the Continuation
of their Intention of marriage & there appearing Nothing that
hindered their answer was they might proceed in marriage between
this and the Next monthly meeting according to Good orders
Collected at this meeting. 00£-16-5

The 18th of Y^e 8th m^o 1760

Was our monthly meeting of women friends held in **Dartmouth**
Deborah Russell and **Elisabeth Gidley** were appointed to talk
with **Susannah Russell** for her Disorderly proceeding **Elisabeth**
Russells Certificate was Read and well accepted no Collection at
this meeting

The 15th of Y^e 9th m^o 1760

Was our monthly meeting of women friends held in **Dartmouth**
where **Joseph Slaid** [**Slade**] and **Deborah Howland** Laid their Intention
of marriage they were Desired to wait for their answer untill
the Next monthly meeting **Kezia Wood** & **Zerviah Howland** are
to make Enquiery into her Clearness & Conversation and make
return to the Next monthly meeting the friends appointed to
attend the Quarterly meeting is **Kezia Wood** & **Sarah Gifford**
this meeting hath made Choise of **Hannah Tucker Alice Anth-**
-ony Elisabeth Smith for to Visit friends families in **apponegan-**
sett the year Ensuing and for **aquishnet Sarah taber Hannah**
Hathaway and **Lois Hathaway Apphia Mott Elisabeth Smith**
is to Draw an Epistle to the Quarterly meeting now Ensuing
no Collection at this meeting

The 20th of Y^e 10th m^o 1760

Was our monthly meeting of women friends held in **Dartmouth**

where **Joseph Slaid** [**Slade**] and **Deborah Howland** both appeared and
Signified the Continuation of their Intention of marriage and there
appearing Nothing that hindered their answer was they might
proceed in marriage between this and the Next monthly meeting
Observing Good orders, No collection at this meeting

The 13th of Y^e 11th m^o 1760

Was our monthly meeting of women friends held in **Dartmouth**
Deborah Haydons [**Haydens**] Certificate was read and well Accepted. No
Collection at this meeting

The 15th of Y^e 12th m^o 1760

Was Our monthly meeting of women friends held in **Dartmouth**
where **Apphia Mott** and **Elisabeth Smith** were appointed to
Draw an Epistle to the Ensuing Quarterly meeting and to answer
the Queries Collected at this meeting   £00-13-10

The 19th of Y^e 1st m^o 1761

Was our monthly meeting of women friends held in **Dartmouth**
No business Presented from the Quarterly meeting no Collection
at this meeting

The 16th of Y^e 2d m^o 1761

Was our monthly meeting of women friends held in **Dartmouth**
where **Weston Briggs** and **Phebe Russell** Laid their Intention
of marriage they were Desired to wait for their answer untill
the Next monthly meeting **Hope Brigs** [**Briggs**] and **Alice Anthony**
are appointed to make Enquiery into the young womans Clearness
and Conversation and make return to the Next monthly
meeting **Ruth Gifford** and **Mary Hammond** have both made
friends Satisfaction for their marrying out of the Good order
of friends no Collection at this meeting **mary Wilber** is Denied
for marry [*sic*] out of the Good order of friends

The 16th of Y^e 3d m^o 1761

Was our monthly meeting of women friends held in **Dartmouth**
where **Weston Briggs** and **Phebe Russell** both appeared
and Signified the Continuation of their Intention of marriage
and they appearing Clear from all others their Answer was
that they might Proceed in Marriage between this and the
Next monthly meeting observing Good orders; **Mary Akins** [**Akin**] hath
made Satisfaction for her marrying out of the Good order of
friends **Apphia Mott** & **Elisabeth Smith** is to Draw an Epistle
to the Ensuing Quarterly meeting the friends appointed to attend
the Quarterly meeting is **Jane Smith** & **hannah Wood** no Collection
at this meeting

The 20th of Ye 4th mo 1761

Was our monthly meeting of women friends held in **Darthmouth**
taken out of the Stock for the use of friends £6-00-00
Apphia Mott Elisabeth Smith and **Ruth Tucker** are appointed
to ballance the accompts of this meeting Collected at this meeting £1-11-3

The 16th of Ye 5th mo 1761

accompts Ballanced and here remains in the Stock £01-09-00

The 18th of Ye 5th mo 1761

Was our monthly meeting of women friends held in **Dartmouth**
Daniel Russell Mary Russell Joseph Gifford & **Hannah Howland**
Samuel Smith Mary Anthony all Laid their Intention of marriage
before this meeting they were Desired to wait for their Answer untill
the Next monthly meeting **Soviah Howland mary Smith** are
appointed to make Enquiery into the young womans Clearness and
Conversation and make returns to the Next monthly meeting
Collected at this meeting £00-7s-9d **Peace Cornwell [Cornell]** hath made
friends Satisfaction for her marrying out of the Good order of friends

The 22d of Ye 6th Mo 1761

Was our monthly meeting of women friends held in **Dartmouth**
where **Daniel Russell** and **Mary Russell Joseph Gifford**
and **Hannah Howland Samuel Smith** and **Mary Anthony** all
appeared at this meeting and Signified the Continuation of their
Intention of marriage & they appearing Clear from all others
their answer was they might proceed in marriage between this
and the Next monthly meeting according to Good orders Establish
ed among friends. the friends appointed to attend the Quarterly
meeting is **Kezia Wood Elisabeth Smith Apphia Mott** & **Elisabeth**
Smith is to Draw an Epistle to the Same Collected at this meeting 0-7-0 we well accepted the Epistle from **Newport** yearly
meeting **Jemima Allen** Certificate was read and well accepted

The 20th of Ye 7th mo 1761

Was our monthly meeting of women friends held in **Dartmouth**
Collected at this meeting £00-4-6

The 17th of Ye 8th Mo 1761

Was our monthly meeting of women friends held in **Dartmouth**
Mary Cornwell [Cornell] Elisabeth Gidly [Gidley] are appointed to make Enquiery
into the Conversation of **Sarah Barker** & **Sarah Anthony**
when Resident among us no Collection at this meeting

The 21st of Ye 9th mo 1761

Was our monthly meeting of women friends held in **Dartmouth**
where **Abigail Shepherd Hannah** ˄Taber [Hannah?] **Allen Eunice Allen**
all their Certificates were read and accepted **Salomy West** and

Alice Gifford and her Daughter **Rachel** are all taken under
the care of friends according to their request **Sarah Wood**
hath maid friends Satisfaction for her Disorderly Proceedings
the friends appointed to attend the Quarterly meeting is **Patience Russell**
Peace Daval [**Davol**] **Elisabeth Gidly** [**Gidley**] no Collection at this meeting
Apphia Mott & **Elisabeth Smith** are appointed to Draw an
Epistle to the Ensuing Quarterly meeting

<hr>

The 19th of Ye 10th Mo 1761

Was our monthly meeting of women friends held in **Dartmouth**
where **Luthan Wood** and **Sarah Tucker** both appeared and
Signified their Intention of marriage they were Desired to wait for
their answer untill the Next monthly meeting, no Collection at
this meeting

<hr>

The 16th of Ye 11th mo 1761

Was our monthly meeting of women friends held in **Dartmouth**
where **Luthan Wood** and **Sarah Tucker** both appeared and
Signified the Continuation of their Intention of marriage and there
appeared Nothing that hindred their answer was they might
Proceed in marriage between this and the Next monthly
meeting, observing Good orders **Nicolas Davis** and **Sarah**
Williams Laid their Intention of marriage before this meeting
they were Desired to wait for their answer untill the Next
monthly meeting **Elisabeth Gidley** and **Susannah Russell**
were appointied to make Enquiery into the young womans
Clearness and Conversation and make return to the Next
monthly meeting no Collection at this meeting

<hr>

The 21st of Ye 12th mo 1761

Was our monthly meeting of women friends held in **Dartmouth**
where **Nicolas Davis** and **Sarah Williams** both appeared
and Signified the Continuation of their Intention of marriage
and there appearing nothing that hindered them their answer
was they might Proceed in marriage between this & the Next
monthly meeting, observing Good orders appointed to attend
the Quarterly meeting **Apphia Mott Hephzibeh Hussey** and
Jane Smith. **Apphia Mott** & **Elisabeth Smith** is appointed
to Draw an Epistle to the Ensuing Quarterly meeting
no Collection at this meeting

<hr>

The 18th of Ye 1st mo 1762

Was our monthly meeting of women friends held in **Dartmouth**
where **Elnathan Eldredg** [**Eldridge**] and **Ann Allen** Laid their Intention
of marriage before this meeting they were Desired to wait
for their answer untill the Next monthly meeting, **Susannah**

Russell & **Lois Hathaway** are appointed to make Enquiery
Concerning the young womans Clearness and Conversation and
make Return to the Next monthly meeting, **Hannah Gidly** [**Gidley**]
Desired the Liberty of Sitting in the monthly meeting her
request is Granted **Patience** & **Rebecka Tuckers** requests is
Granted as to the Liberty of Sitting in the monthly meeting
Susannah Davels [**Davols**] request is Granted as to be taken under
the care of friends Collected at this meeting £00 -11-6

The 15th of Y^e 2^d m^o 1762

Was our monthly meeting of women friends held in **Dartmouth**
where **Elnathan Eldredg** [**Eldridge**] & **Ann Allen** both appeared at this
meeting and Signified the Continuation of their Intention of marri-
-age & there appearing nothing to hinder their answer was they
might Proceed in marriage between this and the Next monthly
meeting, observing Good orders **Humphry Smith** & **Rebekah**
Slocum Laid their Intention of marriage before this meeting they
were Desired to wait for their answer untill the Next monthly
meeting **Alice Anthony Elisabeth Slocum** were appointed to make
Enquiery into the young womans Clearness & Conversation & make
return to the Next monthly meeting, Also **John Akins** [**Akin**]
and **Peace Russell** Laid their Intention of marriage before this
meeting they were Desired to wait for their answer untill the
Next monthly meeting **Hephzibeh Hussey Jane Smith** were
to make Enquiery Concerning the young womans Clearness &
Conversation and make returns to the Next monthly meeting
Ignatious Dillingham and **Deborah Gifford** both appeared at this
meeting and Signified their Intention of marriage they were Desired
to wait for their answer untill the Next monthly meeting, **Hannah**
Tucker & **frances Bowdish** [**Bowditch**] were to make Enquiery into the young
womans Clearness & Conversation & make return to the Next
monthly meeting **Elisabeth Russell** Now wife of **Elisha Russell**
is Denied for marrying out of the unity friends this meeting
is a[d]journed from ye 15th of ye 2^d m^o to ye 22^d of ye Same
Inclusive Collected at this meeting 0-1^s-8^d at the a[d]journment
of this meeting **Henry Russell** and **Mary Bayton** [**Brayton**] Laid their
Intention of marriage they were Desired to wait for their answer
untill the Next monthly meeting

The 15th of Y^e 3^d m^o 1762

Was our monthly meeting of women friends held in **Dartmouth**
where **Humphry Smith Rebecka Slocum John Akins** [**Akin**] & **Peace**
Russell Ignatious Dillingham & **Deborah Gifford** all appeared
at this meeting and Signified the Continuation of their Intentions
of marriage they appearing clear from all others their answer

was they might Proceed in marriage between this & the Next
monthly meeting according to Good orders **Henry Russell**s &
Mary Braytons answer was they might Proceed in marriage
Between this & the Next monthly meeting; **George Sandford** [**Sanford**] and
Rachel Gifford Laid their Intention of marriage before this meeting
they were Desired to wait for their answer untill the Next
monthly meeting **Kezia Wood** & **Mary Smith** were to make
Enquiery Into the young womans Clearness & Conversation
and make returns to the Next monthly meeting

The 19th of Y^e 4th M^o 1762

Was our monthly meeting of women friends held in **Dartmouth**
where the Several Preparative meetings belonging to this meeting
being Called on here appears **Hepzibeh Hussey Jane Smith** for
Ponagansett [**Apponagansett**] none for **acoxet Elisabeth** and **Lydia Maxfeld** Desires
to be taken under the Care of friends

The 17th of Y^e 5th M^o 1762

Was our monthly meeting of friends held in **Dartmouth**
Elisabeth and **Lydia Maxfeld** are taken under the care of friends
according to their Request no Collection at this meeting

The 21st of Y^e 6th M^o 1762

Was our monthly meeting of women friends held in **Dartmouth**
the Several Preparatives meetings belonging to this meeting being
Called on the Representatives are as followeth for **Ponaganset**
Hepzibeh Hussey Elisabeth Smith for **acoaxet Pace Dival** [**Davol**] **Hannah**
Wood Rachel Riders Request is granted and she is taken under
the Care of friends; we Receiv^d an Epistle from the Yearly
meeting at **Newport** which was Read and well accepted **Peace Wood**
Apphia Mott is appointed to attend the Quarterly meeting **Apphia**
Mott Elisabeth Smith are appointed to write an Epistle to the Ensuing
Quarterly meeting **Amey** [**Almy?**] **Slocum** hath maid friends Satisfaction for
her outgoings **Ruth Sowl** [**Soule**] is Denied at this meeting for marrying
from among friends

The 19th of Y^e 7th M^o 1762

Was our monthly meeting of women friends held in **Dartmouth**
the Several Praparative meetings being called on belonging to this
meeting the Represantatives are as followeth for **Ponaganset Hepzibeh**
Hussey Jane Smith for **acoaxet Kezia Wood Dinah Sowl** [**Soule**] **Peace Wood**
Peace Dival [**Davol**] are appointed to Visit friends families in **acoaxet** for
the year Ensuing Several Epistles were read to Satisfaction

The 16th of Y^e 8th M^o 1762

Was our monthly meeting of women friends held in **Dartmouth**
the Sevcral Preparative meetings being Called on here appears for

Ponaganset **Elisabeth Smith Jane Smith** for **acoaxet Peace Dival** [Davol]
Hannah Wood Elisabeth Smith Deborah Haydon [Hayden] **Reliance**
Shepherd Alice Anthony Jane Smith are appointed to visit friends
families in **Ponaganset** the year Ensuing

The 20th of Y^e 9th M^o 1762

Was our monthly meeting of women friends held in **Dartmouth**
the Several Preparat[i]ve meetings being Called on the Representatives
are as followeth for **Ponaganset Hepzibeh Hussey Jane Smith**
for **acoaxet Lydia Mackember** [Macomber] **Peace Dival** [Davol] **Samuel Shove** & **Rebecka Tucker** Laid their Intention of Marriage before this meeting
they were Desired to wait for their answer till the Next
monthly meeting
The friends appointed to attend the Quarterly meeting is as followeth
Penelope Howland Susannah Allen Sarah Gifford Abigail Tripp Apphia
Mott Elisabeth Smith are appointed to Draw an Epistle to the Ensuing
Quarterly meeting; the Queries were Read and answered in this meet-
-ing this meeting is a[d]journed from ye 20th of ye 9th m^o to ye first
of ye 10th m^o 1762   The first of ye 10th m^o 1762 was our monthly
meeting of women friends held by a[d]journment **Lydia Tripp** was Denied
at this meeting for marrying out of ye unity of friends

The 18th of Y^e 10th M^o 1762

Was our monthly meeting of women friends held in **Dartmouth**
the Several Preparative meetings belonging to this meeting
being Called on the Representatives are as followeth for **ponaganset Hepzibeh Hussey Elisabeth Slocum** for **acoaxet Sarah Mosher**
only **Samuel Shove** and **Rebecka Tucker** both appeared and Signified the Continuation of their Intention of marriage and they appearing Clear from all others Respecting marriage their answer was
that they might Proceed in marriage between this and the Next
monthly meeting according to Good order **Adam Mott** and **Rachel**
Rider Laid their Intention of marriage before this meeting they
were Desired to wait for their answer untill the Next monthly
meeting

The 15th of Y^e 11th M^o 1762

Was Our monthly meeting of women friends held in **Dartmouth**
the Several Preparative meetings being Called on here appears
for **Ponaganset Hepzibeh Hussey Deborah Haydon** [Hayden] none appeared
for **acoaxet Thomas Russell** & **Edith Sherman** Laid their Intention
of marriage before this meeting they were Desired to wait for their
answer till the Next monthly meeting **Abigail Briggs** hath
made friends hath made friends Satisfaction for her marrying
out of the unity of friends **Hannah Dival** [Davol] and **Anna Hix** are
taken under the Care of friends according to their Request

The 20th of Ye 12th Mo 1762

Was our monthly meeting of women friends held in **Dartmouth**
the Several Preparative meetings being called on here appears
for **Ponaganset Jane Smith Sarah Howland** for **acoaxet Hannah
Wood Peace Dival [Davol] Adam Mott & Rachel Rider Thomas Russell**
and **Edith Sherman** all appeared at this meeting and Signified
the Continuation of their Intention of marriage their answer
was that they might proceed between this & the Next monthly
meeting Observing good orders **Ebenezar Mosher** & **Jane Craw**
Laid their Intention of marriage before this meeting they were
Desired to wait for their answer untill the Next monthly meet
ing **Apphia Mott Elisabeth Smith** are to Draw an Epistle to the
Ensuing Quarterly meeting this meeting is a[d]journed untill the
first Sixth Day in the Next month the friends appointed to
attend the Quarterly meeting is **Jane Smith Peace Dival [Davol]**

The 17th of ye 1st mo 1763

Was our monthly meeting of women friends held in **Dartmouth**
Where **Ebenezar Mosher** & **Jane Craw** appeared for their
answer and there appeared Nothing to hinder them Respecting
marriage their answer was that they might Proceed in Some
Convenient time between this and the Next monthly meeting
Observing good orders **Lydia Barker**s Certificate was read and
accepted this meeting is a[d]journed untill the Last fourth Day
in the month

The 21st of ye 2d mo 1763

Was our monthly meeting of women friends held in **Dartmouth**
the Several Preparative meetings being Called on there appeared
for **Ponaganset Hepzibeh Hussey mary Russell** and for **acoaxet
Sarah tripp John Dillingham** and **Ruth Gifford Elihu Russell** and
Elisabeth Slocum all Laid their Intention of marriage before this
meeting they were Desired to wait for their Answer untill the
Next monthly meeting **Cyntha Wood** and **Elisabeth Slocum** are
both taken under the Care of friends according to their Request
Rachel Wood ~~and~~ hath made friends Satisfaction for her outgoings

The 21st of ye 3d mo 1763

Was our monthly meeting of women friends held in **Dartmouth**
the Several Preparatives meetings being Called on here appears
for **Ponaganset Jane Smith Elisabeth Slocum** and for **acoaxet
Peace Dival [Davol]**; **John Dillingham** & **Ruth Gifford Elihu Russell**
and **Elisabeth Slocum** all appeared at this meeting and Signified
the Continuation of their Intention of marriage and they appearing
Clear from all others with respect to marriage their answer was
they might Proceed between this and the Next monthly meeting

Observing Good orders **Henry Smith** and **Cyntha Wood** Laid their
Intention of marriage before this meeting they were Desired to wait
for their answer untill the Next monthly meeting; **Zerviah**
Howland Elisabeth Slocum Sarah Gifford are appointed to talk with
Barshaba Gifford upon her Requesting a Certificate from this
monthly meeting, the friends appointed to attend the Quarterly
meeting is **Peace Dival [Davol] Ruth Tucker Elisabeth Slocum Apphia**
Mott Elisabeth Smith Jane Smith are appointed to Draw an
Epistle to the Same this meeting hath made Choice of **Hannah**
Tucker & **Hepzibeh Hussey** for Elders the Queries was read in this
meeting and answered by the **acoaxet** visiters
Likewise the visiters Inform that they have made a general
visit the matter Concerning **Edith Tripp** is Refered untill the Next
monthly meeting **Alice Smith** her Paper is accepted that She Sees it is
read Publickly **Hepzibeh Hussey** and **Jane Smith** are appointed to Draw
a paper of Denial against **Abigail Mackember [Macomber]** and **Zilpha Dival [Davol]** for thar
Scandalous Proceedings this meeting is a[d]journed untill the first Sixth Day in
Next month **Jemimah Davis** hath made friends Satisfaction for her outgoings

The 18th of ye 4th mo 1763

Was our monthly meeting of women friends held in **Dartmouth**
the several Preparative meetings being Called on here appears for **ponaganset**
Mary Russell for **acoaxet Dinah Sowl [Soule] Henry Smith** and **Cyntha Wood**
both appeared and Signified the Continuation of their Intention of marriage
and there appears nothing to hinder their answer was they might Proceed
between this and the Next monthly meeting according to Good orders **Abner**
Shepherd and **Hannah Gifford** Laid their Intention of marriage before this meeting
they were Desired to wait for their answer till the Next monthly meeting
Alice Smith hath made friends Satisfaction for her outgoings **Hannah**
Tucker and **ruth Tucker** are appointed to make Enquiery Concerning
Francis [Frances] Bowdish her Conversation upon her a Certificate from this meeting
Hannah Tucker and **Ruth Tucker** are appointed to make Enquiery
Concerning **Deborah** and **Ruth Dillingham**s Life and Conversation upon
their Requesting a few Lines from this meeting by way of Certificate and
Likewise they are to Draw them; **Sarah Willcox [Wilcox]** hath mad[e] friends
Satisfaction for her outgoings **Edith Tripp**s Paper is accepted if She Sees it read
Publickly **Alice Anthony Jane Smith Elisabeth Smith Sarah Gifford**
Elisabeth Slocum are Chose visiters for the year Ensuing **Deborah Allen**
is taken under the Care of friends according to her request

The 8th of ye 5th mo 1763

all accompts Ballanced and here Remains in the Stock £4-13-0

The 16th of ye 5th mo 1763

Was our monthly meeting of women friends held in **Dartmouth**
where the Several preparative meetings being called on there appeared

for **ponaganset Patience Russell Pheba Slocum**
for **acoxet Peace Dival [Davol] Sarah Tripp Abner**
Shepherd & **Hannah Gifford** both appeared at this meeting and
Signified the Continuation of their Intention of marriage
and they appearing clear from all others respecting marriage their answer
was that they might Proceed in marriage between this and the
Next monthly meeting observing Good order **Sarah Taber** hath
made friends Satisfaction for marrying from among them and She is taken
under the Care of friends **Deborah** and **Ruth Dillinghams** Certificates
were Signed at this meeting **Apphia Mott Elisabeth Smith** and
Kezia Wood were appointed to view the records **Abigail Mackember [Macomber]**
and **Zilpha Divavls [Davols]** Deniel [Denial] was read Publickly Since the Last monthly
meeting

The 20th of ye 6th m^o 1763

Was our monthly meeting of women friends held in **Dartmouth**
where the Several Preparat[i]ve meetings belonging to this meeting being
Called on here appears for **Apponaganset Alice Anthony Elisabeth Slocum**
none appeared for **acoaxet John Ricketson** and **Patience Tucker** Laid their
Intention of marriage before this meeting they were Desired to wait for their
answer untill the Next monthly meeting the friends appointed to attend
the Quarterly meeting is **Susannah Gifford Patience Russell** & **Elisabeth Smith**
Apphia Mott & **Elisabeth Smith** are appointed to Draw an Epistle to the Ensuing
Quarterly meeting we Receivd an Epistle from the yearly meeting at **Newport**
which was read and accepted **Elisabeth Howlands** Certificate was accepted
this meeting is adjourned untill the first Sixth Day in Next month

The 18th of ye 7th m^o 1763

Was our monthly meeting of women friends held in **Dartmouth**
where the Several Preparative meetings belonging to this meeting being
Called on here appears for **acoaxet Dinah Sowl [Soule] Mary Mackember [Macomber]**
    none for
apponagansett John Ricketson and **Patience Tucker** both appeared at this
meeting and Signified the Continuation of their Intention of marriage and
there appearing nothing to hinder them Respecting marriage their answer
was that they might Proceed in marriage between this and the Next monthly meeting according to the good order Established among friends **freeborn**
Riders Certificate was read and accepted

The 15th of ye 8th m^o 1763

Was our monthly meeting of women friends held in **Dartmouth**
the Several Preparative meetings being Called on here appears for
apponaganset Hepzibeh Hussey & **Elisabeth Slocum** for **acoaxet Hannah Wood**

The 19th of ye 9th m^o 1763

Was our monthly meeting of women friends held in **Dartmouth**

Where the Several Preparitive meetings being Called on here appears for
apponaganset Alice Anthony & Deborah Hayden for **acoaxet Sarah Mosher
Lydia Mackember [Macomber] Benjamin Tucker** and **Silvia Ricketson** Laid their
Intention of marriage before this meeting they were Desired to wait for
their answer untill the Next monthly meeting **Kezia Wood** and **Sarah
Gifford** are appointed to attend the Quarterly meeting **apphia Mott** is
to Draw an Epistle to the Ensuing Quarterly meeting this meeting is adjourned
untill the first Sixth Day in Next month

The 17th of ye 10th mo 1763

Was our monthly meeting of women friends held in **Dartmouth**
where the Several Preparative meetings being Called on there appears
for **apponagansett Elisabeth Slocum** none for **acoaxet Benjamin Tucker**
and **Silvia Ricketson** both appeared at this meeting and Signified the Continuation
of their Intention of marriage there appearing Nothing to hinder thar answer
was they might proceed in marriage between this and the Next monthly
meeting observing good orders

The 21st of 11th mo 1763

Was our monthly meeting of women friends held in **Dartmouth** where the
Several Preparative meetings being Called on there appears for **apponaganset
Sarah Gifford & Deborah Willber [Wilbur] Anna Russells** Certificate was
read and accepted

The 19th of ye 12th mo 1763

Was our monthly meeting of women friends held in **Dartmouth**
where the Several Preparat[i]ve meetings being Called on here appears for
apponaganset Deborah Hayden Elisabeth Slocum none for **acoaxet** this meeting
is adjourned untill the first Sixth Day in Next month the friends appointed
to attend the Quarterly meeting is **Alice Anthony & Elisabeth Slocum Apphia
Mott Elisabeth Smith** are appointed to Draw an Epistle to the Ensuing Quarterly
meeting **Chloe Bowen** is taken under the Care of friends according to her
request

The 16th of ye 1st mo 1764

Was our monthly meeting of women friends held in **Dartmouth**
where the Several Preparative meetings being Called on here appears for
apponaganset Jane Smith Patience Russell none for **acoaxet, francis Coffin**
and **Anna Hussey** Laid their Intention of marriage before this meeting
they were Desired to wait for their answer untill the Next monthly
meeting

The 20th of ye 2d mo 1764

Was our monthly meeting of women friends held in **Dartmouth**
where the Several Preparative meetings being Called on here appears
for **apponagansett Jane Smith Susannah Smith** none for **acoaxet francis
Coffin** and **Anna Hussey** both appeared and Signified the Continuation

of their Intention of marriage and there appearing nothing to hinder them
respecting marriage their answer was that they might proceed between
this and the Next monthly meeting according to good orders **Rebecka Cornell**
is taken under the Care of friends according to her request

The 19th of ye 3^d m^o 1764

Was our monthly meeting of women friends held in **Dartmouth**
the Several Preparative meetings being Called on here appears for **apponagan**set
Hepzibeh Hussey none for **acoaxet Joseph Howland** and **Bethsheba Sherman**
Daniel Smith and **Rebecka Cornell** all Laid their Intention of marriage
before this meeting they were Desired to wait for their answer untill the
Next monthly meeting. **Jona Sowl [Soule]** is taken under friends care according to
her Desire **Sarah tripp** and **Susannah Smith** are appointed to attend the
Quarterly meeting **Hepzibeh Hussey Jane Smith Susannah Smith** are appoint-
-ed to Draw an Epistle to the Quarterly meeting.
this meeting is adjourned untill the first Sixth Day in Next month
Elisabeth Gidley Alice Anthony are appointed to talk with **Lilias Russell**
for her Disorderly proceedings

The 16th of ye 4th m^o 1764

Was our monthly meeting of women friends held in **Dartmouth**
where the Several Preparat[i]ve meetings being Called on here appears
for **apponagansett Alice Anthony Deborah Hayden** none for **acoaxet**
Joseph Howland and **Bethsheba Sherman Daniel Smith** and **Rebecka**
Cornwell [Cornell] all appeared at this meeting and Signified the Continuation of
their Intention of marriage and there appeared nothing to hinder respecting
marriage their answer was that they might proceed in marriage between
and [sic] the Next monthly meeting according to good orders **Lydia Cornwell [Cornell]**
is taken under the Care of friends according to her Desire **Elisabeth Howlands**
acknowledgement is accepted and She remains under the Care of friends
We received an Epistle from the Quarterly meeting which was well accepted
Apphia Mott Elisabeth Smith Ruth tucker are appointed to ballance the
meeting accompts the matter Concerning **Amey Hart** and **Lylias Russell**
is refered untill the Next monthly meeting **Deborah Allen Elisabeth Slocum**
are appointed to make Enquiery into the Conversation of **Elisabeth Allen**
upon her requesting a few Lines by way of Certificate

ye 13th of ye 5th m^o 1764

all accompts ballanced and here remains in the Stock £6-13-14

The 21st of ye 5th m^o 1764

Was our monthly meeting of women friends held in **Dartmouth**
where the several Preparative meetings being Called on here appears
for **ponaganset Hepzibeh [Hussey?] Deborah**
Hayden for **acoaxet Hannah Wood Sarah Tripp** this meeting
appoints **Abigail Tripp Hannah Wood** to talk with **Hannah Potter** for

her Disorderly Proceedings in keeping company Contrary to the
orders of friends no Collection at this meeting **Lydia
Sherman** is Denied at this meeting for marrying out of the
orders of friends **Naomy Sisson** is taken under the Care of friends
at this meeting according to her Request

The 18th of ye 6th mo 1764

Was our monthly meeting of women friends held in **Dartmouth**
where the Several Preparative meetings being Called on here appears for
Ponaganset Hannah Tucker Hepzibeh Hussey for **acoaxet Hannah Cornwell
Jona Sowle [Soule]**; **Stephen Hathaway Abigail Smith** Laid their Intentions of marriage before this meeting they were Desired to wait for their answer untill
the Next monthly meeting **Susannah Gifford Hannah Tucker** are appointed to attend the Quarterly meeting. **Apphia Mott Elisabeth Smith** are to Draw
an Epistle to the Same this meeting is a[d]journed untill the first Sixth Day in
Next month

The 16th of ye 7th mo 1764

Was our monthly meeting of women friends held in **Dartmo**
Wher[e] the Several Preparative meetings being called on here appears
Alice Anthony Zerviah Howland for **ponaganset** for **acoaxet Abigail
Tripp Stephen Hathaway Abigail Smith** both appeared at this meeting
and Signified the Continuation of their Intention of marriage and there appears
Nothing to hinder respecting marriage their answer was they might proceed
Between this and the Next monthly meeting according to good orders Establish[d]
among friends **Jemimah Hoxie** and **mary Tucker**s Certificates were accepted
at this meeting we received an Epistle from **Newport** which was re[a]d and
accepted **Hannah Potter** is Denied at this meeting for marrying Contrary
to the order of friends the thing Concerning Choosing overseers is refered
untill the Next monthly meeting this meeting is a[d]journed untill the
twenty fifth Day of this month at the ajournment of this meeting **Elisabeth
Allen**s Certificate was Signed according to her request

The 20th of ye 8th mo 1764

Was our monthly meeting of women friends held in **Dartmouth**
Where the Several Preparative meetings being Called on here appears for
ponagansett Hannah Tucker for **acoaxet Lydia
Mackember [Macomber] Apphia Mott Elisabeth Smith** are appointed t
o Draw ~~an Epistle~~ a Certificate for **Anna Coffin Ruth Eddy** is
publickly Denied for her Disorderly Proceeding

The 17th of ye 9th mo 1764

Was our monthly meeting of women friends held in **Dartmouth**
where the Several Preparative meetings being Called on here appears
for **acoaxet Abigail Kirby** none for **ponaganset** according to the good
orders of friends **Hannah Mosher** is taken under their Care upon her

FIG. 11: *The interior of the Westport Meeting House.*
© Copyright Jean Schnell

Request this meeting hath made Choise of **Hannah Tucker Patience Russell Rebecka Tucker** to attend the Quarterly meeting Next Ensuing **Apphia Mott Elisabeth Smith** are appointed to Draw an Epistle to the Same the thing Concerning Chuseing overseers is refered till the Next monthly meeting Collected 00-02-0 **Anna Coffin**s Certificate was Signed at this meeting this meeting is a[d]journed untill the first Sixth Day in Next month

The 15th of ye 10th m^o 1764

Was our monthly meeting of women friends held in **Dartmouth** where the Several preparative meetings being Called on here appears for **Ponaganset Hepzibeh Hussey Deborah Haydon [Hayden]** for **acoaxet Dinah Sowl [Soule] Jona Sowl [Soule] Benjamin Wing** and **mary Potter** Laid their Intention of marriage before this meeting they were Desired to wait for their answer untill the Next monthly meeting

The 19th of ye 11th m^o 1764

Was our monthly meeting of women friends held in **Dartmouth** where the Several Preparative meetings being Called on here appears for **Ponagansett Hepzibeh Hussey Jane Smith** for **acoaxet Dinah Sowle Susannah**

Cornwell [Cornell] Benjamin Wing and **Mary Potter** both appeared at this meeting
and Signified the Continuation of their Intention of marriage and there appearing
Nothing to hi[n]der them Respecting Marriage their answer was they might
Proceed between this and the Next monthly meeting according to good orders
Established among friends **mary Kirby**s acknowledgment is accepted and
She is taken under friends Care **Meribah Mosher** is taken under the Care
of friends upon her Request Collected at this meeting 00-13-6.
this meeting a[d]journed untill tomorrow at the a[d]journment of this meeting
it was Conclu[d]ed that all offenders Should appear at the monthly meeting
themselves and bring their Confession **Kezia Wood Dinah Russell Elisabeth
Smith** are appointed to talk with **Abigail Bennit [Bennett]** Concerning the writing
she sent to this meeting

The 17th of ye 12th m^o 1764

Was Our monthly meeting of women friends held in **Dartmouth**
where the Several Preparative meetings being Called on here appears for
Ponaganset Hepzibah Hussey Jane Smith None for **acoaxet William
Hathaway** and **Ruth Barker** Laid their Intention of marriage before
this meeting they were Desired to wait for their answer untill the Next
monthly meeting **Hepzibeh Hussey** and **Deborah Haydon [Hayden]** are appointed
to attend the Quarterly meeting **Hepzibeh Hussey Jane Smith Deborah
Haydon [Hayden]** are appointed to Draw an Epistle to the Ensuing Quarterly meeting
no Collection at this meeting this meeting hath made Choise of **Apphia
Mott Elisabeth Smith Alice Anthony Hepzibeh Hussey Ruth Tucker**
for overseers this year this meeting is a[d]journed untill the twenty Sixth
Day of this month **Apphia Mott Elisabeth Smith Ruth Mosher** are
appointed to Receive the Book of Discipline and to peruse it and return
it to the monthly meeting

The 21st of ye 1 mo 1765

Was our monthly meeting of women friends held in **Dartmouth**
where the Several Preparative meetings being Called on here appears for
Ponaganset Hannah Tucker Mary Russell for **acoaxet Mary Wing
William Hathaway** and **Ruth Barker** both appeared at this meeting
and Signified the Continuation of their Intention of marriage and there appear
ing nothing to hinder them Respecting marriage their answer was that they
might Proceed between this and the Next monthly meeting according to
good orders Established among friends **Zerviah Howland Jane Smith**
and **Jemimah Davis** are appointed overseers of ye poor the year Ensuing
taken out of the Stock for the use of friends £02-07 We Received an Epistle
from the Quarterly meeting which was well accepted

The 18th of ye 2^d m^o 1765

Was our monthly meeting of women friends held in **Dartmouth**
Where the Several Preparative meetings being Called on here appears for
Ponaganset Zerviah Howland Jane Smith none for **acoaxet Ezekiel Comstock**

and **Mary Russell** Laid their Intention of marriage before this meeting they
were Desired to wait for their answer untill the Next monthly meeting
Hannah Tucker Hepzibeh Hussey Susannah Allen were appointed to talk with
Elisabeth Cornwell [Cornell] upon her request of being taken under the Care of friends
Abiel Husseys Certificate was read and accepted Collected at this meeting 00-9-0
Elisabeth Smith Jane Smith Alice Anthony are appointed to go and talk with
Lilias Beard

The 18th of ye 3^d m° 1765

Was our monthly meeting of women friends held in **Dartmouth**
where the Several Preparative meetings being Called on here appears for
Ponaganset Alice Anthony Ruth Tucker for **acoaxet Dinah Sowl [Soule] Ruth Wood**
Ezekiel Comstock & **Mary Russell** both appeared at this meeting and
Signified the Continuation of their Intention of marriage and they appearing
clear from all others Respecting marriage their answer was they might
Proceed between this and the Next monthly meeting according to good orders
Established among friends **Elisabeth Cornwells [Cornells]** request is granted and She is
taken under the Care of friends according to her request **Jona Sowle [Soule] Susan-
nah Cornwell [Cornell]** is appointed to talk with **Patience Sowle [Soule]** upon her request
Hepzibeh Hussey Jane Smith are appointed to Draw an Epistle to the Ensuing
Quarterly meeting no Collection at this meeting this meeting is a[d]journed untill
the first Sixth Day in Next month

The 15th of ye 4th m° 1765

Was our monthly meeting of women friends held in **Dartmouth**
where the Several Preparative meetings being Called on here appears for
Ponaganset Deborah Haydon [Hayden] Jemimah Davis for **acoaxet**
Jona Sowl [Soule] Mary Mackember [Macomber] Patience Sowle
[Soule] is taken under the Care of friends according to her request
Charity Sowle [Soule] is Denied for marrying out of the unity of
friends We Received an Epistle from **Newport** friends which was read
and Kindly accepted **Apphia Mott Elisabeth Smith Ruth Tucker** are
appointed to reckon and ballance the accompts of this meeting

ye 13th of ye 5th m°

all accompts Reckoned and Ballanced and here remains
in the Stock £05-13-0

The 20th of ye 5th m° 1765

Was our monthly meeting of women friends held in **Dartmouth**
where the Several Preparative meetings being Called on here appears for
Ponaganset Alice Anthony Deborah Haydon [Hayden] for **acoaxet Abigail Tripp**
Peace Divaul [Davol] Deborah Haydon Susannah Allen Elisabeth Slocum are Chose
overseers for the year Ensuing **Susannah Clarkes** Certificate was read in
this meeting and accepted **Keziah Wood** & **Deborah Slead [Slade]** are appointed to
make Enquiery Concerning **Cibbels Sissons** Life and Conversation upon her
Requesting a few Lines by way of Certificate from this meeting upon

her Removel to the **Oblong** Collected ~~£2-05~~ 2ˢ-7ᵈ taken out of the Stock
£2-5 for to pay recording the book

The 24ᵗʰ of yᵉ 6ᵗʰ mᵒ 1765

Was our monthly meeting of women friends held in **Dartmouth** by a[d]jour-
nment where the Several Preparative meetings being called on here appears
for **Ponaganset Jane Smith Elisabeth Slocum** for **acoaxet Dinah Sowl [Soule]**
Susannah Cornwell [Cornell] Judah Hix Daughter of **Thomas Hix** and **Susannah**
Allen are taken under the Care of friends according to their request
the Epistle was read which came from **Newport** and kindly accepted
Deborah Slead [Slade] and **Ruth Mosher** are appointed to Draw a Certificate
for **Cibbel Sisson** the friends appointed to attend the Quarterly meeting
is **Jane Smith Peace Dival [Davol] Hepzibeh Hussey Jane Smith** are appointed
to Draw an Epistle to the Ensuing Quarterly meeting Collected at this
meeting 0-13-12

The 15ᵗʰ of yᵉ 7ᵗʰ mᵒ 1765

Was our monthly meeting of women friends held in **Dartmouth**
where the Several Preparative meetings being Called on here appears for
Ponaganset Susannah Smith Mary Smith for **acoaxet Mary Wing**
Hannah Dival Zepheniah Anthony and **Wait Allen** Laid their Intention
of marriage before this meeting they were Desired to wait for their answer
untill the Next monthly meeting we Received the Epistle from **Newport**
which was well accepted **Lilias Beard** hath made friends Satisfaction
for her out goings and her paper accepted upon some Consideration

---

The 19ᵗʰ of yᵉ 8ᵗʰ mᵒ 1765

Was our monthly meeting of women friends held in **Dartmouth**
where the Several Preparative meetings being Called here appears for
Ponaganset Zerviah Howland for **acoaxet Peace Dival Zepheniah**
Anthony and **wait allen** both appeared at this meeting & Signified
the Continuation of their Intention of marriage and there appearing
Nothing to hinder them Respecting marriage their answer they [*sic*] might
Proceed between this and the Next monthly meeting according to Good
Orders **Benjamin Dival [Davol]** & **Patience Sowle [Soule]** Laid their
Intention of marriage before this meeting they were Desired to wait
for their answer until the Next monthly meeting **Elisabeth White**
wife of **William White** and **Elisabeth Mackember [Macomber]**
are taken under the Care of friends according to their Request

---

The 16ᵗʰ of yᵉ 9ᵗʰ mᵒ 1765

Was our monthly meeting of women friends held in **Dartmouth**
where the Several Preparative meetings being Called on here appears for
Ponaganset Susannah Smith Anna Howland for **acoaxet Susannah**
Cornwell Hannah Dival Benjamin Dival [Davol] and **Patience Sowle [Soule]** both
appeared at this meeting and Signified the Continuation of their Intention

of marriage and their answer was they might Proceed between this
and the Next monthly meeting according to good orders Established
among friends **Sarah Mosher** and **Sarah Gifford** to attend the Quarterly
meeting **Susannah Smith** & **Anna Howland** are appointed to Draw an
Epistle to the Same this meeting is a[d]journed untill the first Sixth
Day in next month **Phebe Wilber [Wilbur]** is Publickly Denied for her misconduct

The 21st of ye 10th mo 1765

Was our monthly meeting of women friends held in **Dartmouth**
where the Several Preparative meetings being called on here appears for
Ponaganset none for **acoaxet Joan Sowle [Soule] John Howland** and **Hannah
Smith** Laid their Intention of marriage before this meeting they were
Desired to wait for their answer untill the Next monthly meeting
Hannah Russells Certificate was accepted at this meeting

The 18th of ye 11th mo 1765

Was our monthly meeting of women friends held in **Dartmouth**
where the Several Preparative meetings being called on here appears for
Ponaganset Alice Anthony Patience Russell none for **acoaxet John Howland**
and **Hannah Smith** both appeared at this meeting and Signified the Continuation of their Intention of marriage and there appearing nothing to hinder
them Respecting marriage their answer was they might Proceed
between this and the Next monthly meeting according to good orders **Seth
Russell** and **Kezia Walker** Laid their Intention of marriage before
this meeting they were Desired to wait for their answer untill the Next
monthly meeting **Bridget Potter** hath made friends Satisfaction for her
marrying out of their orders **Abigail Slade** hath made Satisfaction for her
Disorderly Proceedings this meeting makes Choise of **Alice Anthony** and
Susannah Smith to Draw a Certificate for **Bridget Potter** and Bring
to the Next monthly meeting

The 16th of ye 12 mo 1765

Was our monthly meeting of women friends held in **Dartmouth**
where the Several Preparative meetings being called on here appears for
**Ponagansett [Apponagansett] Susannah Allin [Allen] Jemimah
Davis** for **acoaxet Hannah Wood Peace Divaul [Davol] Seth Russell**
and **Kezia Walker** both appeared at this meeting and Signified that
they Remained of the Same mind Respecting marriage and their
answer was that they might Proceed between this and the Next
monthly meeting according to good orders this meeting is a[d]journed
untill the first Sixth Day in Next month **Alice Anthony Susannah
Smith** are appointed to Draw an Epistle to the Next Quarterly meeting

The 20th of ye 1st mo 1766

Was our monthly meeting of women friends held in **Dartmouth**
Where the Several Preparative meetings being Called on here appears for

Ponaganset Mary Russell Hepzibeh Hussey none for **acoaxet** this meeting
is a[d]journed untill the twenty Ninth Day of this month athe [at the] a[d]journment of
this meeting **Bridget Potter**s Certificate was Signed

The 17th of ye 2^d m^o 1766

Was our monthly meeting of women friends held in **Dartmouth**
where the Several Preparative meetings being Called on here appears for
Ponaganset Hepzibeh Hussey Mary Russell for **acoaxet Dinah Sowl** [Soule]
Susannah Cornwell [Cornell]

The 17th of ye 3^d m^o 1766

Was our monthly meeting of women friends held in **Dartmouth**
where the Several Preparative meetings being Called on here appears for
Ponaganset Alice Anthony Jemima Davis none for **acoaxet**
Ruth Tripp Rebeckah Tripp Lydia Tripp are taken under the Care
of friends according to their Desire this meeting is a[d]journed untill the
first Sixth Day in Next month **Hepzibeh Russell Jane Smith** are
appointed to Draw an Epistle to the Ensuing Quarterly meeting

The 21st of ye 4th m^o 1766

Was our monthly meeting of women friends held in **Dartmouth**
where the Several Preparative meetings being called on here appears for
Ponaganset Alice Anthony Susannah Smith for **acoaxet Jane Sowle** [Soule]
Susannah Cornwell [Cornell] the friends that Laid their Intention of marriage
before the Last monthly meeting all appeared at this meeting and Signified
the Continuation of their Intention of marriage and there appearing Nothing
to hinder them Respecting marriage their answer they might Proce[e]d between

William Hart this and the Next monthly meeting according to good orders we received an Epistle
& Esther Slade from the Quarterly meeting which was read and kindly accepted **Meriah Smith**s
Laid their Certificate was read and approved of **Amey Hart** hath made friends Satisfac-
intention of tion for her Disorders **Rebecka Russell** is taken under the Care of friends
marriage according to her request **Judah Russell** is taken under the Care of friends
4 mo 1766

Edmund **Alice Anthony Susannah Smith** are appointed to talk with **Patience Russell**
Maxfield & upon her Desire of being taken under the Care of friends **Elisabeth Smith**
Rachel Russell **Ruth Mosher Alice Anthony Susannah Smith** are Chose overseers for the
4 mo 1766 year Ensuing **Easther Slaed**s [**Esther Slade**s] Certificate was accepted

The 13 of ye 5th m^o 1766

all accompts reckoned & Ballanced and here remains in the Stock £4-12-9

The 19th of ye 5th m^o 1766

Was our monthly meeting of women friends held in **Dartmouth**
where the Several Preparative meetings being Called on here appears for
Ponaganset Susannah Smith Mary Smith for **acoaxet Dinah Sowle Sarah tripp**
Edward Wing Eddy Tucker Thomas Smith and **Rebecka Howland** all Laid
their Intention of marriage before this meeting they were Desired to wait
for their answer untill the Next monthly meeting

Patience Russell is taken under the care of friends **Elisabeth Tucker**
Hath made friends Satisfaction for her many Disorders and friends accepts
her under their Care **Susannah Smith** and **Mary Smith** are appointed
to write a Denial against **Susannah Brightman** and bring to the Next
monthly meeting

The 23^d of ye 6th m^o 1766

Was our monthly meeting of women friends held in **Dartmouth**
Where the Several Preparative meetings being called on here appears for
**Ponaganset Alice Anthony Hepzibeh Hussey Edward Wing Edith Tucker
Thomas Smith** and **Rebecka Howland** all appeared at this meeting and
Signified the Continuation of their Intention of marriag their answer was
they might Proceed between this and the Next monthly meeting according
to good orders **William Ricketson** and **Elisabeth Smith** Laid their intention
of marriage before this meeting they were Desired to wait for their answer
untill the Next monthly meeting **Susannah Smith** and **Mary Smith** are
appointed to Draw a Certificate for **Deborah Slaid** and her Children **Kezia Wood
Elisabeth Tucker** are Chose to attend the Quarterly meeting Next Ensuing
Susannah Smith and **Mary Smith** are to Draw an Epistle to the Said
this meeting is ajourned untill the first Sixth Day in Next month

The 21st of ye 7th m^o 1766

Was our monthly meeting of women friends held in **Dartmouth**
Where the Preparative meeting being called on here appears for
Ponaganset Deborah Hix only **William Ricketson** and **Elisabeth Smith**
both appeared at this meeting and signified the Continuation of their Intention
of marriage their answer was they might proceed between this and the Next
monthly meeting according to good orders **Susannah Smith** and **Mary
Smith** are appointed to Draw a Certificate for **Abigail Slaits** and brought
to the Next monthly meeting **Deborah Slaid**s Certificate was Signed at
this meeting

The 18th of ye 8th m^o 1766 --

Was our monthly meeting of women friends held in **Dartmouth**
Where the Preparative meeting being called on here appears for
Ponaganset Alice Anthony Anna Rowland

The 15th of ye 9th m^o 1766

Was our monthly meeting of women friends held in **Dartmouth**
Where the Representatives being called on but none appeared the friends
appointed to attend the Quarterly meeting is **Kezia Wood Ruth Mosher**
and **Mary Smith** is appointed to Draw an Epistle to the Same

The 20th of ye 10th m^o 1766

Was our monthly meeting of women friends held in **Dartmouth**
Where the Representatives being Called on here appear for **Ponaganset
Hannah Tucker Hepzibeh Hussey** we Received an Epistle from the

Quarterly meeting which was read to Satisfaction

The 16th of ye 11th mo 1766

Was our monthly meeting of women friends held in **Dartmouth**
Where **Hepzibeh Hussey** appeared for **Ponaganset Timothy Howland**
and **Susannah Allen** Laid their Intention of marriage before this meeting
they were Desired to wait for their answer untill the Next monthly
meeting

The 15th of ye 12th mo 1766

Was our monthly meeting of women friends held in **Dartmouth**
the representatives being Called on **Deborah Hix** appeared **Timothy
Howland** and **Susannah Allen** both appeared at this meeting and
Signified that they remained of ye Same mind respecting marriage
their answer was they might Proceed in marriage between this and
the Next monthly meeting according to good orders the Queries were
Read and answered **Hepzibeh Hussey Deborah Haydon** are appointed
to Draw an Epistle to the Ensuing Quarterly meeting **Alice Anthony** and
Susannah Smith are Desired to Draw a Certificate for **Abigail Hathaway**
and bring it to the Next monthly meeting **John Williams** and wifes
Certificate was read at this meeting and accepted

The 19th of ye 1st mo 1767

Was our monthly meeting of women friends held in **Dartmouth**
Where the representatives being called on there appears **Anna Howland Sarah
Anthony Elisabeth Russell** is taken under the care of friends according to her request
We Received the Epistle from the Quarterly meeting which was read to Satisfaction

The 16th of ye 2d mo 1767

Was our monthly meeting of women friends held in **Dartmouth**
Where the Representatives being called here appears **Hepzibeh Hussey Deborah
Haydon**

The 16th of ye 3d mo 1767

Was our monthly meeting of women friends held in **Dartmouth**
the meeting being called on here appears for **Ponaganset Hannah Tucker
Mary Russell Thomas Akins Rebecka Russell** Laid their Intention of marriage before this meeting they were Desired to wait for their answer untill
the Next monthly meeting **Alice Anthony Susannah Smith** are appointed
to Draw an Epistle to the Ensuing Quarterly meeting

The 20th of ye 4th mo 1767

Was our monthly meeting of women friends held in **Dartmouth**
this meeting being called on here appears for **ponaganset Hannah Tucker
Alma Barker Thomas Akins Rebeckah Russell** both appeared at this
meeting and Signified the Continuation of their Intention of marriage their
answer was they might Proceed between this and the Next monthly meeting
Timothy Russell and **Hannah Briggs** Laid their Intention of marriage

before this meeting they were Desired to wait for their answer untill the
Next monthly meeting

The 18ᵗʰ of yᵉ 5ᵗʰ mº 1767

Was our monthly meeting of women friends held in **Dartmouth**
this meeting being called on here appears for **ponaganset Hepzibeh
Hussey Deborah Haydon Timothy Russell** and **Hannah Briggs** both
appeared at this meeting and Signified that they remained of yᵉ same
mind respecting marriage and their answer was they might proceed
between this and the Next monthly meeting **Elisabeth Smith** and
Susannah Russell are appointed to talk with **Eunice Kirby** for her
Marrying from among friends it is the Conclution of this meeting
that **Phebe Sisson** Should be Denied for marry from among friends

The 12ᵗʰ of yᵉ 6ᵗʰ mº 1767

Was our monthly meeting of women friends held in **Dartmouth**
this meeting being called on here appears none for **ponaganset
Apphia Mott Alice Anthony** are Appointed to attend the Quarterly
meeting **Phebe Allen** and **Eddy Wing** hath made Satisfaction for their
outgoings **Hannah Tucker** is appointed to assist concerning Setling
this meetings acompts

The 1ˢᵗ of yᵉ 7ᵗʰ mº 1767

all accompts ballanced and here Remains in the Stock £8-0-8

The 22ᵈ of yᵉ 7ᵗʰ mº 1767

Was our monthly meeting of women friends held in **Dartmouth**
this meeting being called on here appears for **Ponaganset Hannah
Tucker Hepzibeh Hussey** we Received an Epistle from the Quarterly
meeting which was read and kindly accepted

The 17ᵗʰ of yᵉ 8ᵗʰ mº 1767

Was our monthly meeting of women friend held in **Dartmouth**
this meeting being called on here appears for **ponaganset Susannah Allen
Jemima Davis Elisabeth Slocum** and **Jemima Davis** are appointed
overseers of the poor for the year Ensuing **Alice Anthony Elisabeth
Smith** are to suppress difficulty if any should arise **Rachel Wilber** is taken
under the care of friends according to her Request.

The 21ᵗʰ of yᵉ 9ᵗʰ mº 1767

Was our monthly meeting of women friends held in **Dartmouth**
this meeting being called on here appears for **ponaganset Elisabeth
Smith Susannah Smith David Anthony** and **Judith Hix** Laid their Intention
of marriage before this meeting they were Desired to wait for their
answer untill the next monthly meeting **Eunice Kirby** hath made
friends Satisfaction for her marrying out of their orders appointed to
attend the Quarterly meeting **Hannah Tucker Sarah Gifford**
the Queries was read and answers accepted the Epistle was read and
approved of

The 19th of ye 10th mo 1767

Was our monthly meeting of women friends held in **Dartmouth**
this meeting being called on here appear **Deborah Haydon** and
Deborah Hix David Anthony and **Judith Hix** both appeared and
Signified that they remained of the Same mind Respecting marriage
and their answer was they might Proceed Between this and the
Next monthly meeting observing good orders **Sharech Dennis**
and **Abiel Hussey** Laid their Intention of marriage before this
meeting they were Desired to wait for their answer untill the Next monthlymeeting

The 16th of ye 11th mo 1767

Was our monthly meeting of womens friends held in **Dartmouth**
this meeting being called on but none appeared **Shadrech Dennis**
and **Abiel Hussey** both appeared and Signified the continuation of
their Intention of marriage their answer was they might proceed
observing good orders Whereas our monthly meeting of women
friends was not held on ye 21th of ye 12th mo 1767 as it should
have been according to course by reason of the coldness of the weather
and we think we may acknowledge there was too much Luke warmness
and Indifferency we therefore have by the advice of ye men friends
called a meeting ye 29th of ye Same month Inclusive of carry on
our Discipline **Hepzibeh Hussey** and **Jane Smith** are appointed
to Draw an Epistle to the Quarterly meeting this meeting is
ajourned into ye 6th of ye 1st mo ye 6th of ye 1st mo was our
monthly of women friends held by ajournment

The 18th of ye 1st mo 1768

Was our monthly meeting of women friends held in **Dartmouth**
this meeting being called on here appears **Elisabeth Slocum Deborah Hix**
we Received an Epistle from the Quarterly meeting which was read
and well accepted

The 15th of ye 2d mo 1768

Was our monthly meeting of women friends held in **Dartmouth**
this meeting being called on here appears **Eunice Allen Elisabeth
Slocum Daniel Ricketson** and **Rebecka Russell** Laid their Intention
of marriage before this meeting they were Desired to wait for their
answer untill the Next monthly meeting

The 21st of ye 3d mo 1768

Was our monthly meeting of women friends held in **Dartmouth**
this meeting Called on **Deborah Hix** and **Sarah Howland** appears
Daniel Ricketson- and **Rebecka Russell** both appeared at this meeting
and Signified that they remained of the same mind and respected marriage
and their answer was they might Proceed between this and the Next monthly
meeting **Benjamin Wing** and **Peace Gifford** Laid their Intention of
marriage before this meeting they were Desired to wait for their answer

untill the Next monthly meeting

The 18<u>th</u> of ye 4<u>th</u> m^o 1768

Was our monthly meeting of women friends held in **Dartmouth**
this meeting being Called on **Elisabeth Slocum Deborah Hix** appears
Benjamin Wing and **Peace Gifford** both appeared and Signified that they remained
of the Same mind respecting marriage and their answer was they might
Proceed between this and the Next monthly meeting **David Allen** and **Hannah
Ricketson** Laid their Intention of marriage before this meeting they were Desired to
wait for their answer untill the Next monthly meeting

The 19<u>th</u> of ye 4<u>th</u> m^o 1768

all accompts ballanced and here remains in the Stock £ 9~12~2

The 16<u>th</u> of ye 5<u>th</u> m^o 1768

Was our monthly meeting of women friends held in **Dartmouth**
this meeting being called on here appears **Elisabeth Slocum Deborah Hix**
David Allen and **Hannah Ricketson** both appeared and Signified the
continuation of their Intention of marriage and their answer was they might
Proceed between this and the Next monthly meeting observing good orders

The 22<u>d</u> of ye 6<u>th</u> m^o 1768

Was our monthly meeting of women friends held in **poneganset**
the Representatives are **Alice Anthony Deborah Hix** both present
Barnabas Kirby and **Elisabeth Allen** Laid their Intention of marriage
they were Desired to wait for their answer untill the Next monthly
meeting **Mary Smith Joanna Mosher Eunice Allen** are appointed
to attend the Quarterly meeting the answers to the Queries red in this
meeting and Likewise the Epistle to the Quarterly meeting and approved

The 19th of ye 7th m<u>o</u> 1768

Was our monthly meeting of women friends held in **ponaganset**
the representatives are **Deborah Haydon** and **Susannah Allen**
Barnabas Kirby and **Elisabeth Allen** both appeared and
signified the continuation of their Intention of marriage their
answer was they might proceed in marriage between this and
the Next monthly meeting observing good orders Established among
friends **William Tripp** and **Elisabeth Maxfeld** laid their Intention of
marriage before this meeting and were Desired to wait for their answer
untill the Next monthly meeting we received an Epistle from the
Quarterly meeting at **Newport** which was read in this meeting and well
accepted **Wesson Briggs** & his wifes Certificate was read in this meeting
Signed from **Sandwich** monthly meeting

The 15th of ye 8th m^o 1768

Was our monthly meeting of women friends held in **Dartmouth**
the representatives are **Hephzibeh Hussey Elisabeth Slocum** both present
William Tripp and **Elisabeth Maxfeld** both appeared and Signified the
continuation of their Intention of marriage their answer was they might

proceed in marriage between this and the Next monthly meeting
Observing good orders Established among friends **Deborah Hix**
Susannah Allen are appointed overseers for this Quarter

The 19th of ye 9th mo 1768

Was our monthly meeting of women friends held in **Ponaganset**
the representatives are **Jemima Davis** & **Susanna Allen** both
present **Caleb Mackumber** & **Rachel Wilber** Laid their Intention
of marriage before this meeting, they were Desired to wait for
their answer untill the Next monthly meeting the answer to the
Queries was read in this meeting and Likewise the Epistle and approved on

The 17th of ye 10th mo 1768

Was our monthly meeting of women friends held in **Poneganset**
the representatives were **Alice Anthony** & **Hannah Mosher** both present
Caleb Mackomber and **Rachel Wilber** both appeared and Signified the continu-
=ation of their Intention of marriage their answer was they might proceed
marriage between this and the Next monthly meeting Observing good orders
Established among friends we received an Epistle from our Quarterly meeting
which was read in this meeting and well accepted **Lucy Howland** is taken
under the care of friend according to her request **Judith Anthony**es acknowledgment is accepted & she still remains under friends care

The 21th of ye 11th mo 1768

Was our monthly meeting of women friends held in **poneganset**
the representatives are **Susannah Allen** and **Sarah Gifford** both present
we Received a Letter from the monthly meeting of friends at the **Ninepartners**
to Desire our meeting to Deal with **Elisabeth potter** for her miss conduct
while she was under their care She being moved away and they not having
Oppertunity to Deal with her themselves and upon that account this meeting
hath appointed **Hepzibeh Hussey** & **Jane Smith** to talk with her and make
their returns to the Next monthly meeting

The 19th of ye 12th mo 1768

Was our monthly meeting of women friends held in **Poneganset**
the representatives were **Hepzibeh Hussey** & **Deborah Hix** both present
Peleg Slocum and **Lucy Howland Barnabas Wing** and **Jane Merrihew** all
Laid their Intention of marriage before this meeting and they was Desired
to wait for their answer untill the Next monthly meeting the answers
to the Queries was read in this meeting and Likewise the Epistle to the Quarter
ly meeting and approved on

The 16th of ye 1th mo 1769

Was our monthly meeting of women friends held in **poneganset**
the representatives are **Hepzibeh Hussey Jane Smith** both present
Peleg Slocum and **Lucy Howland Barnabas Wing** and **Jane Merrihew** all
all appeared and Signified the continuation of their Intention of marriage
their answer was they might proceed in marriage between this and the

Next monthly meeting according to the good orders Established among friends
Bartholomew Taber and **Mercy Bowdish Thomas Amey [Almy]** and **Deborah
Allen** all Laid their Intentions of marriage before this meeting they
were Desired to wait for their answer untill the Next monthly meeting

The 20th of ye 2ᵈ mᵒ 1769

Was our monthly meeting of women friends held in **poneganset**
the representatives are **Deborah haydon** not presen **Elisabeth Slocum** present
Bartholomew Taber and **Mercy Bowdish Thomas Amey** and **Deborah Allen**
all appeared and Signified the continuation of their Intention of marriage
their answer was they might proceed in marriage between this and the
Next monthly meeting observing good orders Established among friends

The 20th of ye 3ᵈ mᵒ 1769

Was our monthly meeting of women friends held in **Poneganset**
the representatives are **Alice Anthony** & **Elisabeth Slocum** both present
James Davis and **Patience Russell** Laid their Intention of marriage
before this meeting they were Desired to wait for their answer untill
the Next monthly meeting **Sarah Gifford** & **Phebe Slocum Hannah Mosher**
are appointed to attend the Quarterly meeting the answers to the Queries
was read in this meeting & Likewise the Epistle and approved on

The 17th of ye 4th mᵒ 1769

Was our monthly meeting of women friends held in **Poneganset**
the representatives are **Susannah Allen Deborah Hix** both present
James Davis and **Patience Russell** both appeared and Signified the continuation of their Intention of marriage their answer was they might proceed
in marriage between this and the Next monthly meeting Observing good
orders. Established among friends **Hannah Tucker Elisabeth Smith** are
appointed to make Enquiery concerning the Life and conversation of
Johanna Mosher & **Elisabeth Tripp** upon their requesting a Certificate
from this meeting **Elisabeth Slocum** & **Lydia Wing** are appointed to
talk with **Rachel Mackumber** upon her requesting a certificate
from this meeting **Dinah Ricketson** hath made friends Satisfaction for
her outgoings an Epistle from the Quarterly meeting was read in this
meeting to Satisfaction **Deborah Hix** is appointed Treasurer

The 15th of ye 5th mᵒ 1769

Was our monthly meeting of women friends held in **Poneganset**
the representatives are **Deborah Haydon Jemimah Davis** both present

The 19th of ye 6th mᵒ 1769

Was our monthly meeting of women friends held in **Poneganset**
the representatives are **Alice Anthony Elisabeth Slocum** both present
Our Esteemed friend **Rachel Wilson** hath visited this meeting with
her Certificate from the monthly meeting of **Kindal** in **Westmorland**
yᵉ 24th of yᵉ 6th mᵒ 1768 with the Concuring meetings from the
Quarterly meetings in **Kindal** for **Westmorland** yᵉ 7th of yᵉ 1 mᵒ 1768

which hath been read to good Satisfaction & her visit kindly accepted
Our Esteemed friend **Sarah Hopkins** hath visited this meeting with her
Certificate from the monthly held at **Haddonfield** in the County of **Glou-
cester** ye 9th of ye 5th 1769 which hath been read in this meeting to good
Satisfaction and her visit kindly accepted: **Elisabeth Potter** hath
made friends Satisfaction for her out goings the answer to the
Queries was read in this meeting and Likewise the Epistle to the
Quarterly meeting and approved on **Jane Smith Deborah Haydon**
are appointed to attend the Quarterly meeting **Mercy Taber Elisabeth
Tripp** and **Rachel Mackumber** Certificates was all Signed at this meeting

7th mo
1769　At a Monthly Meeting of women friends held in
　　　　Dartmouth the 17th of the 7th Month 1769
　　　　the Representatives are **Elisabeth Slocum** Present we
H.
Hussey　Received an Epistle from the Quarterly Meeting which was
　　　　Read and kindly Excepted **Hiphsiba Hussey Jane Smith** and
　　　　Deborah Haydon are appointed to Draw a Sertificate for **Edith
　　　　Wing** and **Jane Wing** if upon Enquiry they think Proper this Meeting
　　　　hath made Choice of **Hiphsiba Hussey** for a Clark to the Meeting this
　　　　year **Apphia Mott Hannah Tucker Elisabeth** ˄smith are appointed to purruse
　　　　the Monthly Meeting Minits to See what part they Shall think proper
　　　　to put on Record

8th mo
1769　At a Monthly Meeting f women friends held in **Dartmouth**
　　　　the 21th of the 8th Month 1769 the Representatives are **Deborah Haydon**
Z. Ricket=　and **Amy Barker Deborah Haydon** present **Abraham Smith** and **Zerviah**
=son　**Ricketson** appeared at this Meeting and Signified theire Intention of
　　　　Marriage they are Desired to weight Untill the Next Monthly Meeting
P　for there answer **Peace Shearman** hath made Satisfaction for her
Shearman　Transgression which was the Sin of Fornication **Amy Barker** & **Jemimah
　　　　Davis** are appointed to Make Inquiry into **Zerviah Ricketson** Clearness
　　　　Respecting Marriage and Conversation and make Report to the Next Monthly
J:　Meeting **Jane Wing** and **Edith Wing** Certificates was both Signed to the
Wing　Monthly Meeting of **Sandwich Apphia Mott Elisabeth Smith Alice Anthony**
E:
Wing　**Deborah Hicks Deborah Allen** are appointed Overseers for one year

9 mo
1769　At a Monthly Meeting of women friends held in **Dartmouth**
　　　　the 18th of the 9th Month 1769 the Representatives are **Mary Smith** and **Han=**
Z　**=nah Mosher** both present **Abraham Smith** and **Zerviah Ricketson** appeared
Ricket　for there answer and we finding Nothing to Hinder there answer was
son　they Might proseed to take Each other in Marriage in Some Convenant
R:　Time between this and the Next Monthly Meeting According to the Good
Wing　Order of friends **John Tucker** and **Roda Wing** appeared at this
　　　　Meeting and Signified there Intention of Marriage they are Desireed
　　　　to weight untill the Next Monthly Meeting for there answer and
R:　**Mary Smith** and **Mary Shearman** are appointed to See into **Roda Wing**
Wing　Clearness Respecting Marriage and Conversation and Make Report

to the Next Monthly Meeting **Deborah Allen** and **Susanna Allen** are
appointed to Make Inquiry into **Elizabeth Gifford** Life and Conver=

E:
Gifford   =sation and Draw a Certificate and bring it to the Next Monthly Meet=
=ing if they think proper the Epistle with the answers to the Queries were
Read in this Meeting and approved and Sent up to the Quarterly Meeting
by our Representatives which are **Alice Anthony Deborah Haydon Sarah**

R:
Wing   **Gifford, Roda Wing** hath Produced a Sertificate from the Monthly Meet=
P: =ing of **Acoaksett** which this Meeting Accepts, **Pheby Sisson** hath made friends
Sisson   Satisfaction for Marrying out of the Unity of Friends

[inserted from the end of the book]

At our Monthly Meeting of Friends held in **Dartmouth** on the
18th of the 9th Month 1769
Our Friend **Paul Russell** Aaquainted This Meeting that he
had it on his Mind to Visit **Pembrook [Pembroke]** Quarterly Meeting
which This Meeting has unity with

A True Coppy of a minute of our S^d Meeting [?]
[?] **Russell** Clerk

---

10 mo:
1769   At a Monthly Meeting of women friends held in **Dartmouth**
the 16th of the 10th Month 1769 **Apphia Mott** Chose Clark for this day

R: **John Tucker** and **Roda Wing** appeared for there answer which was they
Wing   Might Proseed to take Each other in Marriage between this and the next
Monthly Meeting According to the Good order of friends **William**

M: **Taber** and **Martha Hart** appeared at this Meeting and Signified there
Hart   Intention of Marriage and was Desireed to weight untill the Next
Monthly Meeting for theire answer **Apphia Mott** and **Ruth Tucker**
are appointed to See into **Martha Hart** Clearness Respecting Marriage
and Conversation and Make Report to the Next Monthly Meeting **Han=**

R   =nah **Tucker** and **Susannah Russell** are appointed to talk with **Rebecca**
Cornel   **Cornel** Concerning her Request to Come under the Care of friends and
Make Return to the Next Monthly Meeting this Meeting hath Signed a

E: Removal Sertificate for **Elizabeth Gifford** to the Monthly Meeting of
Gifford   **Acoakset Naomy Howland** and **Deborah Hicks** are appointed to Draw
a Sertificate for **Mary Haymond** if upon Inquiry they think proper
and bring it to the Next Monthly Meeting

---

11 Mo:
1769   At a Monthly Meeting of women friends held in **Dartmouth**
the 19th of the 11th Month 1769 the Representatives are **Susanna Smith**

P
Barnard   and **Deborah Allen Susanna Smith** present **Peter Barnard Rebecca**
and   **Hussey, John Wood Dina Hussey, Increas Smith Elizabeth Barker** all
R Hussey
D: appeared at this Meeting and Signified there Intention of Marriage
Hussey   and they are Desireed to weight untill the Next Monthly Meeting
E   for there answer **Catherine Briggs** hath ^maid friends Satisfaction **Naomy**
Barker
C: **Howland** and **Naomy Sisson** are appointed to see into **Rebecca Hussey**
Briggs   **Dina Hussey** and **Elizabeth Barker** Clearness Respecting Marriage and
Conversation and Make Report to the Next Monthly Meeting this Meeting

M:
Haymond Hath Signed a Removal Sertificate for **Mary Haymond** wife of **Thomas Haymond** [**Hammond**]to the Monthly Meeting
This Meeting is Aiourned to the 29ᵗʰ of this Instant

11 Mᵒ. At a Monthly Meeting of women friends held by Aiournment the 29ᵗʰ of
1769 the 11ᵗʰ Month 1769 the Representatives being Called none present
M: **William Taber** and **Martha Hart** appeared for there answer which was
Hart they Might Proceed to take Each other in Marriage Between this and the
Next Monthly Meeting according to the Good Order of friends Received an
Epistle from the Quarterly Meeting which was Read and well Excepted

12 Mᵒ At a Monthly Meeting of woman friends held in **Dartmouth**
1769 the 20ᵗʰ of the 12ᵗʰ Month 1769. the Representatives are **Deborah**
R:H **Allen** and **Mary Smith** both present, **Peter Barnard** and **Rebecca**
D:H: **Hussey, John Wood** and **Dina Hussey, Increas Smith** and **Eliza=**
E:B **=beth Barker**, all appeared for there answer which was that
Each Cupple Might proseed to take Each other in Marriage
between this and the Next Monthly Meeting according to the Good
Order of friends **Eunice Allen** is appointed Overseer of Disorders
Susanna Russell and **Susanna Allen** are appointed Overseers of
the poor the Epistle with the answer to the Queries was Read
in this Meeting and approved **Susanna Allen** and **Anna Hicks**
are appointed to attend the Quarterly Meeting and present the
Epistle with the answers to the Queries Collected £1=2s=4d old ten

1 Mᵒ: At a Monthly Meeting of woman friends held in **Dartmouth**
1770 the 15ᵗʰ of the first Month 1770 the Representatives are **Alice Anthony**
S: and **Elizabeth Slocum** and **Alice Anthony** present **Benjamin Howland**
Smith and **Silvester Smith** Signified there Intention of Marriage and was De=
=sired to weight untill the Next Monthly Meeting for there answer
and **Alice Anthony** and **Deborah Hicks** are appointed to Make Inquiry
into **Silvester Smith** Clearness Respecting Marriage and Conversation and
Make Return to the Next Monthly Meeting Received an Epistle from the
Quarterly Meeting which was Read and well accepted **Mary Cornel** wife
M: of **Daniel** hath Produced a Removal Certificate from the Monthly Meeting of
Cornel **Acoakset** which this Meeting Excepts

2 Mᵒ: At a Monthly Meeting of women friends held in **Dartmouth**
1770 the 19ᵗʰ of the 2ᵗʰ Month 1770 the Representatives are **Jane Smith** and
S: **Susanna Allen Jane Smith** present **Benjamin Howland** and **Silvester**
Smith **Smith** did not appear for there answer by Reason there outward
affairs was not Settled to friends Satisfaction this Meeting is Ajorned
to the 29ᵗʰ of this Instant
This Meeting being held by Ajornment the 29ᵗʰ of the 2ᵗʰ Month
1770 the Representatives being Called both present friends having
H: Sufficiently Laboured with **Hiphziba Shearman** for Marrying out
Shear= of the unity of friends and She had no Mind to make friends Satis=
=man

=faction therefore we do Disone the Said **Hiphziba Shearman** from und=
=er the Care of this Meeting

At a Monthly Meeting of women friends held in **Dartmouth**
the 19ᵗʰ of the 3ᵗʰ Month 1770 the Representatives are **Alice Anthony** &

S:
Smith

Jane Smith both present **Benjamin Howland** and **Silvester Smith**
appeared for there answer which was that they Might proseed
In Marriage in Some Convenant time between this and the next

C:
Russell
C:Gifford

Monthly Meeting Observing the Good order of friends **Caleb Russell**
Jur and **Content Gifford** appeared at this Meeting and Signified there
Intention of Marriage they was Desireed to weight untill the Next
Monthly Meeting for there answer **Jane Smith** and **Elizabeth Smith** are
appointed to See into **Content Gifford** Clearness Respecting Marriage and
Conversation and Make Return to the Next Monthly Meeting **Rebecca**
Cornel is taken under the Care of friends this Meeting has Signed a

P: Wing

Removal Sertificate for **Peace Wing** to the Monthly Meeting of **Sandwich**
the Epistle with the answers to the Queries was Read in this Meeting
and approved and **Sarah Gifford** and **Hannah Mosher** are appointed to
attend the Quarterly Meeting and to Present the Epistle with the answers
to the Queries

---

4 Mᵒ
1770

At a Monthly Meeting of woman friends held in **Dartmouth**
the 16ᵗʰ of the 4ᵗʰ Month 1770 the friends appointed to attend this Meeting are

C:
Russell
C:Gifford

Deborah Allen and **Phebe Slocum Phebe Slocum** Present **Caleb Russell**
Jᵘ and **Content Gifford** appeared at this Meeting for there answer which
was they Might proseed in Marriage in Some Convenant time between
this and the Next Monthly Meeting Observing the good order Esta=

R:
Rotch

=blished among friends **Rebecca Rotch** hath brought a Removal Serti=
ficate from the Monthly Meeting of **Rhod Island** which was Read in
this Meeting and Excepted Received an Epistle from the Quarterly
Meeting which was Read and well Excepeted friends having Sufici=

Sarah
Almy

=ently laboured with **Sarah Almy** for Marriing out of the unity of
friends and She haveing no mind to Make friends Satisfaction there
fore we do Disown the Said **Sarah Almy** from under the Care of this
Meeting Collected at this Meeting £1=15ˢ=0ᵈ old tenner

---

5 Mᵒ
1770

At a Monthly Meeting of woman friends held in **Dartmouth**
the 21ᵗʰ of 5ᵗʰ Month 1770 the friends appointed to attend this Meeting

R:
Macom=
=ber

are **Deborah Hicks** and **Mary Smith** both present **Rachil Macomber**
Hath Produced a Removal Sertificate from the Monthly Meeting of
Acoakset which was Read in this Meeting and Excepted friends have=

R:
Rickit=
=son

=ing Sufficiently Laboured with **Rebecca Rickitson [Ricketson]** for falling into the Sin of
Fornication which plainly appeared by her haveing a Child before Mar=
=riage and She not being in a Disposition of Mind to Make friends Satis=
=faction therefore we do publickly Deny the Said **Rebecca Rickitson [Ricketson]** from
being in unity with friends and from under the Care of this Meeting

Collected at this Meeting £1=13ˢ=0ᵈ old tenner

6 Mᵒ.
1770

At a Monthly Meeting of woman friends held in **Dartmouth**
the 18ᵗʰ of the 6ᵗʰ Month 1770 the friends appointed to attend this Meeting are

M:
Gifford
L:
Shearman
R:
Hathaway

Alice Anthony and **Deborah Allen** both present **Mary Gifford** wife of **Obediah**
Gifford is taken under the Care of this Meeting **Leah Shearman** has Made
Satisfaction **Rhoda Hathaway** has Made Satisfaction the Epistle with the
answers to the Queries was Read in this Meeting and approved and **Amy**
Barker and **Phebe Slocum** are appointed to attend the Quarterly Meeting

M:
Manch=
ester

and to Present the Epistle with the answers to the Queries **Mary Man=**
=chester wife of **Job Manchester** hath Produced a Removal Certificate from
the Monthly Meeting of **Rhod Island** which was Read and accepted **Patienc**

P:
Davis
E
Kirby

Davis hath made friends Satisfaction friends haveing Sufficiently Laboured
with **Elizabeth Cirby [Kirby]** for falling into the Sin of fornication and She not
being in a Disposition of Mind to make friends Satisfaction therefore we
do publickly Disown the Said **Elizabeth Cirby** from being in unity with
friends and from under the Care of this Meeting Collected £1=3=2 old tenner

7 Mᵒ
1770

At a Monthly Meeting of woman friends held in **Dartmouth**
the 16ᵗʰ of the 7ᵗʰ Month 1770 the friends appointed to attend this Meeting
are **Susanna Smith** and **Elizabeth** ₍Smith₎ both present Received an Epistle
from the Quarterly Meeting which was Well Excepted
The treasurer hath Paid **Bethiah Wady** 5ˡᵇ-6ˢ-9ᵈ old tenor for yᵉ use
of the poor

8ᵗʰ mᵒ
1770

Att amonthly Meeting of women friends holden at **Dartmouth**
the 20ᵗʰ Day of yᵉ 8ᵗʰ mᵒ 1770

Mosher
Joanna Gifford
Certif recᵈ

Deborah Hix & **Sarah Gifford** was appointed to attend yᵉ monthly
meeting both Preasent **Johannah Mosher** & her family Sertifcate from
The **Nine Partners** was Read in this ₍meeting₎ and Excepted. **Hephzibah Hussey** and **Sarah**

view minits

Gifford are appointed to look Over the Monthly Meeting Minuts & Record what

Rebec: Bernrd
Certif

Is Necary **Rebaca Barnard**s Removal Certificate was Signed In this Meeting

Hep: Hussey
Clerk

To **Nantucket Hephzibah Hussey** is appointed Clark for another year and **Deborah**

Settle with
Treasurer

Hix is to join the above said Com.ᵗᵉ att the Recording the Book and assist In
Setling with the treasurer and see that the book is ballancᵈ ~ ~ ~ ~ ~

9ᵗʰ m.ᵒ 1770

Att amonthly Meeting of Women Friends Holden at **Dartmᵒ** yᵉ 17ᵗʰ Day of
the 9ᵗʰ mᵒ 1770 – the friends appointed to attend this Meeting are **Susannah**

Lemuel Mosher
proposal of
marriage

Allen & **Susannah Smith** Both Preasant, **Lemuel Mosher** & **Ruth**
Gifford appear-d at this meeting & Signified their Intention of Marriage and
were Desired to wait untill the Next Monthly Meeting for their answʳ

Silvia Smith
paper acceptᵉᵈ

Silva Smith Hath Given In a paper to this Meeting Condemning her Marrying
Out of the Unity of friends which is Excepted, **Elisabeth Smith** & **Neoma Howland**

Inquiry to
be made

are appointed to Inquire into **Ruth Gifford**s Clearness Respecting Marriage
and Conversation and Make Report to the next monthly meeting
The queries hath Bean Read & answʳᵈ In this Meeting together with the

sent to Quar^{ly} *meeting* Epistle and **Susannah Smith Susannah Allen** and **Deborah Haydon** are appointed to attend the quarterly meeting and Present the Epistle with the answ^{rs} to the Queries Collected 5^s:7^d old tenor **Susannah Allen Ebenezer**s wife

overseer of poor is appointed Overseer of the Poor This Meeting Concludes to Deny **Rebaca**

Reb. Briggs to be denied **Briggs** for Marrying Out of the unity of friends being Sufficiently labourd With & making No Sattisfaction

10th m^o 1770- At a Monthly Meeting of Women friends Holden at **Dartm.**^o ye 15th of ye 10.th 1770 **Deborah Allen** and **Deborah Hix** was appointed to Represent this Meeting

Lemuel Mosher answer Both Preasant **Lemuel Mosher** and **Ruth Gifford** appeared att this Meeting & Signified the Continuation of their Intention of Marriage with Each other & finding them Clear to proceed their answ^r was that they take Each other In marriage In Some Some Convenient time between this & the next monthly Meeting Observing the Good orders Established amongst friends

Epistle Rec^d Receiv.^d an Epistle from the Quarterly Meeting held at **Portsmouth** on **Rhodisl[and]** which was Read & well Excepted; **Apphia Mott** and **Elisabeth Smith** are

Han. Winslo^w Request appointed to take a solid opportunity with **Hannah Winslow** upon her Request to come under friends Care and Make Report to the next monthly meeting

Mary Gifford req Certifi This Meeting hath Signed a removal Certificate for **Mary Gifford** wife of **Obadiah Gifford** to the Monthly Meeting at the **Nine Partners** In **Dutches County**

Jenaverah Gifford Case **Patience Russell** & **Susannah Smitts** are appointed to write to **Sandwitch** Monthly Meeting to Inform this Meeting how **Janavereth Gifford** hath Conducted Since She has Resided among them

11th m^o 1770 At a monthly Meeting of Women Friends holden at **Dartmouth** ye 19th of 11th m.^o 1770 The Representatives are **Deborah Haydon** & **Jemimah Davis** both Preasant

Han. Winslow Rec^d **Hannah Winslow** is Taken Under the Care of This Meeting: according to

Treasury Settled appointment we have setled with the treasurer and find in the stock 1^{lb}:16^s:6^d

Lydia Potter denied Old tenor: **Lydia Potter**s Paper of Denial was Read according to appointment which testified against her for the Sin of fornication having been Raboured [Laboured] With in Love but our labour Proving Ineffectual Can Do no less then Deny her from being In unity with us and from under the Care of this meeting

Treasurry Collected 2^{lb}:15^s:0^d old tenor: Taken out of the Stock 2:15:9 o^l. t. for the use

Janaverah Gifford Paper of the poor, **Janeverath Gifford** hath Given in a paper to this meeting Condeming her falling Into the Sin of fornication which this Meeting Excepts Provided Said Paper be Read at the Close of a first Day Meeting for worship: She is Excused from being Preasant at the Reading Said paper by Reason of her being at a great Distance and a lame woman & under low Circumstances in the world

Epistle Rec^d Receiv.^d an Epistle from the yearly meeting of women friends held in **Philadephia** for **Penselvana** and **New Jersey** which was Read & kindly Excepted ~ ~ ~ ~

12th m^o 1770 At a monthly meeting of women friends held at **Dartm**^o ye 17th day of 12th m^o 1770 The Representatives are **Alice Anthony** and **Deborah Allen** both Preasant

Jose Gifford Ju proposal of marriags **Joseph Gifford Jn^r** and **Hannah Winslow** Proposed their Intention of marriage with Each other and were Desired to wait untill the next monthly meeting for their answer and **Hannah Mosher** and **Almy Barker** appointed to Inquire

Janaverah Gifford

Sent up to Quart meeting

Phebe Brigg Certifi

Overseers

Into **Hannah Winslows** Clearness Respecting marriage & Conversation and make Report to the Next monthly Meeting: **Janevereth Gifford**s paper hath been Read according to appointment of last Monthly meeting: The queries hath been Read & answrd – In thir meeting. and Sent up to the quarterly meeting with the Epistle By the Representatives which are **Alice Anthony** & **Deborah Allen** **Hephzibah Hussey**: **Phebe Briggs** Removal Sertificate was Signd. in this Meeting Recommending her to **Swansey** Monthly meeting: **Eunice Allen** is Dismist from being an Overseer of this meeting: **Susannah Smith** is appointed an overseer in the Room of **Eunis Allen** who was Dismist.

At 1 mo. 1771

At a monthly meeting of women friends holden at **Dartmo**. ye 27th of ye 1st m.o 1771 The Representatives are **Sarah Gifford** and **Susannah Smith** both Preasant

J: Gifford answer

Joseph Gifford Jr and **Hannah Winslow** appeared at this meeting and Signified the Continuation of their Intention of Mariage their answ.r was they Might Proceed in taking Each other in Some Convenient time between this and the Next monthly meeting Observing the Good orders Established amongst friends

Epistle recd

Receiv,d An Epistle from the last Quarterly meeting which was Read and

Janaverah Gifford Certifi

Kindly Excepted: **Janavareth Gifford** wife of **Silvanus Gifford** ^Certificate was Signd, In this meeting Recommending her to **Sandwitch** Monthly Meeting

2d M.o 1771

At a monthly meeting of Woman friends holden at **Dartm.o** ye 18th day of ye 2d mo 1771 The Representatives are **Jane Smith** and **Phebe Slocum** both Preasant

3d mo. 1771

At a monthly Meeting of woman friends holden att **Dartm.o** ye 18.th of ye 3d m.o 1771

Dinah Wood Certificate

The Representatives are **Alice Anthony** and **Deborah Haydon** both Preasant **Dinah Wood**s wife of **John Wood** Sertificate was Signed in this meeting Recommed. Her to **Acoakset** Monthly Meeting: **Ann Smith** wife of **Thomas Smith** Produced

Ann Smith certificate

A Certificate from **Nantucket** monthly meeting which was Read & well Excepted The queries was Read & answered In this meeting with the Epistle and Sent up to the

Sent up to Q meeting

quarterly meeting by the Representatives which are **Deborah Haydon Elisabeth Slocum** & **Mary Smith**

4th m.o 1771

At amonthly Meeting of women friends holden att **Dartm.o** ye 15th of 4th m.o 1771-

Jonathan Tucker propo =sal of marage

The Representatives are **Deborah Hix** and **Sarah Howland** both Preasant **Jonathan Tucker** and **Mehetable Mosher** both appeared at this meeting & Signified Their Intention of Marriage and were Desired to wait untill Next monthly Meeting for their answr **Apphia Mott** & **Elisabeth Smith** are appointed To Inquire into **Mehetble Moshers** Clearness Respecting Marriage & Conversation

Epistle recd

and make Report to the next Monthly Meeting: Receiv.d an Epistle from the quartly meeting which was Read and kindly Excepted: **Elisabeth Slocum** and **Mary**

Return from Q meeting

Smith Report that that they attended the quarterly meeting: **Susannah Allen** Wife of **Phillip Allen** Excus,d from being Overseer of the poor and appointed

overseer

Overseer of the Church }. Collected 2lb:2s:2d ½ Old tenor

5th m.o 1771

At amonthly Meeting of women friends holden att **Dartm.o** ye 20.th of ye 5.th Mo 1771 - the Representatives are **Deborah Allen** and **Deborah Haydon** both Preasant

Jonaa Tucker answer

Jonathan Tucker & **Mehetable Mosher** appeared at this meeting & Signified the Continuation of Their Intention of Marriage Thiere appearing Nothing to hinder

Therefore your answr̲ is you May Proceed to take Each other in Marriage in Some
Convenient time between this & the next Monthly meeting Observing the Good

Elisa Shepherd Orers Established amongst friends: **Elisabeth Shephard** Produced a certificate
Certifi from **Portsmouth** monthly meeting for **Rhodisland** which was Read in this

overseer of Meeting & well Excepted: **Judith Russel** is appointed Overseer of the Poor friend
poor Collected 1lb:13s:7½ d old tenor the treasurer is Ordered to Pay **Susannah Allen** 4lb:9s:0d

6th mo 1771 At amonthly Meeting of women friends holden att **Dartm.o** y.e 17.th of 6 M.o 1771 -
the Representatives appointed was **Alice Anthony** and **Sarah Howland** they being

ajournd Called **Sarah Howland** Preasant this Meeting ajorns to 24th Instant

mett This Meeting Met according to ajornment ye 24th Instant the Representatives being

Ann Shearman Called Both Preasant This Meeting Concludes to Deny **ann Sherman** from
to be denied being in unity of friends for marrying out from amongst us altho Precotioned

Abig; Winslow **Abigail Winslows** Paper of acknowledgment was Read according to
paper read

Treasurer report appointment the treasurer Reports She has Paid **Susannah Allen**
4lb:9s:0d old tenor according to Order: The queries hath been Read and

Sent up to answer.d In this meeting with the Epistle and Sent up to the quarterly
Q meeting Meeting By The Representatives which are **Alice Anthony Susannah Allen**

Rachel mac= and **Judith Russel: Rachel Macumber** widow Certificate was Signed
comber In this meeting which Recomends her to **Acaksett** Monthly meeting
certifi We have been favoured with the Company of our worthy friend **Joseph Oxley**

Joseph Oxley at this meeting to our Comfort & Sattisfaction with three Sertificates which
Visit Was Read in this meeting One from the Monthly meeting held at **Norwich Old**
England the 23 day of ye 3d mo 1770 And one from the quarterly Meeting in
the County of **Norfolk** at **Norwich** ye 28th Day of ye 3 Mo 1771 The third
from the yearly Meeting of Ministers and Elders held in **London** by A
journments from ye 2d Day of 6th m.o 1770 to the 11 of the Same Inclusive
Expressing their Unity with this Concern to visit us & were signed by a large
Number of friends Both Men & Women

7th mo 1771 At a monthly meeting of women friends holden att **Dartmo** ye 15th of ye 7th mo 1771
The Representative are **Jean Smith** and **Elisabeth Slocum** being Called not Preasant
Abigail Winslow hath Given In apaper to this meeting (which is as followeth)

Abigail To the monthly meeting of friends to be holden at **Dartmo** ye 18th Day of ye 3 M̲o 1771
Winslow Friends whereas I having had my Education amongst friends but through
acknowledg unwatchfullness I haveing fallen Into the Sin of fornication which I am Sorry
ment for and Do Condemn with all my other offences hoping God will forgive me
and friends Pass it by so far as to lett me Remain under their Care **Abigail**

Epistles **Winslow** Recevd an Epistle from the quarterly meeting of women friends held att
received **Newport.** By the hand of our friend **alice anthony** which was Read & well
Excepted and one Epistle from the yearly meeting in **London** which was
likwise Read and kindly Excepted

8th mo 1771 At a monthly Meeting of women friends held in **Dartmouth** ye 19th of the 8th m̲o 1771
the friends appointed to attend the monthly meeting are **Almy Barker** and

Abig; Tucker denial signd	**Jemima Davis** both Preasant **Abigail Tucker**s Paper of Denial was Signed in this meeting in order to be Read at the Close of a first Day meeting for worship & Said Paper to be Return^d to the Clark to be Rcorded:[22]

Abig; Tucker denial signd — **Jemima Davis** both Preasant **Abigail Tucker**s Paper of Denial was Signed in this meeting in order to be Read at the Close of a first Day meeting for worship & Said Paper to be Return^d to the Clark to be Rcorded:[22]

to d^{r}aw a certifi for Elisa: Potter — **Deborah Allen** & **Jamima Davis** are appointed to draw a Certificate for **Elisabeth Potter** & bring to Next meeting if upon Enquirey She is found worthey: **Apphia Mott** & **Elisabeth Smith** & **Susannah Russel** are appointed to take asolid

Mehitabel and Ann Howlands Request — opportunity of Conference with **Mehithabel Howland** and **Anne Howland** upon their Request to See what the Motive of their Request Springs from & make Return to Next meeting: **Alice Anthony** & **Deborah Allen** are appointed to Confer with **Hannah Gifford** on account of her Making friends Sattisfaction and make Report to Next meeting ----

To Revise minits — **Jean Smith Deborah Haydon** & **Hephzibah Hussey** are appoynted to to Peruse the Monthly meeting Minits and Order what is Propper to

and Settle with Tresurer — be Put on Record: & **Deborah Haydon** & **Hephzibah Hussey** are appointed to Settle accounts with the Treasurer & make Report to

To consider the return of Pernal Thurston Certifi — Next Monthly meeting: **Jean Smith Almy Barker** & **Phebe Slocum** are are appointed to Consider the Return of **Pernal Thuston**s [Thurston] Certificate

Order on Treasu^{er} — and make Report to next meeting: Collected £2.2^s.7^d old tenor and the Treasurer is Desired to bring what money there is in the Stock to the Next meeting

---

9th m^o 1771 — At amonthly Meeting of Women friends holden att **Dartm^o** ye 16th 9th m^o 1771 **Deborah Haydon** & **Deborah Allen** are appointed to attend the monthly Meeting both Preasant **Jean Smith** and **Sarah Gifford** are appointed

Lucy Allen & Mary Howland under dealing — to Confer with **Lucy Allen** & **Mary Howland** for marrying out of The unity of friends and make Report to Next meeting: **Abigail**

Abig; Tucker paper read — **Tucker**s Paper of Denial was Read according to appointment of Last Monthly meeting & Returnd to y^e Clark to Record, ~~and is~~

Elisia Potter certifi — **Elisabeth Potter** wife of Recorded in page 268 **Benj^a Potter** Certificate was Sign$^{d·}$ in this Meeting Recommending her to the monthly ₍meting₎ at **Ninepartners**

Mehitabel & Ann Howland referd — The friends appointed to Confer with **Mihithafel Howland** and and **Anne Howland:** Report that they had an opportunity of conferri with them to Such Satisfaction as to Desire this meeting to Refer The Matter to Next meeting Considering it best not to lay Sudden

Han: Gifford refer^d — hands on None: the friends appointed to Confer with **Hannah Gifford** Report they Receiv^d a degree of Good Sattisfaction but this meeting thought Best to Refer the matter till Next meeting under the Same friends Care and Report to next meeting

Miniuts reviewd — Agreable to appointment **Jean Smith Deborah Haydon** & **Hephzibah Hussey** hath viewed the monthly meeting Minits of the last year

Settled with Treasurer — and ordered what Should Goe to Record & likewise we have Setled with the treasurer & find in stock £3=3^s=8^d old tenor: the Com,^{tt} appointed to Consult **Pernal Thurston**s Certificate Make Report

22. **Abigail Tucker**'s denial appears at the end of the book.

The matter Con=
cerning Parnel
Thurston

They think best to Call in Some Men friends and Pay her avissit therefore **Jean Smith** and **Phebe Slocum** are appointed to vissit her. to See what her mind is in Regard to having a Certificate from this Meeting and make Report to Next meeting; **Mary Spencer** broug[ht]

Mary Spencer
Certifi Rec^d

a removal Certificate from the monthly meeting of women friends in **Newport** which was Read & Excepted: **Hannah Tucker** and **Elisabeth**

To draw a Certifi
for Mary Taber

Smith are appointed to Draw a Certificate for **Martha Taber** wife of **William Taber** and bring to Next meeting Such as She is found

Adjourn^d

Worthy of: This meeting to Attourns to the 4th of Next month

9th month
1771
mett

At a Monthly Meeting of women friends held in **Dartmouth** by Aiournment 4th day of the 10th Month 1771 the Representatives are **Deborah Haydon** and **Deborah Allen Deborah Haydon** present the epistle with the

sent up to
Q. meeting

answers to the Queries was Red and approved and Signed in this Meeting and are Sent up by our Representatives who are at this time **Alce Anthony Judith Russell** and **Keziah Russell** and they to Make Report to the Next Monthly Meeting

10 month
1771

At a Monthly Meeting of women friends held in **Dartmouth** The 21 day of the 10 Month 1771 the Representatives are **Susanna Allen**

Lucy Allen
& Mary How
land referd
Mart: Taber
Certifi

and **Sarah Gifford** both present the Matter Concerning **Lusa Allen** and **Mary Howland** is Referred under the Same friends Care until the Next Monthly Meeting and they to Make Report **Martha Taber** wife to **William Taber** had a Removal Certificate Signed in this Meeting to

Ann Howla^nd
& Mehitabel
Howland
Referd

the Monthly Meeting of **Sandwich** the Request of **Anne Howland** and **Mehetable Howland** is Refered under the Care of **Elizabeth Smith** and **Susannah Smith** and to make Report to the Next

Han. Benni^t.
paper to be
read

Monthly Meeting **Hannah Bennit** paper of acknowledgment was Read and Excepted provided she Cause said paper to be Read at the Close of a first day Meeting She being present and then Return Said paper to the Clark to go on Record **Roda Mitchel** wife of

Rhoda
Mitchel
Certifi accepted

James Mitchel hath Produced a Removal Certificate from the Month= =ly Meeting of **Rhodisland** which was Read and Excepted in this

Return from
Q meeting
Epistle rec^d

Meeting the friends that was appointed to attend the Quarterly Made Report that they all attended & have produced an Epistle from the Same which Read in this Mee^ting and the Contents there in well Excepted it is the Conclusion of this Meeting to Disown **Hope**

Hope
Allen
disown^d

Allen wife to **John allen** of the **Nine Pardners** from being in U= nity with friends and from under the Care of this Meeting for her Marring our of the Unity of friends She being timely precautioned

Collection

but to no affect Collected £0:18^s:6^d old tenner

18 mo 11 1771

At a Monthly Meeting of women friends held in **Dartmouth** The 18 day of the 11 Month 1771 the Representatives are **Amy Bar=** =ker and **Elizabeth Slocum** both present the friends appointed to

Mehitabel & Ann How =land Rec^d   Treat with **Mehetable Howland** & **Anne Howland** made a Rep= =ort which was Excepted and the Said **Mehetable Howland** and **Anne Howland** are taken under then Care of friends

Welthen Spencer request   **Welthon Spe= =ncer** Request to Come under friends Care and **Hannah Tucker** and **Susannah Russell** are appointed to take a Solid opportunity of Conference with the particioner to See if her Motive Sprung from the bottom of true Conviction & to Make Report to the next

order on Treasurer   Monthly Meeting the Treasurer is Desired to pay **Jemima Davis** the ballance of her accompt & make Report to Next Monthly Meeting Collected £1:19^s:8^d old tennor this Meeting Aiourns to 27th Instant

neglect meeting   Friends did not Meet according to ajournment and we would Cha= retably hope it was by Reason of the weather being very Rainny yet there appeard Room to Dout that there was two Much Indiffer= =ency among us which we hope to be more Carefull for the time to Come

---

16 m°12 1771   At a Monthly Meeting of women friends held in **Dartmouth** The 16 day of the 12 Month 1771 the Representatives are **Elizabeth Slocum** and **Alce Anthony** both present the men friends Inform us

Barnabas Russell not to proceed   that they think it is not proper for **Barnibus Russell** to pass to day **Hannah Bennit** paper hath been Red according to the appoint=

Han. Bennit acknowledg =ment   ment of Last Monthly Meeting & is Returned to the Clark to be put on Record & is as followeth To the Monthly Meeting of friends held in **Dartmouth**

15 mo 7 1771 H:ben: :nit   The 15 of the 7 Month 1771 Esteemed friends whereas I haveing had my Education amongst friends but through unwatchfullness I have given way to the Temptation of the Enemy So far as to fall into the Sin of fornication which appears by my haveing a Child So Soon after Marriag which I am Sorry for and do Condemn with all other offences hoping that God will forgive me and friends pass it by So far as to let me Remain under their Care   **Hannah Bennet**

Welthan Spencer received   The friends that was appointed to treat with **Welthon Spencer** Report they found Good Satisfaction So this Meeting thinks proper to Except of her under the Care of friends the Epistle with the answers to the Queries was Red in

Sent up to Q meeting   this Meeting & approved & Signed & Sent up to the Quarterly Meeting by our Representatives who are **Elizabeth Smith Jane Smith** and **Elizabeth Slocum** and they to make Report to the Next Monthly Meeting it is the Concl=

P: Thuston   =usition of this Meeting that **Pernal thuston [Thurston]** Should Remain under the Care of this Meeting agreeable to her Request which augh not to be made a presedent

---

20 mo 1 1772   At a Monthly Meeting of women friends held in **Dartmouth** The 20 day of the first Month 1772 the Representatives are **Amy Barker** and **Phebe Slocum** both Present this Meeting id adjourned

adjound mett   to the 29 day of this Instant this Meeting Met According to adiourn=

Wᵐ Russell proposal of marriage	=ment 29 day of the 1 Month 1772 the Representatives being Called both Present **William Russell** and **Welthon Spencer** Signified there Intention of Marriag and was Desired to Wait untill the
Barnabus Russell proposal of marriage	Next Monthly Meeting for their answer **Barnibas Russell** and **Anne Howland** Signified there Intention of Marriag and was Desired to wait untill the Next Monthly Meeting for their answer **Eliza=**
To inquire into the young womens Clearness	=**beth Smith** and **Susanna Russell** are appointed to Make Inquiry into **Welthon Spencer** & **Anne Howland** Clearness Respecting Marriag and Conversation and make Report to the Next
Return from Q meeting	Monthly Meeting **Elizabeth Smith** and **Jeane Smith** Report that they attended the Quarterly Meeting and have produced
Epistle recᵈ	an Epistle from the Same which was Red and advise
Mary Williams Certifi	therein Contained well Excepted **Mary Williams** hath prod= =uced a Removal Certificate from the Monthly Meeting of **Sandwich** which this Meeting Excepted

2 month 1772	At a Monthly Meeting of women friends held in **Dartmouth** The 17 day of the 2 Month 1772 the Representatives are
The young womens clearness	**Jane Smith** and **Jemima Davis** both present the friends appointed to See into the young women Clearness Respecting Marriag and Con= =versation Report that they found nothing to hinder there proseed=
Wᵐ Russell & Barnabus Russell answer	=ing in Marriag **William Russell** and **Welthon [Welthen] Spencer** **Barnibus [Barnabas] Russell Anne Howland** all appeared for there answer which was that Each Cupple Might proseed to take Each other in Marriag between this and the Next Monthly Meeting according to the Good orders of friends the Committe appointed to Labour with
Lusanna Allen disowned	**Lusanna Allen** for her Marriag out of the Unity of friends Report that they have Discharged them Selves and found no Satisfaction & there Labour proved Ineffectual although She hath been much Labou= =red with & Long waited upon therefore this Meeting being Clear of any further Labour do Disone [Disown] the Said **Lusanna Allen** from being one of our Society & from under the Care of friends this Meeting is Informed from the preparative Meeting that
Mercy Phillips under dealing	**Mercy Phillips** hath fallen into the Sin of fornication which plainly appears by her haveing a Child before Marriag there fore **Jane Smith** and **Anne Smith** are appointed to Labour with her as they find Occation & Make Report to the Next Monthly Meeting this Meeting is Informed from the preparative Meeting
Compl[a]int against Deborah Wilbour	that there is a Scandalous Report about **Deborah Wilber [Wilbur]** therefore we do Appoint **Jane Smith Hephzibah Hussey Deborah Allen** & **Susanna Allen** to Inquire into the above Report and Labour as they May find Occation & Make Report to the Next Monthly Meeting

3 Month 1772 At a Monthly Meeting of women friends held in **Dartmouth**
The 16 day of the 3 Month 1772 the Representatives are
Deborah Allen & **Sarah Gifford** and **Sarah Gifford** present

adjournd This Meeting is ajourned to the 3 day of Next Month and
friends did not Meet the weather being Oncommon Stormy but

meett the 4 day of the Same Month a few friends meet a nuf [enough] to

adjournd ajourn the Meeting this Meeting is ajourned to the 7 day of this Instant

mett At a Monthly Meeting of women friends held by ajournment the
7 day of the 4 Month 1772 the Representatives being Called both present

Mercy Phillips Denied **Jane Smith** and **Anne Smith** Report that **Mercy Phillips** is not in a
Disposissition to Make friends Satisfaction therefore **Jane Smith** and **Hephzibah Hussey** are appointed to draw a paper of Denial against **Mercy Philips**
for falling into the Sin of fornication and bring it to the Next

Deborah Willbor refered Monthly Meeting the Matter Concerning **Deborah Wilber** [**Wilbur**] is Refered
to Next Monthly Meeting under the Same friends Care and then

sent up to Q meeting to Make Report the Epistle with the answers to the Queries was Read
and approved & Signed in this Meeting & **Susanna Smith** is appointed
to attend the Quarterly Meeting & present the Epistle with the
answers to the Queries & to Make Report to the Next Monthly Meeting

---

4 month 1772 At a Monthly Meeting of women friends held in **Dartmouth**
The 20 day of the 4 Month 1772 the Representatives are **Phebe Slocum** and **Jemima Davice** [**Davis**] and **Phebe Slocum** present **Mercy**

Mercy Phillips paper refᵈ **Philips** paper was brought according to appointment and this
Meeting thinks proper to Let it ly [lie] untill Next Monthly Meeting
by Reason this Meeting is Small the friends that have the Care

Deborah Willbor case referᵈ of the Matter Concerning **Deborah Wilber** [**Wilbur**] are not Redy to make
Report therefore it is Continued under the Same friends Care
and they to Make Report when Redy **Rachil Merehew** [**Rachel Merihew**] hath

Rachel Merihew request Requested a Removal Certificate to the Monthly Meeting of **Sand=**
=wich therefore **Hephzibah Hussey** & **Deborah Haydon** are appointed
to Joyn the Men friends and Make Inquiry into her Seircumstances
and Draw a Certificate for her if they think proper and bring
it to the Next Monthly Meeting

---

5 month 1772 At a Monthly Meeting of women friends held in **Dartmouth**
The 18 day of the 5 Month 1772 the Representatives are **Elizabeth Slocum** and **Susanna Allen** and **Susanna Allen** present the friends
appointed to Draw a Certificate for **Rachil Merihew** Report

Refered that her Outward affairs are Not Settled to friends Satisfaction
So it is Refered under the Same friends Care & they to Make

Alice Phillips request Report to Next Monthly Meeting **Alce Phillips** Requested to
Come under the Care of friends therefore we do appoint **Apphia**
Mott and **Mary Smith** to take opportunity of Solid Conference
with her in order to see whether the Motive Sprang from the

botton of true Conviction and Make Report to Next Monthly

Epistle receiv^d Meeting we Received an Epistle from the Last Quarterly Meeting and the advice therein Contained well Excepted, according

Report Concerning Deborah Willbor to appointment we have Laboured with **Deborah Wilber [Wilbur]** Resp= =ecting the Scandelous Report Gone abroad & find her Gilty of takeing Spirituous Liquor two Liberally & got off of her Watch whereby She has fallen into Several Groce Evils and we have Laboured with her in Love in order to Convince her of her Misconduct but finding her in no Capasity to Make Satisfaction, Given forth from your Committe (**Hepzibah Hussey Deborah Allen Susanna Allen**) this Meeting Considering of the Report and finding them Selves Clear from any further Labour do appoint the Same friends to Draw a paper of Denial against **Deborah Wilber [Wilbur]** and bring it to the Next Monthly Meeting

6 month 1772 At a Monthly Meeting of women friends held in **Dartmouth** The 15 day of the 6 Month 1772 the Representitives are **Alce Anthony** and **Jemima Davis** both presen this Meeting is

adjourn^d ajourned to the 22 day of this Instant

mett At a Monthly Meeting of women friends held by ajourn= =ment 22 day of the 6 Month 1772 the Representatives being

Alice Phi= lips accep^d Called both present the Committe Made Such a Report that **Alce Phillips** is taken under the Care of friends

Mary Howland acknow= ledgment rec^d **Mary Howland** wife to **Luthon Howland** her Mis Step In Marr[y]ing out of the Meeting is passed by from a Verbil acknoledg= ment and She Remains under the Care of this Meeting it was permited by Reason friends did not take proper Care in time and not to be Made a president [precedent] for the time to Come **Elizabeth Smith**

To draw a paper of denial against Deborah Willbor and **Susanna Smith** are appointed to Join the Committee in draw- ing a paper of Denial against **Deborah Wilber [Wilbur]** and bring it to Next Monthly Meeting **Alce Anthony** and **Susanna Smith**

Elisa Mosher disorder are appointed to Labour with **Elizabeth Mosher** for Marr[y]ing out of the Vnity of friends and to Make Report to Next Monthly Meeting

sent up to Quarterly meeting the Epistle with the answers to the Queries was Read & approved and Signed in this Meeting & Sent up by **Apphia Mott** & **Joanna Mosher** which are appointed to attend the Quarterly Meeting and present the Epistle with the answers to the Queries & Make Report to

Mercy Phi llip[s] denial Signd Next Monthly Meeting **Mercy Phillips** paper of Denial was Signed in this Meeting in order to be Read at the Close of a first day Meeting & Returned to the Clark [Clerk] to be Recorded

7 month 1772 At a Monthly Meeting of women friends held in **Dartmouth** The 20 day of the 7 Month 1772 the Representatives are **Elizabeth**

Elishib Smith proposal of marriage **Slocum** & **Susanna Smith** both present **Elishub Smith** and **Alce Philips [Phillips]** Signified their Intention of Marriage & was Desired to

wait untill the Next Monthly Meeting for theire answer
& **Mary Smith** & **Naomy Howland** are appointed to Make Enqu=
=iry into **Alce Philips**es Clearness Respecting Marriag & Conversation
& Make Report to Next Monthly Meeting Received an Epistle
from the Last Quarterly Meeting by our Representatives

Return
from Q meeting which was Read & well Excepted and also one from the yearly
Epistles Meeting of women friends held at **Philidelphia** for **Pensylvania**
Receiv^d and **New Jersey** which was Read to Good Satisfaction the
friends that was appointed to Labour with **Elizebeth Mosher** make

Elisa Mosher Report that they have Laboured with her and they do not find
Disown^d her in a Disposistion to make friends Satisfaction for her Marring
out of the unity of friends So this Meeting thinks proper to Deny the

Disownd Said **Elizebeth Mosher** from under the Care of friends **Susanna Smith**
to draw a and **Mary Smith** are appointed to draw a Certificate for **Hannah**
Certifi for **Bennit [Bennet]** to the Monthly Meeting of **Rhodisland** and bring it to the
Han. Benni^t Next Monthly Meeting **Deborah Hicks** has paid **Jemima Davis**
£1=9=6 old tennor according to appointment Collected £3=17=6
and paid out 3:17:6 for the use of poor friends **Deborah Wilber [Wilbur]**

Debr. Willbor paper of Denial was Signed in this Meeting in order to be Read
paper
Signd at the Close of a first day Meeting

---

8 month 1772 At a Monthly Meeting of women friends held in **Dartmouth**
The 17 day of the 8 Month 1772 the Representatives are **Deborah**
Hicks and **Mary Smith** both present the Committe that was to

Alice Philip[s] See into **Alce Phillips** Clearness Report that they dont find any
Clearness thing to hinder there Intention of Marriag **Elishub Smith** and

Elishib
Smith pro= **Alce Philips [Phillips]** appeared for theire answer which was that they might
posal of Proseed to take Each other in Marriage Between this & the Next
marriage Monthly Meeting According to the Good order of friends **Mercy**

Testimony **Phillips** paper of Denial was Read Accoding to appointment
against
Mercy and is as followeth Whereas **Mercy Phillips** wife of **Peter Phillips**
Philips **Junor** haveing had her Education amongst friends and under
the Care of this Meeting yet by Departing from the Testamony
of Truth in her one [own] hart hath so far gone astray as to fall into the
Reproachful Sin of fornication as appears by her haveing a Child
before Marriage and friends haveing Laboured with her in Love
in order to Shew her her Error and Restore her to the way of
Truth but She not Seeing her way Clear to make friends Sattisfa=
=ction and Acknoledg her Transgression friends therefore for the
Clearing of Truth and friends from the Reproach of Such Enormous
Evils therefore this Meeting is Concerned to give this forth as a Pub=
lick Testimony against her Diso[w]ning her the Said **Mercy Philips [Phillips]** from
being one of our Society and from under the Care of this Meeting
Nevertheless if it be agreeable to Divine wisdom that She may

yet find a place of Repentence and by unfained
Acknowledgment of the Evil of her ways Return to the way of truth
Given forth & Signed in & on behalf of our Monthly Meeting of women
friends held in **Dartmouth** the 22 day of the 6 Month 1772

Job Russell   Clark

Hepzibah Hussey   Clark

And **Deborah Wilber [Wilbur]** paper of Denial was Read According to appoint=

Testimony against Deborah Willbor ment and is as followeth Where as **Deborah Wilber [Wilbur]** of **Dartmouth**
in the County of **Bristol** in the Province of the **Massachusetts Bay** in
Newengland having been under the Care of friends and Some times has
Appeared Publickly as a Minister tho' never fully Approved of as a
Minister amongst friends Yet through the Prevailance of the Grand
Adversary of Mankind who Seeks to Devour the Innocent and by de=
parting from the pure Principal of Life & power Wherein alone is
Safety She hath so far fallen & gone Asstray, as to be found in Loose
Company and in takeing too Much Spiritous Liquor whereby She Actively
or passively fell into Gross Debauchery with **Daniel Hathway [Hathaway]** and
Holder Slocum as She Saith who Vilely and wickedly Committed Lewdness
with her whilst in that Condition which Shamful Conduct hath
brought a Reproach on friends who being under a deep Concern and
Excercise of Mind that the Truth and the Holy Profession we bear
May be Cleared & Preserved from Such Odious Scandals & Reproaches
and that Right^eous Judgment may be brought forth and placed
upon the offender According to the Nature of the Offence having
therefore Laboured with her in Love in order for her Recovery and
Restoration from her fall but friends Labour of Love not obtaining
the Desired Effect to the Satisfaction of this Meeting Do therefore
Give this forth as a Publick Testamony Against her hereby Pub=
=lickly disowning her the Said **Deborah Wilber [Wilbur]** from being a Mem=
ber of our Religious Society and from under the Care of this Meeting
yet Desiring if it be Agreeable with Divine pleasure that She may yet
Come to a Clear Sight & discovery of her Error & by an unfeigned Repen=
tance & Acknowledgment of the Same be Restored to the way of truth
and find Mercy Given forth and Signed in and on behalf of our
Monthly Meeting of friends held in **Dartmouth** the 20th of the 7th Month 1772 by

Job Russell ⎱
                 ⎰ Clark
Hephzibah Hussey

Hanah Giffords disorder The Overseers Inform this Meeting that **Hannah Gifford** has Gone
Contarary to the orders of friends in not Riseing at **Ann Gifford** Sup=
plication & Married out of the unity of friends which they have
Laboured with her for it & She hath not Made friends Satisfaction
therefore **Amy Barker Phebe Slocum** and **Hannah Mosher** are ap=
pointed to Labour with her as they find Occation for her Disorders

Hannah Bennet Certifi and Make Report to Next Monthly Meeting **Hannah Bennit [Bennet]** wife of **Robert Bennit [Bennet]** her Certificate was Signed in this Meeting Recommending her to the Monthly Meeting of **Rhod [Rhode] Island** Debo= =rah Hicks **Susanna Allen** & **Deborah Allen** are appointed to Make a

Eliz: Tucker to be Visited Visit to **Elizabeth Tucker** upon the account of the Sencarity of the paper She has Sent to this Meeting and they to Labour as they find Occation and to Make Report when they think proper

---

9 month 1772 At a Monthly Meeting of women friends held in **Dartmout[h]** The 21 day of the 9 Month 1772 the Representatives are **Deborah Hayden** and **Susanna Allen** and not present the Epistle with the answers to the Queries was Read and approved and Signed and Sent

Sent up to Q meeting up to the Quarterly Meeting by our Representatives which are **Amy Barker** and **Susanna Smith** and they to Make Report to the Next

Margret Straton request Monthly Meeting **Margret Straton [Margaret Stratton]** Request to Come under the Care of friends therefore **Hannah Tucker** and **Susanna Smith** are appointed to taks an opertunity of Sollid Conference in order to See if her Request Sprang from the bottom of true Conviction and they to make Report when Reddy **Susanna Russell** and **Keziah Russell** are appo=

Mary Hath= =way disorder =inted to take an Oppertunity of Conversation with **Mary Hathway [Hathaway]** on the Account of making friends Satisfaction for Marriing out of the unity of friends and make Report to the Next Monthly Meeting

Hep: Hussey Clerk **Hephzibah Hussey** is appointed Clark for this year **Hephzibah Hussey Deborah Allen** & **Sarah Gifford** are appointed to Revise

To revise miniuts Settle with Treasurer and Correct the Monthly Meeting Minits to See what part of them are proper to go on Record & they to Settle accounts with the Treasurer & make Report to the Next Monthly Meeting **Alce**

Overseers **Anthony Susanna Smith** and **Deborah Allen** are appointed

Racel Merihew Certifi Overseers of Disorders for the year Ensuing **Rachil Merihew [Rachel Merrihew]** Certificate was Signed in this Meetind Recommending her to the Monthly Meeting **Sandwich** Collected £0=10=7 old tennor

---

10 month 1772 At a Monthly Meeting of women friends held in **Dartmouth** The 19 day of the 10 Month 1772 the Representatives are **Susanna Allen**

Jose: Russell proposal of marriage and **Sarah Anthony** and **Sarah Anthony** present **Joseph Russell** and **Mehe= table Howland** appeared at this Meeting and Signified there Intention of Marriag & they are Desired to wait untill the Next Monthly Meeting for there answer **Hannah Tucker** & **Keziah Russell** are appointed to See into **Mehetable Howland** Clearness Respecting Marriag and Conver=

Han: Gifford acknow ledgment =Sation and make Report to the Next Monthly Meeting **Hannah Gifford** appeared at this Meeting with a paper Condemning her Seting [sitting] at the time of **Ann Gifford** appearing in Supplication which is Excep= =ted of after it is Read at the Close of a first day Meeting She being

Mary Hath way made Satisfaction present the friends appointed to Labour with **Mary Hathway [Hathaway]** Report She Gave them Some Satisfaction and **Mary Hathway** has made friends Satisfaction for Marr[y]ing out of the Good Order of friends the Com=

minites corected	=mitte appointed to Revise & Correct the Monthly Meeting Minits have answered there appointment and there Remains in the Stock
Treasury Settled	£6:4ˢ:0ᵈ old tennor **Deborah Allen** and **Sarah Gifford** are appointed
To draw a Certifi for Deb: Almy	to Draw a Removal Certificate for **Deborah Almy** if upon Inquiry She is found worthy & bring it to Next Monthly Meeting the Overseers
Complaint against Sarah Buf= finton	Inform this Meeting that **Sarah Buffinton** [**Buffington**] has fell into the Sin of forni= cation and they have Laboured with her but there appeared no disposistion

to make friends Satisfaction therefore **Hannah Tucker** and **Amy Barker**
are appointed to Labour with **Sarah Buffinton** as they find freedom and
make Report to the Next Monthly Meeting the friends that was appointed

failled of attending Q meeting	to attend the Quarterly Meeting failed by Reason it was Very Stormy
Epistle & Coppy of miniut Rec	Received an Epistle from the Quarterly Meeting of women friends which was Read & well Excepted and Likewise a Coppy of a Minit of the Last Yearly Meeting
Eliz. Gifford acknowledg- ment	**Elizebeth Gifford William** widow hath presented a paper of acknow= Ledgment for Seting [sitting] in Meeting in the time of **Ann Gifford** appearing

in Supplication **Hannah Tucker** and **Amy Barker** are appointed to
have Some Conversation upon the account of the Sincerity of her
acknowledgment & make Report to Next Monthly Meeting

16 mᵒ 11 1772	At a Monthly Meeting of women friends held in **Dartmouth** The 16 day of the 11 Month 1772 the Representatives are **Deborah**
Jos Russell answer	**Haydon** and **Elizebeth Slocum Deborah Haydon** present **Joseph Russell** and **Mehetable Howland** appeared for there answer and

finding nothing to hinder there answer was that they Might pro=
ceed to take Each other in Marriage Between this and the Next
Monthly Meeting according to the Good order of friends

21 mo 12 1772	At a Monthly Meeting of women held in **Dartmouth** The 21 day of the 12 Month 1772 the Representatives are **Deborah**
Han Gifford acknowledg- ment	**Haydon** and **Sarah Anthony** and **Sarah Anthony** present **Hannah Gifford** paper of acknowledgment was Read according to appoint= ment and Returned to go upon Record,[23] the Epistle with the answers
Sent up to Q meeting	to the Queries was Read and approved and Signed in this Meeting and Sent up by **Alce Anthony** and **Susanna Allen** which are appointed to attend the Quarterly Meeting & present the Epistle with the answers to the Queries and make Report to Next Monthly
Deb: Almy Certifi	Meeting **Deborah Almy** had a Removal Certificate Signed in this Meeting Recommending her to the Monthly Meeting of **Acoakset**

18 mo 1 1773	At a Monthly Meeting of women friends held in **Dartmouth** The 18 day of the first Month 1773 the Representatives are **Deborah**
adjournd	**Hicks** and **Deborah Haydon** and **Deborah Hicks** present this Meeting is a Journed to the 27 day of this Instant

23. **Hannah Gifford**'s acknowledgement is recorded at the end of the volume.

27 mo 1 1773 At a Monthly Meeting of women friends held in **Dartmouth**
mett [*illegible*] by appointment 27 day of the first Month 1773 the Representatives
being Called **Deborah Haydon** present we Received an Epistle from
the Quarterly Meeting by the hands of our Representatives which
Epistle was Read & the Contents therein well Excepted
Rec^d

At a Monthly Meeting of women friends held in **Dartmouth**
15 mo 2 1773 The 15 day of the 2 Month 1773 the Representatives are **Susanna Allen**
and **Phebe Slocum** both present Collected £2 : 2^s : 4^d old tenner [tenor]

At a Monthly Meeting of women friends held in **Dartmouth**
3 month 1773 The 15 day of the 3 Month 1773 the Representatives are **Deborah Allen** and
Deborah Haydon and **Deborah Allen** present the Committee that was appointed
to Labour with **Sarah Buffinton [Buffington]** Report they found no Disposistion in her to
Sarah Buf Make friends Satisfaction for her Transgression so **Alce Anthony Mary Smith** are
finton to be appointed to draw a paper of Denial against her and bring to the Next
denied Monthly Meeting **Hannah Cook** appeared at the preparative Meeting and Like
Han: Cook wise at this Meeting and Desired to Come under the Care of friends therefore
request **Deborah Allen** and **Susanna Allen** are appointed to have a Solid opertunity
with her to See where the Motive Sprang from the bottom of true Conviction
and Make Report to the Next Monthly Meeting the Epistle with the answers
to the Queries was Read and approved and Signed in this Meeting & Sent
up by **Elizebeth Slocum** and **Keziah Russell** which are appointed to
Sent up to attend the Quarterly Meeting and present the Epistle with the answers
Q meeting to the Queries and Make Report to Next Monthly Meeting

4 month At a Monthly Meeting of women friends held in **Dartmouth**
1773 The 19 day of the 4 Month 1773 the Representatives are **Elizebeth**
Slocum and **Phebe Slocum** both present the friends appointed to have
Han: Cook a Solid opertunity with **Hannah Cook** to See if her Request Sprang
Rec^d from the bottom of true Conviction they Report that She Gave them
Some Satisfaction and She is taken under the Care of friends **Susanna**
Susanna **Wing** appeared at the Preparative Meeting and Likewise at this
Wing reques^t Meeting and Signified She had a desire to Come under friends Care
which this Meeting takes Notis of and do appoint **Deborah Allen**
and **Deborah Hicks** to take a Solid Opertunity with **Susannah Wing**
to See if the Motive Sprang from the bottom of true Conviction and
make Report to the Next Monthly Meeting the friends appointed to
Return attend the Quarterly Meeting Report that **Keziah Russell** attended
from Quart^ly and produced an Epistle from the Same which was Read & the advice
meeting therein well Excepted **Sarah Buffenton [Buffington]** paper of Denial was Signed
Sarah Buf= in order to be Read at the Close of a first day Meeting & Returned
finton to go on Record Collected £1 : 2^sd : 11^sd old tenner
Denial signed

18 m^o 5 At a Monthly Meeting of women friends held in **Dartmouth**
1773 The 18 day of the 5 Month 1773 the Representatives are **Amy Barker**

and **Mary Smith** both present **Sarah Buffinton [Buffington]** paper of Denial was

Sarah Buf=
=finton
paper of
denial

Read according to appointment and Returned to be put upon Record
and is as followeth Whereas **Sarah Buffinton [Buffington]** Daughter of **David Gifford**
and **Deborah** his wife of **Dartmouth** in the County of **Bristol** in the
Province of the **Massachusetts bay** in **New England** haveing had
her Education Among friends under the Care of this Meeting yet by
Disregarding the Testamony of Truth in her one [*sic*] breast She hath So
far deviated therefrom as to be found Guilty of the Reproachful
Sin of Fornication as appears by her haveing a Child So Soon after
Marriage and friends haveing Discharged themselves in Labouring
with her in Tender Love to Discover to her the Evil thereof but our
Labour not being Effectual to friends Satisfaction therefore for the
Clearing of truth and friends from the Reproach thereof this Meeting
is Concerned to Give this forth as a Testimony against her and do
hereby Publickly Disown her the Said **Sarah Buffinton [Buffington]** from being
one of our Religious Community and from under the Care of this Meeting
Sincerely Desiring if it may be Agreeable with Divine pleasure
that She may yet Come to a Sense of her out going and by an
unfeigned Acknowledgment of the Error thereof Return to the
way of Truth and find Mercy Given forth and Signed in and on
behalf of our Monthly Meeting of friends held in **Dartmouth**
The 19 day of the 4 Month 1773   **Job Russell** Clark
                                          Hephzibah Hussey Clark

Margret
Stratton
rec^d
Eliz Gifford
paper accepte^d

The Committee that was to Inquire into the Sencerity of **Margaret**
Straton [Stratton] Request Report that She Gave Such Satisfaction as friends
Might Except [Accept] therefore **Margaret Straton [Stratton]** is taken under the
Care of friends the friends appointed to Treat with **Elizebeth Gifford**
William widow Report that She gave them Some Satisfaction and her
Paper of Acknowledgment is Excepted after being Read at the Close
of a first day Meeting She being present and Returned to the Clark [Clerk] to

Susanna
Wing rec^d

go on Record the friends appointed to treat with **Susanna Wing** on the
account of her Requesting to Come under the Care of friends Report they
found Some Satisfaction and She is taken under the Care of friends
Collected £2 : 5ˢ : 0ᵈ old tenner

6 month
1773

At a Monthly Meeting of women friends held in **Dartmouth**
The 21 day of the 6 Month 1773 the Representatives are **Susanna Allen**

Susa: Baker
Certifi

and **Susanna Smith** both present **Susanna Baker** wife of **Rice Baker**
Hath produced a Removel Certificate from the Monthly Meeting of **Acoakset**

Elis: Gifford
acknowledg
ment

which this Meeting accepted **Elizabeth Gifford** her paper is Read accor=
=ding to appointment and is as followeth
To the Monthly Meeting of friends to be held in **Dartmouth**
the 19 day of the 10 Month 1772 Dear friends whereas I have through
Ignorance broke the Good orders of friends in not ariseing at **Ann**

Gifford Supplication and Since have been Informed that I was Disorderly and am Sorry for and do Condem hoping God will for give me and friends So far pass Mine offence by with all other of Mine offences So as to let me Still Remain under theire Care **Elizebeth X**her mark **Gifford william** widow

Sent up to Q meeting   The Epistle with the answers to the Queries was Read and approved and Signed in this Meeting and Sent up by **Elizebeth Wing** and **Elizebeth Sheppard** [**Shepherd**] which are appointed to attend the Quarterly Meeting and present the Epistle with the Answers to the Queries & Make Report to Next Monthly Meeting

7 month 1773   At a Monthly Meeting of women friends held in **Dartmouth** The 19 day of the 7 Month 1773 the Representatives are **Deborah Allen**

Luthan Wood & Benja Sawdy proposals of marriage   and **Sarah Anthony** both present **Luthun Wood** and **Susanna Wing Benjamin Saudy** [**Sawdy**]and **Hannah Cook** all appeared at this Meeting and Signified theire Intention of Marriage they are Desired to wate untill the Next Monthly Meeting for there answer and **Deborah Allen** and **Sarah Anthony** are appointed to Make Enquiry into the youn women Clearness Respecting Marriag and Conversation and Make Report to Next Monthly Meeting

Epistle from Q meeting   Received an Epistle from the Quarterly Meeting which was Read and well Accepted not by our Representatives for they failed Going and Received an Epistle from the yearly Meeting of Women friends held

Philidel: at **Philadelphia** and the advice therein well Accepted and also

London   one from the yearly Meeting held in **London** by aJournment From yͤ 8th Day of yͤ 6th Mᵒ 1772 to yͤ 13th of yͤ Same Enclusive

Order on Trea- surer   was Read & well Excepted the treasurer is ordered to Pay **Joseph Russell** 9ᶠ : 4ˢ : 9ᵈ old tenor Collected 3ᶠ : 8ˢ old tenor

8 month 1773   At a monthly Meeting of women friends held in **Dartmouth** the 16th Day of yͤ 8th Mᵒ 1773 the Representatives are **Deborah Hicks** and **Mary Smith** both Preasant the friends

Susan: Wing & Hanna: Cook clearness   appointed to See into **Susannah Wing** and **Hannah Cook**s Clearness Respecting Marriage and Conversation Report they find Nothing

Luthan Wood Benja Sawdy answer   To hinder **Luthen Wood** and **Susannah Wing Benjamin Sawday** [**Sawdy**] and **Hannah Cook** all appeared for their answer which was that Each Cupple Might Proceed to take Each other in Marriage Between this and the Next Monthly Meeting according To the Good order of friends our Esteemed friend **Cumfort** [**Comfort**]

Comfort Hoegg Visit   **Hoegg** Being Preasant at this Meeting Presented her Certificate from the Monthly Meeting of **hampton** in the Province of **New hampshear** in **New England** Dated yͤ 17 of The 6th Mᵒ 1773 and likewise one from the quarterly Meeting he[l]d in **hampton** yͤ 12th Day of yͤ 7th Mᵒ 1773 which was Read

Dorcas Allen acknowledg= =ment   and well Excepted **Deborah Allen** and **Susannah Allen** is appointed to take a Solid opportunity of Conversation with **Dorkis Allen** Respecting the Cencerity of her Acknowledgement Sent in writing to this Meeting and they

Paper sent to oblong concern =ing Hannah Hammond   to Make Report to Next Monthly Meeting the Com^tt appointed to write to the **oblong** Concern[in]g **Hannah Hammon [Hammond]** braught a paper which was Signed in this

Treasurer Report   Meeting to the **Oblong** the treasurer Reports She hath Paid **Joseph Russel [Russell]** 9^£ : 4^s : 3^d old tenor for the Support of Poor Friends

---

9 month 1773   A[t] amonthly Meeting of women friends held in **Dartmouth** the 20th Day of ye 9th M^o 1773 the Representatives are **Alice Anthony** and **Susannah Smith** both Preasant this

adjournd   Meeting ajourns to ye 21st Instant

mett   this Meeting Met according to ajournment ye 21st Day of ye 9th M^o 1773 the Representatives being called both Preasant the Epistle

Sent up to Q meeting   with the answers to the queries were Read & approved and Signed in this Meeting and Sent up by our friends **Judith Russell Keziah Russell** and **Almy Barker** which are appointed to attend the quarterly Meeting and Presant the Epistle with the answers to the queries and Make Report to next Monthly Meeting

---

10 month   At a monthly Meeting of women friends held in **Dartm^o [Dartmouth]** the 18th Day of ye 10 M^o 1773 the Representatives are **Elice Anthony** and **Deborah Allen** both Preasant this Meeting

adjournd   Ajourns to ye 25th Instant

Mett   This Meeting Met according to ajournment ye 25th of ye 10th Month 1773 the Representatives being Called Both Preasan^t

Dorcas Allen case referd   The committe appointed to have a Solid opporunity with **Dorkes Allen** Make Report they have had an opportunity with ^sd **Dorkes Allen** and find Some Satisfaction but She Not being Preasant it is Refer^d one Month longer under the Same friend Care and then they Make Report. The Representative Report they all

Return from Q meeting Epistle rec^d   attend Except one which was Excused by Reason of being onwell and hav Pro[d]uced An Epistel which was Read in this Meeting and the advice therein well Excepted **Jonathan**

Jonat: Wing proposal of marriage   **Wing** & **Ann Wood** appeared at this Meeting and Signified Their Intention of Marriage & they are Desired to wait untill Next Monthly Meeting for their answer

Enquiry to be made   **Alice Anthon [Anthony]** and **Deborah Allen** are appointed To Make Inquiery into the young womans Clearness Respecting Marriage and Conversation and Make Report to next Monthly Meeting

---

11 month 1773   At a monthly Meeting of women friends held in **Dartm^o** ye 15th Day of ye 11th M^o 1773 The Representatives are **Susannah Smith** and **Sarah**

Dorcas Allen **Anthony** both Preasant **Dorkas Allen** hath Given in a paper
paper accepte^d Condeming her falling into the Sin of fornication which is
provided Excepted with a provisor She Cause it to be Read at the
close of a first d̬.ᵃy Meeting between this and the Next
Monthly meeting She being Preasant

Miniuts The comitte appointed to Correct the Minnits and Settle
Corected
settled with with the treasurer Report they have answered there
Treasurer appointment and find in the Stock 5ᶠ:18ˢ old tenor

Barker Little **Barker Little** and **Elisabeth** his wife hath given in
and wife
acknowledg a paper to this meeting condeming their falling into
=ment The Sin of Fornication which this meeting takes
Notis of and Do appoint **Deborah Hicks** and
Sarah Gifford to take a soled opportunity of Conference
with **Elisabeth Little** for further Sattisfaction of the
cencerity of her Acknowledgment and Make Report
to Next monthly meeting: the overseers Inform that

Meribah **Meribah Russel [Russell]** keeps company with a man Not in
Russell under Vnity with friends for which they have laboured with
Dealling her and She Gave them no Sattisfaction but Persisted
and is Published and this Meeting appoints **Alice Anthony**
and **Mary Smith** to labour with her as they find freedom
and Inform her that If She Proceeds to Marry the Meeting
will Testifie against her

Ann Wood the committe appointed to Inspect into **Ann Wood**s clearness
Clearness Respecting Marriag and Conversation Report they find

Jonathan Nothing to hinder there Proceeding **Jonathan Wing** and **ann**
Wings answer **Wood** appeared at this Meeting and Signified their
in marriage Intention of Marriage there answer was They Might
Proceed to take Each other in Marriage in Some Convenien[t]
time betwen this & the Next Monthly meeting acording

Weston Briggs to the Good order of friends **Wesson Briggs** & his wife
and wife Returned the Same Certificate as they had from hear [here]
certifi Bearing Date yᵉ 17th Day of yᵉ 12 Mᵒ 1770 which was Excepted
return^d again Collacted 1ᶠ : 1ˢ old tenor

---

12 month At a monthly Meeting of women friends held in **Dartm**ᵒ
1773 the 20th Day of yᵉ 12th Mᵒ 1773 the Representatives are
Deborah Allen and **Sarah Anthony** both preasant: the
Comᵗᵗ that was appointed to have A Soled [solid] opportunity with

Elisa Little **Elisabeth Little** Make Report they have had an oppo=
case refer^d =rtunity with her and found Some Sattisfaction so the
Meeting thinks to wait upon her & Rest it under the Same
friends Cear the comᵗᵗ that was appointed to labour

Meribah Russell case referd with **Meribah Russel [Russell]** Report they have laboured with her and found no Sattisfaction but the Meeting thought Propper to wait awhile to See whether She Proceeded in Marriag

Certifi:orderd for Mary Hart **Deborah Hix [Hicks]** and **Sarah Anthony** are appointed To Draw a certificate for **Mary hart** If upon Enquirey She is found worthy and bring to Next Monthly Meeting

Sent up to Q meeting The Epistle was Read and aproved and Sign^d in this Meeting and Sent up to the quarterly Meeting by our Representatives who are **Deborah Allen** & **Silvester Howland** and they to Make Report to Next Monthly Meeting this Meeting

adjournd Adjourns to the 29th Instant this Meeting Met according

mett to adjournment ye 29th Day of ye 12 M^o 1773 the Representatives being Called both Preasant

---

1st month 1774 At amonthly Meeting of women friends holden at **Dartm^o** ye 17th Day of ye first M^o 1774 – The Representatives are

Meribah **Deborah Haden [Haydon]** and **Mary Russell** Both Preasant this meeting Thought Propper to Refer the matter Concerning **Meribah**

Russell Case referd **Russell** by Reason She is Not Married to next monthly meeting under the Same friends Cear [care] and they to Make Report to Next Monthly Meeting: this Meeting hath Signed a certificate for

Mary Hart certifi Epistle rec^d **Mary Hart** to **Sandwitch** Monthly meeting: Receiv^d an Epistle from the quarterly Meeting by the hand of **Deborah Allen** which was Read in this meeting and the Contents thereof well Excepted

---

2 month 1774 At amonthly Meeting of women friends held in **Dartm^o** ye 21st Day of the 2^d M^o 1774: The Representatives are **Sarah Gifford**

Meribah Russell now Arnold is disowned and **Sarah Anthony** both Preasant: the Com^tt Respeting **Meribah Russell** Report that She hath Proceeded in Marriage Contrary to the advice of friends and friends finding themselves Clear from any further Labour Do Deny the S^d **Meribah Arnold** from being in unity and from under the Cear of this Meeting: Collected 3^£:0^s:10^d old tenor

---

3 month 1774 At amonthly Meeting of women friend held at **Dartm^o** 21st of the 3 M^o 1774 The Representatives are **Alice Anthony** and **Deborah Allen Deborah Allen** preasant this

adjournd Mett. Meeting Adjourns to the first Six Day of next m^o This Meeting Met by ajournment y^e 1st Day of y^e 4th Month 1774 the Representatives being Called both

Meribah Arnold aeknowledg =ment Preasant. **Meribah Arnold** Presented a paper to this Meeting Condeming her Marrying out of the unity of friends and this meeting do appoint **Alice Anthony** and **Susannah Smith** to take an opportunity with

her In order to Discover the Cincerity of her Request
and they to make Repor[t] to Next monthly meeting

Elisa Little **The committe appointed to labour with Elisabeth Little** Report
case refer^d they found a good Disposition in her Therefore the Matter is
Referred under the Same friends Cear to next Monthly

Susan Baker Meeting and then to Make Report: **Susannah Baker**
request Request a removal Certificate to **Aquoksett** Monthly
Meeting therefore we Do appoint **Alice Anthony** & **Susannah
Smith** to Draw her one and bring to Next monthly Meeting
If they find things Clear: the Epistle with the answers to the queries

Sent up to was Read and aproved and Sign^d and Sent up to the quarterly
Q meeting Meeting by our Representatives who are **Elsabeth Slocum** and
Sarah Anthony and they to Make Report to Next monthly

Darcos [Dorcas] Meeting **Dorkes Allen**s Paper was Read according to appointment
Allen
paper read and is as followeth

[*bottom half of page is blank*]

---

4 month At Amonthly Meeting of women friends held at **Dartm°**
1774 ye 18th of the fouth M° 1774: The Representatives are **Deborah
Hicks** and **Sarah Gifford** both Preasent The Com^tt Respecting

Meribah **Meribah Arnold** Report they found a good Disposition in
Arnold
case referd her Therefore the Matter is Refer^d under the Same friends
Cear and they to Make Report to Next monthly meeting

Epistle rec^d Receiv^d An Epistle from the quarterly by our Representatives
from
Q meeting which was Read to Good Sattisfaction: **Deborah Allen** and
Deborah Hicks are appointed to Draw Certificates for all

To draw Those friends Remov^d within the Compas of the **Nine partners**
Certificate for
those remov^d Monthly Meeting: Collected 1^£:15^s:11^d old tenor The treasurer is
order on ordered to Pay **Joseph Russell** 12^s:10^d Lawfull Money and to
Treasurer **Thomas Phillips** 1^£:7^s:0^d old tenor

---

5 month At amonthly Meeting of women friends held at **Dartm°** [Dartmouth]
1774 ye 16th Day of ye 5th Mo 1774 The Representatives are **Susannah
Allen** & **Sarah Anthony** both Preasant **Susannah Smith**

Clerk for is appointed Clerk for this Day the matter Concerning
this day
Meribah **Meribah Arnold** is Continued under the Same friends
Arnold
referd Cear for better sattisfaction and Report to next Monthly

Report from Meeting the treasurer Reports She has Paid **Joseph
Treasurer* **Russell** 12^s:10^d Lawfull Money as ordered and also <u>Pd</u>
to **Thomas Phillips** 1^£:7^s:0^d old tenor for the use of the poor

To draw a **Deborah Hix** [Hicks] & **Sarah Anthony** are appointed to Draw
Cer^tific for
Sarah Cornel A certificate for **Sarah Cornel** [Cornell] and bring to next monthly
Meeting: Reiciv^d a few lines from the **oblong** Monthly

Rec^d few lines meeting Concerning **Hannah Hammond** which Signifies
for H^annah
Hammond She hath bean in Some Degree orderly since amongst us

meeting accepts her paper The friends hear that was appointed to make Enquiery in her life and Conversation Report they finde nothing to hinder hur being Reicived therefore this meeting accepts her paper Which is as Falloweth

---

[*next third of page is blank*]

She is rec^d again and She is taken under the Cear of this meeting again

To draw certfic for Han: Hamond **Deborah Hix [Hicks]** and **Susannah Smith** are appointed to Draw a certificate for Said **Hannah Hammon [Hammond]** and bring it To Next monthly Meeting. This Meeting hath Sign^d acertificate

for Jonat: Smith and wife for David Antho^ny wife and Children and all others moved to Hoosuck for **Jonathan Smith** and **Phebe** his wife to the **Ninepartn ers** and also A certificate for **David Anthony** wife & Children to the **Nine Partners. Deborah Allen** and **Deborah Hicks** were Desired to Draw the Remaining Part of The Certificates for the friends Remov^d to **East Hoosuck** and bring to Next monthly meeting

---

6th month 1774 A[t] amonthly Meeeting of women friends held at **Dartmouth** The 20th Day y^e of 6th M^o 1774 **Elisebeth Smith** and **Deborah Allen** are appointed to Attend the monthly

Susan Baker Certificate Meeting Signed a removel Certificate for **Susannah Baker** To **Acoakset** Monthly Meeting and also Signed A removal

Sarah Cornel Certific Certificate for **Sarah Cornel [Cornell]** wife to **Walter Cornel [Cornell]** to the monthly Meeting of **Rhodisland** and likwise

Han: Hamond Certific a removal Certificate for **Hannah Hammon [Hammond]** wife to **Samuel Hammon [Hammond]** To the Monthly meeting at **Oblong** We Receiv.^d Three Certificates on behalf of our Friend

Elisabeth Robinson & Susanna Lightfoot Visit **Elisabeth Robinson** which was Read and well Exiepted In this Meeting and also one in behalf of our friend **Susannah Lightfoot** which was also Read in this Meeting to Good sattisfaction An Eopistle with the answ^rs

Sent up to Q meeting To the queries was Read and approved and Signed in This Meeting and Sent up to the Quarterly Meeting by our Representatives who are **Rebecca Rotch** and **Sarah Gifford** and they to Present the Epistle with the answ^rs to the queries and Make Report to Next

Mary Allen Certifi Monthly Meeting **Mary Allen** wife of **John Allen** Produced acertificate from **Sandwitch** Monthly Meeting which This Meeting Excepts **Hannah Mosher** and

To draw a Certifi for Edith Smith & children **Meriah Smith** are appointed to Draw Acertificate for **Edith Smith** and her Children and bring to Next Monthly If They think Propper

---

7 month 1774 At A monthly Meeting of Women friends held at **Dartm.^o** the 18th Day of ye 7th M.^o 1774 The friends appointed to Attend the Monthly Meeting are **Alice Anthony** &

Meribah Arnold case referd — Susannah Smith both Preasant the Matter Respecting Meribah Arnold is Refer.d to next Monthly Meeting

Edith Smith Certifi not ready — The Com.tt appointed to Draw Certificate for Edith Smith is not Ready.. Rec.d an Epistle from the quarterly

Epistle Recd — Meeting by the hand of Sarah Gifford which was Read and well Excepted Rebeccah Rotch and Susannah

to draw a certifi for Mary Spencer — Russell are appointed to Draw A certificate for Mary Spencer and bring to Next Monthly Meeting If they Think Propper Clement Biddle and Rebacah Cornel [Cornell]

Clement Biddle proposal of marriage — appeared at this Meeting and Signified their Intention of Marriage and were Desired to wait till Next Monthly Meeting for their answer, & Judith Russel [Russell] and Susannah Russel [Russell] are appointed to Enquire into the young womens Clarness Respecting Marriage & Conversation - And Make Report to next Monthly Mating

---

8 month 1774 — At amonthly Meeting of women friend held at Dartm.o ye 15th Day of ye 8th M.o 1774. The Representatives are Susannah

matter of Merebah Arnold refered — Allen and Sarah Howland both Preesent the Matter Respeiting Meribah Arnold is Refered to Next monthly Meeting

To draw a Certifi for Eunice Allen — Jamimah Davis Sarah Gifford are appointed to Draw acertificate for Eunice Allen and bring to Next Monthly meeting If they think Propper: whereas the Monthly Meeting of

The matter concerning Mary Cornel — Acoaksett is oneasie[uneasy] about Some of Mary Cornells Conduct whilst Mongst them and have Chose acom.tt to Joyn us there fore we Do appoynt Deborah Allen Susannah Smith Deborah Hix and Hephzibah Hussey acom.te to Labour with Mary Cornel [Cornell] in the wisdom of truth according the nature of the Case and Make Report to next Monthly Meeting

Hump Smith wife and children Certifi — Signed a removal Certificate for Humphery Smith and Edith his wife and their Children to the Monthly Meeting at the Nine Partners

Mary Spencer Certifi — Signed a Removal Certificate for Mary Spencer Directed to the Monthly Meeting of Greenwich the Committe appointed to Labour with Elizabeth

Eliz Tucker be denied — Tucker Report that they found Little or no Satisfaction therefore Deborah Allen and Deborah Hicks are appointed to draw a paper of Denial a gainst Said Elizabeth Tucker and bring it to the Next Monthly

Rebecca Cornel clearness — Meeting the Committe appointed to Inquire into Rebecca Cornel [Cornell] Clearness Respecting Marriage and Conversation Report they find nothing to

Clement Biddle answer — hinder there proceeding Clement Biddle and Rebecca Cornel [Cornell] appeared for there answer which was that they Might proceed to take Each other in Marriag between this and the Next Monthly Meeting

To draw a certifi for Rebec Cornell — according to the Good orders of friends Susanna Russell and Judith Russell are appointed to draw a Certificate for Rebecca Cornel [Cornell]. after She in is Married and bring to the Next Monthly Meeting

To draw
certifi for
some re=
moved

Susanna Smith Deborah Allen and **Deborah Hicks** are appointed to
Joyne the Men in order to draw Certificates for Some of our Members
that have Moved within the Compas of **Nine Partner** Monthly
Meeting this Meeting Collected £5:17:7 Old tennor

9th month
1774

At a Monthly Meeting of women friends held in **Dartmouth**
The 19 day of the 9 Month 1774
The Representatives are **Susanna Smith** and **Deborah Hicks** both
present after Some time of Consideration and from the Report

Meribah
Arnold
restored

of the Committe this Meeting Concludes to pass by **Meriba**
Arnold offence and take the Said **Meriba Arnold** under the Care

Mary
Cornell
to be deni=
=ed

of friends again the Committe that was appointed to gin **Acoakset [Acoaxet]**
friends to Labour with **Mary Cornel [Cornell]** Make Report they have
had an Opertunity with her and notwith Standing She Sent a
paper of Acknowledgment to **Acoakset** it was not to Satisfaction
So the Committe thought it would be the Most Honour to truth
and Satisfaction to friends to Deny her and that was Submited to
Dartmouth Monthly Meeting this Meeting Concurs with the Report
of the Committe and in Consequence thereof do appoint **Susanna**
Smith and **Deborah Hicks** to draw a paper of Denial against
the Said **Mary Cornel [Cornell]** and bring to the Next Monthly Meeting

Elisa Tucker
Case refer.d

the Committe appointed to draw a paper of Denial against **Elizabeth**
Tucker Report they have had an opertunity with her and She
Desires to be waited upon until next Monthly Meeting So the

Elisa Brigg
request

Meeting Concurs with it **Elizabeth Briggs** Requesting to Come under
the Care of friends and **Mary Smith** and **Sarah Howland** is appointed
to take a Solid Opertunity with her and Make Report when Redy

Ruth Russell
acknowledg=
=ment

Ruth Russell presented a few Lines Condemning her falling into
the Sin of fornication and **Elee Anthony** and **Sarah Anthony** are
appointed to take a Solid Opertunity in order to Labour with
her as they find Occation and Make Report to Next Monthly

Sent up to
Q meeting

Meeting the Queries was Read answered and approved in this
Meeting the Epistle also was Read and approved and Signed and Sent
up to the Quarterly Meeting by our Representatives who are
Elee Anthony Hannah Mosher and **Keziah Russell** and they to

Rebecca
Biddle
Certificate

Make Report to Next Monthly Meeting Signed a Removal Certificate
for **Rebecca Biddle** Recommending her to **Philidelpha [Philadelphia]** Monthly

Han Denis
Lillis Beard
Elisa: Smith
certificates

Meeting Signed Removal Certificates for **Hannah Denis [Dennis] Lillis Beard**
Elizabeth Smith Williams wife and there Children directed
to the Monthly Meeting of **Nine Partners Hephzibah Hussey Deborah**

To Revise
miniuts
& Settle with
Treasurer

Allen and **Susanna Smith** are appointed to Revise and Correct
this Meetings Minits & have them Recorded & Like wise Settle with
the treasurer and Make Report to Next Monthly Meeting this

Adjournd

Meeting a Journs to the 28 day of this Instant

9 month 1774
mett
Shadre^ck
Dennis
Zep: Anthony
certificate

Advice to
women on
Bonnit[?]

Settled with
Treasurer

At a Monthly Meeting held by aJournment 28 day of the 9 Month 1774
the Representatives both present Remov^al Certificates was Signed for
Shadrake Denis [Dennis] his wife and Children and for **Zephaniah Anthony** his
wife and Children directed to the Monthly Meeting at **nine Partners**
it is the advice of this Meeting that for time to Come that women friends
that appears to publish or have there answer or Marry to take of[f] there
bunits or hats at the time of Such appearence Settleed all accounts
with the Treasurer up to the 28 day of the 9 Month 1774 and there Remains
in the Stock the Some of £11-9-10 old tennor

---

10 month 1774

Susan Smith
Clerk

Ruth Russel
[Russell]
Case referd

Return from
Q meeting
Epistle rec^d

Mary Cornell
denial Sign^d

Elisa Tucker
denial
Signd

At a Monthly Meeting of women friends held in **Dartmouth**
The 17 day of the 10 Month 1774
Susanna Smith is Chose Clarke for this day the Representatives being
Called both present the Committe appointed to have Some Conference
with **Ruth Russell** Concerning the Sencerity of her acknowledgment made
Report that they had Some Satisfaction in there Visit to her but they
think it best to wate Some time Longer to See if her Conduct is agreeable
so it is Refered under Same friends Care and **Susanna Allen** is aded
to them and they to Make Report to next Monthly **Alce Anthony** and
hannah Mosher Made Report that they attended the Quarterly Meeting
according to appointment and have Produced an Epistle from the
Same which was Read in this Meeting and well accepted the Committe
appointed to draw a paper of denial against **Mary Cornel [Cornell]** wife
of **Daniel Cornel [Cornell]** have brought one which was Signed in this Meeting
and is to be Read at the Close of a first day Meeting between this
and next Monthly Meeting and then to be Returned to the Clark to
be put upon Record the Committe appointed to draw a paper of
Denial against **Elizabeth Tucker** wife of **Henry Tucker** have done it
agreeable to appointment which was Signed in this Meeting
and ordered to be Read at the End of a first day Meeting and
then Returned to the Clark to be put on Record

---

11 month
1774

Certificate
to be drawn
for Sunna
Russell

Ann Russell
Certificate
to be draw^d
Overseers
Appointed

Ben: Russel
Jedediah
Allen
Certificates

At a Monthly Meeting of women friends held in **Dartmouth**
The 21 day of the 11 Month 1774 the Representatives being Called
both present **Hannah Mosher** and **Ruth Tucker** are appointed
to draw a Certificate for **Susanna Russell** wife to **David Russell**
if upon inquiry She is found worthy and bring to next
Monthly Meeting **Susanna Russell** and **Keziah Russell** are
appointed to draw a Certificate for **Anne Russell** the Widow
and bring to the next Monthly Meeting if upon inquiry She
is found worthy **Susanna Smith Deborah Hicks Deborah Allen**
and **Susanna Allen** are appointed Overseers of Disorders for
the year Ensuing Signed a Removal Certificate for **Benjamin
Russell** his wife and Children and also Signed one for
Jedediah Allen his wife and Children all to the Monthly
Meeting at **Nine Partners**

12 month <u>1774</u>   At a Monthly Meeting of women friends held in **Dartmouth**
The 19 day of the 12 Month 1774 the Representatives being
Called borth present the Committe appointed to have a Solid
Elizabeth   Opertunity with **Elizabeth Briggs** Report they have had Several
Briggs   Oppertunities and found Some Satisfaction therefore She is
Received   taken under the Care of friends the Committe appointed
Anne Russell   to draw a Certificate for **anne Russell** widow Report that
case referd   her Outward affairs is not Settleed to Satisfaction therefore
the Matter is Refered under the Same friends Care as hereto
fore and they to Make Report to next Monthly Meeting the
Sent up to   Queries was Read and the answers & apprved and an Epistle
Quarterly   Signed and Sent to the Quaterly Meeting by our Represen=
meeting   =tatives who are **Elizabeth Slocom [Slocum]** and **Silvester Howland**
and they to Make Report to next Monthly Meeting
Content   **Content Tucker** Request to Come under friends Care therefore
Tucker   **Hannah Tucker Susanna Allen** and **Deborah Hicks** are appo=
request   =inted to have a Solid Oppertunity in order to See if her
Request Sprang from the bottom of true Conviction and
Make Report to next Monthly Meeting the Matter Concerning
Ruth Russell is Refered to next Monthly Meeting under the
Elizabeth   Same friends Care **Elizabeth Little** paper of acknowledg=
Little   =ment is accepted after it is Read at the Close of a first
acknowledg   day Meeting for worship She being present
ment
denials   **Mary Cornel [Cornell]** and **Elizabeth Tucker** papers of Denial was
Read   Read according to the Direction of this Meeting and they to
go upon Record and are as followeth
Mary   Whereas **Mary Cornel [Cornell]** wife of **Daniel Cornel [Cornell]** who was under
Cornel her   the Care of this Meeting by a Certificate from **Acoakset** Monthly Meeting
Testimony   and She Disregarding the Testimony of truth and So far under the
denial   power of antichrist as to Come under the Care of friends in a Hipo=
critical Manner and in Making friends believe that **Timothy
Gifford** was the father of her bastard Child wrongfully and Since that
She hath Given the Said **Gifford** from under her hand that he is Clear
and Still She doth not openly declare who is the father of her Said
Child and for a Long time by her Groce abomination the Innocent
hath Suffered and the Gilty gone free which Shamefull Conduct hath
brought a Reproach on friends who bring under a deep Concern
and Excercise of Mind that the Truth and the holy Profession we
bare may be Cleaned and preserved from Such odious Scandols and
Reproaches and that Righteous Judgment may be brought forth and
placed upon the offender according to the nature of the offence haveing
therefore Laboured with her in order to bring her to a Sight of
her Misconduct but our Labour of Love not having the Desireed
affect to friends Satisfaction therefore for the Clearing of truth

and friends from the Reproach of such practises this Meeting is
Concerned to give this forth against her and do hereby publickly
Disown her the Said **Mary Cornel [Cornell]** from being one of our Society
and from under the Care of friends Nevertheless Desireing if it
be a greeable with Divine pleasure that She may yet beRest=
=ored from the Evil of her way and by unfained Repentance
Return to the way of truth Given forth and Signed in & on
behalf of our Monthly Meeting of friends held in **Dartmouth**
The 17 day of the 10 Month 1774 by   ⎰ **William Anthony Jᵘ** Clark
                                     ⎱ **Susanna Smith**   Clark
                                                for the day

Elizabeth Whereas **Elizabeth Tucker** wife of **Henry Tucker** having been
Tucker under the Care of friends for these Many years and Disregarding
denial the Testimony of truth So far as to fall into the Reproachfull Evil
of taking Spirituous Liquor to Excess as appears by her own
acknowledgment and her other Conduct is not agreeable to
truth and friends having Repeatedly Laboured with her in
Love in order to Restore her to the way of truth but our
Labour of love not having the Desired affect to friends
Satisfaction therefore for the Clearing of truth and friends
from the Reproach of Such Practices this Meeting is Concerned
to give this forth against her and do hereby publickly
Disown her the Said **Elizebeth Tucker** from being one of our
Society & from under the Care of friends Nevertheless Desiring
if it be agreeable with Divine pleasure that She may yet
be Restored from the Evil of her way and by unfained
Repentance Return to the way of truth Given forth at
our Monthly Meeting held in **Dartmouth** the 17 day of
the 10 Month 1774 and Signed in and by order of Said
Meeting by   ⎰ **William Anthony Jᵘ** Clark
                                    ⎱ **Susanna Smith**   Clark
                                                for the day

1ˢᵗ month At a Monthly Meeting of women friends held
1775 In **Dartmouth** the 16 day of the 1 month 1775
Representatives are **Mary Smith** and **Phebe Slocom [Slocum]** both
Ann Russell present no Certificate brought for **anne Russell** we Received
Certificate an Epistle from the Quarterly Meeting by our Representa:
not prepar ᵈ :tives which was Read & the Contents therein well Excepted
Epistle rec ᵈ the Committe appointed to have a Solid Oppertunity with
Content Tuckᵉʳ **Content Tucker** Report they have had an Oppertunity
refer ᵈ with her and She gave them Some Satisfaction but it was
though proper to Refer it til next Monthly Meeting and
under the Same friends Care Signed a Removal Certificate

Susanna Russell
Certificate
Jonathan How=
=land proposal
of marriage

for **Susann Russell** wife to **David Russell** Directed to
the Monthly Meeting at **Acoakset Jonathan Howland**
and **Mary Allen** appeared at this Meeting & Signified there
Intention of Marriage and was Desired to wait till next
Monthly Meeting for there answer and **Susanna Allen** and
Deborah Hicks are appointed to make Inquiry into **Mary Allen**
Clearness Respecting Marriag and Conversation and Make Report

Susan Smith
appointed Cerk
miniutes to be
Revised

to next Monthly Meeting **Susanna Smith** is appointed Clark
for the year Ensuing **Phebe Slocom [Slocum] Deborah Hicks** and
Hepzibah Hussey are appointed to Revise & Correct this Meetings
Minits in order for to be put on Record Collected 3/7 old ten

2 month
1775

At a Monthly Meeting of women friends held in **Dartmouth**
The 20 day of the 2 Month 1775 the Representatives are **Phebe Slocom [Slocum]**
and **Mary Smith** both Present **Hephzibah Hussey** and **Phebe Slocom**

Naomy Sisson
Certificate is
draw[d]

are appointed to draw a Certificate for **Naomy Sisson** and bring it
to the Ajournment of this Meeting the Committe appointed to Inquire

Mary Allen
Clearness
Jonathan
Howland
Answer

into **Mary Allen** Clearness Respecting Marriage and Conversation Report
they find nothing to hinder there proseeding **Jonathan Howland**
Mary Allen appeared for there answer which was they Might
Proseed to take Each other in Marrige at Some Conveniant time
between this and the Next Monthly Meeting observing Good orders

Thomas
Mott:
R: H
proposal of
marriage

Thomas Mott and **Rhode Hathaway** hath Laid there Intention
of Marriage before this Meeting and they was desired to wait
untill the next Monthly Meeting for their Answer **Elizabeth Smith**
and **Mary Smith** widow are appointed to make Inquiry into **Rhode**
Hathaways Clearness Respecting Marrige and Conversation and

Caleb Green
& wife
acknowledg
ment

make Report to next Monthly Meeting **Caleb Green** and **Elizebeth**
his wife hath Sent a paper to this Meeting Condemning there
Marring So neigh in kind and out of the Unity of friends which
this Meeting takes notis of so far as to Appoint a Committe which
are **Elizabeth Smith** and **Deborah Haydon** to gine the men
friends to See if they are Sincear in there acknowledgment
and they to make Report to next Monthly Meeting this

adjournd

Meeting is ajourned to Next forth day Come week

mett

Met by ajournment the 1 day of the 3 Month 1775
the Representatives borth present the Committe appointed

Content
Tucker
Receiv[d]

to treat with **Content Tucker** Report that they find a Good prin-
=cible in her and they think it may be for the best to accept her
therefore She is taken under the Care of friends the Committe appointed

miniuts
Review[d] *&*
settled with
Treasurer

to Revew the Minits inorder to go on Record and to Settle accounts
with the Treasurer Report it is done and there Remains in the
Stock £11=9=10 old tennor **Hannah Tucker** and **Phebe Slocom [Slocum]**

Certificate
Requir^d
Hepzibah
Hussey &
Anna Hussey
proposal
marriage

Naomy Sisson
Certificate

Rebecca
Rotch
request

Certificate Requir^d Hepzibah Hussey & Anna Hussey proposal marriage

are appointed to Gine the men friends inorder to Draw a Certi=
=ficate for **Hephzibah Hussey** her Daughter and Gran Daughter
if upon inquiry they are found worthy and bring it the next
Monthly Meeting **Jonathan Hussey J^o** and **Content Tucker** Laid
there Intention of Marriage before this Meeting and they was
Desired to wait till next Monthly Meeting for their answer
Phebe Slocom [Slocum] and **Sarah Anthony** are appointed to See into
Content Tuckers Clearness Respecting Marriag a Conversation
and Report to next Monthly Meeting Signed a Removal
Certificate for **Naomy Sisson** wife to **John Sisson** to the Monthly
Meeting at **Nine partners Rebecca Rotch** hath informed this
Meeting She is about to make a Visit to **Philidelfia** to See her
Daughter and friends and desires a Certificate to Carry with her
there which was drawed and Signed in this Meeting

---

3 Month 1775

Rhoda Hath= =way Clearness

matter of Elisa Green refer'd

Content Tucker Clearness

Jamima Davis request

Sent up to Qut^{ly} meeting

Tho Mott & Jonat Hussey Answer

Freeborn Rider Recommnded

At a Monthly Meeting of women friends held in
Dartmouth the 20 day of the 3 Month 1775
the Representatives are **Deborah Allen** and **Lidda Barker**
and **Deborah Allen** present the friends appointed to Inquiry
into **Rhoda Hathaway**s Clearness Respecting Marriage and
Conversation Report they find nothing to hinder there
proseeding the Committe appointed to have Some Confer·
:rence with **Elizabeth Green** Report they have not
had an Oppertunity therefore the Matter is Refered under
the same friends Care until Next Monthly Meeting and
then they to Make Report the Committe appointed to Make
Inquiry into **Content Tucker**s Clearness Respecting
Marriage and Conversation Report that nothing appears
to hinder there Proceeding **Jemima Davis** wife to **Joseph
Davis** Request a Certificate to the Monthly Meeting at
the **oblong** and **Susanna Allen** and **Elizabeth Slocom** are
appointed to Make　　Inquiry and if nothing appears to
hinder they are to draw one and bring to the Next
Monthly Meeting the Queries have been Read and answered
and the answers approved and the Epistle Signed and
Sent up to the Quarterly Meeting **Thomas Mott** and
Rhoda Hathaway Jonathan Hussey J^u and **Content
Tucker** all appeared for there Answer which was that
both Cupples Might proseed to take Each other in Marriage
at Some Conveniant time between now and the Next Monthly
Meeting observing the good order Established among friends
Signed a few Lines in this Meeting to Recommend **Freborn Rider**s
publick Testimony and that we have Unity with it to the
Quarterly Meeting of Ministers and Elders this Meeting ajourns
to 29 of this Instant

no Women friends appoited

Met by ajournment 29 day of 3 Month 1775 the Representatives not present there is no friends appointed to attend the Quarterly Meeting at this time and the accounts are

Sent by ye Men adjournd

to be sent up by the Men friends this Meeting is ajoured to 7 day 4 M^o Next

mett

Met by ajournment 7 day of the 4 Month 1775 — the Representatives being Called are not present Signed

J Hussey wife and children Certificate

a Removal Certificate for **Jonathan Hussey** and his wife **Hepzibah** and their Children **Silvenus** and **Rachil Hussey** and their Grandaughter **Elizabeth Hussey** all which are Recommended to the Monthly Meeting at the **Nine partners**

Content Hussey Request a Certificate

Content Hussey informs this Meeting that She is a bout to Remove and desires a Certificate and **Sarah Anthony** and **Deborah Hicks** are appointed to make Inquiry in Regard of her having one and if nothing appears to hinder they to Joyn the Men friends and draw one and bring to Next Monthly Meeting

4 Month 1775

At a Monthly Meeting of women friends held In **Dartmouth** the 17 day of the 4 Month 1775 — there not appearing any Representatives from the Preparitive Meeting the Reason aledged being the Severity

no Represen tatives apeared

of the wether on that day that there was no Meeting neverthe--less this Meeting Concludes to go forward with business as usual yet we fear the Coolness and want of true Zeal for the Cause of truth was too Much the primary Cause of the a for Said Neglect or Omission **Alce Anthony** and

Concerning Elisa Green Acknowledg -ment

Susanna Allen are appointed in the Lieu of **Deborah Haydon** and **Elizabeth Smith** to have a Solid oppertunity of Conferrence with **Elizabeth Green** Concerning of her paper of acknowledgment that She hath Sent to this Meeting and they to Make Report to the Next Monthly

Mary Hart Certificate

Meeting **Mary Hart** hath brought back a Certificate from the Monthly Meeting of **Sandwich** we Received an

Epistle rec^d

Epistle from our Last Quarterly Meeting of women friends held at **East Greenwich** which was Read in this Meeting and the advice Contained therein well accepted

Rhoda Allen request

this Meeting is informed that **Roda Allen** is a bout to Remov and desires a Certificate and **Sarah Anthony** and **Mary Smith** are appointed to Make inquiry and draw and bring one to Next Monthly Meeting if nothing apears to hinder

Jonathan Hussey Jur & wife certificate

Signed a Removal Certificate in this Meeting for **Jonathan Hussey J^{ur}** and **Content** his wife to the Monthly Meeting of **Nine partners** Signed a Removal Certificate for **Jemima**

Jemima Davis certificate	**Davis** wife to **Joseph Davis** to the Monthly Meeting at the **Oblong**

---

5 month 1775 At a Monthly Meeting of women friends held
in **Dartmouth** the 15 day of the 5 Month 1775
the Representatives are **Amy Barker** and **Silvester**
Howland both present the Committe appointed to inspect

E: Green Refered in the Matter Concerning the Sincerity of **Elizabeth**
Greens acknowledgment Report they have had an
Oppertunity with her and She gave them Some Satisfaction yet they
think best it Should be Refered to Next Monthly Meeting under the Same
friends Care and then they to Make Report **Alce Anthony** and **Susanna**

Hannah Hicks request **Smith** are appointed to have a Sollid Oppertunity with **Hannah Hicks** Con=
=cerning her Request to be taken under the Care of friends to find whether
it Sprung from the bottom of true Conviction or not and they to Make

Phebe Allen request Report when Reddy **Phebe Allen** Request a Removal Certificate and **Susanna**
Allen and **Elizabeth Slocom [Slocum]** are appointed to Gine the men friends in
Drawing one for the family if nothing appears to hinder and bring it to
the Next Monthly Meeting the Committe appointed to inspect into the

Ruth Russell be rec^d Sincerity of **Ruth Russell**s acknowledgment Report that She gave them
so Good Satisfaction that they think her paper May be Received and
She to Remain under the Care of this Meeting and in Conciquence thereof
this Meeting accepts her If She Causes Said paper to be publickly Read
at the End of a first day Meeting for worship She being present
and the paper to be Returned again to the Meeting to be put

Rhoda Allen Certificate upon Record Signed a Removal Certificate for **Roda Allen** to the
Monthly Meeting at the **Ninepartners**

---

6 month 1775 At a Monthly Meeting of women friends held in **Dartmouth**
The 19 day of the 6 Month 1775 the Representatives are **Deborah**

James How= land Ju^r proposal of marriage **Hicks** and **Silvester Howland** both present **James Howland Juner**
and **Meribah Shephard [Shepherd]** Laid theire Intention of Marriage before
this Meeting and they were Desired to wait until Next Monthly
Meeting for there answer the Matter Concerning **Hannah Hicks**

Hannah Hicks request refer.^d Requesting to Come under friends Care in Continued another Month
and under the Same friends Care **Susanna Russell** & **Judith**
Russell are appointed to Make Inquiry Into **Meribah Shephard [Shepherd]**

To enquire into Meribah Shepherd clearness Clearness of Marriage and Conversation and Make Report to next
Monthly Meeting **Ruth Russell** paper of acknowledgment hath
been Read agreeable to the Conclution of Last Monthly Meeting
and is as followeth
To the Monthly Meeting of friends In **Dartmouth** to ^beheld
The 15 day of the 5 Month 1775

Ruth Russell acknowledg =ment Whereas I have Given way to the Insinuation of the
adversary so far as to be Guilty of the Sin of fornication as

appears by my having a bastard Child which Reproachfull
Sin I am Sorry for and do hereby Condemn Desiring for=
givness from the almighty and that friends may so far pass
by Mine offence as to lett me Remain under their Care
from your friend　　　　　　　　**Ruth Russell**

*Representa
=tives to
Q meeting* **Judith Russell Deborah Allen Keziah Russell** and **Silvester
Howland** are appointed to attend the Insuing Quarterly Meeting

*Sent up to
Q meeting* the Queries and answers was Read and approved and an Epistle
Likewise and Signed and Sent up to the Quarterly Meeting

*Sarah
Slocum
Certificate
accepted* by our Said Representatives **Sarah Slocom [Slocum]** wife to **Elihu Slocom [Slocum]**
hath brought a Removal Certificate which was Read and
accepted

*Queries &
Epistle to
Quaterly
meeting* The Queries have been read in this meeting, and answered, and the
answers approved, the Epistle likwise hath been read and Signed, all
which are to be Sent up to the Quarterly meeting by our Representatives

*Saʰ Slocum
Certificate* Received a Certificate from **Accoakset** monthly meeting on behalf of
Sarah Slocum Wife of **Elihu Slocum,** which was accepted

Elisaʰ Green The matter conserning **Elisabeth Green**s acknoledgment is refer.d till
next monthly meeting, by reason of the men friends request

Obedi Allen Signed a Certificate for **Obediah Allen** and **Phebe** his wife and their Children
Namely **Ebenezer, Jonathan** and **James** which is directed to the **Ninepartners**
Monthly meeting

*Rebecca
Russell &
Mary Wing
disowned* The overseers make report that they have Precaussioned and Laboured with
Rebecca Russell, wife of **Jethro Russell**: And **Mary Wing** wife of **Giles Wing**
For keeping Company and marrying out of the unity of friends: and in
consequence thereof this meeting thinks they are Clear ~~of~~ without any further
Labur, and do disown the Said **Rebecca Russell** and **Mary Wing** from being
in Membership with us

---

*7 month
1775* At a Monthly Meeting of Women Friends held in **Dartmouth** the 17ᵗʰ of 7ᵗʰ mo 1775
The Representatives are **Mary Smith** widdow & **Lydia Barker** both present

*Meribah
Shepherd
clearness* The Friends that was appointed to make Enquiry into **Meribah Shepherd**s
Clearness and Conversation respecting marriage make report they find nothing
to hinder their proceeding in Marriage

*Jam Howland
Answer* **James Howland Ju** and **Meribah Shepherd** both appeared for their answer
Which was they might proceed to take Each other in marriage at Some Convenant
time between now and next monthly meeting, Observing the good Order
Established among Friends

*Han Hicks
request* The matter conserning **Hannah Hicks** requesting to come under friends
Care is continued a nother month

*Return from
Q: meeting* **Judith Russell, Deborah Allen Keziah Russell** and **Silvester Howland** inform
they all attended the Quarterly meeting according to appointment by whom

*Epistle
receivd* we Received an Epistle from our Quarterly meeting which was read in this
our meeting and kindly Received

Elisabeth Geen — The Committee that was appointed to Inspect the Sinserity of **Elisabeth Green**s acknowledgment condemning her marrying near in kind and from amoung Friends: make Report, that She made them Such Satisfaction as they think she may be Received: In consequence thereof this meeting accepts and continues her the Said **Elisabeth** under their care and in membership

Ann:Condel — **Hannah Tucker** and **Lydia Barker** are appointed to Inspect in the Sencerity of **Anna Condel**s acknowledgment in condemning her marrying out of the unity of Friends and they to make report to this meeting when ready

---

8 month 1775 — At a Monthly meeting of Women Frinds held in **Dartmouth** the 21ˢᵗ of 8ᵗʰ month 1775 The Friends that was appointed to attend the monthly meeting are **Amie Barker** and **Sarah Howland** both Present

Shubel Bunk= =er proposal of marriage — **Shubel Bunker** and **Lydia Gardner** have Laid their Intentions of marriage before this meeting: and they were desired to wate for their answer untill the next monthly meeting ~~for~~ **Judith Russell** and **Keziah Russell** are appointed to ₍make₎enquiry in **Lydia Gardner**s Clearness and conversation respecting marriage and they to make Report to the next monthly meeting

Hannah Hicks Recd — The Comittee that was appointed respecting **Hannah Hicks,** request to See if she was Worthy to come under Friends care, make report, She gave them good Satisfaction and they find nothing to hinder her being received: In consideration there of it is the conclution of this meeting to Receive her under their care and in membership thereof

Ann Condel referd — The Committee appointed to inspect the Sincerity of **Ann Condel**s acknoᵂlegment make report, She gave them pretty good Satisfaction but they think it best to rest Longer

Ann Wing request a cirtificate — **Anne Wing** hath desired our Certificate, Recommending her to **Accoakset** monthly meeting: **Susanna Allen** and **Sarah Gifford** are appointed to make Enquiry in ₍ˢᵈ₎ **Anne** Life and Conversation, in regard to her having one, and if nothing appears to hinder they to Draw one and bring to next monthly meeting

Patie Russell under deal= =ing — The Overseers Inform they have Laboured with **Patience Russell** from time to time for her disorderly proceeding, and she hath not given Satisfaction therefore this meeting appoints **Alice Anthony** and **Deborah Hicks** to make further inspection in the Circumstance, and Labour with her as they shall find freedom, and if no disposition to make Satisfaction, to draw a paper of denial a gainst her if her ofenceᵉ require, and likwise acquaint her with the minniute

---

9 month 1775 — At a monthly meeting of Women Friends held in **Dartmouth** the 18ᵗʰ of 9ᵗʰ month 1775 The friends appointed to attend the monthly meeting are **Mary Smith** Widdow and **Ruth Howland** _ Both Present

Lydia Gardner Clearness — The Committee appointed to make enquiry into **Lydia Gardner**s clearness and Conversation respecting marriage, make report, they find nothing to hinder their proceeding therein

Shubell ₍Bunker₎ ~~Gardner~~ Answer — **Shubel Bunker** and **Lydia Gardner** appeared for their answer: Which was they may proceed to take Each other in marriage at some convenient time between now and next monthly meeting, observing good Orders

Ann Condel referd — The matter respecting **Anne Condel** is refered to next monthly meeting

Mary Potter acknowledgment

Mary Potter hath sent a few lines to this meeting, condemning her being att a marriage consumated contrary to the Order of Friends: It is concluded at this meeting to accept of said acknowledgement and pass by her offence

Complaint against Sarah Wilcox

The Overseers inform this meeting this metting, that there is a Scandelous report Spread abroad respecting **Sarah Wilcox,** and that they have laboured with her for her fault and She hath not cleared it up to their Satisfaction, and they are clear; in Consideration thereof this meeting appoints **Alice Anthony Susanna Allen 2** and **Ruth Howland**, as a Committee to Labour and deal with said **Sarah** as they shall find freedom: and they to make report of their doings to the next monthly meeting

Ann Wing certificate

The Friends according to appointment have brought a few lines by way of Certificat on behalf **Anne Wing**, wife to **Jonathan Wing**, which was Signed in this meeting. Recommending her to **Accoakset** monthly meeting

Patience Russell disowned

The Committee that was appointed in regard of **Patience Russell**s offence make Report, She not having a disposition to make friends satisfaction they have Drawn a Paper of Denyal against her agreeable to their appointment which is Signed in this meeting and to be read at the End of a first day meeting of Worship between this and the next monthly meeting

Queries & Epistle

The Queries have been read and answered in this meeting the answers approved Likewise the Epistle read approved and Signed, all to be sent ᵘᵖto the Quarterly meeting by our Reppresentatives who are **Amie Barker Deborah Haden Deborah Hicks** and **Susanna Smith**

10 month 1775

At a monthly meeting of Women Friends held in **Dartmouth** yᵉ 16ᵗʰ of 10ᵗʰ month 1775 **Alice Anthony** & **Naomie Howland** are appointed to attend yᵉ month meeting both present

Ann Condel referd

The matter concerning **Anne Condel** is refered another month this meeting hath made an addition to the former Committe by chusing **Amie Barker** to inspect the matter concerning Said **Anne** Sencerity, and they to make report to the next monthly meeting

Sarah Wilcox disowned

The Comittee that was appointed to Labour with **Sarah Wilcox** concerning her misconduct report they have had an opertunity agreeable to appointment and found no Satisfaction: In consideration thereof it is the conclusion of and Judg=ment of this meeting to disown her the said **Sarah** from being one in membership with us; and do appoint **Deborah Allen** and **Susanna Allen** to draw a paper of denial against her and bring to the next monthly meeting

Deborah Davis Certificate Recd

Received a removal Certificate on behalf of **Deborah Davis** wife of **James Davis** And one Certificate on behalf of **Sarah Shepherd** wife to **David Shepherd** Juʳ both from **Smithfield** monthly meeting which Certificates are both accepted

Epistle Recᵈ Represenᵛˢ return

Received an Epistle from our Quarterly meeting, which is very acceptable to this meeting: The Representative inform they have attended the Quarterly meeting according to appointment

Comfort Cas= =well disownd

We have been Informed by some of the of the overseers that **Comfort Cassell** Wife of **Daniel** ᴄᵃˢˢᵉˡ hath been Preadmonished before marriage, it not having the desired Effect. She hath married out of the Unity of friends, for which offence

friends have waited long with her, and receive no Satisfaction: In consi=
=deration thereof, this meeting disowns her from being any longer in me^member=
=ship with us: this meeting appoints **Martha Chase** to acquaint her with the
Conclusion of this meeting

Elis Wing
Visit
Received a few lines by way of Certificate, on behalf of our friend **Elisabeth
Wing,** from the **Oblong** monthly meeting Signifying that She hath laid before
them. She had a desire to Visit her friends and Relations in our parts and
their Unity therewith

Freeborn
Riders
minite
Our Friend **Freeborn Rider** informed this meeting that she had an intention
to Visit **Sandwich** Qurterly meeting which this meeting concurs with and gave
her a copy of the miniute

11 month
1775
At a Monthly meeting of Women Friends held in **Dartmouth** y^e 20th of 11th month 1775
There are no Representatives appointed, the reason alleiged is the Weather was
So Stormy that there was no Preparitive meeting

Abraham
Allen propo
sal of mar=
=riage
Abraham Allen and **Phebe Kirby** hath laid their intentions of marriage
before this meeting, they were desired to waite for their answer until next
monthly meeting - **Deborah Hicks** and **Silvister Howland** are appointed to make
Enquiry in **Phebe Kirbys** Clearness and conversation respecting marriage and
they to make report to the next monthly meeting

Ann Condel
referd
The matter concerning **Anne Condels** acknowlegment is ^referd another month

Sarah Wilcox
denial signd
The Committee appointed to draw a paper of denial against **Sarah Wilcok [Wilcox]**
Have don according to their appointment, which Paper is Signed by this
meeting and to read at the End of a first day meeting of Worship between
Now and the next monthly meeting

Patience
Russell paper
of denial
Patience Russells paper of denial hath been read since the Last monthly
meeting and is as followeth

Whereas **Patience Russell** wife of **Stephen Russell** Having had her
Education amoungst Friend and under the Care of this meeting, yet by depart=
=ing from the Testimony of Truth is her own heart hath so far gone a stray
as to fall into the reproachful sin of Fornication as appears by her
having a Child so soon after marriage, and friends having Labour with her
in Love,^in order to restore her to the way of Truth, but our Labour of Love
Not having the desired Effect to Friends Satisfaction: Therefore for the Clearing
of Truth and Friends from the reproach of such a Practice this meeting is conserned
to give this forth as a Publick Testimony agai^st her hereby disowning her the said
Patience Russell from being one of our Society and from under the care of this meeting
Desireing never theless if be agreeable to Divine Pleasur that she may yet find a
place of Repentance, and unfeigned acknoledgment of the Evil of her way return
to the way of Truth

    Given forth and Signed in and on behalf of our monthly   **Wm Anthony Ju^r** Clerk
meeting Held in **Dartmouth** the 18th of the 9th month 1775   By   **Susanna Smith** Clerk

Abigail Rogers
certificate
We Received a few lines by way of Certificate from **Pembrook** monthly meeting
In behalf of **Abigail Rogers** which is accepted

12 month 1775

At a Monthly meeting held of Women friends held in **Dartmouth** 18th of 12th month 1775 The Friends appointed to attend the monthly meeting are **Alice Anthony** and **Phebe Slocum; Alice Anthony** present

Phebe Kirby clearness

The friends appointed to make Enquiry into **Phebe Kirbys** Clearness and conversa= =tion respecting marriage make report they find nothing to hinder their proceeding in marriage

Abraham Allen answer

Abraham Allen and **Phebe Kirby** appeared for appeared for their answer whic which was they might prceed to take Each other in marriage, at Some Convenent time between this and the next monthly meeting observing good Orders

Ann Condel referd

The matter conserning **Anne Condel** acknowledgment is referd another month

Sarah Wilcox paper of denial

Sarah Wilcox paper of denial hath been read, since the last monthly meeting agree =able to the conclusion,^of the meeting: said paper is as followeth

Whereas **Sarah Wilcox** wife of **William Wilcox** having had her Education amongst Friends, but through unwatchfulness and disregarding the Testimony of Truth in her own heart; hath been found guilty of taking Spiritous Licquor to excess and also not attending meetings, all which She hath been Laboured with for and still continuing obstinate: Therefore friends can do no less that testifie against the Said **Sarah Wilcox,** and do hereby disown her from being a member of our Religious Society and from our under the care of this meeting: Desireing if it be Consistant with Divine goodness, She may come to a Sight and Sence of her outgoings, and by unfeigned Repentance be restored to the way of Truth

Given forth and Signed in and on behalf of our monthly **Wm Anthony Jur** Clerk meeting held in **Dartmouth** the 20th of the 11th month 1775 By **Susanna Smith** Clerk

Sarah Morrel acknowledg ment inspect ed

Alice Anthony, **Keziah Russell**, **Deborah Allen**, and **Sarah Howland,** are appointed to inspect the Sencerity of **Sarah Morrell** and **Patience Russells** acknowledgment to find wheither they are Sencear and worthy to be received, and they to make report as Soon as they are ready to this meeting

answers to queries & Epistle sent by Represenvis

The Queries have been Read and answered in this meeting the answers approved And likwise the Epistle read and Signed and Sent up to the Quarterly meeting by our Representa tives **Freeborn Rider Deborah Hayden Elisabeth Ricketson Lydia Barker** and **Deborah Davis**

Aaron Veal & David Sands certificate Recd

Received two Certificates in behalf of our Worthy Friends **Aaron Veal** and **David Sands** both from the **Ninepartners** monthly meeting Bearing date on the 17th day of the 11th month 1775 which was very acceptable amoung us and we ho^pe their Labour may be Serviceable

Apphia Mosher acknowledment

Apphia Mosher brought a few lines to this meeting condemning her going to a disapproved wedding. which was accepted so far as to let her remain under our care

Susanna Smith Elder

Susanna Smith hath some time a go been nominated to be an Elder in the Society, and now Sho^is chosen by the meeting for that Service

1 month 1776

At a Monthly Meeting of Women Friends held in **Dartmouth** ye 15th of 1st month 1776 The Friends appointed to attend the monthly meeting are **Mary Smith 2d** and **Silvister Howland** both Present

Ann Condel
accepted

Anne Condel wife, to **Enoch Condel** hath made the meting Satisfaction for her marrying out from amongst them; and she is in membership with us

Sarah Morrel &
Patience Rus
sell accepted

The Committee appointed to Inspect the Sencerity of **Sarah Morrell** widoe and **Patience Russell** the Sencerity of their acknowledment make Report

They both gave them good Satisfaction, and have freedom for them to be Receiv^d In consideration thereof, it is the Judgment of this meeting and conclusion to pass by both of their offences so far as to let them remain under the care of this meetin and in membership with us; provided Said **Sarah** reads or causes her Paper ₍of acknolegment₎ to be read publickly at the End of a first day meeting of Worship before the next monthly meeting and She be present, and likewise the paper to be returnd to the Clerk to be put on record

The Repre^ves
not attening
Q meeting
except
Freeb^n Rider
Epistle Rec^d

This meeting is Informed that it so fell out by some hendrenes [hindrances] that none of the Representatives attended the Quarterly meeting except **Freeborn Rider,** by whome we received an Epistle therefrom which was read in this meeting and Kind^ly accepted amongst us

Sun Smith
appointed Clerk

Susanna Smith is appointed Clerk for the meeting

2 month
1776

At a Monthly meeting of Women Friends Held in **Dartmouth** the 19th of 2^d month 1776 The Friends appointed to attend the monthly meeting are **Susanna Smith** and **Lydia Barker** both present

John Ricketson
proposal of
marriag

John Ricketson and **Sarah Morrell** hath laid their Intention of marriage before this meeting, and they were desired to waite for their answer untill the next monthly meeting; **Hannah Tucker** and **Lydia Barker** are appointed to make Enquiry into **Sarah Morrell** clearness and Conversation respecting marriage and they to make report to the next month meeting

Sarah Morrells paper of acknoledgment hath been Read according to the Conclusion of last monthly meeting and is followeth

Sarah Morel
paper

To the Preparitive Meeting of Women Friends next to be held in **Dartmouth** the 13th of the 12th month: And to the Monthly meeting the 18th of the Same month

Dear friends; Whereas I have through unwatchfulness fallen into the Reprachful Sin of Fornication, which is Evident by having a child soon after mariage, and marrying from amoungst friends, both of which I ₍condem₎ & am sorrow for Praying to Almighty God to forgive me and Friends to so far pass it by as to Let me remain under your Christian care; this from your friend

Dated in **Dartmouth**   **Sarah Morell**
the 18th day of y^e 12 month 1775

Judith How=
=land ac=
=knolegment

Judith Howland hath made acknow^legment for going and Joyning with a Rude and Licentious Rabble or company, which is contrary to our Principles And in consideration thereof Friends concluds to accept her acknowlegment and pass by her offence, desiring for the futer She may be careful to Shun Such company

3 month
1776

At a Monthly meeting of Women Friends held in **Dartmouth** 18th of 3^d month 1776 The Representatives are **Ruth Howland** and **Mary Smith** 2^d both present *answer to Queries Epistle & represent* The Queries have been Read in this our meeting and answered, the Epistle Read Signed and approved and Sent up to the Quarterly meeting by our represen= tatives who are **Judith Russell** and **Mary Tucker**

Edith Spring er disownd The Overseers Informe this meeting they have Preadmonished and Laboured with **Edith Springer** wife of **Edward Springer**, for keeping company out of the unity of friends: She not regarding their advice, but hath prceeded and Married: For which breach of orders Friends,^think they are clear without any further Labour, and do deny her the Said **Edith** from being in membership with us

Conclution to deny Amie Hart One of the Overseers Informe this meeting that she had some Conversation with **Amie Heart [Hart]** concerning her being guilty of the Sin of fornication but she found no satisfaction, and it is the mind of the meeting they are clear without any more labour with her, and do appoint **Susanna Allen** and **Deborah Hicks** to draw a paper of denial against her and bring it to the next monthly meeting **Elisabeth Smith** is appointed to acquaint her with the conclusion of this meeting

To corect ye minits **Hannah Tucker**, **Ruth Tucker**, **Phebe Slocum**, and **Susanna Smith** are appointed to Review and Corect the miniuts Suitable to be put on record and likwise to Settle accompts with the Treasury and report of their doings when ready

Signed a paper for Ann Gifford Signed a few lines in this meeting Signifying our concurrence with **Anne Gifford**s Intended Visit to **Sandwich** Quarterly meeting

Adjournd This Meeting Adjourns to the 27th of this Instant At a Monthly meeting of women friends held in **Dartmouth** by adjounment on the 27th of the 3^d month 1776. The Representatives are **Ruth Howland** and **Mary Smith 2^d** both present

Sarah Morel Clearness The Friends appointed to Enquire into **Sarah Morrell**s clearness and conversation Respecting Marriage, make report they find nothing materal to hender their proceeding

John Ricket= son answer **John Ricketson** and **Sarah Morrell** appeared for their answer: which was they might proceede to take Each other in marriage at Some conveniant time between now and the next monthly meeting, observing good Orders

Rachel Case request **Rachal Case** hath appeared to this meeting with a few lines desireing to be taken under the care of friends: **Susanna Allen Sarah Gifford** and **Deborah Allen** are appointed to take Suitable oppertunities to inspect the Sencerity of her request Wheither it Springs from the bottom of true Conviction or not; they to make report of their doings when ready

Ann Russell Certificate Signed a Ce^rtificate in this meeting on behalf of our friend **Anne Russell** widdow and her children, Namely **Henry, Ann,** and **Joanna** which recommends them to **Smithfield** monthly meeting

4 month 1776 At a Monthly Meeting of Women Friends held in **Dartmouth** ye 15th of 4 month 1776 The Friends appointed to attend the monthly meeting are **Ruth Tucker** and **Phebe Slocum** Neither of them attended

Epistle Rec^d We Received an Epistle from our Quarterly meeting by **Mary Tucker** one of the Representatives **Judith Russell** did not attend

Mary Wing acknowle= =dgment **Mary Wing** wife to **Giles Wing** hath sent a few lines to ^by way of acknoledgment this meeting condemning her marrying out of the unity of friends in consideration there of we do appoint

Susanna Allen Sarah Gifford and **Anne Gifford** wife of **Daniel Gifford** to make Enquiry and consider on the matter, and take whole Care to Inspect into the Circumstance therof to find if She be worthy to be received; and they to make report to the meeting when ready

Amie Hart paper Signd
Amie Hart.s paper of Denial was Read Sig^{n}ed in this meeting and carried to the mens meeting for concurrance, and assistance to be read at the end of a fist day meeting and to be returned to this meeting to be put on Record

Gid Howland and wife acknoledg ment
Gedion Howland and **Catherine** his wife appeared in this meeting with a paper by way of acknowledgment for being guilty of the Sin of Fornication and Likwise for marrying nearer of kindred than is alowable among friends: for which this meeting appoints **Deborah Haden** and **Judith Russell** a Committee to Inspect the Sencerity of her acknowledgment or Joine the men friends to see wheither they are worthy to remain among friends or not, and they to make their to the meeting when they have done their Service

Meribah Smith under dealing
The Overseers Inform this meeting they have been with **Meribah Smith** concerning her being guilty of Fornication and they think best that the meeting Should appoint some Friends to Visit her; in consideration thereof this meeting appoints **Ruth Howland** and **Silvester Howland** to Joine the Overseers in Visiting Inspecting and dealing with her as they Shall find freedom, and have the matter under their care: and to make report when they are ready

Mary Wing widdow
The men friends desires Some assistance from this meeting on the account of **Mary Wing** widdow: **Mary Smith** and **Sarah Howland** are appointed for that Service

5 month 1776
At a Monthly Meeting of Women Friends held in **Dartmouth** ye 20th of 5th month 1776 The Representatives are **Deborah Hayden** and **Sarah Howland** both present

George Handy proposal of marriage
George Handy and **Mary Potter** hath laid their Intentions of marriage before this meeting and were desired to wait untill the next monthly meeting for their answer; **Deborah Hayden** and **Sarah Howland** are appointed to make Enquiry into **Mary Potter**s Clearness and conversation respecting marriage and they to make report to the next monthly meeting

Mary Wing wife of Giles accepted
The Committee appointed to make Enquiry in regard of the Sencerity of **Mary Wing** wife of **Giles Wing**; and of her Life and conversation, and likwise In Regard of her being married out of the Unity of friends and from amoungst them; make report, they think She may be received again amoung friends In consideration thereof, this meeting accept her acknowlegment and doth take her under their care and in membership again --

Rachel Case accepted
The committee appointed in regard of **Rhachel Case** wife to **John Case** Requesting to come under the care of the meeting Signify they have don according to their appointments and they found pritty good Satisfaction, and think she may be taken under friends care, and it is the Conclusion of this meeting, And they do Receive$_\wedge$^{her} into Membership, and in Society with them

Phebe Beard Certificate
Phebe Baird haith Produced a Certificate from the monthly meeting of **Nan==tucket**, which was read and accepted in this meeting

to draw a Certificate for Mary Wing wife of Giels
Susanna Allen and **Deborah Allen** are appointed to draw a Certificate for **Mary Wing** Wife to **Geiles Wing**, if on enquiry nothing appears to hinder it is to be directed to the **Ninepartners** monthly meeting

Susanna Allen and **Keziah Russell** are appointed Overseers of Disorders

6 month   At a Monthly Meeting of Women Friends held in **Dartmouth** yᵉ 17ᵗʰ of 6ᵗʰ month 1776
1776   The Representatives are **Ruth Howland** and **Deborah Hicks** both Present

adjournd   This Meeting adjourns to the 24ᵗʰ day of this month

Mett   At a monthly meeting of Women Friends held in **Dartmouth** By adjournment
on the 24ᵗʰ day of the 6ᵗʰ month 1776

The Representatives are **Ruth Howland** and **Deborah Hicks** both present

Mary Potter   The friends that was appointed to make Enquiry into **Mary Potter**s clear=
Clearness   =ness and conversation respecting marriage, make report, they find nothing to
hinder their proceeding

George Handy   **George Handy** and **Mary Potter** appeared for their answer; which was they
answer   may proceed to take Each other in marriage at Some convenient time between
this and the next monthly meeting, observing Rules and orders Established among
Friends: **Deborah Hayden** and **Sarah Howland** are appointed to have the
care and oversight of the before mention marriage to See that it is consumated
and carried on orderly; and they to make report to the next monthly meeting

Phebe Yarn=   Received a Certificate on behalf of our Worthy Friend **Phebe Yarnall** from
=all   the Monthly meeting held at **Concord** in **Chester County** in **Pensylvania**
Certificate   Bearing date on the 7ᵗʰ of the 2ᵈ month 1776

Rebecca   And one on behalf of our Worthy Friend **Rebecca Wright** from the monthly
Wright   meeting held at **Chesterfield** on the 2ᵈ day of the 5ᵗʰ month 1776 both which was
Certificate   Read in this meeting and Received with their Labours of Love much to our
Comfort and Satisfaction

Rebeccah   **Alice Anthony** and **Deborah Hicks** are appointed to have Some conference
Russell   with **Rebecca Russell** wife to **Charles Russell** concerning her request to see
request   wheither she is worthy to be received into membership and they to repᵒrt when ready

answers to   The Queries have been read, answered and ~~Likewise~~ approved in this meeting
Queries   Likewise the Epistle, and Signed and to be Sent up to the Quarterly meeting
Epistles &   by our Representatives who are **Judith ~~Smith~~ Russell Keziah Russell Mary**
Representaves to   **Smith Susanna Smith** and **Sarah Howland**
Q meeting

David Farris   Received Certificates on behalf of our Worthy Friends **David Farres** and
and   **John Perry** both from the monthly meeting held at **Wilmington** in the **County of**
John Perry   **New Casel** upon **Delaware** bearing date on the on the 15ᵗʰ of yᵉ 5 month 1776
which was read and Received to good Satisfaction

adjournd   This Meeting adjourns to the 28ᵗʰ of this month

mett   At a monthly meeting of Women friends held in **Dartmouth** by adjournment
on the 26 of the 6 month 1776. **Ruth Howland** and **Deborah Hicks** was
appointed to attend the monthly meeting **Deborah Hicks** Present

Mary Wing   Signed a Removal Certificate for **Mary Wing** wife to **Giles Wing** Recom=
=mending her to the **Ninepartners** monthly meeting

Alice Anthony and **Deborah Hicks** are chosen Overseers of disorders

Amie Harts Paper of denial hath been Read Since last monthly meting; is as follows

Amie Hart   Whereas **Amie Hart** Daughter of **William Hart** and **Mary** his wife of
denial   **Dartmouth** in the **County of Bristol** in the **Province of the Masachusetts Bay** in

New England, Having had her Education among Friends and under the
care of this meeting yet by disregarding the Testimony of Truth
In her own heart She hath so far deviated therefrom, as to be to be found guilty of the
Reproachful Sin of fornication, as ᴬaperd ᵇʸ her having a Bastard Child and friends having
discharged themselves ~~with hin~~ Labouring with her in tender love to discover to
her the Evil thereof but our labour not being effectual to friends Satisfaction
Therefore for the clearing of Truth and friends from the reprach thereof this
meeting is conserned to give this forth as a Testimony against her and do hereby
Publickly disown her the Said **Amie Hart** from being one of our Religious Society
and from under the care of this meeting Yet desireing if may be agreeable with
Divine Pleasure that She may yet come to a Sight and Sense of her outgoing and
by an unfeigned acknowlegement of the Error thereof,ᴬ& return to the way of Truth
and find mercy. Given forth, and Signed in and on behalf of our monthly meeting
of Friends held in **Dartmouth** the 15 day of the 4 month 1776 By

Wᵐ Anthony Juʳ Clerk
Susanna Smith Clerk

7 month *1776*	At a Monthly meeting of Women friends held in **Dartmouth** yᵉ 15ᵗʰ of 7 month 1776 The friends appointed to attend the monthly meeting are **Silvester Howland** preseⁿᵗ
	Deborah Hayden did not attend **George Handy**s and **Mary Potter**s marriage according to appointment by reason she was not well able, **Sarah Howland** informed She was present and the marriag was consumated in an orerly manner
report from *Q meeting*	None of the Representatives attended the Quarterly except **Mary Smith** and ~ **Susanna Smith** by whome we received an Epistle from our Quarterly meeting
Epistles Recᵈ	also we receiver an Epistle from the yearly meeting of Women friends held in **Philidelphia** both were read and received much to the comfort ~~of the~~ and Satisfaction of the Living amoung us
Meribah *Smith*	**Hannah Tucker** and **Phebe Slocum** are added to the former committee in Regard of dealing and Labouring with **Meribah Smith** to bring her to a Sign of the Evil of her ways for her being guilty of the Sin of fornication and they to make report to the monthly meeting
Elder proposed	**Deborah Hayden** is nominated to be an Elder; and it is Left to the consi= =deration, both to the meeting and herself to consider on till the nex monthly meeting
minits *corrected*	The Committee appointed to revise and correct the Monthly meeting mi nits and Settle with the Treasurer report that they have answered their appointment and there Remains in the Stock £11-9-10 old Tennor
8 month *1776*	At a Monthly Meeting of Women Friends held in **Dartmouth** yᵉ 19ᵗʰ of 8ᵗʰ month 1776 The friends appointed to attend the monthly meeting are **Alice Anthony** and **Susanna Allen** both present
Meribah *Smith*	**Deborah Allen** and **Susanna Allen** are appointed to draw a papᴬᵉʳ of Denial against **Meribah Smith** and bring to the next monthly meeting
Mary *Spooner* *disowned*	One of the Overseers Informs this meeting, She hath taken a friend and been with **Mary Spooner** ~~in regard~~ wife of **Simson Spoorer [Spooner]** in regard of her being about

to marry out of the Unity of Friends; and admonished her on that account
But the advice not having the desired Effect, for She went on and married,
and we think the meeting is Clear without any more Labour; and the meeting
disowne her of being any Longer in membership with them

Mary Wing   Signed a paper of denial against **Mary Wing** Widdow which is to be read
at the End of a first day meeting of Worship between this and the next monthly meeting

Elders referd   The matter concerning chusing Elders is referd another month

Mary Trafford   **Alice Anthony** and **Selvester Howland** are appointed to draw a removal
Certificate for **Mary Traford [Trafford]** if on enquiry She is found worthy: and it is to be
directed to **Accoakset** monthly

Susanna Russell is appointed to acquaint **Mary Stoner [Spooner?]** that she is disowned
from among friends

adjournd   This Meeting adjourns to the 2^d day of next week at the 11th hour

mett At a Monthly Meting of Women Friends held in **Dartmouth** by adjournment
on the 26th of the 8th month 1776. The Representatives being called **Alice Anthony** pre^{sent}

Ann Gifford Signed a few lines on behalf of **Anne Giford [Gifford]** Recommending her publick Testimony
Certificate to **Sandwich** monthly meeting to be held at **Falmoth**

List of friend Signed a List of the Names of the members that hath had Removal Certificates
removd From our Meeting to the monthly meeting at the **Ninepartners** and **Oblong**

Job Case Signed a Removal Certificate for **Job Case** and his Children Namely
Certificate **Pardon, A^{b}ner, Elisabeth, Alice, Jonathan, Mary, Sarah, Anna,$_\wedge$^{Roby} Dinah** and
Amie, all which are Recommended to the monthly meeting at the **Olong**

---

9 month At a Monthly meeting of Woman Friends held in **Dartmouth** y^e 16th of 9th month 1776
1776 The Friends appointed to attend the monthly meeting are **Susanna Allen**
and **Mary Smith 2^d** both Present

Ann Gifford Our Friend **Anne Gifford** hath Returned her Certificate that she had
Mary Trafford Last monthly meeting recommending her to **Sandwich** monthly meeting
Signed a Removal Certificate for **Mary Trafford** Recommending her to the
Accockset monthly meeting

Meribah Signed a Paper of denial against **Meribah Smith** which is to be read publickly
Smith at the end of a first day meeting between this and the next monthly meeting

Mary Wing **Mary Wing**s paper of Den^{i}al hath not been read

To Q meeting **Judith Russell Sarah Gifford** and **Deborah Hayden** are appointed to attend the
Quarterly m^{e}eting and they to make report to the next monthly meeting: The Queries
have been read and answered the answer$_\wedge$^{approved} & to be sent up to the Quarterly meeting by
by our Representatives

adjornd This meeting adjourns to the 2^d day of next week at 11 a C^{l}ock

mett At a monthly meeting of Women Friends held in **Dartmouth** by adjournment
on the 23 day of the 9th month 1776
The Representatives are **Susanna A^{l}len** and **Mary Smith 2^d** both present

Gideon It is the Judgment and the Conclusion of this meeting to accept a paper
Howland 2^d of acknowledgment, that **Gidenon Howland** and his wife **Catherine** presented
& wife Provided they Read or cause Said paper to be red publickly at the end of a

first day meeting of Worship between this and the next monthly meeting he the
Said **Gideon** being present: and She excluded of being present by reason of
her Circumstance it is not to be a pesident for the futer.

Elders   **Deborah Hayden** and **Deborah Hick [Hicks]** are are chose and appointed into Service
and place of Elders

Epistle   The Epistle was read approved and Signed in this meeting and to be Sent
up to the Quarterly meeting by our Representatives

---

10 month At a Monthly Meeting of Women Friends held in **Dartmouth** yᵉ 21ˢᵗ of 10ᵗʰ month 1776
1776 The Representatives are **Judith Rusˢell** and **Silvester Howland** both present

A Paper of denial against **Meribah Smith** hath been read Since last
monthly meetⁱng and is ₍as₎ followeth

Meribah   Whereas **Meribah Smith** Daughter of **Benjamin Smith** 2ᵈ and **Susanna** his wife
Smith hath had her Education amoungst Friends but by giveing way to the
denial Insinuation of the Advisary so as to Commit the grose Sin of fornication
as appears by her having a child unmarried and notwithstanding Our Labour
of Love She hath not appearᵉd to make Satisfaction: Now for the clearing of Truth
And Friends from Such a reprᵒachful Sin, do hereby deny the said **Meribah
Smith** from being a Member of our Religious Society and from under the care
of this meeting: Desiring if it may be Consistant with Divine Wisdom She
may Come to a Sight&sence of her outgoings and by unfeigned Repentance be restored
to the way of Truth

Given forth at a Monthly Meeting of Friends held in **Dartmouth** on the 16 day
of the 9ᵗʰ month 1776. Signed in and on behalf of Said Meeting By

             William Anthony Juʳ Clerk
             Susanna Smith Clerk

From Q meet=   The Friends appointed to attend the Quarterly meeting, hath attended
=ing according to appointment: From which meeting we received an Epistle which
was read and kindly accepted amoung us

Abigail   **Abigail Rogers** desires a few lines Recommending her back to **Pembrook** meeting
Rogers **Freeborn Rider** and **Hannah Mosher** are appointed to make Inquiry and if
nothing appear to hinder, to draw and bring a few lines to next monthly meeting

Gideon   **Gedion Howland** and **Catherine** his Wife their paper of acknowledgment
Howland 2ᵈ hath been read Since last monthly meeting – and is as followeth
& wife To the Preparative and monthly meeting of **Poneganset** to be held the 13ᵗʰ & 18 days of 3ᵈ mo 1776
Dear Friends – Whereas We through unwachfulness are fallen into the Sin of For=
=cation as appears by our having a Child so Soon after marriage for which we are
Sorry desiring the Lord may forgive us, and Friends pass it by, together with our
marrying nearer in kindred than is allowable amoung Friends hopeing for the futer
Through Divine assistance we may be Enabⁱed to walk more circomspect that friends
would Still continue us under their care   **Gideon Howland**
Dated this 13 of 3 month 1776   **Cathᵉren Howland**

Susanna   Signed a few lines for **Susanna Allen** Recommending her to the **Ninepartner** month
Allen =ly meeting on a Visit to See her friends and Relations thereabout

11 month
1776

At a Monthly Meeting of Women Friends held in **Dartmouth** yᵉ 18th of 11th month 1776
The friends appointed to attend the monthly meeting are **Naomy Howland** & **Deborah Allen** both ‸present

Sam Howland
proposal of
marriage

Samuel Howland and **Mary Smith** hath laid their Intentions of Marriage before this meeting; They were desired to wait for their answer untill next monthly
Naomey Howland and **Deborah Allen** are appointed to make enquiry into **Mary Smiths** Clearness and Conversation respecting marriage and they to make report to the next monthly meeting

Rebecca
Russell
Receᵈ

The Committee that had the care concerning **Rebecca Russell** wife to **Charles Russell,** requesting to come under friends care, make report, they find nothing to hinder and think her worthy to be receivd; and in consideration thereof this meeting Concluds and doth receive her into membership and under the care of this meeting

Abigail
Rogers

Signed a few lines in this meeting Recommending **Abibail Rogers** back to **Pembrock** monthly meeting

adjouʳnd

This meeting adjourns to next fourth day come week

mett

At a Monthly meeing of Women friends held in **Dartmouth** by adjournment on the 27th day of the 11th month 1776 the friends that ware appointed to attend th monthly meeting are **Naomey Howland** and **Deborah Allen: Deborah Allen** Present

Overseer

Deborah Allen is appointed in the place of an overseer of Disorders for one Quarter by reason that one of our overseers is gone a Journey and need require at present

---

12 month
1776

At a Monthly Meeting of Women Friends held in **Dartmouth** yᵉ 16th of 12th month 1776
The friends appointed to attend the monthly meeting are **Deborah Hayden** and **Alice Anthony** both present

Mary Smith
Clearness

The friends that was appointed to make Enquiry into **mary Smith** clearness and Conversation respecting marriage, make report, they find nothing to hinder their prceeding

Samuel
Howland
Answer

Samuel Howland and **Mary Smith** appeared for their answer; Which was they may proceed to take Each other in marriage at Some convenient time before next monthly meeting advising with the overseers appointed for that purpose who are **Deborah Allen** and **Hannah Mosher,** and they to make report at the next monthly metᶦⁿᵍ

Susan Allen

Susanna Allen hath returned a Certificate She had of this meeting to carry to the **Ninepartners** on a visit

Mary Russel
Lucy Howland
Mar Howlan
papers

Mary Russell Widdow, **Lucy Howland** and **Mary Howland** have each of them Sent a few lines to this meeting Condeming their Purchasing Prize Suger: Which are Refered until the next monthly meeting for further Consideration

adjournd

This Meeting Adjourns to the 30th day of this Instant

mett

Mett by Adjournment of the 12th month
The Representatives are **Deborᵃʰ Hayden** and **Alice Anthony Deborah Hayden** preˢᵉⁿᵗ
Silvester Howland is appointed to attend the Quarterly meeting and to make Return to the next monthly meeting

To the Qatlʸ
meeting

Signed an Epistle to the Quarterly meeting to be sent up by our Representative

1 month
1777

At a Monthly Meeting of Women Friends held in **Dartmouth** ye 20th of 1st month 1777
The Friends appointed to attend the monthly meeting are **Silvester** and **Hannah Mosher**, both Present

Sam Howland married

Deborah Allen Informes that it so fell out that She could not with conveniency attend **Samuel Howland**s marriage according to appointment, **Hannah Mosher** Informes She attend^ed and the marriage was consumated and car^ryed on orderly

Silv^r Howland not attend Q meeting

Silvester Howland Informes She did not attend the Quarterly meeting by reason it was thought not practable on the account of the great Commotions; Nevertheless

Epistle rec^d

We received an Epistle from our said Quarterly meet^ing which was read in this our meeting and kindly received to the Living amoung us

Martha Allen request

Martha Allen appeared ~~in this~~ with a few lines desiring for herself and two daughters to be taken under Friends Care

Hannah Mosher and **Keziah Russell** are appointed to have the matter under their care, and converse with her and her daughters to see wheither ‸the motive Springs from true Conviction, and they Sutiable to be receiv^d amoung Friends and they to make report to this meeting when ready

Mary Russel &c: paper Reced with provisor

Mary Russell, **Lucy Howland** and **Mary Howland** have Sent in a few lines to this meeting condemning their offence in purchasing Prize Sugars[24] which is accepted: Provoided, they do Sign a Testimony that the meeting shall draw For a more fully clearing the Truth: **Sarah Anthony** and **Susanna Smith** Are appointed to Joine the men friends in drawing the before mentioned Testimony

2 month
1777

At a Monthly Meeting of Women Friends held in **Dartmouth** ye 17th of 2d month 1777
There are no Representatives appointed to attend this meeting; by reason that a State of Indifferency so far prevails as to let Small things hinder attending our meetings, so that there was but two Women at our last Preparit[i]ve meeting

Mar Allen

The matter concerning **Martha Allen** is refered under the Same friends care

Mary Russel &c Case referd

The matter concernin those friends that have condemned their purchasing ~~is~~ Prize Suger, is refered until next monthly meeting by reason they are not present at this time

Rebec Shove Certificate

Rebecca Shove Widdow, hath Produced a Removal Certificate from **Swanzey** monthly meeting for herself and Daughter **Rebecca** to this meeting which is accepted

Elisa Russel under dealing

The overseers Inform this meeting that **Elisabeth Russell** appears to be guilty of purchasing Prize Sugar, for which they have Laboured with her for but no Dispossition appears for any Satisfaction; therefore this meeting appoints **Susanna Allen Sarah Gifford** and **Sarah Anthony** a Com^mittee to deal and Labour further to bring her to a sight of so Inniquitous a practice and to let her know that friends proceed against her if She doth not find freedom to make Satisfaction: and said Committ^ee to make report to the next monthly meeting

3 month
1777

At a Monthly Meeting of Women Friends held in **Dartmouth** ye 17th of 3d month 1777
The friends that are appointed to attend the monthly meeting are **Deborah Hayden** and **Silvester Howland** Both Present

Martha Allen

The matter concerni[n]g **Martha Allen** is refered another month under the same friends care

---

24. Prize sugar was sugar seized from a British merchant vessel by an American privateer and offered for sale. Friends viewed purchasing any sort of prize as supporting war.

Mary Russell &c   **Mary Russell, Mary Howland,** and **Lucey How**l**and** hath Signed a Testimony condem= =ning their being concerned in prize ~~goods~~ Suger, and Sent to this meeting which is to be read publickly at the end of a first day meeting of Worship between this and the next monthly meeting; and then the matter will be made up

Elis Russell refered   The matter concerning **Elisabeth Rus**s**ell** is refered Another month under the same friends care

Bethiah Eldredg request   **Bethiah Eldredg [Eldridge]** presented a few lines to this meeting desiring to come under friends care **Deborah Hayden** and **Naomy Howland** are appointed to converse with her and have the mater under their care to find wheither She is worthy of her request and they to make report when ready

Judith Akin   This meeting is Informed that **Judith Akin** is married out of the unity of Friends **Alice Anthony** and **Deborah Allen** are appointed to treat with her for the Same and they to make report to the next monthly meeting

Jonathan Willbor & wife request   **Jonathan Willbor [Wilbur]** and his Wife **Huldah** desire for themselves and Children to be taken under the care of friends care: **Deborah Allen Susanna Allen** and **Susannah Smith** are appointed to Joine the men friends and viset the family to see if they are worthy to be receiveded under the care of friends, and they to Report when ready

Queries answer   The Queries have been read approved and Answered in this meeting

Abigail Russell disorder   We are by the overseers inform[d] that **Abigail Russell** appears to be guilty of pur= =chasing prize Suger which She hath been Laboured with for. but friends not finding Satisfaction: This meeting doth appoint **Hanah Tucker Susanna Allen Sarah Anthony** and **Sarah Gifford** a Committee to treat further with said **Abigail** Concerning her offence and they to make [re]port to the next monthly mee[t]ing

Mary Howland   **Mary Howland** desires a few lines Recommending her to **Accakset** monthly meeting **Mary Smith** and **Sunana Smith** are appointed to draw the Same if nothing on inquery apears to hinder

Abigail Wood Esther Wood   Received a few lines by way removal Certificates on behalf of **Abigail Wood Esther Wood** da[u]gh[t]ers of **Daniel Wood** deceased, fom **Acoakset** monthly meeting Recommending them as members to this meeting which are accepted

Adjournd   This Meeting adjourns to next fourth day come week at the 11[th] hour the meeing to begin

mett   At a Monthly meeting of Women Friends held in **Dartmout[h]** by Adjournment on the 26th day of the 3[d] month 1777 **Deborah Ha**y**den** and **Silvester Howland** was appoint[ed] to attend the monthly meeting both present

To the Qut[ly] *meeting*   The Epistle to the Quarterly meeting was read, approved, and Signed in this meeting and Sent up to the Quarterly meeting by our Representatives who are **Silvester Howland Martha Pabody [Peabody]** and **Susanna Smith**

Elders   **Deborah Hayden Deborah Hicks** and **Susanna Smith** are Recommended as Elders to the Quarterly meeting in the Epistle

Hannah Shearman   **Deborah Hayden,** and **Rebecca Ricketson** are appointed to Draw a Certificate on behalf of **Hannah Shearman [Sherman]** Wife to **Joshua Shearman [Sherman]**, on Enquiry nothing appears to hinde[r] Recommending her to **Sandwich** monthly meeting

4 month   At a Monthly Meeting of Women Friends held in **Dartmouth** y[e] 21st of y[e] 4th month 1777

1777   The Representatives are **Mary Tucker,** and **Barsheba Howland** both present

Martha Allen Rec^d   The Committee that was appointed in regard of **Martha Allen** wife of **Jonathan Allen** Requesting to come under friends care with her two daughters Namely **Mary** and **Isabel Allen**, make report, they found good Satisfaction and think they may be Received; In consideration thereof this meeting concluds to Receive them into Membership with said meeting

Mary Russell Lucy Howland Mary Howland   The Testimony that **Mary Russell**, **Lucey Howland** and **Mary Howland** Signed to be read before this monthly meeting, is not yet read, but is to be before next Monthly meeting; and as many of them as can convenienly are to be present

Elis: Russell   The matter concerning **Elisabeth Russell** is continued anoth_^^{er} month under ye friends care

Judith Akin   The Committee appointed last monthly meeting to Treat with **Judith Akin** have not had oppertunity have not had opportunity [*sic*] according to appointments **Alice Anthony** and **Silvester Howland** are appointed to treat ^with said **Judith** for the Same offence and make reporte to the next monthly meeting

Abigail Russel   The Committee appointed to treat with **Abigail Russell** concering her offence mak^e Report, they have, accordingly to appointment, and found prity good Satisfaction and Likwise She hath Sent a few lines to this meeting condemning the Same. Which this meeting acccepts provided said paper is read publickly at the end of first day meeting of Worship between this and the next monthly meeting She present

Return from Q meeting   This meeting is informed that **Silvester Howland** and **Martha Pabedy [Peabody]** attended the Quaterly meeting according to appointment: **Susanna Smith** was not able By whome we received an Epistle from the Same, which we Kindly accept hoping the good advice contained therein will be more observed for the future

Elis Allen   **Elisabeth Allen** wife of **Eleazer Allen** hath brought a few lines to this ~ meeting condemning her marr[y]ing out of the Unity of Friends; this meeting appoints **Deborah Allen** and **Susanna Allen** to treat with said **Elisabeth** for her offence and find if She is sencear [sincere] in acknowledgment, and worthy to be Continued amoung friends; and they to make report when ready

Mary Howland certificate   Signed a removal Certificate on behalf of **Mary Howland** wife of **Samuel Howland** Recommending her as a member to **Accoakset** monthy meeting

Sarah Slocum widdow & daughters   We are Informed that **Sarah Slocum** Widdow to **Charles Slocum** with her Daug[h]ters are now Residens within the Compass of **Greenwich** monthly meeting And now they have a Title of membership in this meeting: In consideration thereof this meeting drew and Signed a few lines to **Greenwich** monthly meeting desiring they would make Enquiry into their lives and convesations wheither it is agreeable to friends Rules, and deal with th^em if occation on our behalf and Likewise inform us the Circumstance thereof

Penelope Trafford   Ths meeting appoints **Alice Anthony Sarah Anthony** and **Barsheba Howland** to treat and Labour with **Penelope Trafford** concerning Some disordere we fear She is guilty of and let her know that it is inconsistant with our Rules and that friends likely will disown her if she persists therein

5 month 1777   At a Monthly mee[t]ing of Women friends held in **Dartmouth** ye 19th of 5th month 1777 The friends appointed to attend the monthly meeting are **Judith Rus^sell** and **Deborah Hayden** both present

Mary Russell
L: Howland
M: Howland

Mary Russell, Lucey Howland, and **Mary Howland**s paper of acknowledgment hath been read since last monthly meeting according to the conclusion of Said meeting ~ and is as followeth

acknowledg
ment

    To the Monthly meeting of friends in **Dartmouth**
Beloved Friend. We the Subscribers having Inconsideratly Purchashed
Or pertook of Some Small Quantaty of those goods called prize goods taken by
War and Violence, which said Conduct of ours, after a mature Consideration
thereof we do utterly Condemn, and are Sorry for it. Hereby Publickly Testifying
to all people unto whome these presents shall come, that as our conduct is Inconsistant
with the Religious Profession we make, So we would take the repr[o]ach theof to our
Selves and clear the Truth and the professions thereof from the Same, Desireing forgivness
from the Divine Goodness, and that friends would so far pass by this our misco[n]duct
as to let us remain under their care hoping for the future through Divine assistance
to be preserved from the Like misconduct
Dated yᵉ 17ᵗʰ of yᵉ 3 month 1777   From your friends   **Mary Russell**
                                                          Lucy Holand [Howland]
                                                          Mary Howland

Elisabeth
Slocum
Russell

The Committee that was appinted to treat and Labour with **Elisabeth Russell** concerning
her having a hand in purchasing Prize goods, and Likewise her going to a mariage
out of the Unity of friends: mak Report. they have discharged their duty according
to appointment and found no Satisfaction; this meeting thinks they are clear without
any further Labour, and do appoint **Sarah Anthony** and **Sarah Howland** to draw
a paper of Denial against the said **Elisabeth** and bring to the next monthly meeting

Judith Akin
disowned

    The committee that was appointed to treat and Labour wth **Judith Akin**
Wife of **Richard Akin,** for her marriing out of the Unity of Friends make report
they have don according to appointment and they found no disposition in her
to make Satisfaction for her offences and this meeting thinks they are clear
from any further Labour, and do disown her of being any longer in membership with us.

Abiail Russel
Acknoledg=
ment

    Abigail Russells paper of acknowlegment hath been read Since last monthly
meeting accoring to the conclusion of said meeting ~ and is as followeth
    To the Monthly Meeting to be held yᵉ 21ˢᵗ day of 4ᵗʰ month 1777
Wheare as I through unwatchfulness purchased Some of those goods Called
Prize Goods; Which I am sorry for and do Condemn, desireing Friends to
pass it by and Let me Remain under their Care hoping I shall be more carful
for the time to come
Dated 20ᵗʰ day of 4ᵗʰ month 1777   **Abigail Russell**

Jonathan
Willbor
wife and Chil
dren Recᵈ

The Committee that was appointed in regard of **Jonathan Willbor [Wilbur]** and
Huldah his wife and children; concerning their requesting to come under
Friends care make report, that they have according to appointment, and
found a degree of Satisfaction: In Consideration thereof this Meeting
Receives them the Said **Jonathan Willbor [Wilbur]** and **Huldah Willbor [Wilbur]** under
our care, with their Children, Namely. **Benjamin, Abigail, Barsheba**
Huldah, Charlottee Rebecah and **Elizabeth**

complaint against Elisabeth Howland	This meeting is Informed ‸by overseers that **Isaac Howland** complains that his ~~children?~~ Daughter in law **Elisabeth Howland** hath abused him in some respects For which this meeting appoints **Susannah Allen Deborah Allen** and **Keziah Russell** to Inspect into the Circumstace and to Labour and deal with her as need requires for the Same and make report to the next monthly meeting
Deborah Allen overseer	**Deborah Allen** is appointd Overseer of Disorders
Complint against Esther Russell	This meeting is Informd that **Est‸her Russell** hath married out of the Unity of Friends and had a child Soon after marriage, and hath been to a disorderly marriage Since, for which offence. **Deborah Allen** and **Junah Smith** are appoin==ted to labur and deal with her therefor and report to next monthly meeting
Abigail How land deny^d	The Overseers inform they have preadmonshed **Abigail Howland** wife to **Isaac Howland** for proceeding to marry out of the Unity of Friends, She not regarding the advice but persisted therein for which this meeting disowns her from being a member of our society
widow Phebe Russell misconduct	This meeing is informd by the overseers that **Phebe Russell** widow appeares to ‸be guilty of purchasing and peataking of Prize goods for which offence **Susanna Russell** and **Judith Russell** are appointed to Labour to bring her to a Sight of her misconduct therein and they to make report to the next monthly meeting
Judith Akin Abigail Howland	And likwise the Same Committee to Inform **Judith Akin** of her denial and Inform **Abigail Howland** wife of **Isaac Howland** of her denial
6 month 1777	At a Monthly Meeting of Women Friends held in **Dartmouth** ye 16th of ye 6th month 1777. The Representatives are **Alice Anthony** and **Susanna Allen** present
adjournd	This Meeting Adjourns to the 23^d of this Instant
mett	Mett by adjournment ye 23^d of 6th month 1777 ~ Representatives both Present
Elisabeth Howland disownd	The Committee that was appinted in regard of **Elisabeth Howland**s conduct toward her father in law, make report. they have mett according to appointment Laboured and advised according to their capassity but found no Satisfaction. In consideration therof, it is the Judgment and conclusion of this meeting to disown her for her misconduct in Several respect for it appears that some violence was used which was the cause of much pain and Sorrow to him her said father: for which this meeting appoints **Deborah Allen** and **Susanna Allen** to draw a paper of denial against her and bring to the next monthly meeting
Phebe Russel refer^d	The committee that was appointed concerning **Phebe Russell** being guilty of purchasing prize goods: and allowing a marriage in her house out of the Unity of friends make report they found no Satisfaction: only She desires friends to wait another month Signfying she had a desire to make up the matter; which request is granted and the matter ‸to rest under the Same friend care
Bethiah Eldreg Rece	The Committee that was appointed to see into the Sencerity of **Bethiah Eldredg** [**Eldridge**] Requesting to come under friend care report they found pretty good sattisfaction and they think she may be received: And in consideration‸thereof She is admitted into membership and under the care of this meeting
Elis. Russell denial singned	The F[r]iends appointed to draw a ppaper of denial against **Elizabeth Russell** have brought one which was Signed in behalf of this meeting and is to be read

at the End of a first day meeting, between this and the next monthly meeting
and the paper to be returned to be put on Record

Elisa Allen
accepted

The Committee appointed to Treat with **Elisabeth Allin [Allen]** concerning her making
Satisfaction for her marrying out of the Unity of Friends make report She
gave them pretty good Satisfaction: and it is the conclusion of this meeting to
let her remain under their care and in membership with us

Sent up to
[Q?] meeting

The Queries have been read, answered, and the answers approved, and the ~
Epistle read, and Signed in this meeting and Sent up by our Representatives, who
are **Judith Russell, Keziah Russell** and **Elisabeth Slocum** and they to make
report to the next monthly meeting

Esther Russel

The Commttee appointed to Treat with **Esther Russell**, make rep[o]rt thy have not
accompli^{s}hed the matter and it is refered another month

Hanh Sherman
Certificate

Signed a Removal Certificate on behalf of **Hanah Sh^{e}arman** Recommending
her to **Sandwich** monthly meeting

7 mo^{n}th
1777

At a Monthly Meeting of Wome Friends held in **Dartmouth** ye 21st of ye 7th month 1777
Susanna Allen and **Amie Barker** was appointed to attend the mo^{n}thly meeting both presen^t

John Williams
pro^{p}osal of
marriage

John Williams And **Martha Pabody [Peabody]**, Si^{g}nified their Intentions marriage bef[o]re
this meeting and they are desired to waite untill the next monthly meeting for
their answer ~ **Deborah Hayden** and **Keziah Russell** are appointed to make
Enquiry into **Martha Pabody [Peabody]** clearness and conversation respecting marriage
and they to make report at the next monthly meeting

Phebe Russel

The matter concerning **Phebe Russell** is continued another month under
the care of the former Committee with **Alice Anthony** & **Silvester Howland** aded ther^{to}

Elis Russell

The paper of denial against **Elisabeth Russell** hath not been read
The Friends appointed to attend the Quarterly meeting make report they
all have according to appointment except **Elisabeth Slocum**, by whom we receivd

Return from
Q meeting
Epistles rece^d

the Quarterly meeting Epistle with one from the Womens Yearly meeting held
at **Philidelphia** for **Pensylvania**, bearing date the 9th month 1776 with much
Seasonable advice contained therein which was kindly received among us

Esther Russel
case

The Committee that was appointed to Treat with **Esther Russell** wife to **Paul
Russell** make report, they have had an oppertunity, according to their appointment
and found her in no disposion to make Satisfaction; This meeting considering the
report thinks they are with out any further Labour; do appoint the Same Committee
to draw a paper of denial against her and bring to next monthly meeting

Lillis
Maccomber
request

Lillis Maccomber [Macomber] Requests to come under the care of Friends and this
meeting appoints **Deborah Hicks** and **Elisabeth Slocum** to have the matter
under their care, to See $_{\wedge}$$^{if she}$ is worthy and they to make report when ready

Mary Lap=
=ham request

Mary Lapham Wife to **Nicholas Lappham [Lapham]** Desiers to come under the care of
Friends; and this meeting appoints **Alice Anthony** and **Susanna Smith** to have
the matter under their care, to See if She is worthy of her request and they to
make report when ready

Elis. Howland
denial
signd

A Paper of denial was Signed against **Elisabeth Howland**; and to be read
at the close of a first day meeting before next monthly meeting

This Meeting appoints **Deborah Hayden**, **Deborah Hicks**, **Susana Smith**, and **Sarah Anthony**, a Committee to Inspect consider, and determine the matter concerning

Sarah Slocum case **Sarah Slocum**, and her children haveing a ~~Birth~~ right among us of membership and what manner to proceed in the affare that may be to the honnour of Truth And for them to take Such men friends as appears Suitable to assist them in the affairs and draw a paper of Denial against them if need requiren and make Report to the next monthly meeting.

Penelope Trafford disowned The Committee that was appointed to Inspect and Labor with **Penelope Trafford** concerning Some reports that was abroad: Informe, they have had an oppertunity and it appears She hath freequan^tly attended the Priestbeterian meeting for Some considearable times and like drest after their custom and left our meeting which is not agreeable to our profession: For which they Laboured with her For her recovery, but found no Satisfaction; this meeting considering the report think they are clear without any more Labour, and do deny ^her of being a member in our Society

8 month 1777 At a Monthly Meeting of Women Friends held in **Dartmouth** ye 18th of 8th month 1777 The Representatives are **Deborah Hayden** and **Sarah Howland** ~~Daborah Hayden~~ present

Martha Papodys Clearnes The friends appointed to make Enquiry into **Martha Pabodys** [**Peabodys**] clearness and Conversation respecting marriage make report they find nothing to hinder their proceeding in marriage

John Williams Answer **John Williams** and **Martha Pabody** [**Peabody**] appeared for their answer: which was they might proceed to take each other in marriage at Some convenient time between this and the next monthly meeting advising with the oveseers appointed for that Service who are **Keziah Russell** and **Alice Anthony**

Lillis Mac= =comber case referd The Committee that was appointed to converse with **Lillis Maccomber** [**Macomber**] concerning her request: make report, they have had an oppertunity according to appointment and they think best waite longer that She may be better acquainted with ~~friend~~ Principles of Truth before She be Joined in Society, and for the Same friends to have the matter under their care

A Paper of denial hath been read against **Elisabeth Russell**. Since last monthly meeting and is as followeth

Elisabeth Russell paper of denial Whereas **Elisabeth Russell** wife of **Benjamin Russell** Miller haveing had her Education amoung friends and under the care of this meeting, but hath so far departed ~~there~~ from the Simplicity of Truth, and the prof[e]ssion we make as to be found in the pract^ice of buying or purtaaking of those called Prize goods Like wise in going or resorting at a Wedding out of the Unity off friends, all which She hath been Laboured with for in love, in order to Shew her the Evil thereof; but our Labour not obtaining its desired Effect, nor She being free to the Condemning said misconduct to friends Satisfaction: therfore There for the clearing of Truth and friends from the reproach thereof This meeting is concerned to give this forth as a publick Testimony against her Hereby Disowning the said **Elisabeth Russell** from under the care of this meeting Nevertheless Desireing She may come to ^a sight of the Evil of such practices and

Return and be Restored to the way of Truth

Given forth at our Monthly meeting held in **Dartmouth** yᵉ 23ᵈ of yᵉ 6 month 1777

Signed in & on behalf of sᵈ meeting by **Wᵐ Anthony Juʳ** Clerk

Susanna Smith Clerk

Mary Wing paper of denial A Paper of denial against **Mary Wing** was read since last monthly meeting And is as followeth

Whereas **Mary Wing** Some yᵉars past was under Dealing by this meeing as apᵉar by our Records, and altho' She gave in a paper Condemⁿing her misconduct yet the meeting did not receive her in full Unity but Suspended the matter for a proof of her Sincerity, now this meeting of late havin made Enquiry into her conduct and Conversation ~~with~~ and Likwise have had conference with her on that matter and do not find a Sufficient proof of a Sincear Repentance but Reather the contʳary: Therefore this meeting doth deny her the said **Mary Wing** From being a member of our Religious Society, until by Sencarer Repentance and a return from the Evil of her ways, (as a Sure Token thereof) to the way of Truth and well doing

Signed in and on behalf of our monthly meeting   **William Anthony Juʳ** Clerk

Held in **Dartmouth** the 19ᵗʰ of yᵉ 8ᵗʰ month 1777 By   **Susanna Smith** Clerk

A Paper of Denial against **Elisabeth Howland** was Read according to the Conclusion of the last monthly meeting ~ and is as followeth

Elisabeth Howland denial Whereas **Elisabeth Howland** Wife of **Benjamin Howland**, being a member of our Religious Society Through unwatchfulness and disregarding the Testimonʸ of Truth in her own hᵉart, hath fallen into bodily Strife with her father in law **Isaac Howland** and abused him, and hath not made him Sattisfaction, for which misconduct much Labour hath been besᵗowed in love for her recovery But all our labour proveing Ineffectual to friends Satisfaction: Now for the Clearing of Truth, and Friends from Such Groos Evils Do hereby disown the said **Elisabeth Howland** from being a member of our ᷉Religious Society, and from from [*sic*] under the care of this meeing desireing She may come to a hearty Repentaⁿᶜᵉ and find mercy

Given forth at a Monthly Meeting held in **Dartmouth**   ⎫ **Wᵐ Anthony Juʳ** Clerk

this 21ˢᵗ day of yᵉ 7ᵗʰ month 1777   ⎬ **Susanna Smith** Clerk

Signed in and on behalf of Said meeting By   ⎭

adjournd This Meeting Adjourns to next forth day come week

meet At a monthly meeting Women friends held in **Dartmouth** by adjourment this 27ᵗʰ of the 8ᵗʰ month 1777. The Representatives Called upon: **Sarah Howland** present

Phebe Russell **Phebe Russell** hath made this meeting Satisfaction Provided She cause her Paper to be read at the close of Some first day meeting before the next moⁿthly meeting She being present

Sarah Slocum oase refurd The matter concerning **Sarah Slocum** is referd another month under yᵉ same friends ᶜᵃʳᵉ

Jonathan Green Martha Green Received a Removal Certificate from **East Greenwick [Greenwich]** monthly meeting Recommening **Jonathan Greene [Green]** and **Martha Greene [Green]**. Children of **Rufus Green** as members to this meeting which is accepted

Esther Russell
Denied

Signed a paper of denial against **Ester Russell** which is to be read at the Close of a first day meeting before the next monthly meeting

David Sands
Certificate

Signed a few lines by way of Certificate on behalf of ∧our worthy friend **David Sands,** Signifying the Satisfaction we received of his Labour of Love ~~we receiv~~ among us: To the Monthly meeting at the **Ninepartners**

Aaron Lan=
caster
Certificate

Likwise Signed a few lines by way of Certificate in behalf of our Worthy Friend **Aaron Lancaster** Signyfying the Satisfaction we Received of his labour of Love among us: to the monthly meeting at the **O**b**long**

Q meeting
Commitee
request

This meeting is Informed that a Committee from the Quarterly requests That our next monthly meeting may be held the next day after the preparitive meeting, which this meeting concluds to grant according to ther request

---

9 month
1777

At a Monthly meeting of Women friends held in **Dartmouth** yᵉ 11ᵗʰ of 9ᵗʰ month 1777 **Sarah Anthony** and **Silvester Howland** are appointed to attend yᵉ montly meeting both present

John Williams
married

Kaziah Russell Informs She attended the marriage of **John Williams** according to appointment and that it was consumated and carried ᵒⁿ orderly ∧as far as she discoverd **Alice Anthony** did ∧not attend according to appointment

Phebe Russell

Phebe Russells paper of acknowledgment hath not been read but she Signifies She intends to accomplish the matter before the next monthly meeting

Sarah Slocum

The matter concerning **Sarah Slocum** is refered another month by reason we canot find the names of her Children

Esther Russell
paper of
denial

Easther Russells paper of denial hath been read according to the conclusion of the last monthly meeting ~ and is as followeth

　　　Whereas **Easter Russell** Wife of **Paul** has had her Education amongst Friends, yet through unwatchfulness∧and [mist_ing?] yᵉ Testimony of Truth hath so far Given way to the Insinuations of the advesary as to fall into the Goose [Gross?] Sine of Fornication as appears by her having a Child so soon afᵗer marriage, and also married out from amoungst Friends all which She hath been Laboured with for in order to Convince her of the Evil of her ways; but our Labour of Love not having the desired effect to friends Satisfaction; do give this forth as a publick Testimony against her the said **Easter Rus**s**ell,** disowning her from being a member of ∧our Religious Society and from under the care of this meeting. desiring She may come to a Sight of her outgoings and by unfeig[n]ed Repentance be resᵗored to the way of Truth

　　　Given∧forth at our monthly meeting held in **Dartmout** by adjournent this 21ˢᵗ day of the 8ᵗʰ month 1777. Signed in and on behalf of our said meeting By

　　　　　　　　　　　　　　　　　William Anthony Juʳ Clerk
　　　　　　　　　　　　　　　　　Susanna Smith Clerk

To Indulge
none But
our society

This meeting concluds not to Indulge any into this meeting that are not members of the Society for the future, Either at the proposing of marriages or at any other time

To be Sent
up to Qly
meeting

The Queries have been read ansered and approved in this meeting with the Epistle to be Sent up to the Quarterly ~~meet~~ meeting by our Representatives who are **Deborah Haden [Hayden]**, **Sarah Gifford** and **Deborah Allen** and they to make report to the next monthly meeting

To Correct
minites

This meeting appoints **Deborah Hayden Susanna Smith** and **Deborah Allen** to Revise and correct the miniuts and Settle withe Treasurer, and they to make Report to the next monthly meeting

Complaint
against
Katurah
Peckham

We are Informed by one of the Oversers that **Caturah Peckham** appears to be guilty of purchasing prize goods, for which she hath been ~~lab~~ treated with for, but She is not at present in a disposition to make Friends any Satis= =faction, this meeting appoints **Judith Russell** and **Kaziah Russell** to Labour further with her to bring her to a Sight thereof, and they to make report to the next Monthly meeting

Benj: How-
=land 3ᵈ
proposal of
marriage

Benjamin Howland yᵉ 3ᵈ and **Mary Slocum** Declared their Intentions of Marriage at this meeting and they were desired to waite for their answer untill next monthly meeting **Ruth Tucker** and **Lydia Barker** are appointed to make Enquiry into **Mary Slocum**s Clearness and Conversation respecting marriage and they to make report to the next monthly meeting

10 month
1777

At a Monthly Meeting of Women Friends held in **Dartmouth** yᵉ 20ᵗʰ of 10ᵗʰ month 1777 The friends that are appointed to attend the monthly meeting are **Deborah Hicks** And **Sarah Anthony**, **Sarah Anthony** present

Phebe Russell

Phebe Russells paper of ack[n]owledgment hath not been read, and the former comittee are desired to take an opertunity with her and Query what the case is and let her know the meeting waits another month upon her

Sarah Slocum

The matter concerning **Sarah Slocum** is refered another month on the account of the Same ocason as before given

Martha Slocum
Certificate

Received a removal Certificate from **Newport**[?] monthly meeting on behalf of **Martha Slocum** wife to **John Slocum** with her Nine Children Namely **Avis Martha Sarah**, **Benjamin**, **John**, **Pardon**, **William**, **Thomas**, and **Christopher** Recommending them as members to this me[e]ting which is accepted Likewise one born Since they came ~~w~~ Here whose name is **Elisabeth** Said **Martha** desires should be under the care of friend this me[e]ting grants her request and looks on it as a member

from meeting

The friend appointed to attend the Quaterly meeting Inform they attend according to appointment, from which we received an Epistle to good satisfaction desireing the good advice contained therein may be more observed for the future

minites not
Corrected

The committee that was appointed to revise corect the miniuts, and Settle with the Treasurer make report they have not acomplished the matter wʰich is another month under their care

Katurah
Peckham

The Committee that was appointed to Treat with **caturah Peckham** concerning her being guiᵗy of purchasing prize goods, make report they hav had an oppetunity and her not in a disposition to make Satisfaction at present but she desires friends to wait another month which is compᵗied with and left under the same friends care

Marcy
Slocum
Certificate

Received Removal Certificate from the monthly meeting of **Sandwich** held at Talmo[u]th on behalf of **Marcy Slocum** wife of **Giles Slocum** Recommending her as a member to this meeting which is accepted

Mary Slocum
Clearness

The friends that was appointed to make ~~to ma~~ Enquiry into **Mary Slocum**s Clearness and convesation respecting marriage make report they have performed the Same and find nothing to hinder their proceeding in marriage

*Ben How=
land 3
Answer*
Benjamin Howland 3ᵈ and **Mary Slocum** appeared for their answer; Which
was they may proceed to take Each other in Marriage at Some convenient time
between this and next monthly meeting, advising with the Overseers who are **Alice
Anthony** and **Susanna Smith,** and ‸ʳᵉᵖᵒʳᵗ to the next monthly meeting

*Mary How=
land
request*
Mary Howland daughter to **Job Howland** Inform this meeting She is about
to Remove within the Verge of the **Ninepartners** monthly meeting and desires
our Certificate: **Deborah Hayden** and **Lydia Barker** are appointed to make
Enquiry into her Life and conversation and if worthy draw a Certificate and
bring to the next monthly meeting

*11 month
1777*
At a Monthly Meeing of Women Friends held in **Dartmouth** yᵉ 17ᵗʰ of 11ᵗʰ month 1777
The friends appointed to attend the monthly meeting are **Deborah Allen** and **Deborah
Hayden** both present

Phebe Russel
This meeing concluds to waite one month Longer upon **Phebe Russell**

Sarah Slocum
The matter concerning **Sarah Slocum** is continued anothe month

The matter concerning **Caturah Peckham** is referd another month and the Same
Committee are desired to treat with her according to appointment

*Ben Howland:
marriage*
Alice Anthony Informs She attended **Benjaman Howland 3** marriage ~~accor~~
according to appointment and it was consumated orderly as far as She discoverᵈ
Susana Smith was disapointed ‸ᵒᶠ attend by reason her family was unwell

*Lillis Mac=
[co]mber
received*
The Committee that was appointed to Treat with **Lillis Maccomber** on acounᵗ
of her request, make report, they have had Several oppertunities with her and
think best to receive her [*smudge*] Therefore this meeting receives her into membership

*Mary How=
land Certif=
icate*
Sigined a Removal Certificate on behalf of **Mary Howland** daughter to **Job
Howland** Recomending her to the **Ninepartner** Monthly meeting

*12 month
1777*
At a Monthly Meeting of Women friends held in **Dartmouth** yᵉ 15ᵗʰ of 12ᵗʰ month 1777
The Representatives Called **Judith Russell** and **Mary Smith** appeared

*Phebe Russell
acknowledg
ment*
Phebe Russells paper of acknowledgment hath been read Since Last
monthly meeting ~ and is as followeth

　　To the Monthly Meeting of Friends to be held in **Dartmouth** yᵉ 18ᵗʰ of 8ᵗʰ month 1777
Dear Friends ~ Whereas I have Suffered a marriage in my house which was not
according to friends orders, and purchased Some Prize Suggers, all which
Condemn and am Sorry for and hope friends will pass it by so far as to Let
me Remain under their care ~ From your Loving friend **Phebe Russell**

*Mary Lap=
ham recᵈ*
The Committe appointed to Treat with **Mary Lapham** concerning her request
make report, they found pretty good Satisfaction, and that they dont find any
thing to hinder from being received; In Consideration there of this meetᶦng
accept her into membership

Sarah Slocum
The matter concerning **Sarah Slocum** is continued another month

*Katurah
Peckham
disownd*
The Committee appointe to Labour with **Caturah Peckham** for being guilty
Guilty of Purchasing Prize goods, make report that she rather countananced
what She had done: and this meeting thinks they are clear without any further
‸ᴸᵃᵇᵒᵘʳ and do appoint **Deborah Hicks** and **Deborah Allen** to draw a paper of denial

against the ˄sd **Catureh Peckham** and bring to the next monthly meeting **Keziah Russell** is appointed to acquainte **caturah** of her denial

Joanna Gifford Request
Joanna Giford [Gifford] Sent a few lines requesting to come under friends care and her husband requests the Same for their children ~ **Elisabeth Smith** and ~~Hana~~ **Hannah Mosher** are appointed to make Enquiry into their Lives and Conversations, and take Suitable oppertunitys of conference with them the better to unde^rstand wheither they are Worthy, and the motive Springs fro^m true Conviction: and they to make report when ready

To be Sent to Q meeting
No answers prepared at this time ~ Signed an account to be Sent to the ~ Quarterly meeting by our Representatives **Judith Russell, Sarah Anthony Susanna Smith** and **Elisabeth Slocum,** and they to make report to the next Monthly meeting

0-15ˢ-0 to Mart Williams
This meeting desires the Treasurer to pay the Sum of 15ˢ old Tennor to **Martha Williams** which hath been contracted for the Use of Friends

1ˢᵗ month 1778
At a Monthly Meeting of Women Friends held in **Dartmouth** yᵉ 19ᵗʰ of 1ˢᵗ month 1778 The Friend appointed to attend the monthly meeting are **Sarah Anthony** and **Sarah Howland** both Present

Sarah Slocum
The matter concerning **Sarah Slocum** is yet continued another month

report from Q meeting
This meeting is Informd that none of the Representatives that was appoiⁿted to attend the Quarterly meeting but **Elisabeth Slocum** hath performed according to appointment but gave Such reasons as are accepted; we received an

Epistle Recd
Epistle from said Quarterly meeting which was read and Kindly accepted

Treasurer report
The Treasurer Informs She hath paid the Sum of 15ˢ Shillings old Tennor to **Martha Williams** according to the direction of Last monthly meeting

Nic Lapham and wife request
Nicholus Lapham and his wife request that their childrren should be Taken under the care of Friends

This meeting apoints **Deborah Hicks** and **marry Smith** to Joine the men Frind in Visiting the family to find wheither it is agreeable to receive them, and they to make ˄report to the next monthly meeting

Mary Duel Request
Mary Duel Sent a few lines requesting to come under the care of this meeting: **Kaziah Russell** and **Hanah Mosher** are appointed to treat with her the better to understand wheither she is worthy to be received and that the motive Springs from the bottom of true Conviction and they to make report when ready

Content Cornel made satisfaction
Content Cornell hath ˄made the meeting Satisfaction for going to a marrage out of the unity of friends

Katurah Peck denial signd
Signed a Paper of Denial against **Caturah Peckham** which is to be Read at the Close of a first day meeting between now and next monthly meeting

Samˡ Gifford proposal of marriage
Samuel Gifford and **Lillis Maccomber [Macomber]** made proposal of marriage before this meeting and were desired to wᵃite untill next monthly meeting for their Answer ~ **Deborah Allen** and **Elisabeth Slocum** are appointed to make Enquiry into **Lillis Maccomber**s Clearness respecting marriage and Conversation; and make report to next monthly meeting

2 month
1778

At a Monthly Meeting of Women Friends held in **Dartmouth** yᵉ 16ᵗʰ of 2ⁿᵈ month 1778
The Representatives are **Deborah Hayden** and **Rebecca Ricketson: Rebeca** present

Sarah Slocum refer'd

The matter concerning **Sarah Slocum** is continued another month

Lillis Maccom==ber Clearness

The committee appointed to Enquire in **Lillis Maccombers** [**Macombers**] Clarness
and conversation respecting marriage make report, they find nothing
to hinder their proceeding in marriage

Sam Gifford Answer

Samuel Gifford and **Lillis Maccomber** [**Macomber**] appeared for their Answer
Which is they may proceed to take Each other in marriage at some
Convenient time before the next monthly meeting; advising with the
Overseers appointed for that Service who are **Deborah Allen** and **Elisabeth
Slocum** and they to make report next monthly meeting
The Denial against **Katurah Peckham** hath not been read

Rebeccah Rotch request

We are Informed that **Rebecca Rotch** Desires our Certificate Recommending her
to **Nantucket** Month meeting ~ **Deborah Davis** and **Rebecca Ricketson** are
appinted to make Enquiry into her Life and Conversation and if nothing apears
to hinder to Draw a few lines and bring to the nex monthly meeting

3 month
1778

At a Monthly Meeting of Women friends held in **Dartmou[t]h** yᵉ 16ᵗʰ of 3ᵈ month 1778
The Representatives are **Deborah Hayden** and **Mary Smith** both present

Sarah Slocum Case

Susanna Allen Elisabeth Slocum and **Susanna Smith** are appointed to take
an oppertunity to converse with **Sarah Slocum** concerning Some reports that
is S[p]read abroad concerning her and her children and if they appear not to be
deserving to remain among Friends, for them to draw a paper of Denial against
them agreeable to their offence and make report to the monthly meeting

Sam Gifford married

Elisabeth Slocum makes report she attended **Samuel Gifford**s marriage according
to appointment~~ment~~ and it was consumated and carried on with deacency as far
as She discovered

A Denial against **Katurah Peckham** hath been read against her Since last monthly
meeting and is as followeth

Katurah Peckham denial

Whereas **Katurah Peckham** having had a right of membership amoung F[r]iends
and under the care of this meeting, but hath so far departed from the Simplicity
of Truth and the Prfession,ᵂᵉ ᵐᵃᵏᵉ as to be found in the practice ~~of make~~ of buying those
Called Prize goods; and She hath been Laboured with for it in love, in order to ~~Shw~~
Shew her the Evil thereof but our Labour not having its desired effect nor She
being free to condemn it to friends Satisfaction: Therefor ,ᶠᵒʳ the Clearing ᵒᶠ Truth and
Friends from the repr[o]ach thereof this meeting is Concerned to give this forth
as a publick Testimony ,ᵃᵍᵃⁱⁿˢᵗ her hereby disowning the Said **Katurah Peckham** from
under the care of this meeting desiring She may come to a Sigh[t] of the Evil
of Such practices and Returⁿ and be restored to the way of Truth

Given forth at our Monthly meeting held in **Dartmouth** the 19ᵗʰ day 1ˢᵗ month 1778
Signed in and on behalf of Said Meeting by —   **William Anthony Jun**ʳ Clerk
                                                     Susanna Smith Clerk

Elis Johnson Request

Elisabeth Jonson [**Johnson**] desires to come under the care of this meeting with her two
Little daughters, if on Enquiry she is found worth: **Deborah Hayden** and **Eunice**

Taber are appointed to have Suitable oppertunities with ‸her and make enquiry on that account the better to understand Wheither the motive Springs from the bottom of true conviction and they to make report when ready

David Sheherd & son David Request

David Shepherd and his son **David** Signifies they are ab°ut to remove within Verge of **Smithfield** monthly meeting and desires removal Certificates thereto for themselves and families ~ **Alice Anthony** and **Silvester Howland** are appoint^ed to make Enquirey into their Lives and Conversations and if Nothing appears to hinder to Joine the men Friends in preparing Said Certificates and bring to the next monthly meeting

Complaint against Phebe Briggs

The Overseers Informe this meeting that **Phebe Brigg [Briggs]** Widdow to **Weston Briggs** appears to be guilty of Purtakeing or Countena^ncing the use of Prize goods, for ~~whsh~~ which they have Laboured with her for, and She gave no satisfaction **Sarah Giford [Gifford]** and **Mary Smith** are apointed to Labour further with her in order to Restore her and if she gives no Satisfaction, for them to Draw a Testimony of Denial against her and bring to nex monthly meeting

adjournd

This Meeting Adjourns to the 25th of this Instant

mett

Mett according to adjournment ye 25th of 3rd month 1778 Re^presentativs calld both present

Joanna Gifford Rec^d

The Committee that was appointed in regard to **Joanna Gifford**s request make report that they found good Satisfaction and find nothing to hinder her being Received ~ In consideration thereof this meeting receives her into membership with her two daughters Nam^ely **Lillis** and **Joanna Gifford**

To be sent to Qly meeting

The Queries have been read and answered. with the Epistle Signed and approved and to be Sent up to the Quarterly meeting by our Representatives who are **Susanna Smith Sarah Howland** and And [*sic*] **Sarah Anthony**; And they to make report to the next monthly meeting

Sarah Slocum & three daugh ters disownd

The Committee appointed Some time past on account of **Sarah Slocum** (widdow to **Charles Slocum**) And her children, make report, That they have Joined the men friends, and considered the matter and the return from **Greenwich** Monthly meeting; and also had conference with her; and finding their their Lives and Conversations so different from our Profession, as Not attending any of our Religious meeting, with many other disorders not her[e?] mentioned that they think it most for the Honnour of T‸^ruth to disown all them that are come to years of understanding. Which report being accepted Therefore we do disown the Said **Sarah Slocum** and her three Eldest daughters Namely **Margret, Desiah,** and **Mary:**

---

4 month 1778

At a Monthly Meeting of Women Friends held in **Dartmouth** 20th of 4th month 1778 The Representatives are **Susanna Allen** and **Sarah Anthony** both present

Phebe Briggs Referd

The matter concerning **Phebe Briggs** is continued another month

Return from Q meeting

The Friends that was appointed to attend the Quarterly meeting, report they attended according to their appointment, by whom we received an Epistle ‸^read and kindly accepted

Jos Rotch and wife Certificat

Signed a Removal Certificate for **Joseph Rotch** and wife recommending them to **Nantucket** monthly meeting

David Shep= =herd Ju^r Certificate	Signed a Removal Certificate for **David Sheph^rd Junor** [Shepherd] his wife and their two children Namly **Thomas** and **Reliance** Recomending them to **Smithfield** Monthly meeting
Mary Duel Received	The Committee that was appointed Some time past to treat with **Mary Dewel** [Davol?] concerning her Request, Make report they have had Several conferences with her and find pretty good Satisfaction and nothing to hinder her being Received, This meeting accepts s^d report, do receive her into membership with us
Elisabeth Allens Confession	**Elisabeth Allen** Sent a few lines to this meeting condemning her marrying out of the Unity of friends, and being guilty of the Sin of Fornication For which this meeting appoints **Deborah Hayden Deborah Hicks** and **Sarah Gifford** to Treat with her to d_iscover wheither She is Sencear, and worthy to be continued in membership; and they to report when ready
Hannah Woodman disownd	The overseers Inform _this meeting that **Hannah Woodman** Wife of **Robart Woodman** hath Lately married out of the Unity of friends, which they have Laboured with her Sufficiently for, she being obstinate, this meeting thinks they are clear without any further labour (She disregarding their advice) do disown her from being in membership with said meeting
Rebeccah Smith request	**Rebecca Smith** is a bout to remove to **Saratoga** within the verge of the **Ninepartners** monthly meeting and requests a Certificate for her Self and Children: **Sarah Anthony** and **Susanna Smith** are appointed to make Enquiry into their lives and Conversations. and prepare a Certificate for them if nothing appears to hinder and bring to next monthly meeting
Han Woodman to be informd	**Margret Stratton** is appointed to acquant **Hannah Woodman** withe her denial

5 month 1778	At a Monthly Meeting of Women Friends held in **Dartmouth** y^e 18th of 5th month 1778 The Representatives are **Amie Barker** and **Deborah Hayden** both present
Phebe Briggs Referd	The matter concerning **Phebe Briggs** is continued anothe^r month under y^e Sam frinds ^care
Ester Allen disownd	Some of the Overseers Inf_orm that **Esther Allen** Wife of **Robart Allen** hath married out of the Unty of Friends and they laboured with her before marriage, but She not regarding their advice and hath proceeded in marriage This meeting thinks they are clear without any further labour and do deny her of being in membership ~ **Susanna Russell** is appointed to acquaint her of her denial
David Shepherd Certificat	Signed a Removal Certificate for **David Shepher** [Shepherd], his Wife & children under age whose names are **Caleb, Deborah, Gideon, Allen, Elisabeth** and **Lydia**. Recommending them to **Smithfield** monthly meeting
Nic: Lapham Children Rec^d	The Committee apointed to Joine the men friends concerning receiving **Nicholas Lapham**s children under the care of friends, those that are tho not all ready make report they have had an oppertunty and think best to receive them The meeting accepts said report do receive them into membership
Rebec: Smith Certificate	Signed a Removal Certificate for **Rebecca Smith** (Wife of **Daniel Smith**) and her Children, Namely, **Jeremiah, Humphry, Elisabeth, James, Stephen, Abigail** and **Mary**, Recomending them to the **Ninepartners** [Nine Partners] monthly meeting

Jonaⁿ: Sowle proposal of marriage

Jonathan Sowle and **Barsheba Russell** declared their Intentions of marriage before this meeting and were desired to waite for their Answer till the next monthly meeting ~ **Mary Smith** and **Sarah Anthony** are appointed to make Enquiry into **Barsheba Russells** Clearness respe[c]ting Marriage, and her Life and Conversation, and make report the next monthly meeting

6 month 1778

At a Monthly meeting of Women friends held in **Dartmouth** yᵉ 15ᵗʰ of yᵉ 6ᵗʰ month 1778.
    Deborah Hayden Chose Clerk for this day
The Representatives are **Mary Smith** and **Silvester Howland** both present

Silvanus Folger & Georg Folger proposal of marriage

Silvanus Folger and **Avis Slocum** ~ And **George Folge** [**Folger**] and **Rebecca Slocum** Declared their Intentions of marriage before this meeting, and were desired to waite untill next monthly meeting for their Answers
Silvester Howland and **Mary Smith** are appointed to make Enquiry into **Avis Slocum**s Clearness and conversation respecting marriᵃge, and make report next monthly meeting ~ **Deborah Hicks** and **Deborah Allen** are appointed to See into **Rebecca Slocum**s Clearness and Conversation respecting marriage and they to make report next monthly meeting

adjournd

This Meeting is Adjournd to the 22ⁿᵈ day of this month at yᵉ Usual time

Mett

Mett by adjournment this 22ᵈ day of 6ᵗʰ month 1778 Representatives both present

Elis Johnson Recᵈ

The Committee that was appointed Some time past in regard to **Elisabeth Johnson**s Request, make report they found pretty good Satisfaction and think it may be for the best to receive them into membership: In consideration therof this meeting accepts Said report: and do receive her under the care of this meeting with her two little daughters, **Elisabeth** and **Theodate**

Phebe Brigg Case

Phebe Briggs Presented a few lines to this meeting condemning her purchashing Prize Suggar: Likewise the Committee Informs this meeting they have had Several oppertunity on that account, and they are free She Should be Continued among Friends, In Consideration thereof this meeting accepepts [*sic*] Said paper provided She Cause the Same to be read at the Close of a first day meeting of Worship between this and the next monthly meeting She being present when read

David Sand Aaron Lan= kester

Received a Certificate from the **Ninepartners** monthly meeting on behalf of our Worthy Friend **David Sands**: and one from **Oblong** on behalf of our Worthy Friend **Aaron Lankester** [**Lancaster**]; both which are acceable whose labours have been Com= fortable to the living among us

Esther Allen

Susanna Russell Inform this meeting She hath acquainted **Easther Allen** of her deniaˡ

Barsh Russell clearness

The friends that was appointed to make enquiry into **Barsheba Russell** clearness and Conversation respecting marriage make report. they have don acording to appointment and nothing appears to hinder their proceedings

Jonaⁿ Sowle answer

Jonathan Sowl [**Soule**] and **Barsheba Russell** appeared for their Answer; Which was They may proceed to take Each other in marriage at Some convenient time between this and next monthly meeting Advising with the overseers, who are **Alice Anthony Susanna Smith** and they to make report to the next monthly meeting

Elisa Hathway certificate

Received a Removal Certificate from **Swa[n]zey** monthly meeting in behalf of our Friend **Elisabeth Hathaway** and five of her Children Namely **Elisabeth**, **Jonas**, **Lydia**, **Mary** and **George**, all which is accepted *adjournd*   This Meeting Adjourns to the 24th of this Instant

mett   Mett by adjournment ye 24th of the 6th month 1778 Representatives both present

Sent up to   The Queries have been read and answered and the answers approved Likwise
Qualy meeting the Epistle Signed and sent up to the Quarterly meeting by our Representatives

Aaron Lan= Who are **Deborah Hayden**, **Judith Russell**, **Deborah Allen** and **Silvester**
=kester **Howland**; and they to make report to the next monthly meeting
David Sands Signed a Certificate on behalf of our Worthy friend **Aaron Lankester [Lancaster]** to the
Oblong monthly meeting: and one for our Worthy Friend **David Sands** to
the monthly meeting at the **Ninepartners** where they belong Signifying our
Satisfaction with them while amoung us

Reprove   **Alice Anthony** and **Kaziah Russell** are apointed to Joine the men friends
Deserters to treat and labour with those families that are inclin‸ing to freequant or attend
Such meetings as are not in Unity with friends and deal with them as Truth
Shall Require: and make report to the monthly meeting

7 month 1778 At a Monthly Meeting of Women Friends held in **Dartmouth** ye 20th of 7th month 1778
The Representatives are **Phebe Slocum** and **Mary Smith** both present

Avis Slocum   The friends appointed to Enquire into **Avis Slocum**s and **Rebecca Slocum**s
Rebec Slocum Clearness and Conversation respecting marriage make report they have don
Clearness agreeable to their appointment and nothing appears to hinder their proceeding
as they have discovered

Silvus Folger   **Silvanus Folger** and **Avis Slocum** ~ **George Folger Jur** and **Rebecca Slocum**
Geor Folger all appeared for their Answers; Which was they may proceed in marriage at
Answer Some convenient time between this and the next monthly meeting, advising
with the overseers this meeting shall appoint for that Service ~ **Mary Smith**
and **Silvester Howland** are appointed to have the oversight of **Silvanus**
Folgers and **Avis Slocum**s marriage **Deborah Allen** and **Deborah Hicks** are
appointed to have the oversight of **George Folger**s ‸& **Rebecca Slocum**s marriage
and th[e]y all to make report of their proceedings to the next monthly meeting

    Phebe Briggs paper of acknoledgment hath been read according to last
monthly meetings conclusion ~ and is as followeth

Phebe Brigg   To the Monthly meeting ‸of Women friends to be held at **aponeganset**
acknowledg= the 15th day of ye 6 month in the year 1778. ~ Esteemed friends, these lines may
=ment Inform you that I through unwatchfulness have pertook of prize Sager [Sugar]
which is contrary to the Testimony of Friends and the great Profession I am
makeing, for which disorder I am Sorry for, and desire Friends would
Pass it by and Suffer me to Remain under your Care, hopeing to be more
Careful for the time to come ~ From your friend **Phebe Briggs**

Jonathan   The friends that had the oversight of **Jonathan Sowle** and **Barsheba**
Sowle **Russell**s marriage, report that they fulfild their appointment and as far
married as they discoverd it was Consumated Orderly

Return from   **Deborah Allen** and **Judith Russell** report they have attended the Quarterly
Q meeting meeting according to appointment, by whom we received an Epistle from
Said meeting which is kindly accepted

To reprove
deserters

Deborah Allen and **Deborah Hicks** are added to the former Committee that was appointed to treat and Labour further with those member that absent themselves from our meetings and practice going to other meetings

Abigail
Wanton &
Rebec Thra=
=sher disor
der

Susanna Russell and **Hannah Mosher** are appointed to Treat and labour with **Abigail Wanton** and **Rebecca Thrasher** for marrying out of the Unity of Friends and they to make report to the next monthly meeting

Deb Gifford
request

Deborah Gifford presented a few lines to this meeting desireing to to be taken under the care of Friends. This meeting appoints **Sarah Anthony Hannah Tucker** and **Susanna Smith** to Visit the Family the better to understand wheither the motive Springs from the bottom of true Conviction, and they to make report when ready

8 month
1778

At a Monthly Meeting of Women friends held in **Dartmouth** 17th of 8th month 1778 The Representatives are **Deborah Hicks** and **Mary Howland** both pre^snt

Silvanus
Folger &
Geo Folger
married

The Friends that was appointed to have the oversight of the marriage of **Silvanus Folger** and **Avis Slocum,** and **George Folger** and **Rebecca Slocum** make report their marriages was consumated orderly as far as they discovered

Mary
Deborah
Patience
Freelove
Hathway
under dealing

The friends that was appointed to Treat with those members that absent from our meetings make report they have had an oppertunity with **Mary** Hathway [Hathaway] wife of **James Hathway** [Hathaway]; and **Deborah, Patience,** and **Freelove** Hathway [Hathaway] Daughters of **Caleb Hathway** [Hathaway]; and they continue in ^Practice of going to Seperate meetings and Countenancing the Same, for which they have Laboured to

The afore said
friends are
disow
ned

bring them to a sight of their disorder but it not proved effectual they think it for th^e honour of Truth to Testify against them; this meeting accepting said report ^do deny them and app^oint **deborah Allen** and **Deborah Hicks** to draw a paper of denial against them agreeable to their offence and bring to the next monthly meeting

Abigail
Wanton &
Rebecah
Thrasher
disowned

The friends that was apointed to treat with **Abigail Wanton** wife of **John Wanton** and **Rebeccah Thrasher** Wife Sam^uel **Thrasher** for their marrying out from amongst Friends, make report that they have dⁱscharged themselves, as well as oppetunity would admit Some of the overseers have Laboured with them and as the Circumstan^{ce} is think Sufficient care hath been taken. and they Discovered no disposition of their making Satisfaction: In consideration thereof this meeting disowns them the said **Abigail Wanton** and **Rebeccah Thrasher** from being in membership in our Society

Jud[i]th Russell is apointed to inform the above said women of their denial and make report to the next monthly meeting

Edward
Thurston
Case

Wereas the Bounderies between **Swanzey** Monthly meeting and this: hath lately been Settled: and **Edward Thurston** and his wife **Pernal** with their Children falls into the Limmits ^of their Said meeting wherefore we recommend unto them ^the said family as members of their meeting

Naomy
Howland

Signed a Removal Certificate for **Naome Howland** and her daughter **Rebeccah** Recommending them to the Monthly meeting at **East Hoosuck**

9 month
1778

At a Monthly meeting of Women Friends held in **Dartmouth** ye 21st of ye 9th month 1778 The Representatives are **Silvester Howland** and **Mary Smith** both present

Elisa^h Allen acknowledg ment rec^d

The Friends that was appointed to Treat with **Elisabeth Allen** on the account of her being guilty of the Sin of Fornication, make report, that She gave them Such good Satisfaction that they are free Should remain a member in Society This meeting accepting said report, do receive her paper of acknowledgment Provided She cause the Same to be read at the Close of Some firs[t] day meeting for worship between this and the next monthly meeting She being present

Rose Pinkham request

Rose Pinkum [Pinkham] requests a Certificate to **Nantucket** monthly meeting recommending her as a member: **Deborah Hayden** and **Eunice Tabor [Taber]** are appointed to make Enquiry into her life and Conversation while among us, and if nothing appear to hender to Draw one and bring to the next monthly meeting

Bershebah Sowle request

Bersheba Sowle request a few Lines Recommending her to **Acc^oakset [Acoaxet]** monthly meeting as a member: **Mary Smith** and **Silvester Howland** are appoint^{ed} to make Enquiry into her life and Conversation, and if nothing appears to hinde^r to draw a few lines and bring to next monthly meeting

Mary Hath= =way &c denial signd

Signed a paper of denial against **Mary Hathway [Hathaway]** and several of **Caleb Hathway [Hathaway]** daughters which is to be Read publickly at the close of a first day meeting ~~of~~ before the next monthly meeting

Sarah Duel disow[n]ed

One of the overseers Inform this meeting She took a friend and went to Treat with **Sarah Duel [Davol?]** (wife of **David Duel [Davol?]**) before marriage, in regard of her keeping Company out of the Unity of friends, and Laboured with her for the Same but She dⁱsregarding the advice hath gone out in marriage for which this meeing thinks they are clear, and do deny her having any right of membership in Socie^ty amoung ^{us} **Judith Russell** is appointed to acquaint s^d **Sarah** of her denil [denial] and make report to next monthly meeting

Represent^{ves} Q meeting

No answers prepared at this Time; Signed an Epistle to be sent up to the Ensuing Quarterly meeting by our Representatives Who are **Deborah Hayden Eunice Taber Sarah Gifford** and **Kazⁱah Russell**: they to report to the next Monthly meeting

10 month 1778

At a Monthly Meeting of Women Friends held in **Dartmouth** ye 19th of 10th month 1778 The Representatives are **Alice Anthony** and **Mary Tucker** both present

Elis Allen

Elisabeth Allens paper hath not been read according to the conclusion of last monthly meeting

Ann Butts Request

Anne Butts Sent a few lines to this meeing desireing to come under their Care **Susanna Allen Deborah Hayden** and **Sarah Gifford** are appoin^{te}d to take Sutible oppertunities of conferrences on account of ₐ^{her} said request the better to understand wheither She is Sinceare and Worthy to be received and they to make report when ready

Rebeccah Russell request

Rebecca Russell Informs this meeting that She is about to remove within the Verge of **East Hoosu[c]k** monthly meeting and desires a Certi₍ₐ₎ficate, and desires her Little daughter **Amie** to be taken under the care of friends and be recommened **Alice Anthony** and **Susanna Smith** are appointed to make Enquiry into her life and conversation, and to consider the matter concerning her child, and if nothing appears to hinder to draw a Certificate and bring to the next monthly meeting

Rebecca
Folger
request

Rebecca Folger desires a few lines Recommending her to **Nantucket** monthly meeting **Alice Anthony** and **Susanna Smith** are appointed to make Enquiry and if nothing appears to hinder to draw a few lines and bring to next monthly meeting

Return from
Q meeting
Epistle Rec[d]

This meeting is Informed that all the friends that was appointed to attend the Qarterly meeting hath fulfilled their appointment; we received an Epistle from the Quarterly meeting, and one from the yearly meeting of friends at **Phi= =lidelphia** both being read in this meeting and the Seasonable advices contained therein. we hop will be regarded by the Sincear hearted amoung us

Barsh Sowle
Rose Pinkham
Certificates

Signed two Removal Certificates one for **Barsheba Sowle** recommen[din]g her to **Accoakset** monthly meeting

And one for **Rose Pinkham** Recomending her to **Nantucket** monthly meeting

11 month
1778
No Represen[ves]
to this meeting

At a Monthly Meeting of Women Friends held in **Dartmouth** y[e] 16[th] of 11[th] month 1778

There are no Friends appointed to attend the monthly meeting by reason there was no Women friends at the preparitive meeting by reason of an Ind[i]f= =ferency that is much prevailing in this meeting; altho the~~ther~~ wether was very rainny yet we beleive if all our members had been rightly Engaged for the Cause our meeting would not have dropt at that time

Deborah
Gifford &
daugh[t]ers
Rece[d]

The Committee that was apointed Some time ago to treat with **Deborah Gifford** concerning her request to be taken under the [care?] of friends, make report that they fulfilled their appointment and found Such Satisfaction that they find nothing to hinder their being received: In Consideration thereof this meeting Accepts of the Said **Deborah Gifford** and her four daughters Namely **Rachel Edith, Esther**, and **Lydia** into membership with this meeting

Elisabeth
Allens Case

Elisabeth Allens paper of acknowledgment hath not ₍yet₎ been read and this meeting concluds that it Should be omitted untill friends are better Satisfied and do conclude, the Same Committee, **Marcy Slocum** added thereto and they to Labour farther₍ther for her₎ recovery as the Wisdom of Truth shall direct and they to make report when ready

A paper of denial against **Mary Hathaway Deborah, Patience** and **Freelove Hathaway,** hath been read Since last monthly meeting which is returned to the Clerk to go on record ~ and is as followeth

Testimony of
denial
against
Mary Hath=
=way & others

Wheras **Mary Hathaway** (Wife of **James Hathaway**) **Deborah, Patence** and **Freelove Hathaway.** daughters of **Caleb Hathaway,** having a right of membership amongst friends, and having for Some time neglected the attending our meetings, and of Late followed Seperate meetings all which there hath much labour in love to Convince them of their disorderly walking, but our labour of love. not haveing the desired effect to friends Satisfaction: Do hereby disown the said **Mary Hathaway** (wife of **James Hathaway**) **Deborah, Patience** and **Freelove Hathaway** from being members of our Religious Society and from under the care of this meeting hopeing they may yet be favoured to~~ith a~~ come to a Sight and Sence of their Out goings and be restored to the way of Truth

Given forth at our Monthly meeting of Friends held at **Dartmouth**
this 21ˢᵗ day of yᵉ 9ᵗʰ month 1778 Signed in and on behalf of our sᵈ meeting By

Wᵐ Anthony Juʳ Clerk

Susanna Smith Clerk

12 month *1778*	At a Monthly meeting of Women Friends held in **Dartmouth** 21 of 12 mo 1778 The Representatives are **Elisabeth Slocum** and **Sarah Howland** both present
Content Cornell *Request*	**Content Cornel [Cornell]** desires a Certficate to **East Hoosuck** monthly meeting **Elisabeth Slocum** and **Susanna Allen** are appointed to make Enquiry and if nothing appears to hinder to draw one & bring to next monthly meeting
Mary Smith *request*	**Anne Smith** ~~Smith~~ desires a Certificate to **East Hoosuck** monthly meeting for her for herself and Children, **Mary Smith** and **Sarah Anthony** are appointed to make Enquiry and if nothing appears to hender to draw one and bring to next monthly meeting
Avis ~~Slocum~~ᶠᵒˡᵍᵉʳ *Request*	**Avis Folger** desires a Certificate to the Mnthly meeting at **Nantucket Mary** **Smith** and **Sarah Anthony** are appointed to make Enquiry and if nothing apears to hinder to bring one to the next monthly meeting
Sent up to *Q meeting*	The Queries have been read, Answered, and approved, With the Epistle Signed and Sent up to the Quarterly meeting by our Representatives: Who are **Sarah Howland Mary Slocum** and **Kaziah Russell** and they to make report to the next monthly meeting
Abigail Winslow *complaind of*	This meeing is Informed that **Abigail Winslow** appears to be guilty of the Sin of Fornication. for which, **Alice Anthony** and **Deborah Allen** are appointed to Treat with on that account as the Spirit Truth Shall direct, and they to make report to the next monthly meeting
1 month *1779*	At a Monthly meeting of Women Friends held in **dartmout** yᵉ 18ᵗʰ day of 1ˢᵗ month 1779 The Representatives are **Deborah Hayden** and **Silvester Howland** both present
Return from *Q meeting*	**Marcy Slocum** and **Sarah Howland** Informs this meeting they attended the Quarterly meeting accor[d]ing to appointment by whom we received an Epistle which was read in this meeting according to good Satisfaction and we hope the advice ₐᵗʰᵉʳᵉⁱⁿ will be regarded
Abigail Winslow	We dont discover by the report of the Committee that was appointed to treat with **Abigail Winslow** concerning her being guilty of the Sin of fornication that they found much Satisfaction: **Mary Smith** and **Silvester Howland** are appointed to draw a paper of denial a gainst her and bring to the next monthly meetⁱⁿᵍ
Mary Allen *request*	**Mary Allen** desires a few lines by way of a removal Certificate Recommending her to the monthly meeting at **East Hoosuck Mary Tucker** and **Rhod Mott** are appointed to make Enquiry and if nothing appears to hinder to Joine the men Friends in drawing one for the family
Job Sisson *proposal of* *marriage*	**Job Sisson** and **Ruth Shepherd** declared theⁱr Intentions of marriage before this meeting, they were desired to wait for their answer till next monthly meeting **Deborah Hayden** and **Silvester Howland** are appointed to make Enquiry into the young womans clearness and conversation respecting marriage and they to make Report to the next monthly meeting

Complaint against Mary Wood	This meeting is informd that **Mary Wood** Wife of **Abraham Wood** hath Lately married out of the Unity of friends **Judith Russell**, **Silvester Howland**, and **Marcy Slocum** are apointed to Treat with her on that account and make report when ready
Content Cornell and Avis Folger Certificates	Signed a Removal Certificate on behalf of **Content Cornell** daughter of **Danil Cornell**, Recommending her to **East Hoosuck** monthly meeting
	Likewise one for **Avis Folger** Recommending her to the monthly meeting at **Nantucket**
adjournd	This Meeting Adjourns to the 27th of this Instant
mett	Mett by adjournment yᵉ 27th of 1st month 1779 Represenᵛᵉˢ Called **Silvester Howland** peˢᵉⁿᵗ
Slack in Atending meetings	Having Several matters come before this meeting that is Taken under Consideration; That in particular concerning appointing a Committee to Joine the overseers in Visiting those members that are deficient in attending meet=ing, with all other disorders
Removing without Certificates	Likewise it apears that Several of our members have Removed from this meeting without requesting our Certificates Namely, **Anne Mott** and her daughter **Susanna** and **Anne Condel,** all which we think is needful to be Taken care according to the Rules of our Discipline: But the meeting being So Small at this time and so many of our members so Lukewarm and Slack of attending that thare hardly appeared a Sificient number to carry on business

2 month 1779	At a Monthly Meeting of Women Friends held in **Dartmouth** yᵉ 15th of 2nd month 1779 The Representatives are **Deborah Allen** and **Alice Anthony** both present
complaint against Ann Mott.	This meeting is informed that **Anne Mott** with her daughter **Susanna** Hath gone to Reside out of the verge of this meeting without requesting a Certificate: **Judith Russell** and **Kaziah Russell** are appointed to make Enquiry into their Lives and Conversations and if nothing appears to hinder draw Certificats and bring to the monthly meeting
Ann Condel	This meeting is Informed that **Anne Condel [Cundell]** hath removed out of the verge of this meeting without requ[e]sting a Certificate: **Deborah Hayden** and **Kaziah Russell** are appointed to make Enquiry into her life and Conversation and if nothing appear to hinder bring one to the next monthly meeting Recommending her to **Sandwich** monthly meeting
Committee to deal with disorderly members	**Hannah Tucker Deborah Hayden** and **Susanna Smith** are appointed a Committee to Joine the Overseers in dealing with disorderly members and those in perticular that are deficient in attending our meetings and where any appear obstinate to return their names with their offences to the meeting
Than[k]ful Cornel request	**Thankful Cornell** desires to be [~~illegible~~]Taken under the care of this meeting **Elisabeth Slocum** and **Sarah Gifford** are appointed to treat with her on that account to see wheithe She is worthy, and they to make report when ready
Ruth Shepherd Clearness	The Friend that was appointed to make Enquiry into the life and Conversation of **Ruth Shepherd** respecting marriage make report they found nothing to hinder
Job Sisson Answer	**Job Sisson** and **Ruth Shepherd** appeared for their Answer which was they might proceed to take Each other in marriage at some convenient time before

the next monthly meeting, advising with the overseers who are **Deborah Hayden**
and **Silvester Howland** and they to make report to the nex monthly meeting

Bethiah Slocum Case Received a few lines from **Pembrook** monthly meeting desiring our assistance
and advice concerning **Bethiah Slocum**s Life and Conversation Sinc her residence
was here: **Sarah Gifford** and **Hannah Wood** are appointed to Inspect into them
matters and Inform this meeting how things appears when ready

Abigail Winslow Signed a paper of denial against **Abigal Winslow** which is to be read at
the conclusion of a first day meeting of Worship at **Newtown** and then to
Lodge in the Clerks hands to go on record

Ann Smith Certificate Signed a removal Certificate for **Anne Smith** and her Children Namely
Sarah, **Lloyd**, **Paul** and **Barnabus** Recommending them to **East Hoosuck** and
Saratoga monthly meeting

3 month 1779 At a Monthly meeting of Women friends held in **Dartmouth** yᵉ 15ᵗʰ of 3ʳᵈ month 1779
The Representatives are **Mary Smith** and **Lydia Barker** both Present

Ann Mott The matter concerning **Anne Mott** and her Daughters Certificate rests ᴗnder same friend care by
reason the Committᵉᵉ not present

Job Sisson married The Friends that was appointed to have the oversight of **Job Sisson**s marriage
make report they attended and it was consumated and carried on in Some
degree orderly

Abigail Winslow deⁿial This meeting is Informed that **Abigail Winslow**s paper of den[i]al hath been
Read according to the conclusion of last montly and returned to the Clerk as followeth
Whereas **Abigail Winslow** (widdow to **Johⁿ Winslow** late of **Dartmouth** deceased)
having been in membership with us, but by departing from the Principal of Truth
in her owne mind, hath fallen into the Sin of Fornication as appears by her
having Child while unmarried, and friends having Treated with her and
admonish her in Love in order to reclaim her from the Evil of her ways but
our admonitions not being so Effectual as could be desired, this meeting therefore
being Concerned for maintain good Order in the Church, and that friends may
preserved from the repr[o]ach of Such Evil practices, do give this forth as a publick
Testimony against her, and do hereby disown her the said **Abigail Winslow** from
being a member of our Society, untill by unfeig[n]ed Repentance and acknow
ledgment thereof, She Shall be restored to the way of Truth   **Wᵐ Anthony Juʳ** Clerk
Given forth at our monthly meeting held at **Dartmouth**
the 15ᵗʰ of 2 month 1779. and Signed in and on behalf of sᵈ meeing by **Susanna Smith** Clerk

Sent up to Q meeting The Queries have been Read, Considered, and Answered, the Epistle Signed
and Sent up to the Quarterly meeting by our Representatives who are
Deborah Hayden Mary Smith and **Mahetibel Tucker** and they to make
Report to the next monthly meeting

Ann Condel Signed a Removal Certificate **Anne Condell** [Cundell] wife of **Enoch Condell** [Cundell]
Recommending her to **Sandwich** monthly meeting

Bethiah Slocuᵐ The matter concerning **Bethiah Slocum** is continued another month under
Same friends care

John Allen & *wife certifi*te	Signed a removal Certificat for **John** ∧**Allen** and his wife **Mary** with their Children Namely, **Gideon**, **Deborah**, and **Philip**, Recommending them to **East Hoosuck** Monthly meeting.
4 month *1779*	At a Monthly Meeting of Women Friends held in **Dartmouth** ye 19th of 4 month 1779 The Representatives are **Sarah Howland** and **Deborah Gifford** both present
Ann Mott	The matter concerning **Anne Mott**∧**& daughter** Rests under the same friends Care
Adjournd	This meeting Adjourns to next forth [2] day come Week after ye meting Worship Ends
mett	Mett by Adjournment ye 28th of 4th month~~on~~ 1779 Representative Calld **Sarah Howland** present
Clerk	**Mary Smith** Chose Clerk for this day
Return from *Q meeting*	The Friends appointed to attend the Quaterly meeting make report they all attended according to appointment: by whome we received an Epistle which Read and well accepted
Hannah *Willbor* *request*	**Hannah Willbor** [Wilbur] desires to be taken under the care of this meeting if She is worthy; **Sarah Howland** and **Mary Smith** are appointed to take Sutiable oppertunitys of Conferences with her on that account and make report when ready
Ann Mott *referd*	The matter concerning **Anne Mott** and her daughter **Susanna** is refered to next monthly meeting
5 month *1779*	At a Monthly meeting of Women Friends held in **Dartmouth** ye 17th of 5th month 1779 The Representatives are **Alice Anthony** and **Deborah Allen** both present
Ann Butts	**Deborah Hick** [Hicks] is added to the Committee that was appoined to treat with **Anne Butts** concerning her request and they to report when ready
Ann Mott *and daughter*	**Kaziah Russell** and **Judith Russell** was appointted Sume time past to Treat with **Anne Mott** and her daughter **Susanna,** and make Enquiry into their L[i]ves and Conversations; and if nothing apeared to hinder they was to draw a Certificate for them to **Sandwich** monthly meeting; but they have not fulfild according to appointment: **Judith Russell** desires to be dismist from that Service **Susanna Russell** is added in her room [place] and they ∧to make ∧report to the next monthly meeting
Elisa Allen *Meriah* *Hoxcie* *Certificates* *Han Willbor* *request*	Received a removal Certificate from **Sandwich** monthly meeting on behalf of **Elisabeth Allen** Widdow and **Meriah Hoxcie** [Hoxie], Which this meeting accepts **Joanna Mosher** is added to the Committee that was appointed to Treat with **Hannah Willber** [Wilbur] concerning her request and they to make report when ready
Thakful *Cornll* Recd	The Committee that was appointed to treat with **Thankful Cornell** concerning her request; Signify they found good Sattisfaction, and think She may be receivd this meeting accepting Said report, do receive her with her two little Children Namely **Allen** and **Stephen** into membership of said meeting
To revise *Miniuts*	**Deborah Hayden Deborah Allen** and **Susanna Smith** are appointd to Revise and correct the minniuts. and Settle with the Treasurer and they to make report Next monthly meeting
John Allen *certificate*	Signed a removal Certificate for **John Allen** and **Mary** his wife and their Children Namely **Gideon**, **Deborah**, and **Philip**, Recommending them to the **Ninepartners** monthly meeting
6 month *1779*	At a Monthly meeting of Women Friends held in **Dartmouth** ye 21st of 6th month 1779 The Representatives are **Marcy Slocum** and **Mary Smith** both present

miniuts not revised — The Friends appointed to Revise and Correct the minniuts Report they have not fulfild their appointment, they are therefore continued in the Same Service and make report next monthly meeting

Han Sawdy request — **Hannah Sawdy** Request a removal Certificate Recommending her to **East Hoosuck** monthly meeting **Hannah Mosher** and **Martha Allen** are appointed to make Enquiry in her life and Conversation, and if nothing appears to hinder they to prepare one and bring to the next monthly meeting

Solomon Underhill & Jos Walters — Received a Coppy of a minniute from a yearly meeting held at **Westbury** on **Long Island** on behalf of our Eteem͜ed friend **Solomon Underhill**, in company with our friend **Joseph Walters** whose Labour & Service was comfortable and acceptable amoung us

Margret Potter request — This Mee[t]ing is Informed that **Margret Potter** is gone on a Visit among her Friends within Verge of the **Ninepartners** monthly meeting and desires a few lines of Recommendation thereto; **Mary Smith** ͜& **Silvester Howland** are apointed to make Enquiry in her Life and conversation and if nothing apears to hender to prepare a few lines and bring to the next monthly meeting

James Cornell and wife Certificate — Signed a removal Sertificate in behalf of **James Cornell** and **Thankful** his Wife with their two Children, **Allen** and **Stephen**, Recommending to the monthly meeting at **East Hoosuck** or **Saratoga**

Abigail How= land dis owned — The overseers Inform this meeting that they have Laboured with **Abigail Howland** wife of **Isaac Howland** on the account of her disorderly proceedings towards marriage but their Labour not having the desired Effect, She hath marryed out of the Unity ͜of friends for which this meeting denies her from being a member in Society **Deborah Allen** is desireᵈ to acquaint her of her denial and make report to the next monthly meeting

adjournd — This Meeting Adjours to the 24ᵗʰ of this Instant

mett — Mett by adjournment yᵉ 24ᵗʰ of 6ᵗʰ month 1779 The Representatives present

Ann Butt Receᵈ — The Committ appointed to Treat with **Anne Butts** concerning her request make report they found So much Satisfaction they think She may be received the the meeting accepting Said report do receive her into membership with Said meeting

Elis Allen acknowledg= =ment Recᵈ — The Friᵉnds that was appointed to treat with **Elisabeth Allen** concerning her disorderly proceeding make ʳᵉᵖᵒʳᵗ that She gave them cosiderable good Satisfaction and find freedom to receive her again: in consideration thereof this meeting Concludes to accept of her acknowledment Provided she causes it to be read at the Cˡose of a first day meeting of Worship betwen this and next monthly meeting She being present

Mary Wood disownd — The Comittee that was apointed to treat with **Mary Wood** wife of **Abrham Wood** for her marrying out from among friends, make report they have discharged themselves and ͜find her not in a disposition of making friends Satisfaction; in consideration ͜thereof this meeting deny her of any right of mem =bership in Said meeting

To be Sent up to Q meeting — The Qu͜eries have been read, answered, and approved; The Epistle Signed and sent up to the Quarterly meeting by our Representatives ͜who are **Alice Anthony** and **Deborah Allen** they to make report to the next monthly meeting

David Sands and Solomon Un= =derhill Certificates	Signed a Certificate for our Friend **David Sands** to the monthly meeting at the **Ninepartners** Signifying a Satisfactory Vissit Signed a Certificates for our Friends **Solomon Underhill** and **Joseph Walters** to their respective monthly meetings they belong to Signifying their Satisfactory Visits
Anne Mott disowned	This meeting being Informed that **Anne Mott** (wife of **Jacob Mott**) hath Removed herself out of the Compass of this meeting without requesting our Certificate; and likwise that She hath been very Slack in attending our Religious meetings, and in other Respects her life and conduct not agreeable to our Religion: For which this meeting appointed a Committee to Inspect into those matters, and to treat and deal with her as they found occation required Now this said Committee makes report, that they have discharged themselves agreeable to appointment, and She appears to be guilty of the afore said offences And gave no Satisfaction for the Same, for which it is their mind and Judgment, She is no ways Worthy to remain under the care of Friends This meeting accepting Said report do Deny her the said **Anne Mott** from having any right of membership in Society among Friends
7 month 1779	At a Monthly meeting of Women Friends held in **Dartmouth** yᵉ 19ᵗʰ of 7 month 1779 The Representatives are **Sarah Gifford** and **Amie Barker** both present
Miniuts not Revised	The Commtt that was appointed to Revise and Correct the monthly meet =ing minnits have not done according to appointment they are desired to accomplish the Same and mak report to the next monthly meeting
Elis Allen acknoledg ment	**Elisabeth Allen**s paper of acknowledgment hath been read agreeable to the Conclusion of last monthly meeting and is as followeth To the monthly meeting to be held at **Poniganset** 19ᵗʰ of yᵉ first month 1778. Dear friends I have brok a good order of friends by marrying out of the Unity friends & of being gilty of yᵉ Sin of Forn[i]cation as doth apear by my having a child so Soon after marriage all which I con= =demn and am Sorry for; hoping God will forgive me and that friends will so far pass my offences as to Let me remain under their ·care From your friend **Elisabeth Allen**
Benj Sawdy Certificate	Signed a Removal Certificate for **Benjamin Sawdy** and his wife **Hannah** and their Children Namely **Samuel**, **Joseph**, **Elisabeth**, **Thomas Cook Sawdy** Recommending them to **East Hoosuck** or **Saratoga** monthly meeting
Grace Gifford request	**Grace Gifford** desires to be tᵃken under the care of this meeting **Susanna Allen** and **Hannah Mosher** are appointed to inspect into the Sencerity of her so requesting and to find what the motive is; and they to make report to this meeting when ready
Miniutie revised	According to appointment we hav mett, Revised and corrected this meetings minniuts, and also Settleled with the Treasurer and ther rᵉmains in Stock 10£-14ˢ-10ᵈ old Tenner
8 month 1779	At a Monthˡʸ Meeting of Women Friends held in **Dartmouth** yᵉ 16ᵗʰ of 8ᵗʰ month 1779 The Representatives are **Mary Smith** and **Lucey Howland** both present
Hannah Willbor Recᵈ	The Committee that was appointed on account of **Hannah Willbor** [**Wilbur**] daughter of **Content Gidly** [**Gidley**] on her requesting to come under the care of this meeting make report ; they found good Satisfaction and think She may be Received; this meeting accepts Said Report. do receive the Said **Hannah Willbor** [**Wilbur**] into mem= =bership, and under the care of this meeting

Sarah How=
land wife
of Warren
disownd

Some of the Overseers Informe this meeting, that **Sarah Howland** wife of
Warren Howland, hath been Sutiably admonished for her proceeding toward
marriage out of the Unity of Friend, But She disregarding Said advice hath
married out of the Unity and from among Friends; for which this meeting
Denies her the ˄sd **Sarah Howland** from having any Right of membership and from
Under the care of this meeting: **Amie Barker** is desired to Inform her of her denial
and make report to next monthly meeting

Jonathan Clerk
request

This meeting is Informed that **Jonathan Clark** is about to Remove within the
Verge of the **Ninepartners** monthly meeting with his family and desires our
Certificate thereto ~ **Hannah Mosher** and **Martha Allen** are appointed to make
Enquiry, and Joine the Men friends in preparing one and bring to next monthly
If nothing appears to hender

Susan Mott
certificate

Signed a removal Certificate for **Susanna Mott** daughter of **Jacob Mott** Recom=
=mending her to **Sandwich** Monthly Meeting

9 month
1779

At a Monthly Meeting of Women Friends held in **Dartmouth** yᵉ 20ᵗʰ of 9ᵗʰ month 1779
The Representatives are **Deborah Hayden** and **Marcy Slocum** both present

Elis Allen
request

Elisabeth Allen widdow of **Gideon Allen** Informes this meeting that She is
about to remove within˄ᵗʰᵉ verge of the **Ninepartners** monthly meeting and desires
A Removal Certificate thereto: **Hannah Mosher**˄& ᴶᵒᵃⁿⁿᵃ **Gifford** are appointed into her
Circumstances and if nothing appears to hinder they to prepare one and bring
to the next monthly meeting

Phebe Smith
Request

Phebe Smith (wife of **George Smith**) Informes this meeting She hath a desire to come
under the care of Friends: **Deborah Allen** and **Susanna Smith** are appointed to
have Sutiable oppertunities of Conferences with her to See wheither She is
Worthy to be received and they to make report to this meeting when ready

Ann Mott
Informd
Sarah
Howland

Susanna Russell informes ˄ᵗʰⁱˢ meeting She hath acquainted **Anne Mott** wife of
Jacob Mott, of her de[n]ial; **Amie Barker** Informes She hath acquainted **Sarah**
Howland wife of **Warren Howland** of her denial according to their appointment

Jane Smith
Mary Duel &
Elisa Gifford
under
dealing

The overseers with Some of the Committee that was Joined with them to treat with
those members that doth neglect attending our religious meetings make report
that Some of them have visited **Jean Smith Mary Devel [Davol]** and **Elisabeth Gifford**
and Laboured with them for neglecting attending of our religious meetings
and Some of them for going to Seperate meetings held out of the Unity of friends
and Countenancing the Same; for which they gave no Satisfaction for theire Offences
Said Committee finding themselves clear
Therefore this meeting appoints **Keziah Russell Alice Anthony** and **Deborah**
Gifford to treat and Labour further with them for their recovery as best
Wisdom shall direct and they to make report to the ~~next~~ monthly meeting when redʸ

Sent up to
Q meeting

The Queries was read considered & answerᵈ in this meeting the Epistle Signed and
Sent up to the Quarterly meeting by our Representatives, who are **Marcy Slocum Sarah**
Gifford and **Deborah Hayden,** and they to make report to the next monthly meeting

Joseph
Davis Chil=
dren Birth
right

Mary Smith & **Sarah Anthony** are appointed to Joine yᵉ men friends to consider &
Inspect into the matter concerning **Joseph Davis**,s Children; wheither they have a
right of membership among friends, according to the Rules of Discipline and ~~m~~

make report next monthly meeting

10 month
_1779_

At a Monthly Meeting of Women Friends held in **Dartmouth** yᵉ 18ᵗʰ of 10ᵗʰ month 1779
The Representatives are **Deborah Gifford** and **Susanna Allen 2ᵈ** both present
    The Committee that was appointed to treat with those members that appear
dificient and careless on the account of attending our meetings and Joining
with Seperate meetings held out of the Unity of friends make report they

Jane Smith
disown'd

they have had Suitable oppertunity ~~opper~~ with **Jean Smith** and found no
Satisfaction – In consideration there of it is the conclusion of thes meeting
to Testify against her proceedings and disown her the saⁱd **Jean** from
under their care and do appoint the Same Committee to draw a paper of
denial a gainst her and bring to next monthly meeting

others refer'd

    The Committee not all having oppertunity with the aforesaⁱd neglegent offenders
and for Some other circumstances it is refered another month under the Same
friends care, and they then to make report

Return from
Q meeting
Epistle recᵈ

    The friends appointed to attend the Quarterly meeting report they all
attended but **Deborah Hayden,** and She was not able to attend
    Received an Epistle from Said Quarterly meeting which was read ~~and~~ in this
our meeting and well accepted

Grace Gifford

Martha Allen is added~~ed~~ to that Commitee that hath that matter respecting
Grace Giffords request under their care; and they to make report when ready

Elisa Allen
Certificate

    Signed ₍ₐ Removal Certificate for **Elisabeth Allen** widdow to **Gideon Allen**
And one for **Jonathan Clark** and his wife **Susanna** with their Children namely
Lydia, Philip, Elisabeth, Jonathan, and **Ruth,** all the above named are recommended
as members to the **Ninepartners** monthly meeting

11 month
_1779_

At a Monthly Meeting of Women Friends held in **Dartmouth** yᵉ 15ᵗʰ of 11 month 1779
The Representatives are **Sarah Anthony** and **Sarah Gifford** both present

Elisa Gifford
disown'd

    Some of that Committee that was appointed to Labour with **Elisabeth Gifford**
for her Neglecting to attend our Religious meetings, Make report, they have
had an oppertunity and found no Satisfaction, In consideration thereof it
is the Conclusion of this meeting to deny her of any Right in Society, and
do appoint the Same Committee to draw a paper of denial against the Said
Elisabeth and bring to the Next monthly meeting

Mary Duel
[Devol, Davol]
refer'd

    The matter concerning **Mary Duel [Devol, Davol]** is ʳᵉfer'd under the Same friends care,
and they to accomplish the matter and make report to the next monthly meeting

Rhoda Gifford
Recᵈ

    Received a Removal Certificate on behalfe of **Rhoda Gifford** (wife of **Stephen
Gifford**) from **Accoakset** monthly meeting which is accepted

Lydia Hud=
dleston Requ=
est

    Lydia Huddleston (wife of **Seth Huᵈdleston**) desires to be taken under the care
of this meeting – **Joanna Gifford** and **Deborah Hicks** are appointed to inspect
into the Sencerity of her request, So as to discover wheither she is Worthy to be
Received; and they to make report when ready

Ruth Sisson
request

    Ruth Sisson desires a ₍ʳᵉᵐᵒᵛᵃˡCertificate to **Accoakset** monthly meeting **Deborah
Hayden** and **Sarah Gifford** are appointed to make Enquiry, and if nothing
appears to hinder to prepare and bring to the next monthly meeting

Han: Wilcox
Alice Slocum
*under de*ᵃ*ling*

This meeting is Informed that **Hannah Willcox** and **Alice Slocum** appears to be in the practice of resorting to places where undue Liberty is taken: And, Joining with those of a Rude and Licensious Rabble or company contrary to our Principles; For which this disorder this meeting appoints **Susanna Allen 2**ᵈ **Deborah Hayden, Deborah Allen,** and **Susanna Smith** to Labour with and deal with above Said offenders, Indeavoring to bring them off from their disorderly practices and they to make report to the monthly meeting when ready

John Howland
proposal of
marriage

John Howland and **Reliance Shepherd** declared their Intentions of marriag with Each other, before this meeting and were desired to waite for their answer until Next monthly meeting – **Susanna Russell** and **deborah Hayden** are appoined to make Inquiry into the young womans clearness respecting marriage and her conversation; And they to make reporᵗ next monthly meeting

Anna Shepherd
Certificate

Signed a removal Certificate for **Anna Shepherd** daughter to **David Shepherd** Recommending her to the **Oblong** monthly meeting as a member

Jane Smith
denial Signd

Signed a paper of denial against **Jane Smith** which is to be reᵃd publickly at the close of a first ˄ᵈᵃʸ meeting of Worship between this and next monthly meeting

adjournd

This Meeting addjourns to the 24ᵗʰ of Instant

mett

Mettᵇʸ ᵃᵈʲᵒᵘʳⁿᵐᵉⁿᵗthe 24ᵗʰ of the 11ᵗʰ month 1779. The Representatives both present

Debora Haden
clerk

Deborah Hayden Clerk for this day

Elisa Gifford
to be Re-
Visited

As to the matter concerning **Elisabeth Gifford** – One of the Committee not being Present when the report being being made, and appearing not Quite Satisfied this meeting adds **Mary Smith Barsheba Howland** and **Deborah Hayden** to the Committee to make her another visit

Elisa Howland
Sertificate

This meeting received a removal Certificate from **Accoakset** monthly meeting Recommend **Elisabeth Howland** (wife of **Thomas Howland**) and her two Children **Eunicc** and **William** to this meeting as members

12 month
1779

At a Monthly Meeting of Women Friends held in **Dartmouth** yᵉ 20ᵗʰ of 12 month 1779 The Representatives are **Deberah Hayden** and **Mary Smith, Deborah Hayden** present

Alice Slocum
referd

The matter concerning **Alice Slocum** is continued under the Same friends care

Han: Wilcox
*[to]be deny*ᵈ

In regard to **Hannah Wilcox;** two of the Committee Inform this meeting thᵉy have had an oppertunity with her and found her no ways in a disposition to make Sattisfaction: The meeting accepting said report, do deny her any right of membership; and do appoint **Sarah Anthon [Anthony]** and **Susanna Smith** to˄ᵈʳᵃʷ a paper of denial against her agreeable to her offence and bring to next monthly meeting

Jane Smith denial hath been read agreeable to the conclusion of last monthly meeting – and is as followeth

Jane Smith
denial

Whereas **Jane Smith** (wife of **David Smith**) having been a member among us the people called Quakers, and under the care of our meeting, but have So far departed from the Principals we profess as to absent herself from our Religious meetings, Likewise assembles at meetings that are held out of the unity of us the people afore said, and notwithstanding our Labour in love with her to retrect [retract] sᵈ disorders She continues to Justify herself therin; Therefore this meeting is concerned to give this forth as a publick Testimony against her the said **Jane Smith** hereby disowning her ~~the~~ from being a member of our Religious Society untill by unfeigned Repentance and acknoledgment of her misconduct, and shall return to the way of Truth

 Given forth at our Monthly meeting of Friends held in

Dartmouth yᵉ 15ᵗʰ day of yᵉ 11ᵗʰ month 1779. Signed in & on ᴮʸ **Wᵐ Anthony Juʳ** Clerk
               behalf of sᵈ meeting **Susanna Smith** Clerk

Reliance Shepherd Clearness The Friends that was appointed to make Enquiry into **Reliance Shepherd** s~ Clearness respecting marriage and conversation make report they have Enquir'd accordingly and find nothing to hinder their proceedings

John Howland answer **John Howland** and **Reliance Shepherd** appeared for their Answer which was, They may proceed to take Each other in marriage at Some convenient Time between this and next monthly meeting adviseing with the Overseers this meeting shall appoint for that purpos

 Deborah Hayden and **Edith Russell** are appointed to See the above sᵈ marriag Consumated orderly and make report to next monthly meeting

Nat Gifford proposal of mariage **Nathaniel Gifford** and **Mehitable Trafford** declared their Intentions of marriage with each other before this meeting, and were desired to wait for their answer untill next monthly meeting

 Deborah Allen and **Sarah Anthony** are appointed to make Enquiry into **Mehitabel Traford**s clearness respecting and conversation and make report to next monthly meeting

Ruth Sisson Certificate Signed a removal Certificate for **Ruth Sisson** wife of **Job Sisson** Recommend--ing her to **Accoakset** monthly meeting

Phebe Smith Rceᵈ The Friends that was appointed on the account of **Phebe Smith** requesting to come under the care of friend with her Children, make report; they found so good Sattisfaction that they think they may be received: in consideration therof this meeting Receives Said **Phebe** into membership with her children **Abner, Ruth Robe** and **William** and under the care of this meeting

Philip Maccomber and wife request **Philip Maccomber** and his wife hath a desire to come under the care of this meeting with all their children **Sarah Anthony** and **Susanⁿa Smith** are appointed to Joine the men friends to Visit the family so as to discover wheither they are Worthy, and they to make report when ready

adjournd This Meeting Adjourns to the 29ᵗʰ of this Instant

adjournd again There was but one Woman appeared at the adjournment on yᵉ 29ᵗʰ of 12 mo 1779 By reason of the Extremity of the Weather and Said woman ~~and~~ with the assistance of the mens meeting adjours the Womens meeting to the 5ᵗʰ day of next month

mett Mett according to Adjournment ye 5 of first month 1780

The Representatives are **Deborah Hayden** & ~~Mary Smith;~~ **Mary Smith** present

Sent up to Q meeting The Queries have been Read, answered, and approved, the Epistle Signed and Sent up to the Quarterly meeting by our Representatives who are **Susanna Smith Sarah Howland** and **Mary Smith** and they to make report to the next monthly meeting

1st month *1780*	At a Monthly meeting of Women friends held in **Dartmouth** yᵉ 17ᵗʰ of 1ˢᵗ month 1780 The Representatives are **Amie Barke** and **Lucey Howland** both present
Alice Slocum *referd*	The ^matter concerning **Alice Slocum** is continued another month
Lydia Hud- *-dleston* *recᵈ*	The Committee that was appointed on the account of **Lydia Hudleston**s requesting to come under the care of friends of this meeting make report they found pretty good Satisfaction and think She may be received the meeting taking up with said report, do receive her into membership with her little child **Jonathan** and under the care of this meeting
John Howland *married*	**John Howland** and **Reliance Shepherd**,^marriage was consumated Since last monthly meeting: the overseers of Said marriage Inform, they was not able to attend according to appointment~~ment~~
Mehet Trafford *Clearness*	The friends appointed to Enqᵘire into **Mehitabel Trafford**s clearness respecting marriage and conversation make report, they have Enquired according to appointment and find nothing to hinder their proceedings
Elisa Gifford *& Hannah* *Wilcox denial* *signd*	Signed a paper of denial against **Elisabeth Gifford** Widdow of **William Gifford** ~ And one against **Hannah Wilcox** daughter of **Stephen Wilcox** both to be Read publickly at the Close of Some first day meeting of Worship
Return from *Q meeting*	This meeting is Inform'd that **Sarah Howland** attend, the Quarterly meeting By whom we received an Epistle therefrom which was read to Satisfaction the other two gave Such Reasons as are accepted
adjournd	This Meeting Adjourns to the 26ᵗʰ day of this Insᵗant
mett	Mett by adjournment yᵉ 26 of 1ˢᵗ month 1780. Representatives both present
Grace Gifford *Rece-*	The Committee that was appointed concerning **Grace Gifford** requesting to come under the care of this meeting: make report, they found pretty good Satisfaction and think She may be received: In consequence thereof this meeting doth receive her into membership and under the care of this meeting
Nat: Gifford *Answer*	**Nathaniel Gifford** and **Mehⁱtabel Trafford** appeared att this meeting for their answer ~ Which was they may proceed to take Each other in marriage at some convenient time between this and next monthly meeting adviseing with,ʸᵉ overseers who are **Elisabeth Slocum** and **Lucy Howland** and they to make report to the next monthly meeting
Elis: Gifford & *Han: Wilcox to* *be informd*	**Hannah Mosher** and **Edith Russell** are desired to acquaint **Elisabeth Gifford**, and **Hannah Wilcox** of their denial and report to next monthly meeting
2 month *1780*	At a Monthly meeting of Women Friend held in **Dartmouth** yᵉ 21ˢᵗ of 2ⁿᵈ month 1780 The Representatives are **Elisabeth Slocum** & **Sarah Howland** both present The denials against **Elisabeth Gifford** and **Hannah Wilcox** hath been read Since the last monthly meeting ~ and is as Followeth
Testimony of *denial against* *Elisa Gifford*	Whereas **Elisabeth Gifford** Widdow of **William Gifford** late of **Dartmouth** in the County of **Bristol** deceased: Having made Profesion with us as a member of our Society, but hath so far departed from the Sinserity of her profession, and the Practice of faithful friends, into Such a State of Indiffrence of mind as to almost Wholly to forsake ~~our~~ the attendance of our Religious meetings, and friends having frequently visited her in love, and Laboured with her in [muᶜh?] respect

and Tenderness of heart, in order to discover unto her the declined State of mind,
and Inconsistency of Practice that She hath fallen into: But friends Labour
not obtaining the desired end to the Satisfaction of this meetin

   Therefore being concerned for clearing of Truth and friends from the reproach of
Such disagreeable practice and Conduct do give this forth as a publick Testimony
against her the Said **Elisabeth Gifford** hereby disowning her from being a mem-
-ber of our Society untill by a Sincear Repentance and acknoledment of the ~~way~~
Error of her ways She Shall be restored to the way of Truth

   Given forth and Signed in and on behalf of our monthly   }**Wm Anthony Ju^r** Clerk
meeting of friends held in **Dartmouth** ye 17th day of 1st month 1780 by }**Susanna Smith** Clerk

Testimony
against
Han: Wilcox

Whereas **Hannah Wilcox** daughter of **Stephen Wilcox** having having had a birth
Right among friends and under the care of this meeting, But disregarding the
the dictates of Truth in her own heart, hath So fell Short as to be remiss on
the account of asembling at our Religious meeting to perform acceptable Worship
And Likwise She appears to be in the practice of Resorting at places where
undue Liberty is taken such as musick, dancing, and rude behavour contra^ry
to our Principles: For which we have in She might be restored: But our labors
of love not having the desired Effect which appears by her continuing in the
Same Pactices ~ For whis meeting gives this forth as a publick Testimony against
her, the said **Hannah Wilcox,** here by disowning her of any right of membership
among us, and from under the care of this meeting, Until a Sincear acknowledg
-ment of her misconduct and a return to the way of Truth

   Given forth at our Monthly meeting of Friends held in **Dartmouth** the 17th of 1st mo 1780
Signed in and on behalf of Said meeting By   **William Anthony Ju^r** Clerk
                                                        Susannah Smith Clerk

Elisa Gifford
Han Wilcox
not informd

We are Informed that **Hanna Mosher** and **Edith Russell** have not had an oppertun^ity
to Inform **Elisabeth Gifford** and **Hannah Wilcox** of their denial and they are
desired to fulfil their appoint.^ment and make report to next monthly meeting

Nat Gifford
married

This meeting is Informd that **Nathaniel Gifford** and **Mehitabel Trafford**
hath Taken Each other in mariage Since last monthly meeting: The friends
that was appointed to have the oversight of said marriage make report
they did not know when the marriage was nor was not there

Advice on
proceeding
[in] marriage

   It is the advice of this Meeting for the Future young Women be Strictly care
=ful to advise withe overseers, agreeable to the direction of the monthly meeting
when they are Tollerated to proceed in marriage: and likwise that overseers
would be careful to advise, So that deacency and moderation may prevail
Likwise attend their appointment so far as is realy needful to y^e honour of Truth

Philip Mac=
omber Wife
Children
Receivd

   The Committee that was appointed to Joine the men friends in regard of
Philip Maccomber and his family requesting to be taken under the care of
this meeting. Report, they fulfil'd their appointment, and found pretty good
Satisfaction and think they may be received: the meeting accepting said report
do receive **Philip Maccomber** and his Wife **Susanna** with their Children name
-ly **Edith, Gardner, Barnabus,** and **Abraham, Maccombers** under the care of
this meeting and into membership therin

Benj Sawdy
certificate

Signed a Removal Cirtificate for **Benjamin Sawdy** and his wife **Hannah** with their Children Recommending them as members to **Hoosuck** or **Saratoga** monthly meeting

Hum: Russell
proposal of
marriage

Hump^hry Russell and **Bethiah Eldredg** made proposal of marriag to this meeting and were desired to wait for their answer until next monthly meeting

Hannah Tucker ˄Mary Shearman are appointed to make Enquiry into **Bethiah Eldredg** clearness Respecting marriage and conversation, and make report next monthly meeting

Sarah Howland
[o]verser of poor

Sarah Howland is appointed to the place of an overseer of the poor

---

3 month
1780

At a Monthly meeting of Women Friends held in **Dartmouth** ye 20th of 3rd mon^th 1780 The Representatives are **Alice Anthony** and **Silvester Howland** both present

Elisa Gifford
Han Wilcox
not inform'd

This meeting is Inform'd that **Elisabeth Gifford** and **Hannah Wilcox** are not yet Informed of their denial the Same friends are desired to perform their appointment and make report next monthly meeting

Bethi Slocum
certificate

Bethiah Slocum wife of **Jonathan Slocum** hath produced a Removal Certi= -ficate from from **Pembrook** monthly meeting to this meeting: Which is accepted

Han Willbor
certificate

Signed a Removal Certificate for **Hannah Wilbor** Recommending her to the **Great Ninepartners** monthly meeting in **Dutchest [Dutchess]** County

Bethi Eldredg
Cleaness

The Friends that was appointed to make Enquiry into **Bethiah Eldredg**s Clearness Respecting marriage and conversation Report they ˄find nothing to hinder their procee˄ding in marriage

Hum: Russell
Answer

Humphry Russell and **Bethiah Eldre^dg** appeared for their answer Their answer was, They might proceed to take each other in marriage at some convenient time between this and next monthly meeting advising with their overseers who are **Mary Tucker** and **Alice Anthony** they to make report next monthly meeting

Sent up to
Q meeting

The Queries have been read and answer prepared. the Epistle Signed and Sent up to the Quarterly meeting by our Representative who is **Elisabeth Slocum**, and She to make Report next monthly meeting

Louis Shear
man
disown'd

Some of the overseers Informs this meeting that they precaustioned **Louis[e] Shearman** (now the wife of **Andrew Shearman**) against her keeping company out of the Unity of friends, But She persisted therein and married out from amoung friend: for which this meeting denies her any right or claim to mem= =bership or of being under the care of this meeting

---

4 month 1780

At a Monthly Meeting of Women Friends held in **Dartmouth** y^e 17th of 4th month 1780

Deb: Hayden
Clerk

Deborah Hayden Clerk for this day Representatives are **Sarah Howland** and **Mary Smith** neither of them present

Ha:n Wilcox
informd

Edith Russell reports She hath Informed **Hannah Wilcox** of her den^ial

Barna Mosher
proposal of
marriage

Barnabus Mosher And **Ruth Anthony** made proposals of marriage at this meeting and were desired to wait for their answer until next monthly meeting **Silvester Howland** and **Elisabeth Johnson** are appointed to makenquiry into **Ruth Anthonys** Clearness respecting marriage and conversation; and make report next next monthly meeting

adjournd

This Meeting is Adjourned untill to morrow

mett

Mett by Adjournment ye 18th of 4th month 1780. Representatives both present

Hum Russell
married

This meeting is informd that the friends that had the oversight of **Humphry Russell** and **Bethiah Eldredg**ₐmarage have fulfild their appointₐment and that that it was Consumated and Carried on in a good degree orderly so far as they discovered

Elisa Hathway
request

This meeting is Informed that **Elisabeth Hathaway** Widdow hath removed with her family on **RhodIsland** and desires,ₐa removal Certificate for her Self and Daughters Recommening them to the monthly meeting ther to

Lydia Barker
request

Lydia Barker Informes this meeting she is a bout to remove with her family within the compass of the **Ninepartners** monthly meeting and desires a Certificate for herself and daughter thereto

Deborah Hayden and **Sarah Gifford** are appointed to mak enquir into their Lives and conversations and if nothing appears to hinder to prepare Certificates and bring to next monthly meeting

Martha Green
removed

This meeting is Informed that that **Martha Green** is gone to reside within yᵉ verg of **Greenwich** monthly meeting, and agreeable to rule requires a Certificat **Eunice Taber** and **Marcy Slocum** are appointed to make enquiry into her Life and Conversation and if nothing appears to hinder to draw one therto and bring to next monthly meeting

Louis Sherman
to be informd

Ruth Tucker is desired to acquint **Louis[e] Shearman** of her denial

Epistle Recᵈ

Received an Epistle from the Quarterly meeting,ₐred and kindly accepted

Joan: Gifford
overser

Joanna Gifford is appointed overseer of Disorders

---

5 month
1780

At a Monthly Meeting of Women Friends held in **Dartmouth** 15ᵗʰ of 5ᵗʰ month 1780 The Representatives are **Marcy Slocum** and **Hannah**ₐMosher both present

Elisa Gifford &
Louis Sherman
inform'd

Hannah Mosher informs this meeting She hath notified **Elisabeth Gifford** of her denial **Ruth Tucker** Report She hath Informed **Louis[e] Shearman** of her denial

Alice Slocum to
be Received

The Friends appointed to treat with **Alice Slocum** concerning her diₐsorderly Conduct Report that She is in a condesendin disposition, and willing to take friends advice so far that they do receiv her into membership again; prᵒvided Causes her paper of acknowleᵈgment to be read publickly at the close of a first day meeting between this and next monthy meting She being present **Marcy Slocum** is appointed to the place of an overseer

Ruth Anthony
Clearness

The Friends appointed to enquire into **Ruth Anthonys** Clearness respecting,ₐmarrig and conversation, Report they find nothig to hinder their proceeding

Barnabus Juʳ
Mosher
Answer

Barnabus Mosher and **Ruth Anthony** appeared for their Answer their answer was, they may proceed to take Each other in marriage at Some convenient time before the next monthly meeting: advising with the Overseers; who are **Sarah ~~Plow~~ Howland** and **Susanna Smith**: and they to make report next monthly meeting

Elisa Hatha
way Certi-
ficate

Signed a removal Certificate on behalf of **Elisabeth Hathaway** and her Chil= =dren Namely **Elisabeth, Jonah, Lydia, Mary,** and **George** Recomending them to the monthly meeting at **RoadIsland**

Lydia Barker
Certificate

Likwise Signed one for **Lydia Barker** and her daughters Recommending them to the **Ninepartners** monthly meeting, the Childrens names are, **Phebe, Elisabeth, Sarah** and **Rebeckah**

Martha Green *Certificate*	Signed a Certificate for **Martha Green** Recommending her to **Greenwich** ~ monthly meeting
Rose Russell *complined of*	Received a Complaint from the Overseers of the poor, against **Rose Russell**s disorderly conduct in many respects; for which we appoint **Mary Shearman** and **Ruther Tucker** to Joine with the overseers to Labour with her agreeable to her Circumstance and the direction of Truth
Complaint *against* *Apphaer* *Mosher*	Some of the Overseers Inform this meeting, that they have had oppertunity with **Apphia Mosher** concerning her having a Child unlawfully, and her not to present Quallified to make friends Satisfaction: This meeting appoints **Alice** **Anthony** and **Deborah Hayden** to Labour with her for her recovery, and that the The Truth may be cleared from Such Groos Scandels ~ Collected 5ˢ/10ᵈ Lawful mony

6 month   At a Monthly Meeeting of Women Friends held in **Dartmouth** yᵉ 19ᵗʰ of 6ᵗʰ month 1780
1780   The Representatives call'd **Deborah Allen** present
Alice Slocums acknowledgment hath been read Since last monthly meeting, is as follows

Alice Slocum *acknowledg* *ment*	To the Monthly mᵉeting of friends to be held yᵉ 15ᵗʰ of yᵉ 11ᵗʰ month 1780 Whereas I through unwatchfulness have so far gone a Stray as to get into bad Company and going to frollicks all which am Sorry for and condemn, desiring Friends so far to pass it by as to Let me remain under their care and I am in hopes I shall be more careful in future. From your friend **Alice Slocum**
Barrabas *Mosher Juʳ* *marriage*	The Friends appinted to have the oversight of **Barnᵃbus Mosher** and **Ruth** **Anthony**s marriage make report they attended according to appointment and it was consumated and conducted orderly so far as they discovered.
John Lloyd *Certificat*	Received a Certificate on behalf of our Friend **John Lloyd** from a monthly meeting held in **Guined[Gwynedd]** in the County **Philidelphia** in **Pensylvania** bearing date the 25ᵗʰ of yᵉ 4 month 1780. Which ₍ᵂᵃˢ₎ kindly Received with his Labours of Love among us
Ann Almy *Certificate*	Received a Removal Certificate from **Newport** monthly meeting in behalf of **Anne Almy** wife of **Job Almy** which is accepted
Stephen *Buffinton* *Certificate*	Received a removal Certifiate from **Swanzey** monthly meeting in behalf of **Stephen Buffinton** and his wife **Sarah Buffinton** with their Children as members to this meeting
Apphiar *Mosher* *Case*	The Committee that was appointed Labour with **Aphia Mosher** for her being guilty of the Sin of Fornication make report they have fulfilled their appointment and do not find her in a disposi₍ᵗⁱ₎on to make friends Satis- =faction at present, for which this meeting appoints the Same friends to draw a paper of denial against the Said **Apphia Mosher** and bring to the next monthly meeting
Meriah Smith *under deᵃling*	Some of the Overseers informs this meeting that **Meriah Smith** hath been in the practice of attending meetings held out of the Unity of friends for which She hath been laboured with for, but she still countenances the same, this meet= =ing appoints **Hannah Tucker Sarah Gifford** and **Deborah Hayden** to labour fur= ther with her for her disorderly proceeding; and make report next monthly meeting

Mary Taber
& Patience
disorder

This meeting is Informed that **Mary Taber** and her daughter **Patience** have withdrawn themselves from friends meeting, and attend such meetings as are held out of the unity of Friends; and Likwise the daughters dress is no ways agreeable to our principles and Profession: For which **Marcy Slocum** and **Keziah Russell** are appointed a comittee to Labour withem for their help according to the direction of Truth; and they to make report next monthly meeting

Sent up to
Quarterly
meeting

The Queries have been read and answers prepared and an Epistle Signed and to be Sent up to the Quarterly meeting by our Representatives **Alice Anthony** and **Sarah Howland**: and they ˄ᵗᵒ make report to next monthly meeting

Marth Slocum
referd

Martha Slocums Certificate is refered another month

Collected at this meeing 0-4ˢ-10ᵈ LM [Lawful Money]

7 month
1780

At a Monthly meeting of Women friends held in **Dartmouth** yᵉ 17ᵗʰ of 7ᵗʰ month 1780 The Represetatives are **Alice Anthony** and **Deborah Allen** ~ Alice Anthny [Anthony] present The matter concerning **Meriah Smith** is refered under the Same friends care until next monthly meeting

Q meeting not
attended

The friends appinted to attend the Qarterly meeting inform they have not attended and gave Such reasons as this meeting accepts of

Epistles Recᵈ

Nevertheless we received an Epistle from the Quarterly meeting and one from **Philidelphia** for **Pensylvania** and **New Jersey** the latter bearing date the 10ᵗʰ of the Second month 1779 which was read and Kindly accepted

Martha
Slocum
request

Martha Slocum desires a Certificate for herself and children Recommending them back to **Rhod Island** monthly meeting: **Amie Barker** and **Mary Smith** are appoited to make enquiry into their lives and conversations and if nothing appears to hinder they they to draw and bring one to next monthly meetᶦng

Jonathan Hart
& wife Ceertifᵗᵉ

Received a Removal Certificate in behalf of **Jonathan Hart** and his Wife **Experience** and child **Martha** from **Smithfield** monthly meeting ~~wa~~ which is accepted ~ Collected 0-10ˢ-9ᵈ Lawful money

Order on
Treasurer

The Treasurer is desired to answer **Thomas Russell**s accompt which is 1ᵉ1ˢ-0ᵈ and make report to next monthly meeting

Apphia Mosher
denial Signd

Signed a paper of Denial against **Apphia Mosher** which is to be Read publickly between this and next monthly meeting, at the close of a first day meeting of Worship

Mary Taber &
Patience Taber
Case

One of the Committee appointed to treat with **Mary Taber** and her daughter **Patience** for their Neglecting the attending our Religious meetings and freequenting meetings held out of the unity of friends: and Likewise **Patience** dressing dixagreeable to the plainess our profession leads to, make report, She visited the famaly with a Committy of men friends appointed for the Same purpose, and they found no Satisfaction, there fore this meet--ing appoints **Sarah Anthony** and **Sarah Howland** to draw a paper of denial against them and bring to next monthly meeting

8 month
1780

At a Monthly meeting of Women Friends held in **Dartmouth** 21st of 8th month 1780
The Representatives are **Judith Russell** ad **Susanna Allen** both present

Meriah Smith
disowned

The Committee appoin˄ted to treat with **Meriah Smith** concerning her
disorderly prceeding, make report, they have had an oppertunity with her
and She noways Condemns her proceeding, nor gave them any encouragment
of dissisting therfrom: Therefore this meeting denies her of any right
to membership; and do appoint **Sarah Anthony** and **Deborah Hicks**
to draw a paper of denial a gainst her, and acquaint her with the
proceeding of the meeting and bring said paper to next monthly meeting,
Except they discover Some alteration of her mind

Treasurer
report

The Treasurer informs She hath answerd **Thomas Russell** acompt
which is 1£-1s-0d Lawful money

A Paper of Denial against **Apphia Mosher** hath been read
agreeable to the conclusion of last monthly meeting and is as followeth

Testimony
against
Apphia
Mosher

Whereas **Apphia Mosher** daughter of **Joseph Mosher** ˄Deceased and **Joanna** his wife
Having had her Education among Friends, but thro unwatchfulness and
and disregarding the Testimony of Truth in her own heart, hath so far departed
therefrom as to be found guilty of the Repr˄ochful Sin of Fornication as appears
by her having a child whilst in an unmarried State; and friends having
Labour with her in Love in order for her recovery but our Labour˄not having its
desired Effect to friends Satisfaction: Therefore this meeting is concern'd for
the mantaing our Chrstian Testimony and the preservation of ~~our~~ the prfessors
thereof from the reprach of Such practices, Do hereby, publickly disow her
the said **Apphia Mosher** from being a member of our Religious Society and
and from under the care of this meeting untill by unfeigned repentanc She
Shall return to the way of Truth and find marcy with the Lord

Given forth & Signed in and on behalf of our monthly } **Wm Anthony Jur** Clerk
meeting held in **Dartmouth** ye 17th of ye 7th month 1780: By } **Susanna Smith** Clerk

Mary Smith
disorder

This meeting is Inform'd that **Mary Smith** Daughter of **Jonathan Smith**
appears to be in many practices out of the unity of friends that in particurly
of resorting and keeping company with those of pernishious and hurtful
consequencs out of the Truth, and her dressing and fashoning herself out of
Plainess that our principles leads to: Therefore this meeting appoints **Alice
Anthony** and **Susanna Russell** to labour with her in Love to bring her to
a Sight of her iniquitious practices, and they to make report next
monthly meeting or when ready

Martha Slocum
Case referd

The matter concerning **Martha Slocum** having a Certifiate is refered
another month under the Same friends care

Denial Signd
against Wm
Taber & wife
[&] two Children

A paper of denial was Signed in this meeting against **William Taber**
and **Mary** his Wife and their two children, **Edward,** and **Patience Taber** :
Which is to be read publickly at the close of Some meeting of Worship before
next monthly meeting

Appha Mosher
to be informd

Martha Allen is appointed to acquaint **Apphia Mosher** of her denial and
make report to next monthly meeting

[a]djournd	This meeting is Adjourned to the 30ᵗʰ day of this Instant
mett	Mett by adjournment yᵉ 30ᵗʰ of yᵉ 8ᵗʰ month 1780 Representatives both present
Complaint against Elisa Smith	Some of the Overseers Informes this meeting that **Elisabeth Smith** appᵉars to be in the practice of attending Meetings held out of the Unity of friends Therefore this meeting appoints **Hannah Tucker** and **Alice Anthony** to labour further to bring her to a Sight of her disorderly proceedings; and they to make report to next monthly meeting
Mary Duel Case	**Joanna Gifford** is added to the former Committee that was appointed to Treat with **Mary Duel [Devol, Davoll]** concerning her disorderly proceedings and they to make report when ready
Ann Giffor concern to Visit Salem meeting	Our Friend **Ann Gifford** Informes this meeting that She hath a concern on her mind to Visit **Salem** Quarterly meeting: which ˄ᵗʰⁱˢ ᵐᵉᵉᵗⁱⁿᵍ concurs with and Signed a Certificate thereto

9 month 1780	At a Monthly meeting of Women Friends held in **Dartmouth** yᵉ 18- of 9ᵗʰ month 1780 The Representatives are **Elisabeth Slocum** and **Hannah Mosher** both present
Meriah Smith case referd	The matter concerning **Meriah Smith** is refer'd another month under the Same Friends care
Denial to be drawn against Mary Smith	The friends tha Labured with **Mary Smith** for her misconduct make Report, they found no Sattisfaction and think best She Should be denied: This meeting taking up with said report do deny her any right of membership and do appoint **Alice Anthony** and **Deborah Allen** to draw a paper of denial agreeable to her offence and bring to next monthly meeting **Catherine Howland** is appointed to acquaint **mary Sᵐith** of her denial and make report the next monthly meeting
Apphia Mosher inform'd	**Martha Allen** reports She hath acquainted **Apphia Mosher** of her denial
Elisa Smith Case referd	The matter concerning **Elisabeth Smith** is refered another month under the Same friends care
Sent Up to Q meeting	The Queries have been read and answers prepared in this meeting an Epistle Signed and to be Sent up to the Quarterly meeting with our said answers, by our Representatives who are **Marcy Slocum** and **Deborah Allen** and they to make report next monthly meeting ~ Collected 5ᶠ-0-0 old Tenner
Hum: Sherman proposal of marriag	**Humphry Shearman** and **Mercy Lapham** declar'd their Intentions of marriag at this meeting at this meeting and were desired to waite for their answer till next monthly meeting ~ **Deborah Hicks** and **Sarah Gifford** are appointed to make enquiry into the young Womans Clearness respecting marriage and Conversation, and make report next monthly meeting
Report on account of Visiting friends families	The Visiters brought in a report of their prceeding on the account of Visiting the familys of this monthly monthly meeting which this meeting accepts of, and think proper Should go on Record; And is as Follweth

Whereas some time past Some Friends were appointed to assist the Overseers in Treating with Some of our Neglegent members, and Some thus appointed, with Some other Friends, having had a concern on their minds to Joine and make a General Visit to friends families

thᵣouout our Monthly meeting, for the Reviveal of our Antient Discipline
In Stiring up the careless, Lukwarm, Indolent members, to Love and
good works, and haviing Drawings in our minds, not only to the
disobedient, but those that are Setting their faces Zion-ward,ᴧin order to incourage
and Strengthen one another: With desires that yᵉ wast places may yet be
Rebuilt; And by being willing to be obedient our weak minds were Strᵉngthenᵈ
from Time to time through the many Deep Exercisses of mind, in so weighty a
Service; & find Peace and Satisfaction therein, Which is Sificient Reward
 After having accomplishing Said Visit, which in general was well acᶜepted
yet not without Some Exceptions in Some perticurler families

State of the meeting And Now it remains to give Some account of the State of friends in our meeting
We Trust there are Some that are Labouring to do their day's work in the
day time, which we beleive desarves a word of Incouragement, though
the true Seed Seems to be Low, So that it might be truly Said as formerly
By wᴧʰome Shall Jacob, or the true Seed arise, which is in our apprehention
but Small and much pressed down with the many things that are hurtful
Especiᵃly, by the Love of money, Pride, and forgitfulness of God.

 Dated in **Dartmouth** yᵉ 18ᵗʰ of yᵉ 9ᵗʰ month 1780   **Freborn Rider   Thomas Hicks**
                                                            Susanna Smith   Abiel Gifford
                                                            Debrah Hicks

adjournd This Meeting Adjourns to yᵉ 27ᵗʰ of this Instant month

mett Mett by adjournᴧᵐent yᵉ 27ᵗʰ of 9ᵗʰ month 1780 Representatives both present

---

10 month 1780 At a Monthly meeting of Women friends held in **Dartmouth** 16ᵗʰ of 10ᵗʰ month 1780
 The Representatives are **Deborah Hayden** and **Sarah Howland** both present

Meriah Smith Case referd The matter concerning **Meriah Smith** is Refered another month by her
Request and under the Same Committees notice

Mary Smith denial signd & she informd Signed a paper of denial against **Mary Smith** which is to be read pub=
=lickly at the close of a first day meeting of Worship
 Catherine Howland hath Informed **Mary Smith** her denial

Elisa Smith Case referd The matter Concerning **Elisabeth Smith** is continued another month

Return from Q meeting Epistle recᵈ The Friends appointed to attend the Quarterly meeting Inform they attended
agreeable to appointment; Likwise Received an Epistle from the Same
which was read to the real comfort and Satisfaction of the upright hearted
among us

Mehitable Akin disownᵈ The Overseers Informs this meeting that **Mehitabel Akin** now the wife of
Timothy Akin hath latly married out of the Unity of Friends and that they
went Several times before marriage in order to Treat with her but She would
not give them opertunity to Speak with her: this meeting finding themselves
Clear, without any further Labour, do deny her of any right to membership
among friends and do apᵖoint **Elisabeth Ricketson** to acquaint her of her
Denial and inform the next monthly meeting

Marcy Lap= ham Clear= ness The friends appointed to make enquiry into **Marcy Lapham** clearness
respecting marriage and conversation report they find nothing to hinder their
proceeding.

Hum: Shear-
man
Answer

Humphry Shearman and **Marcy Lapham** appeared for their answer
And their answer was, They may proceed to take each other in marriage
at some convenent time before the next monthly meeting Advising with
withe overseers who are **Alice Anthony** and **Susanna Smith** and they to make
report next monthly meeting

Testamony
of denial
against
Wᵐ Taber &
Mary Taber
his wife &
Patience &
Edward their
son & daugh=
ter

A Paper of denial hath been read against **William Tabor** and **Mary Taber**
his wife and their children **Edward** and **Patience Tabers;** and is as followeth
Whereas **William Taber** and **Mary Taber** his wife, and **Edward Taber**
and **Patience Taber** their Son and daughter, all having made profession
with us the people called Quakers and been under the care of this meeting
But hath so far departed from the principles we profess so as to fequent [frequent]
meetings held out of the Unity of our Society, and Join in publick Worship
with them that are disowed by us the afore sᵈ people: and the said **Patience**
also appearing disagreeable in Some of her dress: and friends having
Laboured much in Love to reclaim them from Such practices but our Labours
not having its desired effect to Friends Satisfaction, and they continue to
Justify themselves therein; Therefor for the maintaining the principels we
Profess we are concerned to give this forth as a Testimony against them the
Said **William Taber, Edward Taber, Mary Taber,** and **Patience**ₐᵀᵃᵇᵉʳ hereby
disowning them from being in Unity with us and from Under the care of
this meeting: yet if it Should be agreeable to Divine goodness that they be
Restored to the way of Truth aₐⁿᵈ find Marcy, is our Sincear desire

Given forth and Signed in & on behalf of our monthly ⎱ **William Anthony Juʳ** Clerk
Meeting held in **Dartmouth** yᵉ 21ˢᵗ of yᵉ 8ᵗʰ month 1780 By ⎰ **Susanna Smith** Clerk

Martha Slocum
Certificate

Signed a Removal Certificate Recommending **Martha Slocum** and her
Children back to **Rhod Island** monthly meeting

Ann Gifford
certificate
returnd

Our Friend **Ann Gifford** Returned her Certificate to this meeting which
She hath had to travel to **Salem** Quarterly meeting ~ with their Rᵉception of
her Labour of Love amoung them Indorssed on the back of said Certificate[25]

Freeborn Rider
Minite

Signed a Coppy of a miniut made in this meeting Signifying our ~~Unita~~
Unity and concurrence, with our Friend **Freborn Rider**s intended Visit
to the **Long Plain** Quarterly meeting held for **Sandwich**

Revise ᵗᵒ minits
Settle with
Treasurer

Susanna Smith and **Silvia Smith** are appointed to Revise and correct the
miniuts and Settle with the Treasurer, and make repor next monthly meeting

11 month
1780

At a Monthly meeting of Women friends held in **Dartmouth** yᵉ 20ᵗʰ of 11ᵗʰ month 1780
The Representatives are **Deborah Gifford** and **Ann Butts** both present

Meriah Smith

The matter concerning **Meriah Smith** is continued another month by her requesᵗ

Paper of
[d]enial against
Mary Smith
daughter of
Jonathan

A paper of Denial against **Mary Smith** hath been read agreeable to the
Conclusion of last monthly meeting ~ and is as followeth
Whereas **Mary Smith** Daughter of **Jonathan Smith** and **Silvia** his wife
having had a birthright amoungst us the people called Quakers but hath
So far departed from our principle as to very much absent herself from

25. Ann Gifford apparently was traveling as a minister.

our Religious Meetings; also appearing in Habbit, Conversation, and
Conduct far from that Simple plainess we profess
And Friends having Laboured with her in love to convince her of the
Evil tendency therof, but our labour not having its desired Effect

Mary Smith   nor She manifesting any desire to remain under friends care; ~
Therefore we do hereby disown the said **Mary Smith** from being one in
unity with us, and from under our care; yet that She may be convinced
of the Evil thereof and return to the way of truth is our Sencear desire
Given forth and Signed in and on behalf of our   (**Wᵐ Anthony Juʳ** Clerk
monthly meeting of friends held in **Dartmouth** (**Susanna Smith** Clerk
the 16 day of yᵉ 10 month 1780.

Elisa: Smith   The Committee that had the matter concerning **Elisabeth** ^smith under their Care
disowned   report, they have discharged themselves, and find no Satisfaction; this
meeting,[finds]there hath been Sufficient labour besto^wed, do deny her from
having any right of membership amonung us, and from under the care
of this meeting; and do appoint **Alice Anthony** and **Deborah Hayden** to
Draw a paper of denial against the Said **Elisabeth Smith,** agreeable to
her offence and bring to the next monthly meeting

Mehit: Akin   **Elisabeth Ricketson** Informs that she hath acquainted **Mehitabel Akin**
informed   wife of **Timothy Akin** of her denial

Humphry   The Friends that had the Oversight of **Humphry Shearman** and **Marcy**
Shearman   **Lapham**s marriage make report. they attended and it was consumated
Married   and conducted in a ^good degree Orderly so far as they discovered

Minniuts not   The Committee that was appoint to Revise the minnits and Settle with
Revisd   the Treasurer. have not accomplish'd it they are continued in the Same
Service and make report next monthly meeting

Ruth Sowl   **Ruth Sowle** brought a few lines to this meeting, condemning her
acknowledg-   marrying out of the Unity of Friend: **Hannah Mosher** and **Joanna**
ment   **Gifford** are appointed to take the proper care to Inspect into the Sencerity
of her acknowledgment and make report when ready

Joshua Potter   **Joshua Potter** desires to be taken under the care of this meeting
request   and likwise request for his Small children whose names are **Easther**
Zilpha, Gardner, Phebe, Patience, and **Apphia**; his two Eldest daughters
Request for themselves **Mary** and **Rhoda Potter**
    Hannah Mosher Joannah Gifford and **Martha Allen** are appointed
to Joine the men friends in regard of **Joshua Potter** requesting for
himself and family; to See wheither they are Worthy to be received
amoung Friends; and they to make report when Ready

Epistle   Received a coppy of the last yearly meetings Epistle held at **Rod Island**
Recᵈ   containing good and Seasonable advises wʰich was truly acceptable among us

Robart   **Robert Barker** and **Ruth Tucker** made proposals of marriage^with eacch other before
Barker   this meeting and wear Desired to wait for their answer until next
proposal of   Monthly Meeting; ~ **Deborah Hayden** and **Sarah Gifford** are appointed
marriage

to make enquiry into **Ruth Tucker** clearness respecting_∧^{marriage} and conversation and make report next monthly meeting

Mary [Duel]
disowned
    The Committee that have had the matter under their care concerning **Mary Duels [Devoll's, Davol's]** disorderly walking make report, they have had Several oppertunities with her and_∧^{found} no Satisfaction, She not having any Sight or Sense of her falling Short: therefore this meeting finding freedom to Testify against and do deny her from under their care or right to membership and do appoint **Alice Anthony** and **Sarah Gifford** to draw a paper of denial against the Said **Mary Duel,** and bring to the next Monthly meeting

Miniuts Revisd
Settld with
Treasurer
    The Committee appointed to Correct and Revise this meetings Miniutes, and Settle accompts with the Treasurer report that they have Answered their appointment, and there remain in ye Stock 11^£-2^s-0^d old tennor

12 month
1780
    At a Monthly meeting of Women Friends held in **Dartmouth** ye 18 y^e12^th month 1780 The Representatives are **Sarah Anthony** and **Abigail Shepherd** both present

[El]isab: Smith
[d]enial Sign'd
    The Committee that was appointed to draw a paper of denial against **Elisabeth Smith** have presented one, Which is Signed and to be read at **New Town** at the Close of Some first day meeting of Worship between this and next monthly meeting

[F]reborn Rider
minit Returnd
    Our Friend **Freeborn Rider** hath returned a Coppy of a Minite that she had to Visit **Sanwich** Quarterly meeting: With an Endorsment, Signifying their unity and Satisfaction with her Visit and Labour of Love

Ruth Tucker
Clearness
    The friends appointed to make enquiry into **Ruth Tucker**s Clearness respecting marriage and Conversation make report they find nothing to hinder their proceedings

[R]obert Barker
answer
    Robart Barker and **Ruth Tucker** appearing for their answer, their answer was they might proceed to take Each other in marriage at Some Convenient time before the next monthly meeting: adviseing with the overseers, who are **Hannah Tucker** and **Judith Russell,** and they to make report next monthly meeting

Mary Duel
referd
    Mary Dewel [Devoll. Davol] hath made Some Acknoledgment for her misconduct, which hath Stopt friends proceeding against her; and the matter is Continued under the Same former Committees care, who are **Alice Anthony Deborah Gifford** and **Joanna Gifford** and they to take the proper care to find whether She is Sincear in what She hath offered: which her fruits will make manifest: and they to make report when ready

Adjournd
    This meeting is Ajournd to the 27th of this Instant

mett Mett by adjournment ye 27th of the 12th month 1780 Representatives not present

    The Queries hath been read, and answers prepared and approved: and the Epistle

[Se]nt up to
[Q] meeting
Signed, and _∧^{all} to be Sent up to Quarterly meeting by our Representatives who are **Susanna Smith** and **Sarah Howland;** and they to make report next monthly meeting

[1] month
1781
    At a Monthly meeting of Women Friends held in **Dartmouth** ye 15th of 1st month 1781 The Representatives are **Deborah Hayden** and **Sarah Gifford** both present

    A Denial against **Elisabeth Smith** hath been read agreeable to the last monthly meeting and is as followeth

[E]lisa Smith
[d]enial
    Whereas **Elisabeth Smith** wife of **Joseph Smith** having long made Profession with us the people called Quakers; and of late hath so far departed there from

as to attend meetings held out of the ~~of~~ Unity of our Society and Joine in publick Worship with them who are disowned by us the people afore said: And friends having bestowed much Labour of love to convince her of the Evil tendency thereof but it not having the desired Effect to Friends Satisfaction, and she continuing to Justify herself therein: all which being so contrary to our profession, and these Rules and orders of our Society that friends are consrained to give this forth as a a publick Testimony against her the Said **Elisabeth Smith.** hereby disowning her from being one in Unity with us and from under our care; But that She may be Convinced of the evil of her outgoing is our Sincear desire

     Given forth and Signed in and on behalf of our monthly **Wm Anthony Jur** Clerk meeting held in **Dartmouth** yᵉ 18ᵗʰ of yᵉ 12ᵗʰ month 1780 By **Susanna Smith** Clerk

Robart Barker
Married

     The Comittee that had the oversight of **Robart Barker**s marriage report they have fulfilled their appointment: and so far as they discovered it was consu= =matted Orderly

[H]annah Ben
-nett request
[C]ertif

     Alice Anthony and **Susanna Smith** are appointed to make Enquiry into the Life and Conversation of **Hannah Bennet,** wife of **Robert Bennet** and if nothing appears to hinder to draw a Certificate on her behalf and bring to the next monthly meeting it is to be directed to **Rhod Island** monthly meeting

[com]plaint
[a]gainst
Alice Slo-
com

     This meeting is Informd by one of the overseers that **Alice Slocum** appears to be in the practice of resorting at places where undue liberty is taken of musick and dancing, and keeping company with those that are out of the Unity of friends For which much labour hath been bestowed it not having the desired Effect **Alice Anthony Deborah Hayden** and **Sarah Gifford** are appointed to labour further with her and they to make report to the next monthly meeting

Return from
Q meeting

     One of the Representatives Inform that She attended our Quarterly meeting the other friend informs She did not, by reason of indisposition of body we Received an Epistle from the Same which was read to good Satisfaction to the Honnest hearted among us with desires that the Seasonable advice contained may be observed and put in practice

Phebe Sisson
request

     Phebe Sisson hath desired her Children may be taken under the care of this meeting: **Hannah Mosher** and **Joanna Gifford** are appointed to Inspect into the Circumstance and Sencerity of Said request and make report when ready

Deb Wood
disownd

     Some of the Overseers inform that **Deborah Wood** wife of **Stephen Wood** hath maried out of the unity of Friends; and that She hath been Sutiably and timly admonshed for which this meeting doth deny her from under our care, and from having any Right of membership in our Society and do appoint **Keziah Russell** to inform her of her denial

Nat: Sisson
proposal
of marriage

     Nathaniel Sisson and **Grace Gifford** made proposals of marriage with Each other before this meeting: and were desired to wait for their answer until next monthly meeting **Joanna Gifford** and **Rhoda Mott** are appointed to make Enquiry into the young woman's clearness respecting marriage and conversation and make report next monthly meeting

Nat Gifford
& wife ac=
knowledgᵗ

     Nathaniel Gifford and **Mehitabel** his wife hath made Some acknowledgment to this meeting for their being Guilty of the Sin of fornication: this meeting appoints

Deborah Allen and Deborah Hayden to Joine the men friends to Inspect into the
Sencerity thereof and they to make report when ready

2 month   At a Monthly meeting of Women Friends held in **Dartmouth** yᵉ 19ᵗʰ of 2ⁿᵈ month 1781
1781   The Representatives are **Silvester Howland** & **Mehitable Tucker: Mehitabel** present

Grace Gifford   The Friends appointed to make enquiry into **Grace Gifford**s Clearness respecting
Clearness marriage and conversation make report they find nothing to hinder their proceeding

Nat Sisson   **Nathaniel Sisson** and **Grace Gifford** appeared for their answer; Which was
answer They may proceed to take Each other in marriage at some convenient time
before next monthly meeting, adviseing with the overseers who are **Hannah Mosher**
and **Rhoda Mott**

Joshua Potter   The Committee that was appointed to have the matter under their care concerning
Children **Joshua Potter**s children, make report they found pretty good Satisfaction and think
Recᵈ they may be received: In consideration thereof this meeting Receives them into
Membership and under the care of this meeting, their names being **Mary, Rhoda**
Esther, Zilpha, Phebe, Patience, Apphia Potters

Ruth Sowle &   The friends that had that matter under theⁱʳ care Respecting **Ruth Sowl**s Request
Children =ing for her Self and her three daughter to be taken under friends care, they make
Recᵈ Report, they found good Satisfaction: In consideration thereof this meeting accepts
her acknoʷledgment, and Receives her with her daughters **Susanna, Mary,** and
Thankful, Sowles under the care of this meeting

Alice Slocum   The Committee that was appointed to deal and Labour with **Alice Slocum** for her
to be denied misconduct make report, they have fulfilled their appointment, She not having a
Sight thereof, gave us no Satisfaction: this meeting finding themselves clear
do appoint **Alice Anthony** and **Sarah Gifford** to draw a paper of denial against her
agreeable to her offence and bring to next monthly meeting

Ha:n Bennet   Signed a Removal Certificate for **Hannah Bennet** Recommeding her as a
Certificate member to **RhodIsland** monthly meeting

Mehit: **Mehitable Maxfield** Request to come under ˌᵗʰᵉ ᶜᵃʳᵉ ᵒᶠ this meeting, **Sarah Anthony** and
Maxfielᵈ **Deborah Gifford** are appointed to Inspect the Sincerity of her request, whither
request the motive is from true Conviction; and they to make report when Ready

3 month   At a Monthly meeting of Women friends held in **Dartmouth** yᵉ 19ᵗʰ of 3ᵈ month 1781
1781 The Representatives are **Amie Barker** and **Deborah Gifford** both present

Nat: Sisson   The Committee appointed to have the oversight of **Nathaniel Sisson**s and
Married **Grace Gifford**s marriage report, that they attended said marriage and for
what they discovered it was conducted orderly

Alice Slocᵐ Signed a paper of denial against **Alice Slocum** that is to be read Publickly at the Close
denial signd of Some first meeting of Worship before the next monthly meeting

Sent up to   The Queries have been read, answers prepared, and an Epistle Sign'd and to
Q meeting be sent up to our Quarterly meeting by our Representatives who are **Judith Russell,**
Sarah Howland, and **Silvester Howland;** and they to make report to next monthly
meeting

[D]avid Brooks   We ware favoured with the Company of our Friend **David Brooks** of **deep**
Thoˢ Sattergood **River Gifford** County in **North Carolina**: likwise our friend **John Foreman** at
Visit

Gwinnedd in the Province of **Pensylvania** with **Thomas Scattergood** of **Phlidelphia** with Some lines by way of Certificate with their Labours of love which was truly comfortable to the honest hearted amongst us Likwise the Company of our Friend **Seth Coffin** from a monthly meeting held at **deep river**

Deb: Wood inform'd   **Keziah Russell** Informes this meeting that she hath acquainted **Deborah Wood** of her denial

[S]eth Hart [p]roposal of marriage   **Seth Hart** and **Abigail Anthony** made Proposals of marriage before this meeting and were desired to wait for their answer till next monthly meeting **Deborah Hayden** and **Sarah Gifford** are appointed to make Enquiry into ^the young womans clear -ness respecting marriage and Conversation and make report to next monthly meeting

few lines for Freborn Rider   Signed a few lines on behalf of our Friend **Freeborn Rider** Signifying our Unity with her intended Visit within the Verge of **Sanwich** Quarterly meeting

Abig Devoal Certifi   Received a removal Certificat on behalf of **Abigail Devol [Devoll, Davol]** wife of **Abner Devol** from **Sandwich** monthly meeting which is accepted

Han: Bowdish Certif^te   Received a Removal Certificate from **Swanzey** monthly meeting on behalf of **Hannah Bowdish** wife of **William Bowdish** which is accepted

Prince Potter request   **Prince Potter** and his Wife **Hannah** desires for themselves and for their Children to be Taken under the care of this meeting: **Hannah Tucker** and **Susanna Smith** are ap- -pointed to take the proper care to Visit the family and Joine the men friends to find whether they are worthy to be received into membership and make report when ready

adjourn'd   This Meeting Adjourns to next fo^urth day come week

mett   Mett by adjournment ye 28 of 3 month 1781 Representatives call'd **Deborah Gifford** present

Meriah Smith denial to be draw'd   The Committee appointed to labour with **Meriah Smith** make report they have Laboured with her from time to time, and She continues in the practice of going to Seperate meeting, and gives no Satisfaction: In consideration thereof this meeting ^being clear do appoint **Alice Anthony** and **Barsheba Howland** to draw a paper of denial against Said **meriah** and bring to the next monthly meeting

[E]sther Allen confestion   **Esther Allen** Sent in a paper condemning her marrying out from amoung friends **Judith Russell** and **Susanna Russell** are appointed to Visit said Esther the better to understand whether She is Sincear, and they to make report when ready

Mary Sear= man Jur &c acknolegment   **Mary Shearman, Deborah Sherman, Rhoda Ricketson, Amie Barker** and **Lydia Howland** hath handed in a few lines Condemning their gathering in places where undue liberty is taken which this meeting accepts of provoided they Cause Said paper to be read at the close of Some meeting of Worship on firt day they being present

[A]dam Mott [S]usan Giffod Russell [t]estimony   Signed in this meeting Some Testimonies concerning our Esteemed Friend **Adam Mott Susanna Gifford** and **Paul Russell,** which Testimonies are to be Sent up to our ^next Quarterly meeting at **Smithfield**

[4] month 1781   At a Monthly meeting of Women friends held in **Dartmouth** ye 16th of 4th month 1781 The Representatives are **Sarah Gifford** and **Mary Smith** both present

The denial against **Alice Slocum** hath been read agreeable to the last monthly meetings Conclustion ~ and is followeth

Alice Slocum denial   Whereas **Alice Slocum** daughter of **Peleg Slocum** haveing had a right of member- -ship among us the people called Quakers in **Dartmouth,** and been under the care

of our meeting but hath so far departed from the principles we profess as to be
in the practice of frequenting places where undue Liberty is taken Such as --
musick and Dancing and keeping company with those not of our Society
For which she hath been much laboured with in love to convince her of the
Evil tendency of Such conduck, but our labours not having the desired Effect to
friends satisfaction: therefore for the clearing of Truth and friends from the
reproach thereof, we give this forth as a publick Testimony against her the sd
Alice Slocum hereby disowning her from being one in Unity with us and from
under our care

Given forth and Signed in and on behalf of our monthly ⎫ By ⎫ **Wm Anthony Jur** Clerk
meeting of Friends held in **Dartmouth** 19 of 3 month 1781 ⎭   ⎭ **Susanna Smith** Clerk

Return from The friends appointed to attend the Quarterly meeting Report, they have
Q meeting fulfil'd their appointment; by whome we received an Epistle that was
read to good Satisfaction containing much Seasonable advice therein

Freborn Rider Our Friend **Freeborn Rider** hath returned our Certificate that She had
Certi returnd to Visit **Sandwich** Quarterly meeting: with the concuren͵ce and the Unity
they had whilst amoung them

Mary Sherman **Mary Shearman, Deborah Shearman, Rhoda Ricketson, Amie Barker**
& company and **Lydia Howland**, hath caused their acknowledgement to be read
paper read according to the advice of Last monthly meetinge

Abig Anthony The friends appointed to make Enquiry into **Abigail Anthony**s clear
clearness -ness respecting marriage and conversation make report they find nothing
hinder their proceeding

Seth Harts **Seth Hart** and **Abigail Anthony** appeared for thir answer: which was
Answer they may proceed to take Each other in marriage, at Some convenient time
before next monthly meeting, advising with͵the Overseers who are **Deborah
Hayden** and **Susanna Smith** they to make report next monthly meeting

Meriah Smith Signed a paper of denial against **Meriah Smith** which is to be read
denial Signd Publickly at the close of Some first day meeting of Worship before the next
monthly meeting

Han: Sherman The overseers Inform that **Hannah Shearman** wife of **Caleb Shearman**
disowned hath lately married out of the Unity of Friends, after being precausioned
& to be inform^d In consideration thereof this meeting doth deny her from having any
Right of membership and from under the care of this meeting: and
Alice Anthony and **Barsheba Howland** are appointed to acquaint **Hannah
Shearman** of her denial; and likwise if any thing appears against her
that She was guilty of while under ͵our care, they should draw a publick Denial and
bring to the monthly meeting

Freeborn Rider and **Hannah Mosher** are appointed to Inform **Meriah Smith**
of her denial and make report ncxt monthly meeting

Certi: to be This meeting is Inform'd that **Henry Howland** hath removed with his
prepar'd for Family within the Verge of **Accoakset** monthly meeting: **Alice Anthony** and
Henry How **Sarah Anthony** are appointed to Joine the men friends in preparing Certificats
land and for the family if they find nothing to hinder and bring to next monthly meeting
family

5 month
1781

At a Monthly meet of Women Friends held in **Dartmouth** 21ˢᵗ of 5ᵗʰ month 1781
The Representatives are **Elisabeth Slocum** and **Hannah Wood** both present

Seth Hart
Married

The Committee that had the oversight of **Seth Hart**ₐ & **Abigail Anthony** marriage
Report they attended according to appointment, and that it was consumated
and conducted to Satisfaction

This meeting is Inform'd that the denial of **Meriah Smith** hath been reᵃd
Publickly by the director of last monthly meeting, and is as followeth

Testimony
against
Meriah
Smith

Whereas **Meriah Smith** Wife of **John Smith** of **Dartmouth** having made Pro-
-fession with us the people called Quakers, and been under the care of our meeting
But hath So far departed from the principles We profess as to attend meetings
held out of the Unity of our Society, and Joine in publick Worship with them
that are not own'd by us the afore said people and friends having bestowed
much labour in love to convince her of the Evil tendency therof but our
Labour not having its desired Effect to Friends Satisfaction and She
Continues to Justify herself therein: therefore We are concerned
To give this forth as a publick Testimony against her the Said **Meriah
Smith** hereby disowning her from being one in Unity with us and from under
our Care; Yet that She may so walk as to find marcy is our Sincear Desire

Given forth and Signed in and on behalf of   **William Anthony Jur** Clerk
our monthly meeting of friends held in   **Susanna Smith** Clerk
Dartmouth the 16ᵗʰ day of the 4 month 1781 By

[M]eriah Smith
inform'd

This meeting is Inform'd the Committee hath informd **Meriah Smith** of
her denial according to appointment

[Jo]s: Gifford Ju
[r]equest

This meeting is inform'd that **Joseph Gifford Jur** hath removed with his
family within the compass of **Sandwich** monthly meeting and Desires our Certi-
-ficate thereto **Kaziah Russell** and **Mary Tucker** are appointed to make Enquiʳʸ
Respecting their lives and Circumstances in order to prepare a Certificate if
nothing appears to Hinder and bring to next monthly meeting

[Pr]ince Potter
wife and
[ch]ildren
Received

The Committee that was appointed to have the matter under their care concern
-ing **Prince Potter**s family make report they have had Several oppertunities
and found pretty good satisfaction, and are willing they should be received
In consideration thereof this meeting Receives them under their care, namly
Prince Potter and **Hannah** his wife, with their Children **Elisabeth, Samuel, Seth
Mary, Joseph, Benjamin, Abner** and **Lydia Potters**

[E]dward
Thurston
family
disowned

We are Informed from the mens meeting that they have concluded to deny
Edward Thurton, and **Parnel** his wife with all their Children from under our care
or from any right of membership, if the Womens meeting concurs therewith
which they do

[a]djourned

This Meeting Adjourns to the 30ᵗʰ of this Instant

[m]ett

Mett according to adjournment The Representatives both present

[M]ehitabel
[M]axfield
[r]eceived

The Committee appointed concerning **Mehitabel Maxfield** requesting
to be takeing under the care of this meeting report they found pritty good
Satisfaction and think She may be received into membership; In consideration
thereof accepts the report and receives her under the care of this meeting

[Ph]ebe Slocum [Ju]dith How= [la]nd ac- knowlgt Rec^d	**Phebe Slocum** and **Judith Howland** have Sent a paper to this meeting ac- knowledging and condemning their Joining a company and assisting in prepareing for an entertainment, and going to places where undue liberberty is taken: all which they Seem to be Sorry for: in consideration thereof this meeting takes up with what they have don for Satisfaction

[6] Month 1781   At a Monthly meeting of Women friends held in **Dartmouth** ye 18th of 6th month 1781
The Representatives are **Sarah Gifford** and **Susanna Wood** both present

[Jo]seph Gifford [r]eferd   The Committee appointed respecting **Joseph Gifford Jur** and familys Certifi- -cats Signifie they are not ready to bring one to this meeting

[Es]ther Allen [ac]knowledg [m]ent rec^d   The Committee appointed to Inspect the Sencerity of **Esther Allens** acknow- -ledgment for marrying out of the Unity of friends make report, they found pretty good Satisfaction and are willing She should be received in consideration thereof this meeting receives her under their care and in membership again

[vi]sit of furreign [fr]iends [J]ames Thorn [to]n Samue [S]mith   Received Certificates on behalf of our Worthy friends **James Thornton** from a Monthly meeting at **Abington** in the Province of **Pensyvannia** bearing date the 19th of 3^d month 1781 ~ **Samuel Smith** from a monthly meeting held at **Phi= lidelphia** by adjournment for the Northen district y^e 17 of 4 month 1781

[T]ho: Carring [t]on   **Thomas Carrington** fr^om a monthly meeting held in **New Garden** ₍county₎ in **Pensylvania** held by adjournment y^e 7th of 3^d month 1781 Whose Testimonies with their labours of Love were Eadifying and comfortable to the honest hearted among us

[D]av Cooper   Likewise Our friends **David Cooper** from **Haddington** monthly meeting held at **New Jersey** the 9 of ye 4 month 1781

[Ge]orge [C]hurchman   **George Churchman** from a monthly meeting held at **Notingham** in [?] in **Maryland** the 31 of the 3 month 1781

[W]arner [M]ufflin   **Warner Mufflin** from a monthly meeting held at **Duck Crick** in **Kent** County on **Deliware** by adjournment ye 29 of 4 month 1781
Those three last mentioned friends being Recomended as Serviceable Elders In Unity whose company are truly acceptable

Represeta^{es} to Q meeting   The Friends appointed to attend the Quarterly m^eeting are **Kaziah Russell Ruth Tucker Elisabeth Kirby** and **Mary Tucker** and they to make report to the next monthly meeting

Adjourn'd   This meeting concludes and is Adjourned to the 27th of this Instant
mett   Mett according to adjournment ye 27 of ye 6 month 1781 Representatives both present

Abigail Howland Certificate   Signed a Removal Certificate for **Abigail Howland** wife of **Henry Howlan[d]** and their daughter **Deborah**, Recommending them to **Accakset [Acoaxet]** monthly meeting

Martha Chace Certifi   Received a Removal Certificate fr^om **Swanzey** monthly meeting on behalf of **Martha Chace** wife of **Benjamin Chase**, Recommending her as a member of this meeting, which is accepted

Abigail Allen Certificate   Received a Removal Certificate from **Ninepartners** monthly meeting on behalf ₍of₎ **Abigail Allen** Recommending her as a member to this meeting which is accepted

Epistle to Q meetng   Signed an Epistle to the Quarterly meeting to be sent up by our Repre- -sentatives who are as above mentiond

Jos Gifford *Certificate*	Signed A Removal Certificate for **Joseph Gifford** and his wife **Hannah** with their Children Recommending them to **Sandwich** monthly meeting

7 month
1781 At a Monthly meeting of Women friends held in **Dartmouth** ye 16th of 7th month 1781
The Representatives are **Elisabeth Slocum** and **Silvia Smith** both pesent

Return from
Q meeting
Epistle recd The Representatives appointed to attend the Quarterly meeting Report they all attended said meeting except **Ruth Tucker** by whom we received an Epistle from the same, with a Transcript of an Epistle from the last yearly meeting of Women friends held at **Philidelphia** both containing much good and seasonable advice

Phebe Sisson
Children
Recd The Committee that was appointed Some time past to Inspect into the Sencerity and circumstance of the widdow **Phebe Sisson**s Children, Inform this Meeting, that that they find so much Satisfaction that they are in hopes it will be for the best to receive them: this meeting taking up with said report doth receive them into membership and under the care of friends the daugh- -ter names,are **Ruth** and **Judith Sisson**

8 month
1781 At a Monthly meeting of Women Friends held in **Dartmouth** ye 20th of 8th month 1781
The Representatives are **Mary Shearman** and **Martha Allen** both present

Committee
on Joining
to Sandwich
Quarter This meeting appoints **Freeborn Rider, Deborah Allen** and **Susanna Smith** to confer with a Quarterly meeting Committee of men and women friends Respecting Joining **Ponaganset** and **Acoakset** monthly meetings to Sand- -wich Quarter

Adjourns This meeting Adjournes to the 29th of this Instant month

mett Mett by adjournment ye 29 of 8th month 1781 Representatives both present

Mary Duel
case Our Friends **Martha Allen** and **Hannah Mosher** are appointed to Joine the Committe to treat further with **Mary Deuel [Devol, Davoll]** concerning her acknow- ledgment and they to make report so Soon as may be performed

Phebe Beard
disownd The Overseers Inform this meeting they have laboured with **Phebe Beard** for her keeping company with one that is not of our Society, but she hath so far persested as to be Published out of the Unity of friends, for which She is denied from any right of membership and from being under the care of friends; **Rebecca Hayden** is desired to acquaint said **Phebe** of her denial and make report to next monthly meeting

Adjourd This meeting Adjourns to the 5th day of next month

mett Mett according to adjournment ye 5 of 8 month Reptve **Mary Sharman** present

Allen Russell
proposal of
marriage **Allen Russell** and **Abigail Allen** made proposals of marriage with Each other before this meeting and were desired to wait for their answe till next monthly meeting ~ **Mary Shearman** and **Phebe Slocum** are appointed to make enquiry into the young womans clearness respecting marrage and conver -sation and make report next monthly meeting

9 month
1781 At a Monthly meeting of Women friends held in **Dartmouth** ye 17th of 9th month 1781
The Representatives are **Abigal Shepherd** and **Bersheba Howland** both present

Susan Maccom
ber request a
certificate **Susanna Maccomber** desires a Removal Certificate for her Self and daughters to the great **Ninepartners** monthly meeting, **Sarah Gifford** and **Abigail Shepherd**

are appointed to make Enquiry and if nothing appears to hinder to Joine the
men friends in prepareing a Certificate for the family

Patience Austin request — Patience Austen desires to be taken under the care of this Meeting; **Judith Russell** and **Silvia Smith** are desired to make Enquiry and inspect into the Sencerity of her request and make report when ready

Abigail Allen clearness — The Friends that was appointed to make inquiry into **Abigail Allen's** Clearness respecting marriage and conversation report they find nothing to hinder their proceeding

Allen Russell Answer — **Allen Russell** and **Abigail Allen** appeared for their; Which was, they may proceed to take Each other in marriage before the next monthly meeting Advising with the overseers, Who are **Hannah Mosher** and **Joanna Gifford** they to make report next monthly meeting

To treat with Howland & daughter — **Joanna Gifford** and **Martha Chase** are appointed to treat with **Abigail Howland** and her daughter **Deborah** concerning Some disorders appears in them which hath been the cause that **Acoakset** monthly meeting could not accept a Recommendation on their account

Caleb Serman & wife denial Sign'd — Signed a paper of Denial against **Caleb Shearman** and his wife **Hannah** which is to be read publickly between now and next monthly meeting at the Closs of some publick meeting of Worship

Commtee to Join Q meeting Comteereport — The Committee that was appointed to confer with the Quarterly meetings Committee make report they have had an Oppertunity according to appointment and have brought in their Judgment in said matter, likewise rendread the Circumstances given, which Judgment is accepted by the meeting and Signed therein by the Clerk and to go to the Quarterly meetings Committee

Phebe Beard be inform'd — This meeting Still desires **Rebecca Hayden** to Inform **Phebe Beard** of her denial

Preparitive meeting altered — It is the conclusion of this meeting to hold our next preparitive meeting on ye 26 of this Instant by reason that the meeting for Sufferings is to be held on the Same day our Preparitive meeting comes in corse

Adjourned — Likewise this meeting Adjourns to the Same day

mett — Mett according to Adjournmen: Represenvs Called **Abigail Shepherd** present **Barsheba Howland** not present by reason of indisposition of body

Sent up to Q meeting — The Queries have been read and answer prepared, with an Epistle Signed and to be sent up to our Quarterly meeting by our Representatives who are **Sarah Gifford, Marcy Slocum,** and **Elisabeth Slocum,** and they to make report next monthly meeting

Rhobe Smith Visit — **Rhobe Smith** attended this meeting with a few lines from **East Hoosuck** monthly meeting Signifying her being her being in membership and likewise their Unity with her intended Visit ~ Which we returned back to that said meeting by the bearer thereof with an Indorsment thereon Signifying our reception thereof

10 month 1781 — At a Month meeting of Women friend held in **Dartmouth** ye 15th of 10 month 1781 The Representatives are **Alice Anthony** and **Hanah Mosher** both present

Allen Russell — The Committee that had the oversight of **Allen Russell** and **Abigail Allens** marriage Report they attended said marriage and it was conducted in a good degree orderly as far as they discovered

Commition
Abi Howland
case

The Committee that was appointed to treat with **Abigail Howland** and her Daughter **Deborah** for disagreeable dress and their not attending meetings for Business; are still continued to labour and deal with them as Truth shall direct

return from
Q meeting

The Friends appointed to attend the Quarterly meeting report they attended accordingly by whom we received an Epistle which was read and kindly accepted

Denial against
Caleb
Sheaman
& wife

We are informed that a denial against **Caleb Shearman** and his wife **Hannah** hath been Read agreeable to last monthly meetings conclusion and is as followeth Whereas **Caleb Shearman** (son of **Philip Shearman**) and **Hannah** his wife daghter of **Jacob Russell** deceased, having had a right of membership amoung us the people called Quakers, but through unwatchfulness and by disregarding the Testimony of Truth in their own hearts, have so far deviated thir from as to fall into the Sin of fornication, which is Eviden by their having a Child soon after marriage; and Friends having treated with them in love to Shew the Evil of their Transgression and restore them to the way of Truth But their Labours of love not having the desired Effect to friends Satisfaction Friends are concerned to give this forth as a Testimony against them the said **Caleb Shearman** and **Hannah** his wife; hereby disowning ‸them from being members of our Society and from under the care of this meeting; yet our desire is that they may ‸be come truly Sensible of their Transgressions and be resored to way ‸the of truth Given forth and Signed in and on behalf of men & womens   By   **Wm Anthony Jnr** Clerk

Phebe Berd
informd of
denial

monthly meeting held in **Dartmouth** 17 of 9 month 1781   **Susanna Smith** Clerk

Phebe Beard hath been Informed of her Denial

The Clerk hath Signed a Removal certificate for **Philip Maccomber** his wife **Susanna** and their children Namely **Edith Gardner, Barnabus, Abraham** and **Hannah** Recommend them to the **Nine partners** monthly meeting as members

Overseers

This meeting appoints **Sarah Anthony** and **Hannah Wood** in the place of overseers for disorders

commitee on
dividing
preparitive
meeting

We have considered the matter concerning the dividing our preparitive Meetings, agreeable to the advice of the Quarterly meetings Committy and the requst of Some of the members of our meeting; and do apoint our Friends **Deborah Hick, Susanna Smith, Silvia Smith, Kaziah Russell** and **Judith Russell** to Joine with the men friends agreeable to their miniuts and consider said matter as Truth shall direct & make report to the next monthly meeting

11 month
1781

At a Monthly meeting of Women Friends held in **Dartmouth** ye 19th of 11th month 1781 The Representatives are **Susanna Allen** and **Hannah Wood** both present

Patience
Austin
recd

The Fiends that hath had the matter under their care concerning the Sencerity of **Patience Austins** request, Inform they have had Several Sollid oppertunities with ‸her and She appears Sinceare therein, and they think well of her being received, ~ This meeting accepts of Said report and do Receive her into membership and under the care of this meeing

*Case of **Abigail Howland** & daughter referd*   The matter concerning **Abigail Howland** & her daughte is refer'd under the Same Friends care

Martha Allen request   This meeting is Inform'd that **Martha Allen** is about to remove with her family within the ˄compas of the **Ninepartners** monthly meeting and desires a removal Certificate for herself and two daughter **Mary** and **Isabel: Joanna Gifford Martha Chase** and **Rhoda Mott** are apointed to Inspect into their lives and Circumstance, and if nothing appears to hinder to draw one and bring to the next monthly meeting

Report concern ing preparitive meeting   The comittee that was appointed to take the matter under their care and Consideration Respecting the dividing our Preparitive meeting Report By Reason of so many great weakness prevailing amoung us, perticuly the want of a true Discipline being kept up in Friends families; want of Unity in Some places, and other defects; it is their Opinion that this matter be continued under the care of the Commttee for further Trial This meeting Accepts said report and continues them in their appointment Each one to labour in their ability and the freedom of their minds to Remove all those disorders out from amoung us; and they to make ˄report to next monthly meeting

David Shepherd and Son David Certificates   Received a Certiᶠcate from **Smithfield** monthly meeting on behalf of **David Shepherd** his wife and Children namely **Caleb, Deborah, Gideon, Allen, Elisabeth** and **Lydia**
And one from the Same Monthly Meeting for **David Shepherd Junor** with his wife and Children namely **Thomas Reliance** and **John** Recom= =mending them as members to this meeing, all which are accepted

12 month 1781   At a Monthly meeting of Women friends held in **Dartmouth** yᵉ 17ᵗʰ of 12ᵗʰ month 1781 The Representatives **Mary Smith** and **Rebecca Ricketson** both present

Abigail How land case referd   The matter concerning **Abigail Howland** and her daughter is referd under the Same friends care

Martha Allen Certificate   Signe a removal Certificate for **Martha Allen** wife of **Jonathan Allen** And her two Daughters **Mary** and **Isabel Allen** Recomending them to the **Ninepartners** monthly meeting

Sent up to Quarterly meeting   Answers to the Queries have been read and aproved with an Epistle Signed and to be sent up to our Quarterly meeing by our Reprsentatives who are **Elisabeth Slocum, Martha Gifford, Susannah**˄ˢᵐⁱᵗʰ **Silvia Smith Elisabeth Wood** and **Lillis Gifford** and they to make report to the next monthly meeting

adjourned   This Meeting is adjournd to the 26ᵗʰ of this Instant

mett   Meet acording to Adjournment yᵉ 26 of 12 month 1781 Representatives both present

1 month 1782   At a Monthly meeting of Women Friends held in **Dartmouth** yᵉ 21ˢᵗ of 1ˢᵗ month 1782 The Representatives are **Sarah Gifford** and **Mary Tucker** both present

Abigail Howland case refer   The matter concerning **Abiail Howland** her ˄& daughter is still continued under the Same friends care

Return from Q meeting   We are Informᵉd that the Friends appointed to attend the Quarterly meeting all attended but **Silvia Smith**, who gave the reason of her not attending

which is accepted Received an Epistle which was read to the Satisfaction
of this meeting

Phebe Allens
Acknowledg
ment

Phebe Allen Wife of **Abraham Allen** hath condemned her being at a marriage
Consumated out of the Unity friends which this meeting takes ᴬup with
desireing she may be more careful for the future

adjourned

This Meeting Adjourns to the 30th of this Instant

mett

Mett according to adjournment Representatives Pesent

---

2 Month
1781

At a Monthly Meeting of Women Friends held in **Dartmouth** yᵉ 18th of 2ⁿᵈ month 1782
The Representatives are **Elisabeth Slocum** and **Marcy Slocum** both present

Deb Howland
case referᵈ

The matter is continued another month concerning **Deborah Howland** under the
Same cosiderations

George Folger
Bennet Wing
proposal of
marriage

George Folger and **Rebeckah Shove**; **Bennett Wing** ᴬ& **Rhoda Ricketson** all of
them made proposals of marriage and Each other before this meeting and were
desired to waite for their answer till next monthly meeting; **Mary S**ᴬ**herman**
Bersheba Howland and **Susanna Wood** are appointed to make enquiry into
the young womens clearness Respecting marriage and converˢation and
make report to next monthly meeting

William
Jackson Visit

Our Esteemed Friend **William Jackson** attended this meeting with a Certifi=
=cate from a monthly meeing held at **New Garden Chester** County **Pensylvannia**
Bearing date the 10th of yᵉ 1ˢt month 1781, Whose labours of love was truly
acceptable amoung us to the honnest hearted

Adjournd

This Meeting Adjourns till tomorrow at the Eleventh hour

mett

Mett according to adjournment Representatives both present

Complaint
[?d] against
Silvester
Howland

The Overseers hath handed in a Complᵃint that **Sarah Howland** Exhibeted
against **Silvester Howland**, Seting forth there are Some Scandelos reports
Spread abroad concerning her that she will cheat and Lies, and she Suspecting
Silvester to be the author thereof: Now the Overseers Inform they have labour
=ed to Inspect said matter: and according to their discovery, it doth not
apear that **Sarah Howland** is such a person: and that according to their
apprehention **Silvester** hath not cleared herself from the complaint before
mentioned, Therefore this meeting appoints our friends **Martha Gifford**
Mary Shearman and **Hannah Tucker** to labour further to bring her to a Sight
of the Evil tendency of Such conduct, and likewise for them to deal with
her for the Same, and to Judge of the matter according as Truth may direct
and they to make report when Ready

The matter
concerning
Alice Wood

Received a few lines from **Rhod Island** monthly meeting set[t]ing forth that
Alice Wood hath Sent them her acknowledgment for marrying out of the Unity
of Friends ~ (She now residing in the Verge of this meeting) and they
desireing our assistance; We now appoint **Hannah Tucker** and **Sarah**
Gifford; to have a Soled [solid] oppertunity with her, and make inquiry and
Inspect the Sencerity of said acknowledgment, & Said Committee to make report
to this meeting when ready

Mary Dewel
continued
under frin^d
care

The committee that was appointed to Treat withe **Mary Dewel** concerning Some defects and neglect on account of attending meetings report they have Laboured according to their appointment and found Some Satisfaction and think it may be best that She continues under the care of this meeting, which said report was accepted of for Satisfaction

Henry How=
=land & wife
certificate

Signed a Removal Certificate for **Hnry [Henry] Howland** and **Abigail** his wife and Two of his children under age namely **Prince** and **Beriah** Recomme[n]ding them to **Accoakset** monthly meeting

Complaint
against
Ann Butts

The Overseers Inform this meeting that **Ann Butts** appears to be defective in Several respects, as Refusing the attending Religious mee[t]ings and Justifying the Same, and resorting to places where undue liberty is taken: which the Overseers Inform they have laboured with her for and she not clearing herself therefrom: This meeting appoints our friends **Elisabeth Slocum** and **Deborah Gifford** to restore her therefrom and likewise to deal with her for the Same as T^ruth may direct in the authority there of and they to make report when re^ady

3 month
1782

At a Monthly mee[t]ing of Women Friends held in **Dartmouth** ye 18th of 3rd month 1782 The Representatives are **Mary Shearman [Sherman]** and **Rhoda Mott** both present

Deb: Howland
case refer^d

The matter concerning **Deborah Howland** is continued another month

Concerning
Alice Wood

Elisabeth Slocum and **Susanna Smith** are appointed to Joine the Committee that was appointed to inspect the Sencerity of **Alice Wood**s acknowledgment to **Rhod Island** monthly meeting, they to make report when Ready

Rebe[c?] Shove
Rhoda Rick=
=etson
Clearness

The Friends that was appointed to make Inquiry into **Rebeccah Shove**s and **Rhoda Ricketson**s Clearness respe[c]ting marriage and conversation make report they found nothing to hinder their proceeding ^in marriage

George Folger
Bennett Wing
Answer

George Folger and **Rebeccah Shove**; **Bennett Wing** and **Rhoda Ricke[t]son** appeared for their Answers ~ Which was, they may proceed to take Each other in marriage at some Convenient time before the next monthly meeting Adviseing with the Overseers who are **Elisabeth Slocum** and **Mary Shearman** for **George Folger** and **Rebeccah Shove**: **Sarah Anthony** and **Marey Slocum** for **Bennett Wing** and **Rhoda Ricketson**; the Overseers to make report to next monthly meeting

Adjourn^d

This Meeting Adjourns to the 27th of this Instant

mett

Mett according to Adjournment Representatives both present

Sent up to Q
meeting

The Queries have been read and answers prepared with an Epistle Signed and to be sent up to the Quarterly meeting by our Representatives who are **Judith Russell** and **Hannah Wood** and they to make report to next monthly meeting

Judith
Hathaway
Disowned

The Overseers Inform that **Judith Hath[a]way** wife of **Jethro Hathaway** hath married out of the Unity of friends for which ^She hath been Pre admonished for but she not accepting the advice of friends; therefore this meeting denies her from a Right of Membership and from under the care of this meeting **Sarah Anthony** is appointed to Inform said **Judith** of her denial and She to make report to the next monthly meeting

Report of the matter co[n]cerning Silvester Howland

The Committee that was appointed to treat and labour with **Silvester Howland** have handed in their report with an acknowledgment from **Silvester Howland** and an agreement between the parties: Committees report is as Followeth

To the Committee of Men and Women Friends in the Case of **Silvester Howland** at the Complaint of **Sarah Howland**

Dear Friends Having understood by Sitting in your Monthly meeting That the matter committed to your Charge, was a considerable obstakole [obstacle] in the way of that Service upon which we and other Friends attended your meeting

From Qartly meeting Commite to to mo meeting Committee

we were desireous to see the particurlar parties and neighborhood among whome it Subsisted ~ And now having the Satisfaction to Inform you that with the assistance and concurrance of Several other friends in the neighberhood Those concerned therein have been favoured so far as to lay a hopeful foundation for Reconsiliation and harmony, if their present resolution is abode in

The Substance of which is Set forth in the inclosed paper of acknowled[g]ment Signed by **Silvester** and the agreement Signed by them both; [*smudge*] Which together Set forth the Termes they upon which they have agreed to Settle the Uneasiness; Their particular Connections, and those, who appeared to have entertained favourable opinions of either parties having been parti= =curlarly advised with and approved the Same, and agreed to Join in maintaining love and unity upon those Termes, and Supporting the Discipline in that respect according thereto

Should the above meet your approbation, we propose; wheither it might not be best to report to the meeting, the above acknowledgment and agreement as what might be accepted in Satisfaction, and advise that the acknowledg= =ment be read at the Close of a publick meeting (unless you see Some thing to render it unsuiutable) and the agre[e]ment to be preserved on file and the whole matter be brought to a Close in the meeting as Soon as it can Conveniently be accomplished; as we apprehend the matters, Still being continued in the Meeting will not be so likely a way to gether [gather] Strength after this Settlement as to leave the Sincerity of the acknowled[g]ment and agreement to be proved by time free from any restraint ~ With desires that all may Join to Strengt[h]en the Bonds of Unity ~ We Conclud[e] and remain your Friends **David Steere** [**Stare**?]

Ooziel Wiltinson [**Aziel Wilkerson**?]

Thomas Arnold

monthly meeting Committee concurence

Whereas the Quarterly Meetings Committee having yielded their Assista[n]ce ~~Which~~ In the above Settlement Which we Concur with

		Mary Shearman
Benja Chace	**Benja Slocum**	**Martha Gifford**
Stephen Buffinton	**Wm Wood**	**Peleg Gifford**
Agreeme[n]t is as follows) **Giles Slocum**	**Abiel Gifford**	**James Davis**

Agreement between the parties

We are Sensible the uneasiness between us has given pain and Anxiety to the body of Friends, We do therefore for the peace and Unity of Society hereby agree and engage that by Divine assistance we will not endeavour to Spread or promote the same directly or indirectly: Either to endeavor to enforce the ~~tro~~

truth of said Report on the one part~ or the blame arising therefrom on the
other part, or in any wise endeavor to hurt each others Cherrᵉcter. But we will
Endeavour to the utmost of ∧ᵒᵘʳ power that the same be no longer remembered
amoung Friends, ~ And ∧ᵃˢ a further Confermation of ∧ᵒᵘʳ Sencerity here in we agree
and desire that all Evidences, or other things committed to wʳiteing respect-
=ing the above difficulty Either in the hands of the monthly meetings Commitᵗᵉᵉ
or else where be committed to the fire　　　　　**Silvester Howland**

　　　　Dartmouth 21ˢᵗ of 3ᵈ month 1782　　　　**Sarah Howland**

*w∧ʰich is
accepted
provided*

All which this meeting accepts of, Provided **Silvester** causes her a[c]knowledgment
to be read at the Close of Some first day meeting of Worship before the next
monthly meeting and said acknowledgment handed to the meeting to be put
on record

---

*4 month
1782*

At a Monthly meeting of Woman Friends held in **Dartmouth** yᵉ 15ᵗʰ of 4 month 1782
　　　　Representatives ∧ᵃʳᵉ **Sarah Gifford** and **Edith Russell** both present

*Deb Howland
case referᵈ*

The matter concerⁿing **Deborah Howland** is continued another month

*Jane Williams
Certificate
accepted*

Received a Removal Certificate from **Rhod Island** monthly ∧ᵐᵉᵉᵗⁱⁿᵍ on behalf of
Jane Williams wich is accepted

*Georg[e] Folger
Bennet Wing
marriage*

The Friends appoin[t]ed to have the oversight of **George Folger** and **Rebeccah**
Sh [*ink spot*] **Shoves**: **Bennett Wing**s and **Rhoda Ricketson** marriage make report that
they attended and they were consumated and conducted in some good degree orderˡʸ

Silvester Howland paper ∧ᵒᶠ ᵃᶜᵏⁿᵒʷˡᵉᵈᵍᵐᵉⁿᵗ hath been read according to the last monthly
meetings Conclusion and is as followeth

*Silvester
Howland
acknowledg=
ment*

Dear Friends　　　　　　　　　　To the Monthly meeting ᵒᶠ **Dartmouth**
　　　　Whereas I have ∧ᵘⁿʷᵃᵗᶜʰᶠᵘˡˡʸ been Some Means of Spreading a report which hath
a Tendency to lessen the Character and Reputation of my Sister and nei[gh]bour
Sarah Howland: These are therefore to manifest that I am Sorry for it
and desire her forgiveness therein and Friends to pass it by: and this
Paper is Given up to Friends to be disposed of as best Wisdom shall direct
Dartmouth 2[?]ᵗʰ of 3ᵈ month 1782　　　　**Silvester Howland**

*Return from
Q meeting*

　　　　Our Friends that was appointed to attend the Quarterly meeting [?]
Inform they attended, but by some means the Accounts did not come to Either
of them, so that they mist of them which they Informed the Quarterly meeting
thereof; by whom we received an Epistle therefrom which was read in
this meeting to good Satisfaction

*Judith Hath
=way informᵈ
of denial*

Sarah Anthony Informs that She hath notify'd **Judith Hatʰaway** of her denial

*Ann Butts
disowned*

The Committee that was appointed to deal and labour with **Ann Butts** [no Satisfaction?]
concerning her misconduct make report; they have discharged themselves and found
therefore this meeting denies her from a Right of membership
And do appoint **Marcy Slocum** to draw a paper of denial against her
agreeable to her offence and bring to next monthly meeting

*Joseph Mosher
proposal of
marriage*

Joseph Mosher and **Elisabeth Briggs** made proposals of marriage before
this meeting and they were desired to waite for their answer till the
next monthly meeting: **Phebe Smith** and **Edith Russell** are appointed to

make Enquiry into **Elisabeth Briggs** clearness respecting marriage and Conversation and make report to next monthly meeting

     Marcy Slocum Deborah Allen and **Susanna Smith** are appointed to V^{i}ew and

to correct minites Corre^{c}t the minietes [minutes] and Settle with Treasurer, and make report to the xt Monthly meeting when ready

5 month 1782 At a Monthly meeting of Women Friends held in **Dartmouth** ye 20th of 5th month 1782 The Representatives are **Judith Russell** and **Phebe Smith** both Present

Ann Butts de[n]ial Sign^d   Signed a paper of denial against **Ann Butt[s]** which is to be read at the Cloes [Close] of Some publick meeting of Worship on first day before next monthly meeting **Marcy Slocum** is desired to Acquaint her with her denial and inform the meeting thereof

Martha Green certificate   Receiv'd a Certificate from **Greenwich** monthly meeting in behalf of **Martha Green** which is accepted

Elisa Brigg clearness   The Friends appointed to make Enq[u]iry into the Clearness of **Elisabeth B[r]iggs** Respecting marriage; report they find nothing to h[i]nder their proceeding

[?] Joseph Mosher Answer   **Joseph Mosher** and **Elisabeth Briggs** appeared for their answer which was, They may proceed to take Each other in marriage at some convenient time before the nex[t] monthly meeting, Advising with the Overseers, **Alice Anthony** and **Edith Russell** are appointed to oversee the marriage, tha[t] it is consumated ˄& condu[c]ted orderly, and they to make report to next monthly meeting

Elisa Briggs request certificate   **Elisabeth Briggs** Request a few lines Recomending her to **Smithfield** monthly meeting; the Same Committee are desired to draw own [one] if nothing apears to hinder

6 month 1782 At a Monthly meeting of Women Friends held in **Dartmouth** 17 of 6 month 1782 The Representatives are **Elisabeth Slocum** and **Mary Smith** both present

Adjourned   This Meeting is Adjourned to ye 24th of this Instant

Mett Mett according to adjournment The Representatives both present

Ann Butts denial read and   The Paper of Denial against **Ann Butts** hath been read according to the direction of last month ~ and She informed, And is as Followeth

She inform^d Testimony of denial against Ann Butts   Whereas **Ann Butts** having made profession with us and been under the care of this meeting but have so far departed from the Principles we profess, as to much neglect the attendence of our Religious meetings; also resorts at Places where undue liberty is taken; whc'h she Justifies, and friends having Laboured with her in order to reclaim her from Such practices, but our labours not having the desired Effect to friends Satisfaction: therefore for the clearing of Truth; Friends are concerned to give this forth as a publick Testimony against her the said **Ann Butts**, hereby disowning her from being ˄in Unity with us and from under our care; yet if it be ag˄reeable to divine goo[d]ness She may be restored to the way of Truth as is our Sincear desire

Given forth and Signed in and on behalf of our monthly ⎫   **Wm Anthony Ju^r** Clerk
meeting held in **Dartmouth** ye 20 of 5 month 1782 By ⎰   **Susanna Smith** Clerk

Joseph Mosher marriage Our Friends that was appointed to have the oversight of **Joseph Moshers** and **Elisabeth Briggs** Marriage make ˄report they attended according to appointment and it was consumated and conducted in a good degree orderly

Elisa Mosher
certificate

Signed a ^removal Certificat[e] on behalf ^of **Elisabeth Mosher** Recomending her to **Smithfield** monthly meeting

Adjournd

This Meeting Adjourns to the 26th of this Instant

mett

Mett accor^ding to Adjournment The Representatives present

Sent up to
Quarterly
Meeting

The Queries have been read and ans^wers prepaired and to be sent up to the Quarterly meeting by our Representatives who are **Phebe Smith** and **Edith Russell**; they to make report to next monthly meeting

Judith Russell
& Susanna
Smith dismist[?]
concerning
dividing
prep^rt meeting

Judith Russell and **Su^sanna Smith** hath desired to be dismist from an appoin =tment they have been under concerning dividing the Preparitive meeting which is com^plied with

Committee
to labour
for the reviev
al of plainness

Joanna Gifford, **Martha Chace Martha Gifford** and **Susanna Smith** are appointed to Labour with the Members of this meeting for the Reviveal of Plainness, and other defects ^to Remove as the way oppens to them in the authority of Truth and to Untite [unite] with a Committee of men Friends that are appointed on that account ~ and they ^to make report to the next monthly meeting

Minits cor[r]ec
ted Treasur
ey settled

The Committee appointed hath Revised and Corrected this meetings Minites in order to go on Record; and also Settled with The Treasurer up to the 30th of this Instant month, and there remains in Stock £11=2^s=0^d O[ld] Tennor

~~~~~~

[26]**Abigail Tucker**s Paper of denial should have been Recorded in page **179**. But being neglected, It was thought proper to Record it her[e]; Which is as Followeth

Testimony
of denial
against
Abigail
Tucker

Whereas **Abigail Tucker**, (daughter of **James Tucker**[?] and **Ruth** his wife) Having had her Education amongst Fri[e]nds, and under the care of this meeting yet, by departing from the Testimony of Truth in her own heart, hath so far gon astray, as to fall into the Reproachful Sin of Fornication, as appears by her having a child before marriage: And friends having Laboured with her in Love is order to discover to her the Evil ther[e]of, and to restore her to the way of Truth, but our Labours of Love not proving Effectual to the Satisfaction of this Meeting: Therefor for the Preservation of Truth, and Friends from the Reproach of such Enorm[o]us Evils: This meeting is concerned to give this forth as a publick Testimony against her. hereby disowning hur the said **Abigail Tucker** from being one in our Society, and from under the care of this Meeting; desiring nevertheless if it be agreeable to Divine Pleasur, that She may yet find a place of Repentance, and by an unfeigned Acknowledgment of the Evil of her way return to the way of Truth

Given forth and Signed in and on behalf of our Monthly meeting of Women Friends held in **Dartmouth** ye 15th day of ye 7th month 1771. By

           Hepzibah Hussey Clerk

Hannah Giffords acknowledgment Should have been Recorded in page **191** being omit[t]ed, It is Recorded here, and is as Followeth

---

26. The following two items were intended to be placed earlier in the book. Their corrected location has been previously noted.

To the Monthly meeting of Women Friends to be held in **Dartmouth**
the 19th of the 10th month 1772

Hannah
Giffords
acknowledge=
=ment

Dear Friends   Whereas I ∧have some time past given way so far as to
marry out of the good Order of friends ~ And I said, I would not Rise
at **Ann Gifford**s Supplicat[i]on; and likewise did not Rise at her Supplication
and ∧Since[?] have Consider'd of it, and found I was disorderly, and I am
Sorry for it, and do condemn it, hoping God will forgive me, and friends
so far pass by ∧this my offence with all other mine offences so as to Suffer me Still
to remain under their care   **Hannah Gifford**

[*Insert start*]

At our Monthly Meeting of Friends held in **Dartmouth** on the
p170
18th of the 9th Month 1769
Our Friend **Paul Russell** Aaquainted This Meeting that he
had it on his Mind to Visit **Pembrook [Pembroke]** Quarterly Meeting
which This Meeting has unity with
                    A True Coppy of a minute of our Sd Meeting [?]
                                                    [?] **Russell** Clerk

[*Insert end*]

[*on the opposite unnumbered page is a loose paper pasted in with the following text:*]
        Having accomplished the Recording these
Minites for the Space of Seven years past and
performed the same as well as age, Eye Sight
and ability of body would admitt, being much
disorder'd in he[a]lth ~ And having had occation
in the co[u]rse of these Records so of[t]en to mention the
name of that truly Pious and Worthy Matron
And faithful Labourer in the Vine=yard of whom
a large Testimony could be bourne but[?] only
remains for ∧me to mention her name once more
Deborah Hayden, Who hath lately removed
from hence by death and gone to the world of Spirits
Where She ceaseth from all her Labour and her works
do follow~   Thus Saith
To whom concernd   **William Anthony**
Dartmouth ye 12th of 6th month 1782

INDEX

Page numbers in italics indicate illustrations. Spellings in the minutes are extremely variable, and have been regularized in the index for ease of use. For instance, Willbur, Willbore, Wilber, Wilbor, and Wilbur are all entered as Wilbur. Common name variants are cross-referenced where appropriate. People with the same name are differentiated if they are distinguishable in the context of the minutes. Women are indexed under both maiden and married name if they can be identified as the same person from the context.

THE MINUTES OF
THE DARTMOUTH, MASSACHUSETTS
MONTHLY MEETING OF FRIENDS
1699–1785

*

TYPESET IN ADOBE TEXT

*

PRINTED AT PURITAN CAPITAL
HOLLIS, NEW HAMPSHIRE

*

BOUND AT NEW HAMPSHIRE BINDERY
BOW, NEW HAMPSHIRE

*

DESIGN & LAYOUT BY PAUL HOFFMANN
LANCASTER, NEW HAMPSHIRE